Document Warehousing and Text Mining

Dan Sullivan

Wiley Computer Publishing

John Wiley & Sons, Inc.

NEW YORK • CHICHESTER • WEINHEIM • BRISBANE • SINGAPORE • TORONTO

Publisher: Robert Ipsen
Editor: Robert M. Elliott
Assistant Editor: Emilie Herman
Managing Editor: John Atkins
Associate New Media Editor: Brian Snapp
Text Design & Composition: Argosy

Designations used by companies to distinguish their products are often claimed as trademarks. In all instances where John Wiley & Sons, Inc., is aware of a claim, the product names appear in initial capital or ALL CAPITAL LETTERS. Readers, however, should contact the appropriate companies for more complete information regarding trademarks and registration.

Figures 7.2, 7.3, and 11.9 copyright © 1998–2000 Tennyson Maxwell Information Systems, Inc. All rights reserved. Figures 11.8, 13.4, 15.3, 15.4, 15.5, and 17.2 copyright © Megaputer Intelligence. Figures 16.2 and 16.3 copyright © 10k Wizard Technology, LLC.

This book is printed on acid-free paper. ♾

Copyright © 2001 by Dan Sullivan. All rights reserved.

Published by John Wiley & Sons, Inc.

Published simultaneously in Canada.

No part of this publication may be reproduced, stored in a retrieval system or transmitted in any form or by any means, electronic, mechanical, photocopying, recording, scanning or otherwise, except as permitted under Sections 107 or 108 of the 1976 United States Copyright Act, without either the prior written permission of the Publisher, or authorization through payment of the appropriate per-copy fee to the Copyright Clearance Center, 222 Rosewood Drive, Danvers, MA 01923, (978) 750-8400, fax (978) 750-4744. Requests to the Publisher for permission should be addressed to the Permissions Department, John Wiley & Sons, Inc., 605 Third Avenue, New York, NY 10158-0012, (212) 850-6011, fax (212) 850-6008, E-Mail: PERMREQ @ WILEY.COM.

This publication is designed to provide accurate and authoritative information in regard to the subject matter covered. It is sold with the understanding that the publisher is not engaged in professional services. If professional advice or other expert assistance is required, the services of a competent professional person should be sought.

Library of Congress Cataloging-in-Publication Data:

ISBN 0-471-39959-0

Printed in the United States of America.

10 9 8 7 6 5 4 3 2 1

To my wife, Katherine, who has mastered the art of turning the potential into the actual

CONTENTS

ACKOWLEDGMENTS

The roots of this book extend far and deep through my career, and although there is only a single name listed as author, this book would never have reached fruition without the help of others.

First, I would like to thank my editors Bob Elliott and Emilie Herman at John Wiley & Sons for the talent, patience, and insights that helped to shape this book. Their commitment to this project was evident from the early stages when the book was first proposed through the completion of the final manuscript. This book will no doubt be more useful to readers because of them.

Dr. Karl Haberlandt of Trinity College opened a world of challenges when he introduced me to artificial intelligence and natural language processing seventeen years ago. Karl's disciplined approach to understanding complex ideas showed me that we can take on the hard problems with success. Working with Bob Kuhns gave me my first in-depth exposure to applying computational linguistics. I learned more about building natural language processing systems from Bob than I did in years of graduate study.

I would also like to thank Keith Warman, Craig Warman, Robert Mcaden, and my other colleagues at Computer Resource Team, Inc., for their support while I wrote this book. Keith and Craig have created a company that not only supports but also encourages the development and exchange of new ideas and approaches. Robert, a talented software designer who can also manage clients' demands and consultants' needs, is a rare find. Robert, Craig, and Keith all quietly insulated me from many of the pressures that I could have encountered while writing this book. I would like to especially thank Eric Anderson for his time and effort in reviewing some of the more challenging parts of the manuscript and Roger Gough, who introduced me to Perl and its "there is more than one way to do it" design philosophy. Mike Lynch's and Graeme Cox's technical reviews have significantly improved the quality of this book.

Of all the support I have received, none has been more important than my family's. This project is only one of the many endeavors I could not have considered without the help of my in-laws, Jane and Bill Aiken. Even with their own demanding writing careers, Jane as an art historian and Bill a poet, they always make time to anticipate and attend to the needs of their extended family. I fear my children will expect as much of me.

I cannot have asked for more from my children while writing this book. Nicolas, the nocturnal member of the family, was always ready and willing to forgo bedtime, keep me company, and perhaps squeeze in some late-night tickling. James could always sense how well things were going and knew when I needed to get away with a trip to the pool or a good kickball game. Nicole's deep well of stories about school, her pet birds, and of course her four brothers kept me in touch with the rest of the household even while I was buried in the study. Charles cheerfully awaited the finishing of the manuscript as full of hope as when he waits for Christmas. Kevin kept encouraging me through the entire endeavor and no matter how little I had written on any given night, it was still good progress in his mind. Not only have my children waited patiently while this book was written, they were instrumental in keeping me on an even keel.

Lastly, this book would never have been if it weren't for my wife Katherine. My freelance writing began when she encouraged me to write and publish some of my ideas on design and development. As a former philosophy teacher, she had many more interesting texts to tackle than my mundane writing, but she approached my articles with the same inquiring eye that she brought to Plato and Nietzche. Trying to find someone willing to discuss morphological analysis or the relationship between logic and semantics is no small feat, so having a spouse fascinated by so many different topics was essential to getting this project off the ground. The book was completed only because Kathy was able to juggle the needs of five children, my demanding consulting schedule, and her own writing without missing a beat.

PREFACE

The origin of the idea for document warehousing goes back to 1997 and a relatively obscure paper I presented at a developer's conference on adding documents to the data warehouse. At that time, the biggest issues in data warehousing centered on design techniques and the sometimes slow and painful extraction, transformation, and load processes. Most data warehousing practitioners did not have time to think about making the process even more complex by delving into documents and text mining. Times have changed. We now have a well-developed set of design techniques, flexible extraction, transformation, and load programs, and relational databases that provide functionality specifically for data warehouses. The fundamental work on providing large-scale decision support environments for operation management has been completed and it is now time to move on to the next set of problems. The most pressing of those is to tap the business intelligence potential of text.

Executives, managers, and analysts could spend every working moment reading. They could study status reports, customer complaints, internal procedures, press releases, news stories, legal briefs, patent applications, regulatory agency announcements, and hundreds of other types of documents. There is just too much text. Unfortunately, within that text is valuable information that can shed light on changing customer opinions, shifts in the market, and details about internal operations. The solution to the problem is to integrate documents into the business intelligence infrastructure and provide the means to search for and target specific information the way we now do with numeric data. This book provides a roadmap of that process.

How This Book Is Organized

The book is divided into four sections:

- Part One: Text Analysis for Business Intelligence
- Part Two: Document Warehousing
- Part Three: Text Mining
- Part Four: Conclusions

The first section provides an overview of the importance of textual resources to business intelligence. Part Two moves into a discussion of the design and architecture of a document warehouse. It also includes implementation details, such as programming crawlers to find and retrieve relevant texts for the warehouse. Part Three addresses text mining, which is the process of extracting information from texts. In Part Four, the book concludes with an overview of how document warehousing and text mining can be used today to extend the scope of business intelligence.

Part One consists of three chapters. Chapter 1, "Expanding the Scope of Business Intelligence," describes existing decision support needs that cannot be met by number-centric business intelligence systems. Organizations do not exist in a vacuum, and focusing solely on operational data without an awareness of changing needs of customers, shifts in markets, and other changes in the macroenvironment will never provide a true picture of a business position in the market. In Chapter 2, "Understanding the Structure of Text: The Foundation of Text-Based Business Intelligence," we see that text is not unstructured, as is so often assumed. Language is richly complex and understanding its structure is the key to understanding how to extract information from text. Chapter 3, "Exploiting the Structure of Text," introduces the basic operations of document warehousing and text mining from a business intelligence perspective. With the groundwork laid for understanding why we need to deal with text and what we can expect from existing language technologies, we move to Part Two.

The second part of the book is dedicated to the process and architecture of document warehousing. Chapter 4, "Overview of Document Warehousing," provides an overview for the entire process. Next, Chapter 5, "Meeting Business Intelligence Requirements: More than Just Numbers," delves into understanding the requirements for text-oriented business intelligence, which are sometimes radically different from those of data warehousing. Chapter 6, "Designing the Document Warehouse Architecture," addresses architectural issues and describes how to set up a document warehousing environment. The emphasis shifts in Chapter 7, "Finding and Retrieving Relevant Text," to focus on the process of finding and retrieving texts of interest to users of the document warehouse. Like data warehouses, the information moved into a document warehouse is not always in the desired form and transformations are required. This is covered in Chapter 8, "Loading and Transforming Documents." Document warehouses are driven by metadata. Chapter 9, "Managing Document Warehouse Metadata," discusses the type of metadata that should be kept in a document warehouse and how to organize it. Any application or business intelligence platform requires security mechanisms to prevent compromises and Chapter 10, "Ensuring Document Warehouse Integrity," discusses how to maintain the integrity of the document warehouse. The topic of Chapter 11, "Choosing Tools for Building the Document Warehouse," is choosing tools for the document warehouse. Just as data warehouses require specific tools, such as extraction, transformation, and extraction tools, so too document warehousing has its own tool requirements. Finally, Chapter 12, "Developing a Document Warehouse: A Checklist," offers a checklist of steps and considerations for constructing a document warehouse.

Part Three examines the process of text mining. Chapter 13, "What Is Text Mining?" is something of a look under the hood at text mining, information retrieval, and linguistic processing. The next three chapters examine applications of text mining in business intelligence and related areas. Chapter 14, "Know Thyself: Using Text Mining for Operational Management," looks at how text mining can be used to support internal operations. In Chapter 15, "Knowing Your Business-to-Business Customer: Text Mining for Customer Relationship Management," the topic turns to meeting direct needs of customers. Chapter 16, "Text Mining for Competitive Intelligence" looks into moving beyond internal operations and existing customers to gather market intelligence. Chapter 17 concludes this section with an examination of different types of text mining tools and the role they play in a document warehousing and text mining environment.

Part Four concludes the book with an overview of how document warehousing and text mining can extend the scope of business intelligence to support not only operational management but strategic management as well.

The appendices provide supporting material for the rest of the book. Appendix A includes template documents to aid in the requirements gathering and architectural design of the document warehouse. Appendix B is a list of vendors and other resources for text mining, and Appendix C provides a physical database model for some parts of a simple document warehouse.

Capturing the business intelligence potential of text can provide valuable insights into a business, its competition, its market and more. If this book sheds some light on the process of how to tap into this valuable resource and help you improve your organization's business intelligence systems, then it has accomplished its goal.

Who Should Read This Book

This book is intended for business intelligence designers as well as users. Both audiences will find the first three chapters and Chapter 18, "Changes in Business Intelligence," useful as they lay the foundation of understanding both the need for text-based resources and the basic techniques for extracting key information from those sources. For those responsible for creating and maintaining business intelligence systems, this book will provide a framework for integrating text-based resources into new or existing BI applications. Part Two, "Document Warehousing," will be most useful to designers and developers. Chapter 13, "What Is Text Mining," delves into details of text mining techniques that may be of interest to some developers but is not required to successfully use the tools and techniques described throughout the book. End users will find example applications in Chapters 14 through 16, including supporting internal operations, customer relationship management, and business intelligence. Chapter 17, "Text Mining Tools," will help designers and developers to choose tools appropriate for their specific needs.

What's on the Companion Web Site

The companion Web site to this book contains additional information on document warehousing and text mining, including links to related sites as well as vendor and product information. The site also contains templates to help implement a document warehouse, scripts for basic operations, and example programs for common tasks.

Throughout the book, commercial tools are used to demonstrate how vendors solve a particular problem or implement a technique. Needless to say, tools are changing constantly and new features are being added to these tools as the book goes to press. The Web site will provide links to the latest information on the tools mentioned here as well as other tools that are not mentioned in the book. Text mining is a dynamic arena and there are many more vendors than mentioned in this book, so look to the Web site for other tools as well.

PART ONE

Text Analysis for Business Intelligence

CHAPTER 1

Expanding the Scope of Business Intelligence

For most of us, thinking about business intelligence brings to mind data warehouses, multidimensional models, and ad hoc reports. While these techniques and resources have served us well, they do not completely address the full scope of business intelligence (BI). BI provides decision makers with the information they need to understand, manage, and direct organizations. Unfortunately, we have only touched the tip of the information iceberg. To date, numeric and short character string information has been the sole grist for the BI mill. This so-called structured data excludes the most prevalent medium for expressing information and knowledge: text. Within text we find project status information, marketing reports, details of industry regulations, competitors' advertising campaigns, and descriptions of new technologies in patent applications. We simply cannot get this type of detail from our traditional business intelligence systems.

The Need to Deal with Text

We need to expand the scope of business intelligence to include textual information. Now is the right time to do this, for a number of reasons. First, we now have tools at our disposal for analyzing text and extracting key information to create a document warehouse with distilled, useful business intelligence information. Steady advances in computational linguistics since the 1960s have left us with a wide range of tools for extracting key features, categorizing documents, indexing by topic as well as by keywords, automatically summarizing texts, and grouping similar documents. These tools are the keys to successful integration of text into the business intelligence infrastructure.

Second, the Internet and the World Wide Web are making vast amounts of information easily accessible. With the right tools we can find information about the financial, marketing, and technology plans of competitors. We can track changes in the legislative and regulatory environment that affect our industry and monitor the political and economic conditions of markets around the world. The range of topics that can be researched on the Internet is almost without limit.

A third reason for expanding the scope of business intelligence is that organizations have—since the dawn of commerce and centralized governments—depended upon writing systems of some form to record information. To this point in time, we accumulated 1,000 petabytes of data stored online in mainframes, servers, and client PCs, and that does not even include the Internet (Lycyk, 2000). A significant portion of this information is text-based, and organizations are beginning to realize the need to deal with this text from a decision support perspective. According to research by Survey.com, 81 percent of respondents expect to be supporting free-form text in the data warehouse by 2002 (*Application Development Trends*, February 2000). Our current means of dealing with, or ignoring, text are no longer sufficient to meet the needs of decision makers.

A fourth point to keep in mind is that successful organizations are not just driven by managing core operations such as selling products, tracking changes in quality control measures, or analyzing trends in cash flow. More and more, intangible aspects of organizations, such as knowledge about process management, patented technologies, and methodologies, are fundamental factors influencing the course of a business. "Increasingly, intellectual resources and not physical assets constitute the seeds of marketplace success" (Quinn, 1994). Managers and executives need to understand the competitive advantage created by their intellectual property as well as how the market responds to innovations by competitors. This kind of information is not available by looking at data extracts from transaction processing systems. It is however, available to those who know where to look and how to extract the key information.

Finally, decision makers think strategically. This means that they need information about what is going on outside the organization as well as inside, as depicted in Figure 1.1. They need to understand industry structure and dynamics, which shed light on the competitive environment in which companies operate. Macroenvironmental analysis, another aspect of strategic management, examines the economic, political, social, and technological events that influ-

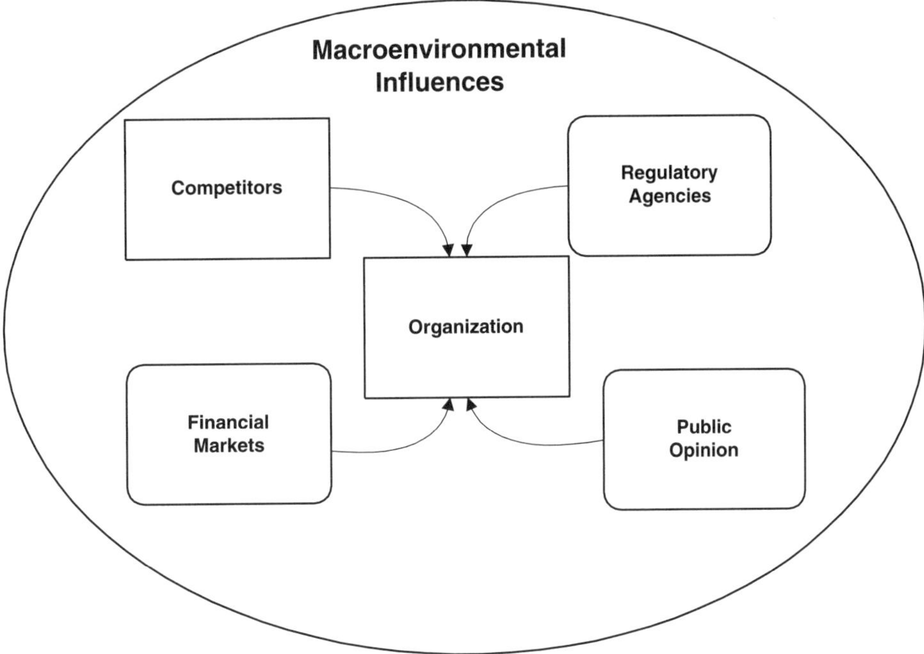

Figure 1.1 Organizations do not exist in a vacuum.

ence an industry. Monitoring the macroenvironment is no small task. As two researchers have noted, "[t]he problem for corporations is that monitoring the macroenvironment is a lot like studying geology—the subject is huge, usually ponderous, but sometimes precipitous; and much of what researchers would like to know is buried under something heavy" (Narayanan and Fahey, 1994). With the aid of document warehousing and text mining techniques, this type of analysis can at least be less ponderous and information far more accessible.

The tools are here, the raw information is available, and organizations have recognized the need for dealing with text. The only question now is, how do we do it? Document warehousing and text mining are the answer. This book will describe the tools and provide the techniques needed to begin mining the rich deposits of information and knowledge available from both internal proprietary document collections and external publicly available sources. This chapter will lay the groundwork for the rest of the book, beginning with a brief description of the wide range of text sources we have at our disposal. It will then examine the limits of the current common approaches to working with large document sources such as the World Wide Web and identify some key benefits of improving this process. Document warehousing and text mining are then introduced as alternate solutions to the problem of managing and using text-based information efficiently.

The term *document* is used throughout this book to refer to a logical unit of text. This could apply to a Web page, a status memo, an invoice, a Supreme Court opinion, or *War and Peace*. Documents can be as complex and long as a new drug application to the Food and Drug Administration or a simple as a short e-mail. Of course, documents are often more than text and can include graphics and multimedia content. For our purposes, we are only concerned with the textual elements of documents.

Growth of Textual Information—The Good News

It is difficult to overstate the impact of the World Wide Web on the dissemination of information. Individuals, businesses, nonprofit organizations, governments, and even terrorist groups have set up shop on the Web so they can effectively share information. Conservative estimates of the size of the Web are over one billion pages at the time of publication of this book. Estimates that include dynamically generated pages from Web databases run as high as 500 times that size.

Not only is the sheer volume of text growing, but the breadth and depth of information available makes ignoring the business intelligence value of text a dangerous proposition. Consider the fact that the Internet started as government-funded research project testing networking between computer science research centers. After computer researchers, other scientists and engineers began using the Internet to share information. The introduction of the World Wide Web as a means for creating hyperlinks between scientific papers opened the door for others outside the strictly technical disciplines to take advantage of Internet. Now we have access to virtually all publicly available information because it is accessible via the Internet.

The range of topics covered by sources on the Web can meet the demand of just about any business. If you want to find the annual and quarterly reports of a publicly traded company, just go to the Securities and Exchange Commission Web site at www.sec.org. If you are wondering what is going on at the Human Genome Project, visit www.ornl.gov/hgmis/publicat/publications.html. If you need to assess the political and economic risks involved in expanding your business into Southeast Asia, the Federal Reserve Bank of San Francisco's Center for Pacific Basin Studies at www.frbsf.org/econrsrch/pbc/index.html is a good place to start. If you are cleaning up a methlybenzene spill and need recovery procedures, try hazard.com/msds. Just about any topic of interest to a business, organization, or government has a place on the World Wide Web.

The Web is not the only growing source of text information. Corporate repositories and document management systems are growing as well. Documents that have never been printed are as important as, or sometimes more important than, their tangible counterparts. Few businesses could or would want to operate without e-mail. Legal departments use case management systems to track depositions, briefs, research, and other textual material. Engineers need access to specifications and project plans. Sales and marketing executives research market conditions and sales prospects and develop their own strategies that are then documented. There is no lack of the written word in the business world today.

Growth of Textual Information—The Bad News

The bad news about this wealth of textual information can be divided into two parts. First, there is no good way to find all the information and only the information we are looking for when we deal with large document collections, such as the World Wide Web. Second, even if we can find a fraction of what appears relevant, it is often too much to read, or even skim. There is just too much information.

Finding Information: It's Not as Easy as It Used to Be

In conjunction with the growth of the Web has been the emergence of search engines. Now, search technology has been around as long as we have had documents stored in information retrieval (IR) systems but Web-based search engines are different from their IR counterparts.

First of all, traditional IR systems are often used to store relatively homogeneous sets of documents, such as news stories, legislation, case law records, and hazardous material safety data sheets. Web search engines confront documents of all kinds, including multimedia documents that span the breadth of human discourse.

Second, IR systems use centrally managed text databases, while the Web is the archetypal decentralized distributed system. There is no single place to go to find all the documents on the Web as shown in Figure 1.2. Search engines work around this by moving from one Web page to the next using hyperlinks to find other documents, but this does not guarantee that every page is found. IR systems, on the other hand, have complete control over the contents of their text database and, therefore, can index the entire set of documents.

Another advantage that IR search engines have is that they can make assumptions about the terms that a user will use when searching for information. For example, if an IR database containing documents on transportation is presented

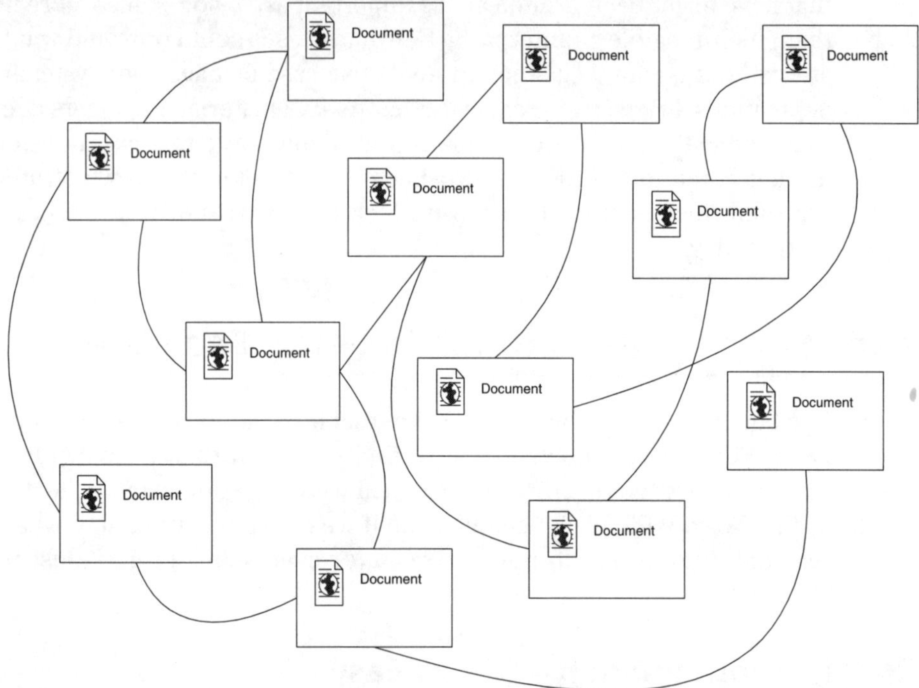

Figure 1.2 The distributed, decentralized nature of the Internet makes it impossible to work from a centralized starting point for indexing the Web.

with a query including the term *fly*, it can assume that the user is interested in air transportation. The query optimizer could expand the query written by the user to include related terms, such as *flight*, to improve the chances that all relevant documents will be found. A World Wide Web search engine does not have the luxury of working with a controlled vocabulary like that. On the Web, *fly* could refer to airline flights, insects, or zippers.

The breadth of the Web makes it more challenging to deal with than traditional IR systems, and to make things worse, we still have to live with problems that have plagued IR systems since their inception: poor precision and recall. Both of these problems deal with how effectively search engines answer a user's query. Precision is a measure of how well the documents returned in response to a query actually address the query. If the IR system returns a large number of documents but most are irrelevant, then precision is low, but if most of the documents are relevant, then precision is high. Anyone who has run a query through a Web search engine only to be left scratching his or her head about how some of those hits could possibly have anything to do with the search has experienced poor precision firsthand. Recall is a related measure. In contrast to looking at the quality of what was returned, recall is a measure of what should have been returned. Since even the largest search engines cannot index every Web page, there will be missed pages for some queries, resulting in poor recall. Better indexing will increase recall, but it will also lead to more text that the end users will have to read through to find the information they are looking for. Pick your poison.

Beware What You Wish for: Finding Too Much Information

The problem we confront today is that we have too much text at our disposal. Imagine if we had databases filled with transactional data but no way to distill the information down into key pieces of information. Even before data warehousing and dimensional modeling were fully developed practices, decision support systems were created that could give a manager or executive an overview of even large transaction sets. Today, most managers cannot get an overview of the contents of a large document collection without enlisting the help of a researcher, analyst, or staff member to review a group of documents, identify the relevant ones, read the text, and summarize the findings. Would any manager today have an employee sit down with a printout of transactions from an accounting system and a calculator and manually add the numbers to find out the state of accounts receivable? Of course not, but we go through a similar process when we need to find key information in text. We do not need to keep working with text in this way, and document warehousing and text mining are the keys to the solution.

The Document Warehousing Approach to the Information Glut

Document warehousing is one approach to dealing with a glut of textual information and is analogous to data warehousing as a method for dealing with large volumes of numeric data. Document warehouses distinguish themselves from data warehouses by the types of questions they are designed to answer. Data warehouses are excellent tools for answering who, what, when, where, and how much questions. They do not do so well with why questions, and these are document warehousing's forte.

Data warehouses, in practice, are often internally focused. We use them to better analyze the operational information of our organizations and rarely include external sources of information. (Demographics data is one common exception.) Document warehouses, though, can gather and process text from any source, internal or external, and this is the key to the document warehouse's ability to support strategic management that looks beyond the internal operation to the external factors that influence an organization. Of course, we could use external sources for data warehousing as well but the work involved in finding and acquiring relevant data in appropriate formats is many times outweighed by the marginal benefit of having the additional information.

There is a price to pay for this branching out though. One has less control over external sources than internal ones. Running an extraction, transformation, and load (ETL) process for a data warehouse will generate well-defined results. Dimensions will be updated, fact tables will grow, and errors will be logged. We may not know the details of the data that is loaded, but we will know its general form. Searching for content for a document warehouse through the Internet can lead to unexpected sources of text. Some downloaded documents may be irrelevant or, worse, inaccurate and misleading. As we shall see in the chapters ahead, one of the most important steps in document warehousing is controlling the document collection process.

Supporting Business Intelligence with Text

Document warehouses are repositories of textual information designed to support business intelligence and decision support operations. The exact nature of textual information actually maintained in a document warehouse can include:

- Complete documents
- Automatically generated summaries of documents
- Translations of documents in several languages
- Metadata about documents, such as authors' names, publication dates, and subject keywords
- Automatically extracted key features
- Clustering information about similar documents
- Thematic or topical indexes

Document warehouses, unlike document management systems, include extensive semantic information about documents, document groupings, cross-document feature relations, and other attributes designed to provide high-precision, high-recall access to business intelligence information.

Data warehouses, especially those built on dimensional models, provide aggregated views of large numbers of transactions. For example, we can easily find the number of laptops sold in the eastern region during the third quarter by a particular salesperson or the total gross revenue for a product line in one store during the Christmas season. Rather than starting with small units of information, such as a transaction, and aggregating along a predefined set of dimensions, document warehouses start with richly complex units—that is, documents—and extract information by applying linguistic-processing and text mining techniques.

Figure 1.3 shows how the data in a large number of transactions can be reduced to a few rows in a fact table and thus provide information, not just data, to end users.

Now, document warehouses have an almost opposite problem. Documents have very high information content (usually). Unlike transactions in an online transaction processing system (OLTP), documents do not follow a relational structure. For example, a simple sales transaction might use a structure like that shown in Figure 1.4.

Document contents are often referred to as free-form text because we cannot fit the contents into a fixed relational structure, at least not a useful one. We can put an entire document into a binary long object and claim victory. This is fine if we are developing document management systems (which are essentially transaction processing systems anyway). It does not help in a decision support environment though. We need to understand what is inside those documents; we need to take them apart, dissect them linguistically, and then make explicit the essential information contained in the text.

We have set the stage for the need for document warehousing, and at this point it is worth developing a formal definition for document warehousing and discussing some of the implications of this definition.

Defining the Document Warehouse

A document warehouse shares some common elements with a data warehouse, so we will first review two definitions of a data warehouse as defined by Bill Inmon and Ralph Kimball. According to Inmon (Inmon, 1995), the four defining characteristics of a data warehouse are:

- Subject-oriented
- Integrated
- Time-variant
- Nonvolatile

Subject-oriented means that data is organized around a particular topic instead of around the processing requirements of the organization's operations. Data warehouses are *integrated* because data is gathered from multiple sources. *Time-variant* means that data in the data warehouse is identified with a particular time period. Finally, the *nonvolatile* characteristic means that data is not removed once it is added to the data warehouse. This last criterion is often

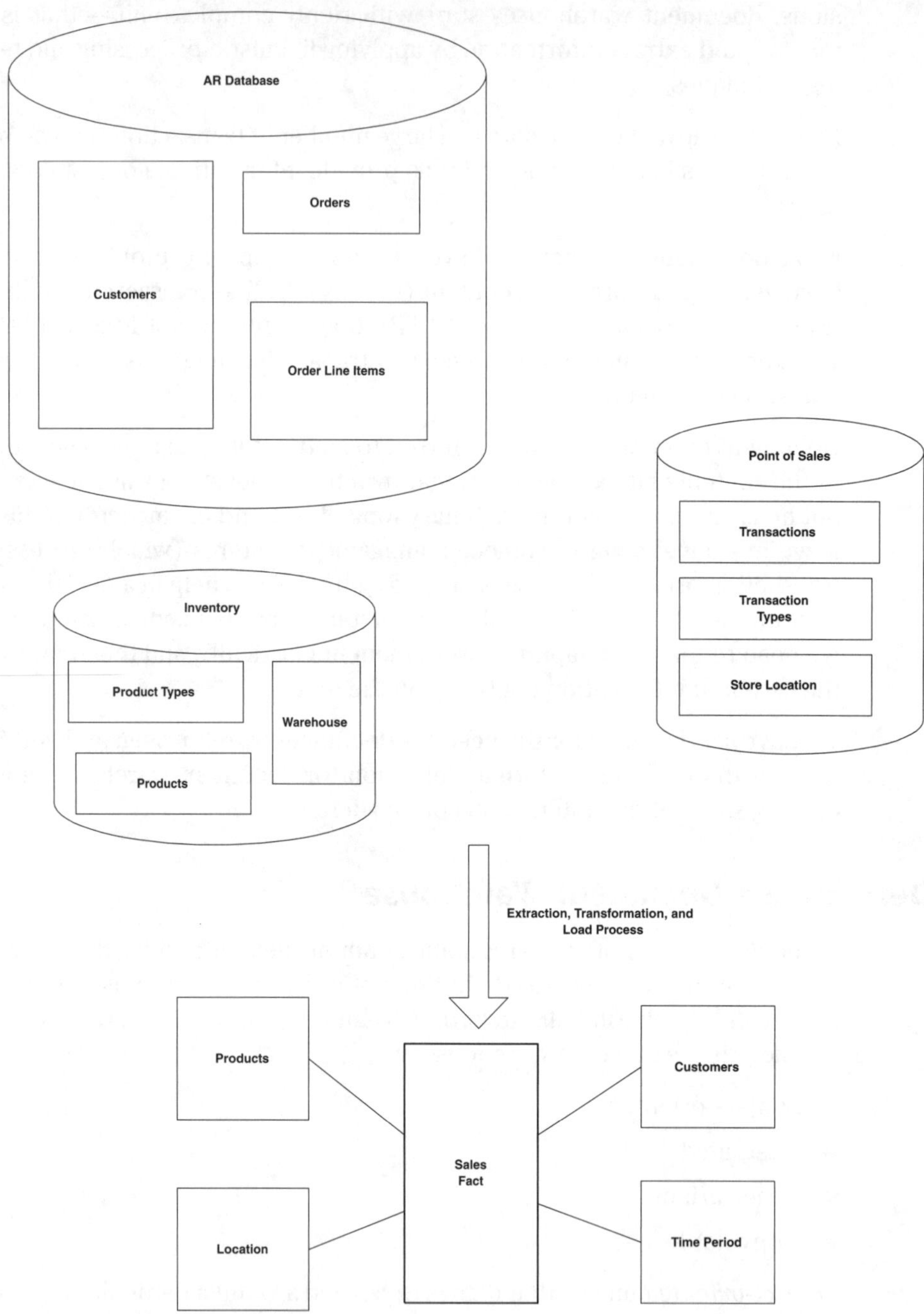

Figure 1.3 Transactional data needs to be structured to provide true decision support information.

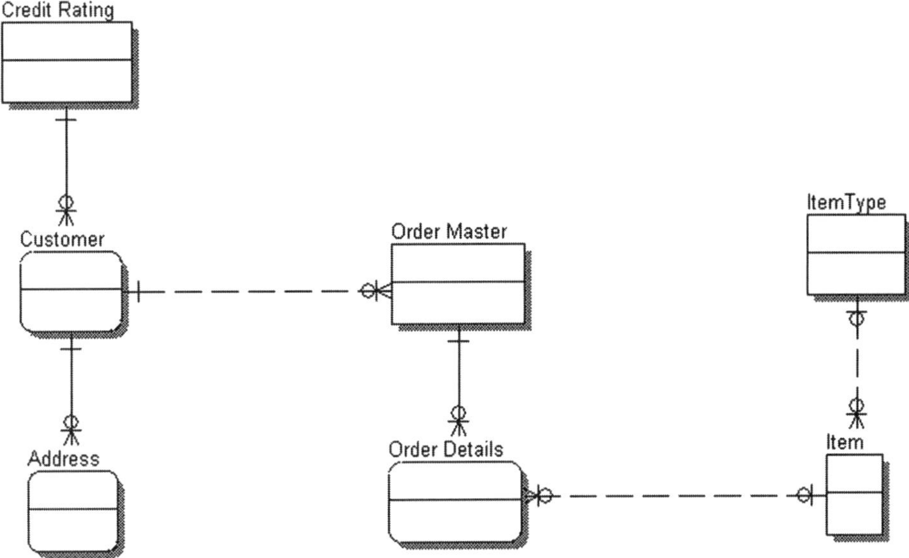

Figure 1.4 Normalized relational models are commonly used to structure transaction processing systems.

relaxed when dealing with large volumes of data. A common practice in such situations is to archive data that is more than three years old.

Ralph Kimball's definition is more concise. He describes a data warehouse as "a copy of transaction data specifically structured for query and analysis" (Kimball, 1996). Here, the emphasis is on restructuring transaction data to make the information entailed in the raw data easily accessible. This is also the key driver in document warehousing.

A document warehouse is characterized by four attributes:

- There is no single document structure or document type.
- Documents are drawn from multiple sources.
- Essential features of documents are automatically extracted and explicitly stored in the document warehouse.
- Document warehouses are designed to integrate semantically related documents (see Figure 1.5).

As we shall see in the next section, these characteristics not only distinguish document warehouses from data warehouses, they differentiate the document warehouse from other document management schemes as well.

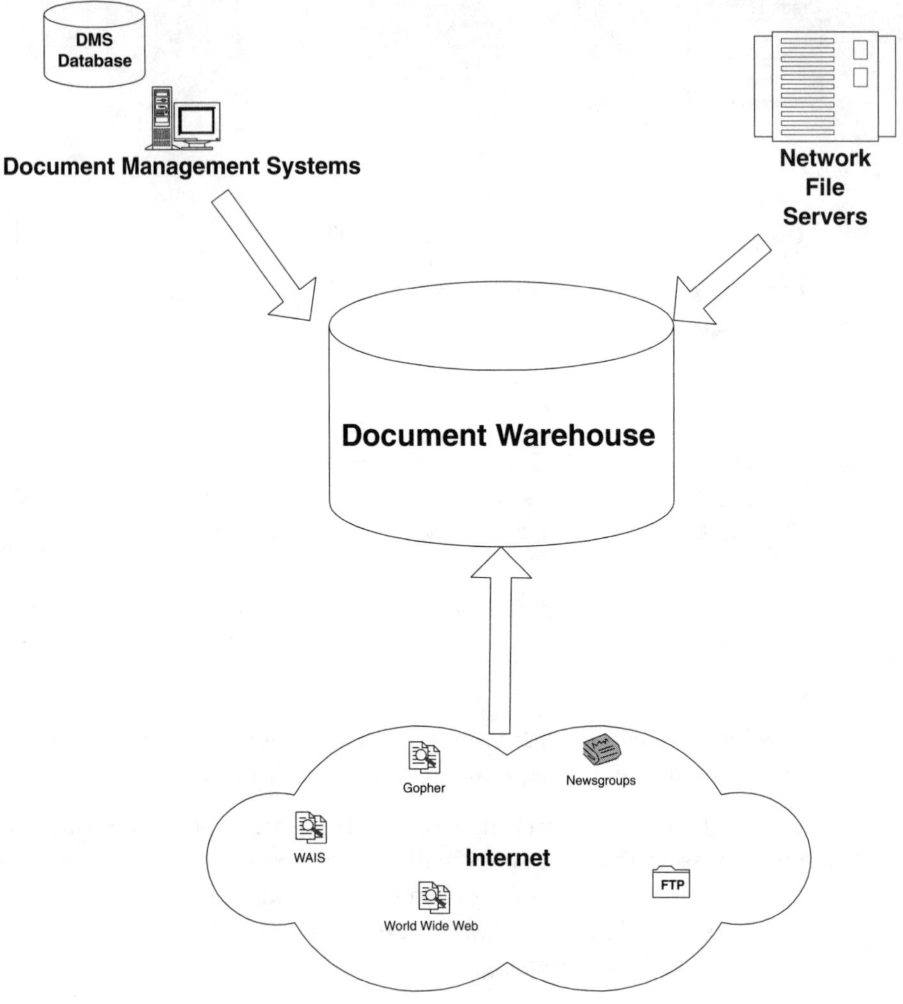

Figure 1.5 Document warehouses draw from multiple sources and work with the meaning of text to organize the repository.

Multiple Document Types

Often DMS applications deal with a single type of document, such as insurance claim forms, material safety data sheets, or bibliographic abstracts. Any type of document can be used in the document warehouse. How documents are processed, however, can vary by type. E-mails, for example, are relatively short and often contain ungrammatical or partial sentences, so there is no point in using automatic summarization techniques with these. When documents are gathered from internal sources, we will generally know the language used to write the document. Text collected from the Web, however, can be in any language. Because of this, the first step is to identify the language of a document, either from metadata contained in the Web page or through the use of a language identification program. If document warehouse users do not generally speak the language, either a human being or a machine translation program should translate it. If we are loading so called semistructured documents, such as a financial report in the eXtensible Business Reporting Language (XBRL), we may first parse the document and analyze only particular sections of it. While a document warehouse will include a wide range of document types, the specific type of processing and information extraction techniques applied will depend upon the individual document type.

Multiple Sources

The second characteristic of document warehouses is that documents are drawn from multiple sources. Organizations have PCs, servers, and storage area networks (SANs) loaded with documents containing key business information. This can include everything from memos about the upcoming Christmas party to confidential legal briefs on pending litigation. Just as we cannot realize the full business intelligence value of transactional data when it is spread across multiple applications and platforms, so too we cannot realize the full value of text the way it is usually stored.

Finding these documents is often a matter of knowing organizational conventions. For example, let's assume that a company keeps all marketing-related documents on the server named MRKT03. Within the server, top-level directories are named after a product line or a consolidated product campaign (unless the information is over two years old, in which case documents are filed under an old convention that is no longer used). From there, subdirectories are named after the lead analyst in charge of the particular marketing project, and then files are named according to some other arbitrary convention. This type of structure reflects one of the problems with fixed file organization for documents. Texts can logically be organized in many different ways but a file system supports only one at a time. What appears as a logical scheme from one perspective is useless from another. The result is that the full business value of textual information is not realized because of the high cost of retrieval. (This is not the only obstacle to fully exploiting text, as we shall see shortly).

Using a document warehouse, we can structure documents to support retrieval and analysis from multiple perspectives based upon the semantic content of the document, not on external attributes such as location and file name as shown in Figure 1.6.

The limit of file-system-based storage is painfully obvious when one needs to work with the contents of documents instead of with just external attributes.

\\server\dir\subdir\filename.ext

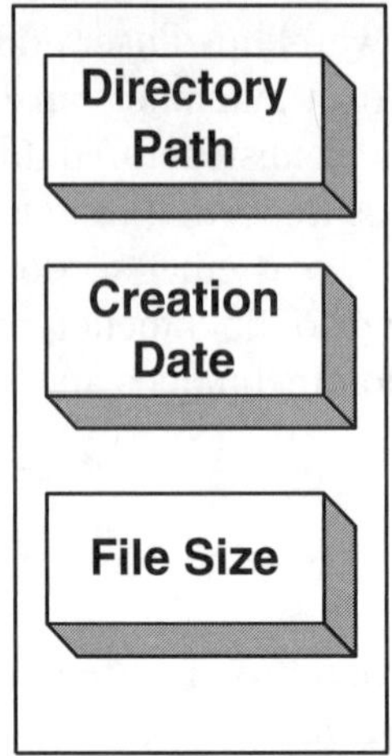

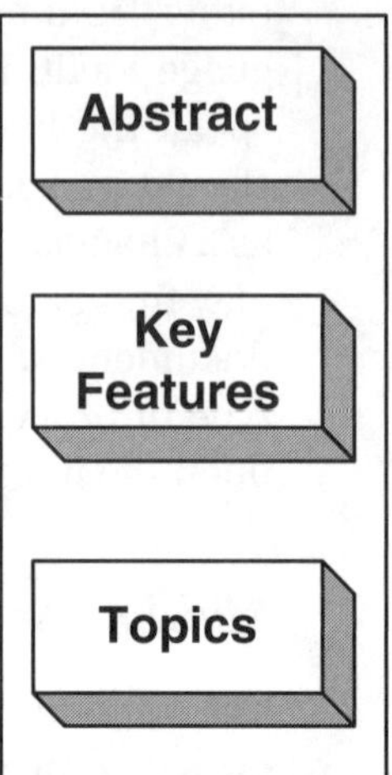

External Attributes

Internal Attributes

Figure 1.6 External attributes are often arbitrary, while internal attributes are derived from the semantic content of documents.

Lawyers, for example, need to track briefs, case law, depositions, research notes, and other text related to a legal proceeding. Textbases, that is databases that are designed to store and index text, are often used in these situations. While they meet the text retrieval needs of many users, they do not extract information or semantically relate it to other documents. Unlike document warehouses that are designed for decision support, these textbases and related document management systems are designed for more transaction-oriented operations, such as finding all documents of a particular type containing a specified phrase. In addition to being extremely useful for these operations, they are also sources of text for the document warehouse as well.

The Internet is the single largest potential source of documents. With all the documents already accumulating within organizations, why would we want more? The answer is simple, the purpose of the document warehouse is to support decision making, and unless a business or organization is an island unto itself, decision makers need to understand their industry and the macroenvironment, as already discussed.

The reason for drawing from multiple sources to populate the document warehouse is the same as for doing so for data warehouses. No single source has all the information we need, and to understand the full breadth and depth of an issue, we must be able to look at it from multiple dimensions.

Extracting Semantic Content

Extracting the semantic content of a document is an essential process in document warehousing. This is done in several ways, including:

- Identifying dominant themes
- Extracting key features
- Summarizing the content

Identifying dominant themes, sometimes called *categorization*, is one way to extract semantic content. This is useful for thematic indexing that allows users to query using topics instead of just keywords. For example, a user interested in stocks would be interested in articles that refer to the same financial instrument as an equity. An analyst assessing the feasibility of relocating operations to Southeast Asia should be able to search on the term *Southeast Asia* and find articles on *Malaysia*, *Thailand*, *Indonesia*, and other countries in the area without explicitly listing them.

Key features of a document include the names of persons, places, and organizations as well as relationships between those entities. Like thematic indexing, key features identify what a document is about but can provide more detail than broad themes can. For example, a document with terms such as *nucleic acid*, *protein expression*, and *polypeptides* might be categorized as a genetic engineering document. Within the broad categories we establish, key features help us differentiate finer-grained topics. Key features also include relationships between terms. For example, "Mary Smith, CEO and cofounder of Alpha Beta Gamma Industries" expresses a relationship between a person and a fictitious company. The ability to extract that kind of relationship from text and put the information into a fixed format in a database can be a valuable technique in many scenarios.

Frequently we do not need to read an entire document and getting the gist of a text is sufficient. A general rule of thumb recognized by researchers in summarization is that the substantive meaning of documents can be found in just 20 percent of the text (so much for 500-page books). Many tools are available now for summarizing by extraction. Basically, these work by identifying the most common words in a text after throwing out frequently used words such as *a* and *the*. Sentences are then weighted according to how many of the most common words are in the sentence and some tuning rules. These tuning rules include weighting the first sentence of a paragraph slightly higher than others and bumping up the weight of a sentence beginning with a phrase like "In conclusion...." Automatic summarization is not always needed. For example, scholarly articles, patents, and long reports often contain abstracts or executive summaries. In general though, automatic summarization can be an effective method of reducing the workload on document warehouse end users.

Integrating Semantically Related Documents

With key contents extracted from documents, it is possible to group documents based upon the topics addressed in the text. There are a few approaches to this task:

- Thematic indexing
- Feature indexing
- Clustering

In the case of thematic indexing, documents can be searched based upon dominant themes in the text. Themes are generally predefined using a controlled vocabulary. For example, documents dealing with international trade might use a controlled vocabulary with terms such as tariff, embargo, shipping, World Trade Organization, and other domain-specific terms. In addition to these terms, related words and phrases are defined, usually in a thesaurus, to include other ways of expressing the same idea. For example, the World Trade Organization is often referred to as the WTO. With thematic indexing, documents

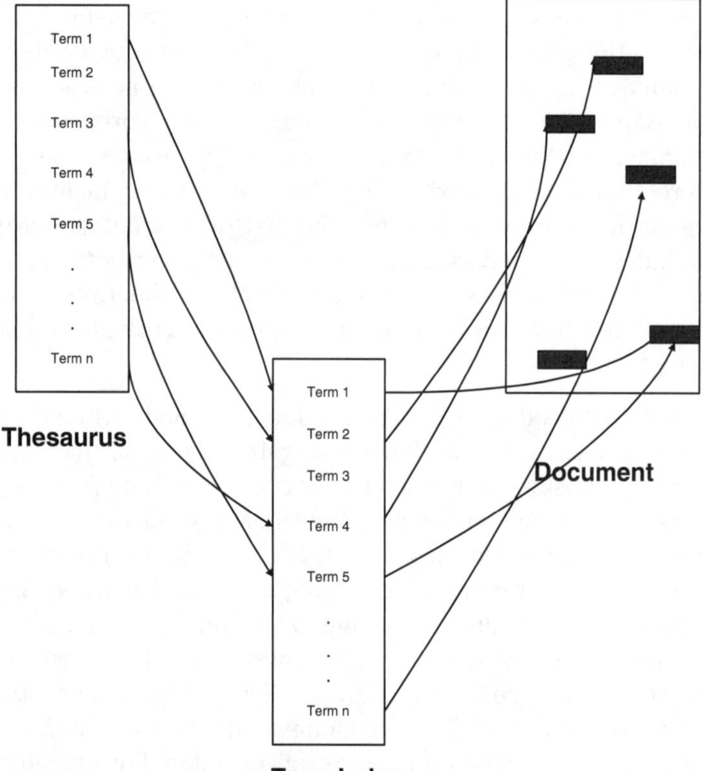

Figure 1.7 Thematic indexing is driven by a controlled vocabulary that represents the set of concepts identified by the system.

about the same topic are related through the index regardless of the specific terms used in the text. This approach works well in domains in which terminology is relatively static, such as economics, finance, and politics, where it is possible to develop a reasonably comprehensive set of terms. Figure 1.7 shows one way to represent a controlled vocabulary.

Feature indexing is similar to thematic indexing, but without a controlled vocabulary. Using feature extraction tools, one can identify significant terms in a document. These terms are then indexed like the controlled vocabulary in the case of thematic indexing. This is especially useful when dealing with a new or changing area, such as genetic engineering, where new or highly specialized terms are frequently used. As shown in Figure 1.8, feature indexing is driven by the contents of the text rather than by the contents of a fixed vocabulary.

Clustering is another approach to relating documents on the basis of semantic attributes. In this case, either themes, key terms, or other shared linguistic patterns are used to group documents. Figure 1.9 shows one type of clustering—hierarchical—in which documents are grouped at differing levels of similarity. This structure allows users to drill down into specific topics of interest by starting with broader categories.

Clearly, the glue that ties documents together in a document warehouse is core-meaning-bearing terms in text, but how are we supposed to figure out what these are? We need to move beyond the traditional set of tools we have become accustomed to in data warehousing. While we still need to gather raw data, or in

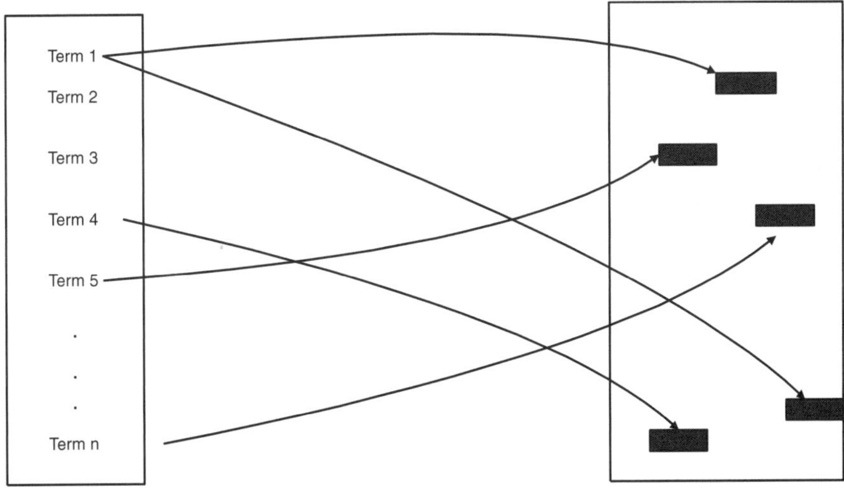

Figure 1.8 Feature indexing extracts key terms to generate the list of words and phrases for indexing.

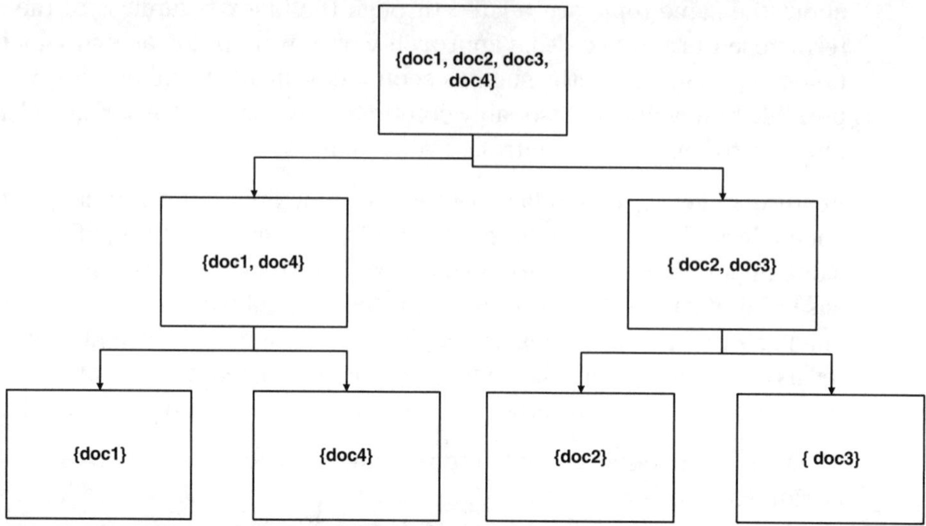

Figure 1.9 Hierarchical clustering relates documents at multiple levels, allowing users to choose the appropriate level of granularity for their analysis.

this case text, transform formats or parse semistructured texts, such as XML documents, and load them into the warehouse, our traditional ETL tools will not meet our needs. Conventional relational database tools, such as SQL and stored procedure languages with string processing support, are not up to the type of semantic analysis that document warehousing demands. We will need several new types of tools, and the most important are those built for text mining.

The Role of Text Mining in Document Warehousing

Text mining is the process of analyzing text to find targeted pieces of information. The key semantic processing operations we have discussed, such as feature extraction, thematic indexing, and clustering are forms of text mining. While document warehouses provide the repository for storing documents, text mining tools extract the explicit semantic content from documents.

There are significant limits to text mining that should be made clear from the outset. First of all, text mining does not entail fully understanding the contents of a document. For close to forty years researchers in Natural Language Processing (NLP), an area of Artificial Intelligence (AI), worked on problems of analyzing sentence structure, devising ways to represent the meaning of sentences, and relating those meanings to construct a model of the meaning expressed in a text. There were many successes in this endeavor. Large, comprehensive dictionaries of words, such as WordNet, have been constructed for representing the meaning of words. Parsers that can analyze the structure of a wide range of sentence types have been constructed. And a variety of knowledge representation schemes have been created to model complex concepts expressed in sentences. However, there has not been a successful integration of these technologies for general use. By the early 1990s, researchers began to shift attention away from the full-blown understanding of single sentences, to a focus on the linguistics of documents and document collections, some times called corpus linguistics.

The object of corpus linguistics is to analyze large collections of texts, not just sentences, to better understand the structure and interrelationships of the syntactic and semantic elements of texts. The result has been a set of techniques based upon both traditional linguistic approaches to analyzing language and statistical methods for studying text. For example, based upon the analysis of extensive texts, we can develop models that predict the part of speech that a word is on the basis of character strings in the word and the location of the word in a sentence. This is especially important in highly specialized domains, where it is virtually impossible to keep a dictionary of terms up to date. While this may not sound like much of an achievement, techniques such as feature extraction and clustering depend upon first having a string of words tagged with their corresponding part of speech, and it is, therefore, critical to text mining.

Text mining, as practiced with commercially available tools, allows us to accomplish several significant tasks in relation to business intelligence. First, it minimizes the amount of text we must read to discover relevant pieces of information. Automatic summarization obviously accomplishes this, but other techniques can guide users to information faster by improving the precision and recall of searches. Second, text mining techniques isolate pieces of information, such as the name of an executive and that person's role in a company. Third, text mining techniques can help us understand the relationship between terms. For example, by studying a large number of patents, we may find the same term occurring in different types of patents. For example, if the term *gene expression* frequently appears in patents with the terms *diabetes screening* and *glaucoma testing*, then this could indicate a potentially common approach to testing for two different disease states. A fourth benefit is that by extracting key terms we can link texts to other systems, such as data warehouses and data marts, that use controlled vocabularies when describing items. For example, dimensional models frequently provide functional descriptions of products, locations, and other structuring elements of the business process. Linking dimensions in the data warehouse to texts in the document warehouse through key terms is one method of integrating the two business intelligence repositories.

Now that the basic structure of the document warehouse has been outlined, it is time to turn our attention to the process of constructing the repository.

Building the Document Warehouse

As Figure 1.10 shows, the basic steps to building a document warehouse parallel the steps in data warehousing. The five main operations are:

1. Identifying document sources
2. Retrieving documents
3. Preprocessing documents
4. Performing text analysis
5. Compiling document metadata

Identifying data sources for a data warehouse is initially done during the requirements and design phases of developing the repository. Unlike those of data warehouses, document warehouse sources are not fixed. Some sources will be known in advance. For example, we can query the United States, European, and Japanese patent offices for details of competitors' technology, we can scan financial and world news sources for particular topics relevant to our organization, and we can obtain details of regulatory issues affecting an industry from government agencies. On the other hand, pieces of unexpected information can be found in these sources and lead to the retrieval of previously unknown or irrelevant documents. For example, the discovery of a document detailing new regulations on the handling of a new class of chemicals could lead to the search for material safety data sheets on the chemicals or a search through the American Chemical Society's database of chemical abstracts available at www.cas.org. Although document warehousing can begin with a set of well-defined sites, either internal or external, the contents of what is found, rather than a list of predefined targets, can direct later stages of document identification.

Document retrieval is tightly linked to document identification. There are generally two types of retrieval operations. Internal document retrieval is largely a fixed, script-driven process. Collecting documents from internal sources, such as file servers and document management systems, can be readily controlled through either shell scripts or, preferably, high-level languages such as Perl or Python. Gathering documents from the Internet entails working primarily with the Web and File Transfer Protocol (FTP) sites. Other types of content management servers have been used in the past, such as the Wide Area Information Server (WAIS), but the Web is largely replacing these. The tool of choice for harvesting documents from the Internet is the crawler, which can be configured to start at a particular site and retrieve linked documents of particular types or to a particular depth. Once the documents are in hand, the preprocessing stage begins.

The objective of the preprocessing stage, like the transformation phase in data warehousing, is to format the information in a consistent manner to support

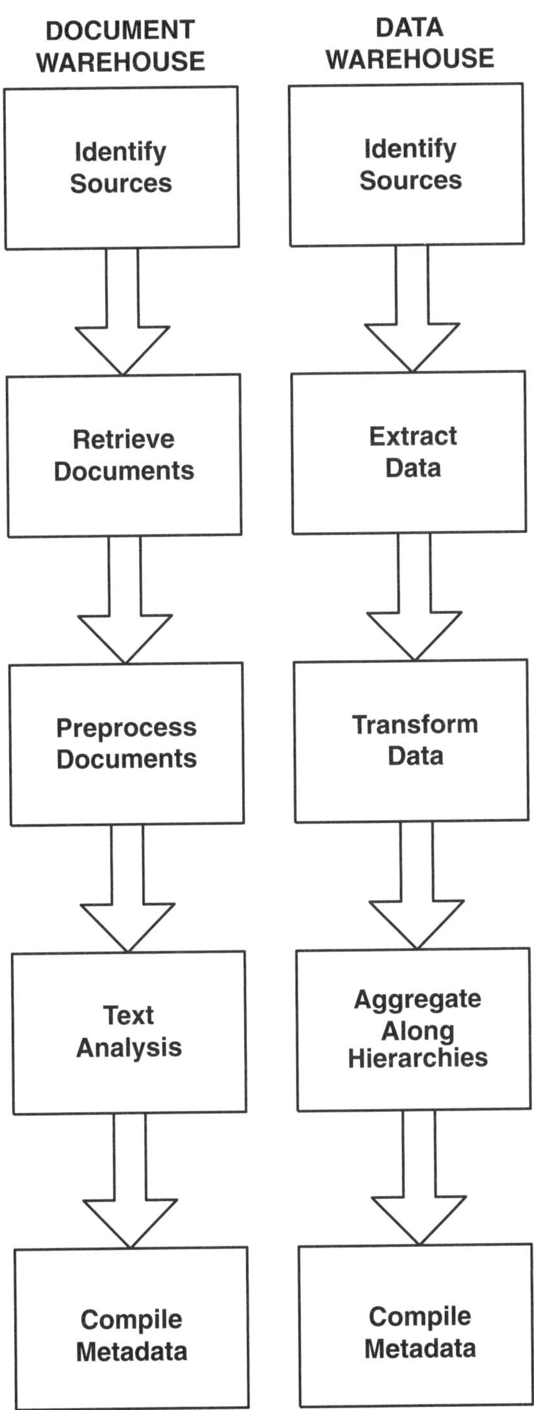

Figure 1.10 The basic steps in document warehouse construction are similar to the tasks in data warehousing.

later operations in the document warehouse process. The key tasks at this point are to make sure that files are in a form suitable for the text analysis tools used in the next step. Some tools expect only unformatted ASCII text, and others work with only certain languages, primarily English. The combination of language identification tools and machine translation systems can provide a preliminary method for addressing multiple languages, but as we shall see, the quality of machine translation is not always adequate for business intelligence needs, and human translation may be required as well.

The next step—text analysis—is the heart of document warehousing. It is here that linguistic analysis is preformed, key features and facts are extracted, documents are indexed by topic, and summaries are generated. Depending upon the type and content of a document, text analysis processes can determine if the entire document should be kept in the warehouse, only a summary, or simply a URL along with extracted metadata.

Compiling metadata is a critical operation because metadata makes explicit, in easily queried form, the essential attributes of a document, such as the key topics, author, source, date of publication, and other factors that can be used to determine its relevancy to a particular issue. For example, a large number of documents might address diabetes screening techniques but only a fraction will have been written after a significant discovery in genetic engineering opened the possibility for a more cost-effective or accurate process. In other cases, the source of the document influences it relevancy. A commentary in a leading financial news daily can certainly sway the opinions of some business executives but the same statements by the chairman of the U.S. Federal Reserve Board could actually change a market. Clearly, not all documents have the same significance to business intelligence users, and the document warehouse accommodates differences through the use of metadata.

The structure of a document warehouse looks similar to Figure 1.11, which shows the final product resulting from the process just described.

Although they have similarities to data warehouses, document warehouses are clearly different. Why should we take on the development of this new business intelligence tool when our well-developed data warehousing practices have served us so well?

Benefits of Document Warehousing

The most significant benefit of document warehousing is that it expands the scope of our business intelligence reach. Whether our focus is improving business operations, sales, marketing, or research and development, unlocking the information in text can provide competitive advantages over those who work

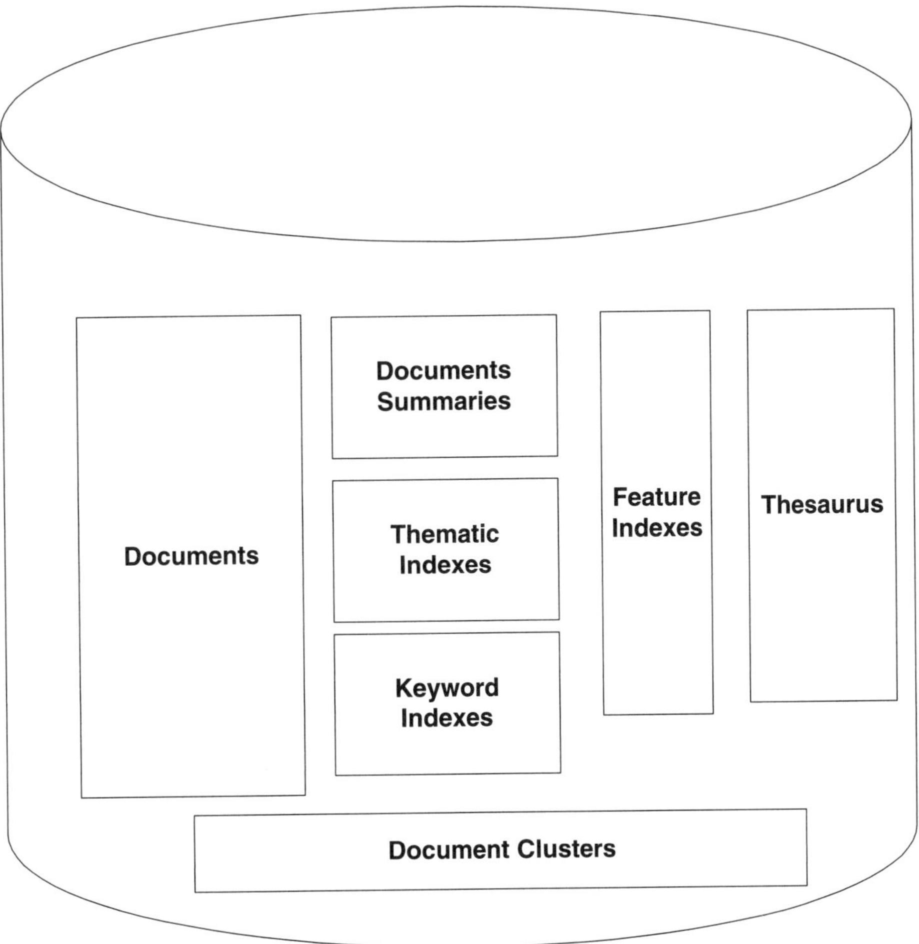

Figure 1.11 Document warehouses are rich collections of semantically related business intelligence information.

with just the numbers. Some of the more specific advantages of document warehousing are:

- Richer operational business intelligence
- Knowing your customers
- Macroenvironment monitoring
- Technology assessment

These benefits are discussed throughout this book but they will be briefly introduced here.

Richer Operational Business Intelligence

Document warehousing provides the ability to move beyond just numeric measures of operational performance. Of course these measures are essential, in fact they are the primary way for managers to track the course of operations but they cannot provide the full picture when something goes wrong. Drops in production or increases in quality control problems can be spotted quickly with ad hoc reporting or OLAP tools but we might not know why they occurred. Production could drop because of delayed shipments of essential components. Is this due to a marketwide shortage or a vendor-specific problem? Could this production drop have been anticipated and avoided if someone had been aware of market forecasts or had tracked this vendor's financial condition? Perhaps, but without automated tools, tracking so much textual information is too labor-intensive for most organizations to justify. By automatically gathering relevant information, reducing it to core facts and features, and making it accessible to decision makers, we can extend the scope of business intelligence about core operations.

Knowing Your Customer

Personalized marketing has virtually replaced mass marketing in some consumer-oriented industries because vendors can track key details about buying patterns, demographics, and personal interests, allowing marketers to craft messages targeted to individuals. Operating in the business-to-business world is a different story, but the same principles apply. If you have enough information about your business customers, they too can be targeted individually. A wealth of information about businesses is available from both public and private sources. Is your customer in a heavily regulated industry, and if so, what are the key problems in that industry? Are there pending changes in the regulatory environment that could create opportunities for or threats to your customers, and if so, how can your company work with them to realize potential gains or avoid possible costs? How is globalization affecting your customers? Are they all affected in the same way, or are there differences? Can your product or service line be adapted to target customers in different positions relative to the changing market? Learning the answers to these questions can require time-consuming research and analysis. Document warehousing will not change that fact, it will just make the process more efficient.

Strategic Management and the Macroenvironment

Strategic management is the art and science of directing companies in light of events both inside and outside the organization. In addition to understanding their own operations, strategic managers must understand the rest of the industry. For example, should a company try to be a low-cost producer or a best-cost producer? How can a company differentiate its product line? Should the focus be on the entire market or on a niche? Without understanding what others are doing, making decisions about these types of issues leads to unexpected results. Again, monitoring the activities of others in the industry can be time-intensive, but with text-oriented business intelligence platforms these operations can be performed more effectively.

Technology Assessments

Rapid changes in technology can lead to the obsolescence of some products or open opportunities for others. Companies can avoid unexpected challenges to their product lines by understanding their relative technology positions in an industry, and this requires detailed knowledge of competitors' technology. Fortunately, publicly available patent information is an excellent source of these details. Tracking current technologies, however, will not target potentially disruptive technologies that could fundamentally change an industry. For example, the Internet could radically change the office copier market by reducing the need for paper-based documents without challenging the copier market industry directly. Keeping abreast of innovation in any market is essential but not easily done without a rich textual component in your business intelligence platform.

Conclusions

We now have the ability to move beyond numeric transactional data to tap the business intelligence potential of text. Data warehouses—especially those built using dimensional modeling—provide easily queried and easily understood models of internal operations through the use of transactional data. Analyzing documents—from status memos, legal briefs, and marketing plans to news releases from regulatory agencies, patent abstracts, and competitor's press releases and advertising campaigns—can provide more comprehensive views of an organization's operations and the broader market.

Beginning with the next chapter, this book will outline one approach to integrating text into the practice of business intelligence. First, we must discuss the structure of language, in Chapter 2—as that provides the key to unlocking the meaning of text. Otherwise, it would be like trying to build a data warehouse without knowing basic mathematical operations such as summing and averaging.

CHAPTER 2

Understanding the Structure of Text: The Foundation of Text-Based Business Intelligence

Text that does not easily fit into a database table is typically considered unstructured, but this is far from the truth. Memos, news stories, project plans, and contracts are all richly structured—just not in the manner we are accustomed to in the world of databases. To see the structure of text, we must move beyond the rows and columns of relational structures and turn to the building blocks of natural language: words, phrases, and sentences. These building blocks are natural structures—that is, ones we are born to acquire and understand. And it does not matter what language we speak—whether it is English, Dutch, Chinese, Bengali, Malay, or Arabic, the building blocks are the same. With an understanding of how words, phrases, and sentences are structured, we can manipulate text and extract information far more effectively than if we rely upon simple string manipulation and pattern-matching techniques.

Our natural language structuring elements do not appear to extend much beyond the sentence level. Fortunately, artificial structures, such as markup languages, have been developed that provide higher-level structures. Texts that use extensible markup language (XML), standard generalized markup language (SGML), and similar conventions are called semistructured documents. For our purposes, we will consider both so-called unstructured texts and semistructured texts in our examination. With an understanding of how natural languages organize the semantic content of texts, we can dispel the myth of unstructured text and build applications that exploit the business intelligence potential of documents.

This chapter will cover a few distinct topics:

- The myth of unstructured texts
- Natural structures described by generative grammar
- Artificial structures used in semistructured texts

First, we will quickly demonstrate the fallacy of unstructured texts, while introducing the elements of language most frequently utilized in document warehousing and text mining. Then the chapter will move to a more in-depth look at the foundations of text mining, the structure of words and sentences as described by theories of generative grammar. Since our models of language are not sufficient to fully understand and analyze the wide range of texts that we encounter in our work, text mining also utilizes statistical techniques to improve performance. These techniques will be discussed as well. Moving from words and sentences into the realm of large texts—for example, business documents and Web pages—we will examine the use of markup languages, such as XML, to provide higher-level structures in semistructured texts. In the end, we will see that from single words to complex webs of hyperlinked documents, structures abound, if we only know how to look for them.

The Myth of Unstructured Texts

First of all, let's dispel the myth of unstructured texts. The term is usually applied to text that does not easily fit into an attribute or value form, such as tabular structures in a relational database. The text *1600 Pennsylvania Avenue* found in a column labeled Address is considered structured because it is a single logical unit with an easily discerned meaning. On the other hand, consider this sentence:

> The President of the United States lives at 1600 Pennsylvania Avenue.

This is generally considered unstructured because attributes—such as the meaning of words and the relationship between words—are not easily manipulated with conventional database or other programming tools. Nonetheless, we understand the sentence to mean the chief executive of the United States resides at the specified address. We are able to understand this sentence because the words are organized according to numerous natural language structures. By comparison,

> The Avenue President United of lives the States 1600 at Pennsylvania

is truly unstructured. We cannot figure out the meaning of this sentence without first unscrambling the words and putting them in proper order. Word order is one of several natural language structuring mechanisms that we will exploit in document warehousing and text mining. Other structuring mechanisms include rules for creating and grouping phrases together, ways of varying the meaning of words by adding prefixes and suffixes, and restrictions placed by verbs on the number and types of nouns that can appear in a sentence.

While many business documents are organized collections of grammatical sentences that comply with the previously cited structuring elements, we also deal with ungrammatical texts. E-mails are a perfect example. Letter writing in the past was frequently a formal process that commanded care on the part of the writer. E-mails are far less formal and often are more similar to verbal conversations, with unspoken assumptions, ambiguous references to other conversations or texts, misspelled words, quickly formulated abbreviations, and incomplete sentences. While text in e-mails and other informal documents is not grammatical at the sentence level, even these ungrammatical texts have enough structure at word and phrase levels to make them amenable to some text mining techniques.

In order to get the most out of text mining, we must first understand how natural language structures operate.

Natural Structures: It's All in Your Head

At the crudest level, natural languages are composed of words and rules for combining words. From a document warehouse and text mining perspective, our task is to develop systems that use language rules and word meanings to produce easily manipulated, categorized, and understood representations of texts. Linguistics, the study of language, and in particular an area called generative grammar, has already identified and classified many of the rules and principals that underlie language; so, we will start there in our investigation into the structure of text.

The Building Blocks of Language

The study of language can be grouped into five main areas:

- Morphology, the study of the structure and form of words
- Syntax, the study of how words and phrases form sentences
- Semantics, the meaning of words and statements
- Phonology, the study of sounds in language
- Pragmatics, the study of idiomatic phrases that cannot be analyzed with strict semantic analysis

We will concern ourselves primarily with morphology, syntax, and semantics. These three areas of linguistics are central to understanding how text mining is able to organize, manipulate, and utilize text. While phonology is of central importance to speech recognition and generation, it plays little role in the text mining focus of this work. Pragmatics is also not useful to text mining at the current time. It is perhaps the most challenging area of linguistics, and is especially important in understanding idiomatic phrases like *sleep tight, kick the bucket*, and *six feet under*. No amount of syntactic or semantic analysis would tell us what these phrases refer to. We simply know from convention and everyday usage the actual meaning of such phrases. Pragmatics may someday help us analyze e-mails and other informal texts more thoroughly but for now we will have to settle for other techniques to analyze those documents. Like phonology, pragmatics is beyond the scope of this book.

Morphology: Words, Words, and More Words

Like atoms composed of subatomic particles, words are made up of subparts called *stems*, *affixes*, and *inflectional elements*. Stems are the core-meaning-bearing elements of words and are often words themselves. For example, eatable has the stem *eat* and the suffix *able* and denotes something that is fit for human consumption. Many words are simply stems and have no affixes or inflectional elements, such as *dog*, *data*, and *document*. Using stems as a starting point, we can build more complex word structures by adding affixes.

The two types of affixes—prefixes and suffixes—vary the meaning of a stem. For example, the prefix *post* usually tells us that the thing described by the stem occurs after something else. For example, a postmortem examination is one that occurs after death. Some of the most common prefixes and suffixes include:

anti-	-ism
post-	-ity
pre-	-ive
un-	-ization
-able	-ment
-an	-ness
-ful	-ous
-hood	

The changes in meaning caused by prefixes or suffixes can be dramatic. *Dispute* implies the existence of a disagreement, while *indisputable* means that there cannot be any disagreement. This variation of *dispute* comes about because the prefix *in* negates the stem. Figure 2.1 shows the hierarchical structure of *indisputable.*

Inflectional elements, the third subpart of words after roots and affixes, change verbs and nouns. For example, inflections are used in English with verbs to distinguish past from present and with nouns to distinguish singular from plural. In some languages, they also show gender in nouns. Take a word as simple as *dogs*. This word is actually a complex symbol constructed of a root or stem, *dog*, and a plural inflection, *s*. As we can see here and in Figure 2.2, something as simple as a single letter can change the meaning of a statement.

This discussion of stems, affixes, and inflectional elements may appear academic at first, but morphological analysis has several important applications in text mining, including:

- Reducing complexity of analysis
- Reducing complexity of representing word meanings
- Supporting other text mining operations

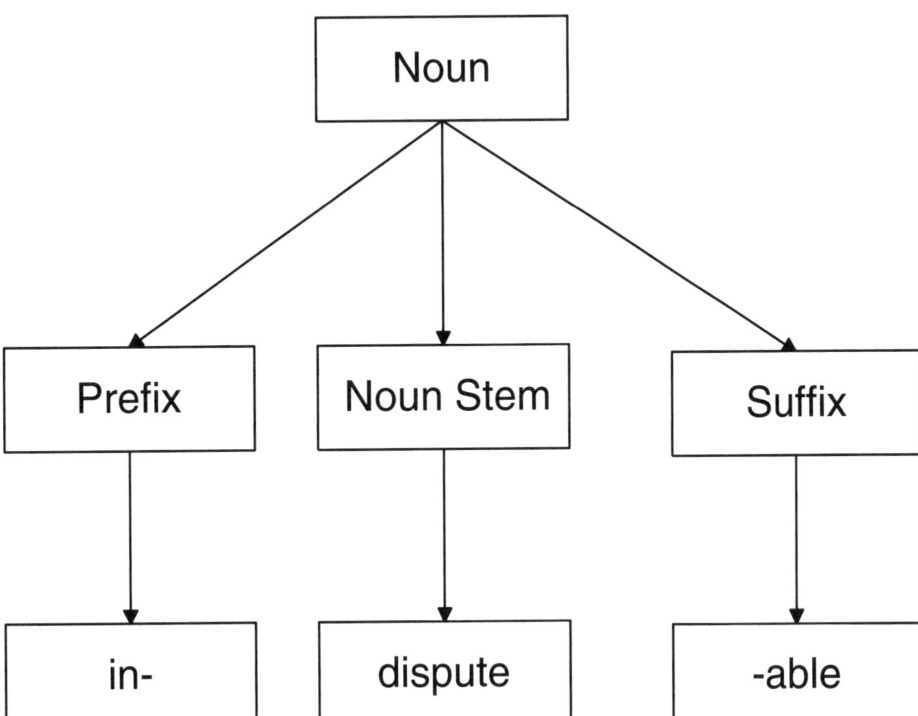

Figure 2.1 Multiple modifications of a word stem increase complexity, but meaning is still easily derived.

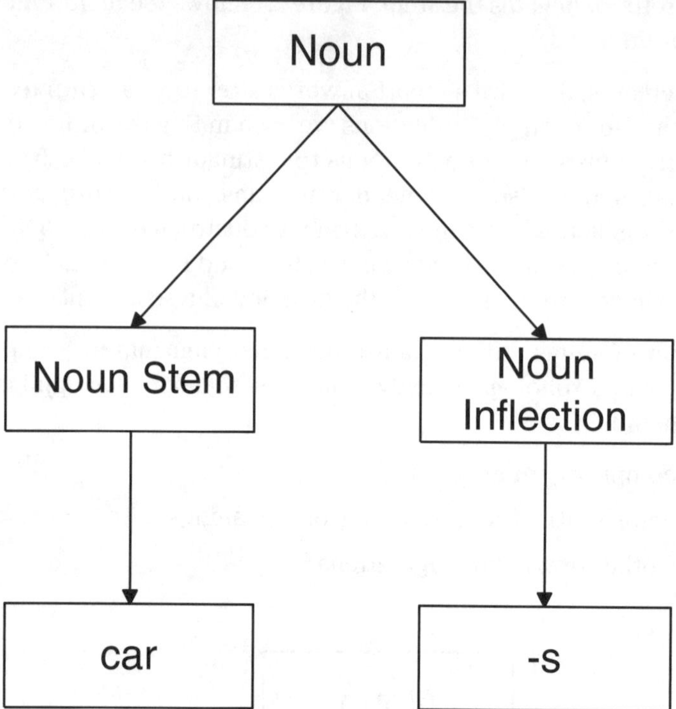

Figure 2.2 Word structure is used to vary meaning.

First, simple variations on words—such as the difference between singulars and plurals—can be eliminated to reduce the complexity of later analysis. This is useful because the number of times a word appears in a document is a good indicator of how important it is to expressing the topic of the document. For example, the words *eat*, *eats*, *eatable*, and *ate* can be considered a single word when counting the number of times each distinct word appears in a text. Counting words may sound like a crude method for assessing the meaning of a document, but it works surprisingly well with some text processing tasks, particularly for generating document summaries.

Second, morphology helps us implement components of text processing tools such as dictionaries, or lexicons. A lexicon is a data structure that stores words according to their meaning, their relationship to synonyms, and their placement in classification hierarchies. With an understanding of morphological analysis, lexicon builders can significantly reduce the number of distinct words that need to be stored. For instance, we no longer have to store the singular and plural form of a noun or the past, present, and participle form of a verb. If lexicons had to store all possible variations of every word, they would rapidly grow to unmanageable sizes.

Another benefit of morphological analysis is that it allows us to build feature extraction programs. During feature extraction, important concepts—especially persons, places, and organizations—are identified. This is a relatively straightforward task when white space, hyphens, and other indicators easily identify terms such as *Citibank*, *Oracle*, and *Congress*. Word phrases, however, are more difficult to determine. Human readers quickly recognize phrases such as *United Nations*, *International Business Machines*, *Food and Drug Administration*, and *London Financial Times* as naming single entities. Morphological analysis, which includes identifying parts of speech, allows text processing applications to correctly identify these noun phrases.

While morphology has practical implications for analyzing words, syntax performs the same role for phrases and sentences.

Syntax: Structuring Sentences

Just as atoms combine to form molecules, words combine to form sentences. The laws of chemistry describe how atoms combine to form molecules, while the rules of linguistics describe valid combinations of words. The resulting combinations can be complex structures like DNA molecules or the 1,300-word sentence in William Faulkner's *Absalom, Absalom!* The syntax of languages describes how words combine into phrases and phrases into sentences.

Phrase Structure

We saw in the last section how knowing the part of speech of a word can help identify larger structures such as noun phrases. It can also identify verb phrases, prepositional phrases, and adjectival phrases. These phrases can combine to form sentences or even more complex phrases. It is syntax that allows us to recognize and utilize phrase structures. Take, for example, the sentence:

> The Federal Reserve Board will curb inflation with higher interest rates.

Using a lexicon for information on parts of speech, a sentence parser (a program that analyzes the structure of sentences) can identify the noun phrase *The Federal Reserve Board*, the verb phrase *will curb*, and the prepositional phrase *with higher interest rates*. Using the rules of syntax, the parser can piece these phrases into the hierarchical structure found in Figure 2.3.

From the sentence structure diagram, we can see that the prepositional phrase is attached to the verb phrase, which tells us that the prepositional phrase modifies the verb phrase. In this case, the prepositional phrase indicates the instrument—interest rates—used to carry out the action of the verb, curbing inflation. Again, this may sound like more dry theory, but it does have practical application. While parsers are identifying phrase structure, they are simultaneously

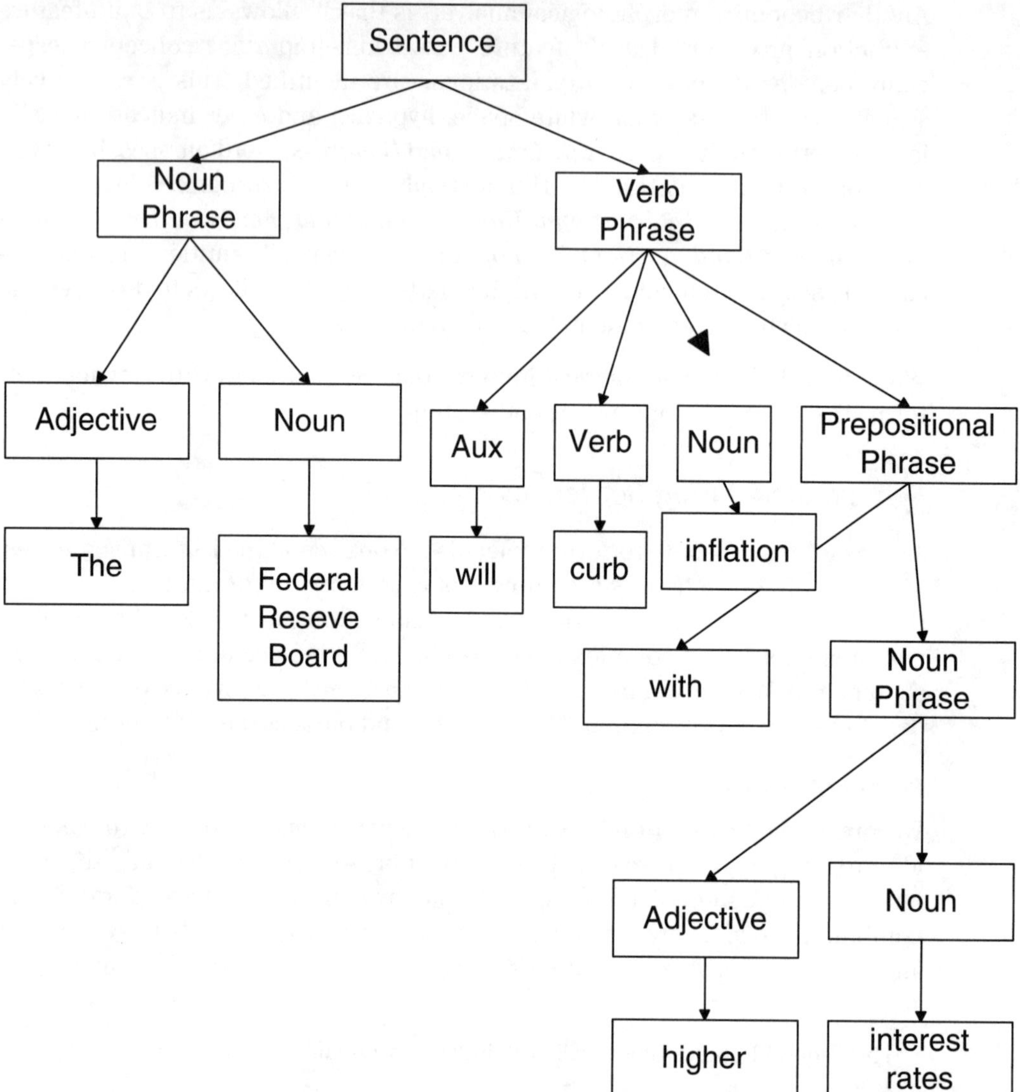

Figure 2.3 Sentences are constructed from phrases.

determining the relationship between phrases—which can be used in later analysis.

Case Assignment

The relationship between verbs and noun phrases is defined by an element of syntax called case assignment. The purpose of case assignment is to identify the role that nouns play in a sentence. In some ways, verbs in sentences act like stems in words. They anchor the sentence and limit the number and types of nouns that can be used in a sentence, just as stems limit the types of prefixes and suffixes that can be added to the base word. For example, if we know the meaning of the verb "to fine," then we know that a grammatical sentence with it will have an agent doing the fining, a recipient being fined, and optionally an amount of the fine as in,

> The Securities and Exchange Commission fined Alpha Beta Gamma Industries one million dollars.

Case assignment information can be stored in the lexicon and used to drive generalized pattern-matching applications. As we will see in the section on the limits of natural language processing, correctly processing case assignment is not always easy.

Using morphological information from the lexicon, syntax rules help us identify structures on the basis of the patterns of words and phrases. Similarly, syntactic analysis—and case assignment information in particular—provides the foundation for the next level of analysis: semantics.

Semantics: The Meaning of It All

Semantics is the study of meaning. In natural language processing, semantics covers both the meaning of individual words and the meaning of sentences and documents. From a text mining perspective, a critical problem is how to represent these meanings. Suitable representations must be space efficient and allow programs to draw conclusions quickly. Several approaches to the problem of representing meaning have been used in Artificial Intelligence (AI) applications—including semantic networks, deductive logic, and rule-based systems. While they all can prove useful in different situations, semantic networks provide the simplest method for capturing the meaning of texts.

Semantic networks use nodes and arcs to represent objects, events, and concepts, and the relations between them. Classification hierarchies, or taxonomies, mentioned earlier, are actually a limited type of semantic network that can represent *type-of* relationships, such as "a sparrow is a type of bird, and a bird is a type of animal." It can also represent *part-of* relationships, such as "Brazil is part of South America." These networks are useful for the classification and generalization of themes that is needed to perform searches by topics instead of just keywords. As Figure 2.4 shows, a program searching for articles on precious metals could be led to search for articles on gold and silver as well. Similarly, searches for articles on gold could return stories about precious metals if the user's search criteria indicated that related concepts should be included.

As a rule, generalized semantic networks with a rich vocabulary of relationships (shown in Figure 2.5) are difficult to build and work only in limited

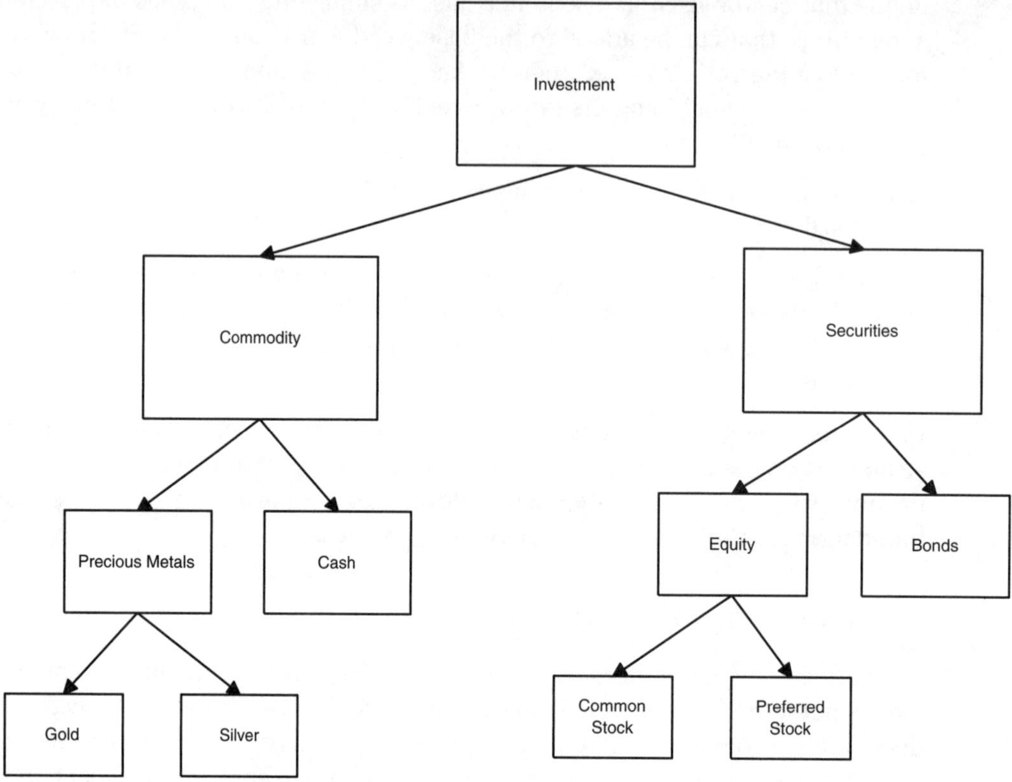

Figure 2.4 Semantic networks represent hierarchical relationships.

domains. While we will see more and more elaborate semantic representations in the future, for now, we must work with classification hierarchies and semantic networks with simple relationship schemes.

Text processing techniques, based on morphology, syntax, and semantics, are powerful mechanisms for extracting business intelligence information from documents. They allow us to find documents on the basis of topics as well as keywords. We can scan text for meaningful phrase patterns and extract key features and relationships, such as "Mary Smith, president and CEO of Alpha Beta Gamma Industries." Furthermore, documents can be stored in a way that allows for easy extraction of both individual elements and many of their relationships. Nevertheless, these text processing techniques are not infallible. In data warehousing we take for granted algorithms guaranteed to give us the correct answer. Counting, adding, averaging, and other aggregations always provide the correct answer when the algorithms are properly implemented. As we will see in the next section, with document warehousing we have to live with

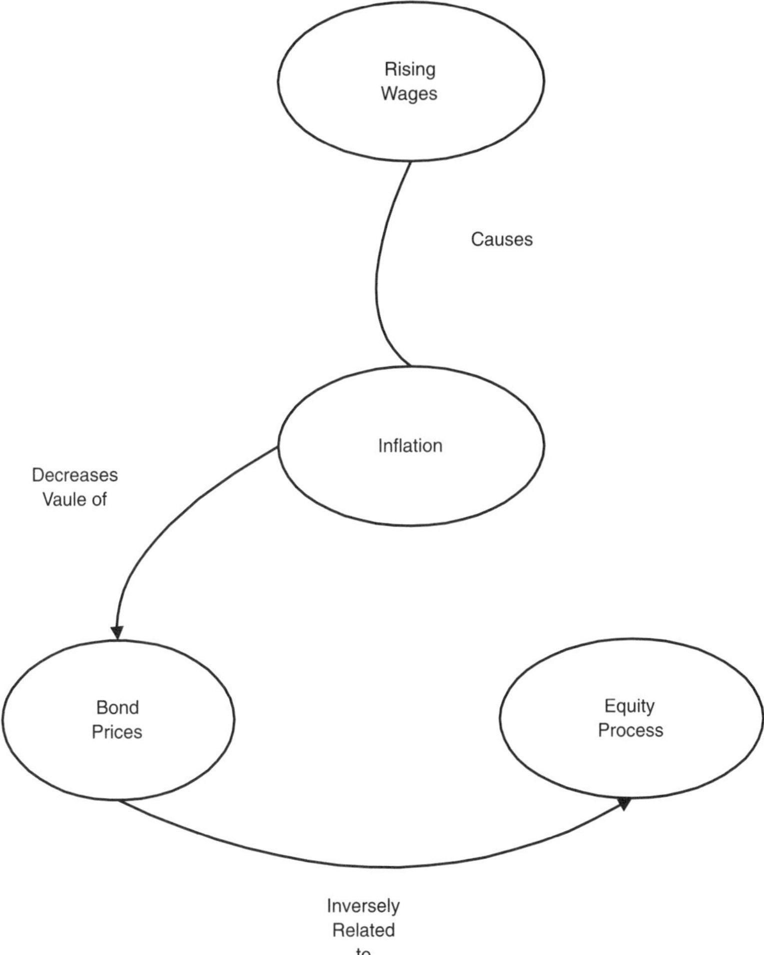

Figure 2.5 Semantic networks can model more complex relationships.

the fact that text mining techniques, even when properly implemented, are not guaranteed to provide complete and accurate answers to our queries.

Limits of Natural Language Processing

While work in natural language processing has yielded text processing techniques that are certainly useful, there are still shortcomings. The most significant problems are:

- Correctly identifying the role of noun phrases
- Representing abstract concepts

- Classifying synonyms
- Representing the sheer number of concepts needed to cover the domain of natural language discourse

Each of these problems increases the difficulty of different types of text mining. Correctly identifying the role of noun phrases and analyzing metaphors affects feature extraction programs. Representing abstract concepts and the extensive number of concepts needed influences how we construct lexicons and taxonomies. Classifying synonyms affects how well we can perform simple tasks, such as keyword searching.

Identifying the Role of Phrases

Some challenges appear relatively simple. Consider the sentence

> I saw the technician with the instrument.

This could mean the subject of the sentence saw the technician, who happened to be carrying an instrument. It could also mean the subject of the sentence used an instrument, such as a telescope, to see the technician. The two possible ways of understanding the sentence are shown in Figure 2.6.

We can choose to ignore the issue of understanding the role of prepositional phrases in these situations. While the problem will crop up in applications that depend upon complex feature extraction and pattern matching, carefully crafted patterns can minimize this kind of phrase attachment problem.

Representing Abstract Concepts

As we already noted in our discussion of semantic networks, some ideas, such as type-of relationships can be easily represented in a hierarchy. For example, a text mining application could show that cost-push inflation is a type of inflation that is in turn a type of economic phenomenon. Compositional hierarchies are also easily represented. The Environmental Protection Agency is part of the Executive branch of the U.S. government, and the Executive branch is part of the federal government. As phenomena become more intricate, however, semantic networks become less apt at drawing conclusions. Delving into areas such as investment risks in relation to political events or the effects of a new drug on the human body requires much more complex representational structures. As the complexity of the representation increases, so does the complexity of drawing deductions from represented facts.

Synonyms and Multiple Terms

Languages are filled with words about common objects that mean pretty much the same thing. A meal can be called a dinner or a repast. Recreation rooms are game rooms, playrooms, or family rooms. In specialized domains, the number of similar terms can grow rapidly when practitioners want to

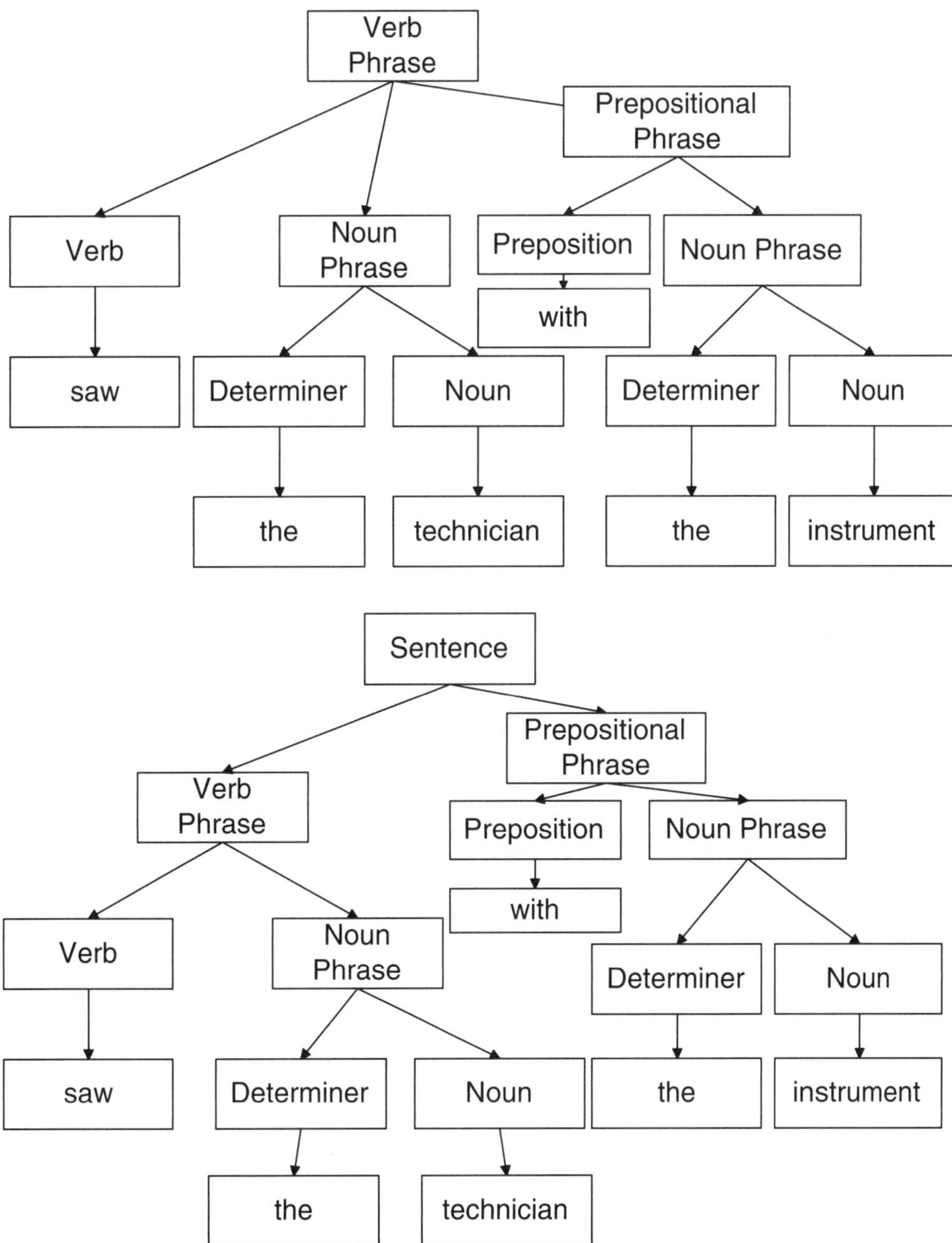

Figure 2.6 Phrase attachment is not always obvious.

make subtle distinctions. A physician might distinguish several types of rhinoviruses that the rest of us just call a cold. Chemists distinguish different types of acids, engineers differentiate among transmitters, economists define different forms of inflation, and the list goes on. As terms are created to make finer and finer distinctions, the problem of representing those distinctions becomes more challenging.

Representing Different Concepts

General news classification systems require tens of thousands of distinct concepts to even begin to approach a reasonable level of accuracy and precision. Take for example the Oracle interMedia Text tool. It uses a classification hierarchy with six top-level categories: science and technology, business and economics, government and military, social environment, geography, and abstract ideas and concepts. Each of these is further broken down into subareas, which in turn are further broken down for several more levels. Clearly the rapid growth in both the breadth and depth of classification hierarchies yields an enormous number of concepts, but even generalized tools like interMedia Text cannot represent every topic that interests us.

One approach to dealing with this problem is to create custom hierarchies for particular applications. A tool for mining scientific articles can skimp on general information about social environment or business and economics and add more terms specific to the scientific areas of interest. Another approach is to learn from example. In this case, programs can be used to analyze a sample set of documents and make a first pass at creating a hierarchy based upon terms found in the documents. At best, these applications provide a rough starting point from which human beings can refine and expand the hierarchy.

The four general problems we've discussed are the some of the significant challenges facing text mining. Some of these can be overcome by improving our natural-language-based techniques, while others require finding alternate ways of dealing with text. We will look at these two options next.

Working with Statistical Techniques

Some of the limits of natural language processing can be addressed by turning to statistical techniques. With this approach, we combine the results of symbolic linguistic analysis with simple statistical measures, such as the number of times different words appear near each other.

A common task in document warehousing is generating document summaries. One approach to this task is to create a semantic network representing the meaning of the text and then find the most significant concepts in the network. An alternate approach—one that avoids semantic networks and their limitations—uses word frequencies to find the most important ideas. As we noted earlier, counting the occurrences of stem words is a crude but effective measure of the importance of a word. Similarly, the importance of a sentence can be estimated on the basis of the importance of the words that make up the sentence. Once the sentences are ranked by importance, generating a summary is just a matter of extracting the most important sentences.

Another approach that combines linguistic with statistical techniques simplifies the construction of semantic networks. In conventional semantic networks, each node in the network represents a word or term, and the arcs correspond to the relationship between the nodes. A simpler approach—and one that lends itself to automatic generation—is to use arcs to represent the degree of correlation between nodes. In this case, correlation measures how frequently words appear near each other. For example, the terms *unit price* and *competition* may occur near each other quite frequently in a group of sales documents—so they would have a high level of correlation. Other terms, such as *Eastern Sales Region* and *plant capacity*, might occur together less frequently, and so would have a lower correlation. While this simple type of representation does not represent the full meaning of the text, it can be used to identify the importance that topics have to each other. Now, instead of just counting the number of times a word appears in text to determine its importance, an application can also take into account other terms it is related to and how strong those relationships are.

Generally, small, grammatical pieces of text, such as news stories, are amenable to analysis using linguistic-based approaches. Statistical techniques such as these work well with both medium-sized documents and large collections of small texts, such as newsgroup archives. They also work well with informal texts such as e-mails. Larger collections of informal texts lend themselves to a combination of linguistic and statistical techniques. As we shall see throughout the course of this book, no one technique will solve all of our problems. Figure 2.7 shows a rough correlation between the effectiveness of different techniques and the size of the text with which we are working. .

Like a piece of plastic stretched too far, even the combination of natural language and statistical techniques can eventually lose its effectiveness when applied to long, complex texts. As documents increase in size and complexity, we need to introduce elements called macrostructures that organize large sections of text.

Macrostructures: Introducing Artificial Structures in Documents

In order to understand the importance of macrostructures, we must first look at the two main problems encountered when analyzing long documents. First, the techniques we have discussed so far treat all parts of a document equally.

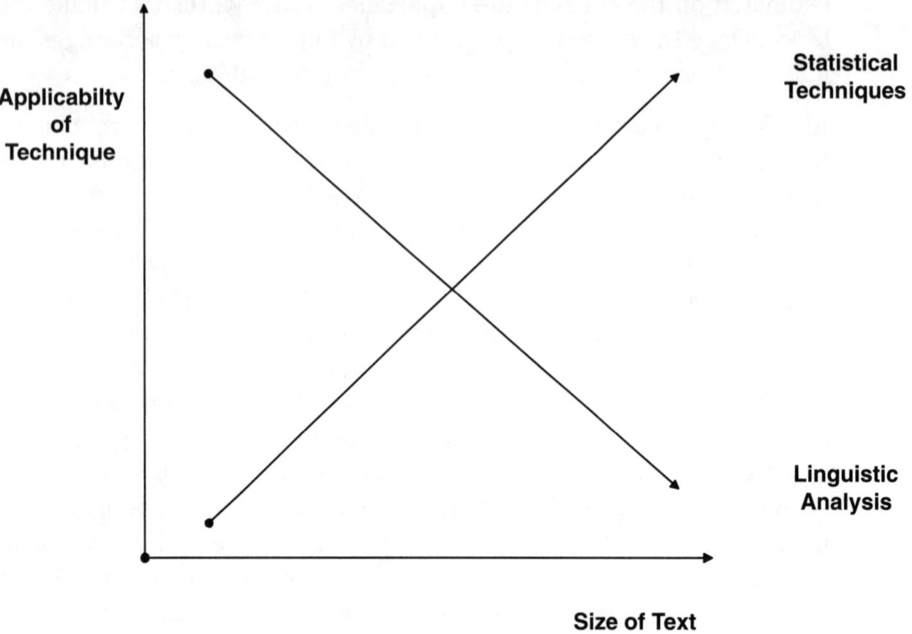

Figure 2.7 Both symbolic and statistical natural language processing (NLP) techniques work well, but for different types of analysis.

For example, a fifty-page business plan may have sections on marketing, finance, and administration. Lets say thirty pages of the document outline the current market, the company's marketing approach, and a description of competition in the market. Another fifteen pages are spent describing the organizational structure and other administrative issues. The final five pages discuss financing. If we create a summary using sentences with the most frequently occurring words, it will include significantly more information about marketing than about finance. Unfortunately, in many real-world applications, some parts of documents are more important than others, regardless of their length. In this case, the finance section may be critical, but it is underrepresented in our summary because it was described with fewer words than the other sections.

Second, the techniques do not take advantage of the fact that many organizations produce the same types of documents over and over again. Examples of commonly used documents include status memos and financial reports. While natural language techniques can recognize terms such *budget status*, and statistical analysis can calculate correlations between terms, neither technique can reliably identify topical sections of a document, such as the paragraphs that describe the budget status. A business unit manager reading these memos may be most interested in the budget status, while the customer's account representative is more likely to track the scheduled completion date. Document warehousing applications should be similarly tuned to focus on key elements of these documents.

Unlike the language structures used at the microlevel, which occur naturally in language, the macrolevel structures we will use have been created explicitly to solve the problems of structuring large, complex sets of data and text.

Hierarchical Conventions from Words to Documents

Markup languages generally serve two purposes—they define structures and describe formatting. For example, XML is widely used for data exchange because it provides a flexible and easily parsed structure for arbitrarily complex data structures. The bulk of Hypertext Markup Language (HTML) tags, on the other hand, support hypertext formatting. Our primary concern is with using markup languages for structure. Markup languages lead to two distinct types of structures: semistructured text and hypertext.

Semistructured texts use markup languages to define logical structures within a document. Unlike natural languages that have predefined elements, such as nouns, adjectives, and verb phrases, markup languages, such as XML and SGML, allow users to define the structuring elements of a document. For example, we could create a standard marketing status report in XML. Here is a sample of such a marketing status report:

```
<?xml version="1.0"?>
 <MarketingStatus>
   <ReportDate>April 10, 2001</ReportDate>
   <MarketingPeriod> Q1, 2001</MarketingPeriod>
   <Region>Northeast</Region>
   <Status>
     This quarter has seen a significant shift in marketing efforts
     away from . . .
   </Status>
   <MarketCondition>
     The market for our products in the Northeast is undergoing
     significant change with the introduction of alternate
     technologies . . .
   </MarketCondition>
   <MarketCondition>
     Another factor effecting the region is . . .
   </MarketCondition>
   <CompetitiveActivity>
     Our main competitor has launched a campaign targeted at . . .
   </CompetitiveActivity>
 </MarketingStatus>
```

In this semistructured text, a top-level structure called Marketing Status is composed of six subordinate structures: report date, marketing period, region, status, market conditions, and competitive activity. For now, the most important thing to note about this type of structuring is that it provides a clear, well-defined structure for topical segments of the document. These allow us to efficiently manipulate each section. Using the previous example, an application can easily retrieve all market condition sections from several documents. Since the beginning and end of these logical sections are clearly marked with start and end tags, there is no need to analyze the content of the text to determine which paragraphs discuss market conditions.

While these markup tags structure single documents, hypertext links provide the means to structure collections of documents. In addition to providing semistructured texts, markup languages allow for the development of hypertext. Hypertext documents contain links to other documents, which in turn may contain links to other texts, and so on. The result is an interconnected network of texts. Hypertext links extend the intradocument structures in that they provide a means for extending structures beyond a single document to a collection of documents. This interdocument structure provides yet another means of guiding the reader, whether the reader is a human being or a machine, to relevant information.

We can now turn our attention to specific markup languages in order to see how semistructured and hypertext documents are organized, so that we can then exploit that organization for text mining and document warehousing purposes.

The Jewel in the Crown: Markup Languages for Arbitrary Structure

SGML and XML, two effective markup languages, offer both flexibility and expressive power and are important for creating semistructured and hypertext documents.

SGML—Extreme Markup Language

SGML has evolved for over thirty years and is the most complex and most powerful markup language in general use today. The goal of SGML is to provide a language for describing the structure of documents so that they may be processed by applications. Today, governments and large corporations manage and structure documents with SGML because the language has realized its design goals so well. There is, however, a price to be paid. SGML is complex and difficult to learn and implement. The benefits of SGML are often outweighed by the cost of using the markup language. In response to this problem, the simpler but still powerful XML has been created.

XML—The People's Choice

XML has been readily accepted by many because of its flexibility and ease of use. We briefly touched on an XML example with the standardized marketing report earlier in this chapter. That example showed how XML could be used to define distinct areas of interest or structure within a document. While we do not need to be XML experts for document warehousing, we do need to understand the basic building blocks of XML and some rules for putting those blocks together.

The building blocks of XML are tags and elements. Tags are markers such as <B>, <I>, and </Title>. These tags are used to mark the beginning and end of elements. For example,

```
<Title>An Introduction to Competitive Analysis for Managers</Title>
```

Elements can be nested within other elements to create more elaborate structures. For example, we could construct a budget status element for our project memo.

```
<Budget Status>
     <Description>
           During the past month . . .
     </Description>
     <Starting Budget>
           $1,000,000
     </Starting Budget>
     <Additional Funds>
          <Additional Amount>
               $175,000
           </Additional Amount>
          <Date Approved>October 30, 2000</Date Approved>
          <Justification>
               Changes in scope have led to several . . .
          . . .</Justification>
     </Additional Funds>
     <Funds Expended to Date>
           $765,000
     </Funds Expended to Date>
     <Estimated Total Expenditure>
           $1,170,000
     </Estimated Total Expenditure>
</Budget Status>
```

As Figure 2.8 shows, XML documents are tree data structures that can grow to arbitrary depth and breadth. By defining increasingly complex elements, we

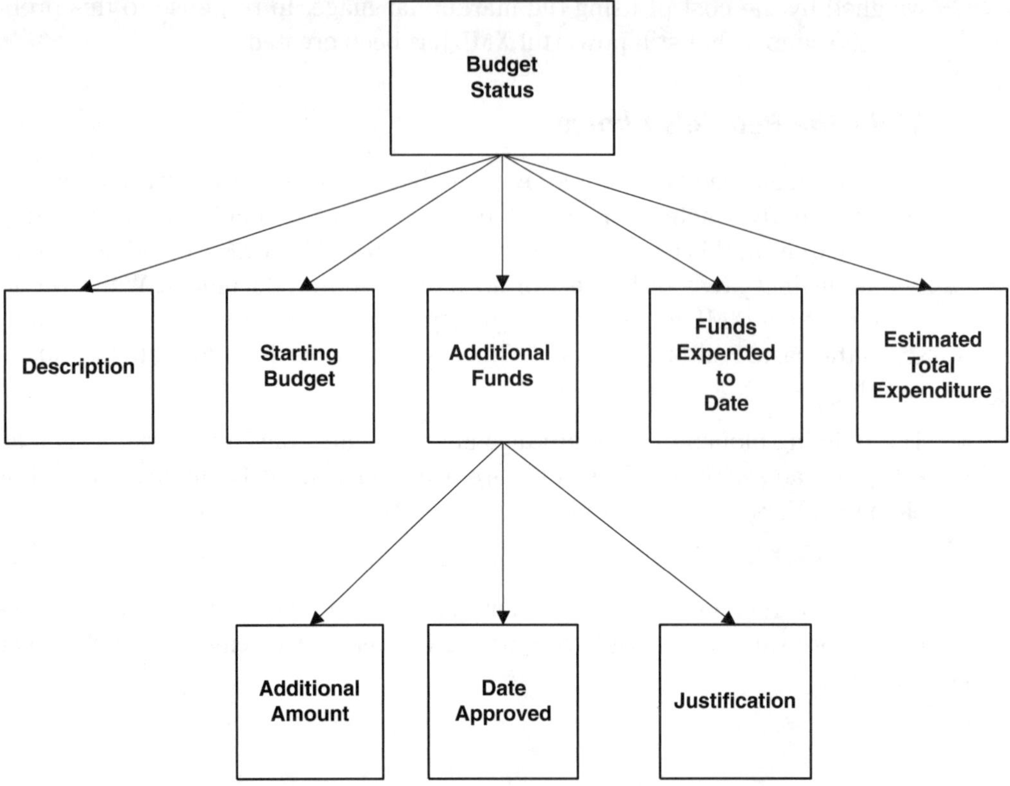

Figure 2.8 A tree representation of an XML fragment.

can create more and more elaborate structuring mechanisms for documents. With that structuring, we provide the foundation upon which to build document-processing applications.

XML does not stop at the boundaries of a single document. We will now turn our attention to XML features for interdocument structures. The two most important features are the XPointer and XML Linking specifications.

XPointer

The XPointer construct is a means of addressing fragments within an XML document, such as the Budget Status section or all the Additional Funding sections of a status report.

The specification describes four types of location terms for addressing elements: *absolute*, *relative*, *spanning*, and *string*. The absolute term describes a specific point in an XML tree without reference to any other point in the tree. The *Root* term is an absolute address and specifies the top level of a document.

Unlike absolute location terms, relative terms describe a node in the XML tree using a starting node and a navigation term such as *child*, *parent*, *ancestor*, *descendent*, *following*, or *preceding*. A spanning location term identifies a subsection of a tree beginning at a starting location term and ending at another location term. The following term selects the second through fourth children below the root of the current tree.

```
root().span(child(2),child(4))
```

The string attribute behaves much like string location functions in common procedural programming languages. Users can specify search strings and substrings within strings as a means of precisely identifying a location.

The Xpointer structure works like a surgical scalpel allowing us to extract with precision fragments of text from larger documents. Finding those documents in the first place is made easier with XML Linking.

XML Linking

XML Linking expands upon the simple linking structure provided in HTML to include several new features:

- Bidirectional linking
- Links that annotate read-only documents
- Additional attributes and descriptive roles for links

Each of these provides an additional structural foundation upon which we can build our text mining operations.

Bidirectional linking is more than a "Back" button on a browser. The link itself actually contains the information identifying the two linked documents. This is important for connectivity analysis, a text mining technique that assesses the importance of a document on the basis of the number of other documents that point to it.

To embed a link in an HTML document, you must have write access to the HTML file. XML Linking avoids this problem by decoupling links from documents. Now, instead of managing links spread out through every document in a collection, links can be managed in a centralized database. One application of this is document annotation. Within the document warehouse, we often need to find a set of documents of interest to a reader. These documents may not have links to each other but we could automatically generate links between them to allow the reader to more easily navigate around these texts.

Another significant advance in XML Linking is the ability to add semantic information to a link. In HTML a link is just a pointer to another resource. The link could be to a subsection of the same logical document, to a related document in another domain, or to something only tangentially related to the contents of the first document. From a corporate home page, we may have links to sections within the company, such as human resources, manufacturing, suppliers, and investor relations. If we are searching for documents on manufacturing, we can use semantic information to limit our search and avoid wasting time analyzing investor relations or other irrelevant pages that just happen to share a common starting point.

It Isn't So Linear after All: Hypertext

So far we have considered text structures primarily from the perspective of a single document. As mentioned earlier, hypertext links build more complex structures by joining two or more documents. HTML's HREF is probably the most popular hypertext link, although the power of XML Linking will fuel its adoption in the near future. Even with HREF's limited unidirectional link we can create elaborately complex document collections.

These links' importance increases when we can analyze groups of links to discover larger structural patterns between documents. These patterns are the highest-level structure we will examine. Although many different patterns of links can occur among hypertext documents, we will only look into two: hub and authority patterns.

Hubs are documents that link to many other documents. Authorities are documents that are pointed to by other documents. Figure 2.9 depicts examples of hub and authority documents.

A document cannot be said to be a hub or an authority in the same definitive way that a word can be classified as a noun or a verb. It is better to think of these as relative terms, with some documents being more of a hub or more of an authority than others. Usually, a numeric score is used to measure the degree to which a Web page is a hub or an authority. Web sites discussing data warehousing often have links to the Data Warehousing Institute home page (www.dw-institute.com); so the Institute's home page would have a relatively high authority score. Similarly, search engines, such as Yahoo!, will have high hub scores by virtue of the many sites to which they link.

Hub and authority scores can be used with other techniques, such as keyword searches, to improve document searches. For example, a simple search algorithm could count the number of times a word, or its stem, appears in a document and rank documents according to that score. A more useful approach is to combine that word count with the document's authority score. If a document has a high authority score, then, as a general rule, we can assume that others find the site useful, and the ranking of the document should be increased. Similarly, if the authority score is low, then others do not recognize this document as valuable, and the relative importance of this document in the search should

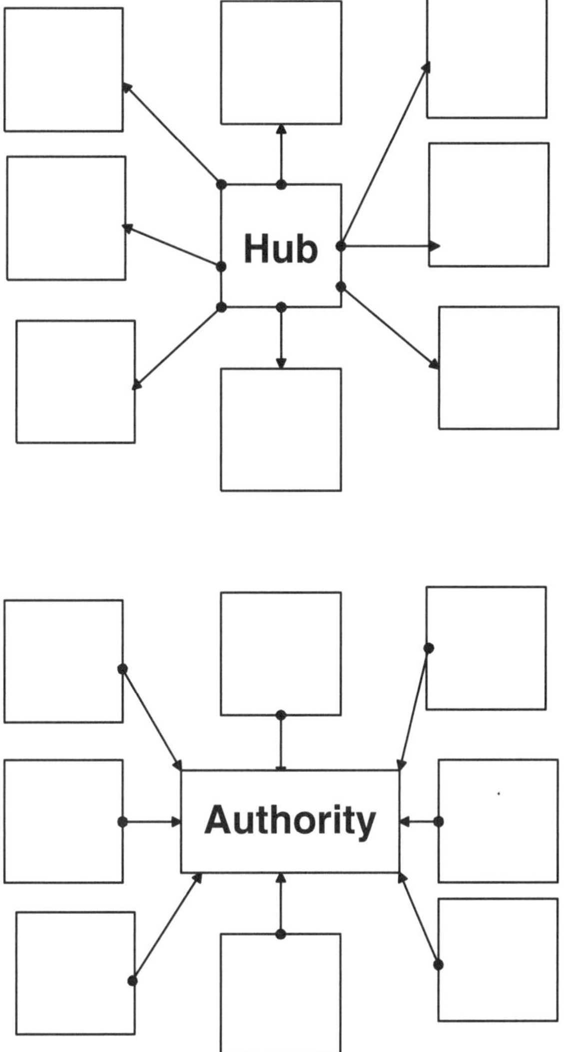

Figure 2.9 Hub and authority documents provide yet another structure we can exploit.

be reduced. The Google search engine (www.google.com) uses authority and hub scores to refine its searches in this way.

Macrostructures that define structures within a document and between documents provide more opportunities for analyzing relationships between documents. Like the natural structures that help us understand the relationship between words and phrases, artificial structures help us understand the relationship between documents and document components.

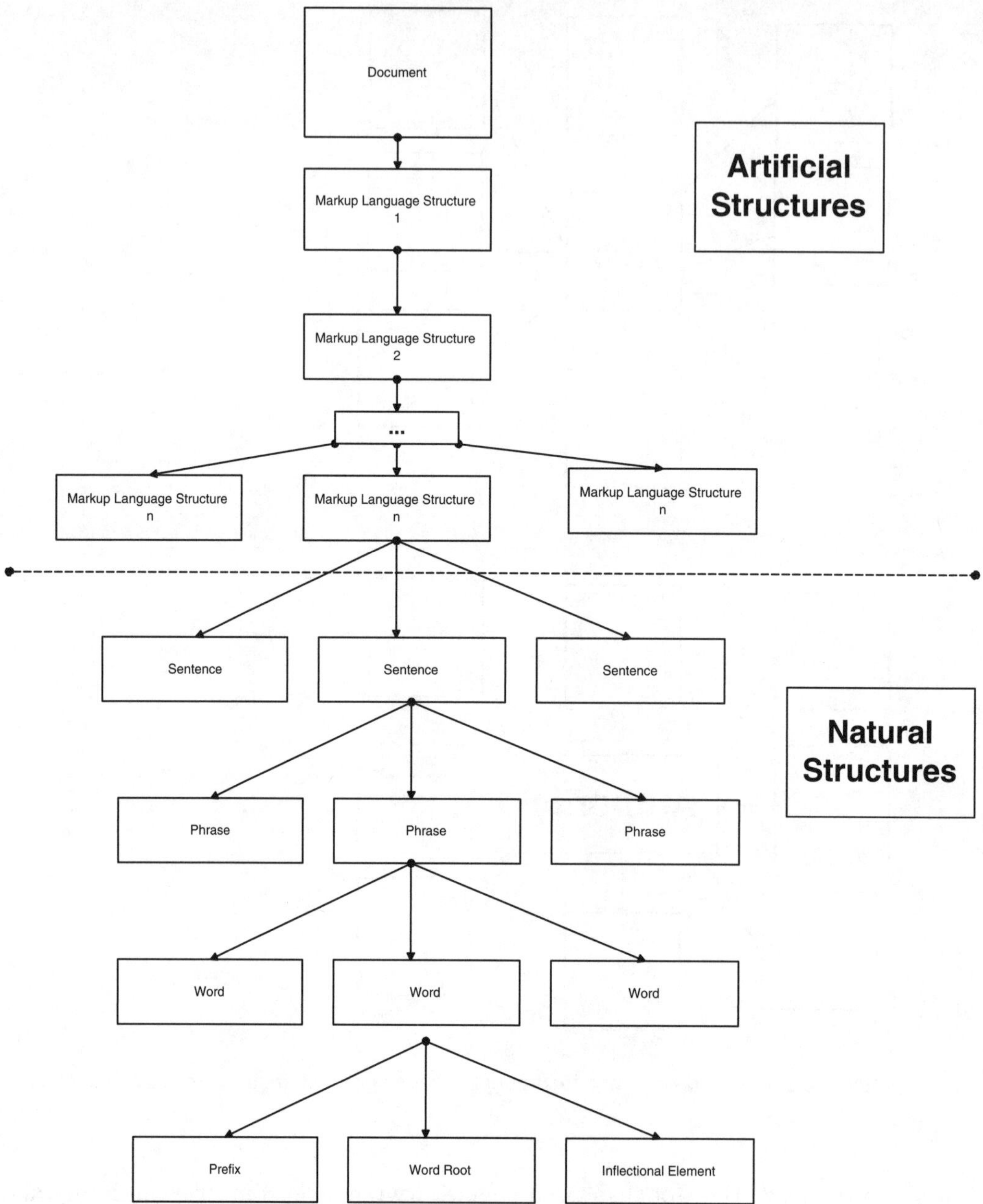

Figure 2.10 Natural and artificial structures used in document warehousing.

Conclusions

From a relational database perspective, text appears unstructured. However, from other vantage points, the structure-rich character of text should now be apparent. As Figure 2.10 shows, we have many types of structures at our disposal for document warehousing and text mining.

Functional models of the structure of language have been developed over the past forty years that illuminate the common ground all languages share, and this is a great asset for text miners. The structures of language give us our first hooks into text processing and understanding. Where natural language structures leave off, artificial structures begin. Unlike natural language structures, these artificial structures are consciously created artifacts with the sole purpose of helping us use, manage, and understand complex texts. Building upon this foundation, we can move on to the main task at hand: creating business intelligence resources and applications that unlock the business intelligence value of documents.

CHAPTER 3

Exploiting the Structure of Text

We saw in the last chapter that even seemingly unstructured texts are organized according to rules and patterns that give us a starting point for analyzing documents. How can we apply these sometimes esoteric principles to daily business problems? That particular question will be answered in this chapter by addressing four more specific questions:

- How do business intelligence analysts work, or wish to work, with text?
- What text analysis techniques support these operations?
- How will text be used with a data warehouse?
- How do we handle different user interests?

The first section of this chapter covers text-oriented business intelligence operations, such as researching a business problem or slumping sales. The second section begins our discussion of text mining techniques, which will be developed in Part 3 of the book. After discussing basic text mining operations, we will look at tying text into data warehouse operations. Finally, we will briefly discuss a particularly challenging issue—modeling user interests. The issues we raise in this chapter are fundamental to document warehousing and text mining, and the remainder of this book will dig into the details of these topics, which we can only begin to introduce here. Chapters 11 and 13 in particular will examine how these operations are implemented.

Text-Oriented Business Intelligence Operations

As we delve into the realm of text-oriented business intelligence (BI), we will quickly see two parallels with more traditional numeric business intelligence operations. First, in both cases we are dealing with large quantities of information. Since 80 percent of all business information is textual, document warehouses will have to deal with massive amounts of raw data.

Second, users need to quickly navigate these extensive information stores to find targeted subsets of information that address particularly pressing questions. The practice of business intelligence is driven by specific questions, such as:

- What were the sales margins for audio products in the eastern region in the last two quarters?
- What patents has our main competitor applied for this year?
- What has the Food and Drug Administration said about the use of linezolid and related drugs for blood infections?
- What are the main points of the latest Agriculture Department crop report?

These questions demand specific, succinct answers.

Third, both types of BI operations depend upon multiple sources of information. Data warehouses are populated with information from point-of-sale systems, production control applications, financial systems, and enterprise resource planning (ERP) systems. Document warehouses are populated with text from internal files, news sources, conference proceedings, market research reports, industry researchers, regulatory agencies, and other government agencies, to name just a handful of sources.

Another obvious parallel is that users' interests constantly change. A top-priority topic one week may be of no interest to an analyst the following week. So, in addition to dealing with large quantities of information from many different sources, designers and architects must support a wide range of subject areas. Data warehouse practitioners have successfully addressed these issues. Fortunately, document warehousing practitioners have effective methods at their disposal as well.

In this chapter, we will examine five methods for managing the complexity of textual information while meeting the needs of business intelligence analysts:

- Summarizing documents
- Classifying and routing documents to interested readers
- Answering questions
- Searching by topic and theme
- Searching by example

For each method, we will examine the objectives of the operation, examples of its use, and an assessment of its effectiveness.

Anarchy, Anarchy! Show Me a Greater Evil!

Now, things are not as bad for document warehousing and text mining as they were for the legendary Greek king who worried so much about anarchy, but we do have our shortcomings in this field. The most important is that we do not have a standard language like SQL for implementing text analysis operations. To date, most applications use proprietary terminology and product-specific tools for manipulating text repositories. So unlike examples of data warehousing operations that can be specified in standard SQL, the document warehouse operations described here sometimes use product-specific syntax. This is not meant to favor one tool over another. If a choice is made between proprietary syntaxes or tools, it is because one may be simpler or clearer for the particular example. Standards will certainly emerge in document warehousing and text mining, but in the meantime we will have to live with a little freewheeling anarchy.

Summarizing Documents

By some accounts, the meaning of most documents can be conveyed using only about 20 percent of the text actually used. This does not say much for writers and their craft, but it is good news for readers. One of our goals in business intelligence is to minimize the amount of data or text that users must examine before finding the information they need. In the case of summarizing, reducing the complexity and length of a document minimizes the text delivered to a reader.

Consider the news described in the 515-word press release from the Joint Economic Committee of the United States, entitled "Federal Reserve Policy Facilitated by Market Price Indicators According to New JEC Study" (www.house.gov/jec/press/2000/10-18-0.htm). It discusses the different types of measures the Federal Reserve Board could use as a basis for policy decisions, including the labor market, output indicators, and market price indicators. One automatically generated summary using about 100 words conveys the gist of the main story.

> According to the study, market price indicators—commodity prices, bond yields, and the value of the dollar—better reflect future changes in prices than do labor market or output measures. The new study, *The Performance of Current Monetary Policy Indicators*, analyzes the effectiveness of alternative monetary policy indicators under a regime of informal inflation targeting, as successfully practiced by the

> Federal Reserve under Chairman Greenspan. The Fed under Greenspan has demonstrated that its policy of informal inflation targeting can reduce inflation, interest rates, and unemployment all at the same time.

Several points should be noted when assessing the effectiveness of automatic summarization. First, the human written narrative flows more smoothly. Although news story summaries tend to read reasonably, other documents, such as marketing reports, regulatory findings, and speeches do not always have a logical flow. Consider the speech by Federal Reserve Board Governor Laurence Meyer entitled "The Challenges of Global Financial Institution Supervision" (www.federalreserve.gov/boarddocs/speeches/2000/20000531.htm). The main theme of the text addresses the difficulty in regulating the risk management practices of large, complex banking organizations. The first few sentences of the summary are:

> I refer, of course, to the development, use, and application of internal credit-risk-rating systems by banks. No less critical is the tying of risk weights to internal risk classifications in such a way as to minimize inconsistencies of capital treatment among banks that have similar risks. Today, our capital regulation, with its one-size-fits-all risk weight for loans, encourages banks to withdraw from low-risk credit markets, or to arbitrage, when regulatory capital requirements exceed levels consistent with an activity's underlying economic risk.

The summary certainly captures the main point of the speech, but the transitions between sentences are awkward and make reference to statements that are not even in the summary itself.

Another common problem is that the important points of an argument, while captured in the summary, appear in the wrong order. For example, we could see a sentence beginning with "Next, the facts also show …" followed by a sentence that leads with "Notice first that …" Regardless of poorly placed sentences and awkward transitions, automatic summarization is an effective tool for controlling the volume of text that a reader must examine before finding needed information.

Furthermore, using the 20 percent heuristic for generating summaries can still lead to long documents. Smaller percentages can be used for very long documents, but anything less than 5 percent will provide poor results.

Automatic summarization is an effective means of reducing the amount of text a reader must analyze to gather relevant information, thus meeting one of our key objectives. Another reduction method is to filter documents before they are delivered to users.

Classifying and Routing Documents

Classifying documents and routing them only to interested readers is a most effective way to minimize the amount of text that we must deal with. We use this technique all the time. When we open our e-mail in boxes, many of us scan the From and Subject attributes to determine what we will read and how we will prioritize it. Most e-mail applications support filters that allow us to automatically screen messages by using keyword and phrase scanning. Document classification allows us to apply similar, but more sophisticated principals to text-oriented decision support.

When readers are interested in a specific set of topics for extended periods of time, document classification will prove useful. Agricultural commodity brokers may want to scan news stories on wheat futures, weather projections, tariffs, and other factors that affect the price of grains. Securities analysts need to stay abreast of SEC filings, corporate press releases, market analysis, and a range of industry-specific publications. Identifying documents that will be of interest to some readers but not others is the key benefit of document classification. The operation has three main components: a classification application, a means of storing user profiles, and a mechanism for updating those profiles.

Classification applications process texts and assign predefined labels to them. For example, the speech by the Federal Reserve Board Governor previously cited could be classified in several different categories:

- Financial services
- Economic risk
- Global finance
- Government regulation

Similarly, the congressional report could be classified with terms such as:

- Monetary policy
- Equity markets
- Market indicators
- Government regulation

Classifying some documents is relatively straightforward. News stories, for example, can be effectively classified with a small number of labels. The Dow Jones news service uses 350 terms in seven categories: industry, market, sector, product, government agency, subject, and region. This categorization works well with news stories but larger, more specific sets of classification terms are necessary for other types of documents.

A thesaurus or subject hierarchy, also called a taxonomy or ontology, is a common component of document classification systems. Classification systems must know that wheat is a type of grain, a tariff is a kind of tax, Microsoft is in the software business, and thousands of other facts. The effectiveness of these programs is limited, in part, by the breadth and specificity of the underlying subject hierarchy or thesaurus. The terms and phrases defined in a subject hierarchy are, in effect, the building blocks for our classification rules. The more terms we have at our disposal, the more tightly we can refine our selection criteria.

Classification applications must balance the need to improve precision with the need to not sacrifice recall. Precision, the ability to correctly classify a document, requires that classification criteria be selective enough to not label texts with categories that really do not apply. For example, a document with frequent references to *interest rates* could be about inflation or the home real estate market, and additional criteria are needed to distinguish between the two. At the same time, we risk making the selection criteria so narrow that we miss documents that should be classified in a particular way, but are not because they are missing a particular keyword or phrase.

Also, in addition to longstanding interests, ad hoc queries will need to be addressed in document warehouse and text analysis applications.

Answering Questions

Sometimes we do not need an entire collection of documents summarized, categorized, thematically indexed, and delivered to our cyberdoorstep; we just need a simple answer.

- What is the capital of Denmark?
- When will Alpha Industries make an initial public offering?
- Where are Malaysia's industrial centers?
- Who is the chief technical officer at Beta Systems?
- How do I connect a scanner to my laptop?

The first four questions can be answered with short, specific answers. The answer to questions such as these can often be found by extracting noun phrases from documents that contain keywords used in the question. For example, a document describing northern European countries might have *Copenhagen* near the words *Denmark* and *capital*, making Copenhagen a possible answer to the first question in the examples above. If the document also identifies countries that border on Denmark, the same program might include *Germany* and *Norway* in a list of possible answers because the application does not fully understand the semantics of the text. Even without a full understanding of a text, question-answering programs can improve performance with some semantic analysis. A relatively easily implemented technique is to identify the type of object we are looking for in an answer. For example, capitals of countries and industrial centers are cities, chief technical officers are persons, and initial public offerings are scheduled for specific dates. Some applications, such as InPlainWords from IaskWeb (www.iaskweb.com), use semantic and syntactic analysis along with other techniques to find specific answers to questions.

Process-oriented questions such as, "How do I connect a scanner to my laptop?" require more elaborate answers. In general, question-answering applications need to return entire documents, or at least summaries, to answer process-specific questions. Since multiple steps, conditional actions, and background information may be required, a simple noun phrase extraction approach will not suffice. Like questions that require short answers, process-oriented questions are often answered with a set of possible answers, and the reader is left to choose among them.

In some cases, questions cannot be answered, so alternate questions are offered by the question-answering system. This is similar to a student not knowing the answer to a test question and offering the answer to another question he does know the answer to—not very effective, but it might help. For example, when posed the question "How do I connect a scanner to my laptop?" the AskJeeves search engine (www.askjeeves.com) could not answer it, but did offer to answer the following:

- How do I get advice on cheap laptops?
- How do I decide between a laptop and a desktop?
- How do I install a wireless communications card on a laptop?
- What are the three types of laptop displays?
- Where can I buy PC notebooks?
- Where can I buy and sell portable computers via online auctions?

State-of-the-art question-answering systems are effective in several areas, such as Web navigation and simple fact gathering. More elaborate questions, such as inquiries about tax laws, investment practices, and political risk assessment, can be addressed by question-answering systems, but users must be aware that these systems do not support elaborate knowledge representation schemes with complex models of these domains. These are simply text processing tools using linguistic rules of thumb for extracting noun phrases and other features from documents, and matching those features with keywords and phrases supplied by user's questions.

When we are looking for a broad base of information and not just a targeted answer, then searching and browsing by topic can improve results over question answering.

Searching and Browsing by Topic and Theme

Searching by topic and theme entails describing the concept we are interested in, not just specifying a few keywords. A closely related variation on searching by topic is browsing using a subject hierarchy.

First, we will look into ad hoc querying by topic, and then we will look at a common example of browsing by topic.

Ad Hoc Searching with Topics

The precision of searches improves significantly when we incorporate support for topical queries. Keyword searches are basically string-matching operations. While this is fine in many situations, the problem of polysemy, or words having multiple meanings, can significantly reduce a search's precision. The word *fly* can refer to a common insect, a zipper, or the act of flying. *Chest* may mean a body part or a piece of furniture. A keyword search engine is just as likely to return documents on one of these topics as the others. If we indicate that we are interested in *fly* as it relates to insects, clothing, or air travel, then we will significantly reduce the number of documents returned by a query and thus improve precision.

Recall can also be improved with topical searches by generalizing and expanding keyword searches to include synonyms. Since there are many ways to say the same thing, searching for one or two words can miss any number of documents that are of interest to the reader. A search for documents on debt should include documents about debt, liability, financial commitment, bills, charges, and accounts receivable and arrears, to ensure that most relevant documents are returned. Automatically expanding keyword searches to include synonyms such as these is a common way to implement topical searches.

For example, Oracle interMedia Text supports the SYN operator (short for synonym), which expands a query to include all synonyms listed in the thesaurus for the specified term. Let's assume that commercial debt instrument has been defined as a synonym for bond, then the clause

```
SYN(bond)
```

is equivalent to

```
{bond} OR ({commercial} AND {debt} AND {instrument}).
```

It is best to think of the SYN operator as a preprocessor operation. Before a query is sent to the query optimizer to develop an execution plan, the synonymous terms are added to the query string. The optimizer is then free to choose the best way to retrieve documents that meet the selection criteria. Alternately, we could let the optimizer handle thematic queries using thematic indexes.

Another way of searching by topic is to examine a thematic index of a document set. Thematic indexing is a form of classification that supports multiple categories for each document. So for each document, we may have many entries in the thematic index. As Figure 3.1 shows, the documents-to-themes association requires a many-to-many relationship. Since a thematic index is

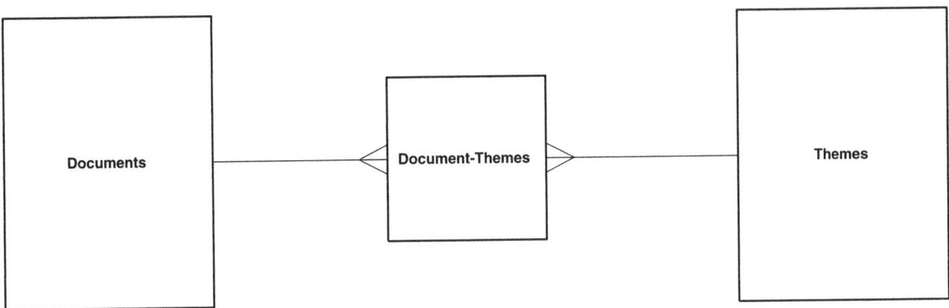

Figure 3.1 Documents may have multiple themes, and themes are found in multiple documents.

available to the optimizer, looking up documents by themes has a slightly different implementation than expanding a query to include other terms.

If a thematic index has already been built, you may find that query performance is better when you use that index as opposed to expanding terms to include synonyms. In general, it is best to avoid OR operations in queries, as with the SYN operator, because of problems optimizers can have with disjunctives.

Browsing by Topic

Browsing by topic is so familiar to us that it is easy to underestimate its importance in business intelligence. The process is similar to searching by topic in that it presumes a thematic index, thesaurus, or some other kind of subject catalog. What differs is how it is used. Rather than specifying an ad hoc query, we start at some point in the subject catalog, usually the root, and navigate into more and more precisely defined areas of interest. Yahoo! (www.yahoo.com) is probably the most widely used directory for browsing by topic. Because this technique is so useful, an increasing number of search engines are supporting it, including Excite (www.excite.com), HotBot (www.hotbot.com), and Google (www.google.com). The top levels of search engine directories categorize extremely wide-ranging topics.

The effectiveness of browsing by topic is dependent upon the breadth and depth of the subject hierarchy. Most Web search engines begin with thirteen to fifteen broad top-level categories. Each subsequent level often has even more topics so that finding very narrow topics can be done quickly. For example, logistics software was found by browsing only four levels in HotBot; information on the North American Free Trade Agreement (NAFTA) and Latin American law was found three levels down at Excite; and companies conducting clinical trials for biotech and pharmaceuticals was only five levels down in Google. Web search engines are a good model for those implementing internal and organization-specific browsing tools. In general, keeping 90 to 95 percent of browseable information within five levels from the root will keep browsing an effective search technique.

Thematic searches and their browsing-oriented kin are the logical extensions of keyword searches. They meet our objective of minimizing the amount of text a reader must analyze to find an answer and are relatively easy to use. Several tools are available to support thematic indexing, categorization, and browsing by taxonomy, including:

- Oracle interMedia Text
- Inxight Categorizer
- SemioMap
- IBM Intelligent Miner for Text Topic Categorization Tool

Some tools, such as Oracle interMedia Text, include a predefined thesaurus or taxonomy. Frequently, the thesaurus can be extended by a user adding his or her own thesaurus. Others, such as SemioMap and IBM's Topic Categorization Tool are built or trained using domain-specific material provided by users.

Another approach to broad searching is to use a document as a prototypical example and have a text-analysis tool retrieve similar documents.

Searching by Example

We have seen that searching by topic or theme can improve precision and recall over searching just by keyword. Another way to accomplish this, and perhaps the easiest to use, is searching by example. In this text operation, we do not have to specify specific terms or concepts, we simply indicate that we want documents similar to a given document. In practice, we usually begin with a keyword search to retrieve an initial document set. In search tools that support querying by example, the initial document set lists each text that satisfies the original criteria and includes an option to search for similar documents.

This technique works well in general searches such as those for *wireless communications*, but it is most effective when dealing with narrow, specific topics that are difficult to distinguish using just keywords. For example, if we were researching optimization techniques for database queries in data warehouses, we could start with a general search such as *query optimization*. The documents returned might describe many approaches to the problem, and one in particular might address very large databases. We could then look for other documents similar to that one.

Searching by example allows us to provide, in effect, a very long selective search criteria without needing to add more and more specific terms. Eventually, though, circular references will catch up with us. Sometimes duplicates appear in result sets within two similarity searches. Often by four consecutive similarity searches, the original document that seeded the process is close to the top of the result set.

Business intelligence application users need to perform several common operations when working with text, including:

- Automatically receiving documents on a specified topic
- Answering questions
- Searching and browsing text repositories
- Finding documents similar to a particular text

Now it is time to turn our attention to techniques that are used to implement these text operations.

Text-Oriented Business Intelligence Techniques

Several text processing techniques can be used to implement the business intelligence operations described in the preceding section. These include:

- Full-text searching
- Directed summarization (feature extraction)
- Undirected summarization
- Document clustering

For each of these operations, we will examine the objectives and purpose of the tasks, provide examples of their use, and finally assess the value of each operation in the decision support environment.

Full-Text Searching: Text Processing 101

Full-text searching is the simplest way to retrieve text information. Anyone who has used a World Wide Web search engine is familiar with the concept of scanning documents looking for specific words. Generally, a user specifies a series of words in a query, and the search engine responds with a list of documents that contain the specified words. Search engines usually rank the results of a search according to the frequency with which the keywords appear in the text and other heuristic rules. While most of our discussion will center around Web-based search engines, full-text searches are supported by many text-based applications, such as legal, news, and academic publication services.

The primary objective of full-text searching is to retrieve text with minimal complexity. However, this ease of use comes at a cost. First, search engines often retrieve documents that are not relevant to the user's query. Second, search engines often miss relevant documents, resulting in poor recall. It is difficult to estimate how many documents should be returned for a query because even the largest search engines only index about one half of the Web. In general, poor recall by search engines is attributed to search engines not having the resources to index all Web pages. A more problematic reason for poor recall is that full-text searches do not account for the fact that there are many ways to describe the same thing. Aspirin might be called an analgesic in one text and a pain reliever in another. We will see how to deal with this problem later when we discuss thematic searching; in the meantime, there are ways to at least improve the precision of full-text searches.

As noted earlier, many full-text search tools do not require a specialized query language but they often support operators that allow us to more precisely describe our query. Some tools, however, use special operators, such as Oracle interMedia Text's CONTANS operator, for text queries. Three common classes of operators are:

- Boolean operators
- Proximity operators
- Weighting operators

The judicious use of these types of operators can significantly improve the quality of search results.

Boolean Operators

Boolean operators include AND, OR, and NOT and are used to specify when words need to occur together in a document, when one or another word should appear in a text, or when a word or phrase should not be in the document, respectively. As in database queries, these operators can be combined to form complex logical conditions.

Proximity Operators

Proximity operators allow users to specify words that should appear near each other. For example, we might want to find all documents with *Food and Drug Administration* or *FDA* near the phrase *clinical trials*. This can be specified in AltaVista as:

("Food and Drug Administration" or "FDA") NEAR "clinical trials"

More advanced text processing tools, such as Oracle interMedia Text, allow users to specify the size of word clumps to search for terms as well the order in which words must appear. For example, to query a document warehouse for texts with *aspartame* within 10 words of *diet*, the following condition would be used:

NEAR((aspartame, diet), 10)

Proximity operators also allow us to specify the order in which words should appear. Oracle interMedia Text includes a Boolean option in the NEAR operator. When it is set to true, the condition will be satisfied only if the words appear within the clump size specified and only if the words in a document are in the same order as in the NEAR clause. So the clause

NEAR((aspartame, diet, soda) 15, TRUE)

will match "... the use of aspartame in popular beverages, especially diet soda, has increased ..." but will not match " today, even more diet sodas use the artificial sweetener aspartame ..." because the three search terms are not used in the phrase in the same order in which they appear in the search clause.

Proximity operators like NEAR are often more useful than Boolean operators because they provide a crude, but effective way of expressing complex ideas, such as the use of aspartame in diet soda. Searching the Web with the keyword phrase

"aspartame" AND "diet" AND "soda"

will return significantly more hits than if a proximity operator had been used.

Weighting Operators

Another way to improve upon Boolean operators is with the use of weighting operators. These operators change the relative importance of words or phrases for a search. Unlike Boolean and proximity operators, which filter documents out of a query result, weighting operators change the relative ranking of a document in the query result. For example, if you are scanning for news stories on agricultural commodities, and wheat in particular, a search with

"commodity AND wheat"

is a good start, but it may return many documents about corn and barley with high rankings. The problem is that "commodity" is a frequently used word in the highly ranked documents returned by the query. To compensate for that, we could indicate the relative importance of *wheat* by specifying a weight, such as

"commodity AND wheat*3"

Wheat is now three times more important than *commodity* from a ranking perspective. Keyword searching, whether in a text database or on the Web, can be an effective technique for finding information, if used effectively. Boolean, proximity, and weighting operators should be used, when available, to improve the precision of searches. Even with precise searches that reducing the number of search hits, some searches will offer too many potential texts with valuable information to read them all. In these cases, we can often get by with just knowing the gist or main points of many of these texts. The next two techniques we will discuss—feature extraction and summarization—can help meet that need.

Directed Summarization (Feature Extraction) Feature extraction is a document-processing operation that finds specific pieces of information in a text. In general, feature extraction applications are pattern-matching programs that identify key phrases in preclassified documents. Once a document is classified, for example, as a terrorism report, a letter of credit application, or a merger and acquisition announcement, predefined pieces of information are pulled from the text and reformatted into a standard form. Let's take a letter of credit application as our first example. Letters of credit are commitments on the part of a bank to make a payment to a seller when the seller meets a set of conditions related to delivering goods to a customer. A bank may receive hundreds of applications a day and want to store a digest of these applications in the data or document warehouse. A bank might receive a letter such as the following:

> Bank of Indonesia
> Jakarta Branch
>
> To Whom It May Concern:
>
> This letter is sent as an application for a letter of credit to be issued within 10 business days in the name of Alpha Industries, Ltd., with offices at Floor 9B, Weiyuan Bldg., Industrial Road 7, Jakarta, Indonesia. Alpha Industries, Ltd., will provide to us, Soccer Goods International, Inc., the following:
>
> 3,000 leather soccer balls, regulation size
>
> no later than 90 days after the date of issuance of this letter of credit with shipping to commence no later than 15 days before the expiration date, and final delivery to be made to port of Seattle, WA USA .The purchase price is USD 17,500. Buyer will provide insurance and will collect freight at the port.
>
> Please debit our account, 17877345, the total cost of this transaction.
>
> Regards,
>
> Purchasing Agent
>
> Soccer Goods International, Inc.

What the bank really wants is a structured form containing only the relevant information, as shown in Table 3.1.

The process of identifying relevant information such as this is the role of feature extraction. There are several layers of processing involved, including noun phrase identification, pattern matching, and template fulfillment.

Table 3.1 Examples of Extracted Information in a Structured Form

ATTRIBUTE	VALUE
Receiving Bank	Bank of Indonesia, Jakarta Branch
Beneficiary	Alpha Industries, Ltd.
Purchaser	Soccer Goods International, Inc.
Address	Floor 9B, Weiyuan Bldg., Industrial Road 7, Jakarta, Indonesia
Amount	17,500
Currency	USD
Expiration Date	90 days from the date of issuance
Latest Shipping Date	15 days before the expiration date
Ship From	Jakarta, Indonesia
Ship To	Seattle, WA USA
Freight	Collect
Insurance	By buyer
Goods	3,000 leather soccer balls, regulation size

Noun phrase identification is an essential element of feature extraction and requires a preprocessing operation to identify the part of speech of each word in a text. Noun phrases are then identified according to linguistic rules that describe allowable patterns of different parts of speech. Table 3.2 shows some common noun phrase forms and related examples.

In addition to terms generally found in dictionaries, frequently used proper nouns are often specified in a feature extraction dictionary to improve accuracy. These lists generally include well-known terms, names of companies, geographic entities, and government institutions.

Once noun phrases have been identified, they can act as building blocks for broader sets of information. Keywords and phrases can trigger the search for

Table 3.2 Examples of Common Noun Phrase Structures

NOUN PHRASE TYPE	EXAMPLE
Receiving Bank	Bank of Indonesia, Jakarta Branch
Noun-Noun	Data Warehouse
Adjective-Noun	Social Security Administration Security Exchange Commission
Prepositions and Conjunctions with Nouns	Federal Bureau of Investigation

particular patterns. For example, the phrase *in the name of* in a letter of credit application is most likely followed by a noun phrase identifying the recipient. Message processing systems, such as those described in Riloff and Lenhert (1994), scan stories with patterns such as:

"in the name of " OR "made out to" + (RECIPIENT: noun-phrase)

to find phrases that identify expected pieces of information.

Since feature extraction serves the purpose of directed summarization, a fixed pattern or template must guide it. In the letter of credit example, we expect to find a beneficiary, a purchase amount, a description of goods, and other shipping details. Merger stories name two or more companies, an amount of money, and possibly a reference to regulator approval. Developing these patterns is difficult, and to date the practical application of this type of summarization has been limited to high-volume or critical applications, such as those found in the military or intelligence services. The benefit of using a custom-developed feature extraction program is that it is more likely to provide the key elements than an undirected summarization program that uses word frequency or other heuristics to identify the most important information.

Undirected Summarization

Undirected summarization does not use patterns like those found in feature extraction. Instead, entire sentences or paragraphs are copied from the original document in an attempt to build a shorter text that still conveys the key ideas of the initial document. This is called summarization by extraction. Undirected summarization does not work the way humans summarize, by assessing its meaning and then writing a short document highlighting the main ideas of the original text, which is called summarization by abstraction. Artificial Intelligence (AI) researchers have made some inroads in this area but creating summaries abstraction is not a practical option today.

Summarization by extraction is based upon measuring the relative importance of words in a document. Some words occur so frequently that they are of no help in distinguishing the meaning of texts. Words like *a, and, the, and but* are called stop words and are ignored. Other words are analyzed to identify their stems, and the frequency of these stems is an indicator of their importance. For example, *merge, merger*, and *merged* would all be considered the word *merge* for the purpose of determining relevance. While a simple counting of word stems can work well in some cases, other clues are frequently available to improve the process.

For example, some commonly used heuristics are the following. First, keywords found in a title are weighted more heavily than other words. Second, important sentences are assumed to appear near the beginning and end of documents. For example, the first sentence in a news story is almost always included in summaries. Third, indicator phrases, such as *In this report . . .* or *To conclude . . .* identify important sentences. Finally, cue words such as *greatest* and *most important* indicate sentences that should be included, while stigma words such as *hardly* and *impossible* identify sentences that should not be included in a summary.

Regardless of the specific algorithm used, most summarization programs work reasonably well, and summarization by extraction is one of the most reliable text analysis techniques available to us. Another well-developed technique that also builds upon morphological and statistical analysis is document clustering.

Document Clustering

Clustering is a useful technique when we want to group similar documents together. We've seen that searching for similar documents is one way to make navigation easier for end users. We've also seen that classification reduces the number of documents readers must wade through before finding interesting text. Clustering serves a similar purpose to classification in that comparable documents are grouped together, but unlike classification schemes, clustering does not use a predefined set of terms for a taxonomy to create the groups. Grouping is based solely on the features of the documents to be clustered.

The basic clustering process works as follows: First, a simplified description of the document is created for each text being added to the clusters. The descriptor is usually a feature vector, or a list of dominant themes or keywords and a measure of the relative importance of each theme in the document. Table 3.3 shows a simple feature vector for a news story about an auto parts manufacturer issuing bonds to build a distribution center in North Carolina.

The next step is to determine the proximity of two documents based upon their feature vectors. When clustering numeric data, this is usually done by assuming that the weights of a feature vector define a point in space and finding the distance between two points. With documents, conceptual similarity measures are used that measure the distance in a subject hierarchy. For example, bonds are relatively close to investment instruments but farther away from currency exchanges in the subject hierarchy depicted in Figure 3.2.

Table 3.3 Document Feature Vectors Describe the Relative Importance of Document Topics

FEATURE	BONDS	DEBT INSTRUMENTS	COMMERCIAL INVESTMENT	AUTO INDUSTRY	MID-ATLANTIC (US)	AUTO PARTS SUPPLIER
Weight	0.90	0.86	0.77	0.75	0.50	0.42

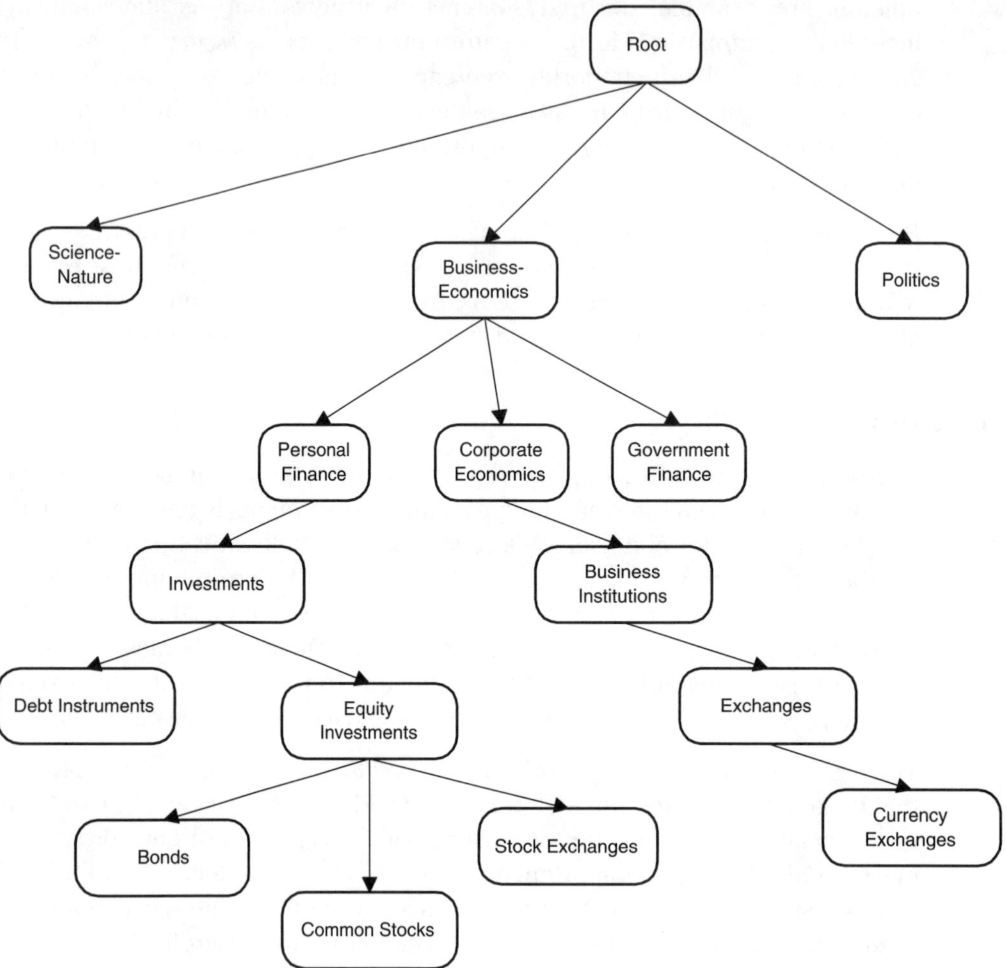

Figure 3.2 Subject hierarchies are the foundation of conceptual measures.

Conceptual similarity measures are generally based upon a function of the distance between topics in the subject hierarchy and the weights of those topics in the documents. Once the distance between documents is calculated, they can be grouped in several different ways.

Hierarchical clusters use a tree structure to group documents. The root of the tree is a cluster with all the documents in the original set. Each leaf node of the tree has only one document, representing the simplest clusters. The intervening levels have groups of documents that become more narrowly focused as you move deeper down the tree.

Partitioning, or binary, clusters use a predefined number clusters. Unlike hierarchical clusters that have nested sets of clusters, each document in the partitioned scheme is added to only one cluster. A cluster is chosen for a document so that the average distance between documents in a cluster is minimized, while the average distance between clusters is maximized.

Fuzzy partitions also use a predefined number of clusters but assume that all documents belong to all clusters to varying degrees. The idea behind fuzzy partitions is that sometimes hard, fixed distinctions do not work well. For example, if we were using partitioning clusters, should we add a document about an airline merger to a cluster that has banking and telecommunications industry mergers or to a cluster that has news stories about pilot strikes and airport congestion? Fuzzy partitions avoid the problem by including the document in both partitions, perhaps with different degrees of membership. Let's assume we have created a fuzzy partitioning of a group of news stories that cover the airline, auto, and telecommunications industries. As Table 3.4 shows, cluster 1 is dominated by airline industry stories, cluster 2 is primarily, but weakly, about mergers, and cluster 3 is primarily about the auto industry.

Regardless of which clustering technique is used, it is important to validate the usefulness of the clusters. The utility of this technique is due in large part to the logical cohesiveness of the document set to be grouped. If a wide range of topics is addressed, the resulting clusters will reflect this range and may not appear cohesive. In these situations, a larger number of clusters will be required to ensure a logical cohesiveness.

Keyword searching, summarization, both directed and undirected, and clustering can help us meet the business objective needs outlined earlier. These techniques reduce the amount of text users must read to find salient information, and they make search and retrieval more efficient. Text is not an island unto itself. Certainly a great deal of business intelligence information is locked inside corporate documents and Web pages, but there is also a wealth of information in data warehouses. Linking text to the warehouse is the last step in fully exploiting the business intelligence potential of text.

Table 3.4 Fuzzy Clusters Use Degrees of Membership Instead of Assigning Documents to a Single Cluster

	CLUSTER 1	CLUSTER 2	CLUSTER 3
Airline strike	0.90	0.49	0.19
Airport congestion	0.82	0.30	0.15
Airline merger	0.74	0.81	0.23
Auto plant construction	0.11	0.18	0.95
Telecommunications mergers	0.23	0.70	0.09

Integration with the Data Warehouse

If anything, data warehousing has taught us that information integration is an essential element in effective business intelligence. Since the dimensional model and star schemas are so widely adopted, we will begin our examination of data warehouse and document warehouse integration there.

Dimensional Models: A Quick Refresher

Dimensional models, such as the star schema and its snowflake variation, are designed around two basic types of entities: fact tables and dimensions. Fact tables are used to store information about particular measurements of a business process such as sales margins, inventory levels, gross expenditures, and other core pieces of information. Dimensions are used to organize facts. For example, a sales margin is a fact about the sales of a particular product at a specific time, in one location, and by a single salesperson. Figure 3.3 depicts a simple star schema representation of such a model.

For our purposes, the dimension tables are the starting points of document warehouse integration. Dimensions contain a great deal of descriptive information. A

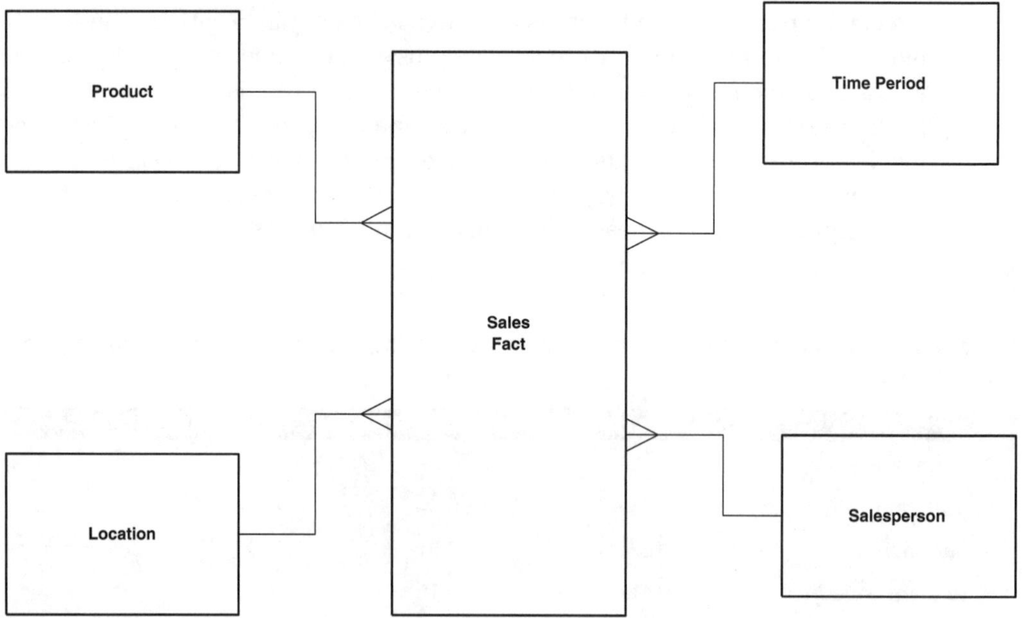

Figure 3.3 A simple sales star schema.

product dimension could contain descriptions of products, product categories, related parts, and subcomponents. Location dimensions describe physical locations, marketing regions, advertising areas, and other geographic-based information. Each dimension attribute that describes some feature of a measure is a bridge between data and text.

Integration Example: Slumping Sales

Let's take, for example, a sales performance data mart used to track sales revenues and margins. We will also assume a document warehouse containing internal documents about products, advertising campaigns, marketing strategies, and competitive analysis as well as industry related news and analysis. Now an analyst may find that sales of wide-screen televisions have fallen below projections in the first quarter of the year. Drilling down, the analyst finds the gap between projected and actual sales is a general trend across manufacturers but appears limited to several regions within major metropolitan areas. The data mart figures clearly point to a problem and describe what is happening but cannot help us answer the question, "why?"

To move beyond simply describing the problem to understanding the bigger picture, we need to move into textual descriptions. The first step is to search for documents about the product line in trouble. Now, the poor sales are showing up across manufacturers' product lines, so thematic searching based upon product category descriptions is the best starting point. Drilling across from a data mart, we need to search the document warehouse using the product category (wide-screen television) and the period in question (first quarter of the current fiscal year). Since the phrase wide-screen television may have many synonyms, such as big-screen TV, 32" television, 34" diagonal television, and others, searching by topic will ensure the best recall. We have also defined metadata with each text as it is added to the document warehouse, including the date the document was created, so that we can further restrict our search to the first quarter, plus or minus some marginal period. At this point, it is not clear why some metropolitan regions have slumping sales but not others, so location is not a factor in the initial search. Topical searching with the restricted date range creates a result set with:

- 12 product fact sheets with technical information on different wide-screen televisions
- 3 advertising department internal documents on newspaper ad layouts for an electronics sale
- 4 marketing memos on redefining strategies to accommodate new technologies, such as high-definition television
- 7 competitive intelligence documents about other retailers' advertising campaigns
- 2 industry analysis white papers on high-definition television (HDTV)

Just by scanning the list of documents returned, the analyst conjectures that the problem may lie in increased competition from alternate products cutting into the demand for wide-screen TVs or from increased competitive pressure.

Our user proceeds to review summaries of the four marketing memos on new technology strategies, the two industry analysis white papers, and the competitive intelligence reports. The competitors' campaigns are not radically different from what the analyst has seen before, and there is no indication that competitors have opened new stores in the affected areas, so the analyst assumes that direct competition is not the cause of the slumping sales. She then proceeds to delve more deeply into the marketing memos and discovers that analysts in the marketing department have been concerned about high-definition television becoming available and displacing the demand for home entertainment centers that use current broadcasting technologies. The analyst reads the shorter of the two industry analysis reports and finds supporting facts for the marketing group's concerns. She then searches for documents similar to that industry analysis and finds several documents, including one that discusses the availability of HDTV broadcasts in several major U.S. media markets. With clear indications that high-definition televisions are cutting into older technologies, the analyst moves back to the data warehouse to assess the sales of their HDTV product lines. Depending upon her findings, the retailer may need to increase its marketing and advertising of high-definition televisions in selected areas and adjust projections for several product lines. Figure 3.4 depicts how this type of data mart and document warehouse analysis can proceed.

In general, data found in the data warehouse can trigger questions that cannot be answered by the data in the data warehouse. Linking data and document repositories can help us understand the details of an organization's sales, internal operations, market, and other external factors. As we saw in the example, analyzing information in a document warehouse can lead to a hypothesis that can be tested, at least to some degree, using information in the data warehouse. Neither the data nor the document warehouse can answer every question, but working with both can provide deeper insight than can working with either alone.

Integration with the World Wide Web

No matter how large our document warehouses become, they will never come close to matching the extent of the World Wide Web, and they do not need to. Document warehouses, by their very nature, need to be closely integrated into the Web and other Internet resources, such as FTP sites and Gopher servers. There is no fixed formula to integrating the Internet and text repositories but there are several issues that must be addressed:

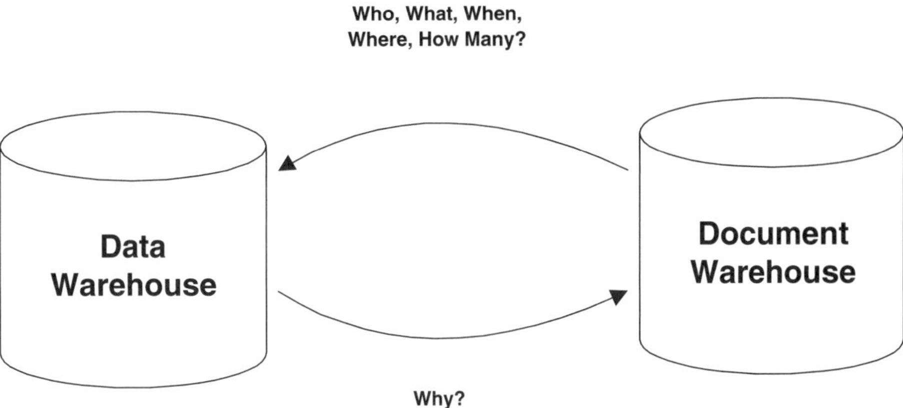

Figure 3.4 Analysis moves back and forth between the data warehouse and the document warehouse.

- What documents should be copied into the repository and which should be referenced by URL?
- How should Web and repository searches be integrated?
- What limitation do copyrights place on incorporating Web documents into the warehouse?
- Can automatic retrieval programs, such as Web robots (bots), be used on key Web sites?

Deciding what to include in the document warehouse is probably the most challenging issue facing architects, designers, and users. At first blush, it may appear that one can limit documents to a specific domain, such as bioinformatics, insurance fraud, or agricultural commodity news and reports. Unfortunately, there are no clear lines demarcating these subject areas, and the volume of text on any one of these areas could be enormous. Another issue that must be considered is the need to control the document. Web sites change constantly, and a critical news story from your perspective may be a marginal article from a Web administrator's point of view, so it may not remain available for long. In the following chapters, we will examine specific techniques for managing the text selection and loading process.

Adapting to Changing User Interests

The topics that interest users change with time. Sometimes, interest is driven by a changing market condition, a tactical move by a competitor, a shift in regulatory oversight, or other external influence. Sometimes a user's job responsibility changes or his or her research projects finish and new ones start. For whatever reason, document warehouse designers need to assume that interests are dynamic.

We can deal with this change in several ways. First, individuals can develop their own interest profiles. Web-based news services, such as CNN, offer custom news pages like myCNN.com, using interest profiles. Second, groups of individuals with similar functions can use a single group profile. For example, oil industry analysts will most likely want to read similar types of documents as others in their field. A third and more challenging approach is to monitor the types of documents users retrieve and adjust their profiles automatically. Chapters 5 and 6 will discuss how to define these profiles and then adjust them using machine learning techniques.

Conclusions

Improving business operations, sales, and marketing demands more than numbers. Vast amounts of business information are found in texts ranging from status memos to new drug applications. Document warehouses are an essential building block of enterprise-based business intelligence operations. Like data warehouses, they help users understand internal operations, market conditions, strategic directions of competitors, and regulatory environments.

Text-oriented business intelligence operations efficiently provide relevant information to users while filtering or reducing nonessential information. The hallmark of a successful decision support system is the ability to provide users with the information they need, when they need it and in an easily accessible form. Summarizing and routing documents and searching by topic and example are as fundamental to business intelligence as drilling down into an OLAP cube or manipulating a pivot table is in an ad hoc query tool.

As we noted at the beginning of the chapter, we could only introduce some of the key topics of document warehousing and text mining here. Now, it is time to look at the details of building the document warehouse.

PART TWO

Document Warehousing

CHAPTER 4

Overview of Document Warehousing

If the Web is the mine from which we extract raw material, document warehouses are the mills and refineries through which we turn text resources into usable business intelligence and distribute it to the ultimate customer. As we will see in this chapter, document warehouses are dynamic repositories, constantly adapting to the changing needs of their users while keeping essential, but proprietary information in-house.

In this chapter, we will briefly look into some requirements of document warehousing, including understanding what content our users need, when it is needed, and where it can be obtained. The second section of the chapter describes the architectures of document warehouses. Specifically, we will examine document sources, text processing servers, database and other storage options, and metadata repositories because they provide the basic building blocks of the document warehouse infrastructure. The third section discusses the document warehousing process, including document identification and retrieval, text analysis, and end-user support providing an overview of the steps required to meet the text-based business intelligence needs of users.

Meeting Business Intelligence Requirements

To understand text-oriented business intelligence requirements, we first need to ask the following questions:

- Who are the end users?
- What information do they need?
- When is it needed?
- Where can the needed information be found?

End users define the requirements and, therefore, drive the development of the document warehouse. Having identified the end users, we must identify what they need, when they need it, and where the warehouse processes can find it.

Who Are the End Users?

The first step in document warehousing is to understand your users' interests and their roles within the organization. Depending upon your company or agency, your end users could be a homogeneous group of analysts focused on single, narrow domains such as prescription allergy medication or home heating oil production. Or you may have wide range of executives, managers, and analysts concerned with broad areas such as wireless communications or consumer foods. In addition to understanding their area of interest, document warehouse designers need to understand their users' functional needs. A research scientist studying prescription allergy medicines requires radically different information from the analyst assessing the market for the same type of product. With an understanding of their function and interest, we can begin to understand what documents and text they need.

What Information Is Needed?

Users may view text mining with a variety of perspectives and objectives, but they frequently share a need for the same types of documents. Marketing, sales, and product development may all need competitive intelligence information. Finance and legal departments overlap in their need for contract information. Production management, project management, and personnel frequently need access to government regulations. Here are just some of the most common needs found in commercial enterprises, grouped by function:

- **Marketing:** Market analysis, competitive intelligence, and regulatory information

- **Sales:** Marketing plans, advertisement campaigns, and competitive intelligence
- **Product development:** Market analysis, production capacity, and planned capital investments
- **Finance:** Purchase and sales contracts, and budget justifications
- **Production management:** Status memos, quality control reports, and employee evaluations
- **Project managers:** Status reports, design documents, and test plans

In addition to these specific document types, many users will need access to e-mails, memos, meeting notes, transcripts, and other texts spread throughout an organization.

When Is It Needed?

"You want it when?" begins many jabs and jokes decorating coffee cups and cartoons seen around corporate offices. The value of information is often determined by when someone sees it. Breaking market news or government production estimates can influence stock markets when first publicized. The next day, the same information would be useless to an investor. Take for example research services that provide vital information to their clients. Some investment research services provide market analysis several times during the day, with information from different markets around the world. The value of this type of information dissipates quickly, so communications from these firms must be distributed immediately. Other consulting services, such as industry analysts, provide assessments and projections for broad sectors and provide information that retains its value months after the original publication. Understanding the time-related value of information is essential in text mining and document warehousing.

Time influences the business intelligence value of text in three ways. First, market conditions or other external factors can determine the value of a document. The Eddie Murphy movie *Trading Places* depicts two crooked traders who try to corner a commodity market by getting government production estimates before everyone else. Once those numbers were released and everyone had them, they provided no competitive advantage. You do not need to be a Wall Street trader to know the value of getting information on time. Within any organization, the impact of delays can ripple through entire departments and project teams, as actions are held pending while people wait for information.

Second, the text itself contains information that effectively limits its value. For example, a bid or proposal may stipulate an expiration date. Letter of credit applications specify when goods will be shipped, so those applications must be processed before that date to ensure the customer's needs are met in time.

Third, assumptions underlying the information in a document affect the importance of the text. For example, a contract to provide five tons of winter wheat to a consumer food manufacturer is virtually useless if the customer files for bankruptcy protection. Keeping abreast of changing conditions is one of the fundamental needs addressed by document warehousing.

Where Is the Information Found?

Searching out the source of document warehousing texts can be as slow and arduous a task as identifying and understanding data that populates data warehouses. Where does one find the documents, short texts, and other items for the document warehouse? The short answer is that one finds them on enterprise file systems, the World Wide Web, and external services, such as news feeds and research services.

If we were to collect all the files stored on enterprise file servers, mainframes, and storage area networks (SANs), we would end up with about 1,000 petabytes of information (one petabyte is equivalent to 1,024 terabytes). Text composes an estimated 80 percent of all business information, so we are looking at a potential for 819,200 terabytes of text in internal corporate repositories. These include word-processing files, presentations, the contents of document management systems, and e-mails, to name just a few sources. Internal file systems alone are a rich source of textual information.

The World Wide Web is an obvious source of raw material for text mining and document warehousing. Like internal sources, the Web has much to offer but finding what you need without being inundated with useless information requires searching with precision. In fact, one of the most time-consuming parts of document warehousing is defining what should be included and what should be excluded from the repository.

Third-party providers, such as news feeds and research services, provide another important source of textual information. Unlike Web-based information, this text is delivered to end users and generally covers known areas of interest to the user.

The Role of the Document Warehouse in Business Intelligence

With so much information available on the Web and internal storage systems, why add more complexity to an organization by building a document warehouse? Document warehouses provide several benefits not found in a fully distributed system such as the Web.

First, a document warehouse integrates internal and external sources. The value of data warehouses becomes abundantly clear when information from several sources is integrated and analyzed together. Similarly, internal documents on sales and marketing combined with market reports, industry analysis, and projections are far more valuable than any one of those alone.

Second, text mining can extract essential information through feature extraction, summarization, and related techniques. Some text mining operations are computationally expensive, and their results should be saved and made available to other users.

Third, document warehouses are a clearinghouse for metadata about documents and document sources. This is especially the case with quality control information. While the Web is filled with information, no one can say how much is accurate, how much is somewhat informed, and how much is junk.

Before beginning a document warehouse project, it is essential to understand the target audience and ensure that you choose a reasonably sized group of users. Do not attempt to meet the document warehousing needs of everyone in your organization at once. Like data warehousing, it is often best to start with a limited scope and address a limited set of needs and then build incrementally.

A common error in the early days of data warehousing was to assume that we could meet the needs of an entire enterprise if we just did enough analysis and built a expansive enough warehouse. We have learned that this "Big Bang" approach often failed because it delivered too late and cost too much. And to add insult to injury, the requirements usually change during the development of the data warehouse. Monolithic data warehouses were constructed over the course of 18 to 24 months, cost \$2–3 million, and often ended by producing a warehouse that met two-year-old needs. The practice of incrementally constructing data warehouses, using techniques such as Kimball's Data Bus Architecture, have led to the rapid construction of focused sections of the warehouse. Document warehousing will do well to follow suit.

With an understanding of our end users' needs, we can now turn to an overview of the structure and components of the document warehouse.

The Architecture of the Document Warehouse

There are several primary components of the document warehouse:

- Document sources
- Text processing servers
- Textbases and other storage repositories

- Metadata repositories
- User profiling

In this section, we will examine the role of each of these and briefly discuss options for each.

Document Sources

Finding documents to populate a document warehouse is never a problem. We are surrounded by text. In general, we can think of three distinct types of sources: internal sources, the Internet, and subscription services.

Internal Sources

Within an organization, documents and other texts, such as e-mails, are spread throughout the organization on file servers, in document repositories, and in document management systems. While these systems meet many of our file management needs, they do not provide the integrated text analysis features need in text mining and intelligent information retrieval.

Departmental file servers store the bulk of enterprises' text with very little support for document management. In general, file servers provide storage and crude navigation and search services. The Windows Explorer's treelike navigation tool is widely recognized. It exploits the advantages of hierarchical storage systems by allowing us to quickly navigate to areas of interest, assuming that we know exactly where we want to go.

When we do not know the exact location of a file, we turn to search utilities. Basic search operations are supported in most file systems. The Windows operating system provides a Find File tool that provides for simple pattern matching on file names and searches for strings within documents. UNIX tools such as grep and fgrep, support more flexible searching, using regular expressions. Users requiring more sophisticated file management and searching features often turn to scripting languages such as Perl to meet their needs. In general operating systems provide only the most basic document management features, and we need to turn to other tools for better text support.

Document repositories, such as Lotus Notes, are popular in large, distributed organizations. They provide more elaborate search facilities and are generally easier to navigate. One of the key benefits of Lotus Notes over file system repositories is that users can create customized views and folders to organize documents. Navigation tools within Lotus Notes can also display descriptions and other metadata about documents.

While document repositories provide the means to store and retrieve a wide range of file types for a variety of uses, document management systems focus on large volumes of similar documents. These management systems often combine text storage with workflow features to support specific document-processing tasks.

Although these internal systems provide different services, they cannot provide the rich set of text analysis and information retrieval support of the document warehouse.

Internet

The Internet is the largest single integrated source of text available to us. As we will see later, this is something of a mixed blessing. However, first we will examine some of the different types of text repositories on the Internet, including the World Wide Web, Gopher servers, and FTP servers.

World Wide Web

It is difficult to categorize the entire contents of the World Wide Web into a few areas but for building document warehouses to support enterprise operations, we will look into three broad types of Web sites:

- News sites
- Industry-specific sites
- Government information sites

Some news sites, such as CNN.com, WashingtonPost.Com, and MSNBC.com, provide general news of broad interest. Depending upon your organization's focus, general news sites will vary in their usefulness. Smaller, single-product-oriented firms will find less that is pertinent in these sources than will larger conglomerates with extensive holdings and product lines. Broadly speaking, general news sources are some of the best sources for information on factors outside normal markets that can effect an industry. For example, international investment decisions are influenced by political risk assessments. Given a choice of three sites throughout the world for building a factory, which is the most stable? Have there been any unusual events in the major OPEC countries in the past six months? How has the NAFTA treaty affected border states in the United States? Of course, precise expert answers to these questions are not likely to be found on the Web but the background information necessary to draw your own conclusions is there.

Business news sites provide narrower ranges of information, often focusing on business and economic news. *The Wall Street Journal* (www.wsj.com), *London Financial Times* (www.ft.com), and Bloomberg (www.bloomberg.com) all provide extensive coverage of the business world. Other sites tend to focus on specific regions, such as Japan Financials (www.japanfinancials.com) or on particular types of investments, such as Mutual Funds in the World (www.qualistream.com/eng/opcvm.html). These sites provide more business-oriented information than general news sources do and often cover these issues in more depth as well. For detailed coverage of a particular market, industry-specific sites frequently provide the most specific coverage.

Industry-specific sites can range from broad professional associations, such as the Metals Industry Trade Associations (www.ita.doc.gov/metals/assoc) to member only sites providing proprietary information, such as the Pharmaceutical Research and Manufacturers of America group. (www.phrma.org). These sites often serve as hubs with links to industry firms, suppliers, regulatory agencies, and service providers, which themselves can be rich sources of market and competitive intelligence information.

Government information services provide valuable information often not available elsewhere. With the power to legislate reporting requirements, governments have become the de facto keepers of key industry information. For example, the U.S. Department of Agriculture regularly publishes grain projections, cattle inventory data, and market prices for crops and livestock. The Security and Exchange Commission maintains the EDGAR database of the SEC filings required of all publicly held U.S. corporations. Employment and wage data is available from the Bureau of Labor Statistics. Similar information is available from the European Union and other industrialized nations as well.

Gopher

The Gopher protocol, developed at the University of Minnesota, was an early means of hierarchically organizing text on the Internet. The purpose of Gopher was to allow users to easily find and navigate documents distributed across the Internet. Today, relatively few sites use the Gopher protocol, which has been largely surpassed by the World Wide Web. Some Gopher sites, primarily at universities, are still available.

If you do decide to search Gopher sites for information, then you will want to find a Veronica or Jughead server. Veronica is a spider that searches Gopher sites, much as WWW search engines crawl the Web to index HTML documents. To query Veronica, users log into a server that supports the indexing application, using Telnet. A command-line interface is then used to search all Gopher servers on the Internet, sometimes called Gopherspace. A similar, but less sophisticated Gopher search tool, Jughead, is used to search smaller areas of Gopherspace. Many users find Jughead faster than Veronica.

FTP

The File Transfer Protocol (FTP) is the primary means of file transfer across the Internet. FTP servers allow users to log into the server, often anonymously, to copy files to and from the server. Unlike Gopher, which has been largely replaced by the HTTP protocol, FTP is still frequently used.

Archie, a spider that indexes FTP sites, serves the same purpose as Veronica in Gopherspace and search engines in the World Wide Web. Archie is a command-line application accessible to users who have logged into an Archie server via Telnet. A WWW interface called ArchiePlex is also available for searching FTP sites from the Web.

Services

Subscription services provide access to proprietary databases their for their customers. Such services are often industry-specific—for example, providing access to legal cases or market analysis. Other services offer news archives for historical research. In the past, these services were often accessed through dial-in servers or via satellite for continuous feeds. The widespread adoption of the Internet and the World Wide Web, and e-mail in particular, is largely replacing these other means of providing subscription services.

Text Processing Servers

Within the document warehouse environment, there are four distinct types of servers:

- Document collection servers
- Text analysis servers
- Publishing and distribution servers
- Storage servers

Although we discuss these servers as if they were distinct machines, the same physical server can perform two or more operations. In general, our distinction between servers is a logical and functional one and may not mirror your physical implementation.

Document Collection

Document collection servers gather and preprocess texts. The collection process can occur in three ways.

- Processes gather texts using a predefined list of sources for direct automatic collection.
- Processes gather text using predefined lists of topics for direct searching.
- Documents are manually submitted.

Each process serves a distinct document collection need.

Predefined Direct Collection

Most documents enter the document warehouse through predefined direct collection. In this scenario, a list of sources is maintained in a database, and a collection program, or set of programs, actually copies the files to the document warehouse.

The database of sources needs to maintain at least three core attributes. First, we must know where the targeted file is located. Internal documents can be collected simply by using copy or FTP commands. Internet resources will be collected according to their protocol. Web robots, programs that act as agents to perform tasks such as document collection, are used to retrieve both HTTP and FTP resources. Customized scripts can be used for Gopher retrieval.

Second, direct collection processes require information on collection times and refresh rates. Industry news sites may be visited every night, while the SEC's EDGAR database may be queried on a weekly or monthly basis. Some documents, such as the federal government's reports on housing or unemployment, are collected on specific calendar dates and times.

Third, document collection must be prioritized. Like extraction, transformation, and load processes in data warehousing, we may have limited time windows in which to perform document collection. Limited bandwidth is an obvious potential bottleneck but the computational demands of text analysis can also limit the number of documents that can be processed within the time available.

Predefined Topic Search

Of course, we cannot know ahead of time all possible documents we will want in our repository. If a primary application of our document warehouse were competitive intelligence and analysis, we would want to monitor news and press release sites for stories on our competitors. A firm providing consulting and market analysis to the oil industry may regularly search for information on energy prices, political events in OPEC countries, and changes in environmental regulations, tariffs, and exports restrictions.

Since search engines are notorious for returning huge numbers of hits for relatively simple queries, predefined search topics should be as specific as possible. When large numbers of documents are returned, processes should be parameterized to retrieve only a fixed number of documents or to retrieve documents based upon the relevancy ranking provided by most search engines.

Manually Submitted Documents

Some types of documents, especially internal legal findings, strategic assessments and other types of restricted information, should not be open to automatic inclusion in a document warehouse. At the other end of the spectrum, some topics are so broad ranging, such as financial news, that most users do not automatically search for those. However, sometimes a news service's in-depth studies into timely economic and political issues or government reports on topics germane to the organization are worth having for reference purposes. In these cases, users should have the option of manually including texts in the document warehouse.

Text Analysis Servers

Text analysis servers provide two operations:

- Preprocessing
- Primary processing

The job of preprocessing servers is to identify document formats and, if necessary, convert the document to a format acceptable to other text processing tools. Some tools processes only text files, and some work better if markups, such as HTML tags, are removed. The language of the text is also identified and, again, if necessary, translated into an acceptable target language.

The goal of the primary processing servers is to distill text into a form suitable for efficient retrieval and text mining. These operations include keyword indexing, thematic indexing, clustering, feature extraction, and summarization. We have touched on these topics in the previous chapter and will examine them further in subsequent chapters as well.

In general, the primary processing operations are the most computationally demanding in the document warehouse, and servers should be sized accordingly. Again, later chapters will address this topic more thoroughly.

Publishing and Distribution

"Build it and they shall come" is an anathema in document warehousing. Often the value of business intelligence information is lost if it is not distributed to the right people or not published in a timely manner. To preserve the value of textual information, it must be presented to users in a content-dependent manner. High-priority information or news can be e-mailed or delivered to a wireless device, such as a Wireless Application Protocol (WAP) handheld computer. Less urgent information can be delivered through dynamically generated links in an intranet portal or simply added to a hierarchical subject index for later retrieval. How these steps in the document warehouse process are handled is the responsibility of the publishing and distribution servers.

The publishing and distribution servers must accomplish specific tasks:

- Monitoring the contents of the document warehouse
- Maintaining user profiles and preferences; for example, what is high-priority information and how should it be delivered?
- Interfacing with delivery services, such as e-mail systems.
- Formatting summaries and category lists for the appropriate device (for example, Web browser or WAP microbrowser)

The ability to accomplish these tasks is closely tied to the features of the database used to store the text, metadata, user profiles, and other necessary information.

Text Databases and Other Storage Options

We have several options for storing text in a document warehouse. They include:

- Textbases
- Databases with support for support for text
- File systems
- Combined file system/database repositories

Textbases, such as Lotus Notes, have been widely adopted in large organizations. The key benefits of these applications are easily configured interfaces, a rich set of text-searching features, flexible programming tools, and scalable architectures.

Databases with support for text, such as Oracle and Thunderstorm's Texis, combine the benefits of a relational database, such as SQL support, with extended data types for text and text retrieval operators. This option has several appealing features. Integration with other relational database applications is straightforward. Scalability and portability is not an issue with any of the major relational database vendor's core products. Many of the features developed for OLTP and data warehouse applications, such as partitioning, high-performance loader tools, and parallel query processing are valuable in the document warehousing environment as well.

File systems are also an option for a text repository. Many text processing tools work directly with files, so there are no real disadvantages to this approach during the loading and text processing stages. Maintenance, however, is more challenging with file systems than with databases or textbases. Since a database is required to manage user preferences and metadata regardless of the where the text is stored, there is little savings in administrative overhead. Some tools, such as Oracle and Texis, give administrators the option of storing text in the database or in a file system. One disadvantage of this is that the database cannot control changes to operating system files and inconsistencies can creep into the warehouse. For example, a summary and list of categories may be generated for a document and stored in a database or other file. If another user inadvertently overwrites the source text or changes it in some other way, the summary category list will not be automatically updated. Within a database, triggers can regenerate the summary and reclassify the document automatically.

A fourth alternative, Oracle's iFS combines the features of database storage with file system storage. While maintaining many of the features of file systems, such as hierarchical collections of directories and files, these systems offer database services as well.

Metadata Repositories

Metadata is information describing documents and texts and is a critical piece of the document warehousing environment. Metadata serves several purposes:

- Improves search precision and recall
- Allows for extended searching options, such as by author, date of publication, and so on
- Categorizes texts
- Indicates relative levels of quality, reliability, and timeliness

Metadata standards have emerged from two directions. First, software designers and developers have backed the creation of data and system modeling metadata standards such as the Common Warehouse Metamodel (CWM) and the Open Information Model. Alternately, library and information science professionals have developed standards, such as the Dublin Core, that move beyond traditional cataloging schemes for printed materials to categorize any content bearing data or objects. Document warehousing will draw from both schools of thought.

For example, the Open Information Model, version 1 (which has merged with the CWM), includes a Semantics package for organizing information in a semantic model. The Common Warehouse Metamodel includes support for transformations and business nomenclature. The former can be adopted to fit the needs of text mining transformations, such as summarization and feature extraction. Business nomenclature models business structures with entities such as taxonomies, glossaries, terms, and concepts.

Several initiatives have emerged from cataloging projects such as:

- The Text Encoding Initiative
- Machine Readable Cataloging
- Global/Government Information Locator Service
- Dublin Core

The Text Encoding Initiative (TEI) began in 1988 with an emphasis on academic texts. Machine Readable Cataloging is a popular library format used in many countries with some national variations. The United States and Canadian governments use the Global/Government Information Locator Service (GILS). Librarians and information scientists developed the Dublin Core to describe Internet resources more precisely and to improve search engine precision. With its emphasis on Internet resources, the Dublin Core is of most interest to us.

The Dublin Core supports 15 data elements (see Table 4.1).

These metadata standards provide an excellent starting point for us, but they will need to be extended to support quality measures in particular. Since information gathered from the Internet is not always accurate, we must provide a means to distinguish reliable sources from others. Integrity marking has been used in database systems to classify data according to a fixed set of measures, such as correct, acceptable, wrong but usable, and unusable. Similar classification schemes are needed in the document warehouse to ensure that users understand the quality of the information they are reading.

User Profiling

End users interests tend to fall into two categories. First, they have short-term specific needs. What did the marketing plan call for? What have economists said about exchange rates and their effects on the energy prices? Is our main competitor increasing advertising in the Chicago area? These needs tend be focused and ad hoc. Other interests tend are longer term and consistent. For example, product managers are interested in the current sales of products, marketing and sales plans for the products, information about competitive alternatives, market conditions, and other factors that may affect sales. Analysts in the chemical industry might want regular information about changes in government regulations, political risk analysis on nations providing raw materials, or market demand and other conditions that influence sales. To support these

Table 4.1 Data Elements Supported by the Dublin Core

DC.Title	Title of the resource
DC.Creator	Author
DC.Subject	Subject keyword
DC.Description	Annotation or summary
DC.Publisher	Publisher
DC.Contributor	Contributing person or institution
DC.Date	Date
DC.Type	Resource type (according to a list of accepted terms)
DC.Format	Format, file type, or physical medium
DC.Identifier	Resource identifier: URL, URN, ISBN, etc.
DC.Source	Resource (physical, digital) from which the current resource was derived
DC.Language	Language of the resource
DC.Relation	Relationship to other works
DC.Coverage	Geographic or temporal coverage
DC.Rights	Copyright information

longer-term interests, the document warehouse provides for user profiles that support three methods for describing interests.

- By subject
- By source
- By keyword

Profiles map specific interests to concepts supported by subject hierarchies used in the document warehouse. For example, specifying an interest in retail sales will direct the publication and distribution servers to forward stories on department stores, convenience stores, discount stores, and supermarkets to an end user. In this way, users can regularly receive information germane to their work.

User profiles should allow users to specify that particular resources be monitored. These can include internal directories—for example, the mid-Atlantic sales report directory, as well as Internet resources, such as an industry trade publication or new source.

For fine-grained searches, keywords can be specified along with specific sites to search. For example, a product manager in the wireless industry may want to monitor technical publications, such as the Institute of Electrical and Electronics

Engineers (IEEE), for terms such as active sensing, microwave degradation, or WAP.

In addition to the structure of the document warehouse, it is essential to understand the process of document warehousing.

The Process of Document Warehousing

The main processes of document warehousing are closely aligned with its architecture. We will specifically look into:

- Identifying document sources
- Document retrieval
- Preprocessing operations
- Text analysis operations
- Managing the document warehouse
- Supporting end-user operations

The first three steps parallel the extraction, transformation, and load process in data warehousing, while the last two, managing the document warehouse and supporting end-user operations, address the same fundamental issues we find in maintaining a data warehouse. Text analysis, as we shall see, is a document-warehouse-specific operation.

Identifying Document Sources

The first step in document processing is to identify what documents are to be included in the warehouse. Previously, we described three ways of identifying particular documents: with resource lists, searches by keywords, and searches by topic. Presumably, the searches could be done across the Internet as a whole, without regard to the particulars of a Web site. This approach is problematic from a quality control standpoint. Given, a broad search, how are we to assess the quality of the information provided by the identified Web sites?

Finding Potential Document Sources

Of course starting with broad Web searches is the most common way of finding potential document sources but there are other techniques that, as a general rule, will provided higher-quality results. These techniques are based upon several heuristics:

- Reliable sites link to reliable sites
- Web taxonomies group comparably reliable sources together
- Searching for similar documents yields similar quality documents

Again, these are rules of thumb that provide a starting point, and they are by no means infallible.

The first heuristic often applies when dealing with commercial sites, such as industry portals. A livestock exchange will link to feed providers, trucking, rail, and other transportation sites and market news sources. News sites are definitely tricky though. This heuristic does not apply to them. While we would not expect the *New York Times* to link to a newsstand tabloid as an alternate source of information, it may link to Web sites of organizations covered in one of their stories. A story about a mass suicide in a cult may include a link to the cult's Web site to provide readers with more background information on the group. This is clearly not an endorsement on the part of the news service, and we cannot presume that.

Web taxonomies, such as Yahoo!, offer logical groupings of Web sites. Here we can find categories on business-to-business software, government sites, corporate investments, foreign relations, and on and on. Taxonomies themselves provide no quality measure, only a rough grouping of comparable quality documents.

Our third heuristic, searching for similar documents yields similar quality documents, is the weakest of the three heuristics and should be used carefully. The idea behind this rule of thumb is that search engines, such as Google and Excite, which provide a similar document feature, base their results on word frequencies and other lexical measures. The primary problem here is that individual words, or sets of words, do not always describe the same thing, and the distinction is often subtle. For example, a document on funding NASA SETI (Search for Extraterrestrial Intelligence) may share high-frequency words, such as *life, planet, contact, radio wave, probe* with a "Greatest Alien Abductions of All Time" site.

Document warehouse administrators must balance the need to control the quality of the content in a document warehouse with the cost of manual intervention.

Assessing Quality

There is no substitute for quality control information. In general, there are three distinct measures we presume when discussing quality in the document warehouse. First, is the information in a document accurate? A news story about the stock market that does not have the right numbers is worse than useless; it is harmful.

The second measure, is the scope of the information. A story in the local paper on World Trade Organization policies may be accurate but not very in depth. Specialized sources, such as the *Wall Street Journal* or *The Economist* may cover the same story but provide much more information.

Third, we must understand if the information is objective—that is, if it describes objects and events as they actually occur—or subjective—that is, personal opinion and interpretation enter into the assessment. (There are entire schools of thought centered on postmodernism that argue all writing and speech is subjective, but we will ignore that intellectual game for now and assume that we can distinguish objective from subjective texts). Now, there is nothing wrong with subjective texts. In fact, we often go out of our way and pay significant costs to get subjective assessments. If a leading Wall Street investor recommends a stock, many people will rush to buy it. Information technology (IT) organizations regularly retain the services of market research firms, such as the Gartner Group, Forrester Research, and others, to have access to their opinions on market trends. We just need to provide explicit information to users so that they understand where a text falls on the objective-to-subjective spectrum.

Site Metadata

Once we have made assessments of Web sites or other resources, the information should be preserved. In addition to the document metadata we discussed earlier, we may also want site metadata that includes quality assessments. Site metadata will be of use to both end users evaluating the information provided to them by the document warehouse and to warehouse processes responsible for document retrieval.

Document Retrieval

The document retrieval process is analogous to the extraction phase in data warehousing. Once we have identified the source of our documents, we need to schedule their retrieval. As we saw when discussing the architecture of the document warehouse, retrieval servers act as agents to gather the documents and load them into the warehouse. Unlike data warehousing, we do not have specialized tools like those provided by Informatica, Sagent, and other vendors that are designed exclusively for loading text into the document warehouse. In general, we will find that scripting languages with rich support for pattern matching are excellent tools for working with internal data sources. Web robots and crawlers are excellent tools for retrieving Web-based information.

There are several factors to consider when developing a document retrieval schedule.

- Bandwidth availability
- Retrieval rates of targeted Web sites
- Backup schedules of internal file servers
- Priority of targeted documents

Bandwidth availability will determine how much text can be pushed into the document warehouse in a given time period. For example, a company with a T1 connection can expect about a 1.4 MB/sec rate of transfer under ideal conditions. Unfortunately, conditions are hardly ever ideal. The company may have satellite offices or stores that upload data to mainframes every night over the T1. The data warehouse might make heavy use of the network at the same time for its extraction, transformation, and load processes. Network architectures are often segmented to localize traffic as much as possible, and therefore minimize the total bandwidth taken up by a single transfer, but other jobs must still be considered.

Regardless of your connection speed to the Internet, the target location may have a slow response time. This could be due to the fact that the target site has a slow Internet connection or that the site is quite popular, and it is serving a large number of requests. Anyone making a number of requests to the same Web site should space their requests sufficiently so that a single user does not overly tax the target server at the expense of others.

When retrieving internal documents, one should schedule loads around backup schedules so as not to put additional demands on file servers. Backups often have a limited window of opportunity in which to finish, and additional loads on a server may prevent the processes from completing in time.

The most important scheduling issue in document retrieval is how to prioritize appropriately. Not all documents are as important as others. Core documents, such as internal documents and pages from subscription services, should be processed first. Visits to industry Web sites with timely information should come next, followed by topic and keyword searches for new material.

Another point to remember is that all documents retrieved should be processed before the next retrieval cycle begins.

Preprocessing Operations

Prior to fully processing documents in the warehouse, three basic preprocessing steps should occur:

- Character set identification
- Format conversion
- Language identification and machine translation

The need for these steps will vary with the types of document retrieval used in the document warehouse. The more unconstrained the searching, the higher the likelihood that foreign language documents and varying character encodings will appear in the document warehouse.

Character Set Identification

Many of us are accustomed to working with the ASCII character set. Along with EBCDIC, a predominately IBM creation, these two character sets have been the predominate methods for representing characters in computer applications. A newer standard, UNICODE has emerged to surpass other encoding schemes because of its ability to represent far more characters than either ASCII or EBCDIC. Unicode will eventually replace the older character sets but in the meantime we might need to identify the character set of a document, and if necessary, convert it to an appropriate character set for later processing tools.

Format Conversion

Documents come in a myriad of formats. There are several common word-processing, spreadsheet, presentation, and drawing formats, along with the Portable Document Format (pdf) and PostScript (ps) that many of us deal with every day. Again, depending upon the processing tools that will be used in later steps, these documents might need to be converted to a target format acceptable to those applications.

Language Identification and Machine Translation

Some tools, such as morphological analysis categorization tools, are language-specific, so identifying the language used in a document is important. Documents with markup tags sometimes specify the language using a metadata tag; other times a language identification program must be used. If a document is highly valued but not in a language suitable for text processing tools, then it must be translated.

Machine translation is not to the point where we can depend upon it for correctly translating all texts. A rough translation may be enough in some cases, while human review and correction may be needed for others. In the latter case, a translation queue is set up in the document warehouse to store the documents pending final translation, after which they can continue to be loaded along with other texts.

Text Analysis Operations

Once the preprocessing operations have been completed, the real work begins. We have touched on these steps in the previous chapter and will expand upon them further in later chapters but briefly, the key operations are:

- Indexing
- Feature extraction
- Categorization
- Summarization
- Clustering
- Machine translation

These are computationally demanding processes with a variety of implementations. As we shall see in future chapters, some tasks, such as machine translation, cannot be fully automated, while others, such as summarization, work quite well without human intervention.

Managing the Document Warehouse

Now that we have created a document warehouse and unleashed it upon the Web and the rest of our organization, we must manage and attend to it on a regular basis. In addition to the processing tasks described previously, document warehouse administrators will find themselves with several basic tasks, including:

- System maintenance
- Metadata maintenance
- Archiving
- Trimming and purging

System maintenance includes space management, backup and recovery, user administration, and related care and feeding operations.

Metadata maintenance is primarily the responsibility of domain experts. The primary tasks here are assessing document source quality measures, identifying new document sources, removing sources from search lists, and maintaining lists of topic searches.

Archiving will eventually be required in large document warehouses. Documents can accumulate rapidly, and rates of growth are difficult to estimate.

Most data in a data warehouse comes from internal sources, and their growth can be estimated based upon projected increases in the size and scope of source systems. Document warehouses retrieve much of their raw material from outside sources, where the growth rates of particular topics are difficult to measure. For example, how many documents on human genomes will be available in one year? Without strict controls on the document retrieval process, the input stream to the warehouse can grow in unexpected bursts.

In addition to archiving, two other processes can control growth. The first is trimming, or replacing a full document with a smaller representation. While we may want to keep information about documents in the warehouse for extended periods, we may not need all the details. Our options for reduced forms include keeping some combination of a summary, a list of categories, a URL, and some basic metadata. Occasionally duplicate files may be loaded in the document warehouse or multiple versions of a text may be stored intentionally. In either case, purging is the process of removing duplicates and multiple versions.

Supporting End-User Operations

End-user operation, in many respects, is the most important operation of the document warehouse. The documents have been gathered, converted, and translated as necessary, then thematically indexed, grouped into similar clusters, summarized, routed to interested readers, and finally stored in the document warehouse. Now end users, from analysts working on a marketing plan to strategic planners looking into competitive intelligence issues to front-line associates trying to resolve a customer complaint, are relying upon the document warehouse to support their tasks. In later chapters we will delve in detail into the issues surrounding end user presentation, navigation, and ad hoc querying of the document warehouse.

Conclusions

We have now come full circle. We started this chapter with a discussion of business intelligence needs, and that is where we shall end. End users are the driving force behind the document warehouse. The purpose of this repository is not to store documents in a mausoleum-like edifice but to make them accessible and usable by the broadest audience possible. With the correct infrastructure and the proper set of processes, we can reach our goal of meeting the textual demands of business intelligence users.

In the next chapter we will delve more directly into how document warehousing can support business intelligence operations by looking at specific problems, how they relate to end user requirements, and how we can craft a project plan to meet those needs.

CHAPTER 5

Meeting Business Intelligence Requirements: More Than Just Numbers

Business intelligence (BI) is as much an art as a science. On the science side, we have well-defined organizational structures and processes that can be measured with numbers. We have core facts, such as the number of full-time employees, gross revenues, percent of products failing quality control checks, and units produced in a given time period. From these we derive other measures, such as marginal revenues, levels of productivity, and quality control measures. We also have projections. Using sometimes simple and sometimes complex models of production and market demand, enterprises can estimate future conditions and profits. Even with all the numeric facts, measures, and projections, we cannot describe the complete state of an organization or market. Not all business intelligence is reducible to numbers. This is where the art of business intelligence is needed. For example, what problems are causing delays in the development of a new product? Why has employee attrition risen in the engineering group in the last six months? Some numbers do not need detailed explanation. If product sales drop sharply after a competitor releases a higher-quality, less-expensive version of our cash cow, we do not need a BI system to understand why. In this case, what was needed was a text-based system that could have monitored competitors' marketing efforts, patent applications, business alliances, and other activities and offered predictive information about their intentions.

In this chapter, we will examine how to meet the text-based business intelligence requirements of an organization. We will begin with a look into several types of problems that are solved with text analysis techniques. Next, we will develop techniques for defining BI requirements and understanding user needs. We will then discuss developing a project plan for a document warehouse as well as the design, development and testing of the repository, and related processes. The chapter concludes with a description of templates for document warehouse requirements gathering.

A Variety of Problems to Choose From

With so much business information in text form, it is not difficult to find sample problems. In this section, we will concentrate on four:

1. Intelligent document management
2. Historical reporting and trend analysis
3. Market monitoring
4. Competitive intelligence

These examples are certainly not exhaustive but provide a representative sample of the problems that can be addressed with text analysis.

Intelligent Document Management

Document management is the process of organizing, storing, and managing the processes associated with the life cycle of documents. In some cases, document management is used to support fixed processes, such as insurance claims processing. In that area, a large number of documents are moved through a relatively small number of possible paths through an organization. It has also been used in less structured knowledge management applications. Knowledge management systems (KMS) are not restricted to tightly controlled processing but allow for more flexible grouping and retrieval of documents. KMSs tend to be more topic-oriented than process-oriented and are more likely to be used in an ad hoc fashion than in fixed-process workflow systems.

As Figure 5.1 shows, as the formal structure of the document management process decreases, the need for metadata increases. This is due in part to the fact that much of the data in a workflow systems is highly structured. Names, addresses, policy numbers, and the specifics of a claim are found in predefined fields on a claims form. The information in these fields controls how the claims are routed and processed. Documents without predefined high-level structures, such as white papers, customer solicitations, marketing brochures, and memos need more metadata to properly classify the texts within a document manage-

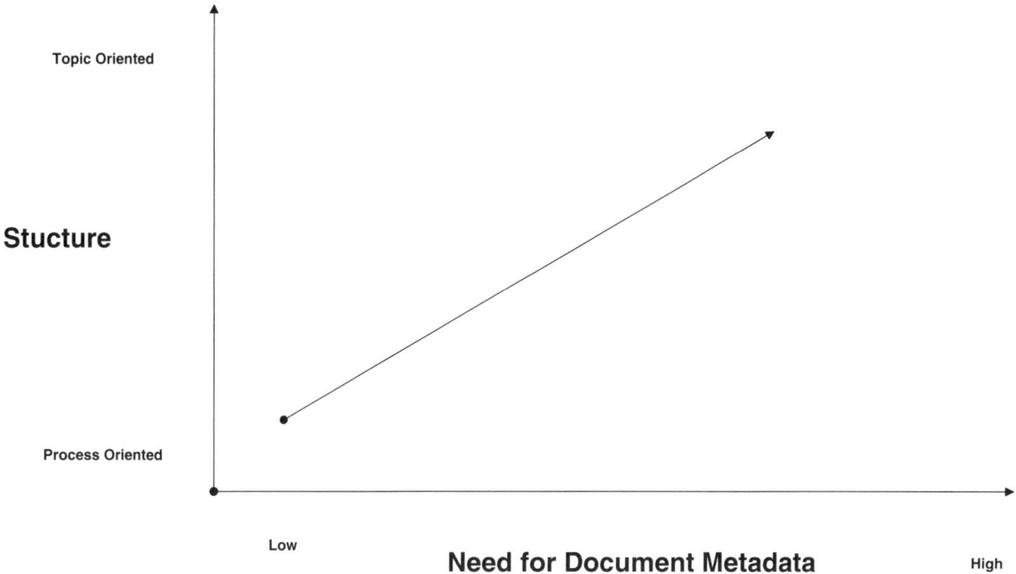

Figure 5.1 The need for metadata increases as the process structure decreases.

ment system. The metadata often includes the author, dates of original publication and revisions, key topics, disposition, and domain specific features, such as document type. Frequently, this information is maintained manually.

Intelligent document management reduces manual maintenance by extracting metadata from free-form documents. A classification tool, such as IBM Intelligent Miner for Text, can extract the main themes of a document, while feature extraction tools can identify persons, places, companies, and other organizations prominent in a text. Language identification tools can automatically identify the language used to write a text, which is quite important for multinational corporations and others with international dealings.

Historical Reporting and Trend Analysis

Publicly traded companies are required to disclose detailed information about their operations. Much of this data is numeric, such as income, cash flow, stock value, and other performance measures. This type of data has long been used for historical reporting and trend analysis but it is not the only type of information that provides insights into historic patterns and trends. The text that accompanies numeric data in securities reports describes essential aspects of a corporation and the challenges they face. Changes in key areas of an organization can be tracked by monitoring topics such as:

- Key market segments
- Products and services
- Forward-looking statements
- Revenue and economic conditions
- Contingency plans
- Restructuring efforts

These and other topics are regularly reported in mandated reports such as the Security and Exchange Commission's 10-K Annual Reports and 10-Q Quarterly Reports in the United States. Regulatory agencies, such as the Food and Drug Administration (FDA) and the Federal Communications Commission (FCC) in the United States, are a source of other historical reports that lend themselves to text analysis. Within the text analysis framework, summarization and feature extraction are the most useful techniques for historical and trend reporting.

Using summarization techniques, the key segments of reports, such as forward-looking statements, can be reduced to their essential statements making comparisons between those statements and subsequent company conditions easier. Multiple restructuring efforts warrant close review but a quickly read summary of such statements may provide enough information to an analyst to identify substantial management problems within a company. When utilizing historical reporting and trend analysis, summarization works well when combined with other information such as numeric data that precisely describes key measures, such as income growth and cash flow. It also works well with feature extraction.

One can get an understanding of changes in markets, products, and services by detecting differences in the persons, places, organizations, and other groups mentioned in securities reports, marketing material, press releases, and other publicly available documents. Feature extraction tools, such as Oracle interMedia Text's thematic indexing, provide the means to identify these attributes of texts.

Market Monitoring

Understanding market conditions requires, at minimum, an understanding of the demand for a set of products and the supply of the products. Take for example, the prescription drug market. The demand for specialized prescription drugs is limited to a relatively specialized market, such as those suffering from diabetes, coronary heart disease, or particular forms of cancer. Many projections of a disease's rate of growth and its composition among different demographic groups are available from groups such as the World Health Organization and the U.S. Centers for Disease Control. Much of this data is numeric and does not require text mining techniques to utilize it. The supply side is another story.

Of course information on the sales of current drugs is also readily available. Emerging treatments and new techniques are not easily quantified and categorized into preexisting classifications, so the numeric data that is available on potential new drugs is limited. However, a great deal of information is available in New Drug Applications to FDA and scientific journals. Summarizing and categorizing this type of information is essential to effectively harnessing it. Feature extraction can also be used to identify parties in a business relationship.

Competitive Intelligence

Competitive intelligence (CI) is the art of gathering information about competitor's activities and general market trends. From a business intelligence perspective, CI is the means of gathering and assessing external data on external factors influencing an organization. Traditional business intelligence typically concentrates on internal data sources, such as enterprise resource planning systems, point-of-sale systems, and financial and budget applications. Occasionally, BI applications will include external data on consumer behavior and household characteristics, especially in consumer retail markets. CI is much more oriented to external information since the goal is to describe extraorganizational influences.

In highly competitive markets, text analysis techniques provide the foundation for developing competitive portfolios. A competitive portfolio is a collection of information—some textual, some numeric—describing the state of a competitor with regards to current market conditions. Competitive portfolios consist of two main parts: strategic plans and tactical operations.

The strategic plan section is composed of financial data, product information, organizational structures, and market status. Financial data is gathered from any number of sources, such as regulatory filings and news sources. Product information is gleaned from obvious sources, such as catalogs and Web sites as well as more useful sources, such as patent and trademark applications, announcements of business partnerships or alliances in a vertical market, and mergers and acquisitions. Understanding a competitor's growth is essential. Market penetration can be measured quantifiably after the fact, but knowing that a strategic move is underway is far more useful. When a competitor issues debt instruments such as bonds, opens operations in new areas or forms alliances with new distributors, tracking this information can ultimately lead to piecing together the bigger picture of your competitors' long-term plans.

Day-to-day operations of competitors are more dynamic than strategic plans, but tracking operations can be just as useful. Short-term information on competitors often comes from advertising and sales information published by the competitor. With this type of information, feature extraction and classification are most useful. However, the value of this type of information has a much narrower time window than strategic information. Sales and advertising texts are not likely to provide new information to an analyst familiar with the market, so summarization is not necessary.

The four areas discussed here, intelligent document management, historical trend analysis, market monitoring, and competitive intelligence, can provide some idea of how text analysis can be used in the business environment, but to truly appreciate its value you must understand the business objectives of your own operation.

Defining the Business Objectives

For many potential applications of document warehousing and text mining, precisely defining business objectives will ensure that your efforts do not drift from one target to another without delivering on any. Some questions to keep in mind while defining your objectives are:

- What do you want from your text?
- What kinds of business questions need to be answered?
- Who will use the system?
- What types of information should be extracted?
- How should information be organized for browsing?

The following sections will address each of these questions in greater detail.

Getting What You Want from Your Text

Answering the question, "What do you want from your text?" sets the scope of your document warehousing project. Your answer can be relatively simple:

Users need access to all contracts, memos, and legal briefs concerning litigation currently under consideration by the legal department.

Or the answer can be quite expansive:

Users need summaries of internal documents, including white papers, reports, contracts, memos, and studies, along with external documents such as news stories, press releases, government reports, case law, administrative findings, and federal and state regulations. Users will search by keywords and topics and need to find documents similar to a given document. Each document must be categorized according to a specialized taxonomy defined by end users. Users will pose ad hoc questions and expect to receive a set of documents that best answer the question, prioritized by their relevance to the question. Internal documents must be available to users within 3 hours of publication; external documents must be available to users within 24 hours of publication.

Defining what we want from our texts requires that we know what types of documents we are dealing with, how they will be used, and when we need them.

Document Types

It is clear from both objective statements that one of these defining characteristics of a document warehouse is the type of document that is stored in the warehouse. Different document types will have different requirements for how to store and manage them. The following are some common document types and their requirements:

Contracts. Executed contracts are legally binding, while pending contracts are not, so the distinction between the two must be clear in the document warehouse. Contracts are generally highly structured and each sentence can be important. Revisions are frequently made in the form of addendums that may be tracked as separate documents. Summarization may be useful for sections of a contract but must be used carefully. Metadata for contracts should include the parties involved, effective dates, jurisdiction, and type of contract. The full text of contracts should be kept in the document warehouse.

Correspondence. Letters and e-mails with customers, suppliers, contractors, and others constitute a significant portion of the text generated in many companies. These documents are relatively short, so summarization is not appropriate. Depending upon the length of the text, categorization programs may not be able to accurately classify these texts. Keywords combined with metadata searches work best when retrieving short correspondence.

Material safety data sheets (MSD). MSD documents describe chemical substances found in industrial complexes, including procedures to handle the substances and treat accidental exposures. In the United States, these are relatively structured documents making categorization and feature extraction easier than usual. Like contracts, every sentence can be important, so summarization is not appropriate.

News stories. These texts are generally short external documents. The relevance of a news story varies over time and depends upon the topic. Market condition news stories have a relatively short useful time span, others, such as project demand for winter wheat, have longer useful life spans. News stories are not revised. Summarization, feature extraction, and categorization can be used effectively with news stories. The full text need not be kept in the document warehouse; a summary and URL are often sufficient. Images associated with news stories need not be stored in the document warehouse if they are available with the original text.

Policies. Corporate policies describe rules governing common situations in an organization, such as dealing with customers, accumulating and using leave time, and submitting travel expenses. Categorization and keyword indexes are useful for finding particular pieces of information. Summarizations are useful in some cases, but frequently a full description of a particular situation is needed. For example, under what circumstances can an employee carry over vacation accumulated in one year into the following year?

Project plans. These are internal documents describing projects undertaken by an organization. For some companies, such as consulting and construction businesses, projects are the main production processes. For other firms, such as manufacturers, projects are ad hoc tasks outside of standard operations. For the former, metadata about project plans include client information, schedule, and cost. For the latter, metadata about projects describe the objective of the project and standard operating procedures related to the project. Both would include metadata about the project manager, executive sponsor, schedule, and cost. Summarization techniques may be used to create executive summaries of project plans. Categorization and feature extraction can also be used to improve precision and recall of ad hoc queries.

Reports. Reports are generally long, in-depth studies of a particular issue or event. They originate form both internal and external sources. Reports may be revised, and drafts are common. Categorization and summarization of distinct sections works well. Reports are useful for extended periods and should be kept indefinitely. The full text of the report should be kept in the document warehouse. Reports may contain multimedia elements, such as drawings, images, video, and sound clips that should be included in the warehouse as well to maintain the integrity of the report.

Standards documents. These are common in many organizations, especially in Information Systems (IS) departments. Standards documents include descriptions of standard operating procedures, coding conventions, and documentation requirements, as well as sample and template documents. Standards documents should be kept in their entirety. Summarization works well in general with these texts.

This is not an exhaustive list of document types by any means. Also general statements, such as "correspondence is short," are not true in all cases, so corollary statements, such as "summarization does not work well with short texts such as correspondence" are not true in every situation. These examples should be considered broad-brush guides. As we will see later in the chapter, part of the requirements and analysis phases of document warehousing is spent assessing the particular features of the texts that will eventually populate the repository.

Document Usage

The same document can be used in several different ways, depending upon the end users' needs. For example, a reader may need to:

- Answer a particular question
- Understand a longstanding client relationship
- Become familiar with the details of a contract

Each case requires a somewhat different approach to meeting the need. In the first case, a user has a specific question that needs to be answered. This could be as simple as, "What is the payment schedule for the Alpha Industries project?" In this case, the work order, project plan, or contract could be used to answer the question. A keyword search would probably work well enough to answer the question but an index of extracted features could improve precision.

For an in-depth understanding of a particular topic, such as a client relationship, project history, or plan to market a new product line, no single document will provide all of the necessary information. Some key documents, such as project and marketing plans, will be read in detail. Contract metadata may be skimmed for particular details such as execution dates. Summaries of status memos provide a chronology of events in a project life, which is especially useful when projects go over budget and beyond schedule.

Sometimes the reader of a document needs to understand the details of a particular text. In this case, ease of retrieval is one of the most important services provided by the document warehouse. Draft versions of a document can also provide insight into the history of the document and highlight areas of dispute or concern in previous versions. Navigating to related documents can also provide more background into the topic discussed in the document under investigation.

Document Availability

The problem of document availability includes both how to ensure that the document is accessible when it is needed and how to ensure that it does not consume resources when it is no longer needed.

The first issue can be rephrased as, "When should the document be loaded?" Users may want government reports on crop production, trade and exports, or other economic indicators as soon as they are available. Internal documents that are produced on a regular schedule, such as status memos, may be loaded at a fixed time every week. Some documents may only be loaded on demand. For example, if a company that has been doing business within the European Union is considering expanding into non-EU countries in Europe, then an analyst may request reports and news stories dealing with political risk in Eastern European countries. Once these are loaded they may be kept for indefinite periods.

The question of when to purge the document warehouse is a tricky one. Data warehouses are historical repositories where data is never (in many cases) deleted. Document warehouses are slightly different. Documents can have several different representations within the document warehouse. We might store the original document, a summary of the document, or multiple translations of the full or summarized text. We could also reduce the level of detail retained and store a URL to a source document. This process of reducing the amount of detail kept on a document is called pruning. Of course, using URLs is done with the understanding that we are at the mercy of an external organization to maintain the text at that location. A middle ground option is to store metadata along with a URL to provide minimal details in the event that the original text is no longer available.

Ideally, all documents and their corresponding metadata can be kept indefinitely but when resource constraints impinge on the ability to grow the document warehouse, selective pruning is called for. Summaries of market news stories may be kept for several months after which only a URL, metadata, and categorization information are stored. Contracts, policies, and other legal documents may be kept indefinitely. Correspondence may also be kept indefinitely.

Answering the Right Business Questions

Question answering is to document warehousing as ad hoc querying is to data warehousing. Questions can generally be divided into two types: "Wh…" questions and Yes/No questions.

Who, What, When, Where, and Sometimes Why

"Wh…" questions include:

- Who is the current president of the European Union?
- When will the letter of credit application become finalized?

- What is the exchange rate between the Japanese yen and the British pound?
- Where did the shipment of cellulose acetate used in batch 784357 originate?

Technically, the list should include a "why" question such as, "Why is the actual revenue from District 7 below budget?" but the answer to that is much different from the answer to the other four sample sentences. We will return to "why" questions in a moment.

Question answering can be done in two ways. First, particular answers can be extracted from a set of texts and provided in isolation to the end user. This technique works well with small document sets, such as the contents of a Web site, or in limited domains, such as documents about international politics in the last five years. The second approach is to provide a set of documents likely to contain the answer. Although users will be required to read more to find the answer, additional background material is provided that may prove relevant to the broader issue the reader is addressing.

"Why" questions are problematic in that they do not simply require the extraction of a single piece of information like the other "Wh…" questions. "Who" questions are answered with the names of persons or groups, when questions are answered with dates or times, "what" questions are answered with objects, and "where" questions are answered with locations. "Why" questions are answered with explanations and logical chains of reasoning or sequences of events. At this time, the generation of a logical line of argument is beyond the scope of text mining and document warehousing, so the second approach is the only choice for why questions.

Yes or No Questions

Yes or no questions look simple on the surface, but like "why" questions, they can lead to a great deal of implicit reasoning. A simple question, such as, "Is Rome the capital of Italy?" is straightforward to answer by translating the question into a canonical form such as

CapitalOf(Italy,Rome)

and then querying a logic database. Another option is, assuming users are severely restricted in the syntax of questions that can be asked, to translate the question into a database query such as:

```
SELECT
     Captial
FROM
     Countries
```

```
WHERE
      country_name = 'Italy'
```

The second option is the type of operation used with natural language front ends to relational databases. This type of querying is suitable for work with relationally structured metadata. In general, when working with document collections, yes/no questions are best handled by retrieving documents or summaries that contain the answer. The advantage here is that the additional text may include additional information or indications that the question was understood. In this way, the chance of misinterpretation or unanticipated ambiguity is unlikely.

Determining Who Will Use the System

In addition to understanding types of documents and general patterns of use, it is important to understand and model the particular interests of individual users. You should keep in mind several things when developing an understanding of user's interests.

First, user interests vary over time. Sometimes, an interest in one topic can expand to include related topics, while at other times, an interest may become more specialized. Sometimes interests shift completely. In the most challenging circumstances, there does not appear to be well-defined areas of interest, as often occurs with ad hoc querying.

Second, because interests change over time, users will need some way to adjust their profiles. Depending upon the rate of change of someone's interests, this could be a significant task. One approach to minimizing the burden of these tasks is to use machine learning techniques in which users provide examples of items that interest them as well as things that do not. This type of approach can require a significant number of examples. If the examples are inconsistent or if our description of document topics is not precise enough to distinguish texts that a user distinguishes, then our description of user interest will be inaccurate.

The previous point brings up another issue. How we categorize and classify documents will limit how well we can define a user's interest. Our taxonomy or category list is our language for describing user interests. Our set of categories may need to change over time to accommodate user preferences.

A final point to remember is that using topics is not the only way of identifying interesting documents. We often reuse texts we have read before, going back to find a book, a passage, or a Web site with some bit of information we once saw. Past usage patterns may also need to be modeled. This can be as simple as browser-based bookmarks. It can be as complex as a generic model that can handle attributes ranging from document size and the last time a text was referenced to information about where it came from, links to the e-mail it was originally attached to, and the color of the book cover. Complex models have been developed in research environments but it may be some time before we see comparable levels of flexibility in commercial offerings.

Extracting the Right Information for Future Processing and Searching

Another area that must be addressed when gathering business intelligence requirements is the need to extract key pieces of information that often end up in a relational structure. The two main types of data that are extracted from text are features and metadata.

The features that should be extracted from a text will vary with the document type. The most common are:

- Company names
- Persons
- Organizations
- Places
- Dates
- Amounts of money
- Relations

By extracting these pieces of information and storing them in a table, we gain the benefits of dealing with a relational database, including fast indexed retrieval. Also, semantic processing and pattern matching is done only once, and the results stored for multiple uses.

Specific pieces of metadata also need to be defined. In general, a well-developed standard, such as the Dublin Core (described in Chapter 6), should serve as a starting point, but domain-specific attributes can be added as needed. Quality information, perhaps based on the particular document or the source of the document, should also be kept if there is any possibility of retrieving text with questionable information.

Classifying Documents for Browsing

The final issue in defining the business objectives of the document warehouse is to understand how documents should be classified. We have two broad options, a general taxonomy or a domain-specific taxonomy.

General taxonomies, such as Yahoo!'s classification scheme or Oracle interMedia Text's knowledge base, are examples of general taxonomies. These include categories such as science and nature, business and economics, government and politics, and geography, as well as arts and humanities. These taxonomies work well with broad-based document warehouses but those with a narrower focus would do well to use domain-specific taxonomies.

While general taxonomies can classify a wider range of documents, their lack of precision can limit their effectiveness. A company dealing with computer science, biotechnology, agribusiness, or land use controls may have a disproportionate number of documents classified under a small area of a general taxonomy. Take IT for example. A general taxonomy for IT might include the following categories:

- Software engineering
    - Methodologies
    - Case tools
    - User interfaces
    - Data management
    - Online transaction processing (OLTP) system
    - Decision support
        - Data warehouses
        - Document warehouses
- AI and expert systems
    - Tools
    - Techniques

Users doing work in Artificial Intelligence (AI) need a finer-grained distinction than the AI and Expert System category provides. A better taxonomy for them is:

- AI and expert systems
    - Tools
        - Programming languages
            - Functional languages
                - Lisp
                - Scheme
            - Logic programming languages

        - Prolog
        - Godel
- Techniques
    - Symbolic
        - Knowledge representation
            - Production systems
            - First order logic
            - Frames
- Connectionist and other neural network
    - Training algorithms
        - Back propagation
        - Simulated annealing

As this example shows, the domain-specific taxonomy can extend the number of levels in a general taxonomy to increase the depth of the classification tree as well as increasing the branch points to widen it.

While general taxonomies are good starting points, users will need to refine and extend them to ensure that documents are precisely classified.

Setting the Scope

As Gause and Weinberg point out in *Exploring Requirements: Quality Before Design* (Gause and Weinberg, 1989), defining requirements entails identifying what will be included in a system and what will be excluded. In the case of document warehousing, we are concerned primarily with:

- Defining the what information the user needs
- How to organize the documents
- The time and space requirements for the document warehouse
- Creating the project plan
- Designing and developing the document warehouse

The first two issues were addressed earlier in this chapter, and we will now turn our attention to determining how long it takes to load and process documents and how much space they will require. Next, we will briefly examine how to plan the process, and finally we will provide some templates to aid in the design and development of the document warehouse.

Time Requirements

The time requirements we are concerned with here are related to the time needed to gather documents, preprocess them, and analyze them. The total time required to load and processes documents is a function of the number of operations that are preformed on the document. The following are the most common operations:

- Retrieving
- Converting the format
- Classifying
- Clustering
- Extracting features and metadata
- Summarizing

In general, the total time required to perform these operations is directly related to the size of the document. Retrieving is often the longest operation.

Less common operations that may need to be performed include:

- Language identification
- Document translation

Language identification can be done by sampling a text and does not necessarily take a longer time for large documents. Translation, of course, requires analyzing the entire text, and so the time required is a function of the length of the document.

Since tools vary so widely in their approach to specific tasks such as extracting features and clustering groups of documents, the best way to determine the time requirements for the expected volume is to analyze sample sets of documents. When choosing a sample, make sure to include:

- Documents from multiple sources, both internal and external
- A range of document sizes
- All expected formats
- All expected languages
- Documents with special preprocessing requirements, such as the need to extract tabular data

For accurate timings, be sure to balance the samples to reflect the actual workload. If a legal department will be working primarily with long contracts, do not weight the sample with a large number of legal briefs and memos.

Space Requirements and Sizing the Document Warehouse

Sizing the document warehouse requires that we assess the space requirements of several components including:

- Document size
- Summary size
- Metadata
- Extracted features
- Number of categories

When estimating document size, we must determine whether the entire document will be stored in the warehouse. It is quite conceivable to create a warehouse with no full documents, only references to external resources and their associated metadata. On the other hand, some documents may be so important that complete control within the document warehouse environment is required, and the entire text of all documents is stored. To estimate the size of document storage required use the following formula:

```
(Number of Documents Stored Completely * Average document size)
+
(Number of Document Summaries * (Average document size * 20%))
+
(Number of Documents stored using URL/File Path * 100 bytes)
+
(Average Number of Categories * Number of Documents * 30 bytes)
+
(Number of Documents * 1000 bytes of Metadata)
+
(Number of Documents * Average Size of Extracted Features)
+
(Number of Translated Documents * Average Document Size)
```

The average document size refers to the size of the documents after any format conversion. Average document size and average size of extracted features will vary by application and need to be determined on a case by case basis. The average number of features will vary depending upon the tool used. Some categorization tools return a fixed number of categories—for example, the top ten—others return as many categories as needed. Depending upon the particular metadata needs, the 1,000 bytes for metadata factor may need to be changed. Clearly, this formula provides a rough estimate of the size of the document warehouse needed just to store basic data. Indexing in a relational database can require another 10–15 percent of space. Again, tools vary in their implementation, and some indexing techniques, such as Microsoft SQL Server's cluster indexes or Oracle's bitmap indexes, can save significant amounts of space.

Creating the Document Warehouse Project Plan

The first step in document warehousing, as in just about any other IT task, is developing the project plan. This does not have to be an elaborate or complex paper; it just needs to cover the basic tasks, resources, and schedule.

The task section will include steps such as:

- Gathering requirements
- Developing the document warehouse architecture
- Designing the document warehouse and related applications
- Testing and evaluating the warehouse
- Formulating a maintenance plan
- Training

Resources will include both human resources, such as end users and developers, and hardware and software infrastructure. During pilot projects, resources can be limited. For example, a single end user may act as the domain expert to identify requirements, while one or two IT developers utilize existing servers to implement a small document warehouse with a small set of text processing tools. Full-scale development efforts will require several end users to identify requirements, an architect to design and size the hardware infrastructure, designers to build data and process models, and developers to develop document load programs.

Schedules are essential to successful document warehouse projects. Like data warehousing, there is so much we could do that if we do not place a limit on the time spent on particular pieces, the project can become stuck in common traps such as scope creep and analysis paralysis. As Kimball and others have shown (Kimball et al., 1998) in data warehousing, it is possible, indeed preferable, to build incrementally.

Design and Development

Much has been written on the topic of system design and development, and I will not try to expand upon what has already been done. Instead, this section will provide some basic templates for use when developing a document warehouse. In particular, we will look at:

- Requirements
- Architecture
- Testing and evaluation

These templates do not constitute complete documents but simply provide a starting point for addressing document-warehouse-specific issues. Appendix A lists each of the three templates.

Conclusions

Meeting the business intelligence needs of our users is a complex task. While in the past we have focused on numeric information, we now have the tools at our disposal to tap textual sources as well. In this chapter we examined some sample applications as well as some of the issues that must be considered when developing a document warehouse. While well-tuned databases and high-performance tools are an important element in a successful document warehouse, understanding user requirements and formulating a project plan are the essential first steps. The next step, then, is to understand the architecture of a document warehouse.

CHAPTER 6

Designing the Document Warehouse Architecture

Document warehouses, like their data warehouse brethren, have distinctive architectures different from online transaction processing (OLTP) systems. In this chapter, we will examine the components that make up the document warehouse. The key constituent components of a document warehouse are:

- Document sources
- Text processing servers
- Document storage options
- Metadata repository
- End user access and user profiles
- Support for data warehouse integration

In the next chapter, we will begin to delve into the processes that occur within the document warehouse, but our focus now is on the "what" and not the "how" of document warehousing.

The document sources provide the raw material for the warehouse. Text processing servers analyze the text and extract salient information. Thanks to the large, high-performance demands of data warehouses and online transaction processing systems, we have a number of storage architecture options that we

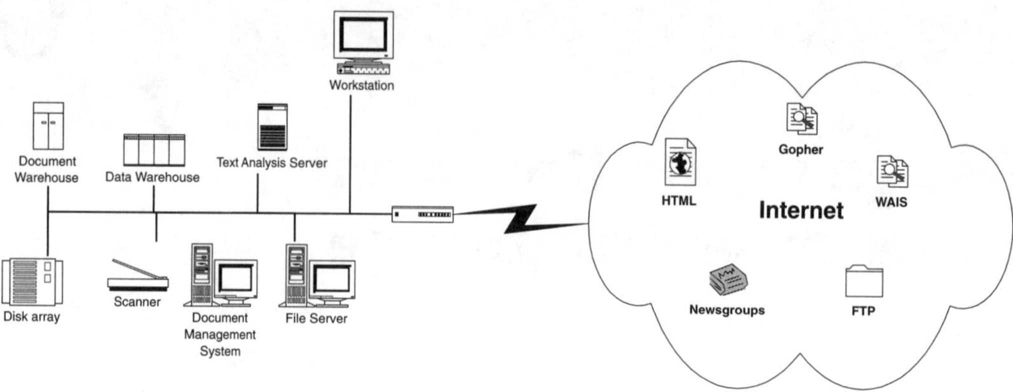

Figure 6.1 The architecture of a document warehouse.

will examine in detail. We will also look into the logical structure of document warehouses, including ways of managing metadata. Finally, the components that will ultimately provide end user access to the document warehouse will be presented. Figure 6.1 shows a general example of a document warehouse environment.

Document Sources

Document warehouses are populated from multiple sources, including:

- File servers
- Document management systems
- Internet resources

Clearly, there are overlaps in these areas. Document management systems and intranets both use file servers to manage files. However, based on their differences at their highest levels, we will consider them distinct.

When we look at each document source, we will ask several questions. What types of documents are available? How are the files accessed? What limitations of these document sources will affect the document warehouse? What features can be exploited for the benefit of the warehouse? The answer to these questions will affect how we design document retrieval programs and how we extract metadata. We will start with the simplest document source, the local file system. Figure 6.2 shows the key focal area of this section.

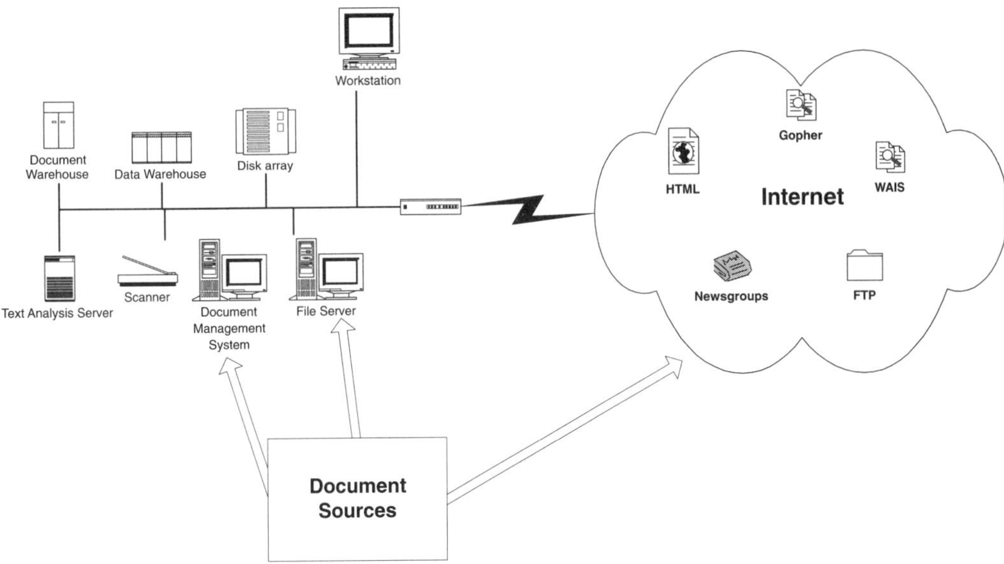

Figure 6.2 Document sources in the document warehouse environment.

File Servers

File servers are ubiquitous in the networked organization. In this section, we will briefly discuss the functional features of file servers and then various configurations to support a range of document-processing requirements.

File Server Functions

The primary purpose of these servers is to provide organized storage for a broad range of documents with as few restrictions as possible. For example, in UNIX file systems, files are treated simply as a stream of bytes. This simple assumption makes it very easy to store a variety of types of files, from text and spreadsheets to graphics and computer-assisted design (CAD) documents. With so few assumptions about the structure of a file, operating systems are able to provide only a few basic operations such as:

- Copying
- Deleting
- Versioning
- Purging
- Linking

Copying and deleting are common to all operating systems. The ability to store multiple versions of a single file is available in some operating systems, such as OpenVMS, along with the ability to remove old versions by using purge commands. Linking is the ability to create pointers to a file to make a virtual copy, which allows one to store a single copy of a file yet have it appear in multiple directories. This is another useful feature, but it is limited to only some operating systems, such as UNIX.

File servers are the wide-open ranges of document warehousing. The vast majority of an organization's documents are stored on file servers that are not themselves readily available from the Internet, or on specialized applications such as document management systems. The key benefit here is that documents are easy to retrieve for inclusion in the warehouse by using operating-system-level commands. Since most operating systems provide scripting languages and support even more powerful file manipulation tools, such as Perl and Python, extracting and loading documents from a file system is trivial. (Perl and Python are both full-blown programming languages useful for many different programming tasks, but their support for file manipulation makes them ideal tools for the extraction, transformation, and loading phase of document warehousing.)

Like a double-edged sword, the reasons that file systems are so easy to work with are also the reasons that they present difficulties for document warehousing. First, since most operating systems lend themselves to naming conventions, but do not enforce them, we can run into problems if we depend on file names to distinguish file types. As long as everyone agrees to save all word-processing files with a .doc extension, then there is no problem finding such files. More importantly, regularly produced documents may be named according to a complex scheme. For example, a consulting company may have a directory for projects with subdirectories for each individual project. Within each subdirectory, each file may be named according to its type—for example, status report, invoice, or proposal. Extracting all project status reports from the file system is then just a matter of searching each subdirectory, assuming that the naming convention has been followed. Without enforcement of these conventions, though, we could easily miss documents that should be included or include those that should be excluded.

Another limitation of file systems is that they do not store rich metadata about documents. All operating systems store some information about a file, such as creation date and time, last access time, and attributes such as archive flags. They do not include higher-level metadata such as author (although some have the username of the file owner, this is not the same), keywords, and description of purpose.

So far we have addressed the logical functions of file systems, but now it is time to turn our attention to the storage configuration options of these systems.

Storage Configurations

Broadly speaking, storage devices are generally configured in three different ways:

- Disk off server
- Network attached server
- Storage area network

Each configuration offers different benefits, and which on you choose depends on the particular needs of your document warehouse. While we are discussing storage configurations with regard to data sources in this section, the same points apply to storage for the document warehouse itself.

Disk off Server

The disk off server is the simplest configuration. In this scenario, disks are physically attached to a server using a high-speed bus such as the 160 MB/sec Ultra3 SCSI. The server itself is a node on a subnetwork shared with other servers and client machines as depicted in Figure 6.3.

With this configuration, storage is managed as part with the server thus minimizing additional administration overhead. The drawback is that the storage device is dependent upon the server, which may support other tasks as well. Connecting a storage device directly to the network, as with network attached servers, can eliminate that problem.

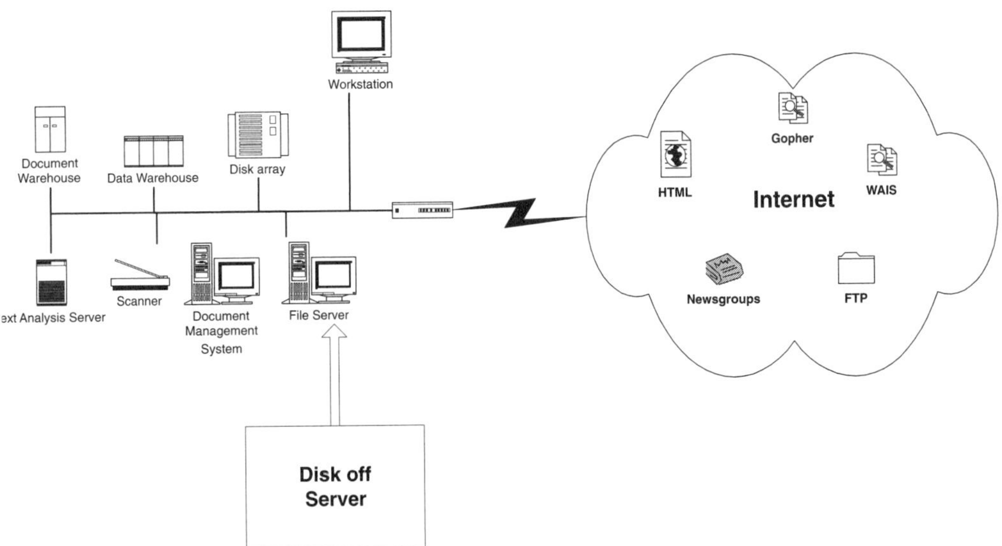

Figure 6.3 Disk off server configuration depends upon the server's network connection.

Network Attached Servers

Network attached servers (NASs) consist of disk arrays and other storage devices that connect directly to a network through their own network interface. NAS devices generally use 10-Mbps or 100-Mbps Ethernet or other high-speed network connections and, again, share subnetworks with servers and client devices. As Figure 6.4 shows, multiple devices are managed separately within NAS environments.

Because these devices are connected directly to the network, a down server or the load of a multipurpose server does not adversely effect its ability to provide file access.

Storage Area Networks

Storage area networks (SANs) are subnetworks connecting multiple storage devices, such as RAID (redundant array of independent disks) arrays and backup devices. The major benefits of SANs include high-speed, alternate paths between devices, redundancy, and reduced local area network (LAN) traffic. SAN devices are connected over Fibre Channel devices that can range in speed from 133 Mbytes/sec to 1.0625 Gbits/sec and span distances up to 10 km. While SANs support both point-to-point and switched topologies, the Fibre Channel-arbitrated loop (FC-AL) is used most often because of its ability to provide any-to-any connectivity. As the name implies, the storage devices on a SAN are on a separate subnetwork of the LAN as we can see in Figure 6.5.

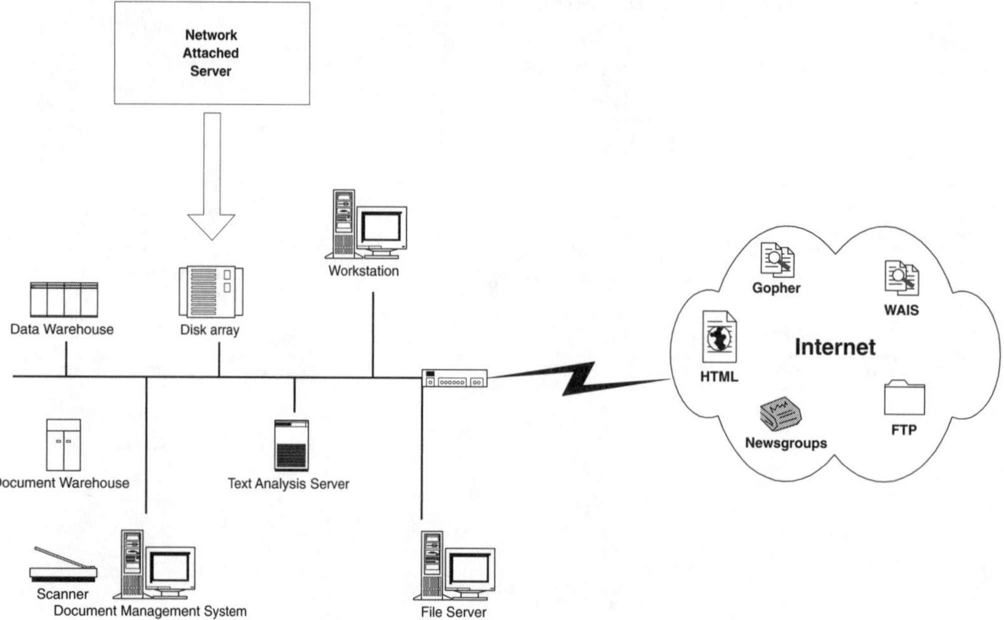

Figure 6.4 The NAS configuration connects storage devices directly to the network.

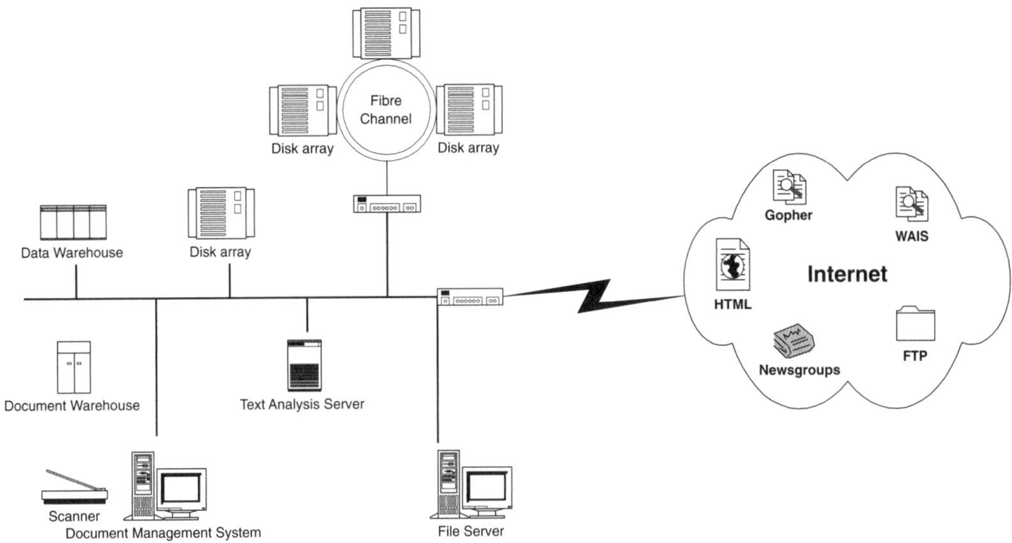

Figure 6.5 SANs minimize storage device to storage device traffic on the LAN.

Additionally, SANs provide centralized management for the storage devices within the subnetwork.

The benefits of using SANs include high-speed data access, ease of management, and reliable storage services due to redundancy in both the disk systems and the communication channels. For high-volume document or data warehouses, SANs provide the best option for maintaining scalable and reliable performance.

While many documents that will be loaded into the data warehouse exist simply as files on a file server, many other are housed within document management systems.

Document Management Systems

Document management systems have a long history in document-intensive organizations, such as insurance companies and government agencies. In addition to basic operations, such as image storage and conversion of text through optical character recognition (OCR), document management systems have moved into the realm of workflow and knowledge management. Delving into the details of document management is well beyond the scope of this book, but see Michael Sutton's *Document Management for the Enterprise: Principles, Techniques and Applications* (Sutton 1996) for a comprehensive reference on the subject. Figure 6.6 shows an example of a basic document management system.

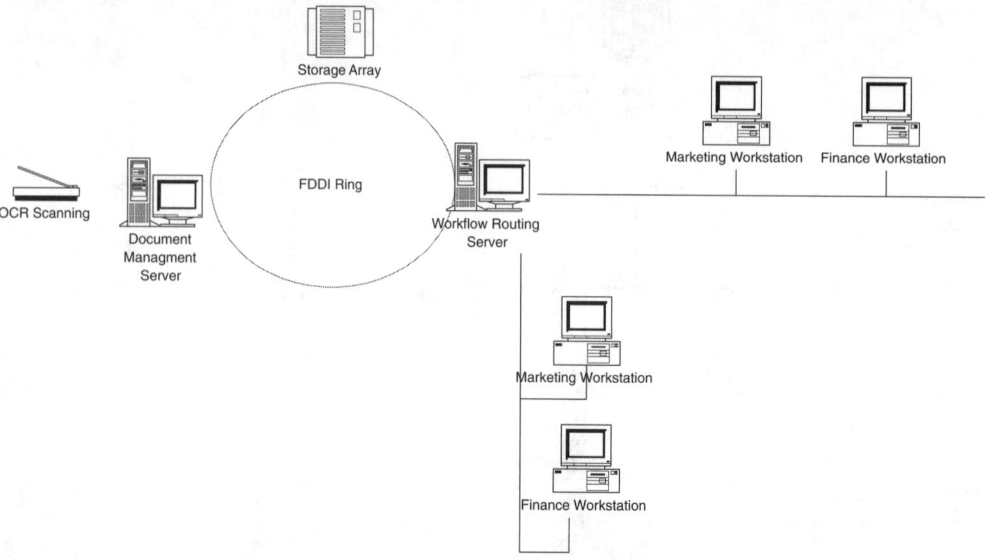

Figure 6.6 A document management system can include scanning, storage, and workflow routing functions.

For our purposes, we are primarily concerned with extracting documents and related metadata from document management systems for long-term inclusion in the document warehouse. The rising popularity of document management systems, which often operate at a departmental and not enterprise-wide level, has led to a proliferation of a number of different document management systems that need to interoperate. The document management industry has responded to the need by developing standards and programming interfaces to these systems. At the same time as document management vendors were wrestling with the interoperability problem, Web developers we addressing similar problems with content management on HTTP servers. The Internet Engineering Task Force (IETF) has developed a distributed authoring standard that is proving useful in the document management arena as well. We will now briefly turn our attention three of these standards:

- Open Document Management API
- Document Management Alliance
- WebDAV

Each standard provides a distinct approach to the problem of document management. The first two grew out of the document management industry, while WebDAV is an Internet standard that provides many of the benefits of the others while offering a widely adopted standard.

Open Document Management API

The Open Document Management API (ODMA) standard is a platform-independent application programming interface that provides a client application interface to document management systems. Widely used desktop applications support the ODMA—including Microsoft Word, Corel WordPerfect, and Visio's diagramming product. The goals of ODMA were to minimize the burden on application developers dealing with document management systems and to provide platform independence. To that end, ODMA addresses:

- Unique document identifiers
- Error handling
- Connections and a connection manager
- Document format names
- File system dialogs
- Character sets
- Application interfaces
- Document management system querying

With our focus on extracting documents, the query support ODMA provides is especially important. First of all, ODMA provides a number of functions to manipulate documents within the document management system, including:

- ODMGetDocInfo: This function returns information about the document from the document management system.
- ODMOpenDoc: This function makes a specified document available to the application.
- ODMQueryCapability: This function is used by clients to determine if a document management system provides support for a particular ODMA function.
- ODMQueryExecute: This function has a document management system parse a string representation of a query and return a query ID that is used by ODMQueryGetResults to retrieve document identifiers.
- ODMQueryInterface: This function is used to get a COM interface from an ODMA provider.

Some of these functions, such as the ODMGetDocInfo and Select queries can use specific attributes supported by ODMA. Some of the most important are:

- ODM_AUTHOR: Author of the document
- ODM_CONTENTFORMAT: Format name string indicating the contents using either MIME Content Type or Windows file type or extensions

- ODM_CREATEDBY: Username of person who created the document
- ODM_CREATEDDATE: The date and time the document was created
- ODM_DOCVERSION: The document version string
- ODM_LOCATION: The logical location (e.g., folder)
- ODM_KEYWORDS: A comma-separated list of keywords assigned to a document
- ODM_NAME: A descriptive name of the document but not the file name
- ODM_OWNER: The document owner
- ODM_SUBJECT: A string describing the contents of the document
- ODM_TITLETEXT: A short descriptive title of the document, possibly compiled from a document's profile
- ODM_TYPE: The type of the document, such as a memo, contract, status report, and so on
- ODM_URL: The Universal Resource Locator of a document

These attributes are used in Select statements that are at the heart of queries. For example, to find the author and location of all contracts, we could use the following statement:

```
Select
     ODM_DOCID, ODM_AUTHOR, ODM_LOCATION
Where      ODM_TYPE = 'contract'
```

For extracting documents from a document management system, ODMA provides many of the features needed to program extraction routines using a portable interface. While ODMA focuses on the function and COM level interaction between client applications and document management systems, another standard, the Document Management Alliance standard, addresses broader architectural issues.

Document Management Alliance

A consortium of over fifty commercial users, vendors, integrators, and government organizations formed a working group, the Document Management Alliance (DMA), to address interoperability in document management systems under the auspices of the Association for Information and Image Management (AIIM). Some of the key features of the DMA standard are:

- Automatic location of document repositories
- A common mapping for attributes across document management systems
- Support for document versioning

- Support for folders
- Support for Web browsers
- Support for multiple renditions of a document
- Automatic discovery of document classes and properties
- Support for the UNICODE character set

The DMA standard works with the ODMA function set, but also provides additional features to hide implementation-specific characteristics of the document management system. The resulting goal of the DMA standard is to provide true many-to-many interoperability between document management systems. True many-to-many interoperability comes at a cost, though, because the DMA standard is more complex than the ODMA. A third alternative, which again can operate with or independently of DMA, is the WebDAV standard.

WWW Distributed Authoring and Versioning

While ODMA may be too low level a standard for some, and the DMA standard may be too complex for others, the WWW Distributed Authoring and Versioning (WebDAV) standard provides something of a middle ground. WebDAV grew out of the needs of Web developers to better manage Web sites with features such as remote editing and loading and saving of documents and other media types. Some of the key features of WebDAV, defined in Internet Engineering Task Force (IETF) documents RFC 2291 and 2518, include:

- Document properties
- Typed connections called links
- Locking
- Reservations of documents
- Partial writes
- Name space manipulation
- Collections
- Versioning
- Security
- Internationalization

Furthermore, these features operate across replicated distributed servers. Since many of the features important for Web administration are also found in document management systems, it is not surprising that WebDAV has been adopted for some applications. WebDAV is the protocol behind Microsoft Office 2000

Web Folders and the interface to the Microsoft Exchange 2000 Web Storage System. WebDAV is also supported in the Apache Web Server, the Perl programming language through the PerlDAV module, and Adobe's GoLive product.

DAV Searching and Locating (DASL) adds improved functionality to WebDAV. The purpose of this standard is to extend the search capabilities of DAV to include:

- Finding resources of a particular kind
- Finding resources of a particular language
- Using content and property searches
- Word stemming
- Word proximity searches
- Query by example

DASL will also work with taxonomies and thus brings key text mining operations within the realm of a widely implemented Internet standard.

Through WebDAV and DASL, we can see how document management systems and the Internet may converge more tightly and blur the lines of distinction between what lies within and outside of a document management system. For the time being though, we will continue to treat them as distinct entities, since standards such as ODMA and DMA are implemented in existing systems, and the new DASL standard is still emerging.

Internet Resources

As we saw in Chapter 4, the Internet is a rich source of documents for text mining and the document warehouse. One way to look at the logical structure of the Internet is through the protocols it supports, and here we will consider four protocols as indicative of important architectural elements for document warehousing. The protocols we will consider are:

- HTTP
- FTP
- Gopher
- WAIS

HTTP is the most popular and is the base protocol for the World Wide Web. XML Linking and Pointing, the newest of the protocols, is quickly addressing some of the shortcomings of HTTP, and is commonly used for transferring files, while Gopher and WAIS have, to some degree, been eclipsed by HTTP. Next, we will briefly discuss the role played by these protocols, and in the next chapter we will look in greater detail at how to exploit these tools when searching for document warehouse sources.

HTTP

The Hypertext Transfer Protocol (HTTP) protocol provides the means to link documents and other resources. When we think of text mining, we usually mean text mining in a hypertext environment using either HTML or XML Pointing and Linking. Both build upon HTTP. Along with Universal Resource Locators (URLs), it provides the building blocks for retrieving documents from the Internet, intranets, and extranets.

FTP

The File Transfer Protocol (FTP) provides Internet-based access to hierarchically organized file systems or parts of file systems. One of the key benefits for document-loading processes is that document-loading programs built on FTP become portable across file systems. Of course some file system idiosyncrasies may need to be attended to, but for the most part the core command set is the same across server types.

Gopher and WAIS

Gopher provides a hierarchical organization of text on the Internet, while the Wide Area Information Servers (WAIS) support searching for text on topically organized WAIS servers. Neither protocol is as widely used as HTTP or FTP but some early sites still support them.

From Document Sources to Text Analysis

Finding documents is the first step in the document warehousing process, and our main sources are file systems, document management systems, and the Internet. Each type of source has its own distinct set of architectural features and processing issues that we must bear in mind when designing the document warehouse. For example, file systems have relatively straightforward utilities and commands for manipulating documents, the Internet provides several protocols, reflecting different organizational structures, and document management systems may require the use of a proprietary API or one of a few standard interfaces to their document repository. In any case, once the means of extracting the documents have been defined, we will need to get them to servers for text analysis.

Text Processing Servers

Text processing servers are responsible for getting documents, analyzing them, and distributing them as needed. We will first examine how documents can be retrieved using agents and crawlers and then look into how to configure text analysis servers to appropriately balance the workload in a document warehouse. Figure 6.7 depicts text processing servers in the middle of the document warehouse, reflecting their central importance to text mining operations.

Using Crawlers and Agents to Retrieve Documents

Agents and crawlers are programs designed to work in a networked environment. Crawlers are programs that run on a single server and retrieve resources—such as Web pages—and use information within that resource to find other resources. In document warehousing, an agent is a program that may run on different servers in a network environment to carry out a specific task, sometimes communicating with other agents.

Crawling the Web

Anyone who has used a search engine has benefited from the use of crawlers. These programs are fairly straightforward. An indexing crawler is given a start-

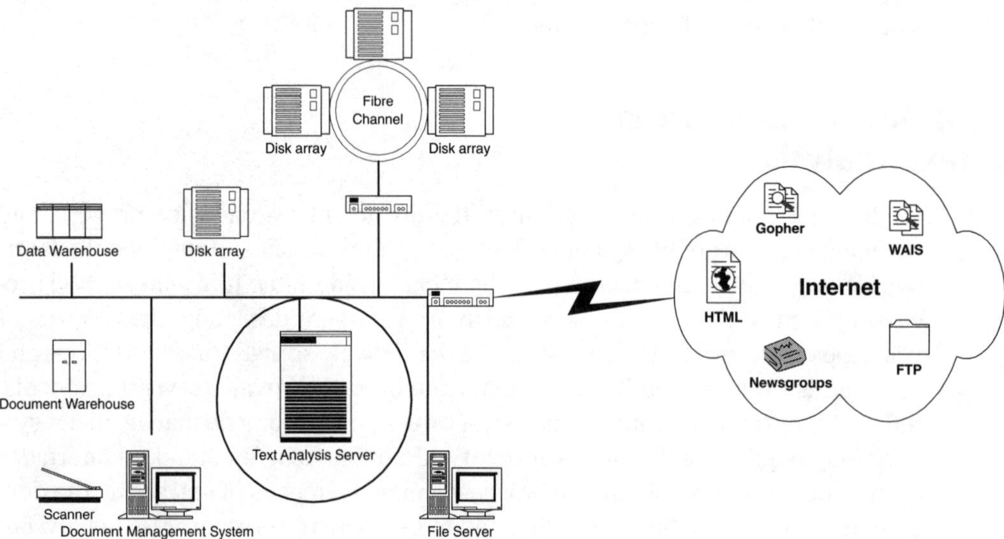

Figure 6.7 Text processing servers are the heart of the document warehouse.

ing point, usually in the form of a URL. The crawler downloads the document at the specified URL and then extracts all of the hypertext links to other resources from that page. The crawler then repeats the fetch and extract processes, collecting documents as it goes.

Not all crawlers are strictly for searching and indexing. Crawlers exist for extracting specific pieces of information, such as the cost of a book or the times of airline flights. These programs are frequently called agents, but here we will reserve that term for a more complex type of system. Rather than extract hyperlinks, these programs fetch a Web and extract particular pieces of information, such as product descriptions and cost or scheduled departure and arrival times of flights. The principles and functions of search and index crawlers remain the same. Custom crawlers can be designed for document warehouses and other decision support environments with specific needs. For example, an energy industry analyst may want to gather crude oil price projections from a number of different sources for comparison. In this case, as with crawlers designed for comparison shopping over the Internet, a number of specific sites are visited, and targeted information is extracted. Exactly how the information is extracted is dependent upon the document retrieved. XML documents can be easily parsed, while free-form text must be more carefully analyzed to extract relevant information with custom routines.

Crawlers are uncomplicated but powerful programs. Although each step is simple, when done over and over in a richly interlinked environment, the collective results can be an expansive search of the hyperlinked environment. Another way to effectively search a distributed network of documents is with agents.

Agents in Action

Agents differ from crawlers in several significant ways. First, agents are directed to accomplish a specific task, such as retrieving information about a particular topic. Search crawlers, on the other hand, move from document to document through links without regard for a reader's topic of interest. Second, agents can interact with other agents to share information, while crawlers work independently. A key benefit here is that an agent can acquire information, such as a list of interesting sites, from another agent and thus avoid having to compile the list itself. Third, because agents interact, more complex architectures can be developed on the basis of specialized agents. For example, some multiagent systems found in information retrieval use producer information for other agents, consume information and deliver it to end users, and organize tasks. Yet another distinction is that agents can persist over time, continuing to look for information. Agents with long lifetimes, such as weeks or months, become "Smart Browsers," continually browsing the network looking for topics of interest, perhaps revisiting sites and constantly sending back new information (Marsh and Masrour

1997). While a number of different approaches have been developed for implementing multiagent information retrieval systems, they share a common general architecture, which we will discuss next.

Multiagent Architecture

Both commercial systems such as MCC's InfoSleuth (www.mcc.com/projects/infosleuth), and research projects, such as Marsh's ACORN (Marsh and Masrour 1997) and Decker et al.'s MACRON (Decker, et al. 1995), share enough common architectural features that we can generalize a basic multiagent architecture for information retrieval. It should be noted that these applications are designed for discovering and retrieving information but not necessarily for a document warehouse or for text mining purposes. Figure 6.8 shows the basic multiagent architecture.

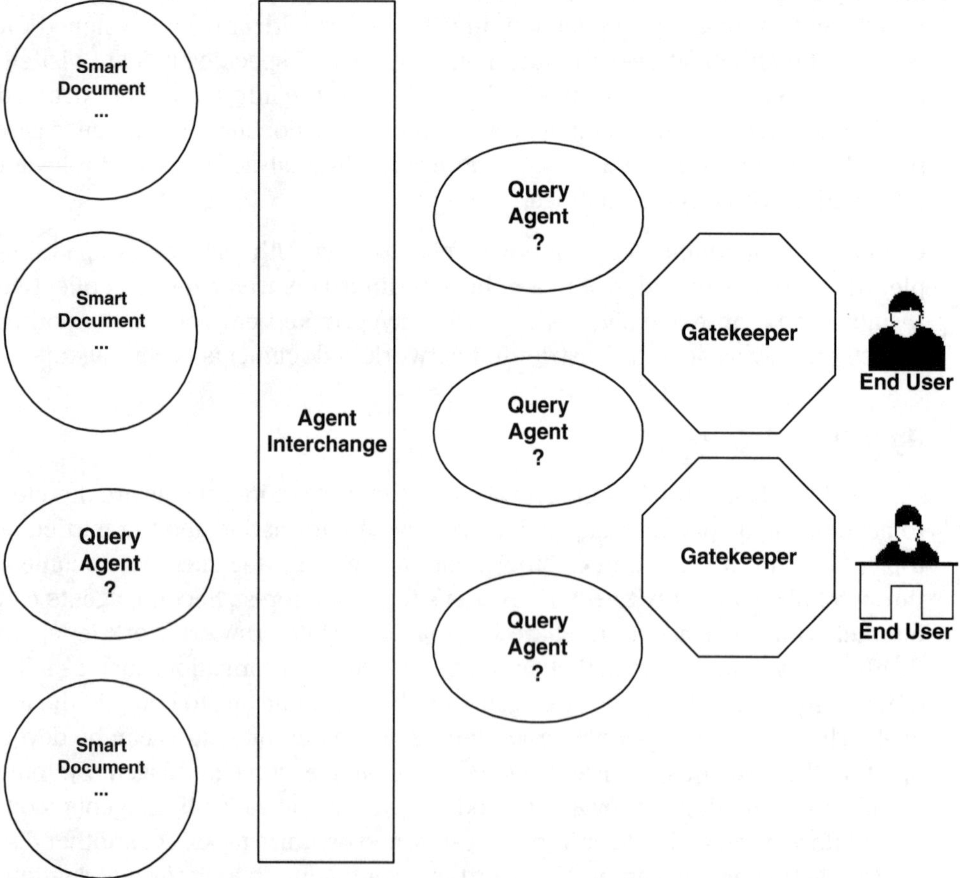

Figure 6.8 A generalized multiagent architecture for information retrieval.

The basic components of multiagent systems include:

- Consumer or query agent
- Producer or smart document agent
- Agent interchange
- Gatekeeper agent

Consumer or query agents represent a user's area of interest, such as the rate of production of crude oil and natural gas. The representation could be a simple list of keywords, a set of terms from a taxonomy, or a query in a more complex language such as the Knowledge Query Manipulation Language (KQML). The goal of consumer agents is to find producers representing documents that match the consumer's interest. Frequently, a consumer will start with a list of potential sites that may have the information sought. Consumer agents generally have limited lifetimes, after which they cease to search for information.

Producer agents represent documents similarly to the way in which consumers represent queries. In the case of the ACORN system, the Dublin Core metadata set (which includes description, type, and subject keywords among other attributes) is used to describe a document. InfoSleuth uses KQML and a built-in taxonomy to describe the contents of a document. InfoSleuth also uses another type of agent, the ontology agent, to map terms into a common language for querying between agents. Just as consumers start with a list of potential sites that may have relevant information, producers act as active publishers of information, distributing it to a starting list of readers who may find it of interest. Like consumers, producers can have limited lifetimes. In most cases, the information is archived before the agent expires so that it is still available in a central repository such as a document warehouse. Some multiagent systems perpetuate the life of agents if the information is useful to a large number of consumers, and in some cases, the agent is duplicated to make its information more widely available.

An agent interchange, called a café in ACORN and a broker in InfoSleuth, match consumers and producers. When a consumer finds a producer agent that may be of interest to the consumer's reader, the producer is directed to send the information to the consumer's home server. At the home server, a gatekeeper agent may be used to determine if the information is still relevant to the reader and, if so, add it to the reader's collection of resources.

The use of agents in commercial environments is still limited but we can expect their use to grow. They provide a more flexible architecture that can exploit the processing resources of a distributed network of computers and thus avoid resource bottlenecks on single servers.

Text Analysis Services

Crawlers, agents, and other document retrieval mechanisms will provide the grist for the text analysis mill, which is implemented on text analysis servers. As we have noted in previously, while we make a logical distinction between text analysis tasks, some of them can—and often are—performed in tandem on the same server. Not all document warehouses will need all text analysis services, but the core operations are:

- Character set conversion
- Format conversion
- Machine translation
- Full-text indexing
- Thematic indexing
- Feature extraction
- Summarizing
- Clustering
- Question answering

Character set conversion and format conversion are really preprocessing steps that provide the document in a form suitable for the chosen text analysis tools. Machine translation is a particularly challenging area, and we will leave that for Chapter 8, when we will examine in detail the various options and tradeoffs with machine translation and machine-aided translation techniques. Full-text and thematic indexing and feature extraction tend to overlap but they provide the basis for the most common representation scheme used in information retrieval—the vector model. Once these three operations are performed, we will have an efficient representation of a document for the warehouse. In addition to indexing by the main features, it is often useful to maintain in the warehouse abstracts or summaries of documents. Once documents are represented in the warehouse, we can group them together with clustering techniques. The last operation, question answering, is akin to ad hoc querying in data warehousing.

With these operations in mind, we need to understand key architectural issues such as:

- Given a set of text analysis tools, what preprocessing must be performed?
- What services are bundled together, for example character set conversion and format conversions?
- Given the business intelligence requirements of the project, what text analysis is required and how soon after loading does it need to be done?

Some text analysis tools have preprocessing functions built in directly. Oracle's interMedia Text and AltaVista's Discovery tool can process a wide range of document types, while others require plaintext files.

Some services are bundled together. For example, some tools will generate a full-text index while a document is loaded, and the loading process itself may entail a character set conversion and a format conversion. The benefit of a bundled approach is that there are fewer tasks for the warehouse manager to attend to, but this comes at the expense of not being able to partition the workload by task. In general, only core operations, such as conversions and full-text indexing, are bundled. Optional text analysis tasks and the more computationally expensive operations, such as summarization and clustering, can be run on separate servers or as distinct processes with appropriate operating system priorities.

The other main decision that must be made in determining the appropriate architecture for text analysis servers, is how soon operations need to be performed. Certainly, new documents need to be loaded and indexed as soon as possible. What if summaries were performed for only some documents and then did not finish until well after the core operations? Can clusters be developed over time, perhaps running at a low priority and thus only when no other operations are taxing a server? If some operations can be performed at a slower pace or over a longer time, then fewer computational resources are required than if a faster turnaround time were required.

Document Warehouse Storage Options

Another decision in the design process with a number of good options is how to store the documents and related attributes of the document warehouse. In effect, we have three main choices:

- Databases
- File systems
- Distributed storage

Databases traditionally have focused on numeric and string data, but not text. Fortunately, this is changing, and major database management systems (DBMSs) are providing support for text, multimedia, and other binary large objects. Files systems still provide an alternative for storing at least the documents of the warehouse, but there are some disadvantages to databases that we will discuss. Finally, the potential size of a document warehouse may become prohibitive if we intend to store every document directly in the warehouse. Keeping only metadata and extracted features, including indexing information, and storing the URLs of Internet documents instead of the full text to maintain a distributed document warehouse over the Internet, is one approach. Again, there are advantages and disadvantages that need examination.

Database Options

When we think of databases, we often think of relational database management systems (RDBMSs) such as DB2, Oracle, SQL Server, Informix, and Sybase. These certainly dominate the database market, and the data warehousing market in particular, but there are other options. We will consider the three most readily available options for database storage:

- Object databases
- Textbases
- Relational databases

Object databases offer a hierarchical alternative, while textbases treat the document and its attributes as the basic data types. Textbases have evolved to accommodate the needs of text management systems that, at least in the past, have not been well supported in other models. Relational database support for text centers on the basic entity and attribute model so familiar in systems design. Our concern here is not to delve into the details of each database design strategy (that is well documented elsewhere), but to weigh the pros and cons of each type of database as the backbone of the document warehouse.

Object-Oriented Databases

Object-oriented databases use a hierarchical model as the basis for their design. These databases are popular in applications that have a natural hierarchical structure, such as engineering design, where a component may be a part of another component, which in turn is part of another large component, and so on. For document warehousing, object-oriented databases have two features that are particularly appealing.

First, these databases support classes and instances. A class is an abstract description of an object, such as an SEC report, a news story, or a regulatory agency requirements document. Classes allow us to define the structure of a document and use it to create specialized versions in the form of more specific classes, such as financial news story specialized to merger news story, earnings news story, or product announcement news story. Instances of these classes are the actual documents in the warehouse. The support for classes and instances is a natural fit in some document warehousing applications, especially in multidimensional taxonomies that categorize documents along several different themes or dimensions.

Second, object-oriented databases have long provided support for binary objects. Since documents in the warehouse still need to maintain formatting and rendering information, the most efficient method is to store that data along with the document itself, and binary objects are the best way to do that.

Another advantage of object-oriented databases, at least in some cases, relates to the Document Object Model (DOM). DOM is an object model for documents that provides an object-oriented API for managing XML documents. This language-independent descendent of HTML is a natural fit with object-oriented databases.

Textbases

Textbases, such as Lotus Notes and Domino, provide a platform for developing document-centric applications. These applications tend to support a range of information retrieval options, such as complex searches, as well as document-oriented design features, such as folders and electronic file cabinets. The advantages of textbases are their native support for text operations and their ease of use.

Support for text operations often includes more than full-text searching and indexing. Some tools provide for document hierarchies, allowing users to track threads, such as Note's main document, response document, and response-to-response document. Navigation tools for exploring the textbase are also common and in some cases customizable, adding to the tool's ease of use.

Relational Databases

The relational database is the king of the DBMS mountain. With a proven track record for scalability and flexibility in design, RDBMSs are the best choice for document warehousing for several reasons.

First, a broad range of designs can be supported, from generic data models to application-specific models, such as dimensional models in data warehousing. David Hay's *Data Model Patterns* (Hay 1995 demonstrates the flexibility of generic data models in several areas, including document management. Ralph Kimball's *Data Warehouse Toolkit* (Kimball, 1996) and Kimball et al.'s *Data Warehouse Lifecycle Toolkit* (Kimball 1998) develop commonly used techniques for dimensional models that provide for efficient and easily navigated data warehouses.

A second benefit of using an RDBMS is that we can support multiple types of text indexing structures, such as full-text indexes, thematic indexes, and multidimensional taxonomies, using the same basic RDBMS features.

Third, and perhaps most importantly, with text mining and document warehousing, we are not just interested in treating documents as a monolithic unit or a hierarchy of subdocuments. We want access to the semantic content of the document, and to get this we must have a way to store and access the key attributes about the document such as its:

- Main topics
- Names of companies, government agencies, or individuals mentioned
- Relationships between those organizations and individuals
- Other metadata

All of these items easily fit the tabular model of relational databases. In addition, the demands of data warehouses have pushed relational database vendors to develop systems that can manage large (terabyte-plus-sized) databases. Now, we have the benefits of a natural fitting model with the scalability and performance needed for large document warehouse projects.

The Metadata Repository and Document Data Model

In addition to storing documents, which could fit into any of the three database models just discussed, we need to store information that describes those documents and that has been extracted from those documents. This information constitutes the metadata about the document and comes in four types:

- Document content metadata
- Search and retrieval metadata
- Text mining metadata
- Storage metadata

Document content metadata generally follows one of the document metadata standards such as the Dublin Core or the Text Encoding Initiative. Search and retrieval metadata contains information about when documents were added and how they were found. Text mining metadata is basically the output from text mining operations. Storage metadata is used for managing the contents of the document warehouse.

Document Content Metadata

While a document warehouse designer can arbitrarily define the document content metadata for the warehouse, it is strongly suggested that you use one of the widely adopted standards as a basis. The main reason for this is that there is a growing awareness for the need for metadata on the Web. Organizations are adding more metadata to the content of their Web sites to ease *their own* content management problems. As intranets grow within organizations and sometimes merge, they become more difficult to navigate and searching with standard tools still brings on the problems of poor precision and recall. As a result, there is a heightened interest in using metadata to improve the value of intranets and the Web in general. The Dublin Core metadata standard was developed with Internet resources in mind and is the best option for most document warehouses. If your warehouse will be integrated with other systems that depend upon other metadata standards, such as geographic information systems, then by all means use those standards. Regardless of the standard used, when collecting documents from sites that use the same standard as you do, the metadata can be easily extracted and categorized within the document warehouse.

Here is a basic list of attributes to start with when designing content metadata:

- Creator
- Subject
- Title
- Description
- Publisher
- Contributor
- Published Date
- Revised Date
- Type
- Format
- Language
- Rights

Search and Retrieval Metadata

As we will see in Chapter 8, the process of managing the search and retrieval process is dependent upon metadata about what types of documents to look for. Unlike document content metadata, which describes the features of a particular document, the search and retrieval metadata describes:

- How the document came to be in the document warehouse
- What kind of source it came from
- How to manage multiple versions

How documents come into the warehouse is defined by source metadata that includes URLs for online sources or file system pathname for local files, frequency of searches, regular expressions specifying search criteria, and crawler- or agent-specific information that controls the search processes. For example, some crawlers allow users to specify a time interval between requests to servers. This is especially useful when searching sites that could easily be taxed by rapid page hits.

Not all sources are the same, and users of the warehouse will need information about where documents came from. The most important attribute about a source is its quality. For document-centric applications, this can be distilled down to timeliness and veracity. News sources are in constant competition to deliver breaking news, so they are generally very timely sources. On the other hand, some checkout counter tabloids may be timely, but the accuracy of their content is questionable. For complex issues, such as those warranting government investigations, such as airline crashes, accuracy is more important than timeliness when measuring quality. Timeliness and veracity are the two core measures for quality but you may find the need for others, depending upon your applications.

Another issue that should be dealt with during the search and retrieval process is versioning. Frequently, one will repeatedly find the same document at a source. Checking the timestamp of the source is the simplest way to determine if this is a new version and should be downloaded. Operating systems that support versioning will provide other means for detecting changes in versions as well. In some cases, as with draft documents, contracts, position papers, or other evolving texts, you may want to store all versions of the document instead of replacing the existing version in the warehouse. (This raises a distinction between data warehouses, where data is rarely, if ever deleted, and document warehouses, where some texts do not warrant perpetual storage. There will be more on this topic in Chapter 9.)

Here is the basic list of search-and-retrieval metadata to begin with:

- Source Type
- URL Pattern
- FilePath
- Depth
- Span Site Indicator
- Number of Tries
- Time out
- Wait between Retrievals
- HTTP UserName

- HTTP Password
- Proxy UserName
- Proxy Password
- Reject List
- Include Directories
- Exclude Directories
- Search Engine

With this set of search and retrieval metadata one can precisely control the document collection process.

Text Mining Metadata

The content of text mining metadata is driven by the specific needs of the document warehouse users. The most basic elements of text mining that metadata will include document:

- Features, such as keywords and topics
- Summaries
- Relations

Features identify the main points of a document. Depending upon the tools used, features may be automatically stored in a database and managed behind the scenes, much like indexes in a relational database. In cases where they must be dealt with explicitly, keywords can be stored as attributes of a document along with a measure of their frequency within the document. Topics similarly are stored along with a measure of the importance of the topic to the overall document. In most cases, documents will have multiple keywords and topics.

Depending upon the expected use of certain document types, summaries can be generated after the documents are loaded into the warehouse or on an as-needed basis. Since summaries describe the content of a document, they are, by definition, metadata, although metadata generally falls into more of a conventional attribute value form.

Relations describe the relationships between persons, places, and things in a document. A financial news story that includes text such as:

> Mary Smith, president and CEO of Alpha Industries, announced the acquisition of Gamma International of Montreal at a press conference today.

Identifies two relations directly, as shown in Table 6.1.

Table 6.1 Relations Describe Roles and Attributes of Entities within a Text

ENTITY1	RELATIONSHIP	ENTITY2
Mary Smith	President and CEO	Alpha Industries
Gamma International	Location	Montreal

Feature extraction programs can identify these relationships as well as data and time expressions, ages of persons, proper names, and others. The fact that a precise relationship can be established allows users to search the metadata of relations with precision rather than having to search text with criteria such as "Mary Smith" AND "president."

Document features should be tied to a taxonomy of features to allow the greatest search and navigation flexibility within the document warehouse. A taxonomy, sometimes called a ontology to distinguish it from navigational taxonomies such as Yahoo!, is a knowledge representation scheme for organizing relationships between terms. Terms relate to each other as either broader terms or narrower terms. Taxonomies can also be represented as thesauri (see Chapter 8), which add support for preferred term relations. A single concept can be expressed in several forms, for example the terms *President*, *President of the United States*, *Chief Executive*, and *Commander in Chief* all refer to the same position. Rather than integrate all of these terms into a taxonomy, a single term is chosen as the preferred term used in the taxonomy. The synonymous terms are mapped to the preferred term during indexing.

Storage Metadata

Storage metadata describes how a document should be handled once it has been retrieved and analyzed. The main types of storage metadata deal with how to represent the document in the warehouse and when to change representations.

Let's describe the possible representation schemes. First, we can store the entire document. That sounds pretty straightforward, but like everything else in the world of IS, things are not as simple as they first appear. Documents may need to be translated and reformatted. Should the original document be kept along with the translated version? How many different translations should be kept? Should only summaries of the translation be kept? Machine translation, while reasonable, is not perfect, as we shall see in Chapter 8. Should we keep a machine-translated version of the document until a human translator reviews and corrects it? Depending upon the specific needs of your text mining applications, additional storage metadata may be required. In general, though, the issues will center on how to handle multiple representations of the same content.

Instead of storing the entire document, we may decide, for reasons of balancing storage with document priorities, that not all documents need to be stored in their entirety. We could store only summaries or just a URL. In the later case, we should specify when the URL should be verified to ensure that it still exists.

In some cases, the timeliness of some documents may require that they be stored in the document warehouse at first but after a period of time can be effectively archived. One approach in this situation is to store the entire document at first and then store only the summary and eventually just a URL or other reference to its location. As mentioned previously, this process of reducing the document representation within the warehouse is called pruning and can be an effective strategy for balancing the need for controlled access with the need to manage storage.

Here is the basic list of storage metadata to begin with:

- Store Entire Document Indicator
- Store Summary Indicator
- Store URL Indicator
- Store Pathname Indicator
- Prune Full Document
- Prune Full Document after
- Prune Summary Indictor
- Prune Summary after
- Keep Full Translations
- Keep Summarized Translations
- Translation Review Required

Storage metadata such as this is associated with a set of documents, such as particular document types, documents from a specific source, or those found by using particular search criteria.

Document Data Model

With the discussion of document metadata, we have made a transition from the physical architecture of the document warehouse to the logical design considerations. The document data model is at the heart of the logical model of the warehouse. As Figure 6.9 depicts, the document warehouse logical model has similarities to the star schema architecture used so often in data warehouses.

Content, source, search, and storage metadata correspond to dimensions in a dimensional model. Although specific content metadata will often relate to only

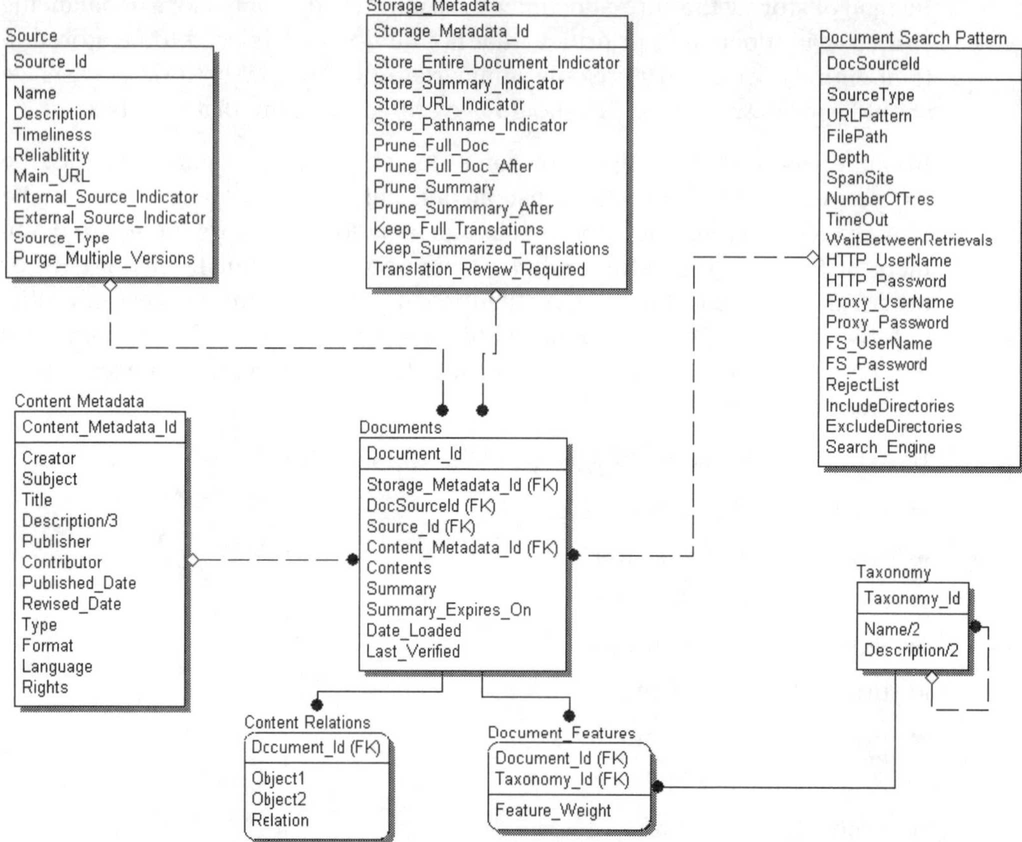

Figure 6.9 A basic model for the document warehouse.

a single document, when multiple versions are stored, it may relate to several documents. Documents have a many-to-one relationship with content relations and document features. Features ideally correspond to the preferred terms used in a thesaurus or taxonomy.

The text of a document is stored, along with optional summary, in the documents table. Versions are tracked as well at this level. Since documents may be pruned or deleted, expiration dates are also tracked. Finally, if only a URL is kept in the documents table, a record is kept of the last time the URL was verified. For a detailed listing of this model, see Appendix B and the companion Web site.

User Profiles and End-User Support

While many users have one-time questions that can be answered by ad hoc queries to a data warehouse or a by a question-answering system in a document warehouse or over the Internet, these same users often have long-term interests as well. End-user profiles are commonly used to represent the long-term interests of users. By keeping a long-term record of a person's interests, we can utilize information-filtering techniques, such as agents, to improve the quality of information provided to our users. The key issues in user profiles are:

- How should we represent user's interests?
- How should we create a user profile?
- How should we maintain a user profile?

Finding a way to represent a user's interest is perhaps the most important issue, for the profile must be capable of expressing the domains of interests while eliminating topics that are irrelevant. Creating a user profile depends upon the representation scheme utilized and the method for gathering initial information. Finally, maintaining a profile over time requires us to recognize when interests change and to adjust the profile in such a way as to cover new interests and eliminate old interests without adding too many new topics or removing others still of genuine interest to the user. In many ways, these three issues boil down to the classic problem of information retrieval, how to balance precision (getting only documents of interest) with recall (not missing documents of interest).

The most common way of representing a user's interests is to use a list of terms. This is similar to the list of terms that is used to represent documents in the vector model of information retrieval. Generally, terms are weighted so that those that are more important have larger weights than those of less importance. For example, someone interested in document warehousing may have a list such as the one in Table 6.2.

Table 6.2 Weights Are Used to Indicate the Relative Importance of Different Topics to Users

TERM	WEIGHT
Agents	0.72
Data Warehouse	0.74
Document Warehouse	0.95
Hypertext	0.48
Information Retrieval	0.60
Latent Semantic Indexing	0.57
Morphology	0.63
Text Categorization	0.82
Text Mining	0.98

Another approach to representing user interests is through filtering rules. These generally take the form of "IF <condition> THEN RELEVANCY = <value>". The condition specifies a known attribute about the user, such as the department she works for or her position within the organization, or attributes about documents, such as the extracted features or a metadata item (for example, the author's name):

```
IF features = { hypertext and information retrieval and XML }
THEN RELEVANCY = 0.67;
```

In both representation schemes, the same key words or features that represent documents are used in user profiles, so matching documents with interested users becomes a matter of matching common terms and weights. These representation schemes can be used in a number of different types of user profiles. Researchers in user profiling (Kuflik and Shoval 2000) have identified six methods for user profile creation:

- User-created profiles: With this method a user specifies key areas of interests and optionally provides weights for each domain. Customized news services, such as myCNN.com, use this approach.
- System-created profiles by automatic indexing: Users specify a group of documents that they deem interesting, and the system identifies the most frequent and meaningful terms to use as the basis for the profile.
- System plus user-created profiles: In this method, an initial profile is created by automatic indexing, and then the user modifies the results.
- System-created profile based on learning by neural networks: With this method, a neural network is trained using a set of documents judged relevant by a user. The network is then used with other documents to determine their relevance relative to the training set of documents.
- User profile inherited from a user stereotype: This method assumes that an administrator has defined templates of common interests; for example, for financial analysts, quality control engineers, competitive intelligence analysts, and so on.
- Rule-based filtering: This approach builds a set of rules on the basis of a set of standard questions posed to a user about his or her information needs. This technique may be combined with user stereotypes to provide a starting set of rules that is then modified according to user specifics.

Again, for our purposes of answering questions about the architecture of the document warehouse, we need to decide what approach is the best for a particular document warehouse. User-created profiles, system-created profiles by automatic indexing and system plus user-created profiles are the easiest to implement. Full-blown rule-based filtering requires a rule processing engine that can resolve conflicts between rules and prioritize rules. The additional overhead is probably not worth the improvement, if any, in precision and recall over other methods. Keeping two metaobjectives in mind—that is, the document warehouse must be easy to use and it must be fast—we should opt for weighted term vector models for representing user profiles. They will be easier to utilize in a production environment.

End-User Profiles

As Kuflik and Shoval have shown, there are several ways to represent user interests. At this point, we shall briefly turn to the basics of modeling user interests.

User-Created Profiles

User-created profiles are the easiest of the several techniques mentioned previously. User-created profiles often begin with simple checklists based upon taxonomy entries as shown in the following list.

A SIMPLE CHECKLIST TAXONOMY FOR CREATING USER PROFILES

- □ Business
  - □ Finance
  - □ Marketing
  - □ Accounting
  - □ Sales
- □ Science
  - □ Physical Science
  - □ Astronomy
  - □ Chemistry
  - □ Meteorology
  - □ Physics
- □ Biological Sciences
  - □ Anatomy
  - □ Genetics
  - □ Marine Biology
  - □ Physiology
  - □ Zoology
- □ Social Sciences
  - □ Politics

- International Relations
- Federal Government
- Law and Judiciary

- Regional Politics
  - Economics
  - Macroeconomics
  - Fiscal Policy
  - Monetary Policy
  - Microeconomics
- Stock Markets
  - Bonds and Debt Instruments
  - Sports
  - Baseball
  - Golf
  - Football

As the above example illustrates, user-created profiles can be based upon a hierarchical structure and thus tied to a taxonomy. The data model required to support this type of profile is extremely simple and is shown in Figure 6.10.

Rule-Based Profiles

The list-of-terms model for user interests can be captured in a data model similar to the one depicted in Figure 6.10. Filtering rules based upon conjunctive and disjunctive Boolean conditions can also be modeled with minor modifications. For example, the following rule provides for individual weighting of each term.

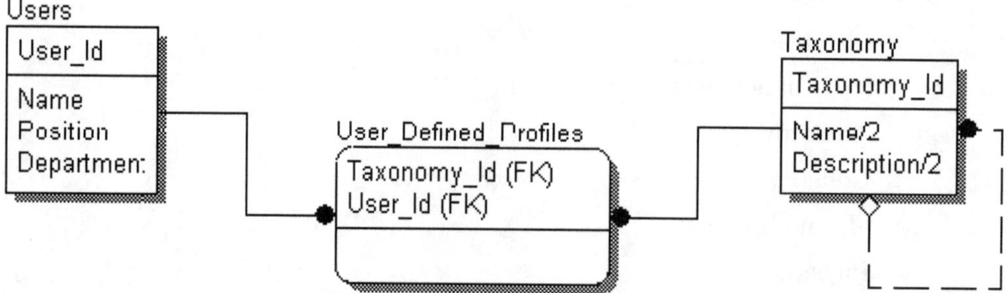

Figure 6.10 Modeling a user-created profile requires as few as three tables.

```
IF (hypertext > 0.68) AND
   (information retrieval > 0.50) AND
   (XML > 0.3)
THEN RELEVANCY  = 1;
```

This row, would require three rows in the User_Interests table. The taxonomy_id in each row would correspond to either hypertext, information retrieval, or XML. The minimum_weight is simply the weight specified in the Boolean condition. Interest_Group_Id is a unique identifier allowing us to group the three conditions together. Disjunctive conditions can be similarly be represented by using additional interest groups.

This type of rule representation does, however, have its limits. First, it assumes that all rules will be composed of simply a set of minimal weights for particular features. Second, disjunctive rules must be represented as distinct rules, so that a rule of the form

```
IF (hypertext > 0.68) OR
   ((information retrieval > 0.50) AND
    (XML > 0.3))
THEN RELEVANCY = 1;
```

will require two separate interest group sets, one with hypertext and information retrieval, and one with hypertext and XML. In spite of these limits, if a rule-based approach is considered, the simpler it is, the better.

User interests are not always linked to text. We saw in Chapter 1 that data warehouses cannot meet all the business intelligence needs of decision support system users. Document warehouses cannot meet all their needs either, as the importance of data warehouses can attest.

Data Warehouse and Data Mart Integration

Document warehouses will frequently coexist with data warehouses. As we saw in Chapter 3, analysis in a data warehouse environment can lead to questions that cannot be answered by looking at numbers. This can lead users to the document warehouse in search of text on a particular subject, which may in turn raise questions or theories that must be checked against the data warehouse. As Figure 6.11 shows, business intelligence operations often move between the realms of text and numbers.

As we address design issues relating to the integration of data warehouses and document warehouses, we will work on three topics:

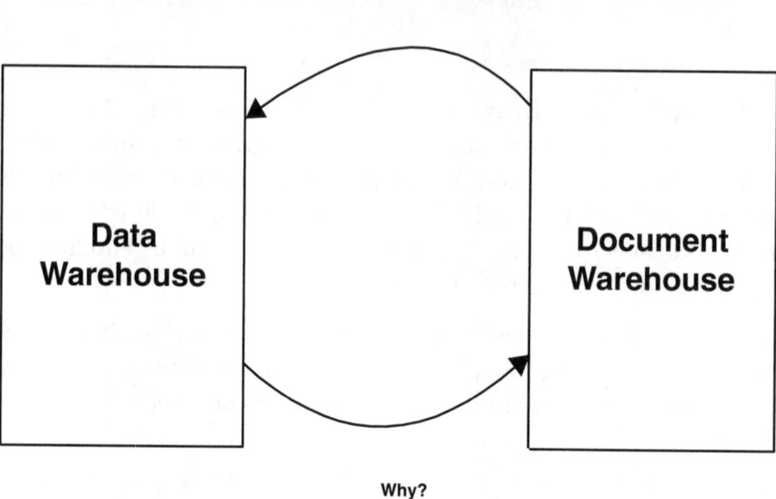

Figure 6.11 Analysts need both text and numeric data to form a complete picture of a business situation.

- Linking numbers and text
- Integration heuristics
- Limits of automated integration

Linking numbers and text is our primary goal. To meet this objective, we will consider how metadata can be used to serve integration and discuss some heuristics, or rules of thumb, for exploiting the features of dimensional models to link the two types of warehouses. Finally, we will examine the limits of these automated techniques.

Linking Numbers and Text

Data warehouses are filled with measurements about sales, revenues, production quotas, budgets, and other business processes and entities. Dimensional warehouses allow us to quickly and easily target measures to particular aggregated areas of interest, such as the sales figures of kitchen appliances in the northeast region last summer or particular measures such as the revenues from the sale of 19" Sony televisions in store number 874 last week. Now, it is not likely that we will find detailed documents about the sale of 19" Sony televisions in store number 874 last week or at any other time. We will, however, find documents about the product type, such as electronics and the region of the store. And this leads to a general principal about linking numbers and text: The precision of numbers will outstrip the precision of text.

Table 6.3 Basic Attributes of a Product Dimension in a Data Warehouse

ATTRIBUTES	EXAMPLE VALUES
Product_Id	378456
Product Category	Consumer Electronics
Product Class	Televisions
Product Type	19" HDTV
Manufacturer	Sony
SKU	338764531
...and others	

To adequately link numbers and text, we must generalize from specific items, such as 19" Sony televisions or store 874, to higher levels within data warehouse dimensions.

For example, a product dimension in a dimensional data warehouse may have the attributes shown in Table 6.3.

For the purposes of finding related documents, the keywords and topics are *consumer electronics*, *televisions*, and *HDTV*. Combining these with similar types of attributes from other dimensions, such as geographic regions, can provide the starting point for linking the document warehouse and the data warehouse.

Integration Heuristics

In data warehousing operations, we are accustomed to dealing with algorithms—that is, a sequence of operations that produce a well-defined result. The wonderful thing about algorithms is that, once implemented correctly, they always produce the correct result. Heuristics, on the other hand, are general rules of thumb that work in many cases, but not all and so, on occasion, they produce incorrect or poor results. When it comes to integrating data warehouses and document warehouse, we are limited to heuristics. Three generally applicable rules for generating keyword descriptors to link the two warehouses are:

- Ignore numeric measures from descriptions.
- Weight keywords proportionally to their depth in the hierarchy.
- Make sure words used in descriptions are in the taxonomy.

Dimensions in a data warehouse are loaded with descriptions. Some are very detailed and others quite broad, depending upon the level of the dimension hierarchy that is being described. Frequently the most detailed descriptors contain numeric measures, such as 19" television, that can be ignored since they do not typically lead to significant improvements in precision or recall. Note that this does not include model numbers, such as a GM Suburban 1500 LT, which can be used for more precise searching in the document warehouse.

When searching for related documents, weighting precise descriptors more heavily than general labels, such as consumer electronics, will also improve precision and recall. Since the general labels can apply to so many different documents, especially in thematically indexed warehouses, weighting less frequently used terms more heavily will rank documents with these terms higher than if the weightings had not been used.

Finally, because terms used in dimension descriptions are the basis for keyword or topical searches in the warehouse a common vocabulary will improve integration. Taxonomies are frequently used in text mining tools to support topical searches and browsing. Terms used in dimensional descriptions should be included in the document warehouse taxonomies as well.

Conclusions

Designing a document warehouse entails a range of decisions—where to get documents, how to get them, what to do with them, how to manage what you get, how to help users get what you have to offer. The key decision points to keep in mind when designing the warehouse are:

- Where do we find the documents that meet the users' requirements?
- How should the documents be extracted?
- What transformation and text mining operations should be applied?
- How should different classes of documents be handled in terms of storage and analysis?
- How do we provide support for long-term user interests?
- How do we integrate the document warehouse with the data warehouse?

Some of these issues can be addressed relatively quickly, such as how to extract documents once their source has been identified. Others, such as integrating data and document warehouses, will likely evolve over time. Document warehousing and text mining are relatively young disciplines in organizational settings, and in time more heuristics and other design principals will emerge. In the meantime, addressing the six main design issues described above will put the document warehouse on a firm foundation for growth.

CHAPTER 7

Finding and Retrieving Relevant Text

The task of retrieving documents is relatively easy once we have identified documents that are worth adding to the warehouse. Even with easy tasks, however, issues can arise—so in this chapter we will look into problems that can crop up during retrieval. In identifying relevant text, we do not necessarily need to answer specific questions or target particular documents; rather, we are more concerned with groups of potentially interesting documents. The last part of this chapter will discuss some techniques for representing users' areas of interest and improving the quality of the document warehouse by learning which documents users find useful and which they do not. The key topics for this chapter are:

- Manual retrieval methods
- Automatic retrieval methods
- Tradeoffs between the two methods
- Text management issues
- Improving performance

With regard to manual retrieval methods, we will discuss end-user tools that support document searching, both on internal files systems and over the Web. Automatic retrieval methods include crawlers and agents, which were introduced in the last chapter. Now, it is time to dig into some of the details of how to use these tools. Any time we make a choice there are tradeoffs, so the key benefits and disadvantages of each retrieval method will be covered next. Text management issues include the common problems of dealing with duplicates, version control, and reliability of sources. To improve performance, we will look into ways to effectively represent users' areas of interest so that a document warehouse system can adjust these representations over time to better adapt to the users' needs.

Manual Retrieval Methods

No matter how many file retrieval scripts we write or Web crawlers we run, programmatic searching will never get everything we should have in the warehouse. Ad hoc additions to the document warehouse are commonplace. Users, for example, will find interesting news stories or e-mails that may be of interest to others that are not included in automated searches. One-time or infrequently created documents, such as annual reports, budgets, and audit reports should be in the warehouse, but new versions of these documents are so infrequent that they do not warrant automated collection. Also, the documents created for projects should be added to the warehouse at the end of the project, if not sooner. Of course some users have favorite sites that they frequently visit but these are not included in automated searches because the sites do not yield interesting material often enough. In such cases, it is best to depend upon the users to select material from the site for inclusion in the warehouse.

Manual retrieval methods can be as simple as a copy command or as elaborate as Web farming with sophisticated search and navigation tools. No matter what tools are used for manual document retrieval a file staging area should be used to store the documents as depicted in Figure 7.1. From there, a document warehouse process can load them into the warehouse.

Two types of staging areas can be used. First, a user can simply copy a file to a staging directory, where a document loading process will find it and add it to the warehouse. Once in the warehouse, it will be indexed, clustered, summarized, and otherwise analyzed according to a default policy for manual documents. In this scenario, budget documents, news stories, press releases, product catalogs, government regulations, and legal briefs are all treated identically. In some cases this may be sufficient. If different types of documents are to be treated differently in the warehouse, then document metadata to control the transformation process is required.

When only metadata is used, information about the document is kept in a database table, and this information, in turn, drives the document loading process. Some of the information that might be included is:

- File location
- Author

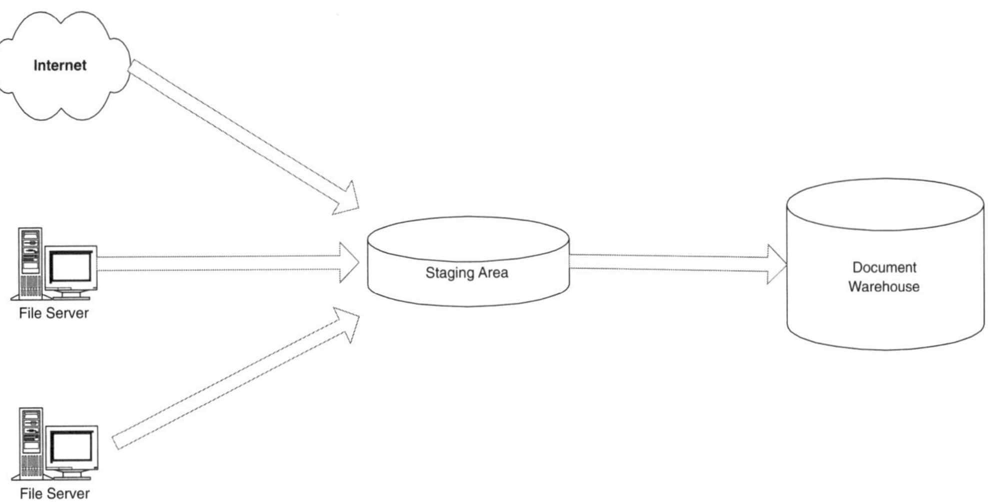

Figure 7.1 A document staging area is used to store documents before they are loaded into the warehouse.

- Document type
- Subject
- Contributor

Generally, this should be enough to drive the analysis processes—but other metadata elements from the Dublin Core or other metadata standards can also be used.

Search Tools

Document search utilities have steadily evolved as the size of document sets has increased. From regular expression searches in operating system tools to GUI utilities found in Windows to Web search engines such as Google and AltaVista, users have an array of tools to choose from. Since these tools are so well understood, there is no need to address them here, but the next step in the evolution of search tools beyond operating system utilities and search engines is worth discussing. Personal search tools, such as AltaVista Discovery are especially useful to those who do extensive document searching or manually populate a document warehouse.

In this section, we will discuss AltaVista Discovery (discovery.altavista.com) as an example of this new type of tool and look at specific features that make it a useful application in the document warehouse process.

The features of particular interest to us are:

- The ability to search both local files and e-mails as well as the Web
- The ability to restrict searches to specific Web sites
- Automatic indexing of browsed pages
- Find Similar Pages feature
- Find Referring Pages feature
- Document Summarization feature
- A visualization tool for mapping Web sites

Each of these features makes searching a little easier, and together can make it much easier.

Within AltaVista Discovery, users can define search spaces such as local and network drives, e-mail systems, favorite Web sites, discussion groups, and previously browsed pages. When searching for keywords, the user can identify the search space to examine. If the local and network drives are searched, then a local index, maintained by AltaVista Discovery, is used to find relevant documents. Similarly, when a select list of Web sites is searched, then a local index is used as well. For Web and newsgroup searches, the AltaVista search engine is used.

Another useful feature is the automatic indexing of browsed pages. Loading a document into a browser triggers the document's indexing. Anyone who has ever tried to remember where a particular page was located or where they saw some important bit of information will appreciate this option. For users manually loading documents in a warehouse, this features allows them to search by keywords, by similar documents, and by referencing referring links, while maintaining a running history of where they have been. When the search process is done, the user can use keyword searches within the browsed pages to choose documents worth saving in the warehouse.

Along with automatic indexing of browsed pages, the Find Similar Pages feature allows searchers to quickly find related documents that can then be added to the warehouse. Two additional features allow users to assess the content of a Web site quickly. First, the document summarization tool generates a summary of the currently browsed document. This is especially useful with news stories and other documents that may or may not have interesting information. The second feature is a visualization tool that generates an easily navigated map of an entire Web site. With this tool, users are no longer limited to just browsing by content; they can navigate by Web site structure.

Tools such as AltaVista Discovery are most useful for analysts or researchers with targeted interests. They can quickly hone in on texts of interest to them, find similar documents and assess entire Web sites. Since the automated indexing of browsed pages keeps a history of the analyst's browsing, others can have access to his or her research, even if the analysis never saved a document. For example, searching the browsed index for keywords, such as *text mining* returns an HTML page with links to Web sites. How should all those documents be retrieved? This is where the automated methods come into play.

Automatic Retrieval Methods

The automatic methods for gathering documents discussed here deal with both the Internet and internal documents. Internet documents are gathered with crawlers (which were introduced in Chapter 6), while internal document gathering will require custom scripts. First, we will begin with a discussion of data-driven searching and then move to a detailed discussion of crawlers. From there, we will turn our attention to internal document processing with an emphasis on retrieving documents from file systems and document management systems.

Data-Driven Searching

All automated search techniques require a repository of search control data to drive the process. Specifically, these techniques require the following data that should be maintained in a search control table:

- Internet sites or internal drives to search
- File name patterns to search for
- File name patterns to exclude
- Keywords for keyword-driven Internet searches
- Control parameters, such as times to search, intervals between searches, authorizations, and so on.

Depending upon the source, not all of these elements are needed. For example, file name search patterns are not required for Internet searches.

Core Features of Automated Searching

Designations for Internet sites or internal drives to search are the core pieces of information needed for automated retrieval. These are stored either in URL format or as fully qualified pathnames for the local file system.

Since our goal is to retrieve interesting text, we are primarily concerned with HTML, PDF, and other document formats commonly found on the Web. Within internal sites, we are interested in the same document types as well as word-processing documents, presentations, and other types of text files frequently used in organizations. (Certainly, any type of document can be found in either the Web or internal sites; these are just mentioned for illustrative purposes). The file patterns we specify to retrieve will primarily focus on text-oriented documents, and the excluded patterns would include video and audio files commonly found on the Web. Graphics files on the Web are frequently integral parts of a document, so you will need to determine, on a case-by-case basis, whether or not to download these as well. Compressed files, such as ZIP files, may contain valuable text, but the crawler cannot identify the contents of such files. Deciding when to download compressed files, again, needs to be done on an individual site-by-site basis.

Searching Internal Networks

Searching for files within a local file system is a common task. The specifics vary by operating system and network configuration, but the basic navigation tools of hierarchical file systems are common to most systems. Since this task is so well understood, it does not need elaboration here. The only suggestion offered is that a portable scripting language, such as Perl or Python, should be used to write internal file system search programs. These languages are both mature robust programming languages that are easy to learn and full-featured. Best of all, they have been implemented on many different platforms and are freely available under open source licenses. Perl is available from www.perl.com, and Python from www.python.org.

So Whose Document Is This Anyway?

We should all beware of copyright issues when downloading files. The intention of most hits on a Web site is to download a file (perhaps dynamically generated) to a user. Search engine crawlers regularly visit sites to index their contents. For the most part, these downloaded documents are not stored for extended periods of time, and this type of use does not seem to violate any copyright laws (at least no one seems to be complaining). If the document warehouse stores only a URL to the document, along with keyword indexes, thematic indexes, and other metadata, then the warehouse behaves like a minisearch engine. If the documents are kept in their entirety, then it might be considered a copy and could violate a copyright. Copyright laws were not developed with the Internet in mind, and they will certainly adapt to meet the needs of the digital world. In the meantime, we will need to understand the limits to our use of someone else's intellectual property.

Keyword-Driven Searching

In addition to searching specific sites, we might want to automatically search for particular topics of interest to users. In this case, a search engine along with a search expression is stored in the search control table. The complexity of the search string will depend upon the type of the search. Searching for the words *text* and *mining* can be done at many search engines with the expression *text+mining*. The phrase *text mining* can be found with the expression *%22text mining%22* (search engines often substitute *%22* for the quotation mark). For more complex expressions, such as those using Boolean operators, you will need to experiment with particular Web sites, since the expression syntax is not standardized across search engines.

Once you have identified the appropriate expression for a search engine, that search expression will need to be appended to the search engine's query URL. In AltaVista's case, it is www.altavista.com/cgi-bin/query/q?=, while HotBot uses http://hotbot.lycos.com/?MT=. So to search AltaVista for text mining articles, we would use the URL:

www.altavista.com/cgi-bin/query/q?=%22text mining%22

Some search engines allow for special features, such as translation in AltaVista and searches limited to specific Web sites in Google. These are usually specified by using additional expressions appended to the end of the search URL. Again, since search engines vary in their features and syntax, experimenting with your favorite engine is the best way to find the appropriate incantation for your specific searches.

Configuring Crawlers

In addition to compiling a list of sites to search, we will need to specify crawling options for each target. Crawlers will support different options, and some with have proprietary performance features but here are some basic feature categories that are used in document warehousing operations:

- Logging
- Download options
- Directory specifications
- Protocol options
- Recursive retrieval options
- Accept/reject options
- Timestamping

Each of these categories includes several features, which we will discuss now. wget, a freely available crawler provided by the GNU Project (www.gnu.org)

distributed under the GNU General Public License, will be used be used in the following examples. Like the scripting languages Perl and Python mentioned earlier in the chapter, this tool is mature and runs on multiple platforms.

Logging

Since most retrieval will be done in background processes, often during off-hours, creating log files is essential for monitoring the success or failure of a process. A crawler should at least allow users to specify a log file and directory. Some offer the option to append to an existing file and change the level of detail saved to the file.

Download Options

Download options control several aspects of the download process including the following: Users should be able to specify the number of times to try to download a file and the time to wait for a response from a server. This is especially useful with slow or heavily used servers. When dealing with slow servers, you should increase the time between requests to the server so that the document warehouse processes do not overburden the server. For example, in wget the following command would mirror the entire site, waiting up to 120 seconds for a response from the server and then waiting 20 seconds between requests, with up to three retries for each file:

```
wget -wait 20 -tries 3 -timeout 120 www.veryslowserver.org
```

Since sites may be visited repeatedly, the crawler will need to know if it should overwrite existing files in the local staging area. This is also useful if the retrieval process must be restarted after a site has been partially downloaded and you do not want to overwrite everything already downloaded.

Downloading all the document from a site can easily lead to retrieving more files than expected, so specifying an upper limit on the amount of data retrieved should be done regularly. In wget, the command

```
wget -quota 2m www.verylargesite.org
```

limits the total size of all files retrieved to 2 MB. Once the quota is exceeded, the process aborts.

Directories

Directory options allow users to specify where files will be saved and how the directories will be named. The most important directory options are the ability to specify a target directory and whether to store all files retrieved in a single directory or create a directory hierarchy mirroring the Web site's. In wget, the command

```
wget -no-directories -directory-prefix /alldocs www.verysmallsite.org
```

will not create subdirectories and will place all retrieved documents in the /alldocs subdirectory.

Protocol Options

Both HTTP and FTP support protocol-specific options that may be useful in retrieval processes.

HTTP-Specific Options

The most commonly used HTTP option is username/password. If a crawler does not support an option for the username and password, then users can specify the parameters in the URL using the following format:

```
http://user:password@host/path
```

(Similarly, ftp://user.password@host/path can be used with FTP). This username/password combination provides access to an HTTP server. If a proxy server requires a username and password as well, that will need to be specified separately. In wget, the following command does that:

```
Wget -proxy-user dsulliv -proxypasswd textmine www.goingthroughproxy.org
```

User agents, such as crawlers can identify themselves to Web sites. This allows sites to control the number of crawlers when resources are limited. By default, crawlers often identify themselves by the name of the program, such as wget or Teleport. With an HTTP option, users can specify a more specific string to identify themselves.

FTP-Specific Options

Two FTP-specific features may be required for some sites. First, UNIX supports symbolic links between files, allowing files to appear in multiple directories even though a only a single copy of the file is actually stored on the file system. When retrieving documents, the crawler should copy the actual file and not just create links locally.

Sometimes firewalls create problems for FTP retrieval. In these cases use passive FTP to allow the client to initiate a connection.

Recursive Retrieval

With recursive retrieval, a search process can start at a specific URL, then fetch all hyperlinked pages from that page, and then all hyperlinked pages from those pages, and so on. Clearly, this can get out of hand if limits are not set. The two most important parameters to control recursive retrieval are the depth to search and whether or not to span domains.

Specifying an appropriate level of searching is essential to preventing enormous retrievals. If a site has an average of five links per page, then searching to two levels will retrieve six documents, the starting page and the five pages hyperlinked to that page. If the search level is three, then the process will pull in 31 documents, the six from the first two levels plus the 25 pages linked to the five second-level pages. Going to four levels brings the total to 156. If the average number of links is greater than five, and it often is, then these figures grow even faster. Whenever recursive retrieval is used, it is a good idea to set a quota on the total size of a download.

Since hyperlinks can go outside of a domain, you may find yourself retrieving files from sites you have never heard of. This could help users find new sources of valuable information, and it may be exactly what you want. On the other hand, it could lead the retrieval process off on tangents, wasting time and resources. It is recommended that if you do allow the crawler to span domains, you keep the recursion level relatively low, certainly not more than four for well-linked sites. This combination will allow users the chance to examine a sampling of the contents of other sites without loading too much extraneous material.

Accept and Reject Options

Accept and Reject options allow users the option of specifying the types of files and directories to retrieve and search. Most accept and reject options take regular expression patterns, such as *.html, *.htm, *.pdf to specify all HTML and PDF files. Similarly, directory names can often be specified using wildcards to pinpoint directories to search and others to avoid.

Timestamping

The ability to control document retrieval on the basis of file timestamps is critical in document warehousing processes. Without this feature, controlling duplicate documents in the warehouse becomes much more difficult.

In general, document retrieval processes will want to download documents when a file does not exist in the warehouse and when a newer version is available. HTTP provides two ways to implement timestamping, using the If-Modified-Since request or checking the Last-Modified header and comparing it to a local file. To ensure that timestamping works correctly, make sure that files keep their modification date when downloaded, and when retrieving make sure timestamp checking is enabled. In wget, the command

```
Wget -timestamping www.timestampsite.org
```

turns on timestamp checking.

Batch versus Interactive Retrieval

The examples provided so far have assumed that that the crawler is a command-line utility that will be invoked on a regular basis to retrieve documents for the warehouse. While this will work in many cases, it is often useful to download sites on an ad hoc basis. In these cases, interactive crawlers are more useful. While they have similar features to their command-line counterparts, they offer a better option for the occasional user.

Interactive crawlers often provide Explorer-like interfaces, as in Figure 7.2, which depicts the main form from one such tool, Teleport Pro. This tool also allows users to configure specific projects, including many of the options discussed above. Figure 7.3 shows a dialog box for controlling recursive retrieval and authentication in Teleport Pro.

Whether you use a batch or interactive process will depend on the type of retrieval you do. For regularly visited sites, command-line tools combined with scripting languages are the better option. For more exploratory and ad hoc retrieval, interactive tools provide an easily learned alternative.

Restrictions on Web Agents

For document warehouse builders, Web crawlers are essential tools. For some Webmasters they are a headache. Crawlers can easily tax an HTTP server by

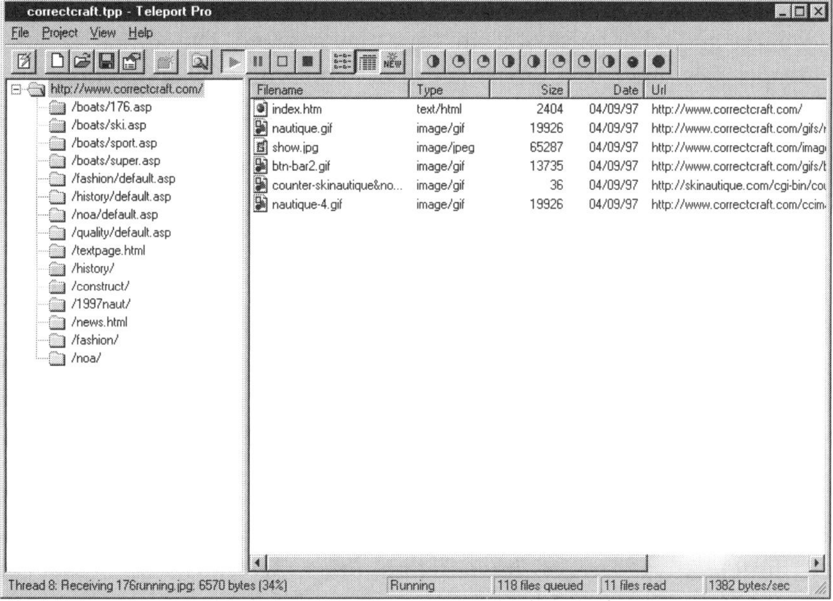

Figure 7.2 Interactive crawlers provide easily navigated interfaces.

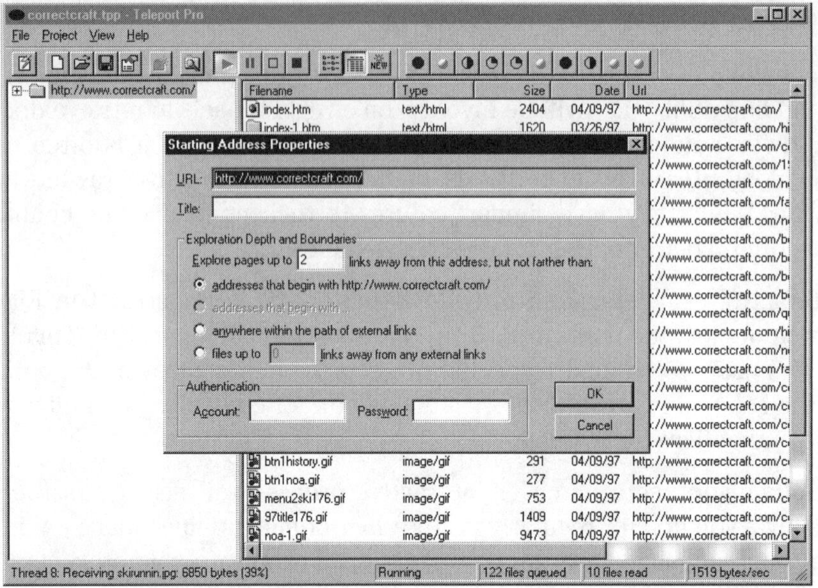

Figure 7.3 Crawling options are set through dialog boxes rather than command-line options in interactive tools.

making a barrage of requests, and when multiple crawlers hit at the same time, the problem grows accordingly. In response to this problem, the Robot Exclusion standard was developed as a means of controlling what crawlers were allowed into a site and what parts of a site they may retrieve. The Robot Exclusion standard specifies that a text file named robots.txt with exclusion criteria should be placed on the root directory of a Web server to limit crawler use of the site.

The contents of the file are one or more records separated by blank lines. Each record uses the following format:

```
<field>:<optionalspace><value><optionalspace>
```

Each record starts with one or more User-agent lines followed by Disallow lines. The User-agent specifies the name of an agent, such as a search engine or a general-purpose crawler such as wget. An * matches any agent that does not match any other User-agent name in the robots.txt file. Disallow lines specify a partial URL describing areas that cannot be visited. For example

```
Disallow: /internal
```

means that the corresponding user-agent should not visit or retrieve the /internal directory or any of its subdirectories. It also means that files like internal.html should not be retrieved either. To limit exclusion to directories only, and not file names be sure to use a / at the end of the pattern, as in:

```
Disallow: /internal/
```

An empty URL following disallow means that the entire site may be visited. The following specification blocks all crawlers from the entire site:

```
User-agent: *
Disallow: /
```

Many sites do use the robot exclusion standard, so if your crawler is configured to abide by the standard, then you should have no problem searching and retrieving from the site. Some crawlers allow users to specify arbitrary names to get by explicit exclusions, and some will ignore the robot exclusion directives altogether if you specify that choice. Since this standard is a voluntary protocol for behavior and not an enforced control mechanism, you could ignore the intent of the Web site's managers and gather documents as you like. This is not recommended. Agents and crawlers are powerful mechanisms, and we should use them as much as possible in document warehousing, but we should not use our tools in a manner detrimental to the Web sites that we find so valuable.

Retrieving from Document Processing Systems

The bulk of our discussion has centered on collecting documents from either local file systems or from the Internet. In some document warehouses, these will be the sole source of documents but for others, document management systems (DMS) will have a role as well.

As discussed in Chapter 6, DMSs are transaction-processing-oriented systems geared toward managing large collections of documents. Usually, these documents are added, modified, retrieved, and deleted using application-specific tools. For some tasks, such as populating the document warehouse, the contents of the DMS must be extracted. This is done with a proprietary tool or through one of the industry standard APIs mentioned in the previous chapter. As with data warehousing, there are no good generalizations to be made about extracting data beyond the use of APIs. Since APIs can be used to extract files from a DMS and place them into a file system, the general discussion about loading from file systems applies to extracted DMS documents as well.

Tradeoffs between Manual and Automatic Retrieval

Given the option of using manual or automatic retrieval methods, how should we choose? In most cases, document warehouses will be populated through a mixture of both. The four main criteria for evaluating how to balance the two are:

- Precision
- Recall
- Cost
- Effectiveness

Precision, relevancy, and cost measure independent dimensions for assessing the value of a document retrieval strategy, while effectiveness provides an indication of its overall worth.

Precision

Precision is the measure of what percentage of documents identified as relevant by an information retrieval tool are actually relevant in the opinion of the end user. When we look at precision from the manual retrieval perspective, we do not want to try to measure this criteria based on the number of documents someone saves. If a user is searching the Web and he or she saves a document, then it must be relevant. A better indication of precision is how many documents a user had to read before determining its relevancy.

Consider this example. A searcher uses two tools to retrieve documents either from the Web or from another document collection. The user enters search criteria into each tool, and the tools respond by displaying information about a set of documents. This information could include the first few lines of text as well as metadata such as the author and subject. The tool that is more precise is the one that provides enough information to the reader so he or she can accurately decide if a document is relevant without retrieving the entire document. If one of these tools is an automated search tool, then the user will not be evaluating the preliminary information; instead the document is simply retrieved. If the other tool is interactive and allows the user to evaluate the preliminary information, then some documents can be evaluated and eliminated as irrelevant before retrieval, thus improving precision.

The ability to evaluate preliminary information is essential to maintaining high precision but that does not fit into the automatic retrieval process. If precision is the top priority, then manual retrieval methods may need to be used. Techniques presented at the end of this chapter also help in these cases.

Recall

Recall is a measure of how many documents were returned versus how many documents should have been returned given a search criterion. For example, if someone is searching for information on painkillers, and the search tool does not retrieve documents about morphine that are in the searched area, then recall is lower than it would have been if the morphine documents were returned. Traditionally, steps that lead to improved precision (that is, eliminating irrelevant documents) have lowered recall. Conversely, improving recall frequently leads to decreased precision. The same phenomenon can be seen in the automated versus manual tradeoffs.

An automated search can blindly follow links returning every document in its path. Manual searching on the other hand is slower since documents are evaluated before they are retrieved. Think about the times you searched for something on the Web and got hundreds of hits. How do you decide which links to follow from the search results? By assessing the brief text returned with the URL, by considering the source (for example, is it a major news source, research agency, government office, etc.?), and by judging the title of the page. This conscious evaluation process will slow retrieval down and thus decrease recall but at the same time it will improve precision.

Cost

Cost is actually very difficult to measure. Using the total number of documents retrieved versus the total cost of the retrieval operation is one way. Unfortunately, this does not take into account the quality of the documents retrieved. A document warehouse filled with irrelevant texts is expensive by any account. Manual processes will appear costly at first blush while automated retrieval programs appear cost-effective. In general, comparing expenditures versus number of documents retrieved is an extremely poor measure. What we really want to know is the effectiveness of our retrieval strategy.

Effectiveness

Effectiveness is the measure of how useful end users find the set of documents available to them in the document warehouse. Remember the document warehouse serves two general purposes. First, it is a repository of documents known to be of value to an organization. These include contracts, press releases, process descriptions, and other intellectual property. It also contains documents of general interest to the organization such as new stories about the company's industry, government reports and regulations, market condition assessments, other companies' press releases, and related material from competitors. The general-interest documents provide breadth to the warehouse and offer a glimpse of what might be of interest to end users. It is these documents that provide the grist for the text mining mill. As with data mining, you do not know ahead of time everything you are going to find, but without enough raw materials to work with, the chance of finding valuable pieces of information is limited.

To maintain effective document warehouses, use both manual and automated retrieval methods. Save the manual methods for targeted research such as the market conditions in the European Union wheat market or the evaluation of the clinical trials of a competitor's new drug. Automated methods work best with broader topics such as political risk assessment, competitive intelligence gathering, or industry newsgathering. Using the right tool for the right job is the key to a successful retrieval strategy.

Text Management Issues

Once a document retrieval strategy is set, there are still some issues that need to be considered. Three of the most important issues are:

- Avoiding duplication of documents in the warehouse
- Accommodating document revisions and versioning
- Assessing the reliability of sources

Avoiding Duplication

Repeated visits to Web sites by crawlers can easily lead to multiple copies of the same document being loaded into the warehouse if the retrieval program is not configured correctly. The same problem can occur with local file system retrieval as well as document management system extractions. The single most effective way of avoiding duplication is to use timestamping.

Every document that enters a warehouse needs to be tracked with a file name, source (either URL or fully qualified pathname) and time and date of last modification. With that information, crawlers and loader programs can determine if a newer version of the file has been created and retrieve only new or updated documents.

If a new version of a previously loaded document is available, then we have two options. First, the original document can be deleted from the warehouse. Unlike data warehouses where keeping a consistent record of historical data is a major advantage to business intelligence applications, document warehouses need not keep every version of every document ever created in the organization. When data is loaded into a data warehouse it generally reflects a completed process, such as the sales figures for the past month or yesterday's production details. These numbers are not going to change. Documents on the other hand can enter the document warehouse when they are still evolving drafts or works in process. Documents represent ideas or descriptions of events, entities, and processes that change over time. For example, this chapter is written over several days, and it could be retrieved for addition to a document warehouse every night but there is nothing sacrosanct about each nightly version. The only version worth keeping is the final version. That said, there are times when multiple versions should be kept.

Accommodating Document Revisions and Versioning

Some documents are so significant or their development is so important that every version should be kept. In this case, these documents are like the numbers loaded into a data warehouse. Each version is an important end product in itself unlike the half-finished chapter mentioned in the previous example. Documents that require versioning can be handled in two ways.

First, versioning can be addressed outside the document warehouse and in the production stage. In this case, distinct copies of the document are saved under different names or versions, if supported by the file system.

The second option is to partition documents that require versioning from those that do not, during the document loading process. The former group could be loaded directly, while the latter group could be controlled for duplicates by using timestamping or other techniques.

Assessing the Reliability of a Source

Knowing the reliability of a source is essential anytime we make decisions based upon information. Anyone who has ever found a mistake in a decision support system knows how long it takes to regain confidence in the application. The same applies to document warehousing and text mining systems.

Reliability of sources is less of an issue with manual retrieval since users are, at least implicitly, weeding out poor quality sources along with irrelevant information. Automated retrieval processes can easily collect documents from unknown or unreliable sources. Both keyword searching and crawling beyond the domains specified for search can lead into uncharted waters. There are no good options for dealing with this problem. If we limit ourselves to known sites and do not automatically search for new sources of information, then the growth in the breadth of the warehouse will be impeded. If we allow documents from any site, we have lost control of document quality. Ultimately, the end user will have the final say in the matter.

The document warehouse should maintain metadata information about sources as well as about documents. As new sources are discovered, users can be called upon to evaluate the reliability of the source. Certainly, this is not a trivial task but once a site has been evaluated, it can be added to the list of sites to crawl if the site is useful, and documents from that site can be excluded if the site is found to be unreliable. In practice, there will be too many sites to evaluate them all, and users will end up making some valuation judgements on their own when reading the documents.

Improving Performance

With effectiveness as our primary goal, we can now ask, how can we improve performance? If we have compiled lists of sources that are regularly searched, and we have created keyword searches to find new sources, and the effectiveness of our strategy is still lacking, we need to move to the next step, which is creating a better representation of user' interests.

Understanding what interests a user requires four things:

- A language for describing interests
- A data store for these descriptions
- A means of creating the interest specification
- A method for using the interest specification to drive the search process

While developing a language for describing interests and storing them is relatively straightforward, automatically modifying interest specifications is difficult to do effectively. However, if we design our interest specification correctly, it will easily map to specifications for searching.

Representing Users' Areas of Interest

Users' interests can be represented in two ways. First, we can use a weighted list of keywords or topics that describe a user's area of interest. For example, a political risk analyst interested in Southeast Asian economies could be represented by using the topics in Table 7.1.

Table 7.1 Sample of Weighted Keywords to Represent a User's Area of Interest

TOPIC	WEIGHT
Politics	0.93
Economics	0.91
Asia	0.90
Malaysia	0.8
Thailand	0.8
Vietnam	0.75
World Bank	0.6

Similarly, additional keywords or topics could be used to describe other areas of interest to this user. There are several advantages to this representation scheme. First, keywords and topics are easily extracted from documents. Weights are also easily calculated on the basis of the number of times words occur in a document, adjusted for the number of times those words appear throughout all documents. This provides a means for reducing the weight of frequently used words in a document if they also frequently occur in other documents. A second advantage is that this representation is space-efficient. Entire documents can be reduced to lists of terms and weights. Third, multiple weighted keyword or topic lists can be used to represent distinct concepts of interest to the reader. A fourth reason to use this representation is that it can be created automatically using machine learning techniques. If a user were to provide examples of documents that were of interest, then machine learning algorithms could be used to find the best set of weights for a keyword or topic list.

The second technique uses prototype documents to represent users' interests. In this case, rather than extract keywords or topics, a set of documents is actually stored as prototypical examples of what interests the user. This technique uses a strategy known as case-based reasoning. There is nothing unusual about this approach, we use it all the time in our everyday lives. Lawyers argue on the basis of past legal cases, business schools teach with case studies, and programmers develop applications using design patterns. Since an entire set of documents is stored to represent a users' area of interest, the weighted keywords or topics can be derived from the example set if needed. Another benefit is that the documents can be used for similarity searches with major search engines. Finally, since these texts that are of particular interest to users of the document warehouse, they will be stored in the warehouse anyway, so there is relatively little additional storage cost associated with this approach.

Data Store for Interest Specifications

Data structures for managing interest specifications are relatively simple. We will first look into weighted keyword representations and then move to prototypes.

For weighted keyword representations, we will turn to the staple of dimensional modeling: the star schema. Ralph Kimball and others have promoted the star schema as a solution to the main challenges of data warehouse design: making it fast and making it easy to use. We adopt it here for similar reasons.

Figure 7.4 depicts a simple star schema that includes three dimensions: User, Keyword, and Interest Area. The fact table measures the relative importance of that keyword to the specified user and that particular area of interest.

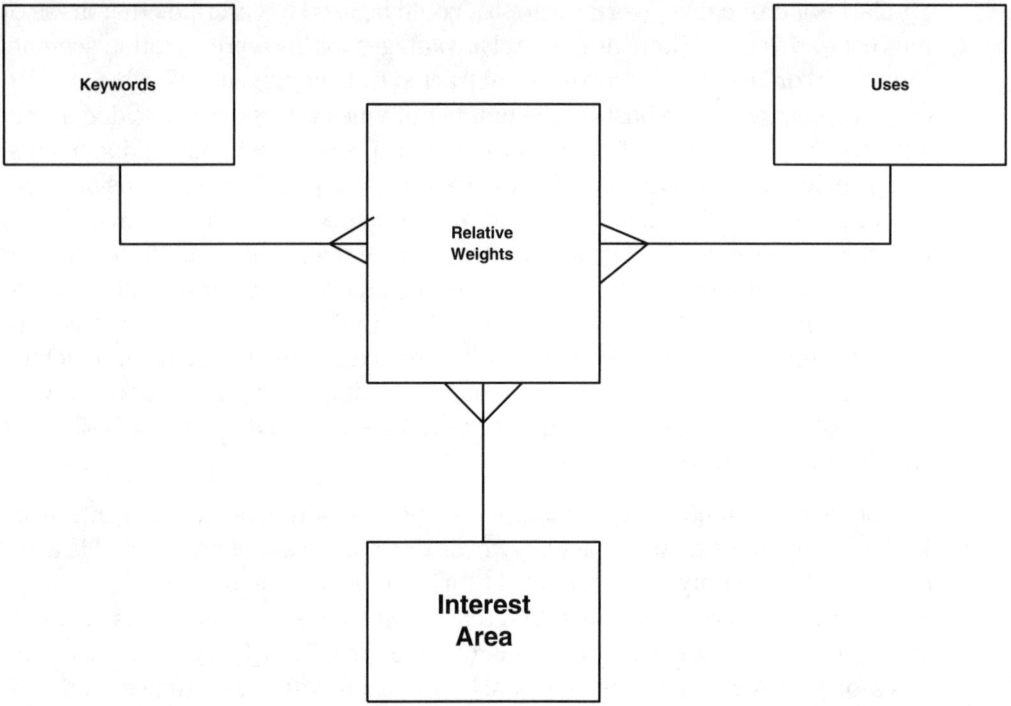

Figure 7.4 A simple star schema can represent user interests.

Using this scheme, a single user can maintain multiple interest sets. This is important because users may have areas of interest that are relatively disjointed—for example, Southeast Asian political risk analysis, European Community trade policy, and currency exchanges. Trying to create a single interest representation that captures all of these areas could lead to an extremely broad set of keywords that yields poor precision when used in practice.

A similar structure can be used for prototype documents, changing the keyword dimension to a prototypical document dimension as shown in Figure 7.5. Again, interest areas are kept distinct to improve precision.

Creating Interest Specifications

The basic process for creating weighted keyword representations consists of five steps:

1. A user defines an area of interest, such as currency exchange rates.
2. The user identifies a representative set of documents that describe as many aspects of the area of interest as possible.

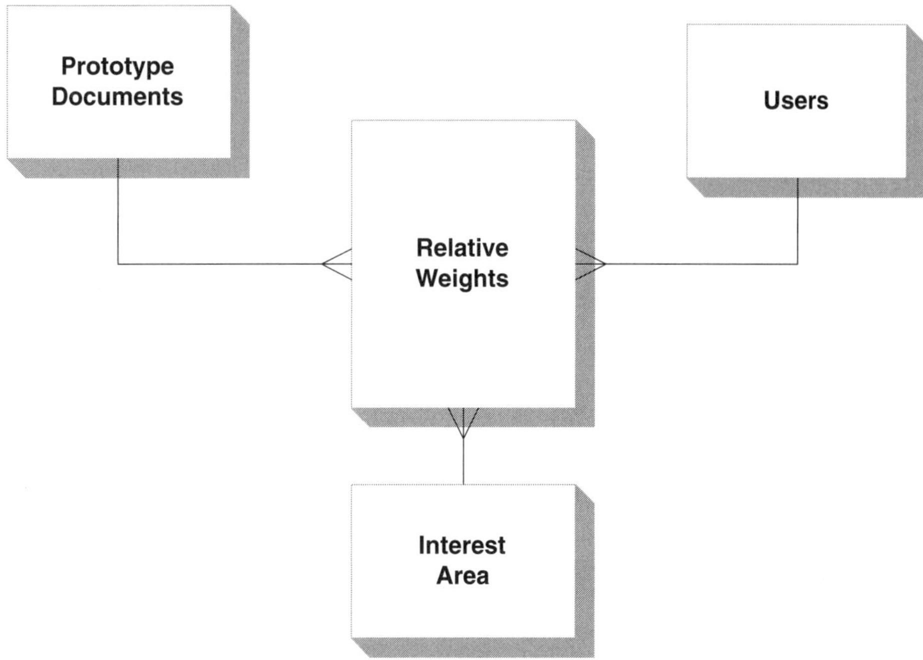

Figure 7.5 A slight variation in the dimension allows the same basic design to work for prototype representation schemes.

3. For each document in the interest set, the user assigns a relative degree of interest.
4. Automatically extract keywords from each document.
5. Using a classification algorithm (discussed later), the user develops a set of classifiers.

The first two steps are self-explanatory. When assigning degrees of interest, it is best to keep the number of distinct values low, for example two to four. The reason for this is that in the last step the classification algorithm will produce a rule or a classifier for each distinct degree of interest. For example, the following trivial rules could be generated if the degrees of interest were High, Moderate, and Low.

```
If  (Euro > 0.78) AND
     ((Interest Rate > 0.6) OR
            (Bundesbank > 0.3)) Then High

     If  (Swiss Franc > 0.5) OR
      (British Pound > 0.43) Then Moderate

     If  (Federal Reserve Bank > 0.7) AND
       (Yen > 0.8) AND
       (European Union > 0.2) Then Low
```

These rules now provide us the critical keywords that help us identify interesting documents. The sample set of documents may have a large number of keywords with no obvious pattern but that is where the classification algorithms come in. These algorithms examine all of the data and methodically search for rules that best describe the data set. For a detailed discussion of these and other data mining algorithms see Barry and Linoff's *Data Mining Techniques for Marketing, Sales and Customer Support* (Barry and Linoff 1997).

Interest Specifications Drive Searching

Once interest specifications have been defined, they can be used to generate search strings that in turn are sent to search engines using a crawler. Prototype representations do not require that keywords be extracted, so their mechanism for driving searching is slightly different.

Weighted-Keyword-Driven Searching

With a set of classification rules developed, the same basic crawling mechanism described previously in this chapter can be applied, using the rules generated by the classification rules. Here is the basic algorithm:

```
1 For each area of interest Do
2     Create search string with keywords of interest
3     Submit search string to search engine
4     For each hit from search engine
5          Retrieve page
6          Extract keywords and relative weights from page
7          Apply classification rule to extracted keywords
8          If classification rule applies
9               Then Save Document
10               Else Discard
11     End For each hit loop
12 End For each area of interest loop
```

In line 2, the string of keywords follows the same form as the condition used in the classification rule. For example, the rule

```
If  (Euro > 0.78) AND
          ((Interest Rate > 0.6) OR
        (Bundesbank > 0.3)) Then High
```

would map to the search string

```
Euro AND ('Interest Rate' OR Bundesbank)
```

where the syntax of the string is driven by the search engine that is used to retrieve documents.

Line 3, submitting the search string to a search engine requires the use of a crawler. For example, the following command uses the wget crawler to search AltaVista for documents about the Euro and either interest rates or the Bundesbank. When the resulting page is returned, the crawler will recursively search down one level—that is, to the pages that meet the criteria.

```
Wget -r -l 1 www.altavista.com/cgi-
bin/query?q=Euro+and+%28%27Interest+rates%27+or+Bundesbank%29
```

When the documents are returned, a text analysis tool is used to extract the keywords and compare them to the classification rule. Depending upon the outcome of that comparison, the document is either saved in the warehouse or discarded.

Prototype-Driven Searching

Prototype-driven searching follows the same basic pattern as keyword-driven searching, but with fewer steps. The basic algorithm is:

```
1 For each area of interest Do
2     Create string using document URL and similarity options
3     Submit search string to search engine
4     For each hit from search engine
5          Retrieve page and linked pages
11     End For each hit loop
12 End For each area of interest loop
```

In line 2, the search string created specifies the URL of the prototype document and indicates to the search engine to use the similar search option. In Google, the command would look like: http://related google.com/search?q=related:www/somesite.com/interesting.html.

Lines 4 and 5 specify that each similar page should be retrieved and that recursive retrieval should be used to find pages linked to the page similar to the prototype. The following command would find pages similar to www.somesite.com/interesting.html and retrieve them along with all linked pages up to two levels deep.

```
Wget -r -l2
http://related.google.com/search?q=related:www.somesite.com/interesting.html
```

Improving search precision and personalization are active areas of research, and the two methods are just the beginning of possible solutions to the problem. The heuristics presented here should be considered starting points for experimentation.

Conclusions

Gathering documents for a document warehouse is a challenging task. We have tools at our disposal that make the process of retrieving documents almost trivial. The real work is identifying relevant documents, finding new and reliable sources of documents, and maintaining a repository of timely and relevant documents for the warehouse's users. Now that we have the ability to target and retrieve documents, we will turn our attention to applying transformations to those texts to make their content more accessible to business intelligence users.

CHAPTER 8

Loading and Transforming Documents

It is now time to turn our attention to the workhorse issues of document warehousing: loading and transforming documents. At this stage, documents are preprocessed, if necessary, to ensure that they are in a character format and language appropriate for the tools that will later perform text analysis. Documents are then indexed for both full text and themes. Depending upon the needs of document warehouse users, documents may also need to be classified, grouped with similar documents, and summarized. This chapter will examine each of these steps in the following order:

- Internationalization and character set issues
- Translating documents
- Indexing texts
- Classifying documents
- Clustering documents
- Summarizing text

We will examine language differences in the first two topics, with an emphasis on the importance of the Unicode standards and on the uses—and limits—of machine translation. Since the basics of full text and thematic indexing have already been discussed in Chapter 4, we will now look into customizing indexing with specialized thesauri and stoplists. Classification of documents can be done in

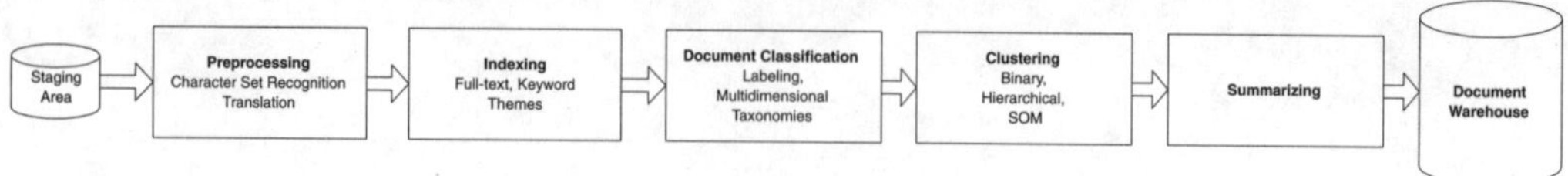

Figure 8.1 An overview of document loading and transformation.

two ways, using single labels or using multidimensional taxonomies. Similarly, the problem of grouping documents into clusters can be approached in at least three distinct ways, and we will examine those and discuss their appropriate uses as well. Finally, we will look in detail at different approaches to text summarization. Figure 8.1 shows the basic steps in the loading and transformation process. First, preprocessing steps are performed to ensure documents are in a form suitable for text analysis. Then full text and thematic indexing is done followed by higher level text analysis operation, such as classification, clustering, and summarization.

Internationalization and Character Set Issues

Rapid globalization of economies is bringing new issues right into the middle of many businesses operations. The European Community has had to deal with it since its inception, and has found the cost of publishing every official document in 11 different languages simply astounding. What does this mean to document warehouse practitioners? Mainly that they will now need to meet several different types of multilingual needs, including:

- Business intelligence sources in multiple languages
- Translations of internal documents, such as procedure manuals and user guides
- Government publications, including regulations and advisory notices
- Contracts and other interbusiness documents

Business intelligence sources in different languages are essential for a business with operations in multiple countries. If we depend upon domestic sources for information about a foreign business climate, then we run the risk of missing details not covered by the domestic press. There is also the problem of relevant cultural differences that may be uncovered from resident sources that are lost in local coverage.

Multinational companies have always had to deal with multiple translations of documents. The document warehouse does not create additional problems, it just brings some issues to the forefront. For example, if all documents within the warehouse should be equally accessible (assuming appropriate security controls), then the warehouse will need to store, and client applications will need to render, multiple alphabets.

Managing operations across borders also requires the ability to track and abide by the laws of each host country. While international agreements—such as the European Union regulations and the North American Free Trade Agreement—have eased international business, local regulations must also be tracked. Some nations, such as Germany, have more extensive laws governing commerce than other countries. In these cases, not only do the local divisions of a company need to understand these laws, but other divisions that work with them should know them as well. For example, if a manufacturer's facility in Ireland is planning on increasing production, it could affect distribution centers in Germany. Will the German center need to increase staff or make capital investments because of limits on hours of business operations? While the details of such questions will probably need to be addressed by the local division, understanding the operating environment of business units in other nations could prove to be an advantage.

Of course, government regulations are not the only source of international documents. Business-to-business dealings will generate plenty of contracts, agreements, and other documents that should be managed within the document warehouse.

Meeting these and other needs will require that document warehouse designers and developers deal with two language-related issues: character sets and machine translation.

Coded Character Sets

Coded character sets are used to represent alphabets in computers. Since digital computers fundamentally represent all information using binary numbers, characters need to be mapped into a numeric representation. The two most commonly used are ASCII and Unicode. The former is the older of the two and has long been used in countries with the Latin alphabet. Unicode was developed in response to the need to represent other types of alphabets. Syllabaries use a single character to represent a syllable, such as the kana system used in Japanese to supplement the Chinese characters used in the language. Another alphabet form is ideographic. These systems, such as Chinese, use a single text element to represent an entire word. As Figure 8.1 depicts, modern-day writing systems have evolved and branched off from a variety of earlier systems. The design goal of Unicode was to represent any text element from any language; consequently it is a much richer character set than ASCII.

ASCII Characters

The American Standard Code for Information Interchange (ASCII) was originally a 7-bit character set able to represent 128 letters, numbers, and symbols. The current de facto standard is 8-bit ASCII, which can represent 256 characters. The high-byte characters (from 128 to 255) do not have a standardized character mapping and have been used for formatting features, such as italics, graphics, and non-Latin characters. Unfortunately, 256 possible characters are not enough to represent all the needed symbols, so Unicode was designed to address this shortcoming.

Unicode

The Unicode coded character set was developed with three design goals in mind:

- Universality
- Uniqueness
- Uniformity

The code was designed as a universal representation system for all written languages, modern and ancient. Each text element has one and only one encoding in Unicode. Also, all characters are represented uniformly in a fixed width representation. The default 16-bit encoding provides for the representation of more than 65,000 characters. Almost 50,000 characters, symbols, and ideographs have been assigned Unicode codes. An extension to Unicode, UTF-16, is a mechanism for providing representations for up to one million more characters. Unicode also uses a single encoding for characters shared across languages, such as those in Chinese, Japanese, and Korean.

It should be noted that Unicode represents abstract characters and does not specify how those characters should be rendered on paper or an electronic display. A glyph, or rendering of a text element, is outside the scope of Unicode.

Most new computing standards, such as XML, and major computing vendors have adopted Unicode. Since the Unicode character set uses the same numbers to encode the Latin alphabet as ASCII, conversion between the two is relatively straightforward. Document warehouse developers will primarily need to concern themselves with ensuring that client browsers support the character sets needed to display the languages found in the warehouse.

Translating Documents

If documents may be added to the warehouse from multiple languages, then designers will need to address translation and language tracking issues. There are basically three issues that need to be addressed:

- Language identification
- Language translation
- Document storage options

Language identification is the first step in managing language issues. There are several options in language translation, and—as usual—your choice depends upon your particular needs. Finally, since translations yield new documents, warehouse designers will need to specify how these new documents are treated within the warehouse.

Language Identification

The three main ways in which language is identified in document warehousing and other text mining operations are:

- Language identification programs
- Search engine restrictions
- Document metadata

Each method has its advantages, and all three can be used reliably in the document warehouse.

We humans can quickly identify text written in our own language, even if we do not understand the content. Take the following example from *Gray's Anatomy*:

> The part of the choroid plexus seen in the descending cornu is formed in exactly the same way, viz, by an ingrowth of the vessels of the pia mater into the cavity, pushing the ependyma before it, at a part of the wall of the horn where there is a similar absence of nervous tissue where it consists simply of pia mater and ependyma in close contact. (Henry Gray. 1977. *The Classic Collector's Edition Gray's Anatomy*, New York: Bounty Books)

Although many of the terms are foreign to most of us, there are enough linguistic clues to know that this is English. First, the Latin alphabet is used. Second, common English words such as *the*, *in*, *at*, *of*, *there*, and *where* appear throughout the passage. Finally, there are morphological clues. The word *formed* ends in *-ed*, making it likely a past tense verb. It is closely followed by a word ending in *-ly* making that word a likely adverb and increasing the likelihood that the word ending in *-ed* is in fact a verb. Just as humans can identify a language without understanding the text, so can text analysis programs.

Language identification programs are generally trained with a sample set of documents in a particular language. Using frequently occurring words and character sequences, these programs can develop profiles of languages and reliably identify a document's source language. The language identification tool in the IBM Intelligent Miner for Text suite, is preconfigured to identify 14 languages:

Brazilian

Catalan

Danish

Dutch

English

Finnish

French

German

Icelandic

Italian

Norwegian

Portuguese

Spanish

Swedish

The statistical techniques that are used with language identification tools generally allow for users to develop identification profiles for other languages. This process usually entails creating training sets of documents in the target language and running the language identification program in a training mode.

The second method for identifying languages is to take advantage of search engine options to restrict searching to a specified language. All documents that are returned from those searches are guaranteed to be in the selected language. Of course, this technique does not help when dealing with internal documents but a similar principal applies. Extraction programs that collect documents may be written to target servers where a single language predominates. For example, a multinational firm can use different processes to collect documents from their London, Rome, and Amsterdam sites so that documents in different languages are kept partitioned before being loaded into the warehouse.

The third method is to use document metadata. The Dublin Core metadata standard includes a language specification for the specified document. For example, a fictional introduction to text mining might include the following metadata specified by the Dublin Core and implemented using the Resource Description Format (RDF)

```
<?xml version="1.0"?>
  <rdf:RDF
       xmlns:rdf="http://www.w3.org/1999/02/22-rdf-syntax-ns#"
         <dc:title> Introduction to Text Mining</dc:title>
      <dc:creator> Mary Jones </dc:creator>
      <dc:creator> Bob Smith </dc:creator>
        <dc:subject>
              Text Mining;
```

```
            Classification;
            Clustering;
            Summarization;
            Feature Extraction
       </dc:subject>
        <dc:publisher> Association of Text Miners </dc:publisher>
        <dc:date> 2000-08-15 </dc:date>
        <dc:format> text/html </dc:format>
        <dc:language> en </dc:language>
     </rdf:Description>
   </rdf:RDF>
```

The XML entity `<dc:language> en </dc:language>` identifies English as the document's language. Now, it should be noted that the metadata could be specified in other than the language of the document. For example, the tag `<rdf:li xml:lang= >` identifies the language of the metadata, allowing document creators to describe the contents of the document in multiple languages, thus aiding searchers using those other languages.

Language Translation

If language translation is supported in a document warehouse, additional processing and flow of control support is required. As Figure 8.2, shows, once documents have reached a staging area the following steps must be performed:

- Identify the language of the document.
- If the language is to be translated, determine if manual or machine translation will be used.
- If manual translation is selected, add the document to the manual translation queue for the document's language.
- If machine translation is selected, execute the translation program.

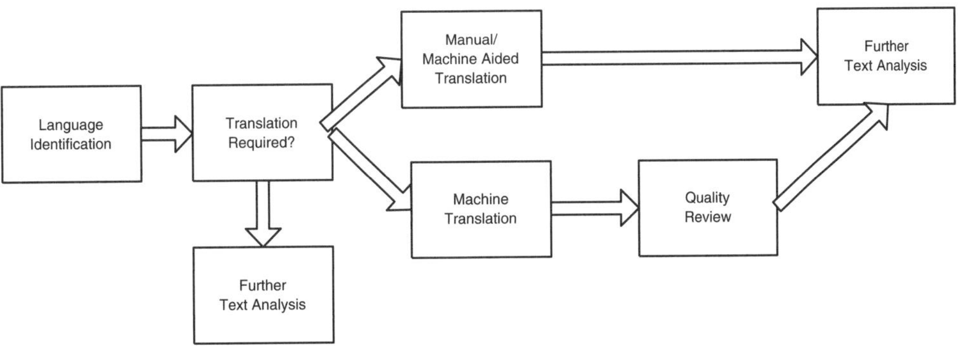

Figure 8.2 Translation adds several steps to processing the document stream.

- If the full document is to be stored, add it to the document stream for further processing.
- If only a summary of the translated document will be stored, execute a summarization program and add the summary to the document stream for further processing.

Of all these steps, the choice of manual versus machine translation is perhaps the most important. Manual translation offers the best quality translation but is slower and significantly more costly than automatic translation. Machine translation is generally faster but, in general, the reader will only get the gist of the document without a thoroughly accurate translation.

An alternate methodology to the one described above is to store documents in their native language, translate queries, and then provide summaries in the language of the query. If the document is of sufficient interest to the reader, then it can be completely translated. This approach is most appropriate when automated translation is of insufficient quality, and the cost of translating a large volume of documents is prohibitive.

Manual Translation

Manual translation is sometimes the best option for ensuring high-quality information in the document warehouse. Machine-aided translation (MAT) provides some automated support for humans through the use of online dictionaries, morphological analysis, and other text processing tools. In the case of MAT, human translators can increase productivity while still controlling quality.

Another option with regard to manual translation is to let a translation program make a first pass at the translation, and then have the human translator finalize the translation. Again, the final quality assurance measures rest with the human translator. As Figure 8.3 shows, there are different options for configuring a manual translation environment.

Machine Translation

The early and persistently elusive goal of machine translation is fully automatic high-quality translation (FAHQT). The ideal translation system works independently of humans yet produces translations at least as good as a human translator. To accomplish this task, the translation system must deal with ambiguity, polysemy, and idioms, among other challenges. Needless to say, we have not yet achieved FAHQT. What has been discovered, however, is that there is a definite tradeoff between the complexity of the translation system and the quality of the translation. Three general approaches, in increasing level of complexity, are:

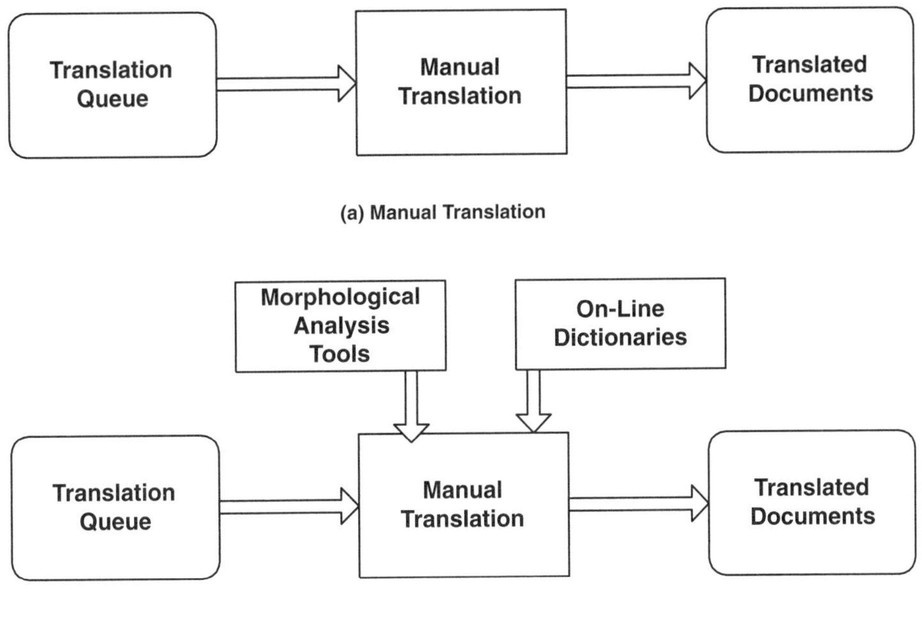

Figure 8.3 Manual translation can be done independently (a) or with the use of machine-aided translation tools (b).

- Direct translation
- Transfer approach
- Interlingua approach

Direct translation was the earliest, and continues to be the most common, design strategy. The transfer approach and interlingua approach were both developed to overcome limitations of earlier approaches.

Direct translation uses a word-for-word approach to translation. As Figure 8.4 shows, a text in a source language is mapped to a target language, using a bilingual dictionary and basic rules for reordering phrases.

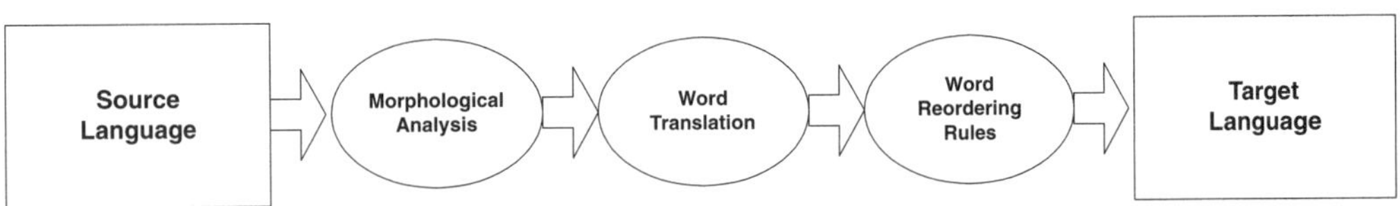

Figure 8.4 Direct translation is the most basic translation technique, using only a dictionary and some rewrite rules.

Table 8.1 English-to-Spanish Substitution Rules

ENGLISH PHRASE	CORRESPONDING SPANISH PHRASE
Adjective Noun	Noun Adjective
Noun1 Noun2	Noun2 "de" Noun1
Adjective1 Adjective2 Noun	Noun Adjective2 Adjective1
Adjective Noun1 Noun2	Noun2 Adjective "de" Noun1

Although fast and efficient, direct translation does not perform any analysis of content or try to resolve ambiguities. It has been successfully used with languages that have similar grammatical structures, for example, English and Spanish. One study of a commercial machine translation program (Gimenez and Forcada 1998) found the substitution rules in Table 8.1 were used in an English-to-Spanish translation program.

The transfer approach improves upon the basic dictionary lookup philosophy of the direct approach by adding syntactic analysis. As Figure 8.5 shows, the second step of this method—the transfer—uses syntactic rules to determine the sentence structure of the target sentence. In the final phase, morphological rules are applied to create the final word forms in the target language, and grammar rules are applied to determine the appropriate phrase and sentence structures. Like the direct approach, the transfer method works only on a single sentence at a time and does not perform semantic analysis. The technique with the most emphasis on semantics is the interlingua approach.

The interlingua approach uses a special language-neutral stage, called the interlingua. The purpose is of the interlingua is to act as a universal semantic representation scheme. Rather than mapping words from the source language onto words in the target language and then rearranging word order according to the grammar of the target language, the interlingua represents the meaning of the source text and then synthesizes text in the target language. Figure 8.6 shows the basic structure of the interlingua approach.

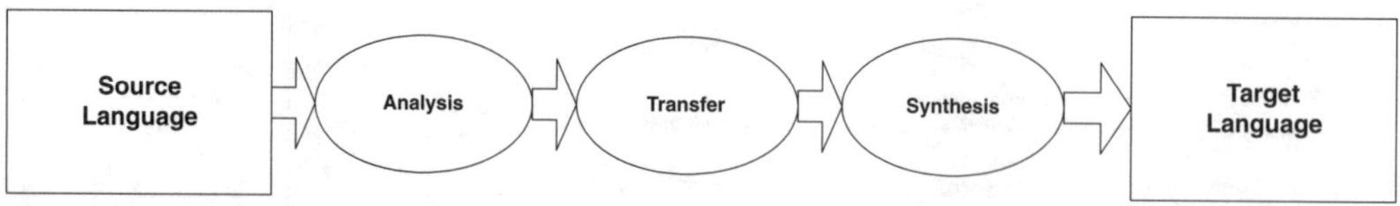

Figure 8.5 The transfer approach includes syntactic analysis and source-to-target language transfer rules.

Although theoretically appealing, this method has not yielded significant results (Hausser 1998). The most significant problem has been finding a suitable interlingua. Proposals include a logic-based language, an artificial language such as Esperanto, and a set of semantic primitives. The use of both logic-based languages and semantic primitives have been extensively studied in Artificial Intelligence (AI), but a comprehensive representation scheme built on these approaches has yet to be developed.

Partial Translations of Structured Texts

In addition to translating entire texts, semistructured texts lend themselves to partial translations. For example, in a financial report it may be sufficient to translate only column and row headings used in tables of financial data. For longer documents, abstracts or executive summaries could be translated by machine to provide the main gist of the document to the reader, while leaving the rest of text to be translated only if there is a specific need.

Limits of Machine Translation

Whether you choose full or partial translation, there are limits to the quality of the translation that end users should be aware of.

First, not all terms used in a source document will have entries in the bilingual dictionary. This is especially true for scientific and technical terms. Many software packages do, however, allow users to add additional terms for specialized vocabularies.

Second, outside of restricted language domains, translation requires some semantic understanding. For example, machine translation systems have been successfully used in Canada to translate weather forecasts, a domain with a limited scope, from English to French. A similar attempt to develop a machine translation system for aviation hydraulics was abandoned after three years. (Klein 1999).

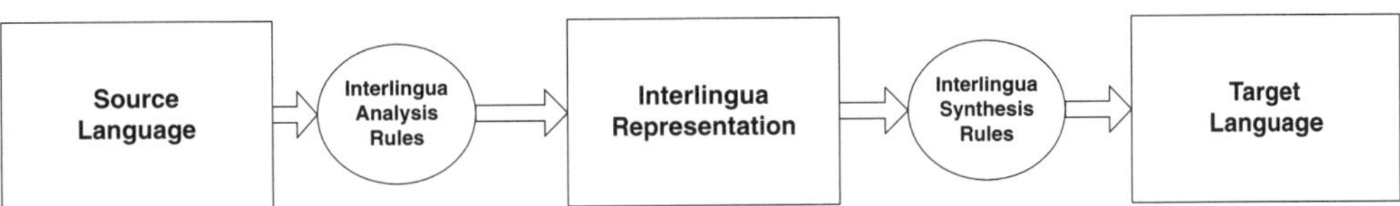

Figure 8.6 Semantic representation in a common meaning representation scheme distinguishes the interlingua approach from the direct and transfer methods.

A third problem with machine translations is known as lexical gaps. This occurs when one language has a single word that can be translated into two or more words in a target language. For example, the English word *know* translates into both *savoir* and *connaitre* in French and into *wissen* and *kennen* in German. Determining the correct translation requires a semantic understanding not usually found in current machine translation systems. One approach to dealing with this problem is to allow a user to choose among alternate translations.

Document Storage Options

Translated documents add another dimension of complexity to the document warehouse. We now have multiple versions of the same document in the sense that each translation conveys the same semantic content. Some of the options that warehouse designers have are:

- Storing the original text and all translations
- Storing the full text of the original and only a summary of the translated document
- Storing only a summary of all versions, including the original
- Storing the translation but not the original

How you choose between these and other options depends upon the importance of the document, the cost of retranslating if necessary, and any potential quality control and legal issues.

- The simplest solution—from a design perspective—is to store the full text of the original document as well as all translations. The advantage of this choice is having the original on hand in case there are questions about the translation at a later time. It also provides translations of the full text, so readers would not need to translate the entire document if only a translated summary was stored.
- Storing the full text of the original and translations of the document summary is another option. In this scenario, space use is optimized, and readers can still get the gist of a document from the summary. Since only summaries are translated, this could reduce the translation load by as much as 80 percent. Similarly, the original document may not be important enough to warrant storing the full content in the warehouse, and in this case, a summary-only scenario is appropriate.
- Finally, having news stories, press releases, and other noncritical documents in the original language may not add any substantive value to a doc-

ument warehouse. A mobile phone manufacturer announcing a new line of products in Finnish may not need to be included in the warehouse when an English version meets the needs of end users.

- In general, the most important documents—such as contracts, legal opinions, and government regulations and reports—warrant multiple language versions in a document warehouse, especially when machine translation techniques are used. Readers may get the main point of a document from a machine-translated rendition, but details and subtle points can easily be missed or misrepresented in an automatically generated translation. Because of these limitations, it is important for users to understand how the document was translated and any shortcomings of that method.

Indexing Text

Indexing text allows us to efficiently search for documents relevant to a query without examining entire documents. In this way, text indexing is similar to conventional database indexes, which allow us to forgo full table scans for more efficient retrieval of rows of data. The two types of indexing we are primarily concerned with are full text indexing and thematic indexing.

Full Text Indexing

Full text indexing occurs automatically in many text analysis tools when documents are loaded. Indexes will generally record information about the location of terms within the text so that proximity operators, as well as Boolean operators, can be used in full text queries. The most common operators in text queries are:

- Boolean Operators
  - AND
  - OR
  - NOT
- Proximity Operators
  - NEAR
  - WITHIN

Indexing supports Boolean operators by allowing those operations to be performed on the indexes without full document searching. Since the indexes maintain information about the position of words within a text, proximity operators can also make use of indexes. The NEAR operator can be implemented in several ways. First, it can return a score relative to the distance between two specified terms. It can also be limited to searching for pairs of words with a maximum number of words between them. Finally, the order of terms in a NEAR query may or may not be relevant.

To maintain the efficient implementation and use of full text indexes, frequently used words, called stop words, are often ignored. Stop words appear so commonly in discourse that they do not add any value to document searching and can be safely ignored.

Some tools, such as Megaputer's Text Analyst automatically calculate the lexical affinities that measure the co-occurrence of words. Words that appear together such as *real estate*, *mortgage rate*, and *data warehousing* will be identified as lexical affinities. Using lexical affinity measures can improve full text searching by helping to disambiguate words with multiple meanings such as *bed* in *flower bed* or *queen-sized bed*.

Thematic Indexing

Thematic indexing depends upon the use of thesauri. A thesaurus is a set of terms that define a vocabulary and are organized using relationships. It provides a hierarchical structure that allows text mining tools to quickly find generalizations as well as specializations of specific terms. The ISO-2788 standard for monolingual thesauri is the most commonly used standard for thematic indexing and consists of four main components:

- Thesaurus
- Indexing term
- Preferred term
- Nonpreferred term

Indexing terms are either a single word or a compound term representing a concept in the thesaurus. Preferred terms are the terms used when indexing concepts. For example, *automobile* could be the preferred term for *car*, *van*, and *minivan*, which are considered nonpreferred terms.

Preferred terms are organized hierarchically. Nonpreferred terms are tied to the hierarchical structure by their reference to a preferred term. Preferred terms are related to each other by relations that define the hierarchy. The ISO-2788 standard defines the following relations:

- USE: The term that follows is a preferred term.
- UF: The term that follows is used for a preferred term.
- Top term: This specifies the name of the broadest class to which a term belongs.
- BT: This defines a broader, generalized term for a specified word.
- NT: This defines a narrower term that specifies another term.
- RT: The related term operation associates words that are not synonyms or quasisynonyms of a given term.

Some tools, such as Oracle interMedia Text, are preconfigured with a thesaurus and can be used immediately to thematically index text. Others tools—and some text mining applications—will require custom thesauri. Figure 8.7 shows a sample thesaurus using standard terms and relations.

With a thesaurus, applications will be able to search by topic as well as by full text. It is highly recommended that all document warehouses provide this basic service. Thematic indexing reduces the poor precision and poor recall associated with polysemy (words having multiple meanings) and synonymy (multiple words for the same meaning).

Company
NT Corporation
NT Sole Proprietorship
NT Limited Liability Partnership
SYN For-profit Organization
Organization
NT Company
NT Non-profit Organization
NT Government
Government
NT Federal Government
NT Regional Government
NT Municipal Government
Regional Government
SYN State Government
SYN Provincial Government

Figure 8.7 A sample thesaurus in ISO-2788 format.

Document Classification

Full text and theme indexing are usually implemented to support ad hoc searching, but they also provide the basis for document classification. By looking at the pattern of words and themes, we can develop a rough partitioning of documents into a predefined set of groups. Examples of such groups include:

- Industry sector news stories
- Regulatory notices
- Project-related documents
- Product-specific technical documentation and manuals
- Financial reports

These rough partitions can be further refined as necessary. For most document warehouses, two types of classifications will be used: labeling and multidimensional taxonomies.

Labeling

Labeling is the process of assigning a dominant theme or topic descriptor to a document. The labels chosen may be domain dependent or in general categories— such as the ones found in Oracle interMedia Text's knowledge catalog. For finer classifications, multiple labels can be assigned along with weights. For each document, a list of labels and weights are assigned:

$$\text{Document} \rightarrow [\ (\text{label}_1,\ \text{weight}_1),\ (\text{label}_2,\ \text{weight}_2),\ \ldots\ (\text{label}_n,\ \text{weigth}_n)\ ]$$

The labels and weights can be used with text querying tools to specify minimum thresholds when looking for documents. For example, the following code can be used to return the document identifier and title of documents about currency exchanges with at least a weighting of 0.5:

```
SELECT
  Document_Id, Title
FROM
  Documents
WHERE
  ABOUT(text_column, 'currency exchange') >0.5
```

Labels without weights can also be used to populate the SUBJECT field of the Dublin Core metadata set kept for document. Ideally, the document creator will specify subject labels, but if these lables do not exist or do not conform to the preferred terms used in the document warehouse thesauri, then classification labels can be assigned.

Labeling—How It Works

Successful labeling depends upon three types of data:

- Word frequency statistics
- Morphological knowledge
- Type-specific terms

Two word frequency statistics are necessary: relative frequency and absolute frequency. Relative frequency measures the number of times a word appears in a document. Absolute frequency measures the number of times a term appears in a set of documents. Depending on the classification tool, absolute frequency might be calculated over a broad range of documents and the statistics provided along with the tool. In other cases, tools can be trained by using sample documents provided by document warehouse designers and text miners.

Morphological knowledge is used to determine the preferred (or canonical) representation of a term. For example, the canonical form of *eat*, *ate*, *eats*, and *eating* is *eat*. Morphology is used to eliminate the variations that occur in language such as tense, plurality, and, in some languages, noun declinations and verb conjugations. So no matter how the root of the word is modified to meet the grammatical rules of the source language, it will be identified as a single term.

Type-specific terms are used to augment general lexicons and thesauri. These extra terms include names of cities, states, provinces, and other geographic references as well as common abbreviations, names of clients and customers, and other company- or domain-specific terms.

Once morphological analysis renders words into a standard canonical form, relative frequencies can be calculated. The most common measure for determining the weight of a term in a document is the inverse document frequency measure. The basic idea behind the measure is that high weights should be assigned to terms that appear in few documents because these are good discriminators. Since relative frequency measures the number of times a word appears in a document, its weight will be proportional to the relative frequency. Terms that appear in many documents have a high absolute frequency and indicate poor discriminators. In these cases, the weight is inversely proportional to the absolute frequency.

The combination of terms and weights has proven to be a powerful technique for classifying documents. One limitation of labeling, though, is that it does not generalize. For example, a document labeled *automobiles*, *trucks or buses* or *rail transportation* is also about *ground transportation*. Without the use of a taxonomy one cannot easily query for generalized concepts such as ground transportation.

Multidimensional Taxonomies

The idea of a multidimensional classification structure is well known to data warehouse practitioners. Ralph Kimball and others have developed the multidimensional model into an effective tool for organizing large quantities of numeric data in data warehouses. Multidimensional models allow us to quickly and easily target a subset of the database that interests us, using major structural categories, such as time period, customer, product, and location. Similarly, with multidimensional taxonomies, we can quickly and easily target a subset of a document set by using classification categories, as shown in Figure 8.8.

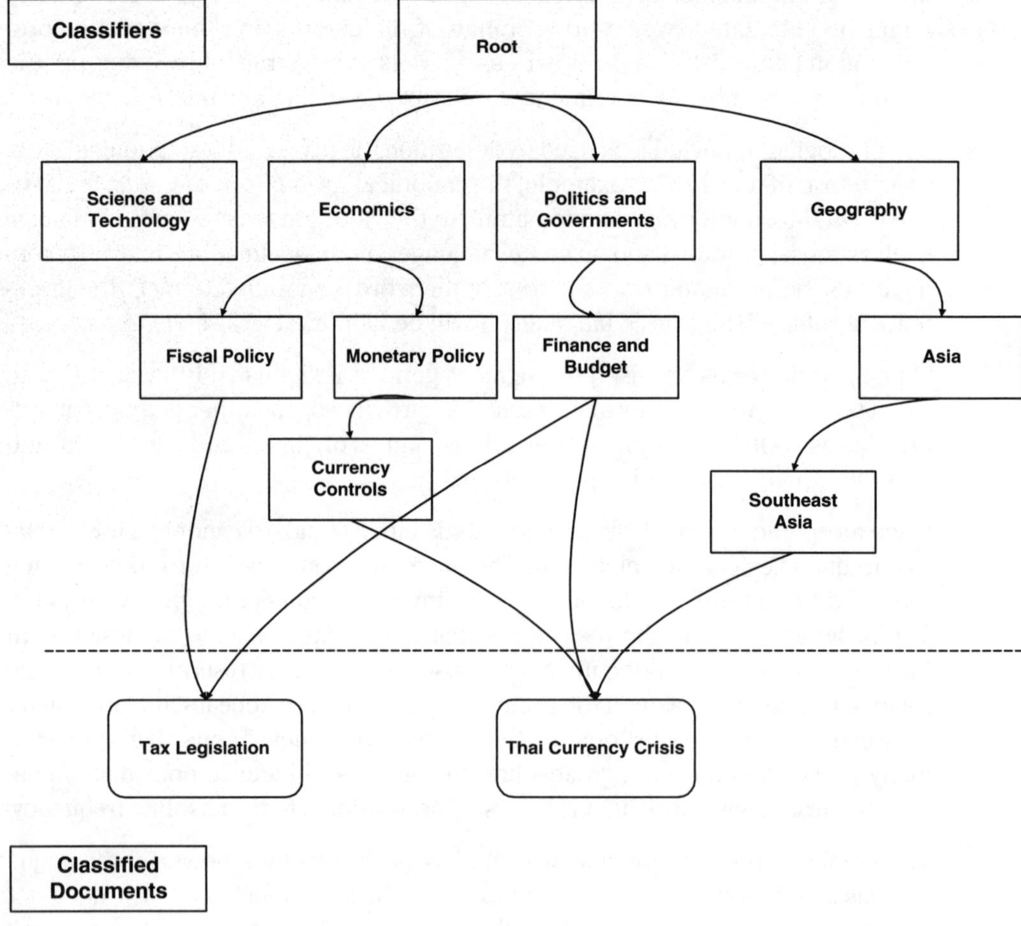

Figure 8.8 A partial sample taxonomy for classifying a broad range of documents.

Taxonomies can be created using specialized taxonomy-generation tools or with a combination of clustering and feature extraction, as described in Muller et al. (1999). Given a taxonomy, we can classify documents with both specific terms, as in the case of labeling, and hierarchical categories. The net effect is equivalent to drilling-up hierarchies in a multidimensional data warehouse. Thus, we can query for documents about *ground transportation*, and we can find documents about *automobiles* and *rail transportation*.

When dealing with taxonomies, it is useful to distinguish two concepts: the intention of a term and the extension of the term. The intention of a term describes the term abstractly, by relating it to other abstract terms. For example, *automobile* is a type of *ground transportation*. The extension of a term is the set of documents (in our case) that are about that particular term. For example, the extension of the term *automobile* might be documents with document IDs 1001, 2387, 11183, and 93321. The extension, thus, points to actual documents which instantiate the concept of *automobile*. With these definitions in hand, we can now proceed to discuss how multidimensional taxonomies are used within the framework of the document warehouse.

From the classification problem perspective, multidimensional hierarchies classify particular documents (the extension) into multiple categories at multiple levels of generality (the intention)—thus providing a richer classification scheme than labeling alone.

Document Clustering

Document clustering may be useful for some applications, such as quickly finding similar documents and exploring the macrostructures of a large collection of documents. Clustering can also help identify duplicate documents in the warehouse so they may be removed. Unlike classifications, clustering does not presume a preexisting set of terms or a taxonomy that is used to group documents. Instead, groups are created on the basis of the features of documents within the set of documents being clustered. Although this technique is not as common as thematic indexing or summarization, it may prove useful to some.

Many techniques have been developed for document clustering, but we will concentrate on three main types:

- Binary relational clustering
- Hierarchical clustering
- Self-organizing maps (SOM)

Binary relational clustering partitions a set of documents into groups, with each document in a separate group. Hierarchical clustering groups documents at multiple levels, providing drill-up and drill-down navigation. Self-organizing maps are especially useful for document sets covering a broad range of topics, such as e-mails.

Binary Relational Clustering

Like other clustering techniques, the main objective of binary clustering is to group documents so that the similarity measures between documents in a cluster is maximized, while the similarity between documents in different clusters is minimized. The dominant features of binary relational clustering are:

- Clusters are flat.
- Documents are in only one cluster.
- Clusters correspond to a single topic.

Binary relational clustering works by assigning documents to a single cluster, much as labeling assigns one classification to a document. Like labeling, each cluster corresponds to one topic, which is basically the set of common features shared by all documents in a cluster. For example, a cluster with documents about Windows NT, Windows 95, DOS, VMS, UNIX, and Linux corresponds to an operating system cluster. As Figure 8.9 shows, binary relational clustering groups documents on the basis of similarity threshold and a predefined number of clusters, and does not guarantee a balanced distribution of documents over all clusters.

Hierarchical Clustering

Hierarchical clustering groups documents together according to similarity measures in a tree structure. As Figure 8.10 shows, documents can be in multiple clusters in a hierarchical clustering scheme. Rather than finding the single best match between a document and a cluster, hierarchical clustering algorithms iteratively group documents into larger clusters.

The basic algorithm works as follows: First, assign each document to its own cluster. These are the leaves of the tree. Then create the second level of the tree by merging two clusters at a time, grouping them according to similarity. Create the third level by grouping pairs of clusters from the second level, and so on, until all groups have been merged into a single cluster at the root of the hierarchy.

One of the advantages of hierarchical clustering is that it supports browsing by drill-down and drill-up operations.

Self-Organizing Map Clustering

A third clustering technique uses a neural network to map documents in document sets that have many possible topics (that is, the document space is highly

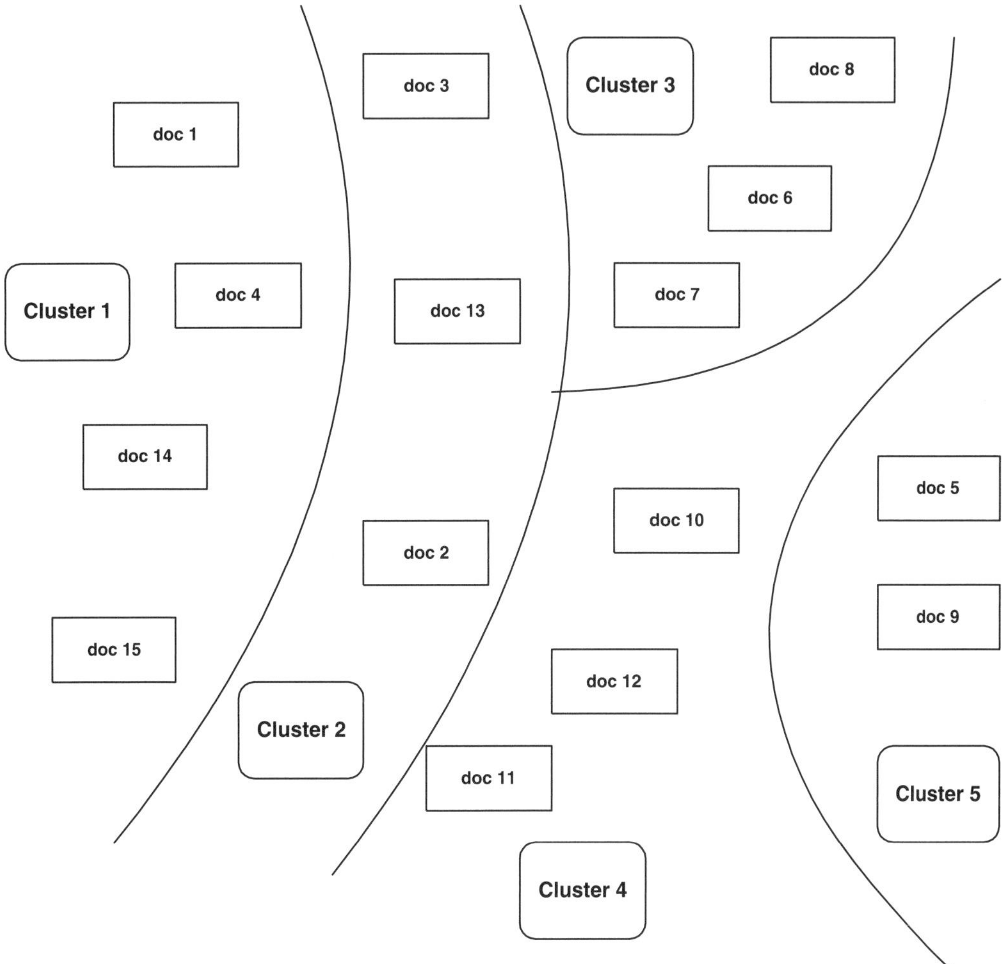

Figure 8.9 Binary relational clustering renders a flat partitioning of a set of documents.

dimensional), where each document has only a small number of those topics (that is, the document space is sparse).

Like the other clustering technique, self-organizing maps (SOMs) depend upon a similarity measure. Unlike the other techniques that compare documents to each other, SOMs compare the similarity of a document to a point on a two-dimensional grid, as depicted in Figure 8.11. The grid is created initially and populated with weighted feature vectors. The similarity measure compares the distance between a document and each the feature vector, corresponding to the point on the grid. After finding the closest match, the algorithm adjusts the weights of the feature vectors at the grid point to move it a little closer to

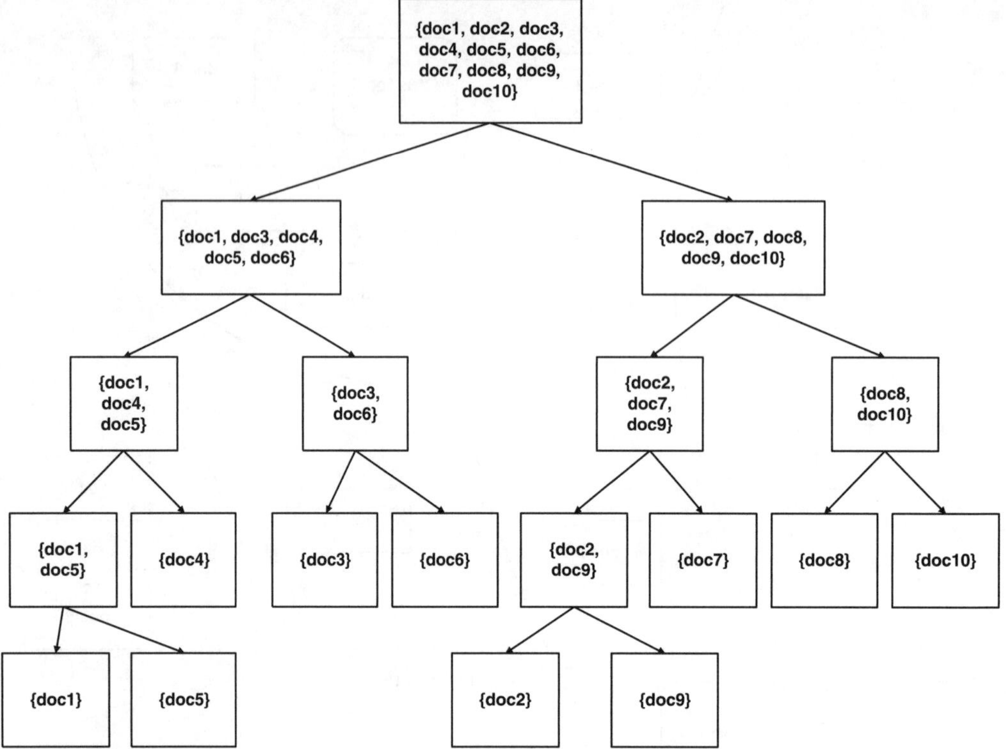

Figure 8.10 Hierarchical clustering groups documents into multiple clusters.

the document just added to the cluster. The amount of adjustment is controlled by a rate of learning parameter specified when the clustering program is run.

SOMs have been used successfully with large newsgroup collections, which are generally considered difficult to analyze because they are frequently filled with short, ungrammatical pieces of text (Kohonen 1998).

Clustering techniques will prove useful when trying to understand the overall structure of a document set and for some maintenance operations, such as detecting duplicates.

Summarizing Text

The goal of summarization is to reduce the length and complexity of a document while maintaining its meaning. The two basic methods of summarization are summarization by abstraction and summarization by extraction. When we humans summarize, we generally read the entire text, develop an understanding of the main ideas, and then write a coherent summary of the text. This is

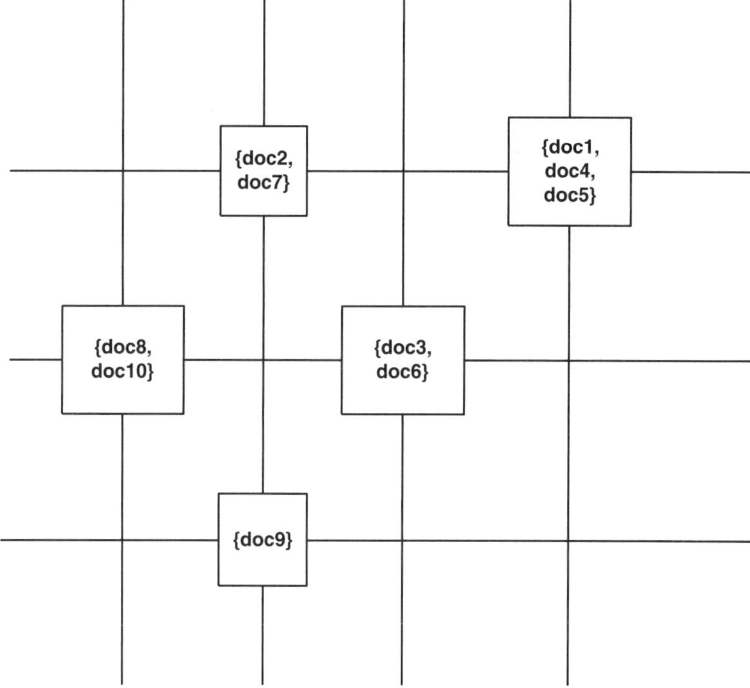

Figure 8.11 Self-organizing maps use two-dimensional grids to organize the clustering of documents.

summarization by abstraction and is beyond the abilities of automated methods. Summary by extraction works by taking key parts of the text and building a summary without understanding the meaning of the text. Three distinct approaches to summary by extraction have been proposed:

- Paragraph extraction
- Sentence extraction
- Sentence segment extraction

Each technique has distinct advantages, as we shall now discuss.

Basic Summarization Methods

All three methods determine the most important terms using the same techniques used for document classification and clustering. In the case of paragraph extraction, entire paragraphs are ranked according to the presence of important terms in them, and the most important paragraphs compose the summary. The primary advantage of this method is that the summaries are the most rhetorically coherent of the three approaches.

Sentence extraction works similarly, but at the sentence level instead of the paragraph level. In this approach, less text is retained in the summary since unimportant sentences within a paragraph are discarded. Sentences are usually ordered according to their relative weights, so it is not uncommon to lose rhetorical consistency. For example, a sentence that begins with *In conclusion* … could appear before a sentence that begins, *First, there is the issue of…*' This problem can be avoided by ordering sentences in the same order in which they appear in the document, rather than by their weights.

Sentence segmentation drills down even farther to work at the clause level. With this technique, a sentence is divided into segments by looking for cue phrases. Each segment conveys a single idea, such as *interest rates are rising.* Segments are separated by cue phrases like *because* or *that,* as in *interests rates are rising because the Federal Reserve is concerned about inflation.* The primary advantage of sentence segmentation is that is removes clauses within sentences that do not convey important information. Like sentence extraction, this technique can suffer from poor rhetorical cohesion.

Dealing with Large Documents

While all three methods for summarization by extraction will produce suitable summaries for most texts, there are special issues that must be addressed with large documents. Prior to summarizing, large documents may need to be preprocessed in one of several ways, through:

- Document partitioning
- Tabular data extraction
- Targeting structured elements

Document partitioning uses knowledge of document types to identify semantically distinct sections of document. Many business and government documents contain both text and numeric data that is essential to understanding the meaning of text and needs to be addressed when summarizing. Finally, semistructured texts can provide additional clues about important elements of a document and may need to be extracted during document parsing.

Document Partitioning

Large documents are usually divided into logical sections. For example, a business plan will provide a discussion of the business organization, financial plans, and marketing information. Project plans might describe the business problem solved by the project, the proposed team structure, duration, and funding. Summarizing across logical boundaries can cause problems when the relative importance of a document section is not reflected by the section's length.

Recall that the importance of a term is measured by its relative frequency in a document and measured inversely proportional to the term's appearance in the larger document set; thus, the number of times a term appears in a document will control its measure of importance. For example, the marketing section of a business plan may be a dominant section of a business plan so terms such as *market segment* appear frequently. Since this is a relatively uncommon term across all documents, it will have a low absolute frequency and thus be considered an important term in the document. Now a term such as *long-term debt* may appear just as infrequently over the set of all documents and, thus, have a similar absolute frequency to the term *market segment*. However, if the financial plan section comprises primarily short texts and tabular numeric data, then terms such as *long-term debt* will have a low relative frequency, making their appearance in the summary less likely.

To avoid this problem, semantically independent document sections may need to be separated into separate documents before summarizing. The result of the individual summarization operations can then be merged to create a semantically adequate document summary. XML is an ideal tool for document partitioning.

Tabular Data Extraction

Since numeric data can often explain a fact much more concisely than a verbal description, tables of data are often embedded within documents to help convey a point. Summarization techniques are not designed to deal with numeric data, so it is best to extract these tables before summarizing and merge the extracted tables with the summarizer's output.

Table extraction can be done either with generic programs for report reformatting (sometimes called "screen scrapers") or with custom programs. If the tabular data is relatively well structured and consistent across a large number of documents, then the screen-scraping approach may be the most efficient. If tabular data will vary in location and complexity, then a scripting language with strong support for regular expressions, such as Perl or Python, can provide the flexibility needed to build a robust extraction routine, but at the expense of writing and maintaining a custom program.

Targeting Structured Elements

With the increasing popularity of XML and derived standards, we can expect to find more and more documents in the warehouse with these structuring elements. Document warehouse designers can take advantage of these elements in several ways.

First, rather than using a summarization by extraction program to create a summary, one could extract salient entities from the XML document, such as an executive summary and the conclusion. Multiple summaries could also be created targeted to different audiences. Financial analysts could be provided with an executive summary and key financial indicators, while marketing executives might prefer the executive summary and an automatically generated summary of the other major sections.

Second, only particular sections of the document might be summarized. This could lead to some improvement in the quality of the summary but it could also significantly reduce the amount of text that must be analyzed by the summarizer.

Third, summaries can replace the contents of some sections of the XML document and thus keep the benefits of the semistructured document, while reducing the size and complexity of the document. This approach is useful when some entities are significantly longer than their relative importance warrants.

Conclusions

Loading and transforming documents is a critical and complex operation in document warehouses. The initial steps begin with preparing for documents in multiple languages and in multiple character sets. Preprocessing steps might include converting character sets, translating documents, extracting tabular data and identifying key entities in semistructured texts.

Main processing steps include indexing documents, both by full text and by theme or topic. Document metadata can then be augmented by adding topic labels to support metadata-oriented searching. Since documents cover multiple topics, the use of multidimensional taxonomies can greatly improve browsing by end users.

Summaries are an important aid to end users because they reduce the complexity of texts without losing significant amounts of information. Automatic summarization is not without its limits, but preprocessing large documents and documents with significant amounts of text can improve the quality of the final summary.

Classification and clustering do not strictly transform documents but augment what is known about documents by making implicit features, explicit. The end result is that users have explicit representations of implicit relationships between documents.

A number of operations are required during the load and transformation stage—managing these operations, and others, is the topic of the next chapter.

CHAPTER 9

Managing Document Warehouse Metadata

In Chapter 6, we looked at metadata to understand one way of logically modeling it. In this chapter, we will look into the details of metadata and explain what it is, why we need it, and how to maintain it. Briefly, metadata is information about the contents and processes of the document warehouse. It can be roughly broken down to three main areas:

- Content metadata
- Technical metadata
- Business metadata

Content metadata describes the subject of a document as well as its origin. This is particularly important to users of the document warehouse because it provides a key mechanism for improving the precision and recall of document searches.

Technical metadata is set up by document warehouse administrators to help manage the warehouse. Common operations like data loads and transformations should be explicitly described in technical metadata. With the potential for large numbers of document retrieval processes—each with its own objectives and constraints—a warehouse administrator cannot simply create custom extraction, transformation, and load (ETL) programs for each task. To keep the document warehouse manageable, the document loads and transformations should be driven by common programs that use metadata as the driving parameters.

Business metadata bridges the world of end users who are primarily served by content metadata and administrators who depend upon technical metadata. While content metadata is focused on a single document and technical metadata operates at the warehouse level, business metadata focuses on midlevel structures, such as the quality control of document groups and access control to parts of the document collection. Figure 9.1 shows the role of each type of metadata relative to those who use it.

Although the needs of a document warehouse are specific to its domain, we have much to learn from developments in data warehousing metadata and in information retrieval and library sciences metadata. The former is well represented by the Common Warehouse Metamodel. From those concerned with cataloging, information management, and resource discovery, we have the Dublin Core as a prime example of a metadata standard that can serve our needs for content metadata. Standards from both the data warehousing realm and the information management arena contribute to the final metadata model proposed here for document warehousing.

This chapter will begin with a discussion of current metadata standards. Combining elements of both data warehousing metadata and information management metadata, we will proceed to address the key needs of document warehousing metadata: content metadata, technical metadata, and business metadata.

Metadata Standards

Metadata standards have developed in a number disciplines, ranging from astronomy and geography to data warehousing and Web searching. The com-

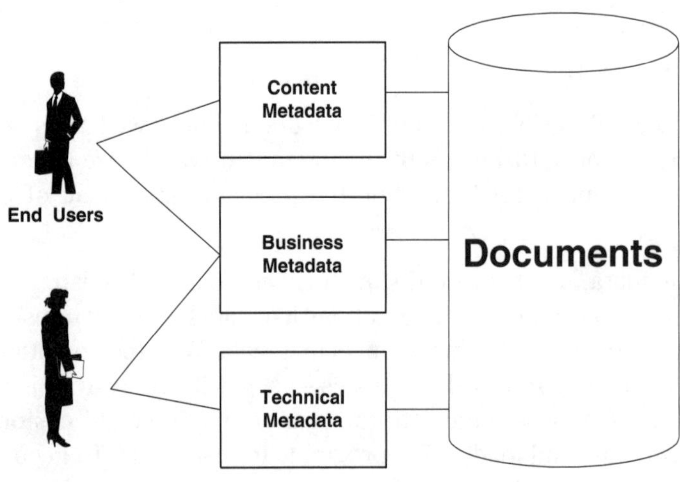

Figure 9.1 Business metadata is needed by both end users and administrators.

mon purpose of all metadata standards is to provide a common description of the contents of a resource, such as a document, a data set geographic information system's feature layers, or a video or audio clip. The author or producer of a resource generally creates metadata. The exact contents of the metadata can vary even within a single discipline, and one objective of metadata standards is to create a common vocabulary that will improve interoperability.

In data warehousing, the need for interoperability has been particularly strong. Many tool vendors have participated in the development of the Common Warehouse Metamodel. Another metadata standard, the Open Information Model initially began as a separate initiative but joined the Common Warehouse Model development program. By sharing information about databases, ETL processes and dimensional model tools built with the Common Warehouse Metamodel in mind are better able to integrate into the large data warehousing environment.

Resource discovery—the processes of finding information—on the Internet can be greatly improved with the use of metadata. When authors describe in well-defined vocabulary the subject area of their documents, how it relates to other documents, and the time period or location the document applies to, the precision of document searching increases.

In this section, we will examine the development of two significant metadata standards:

- Common Warehouse Metamodel
- Dublin Core Metadata Initiative

The Common Warehouse Metamodel describes essential data warehousing processes and objects. The Open Information Model—now incorporated in the Common Warehouse Metamodel—originally developed a distinct metamodel, encompassing data warehousing as well as other software engineering efforts. Since our objective here is to understand existing metadata models as well as how they can evolve to support document warehousing, we will consider the original Open Information Model separately from the Common Warehouse Metamodel. The Dublin Core Metadata Initiative does not concern itself with processes of text mining or document warehousing; rather, it focuses on succinctly describing the contents of an Internet resource. Metadata in the document warehouse will flow from both data warehousing standards and resource discovery standards.

The following discussion of metadata standards is aimed at those with an interest in the details of metadata design. Since the Common Warehouse Metamodel standard was developed with data warehouses and other software systems in mind, some of the details do not apply directly to document warehouses. In any case, if you are not a metadata maven or have only a passing interest in metadata issues, you can easily pass over this section without loss.

Common Warehouse Metamodel

The Common Warehouse Metamodel (CWM) is an Object Management Group (OMG) standard developed by IBM, Oracle, Hyperion, Unisys, NCR, and other data warehouse vendors. The model describes 11 distinct types of metadata along with foundational elements of the model:

- Relational data sources
- Record data sources
- Multidimensional data sources
- XML data sources
- Data transformations
- Online analytic processing (OLAP)
- Data mining
- Information visualization
- Business nomenclature
- Warehouse process
- Warehouse operations

Each of these areas will be briefly described after discussing foundation of the CWM. We will then turn our attention to a more detailed look at the areas most relevant to document warehousing.

Foundations of the Common Warehouse Metamodel

The main sections of the model are organized into hierarchical packages. The four primary packages are:

- Foundation
- Resource
- Analysis
- Management

The Foundation package, shown in Figure 9.2, includes Business Information, Data Types, Expressions, Keys and Indexes, Software Deployment, and Type Mapping packages. The Resource package encompasses the Object-Oriented, Relational, Record, Multidimensional, and XML packages. Analysis includes the

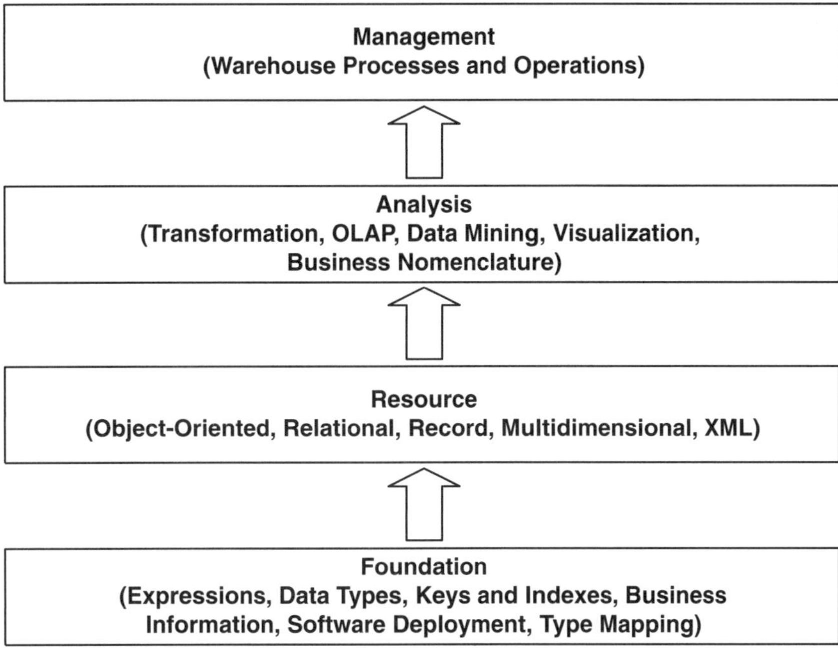

Figure 9.2 The Common Warehouse Metamodel builds upon foundational elements.

Transformation, OLAP, Data Mining, Visualization, and Business Nomenclature packages. Finally, the Management package contains the Warehouse Process and Warehouse Operation packages.

Business Information

The Foundation package provides the means of expressing business information about other elements within a metadata model. For example, the Business Information package describes offline documentation, persons responsible for particular parts of the system, and contact information for those responsible parties.

Data Types

The Data Type package gives designers the means to specify data types used in a model. The CWM does not assume a predefined set of data types, so designers and architects are free to construct their own. The CWM does however provide a group of data type classes as building blocks. These include:

- Any
- Enumeration
- Enumeration Literal

- Extent
- Float
- Query Expression
- Type Alias
- Union
- Union Member

The Any class allows an object to take on the value of any defined data type.

The Enumeration class allows for the creation of lists of allowed values that a data type can take on. Enumerations may or may not be ordered. Enumeration Literals define the identifiers used in enumerations. Enumeration Literals are also used to express more complex types (such as ranges, with Enumeration Literals specifying the beginning and end of the range).

Extents create collections of instances of particular types. This class is used primarily to link concrete examples of a type to the type itself. For example, in the multidimensional taxonomies used in document warehouses, Extents would link documents to the descriptor nodes in the taxonomy that classify those documents.

The next two classes are probably well known. Floats are used to specify floating point numbers. Query Expressions allow for the creation of language-dependent query statements, such as SQL's SELECT.

The Type Alias provides the means to describe scenarios in which renaming a class effectively creates a new class.

Union classes support both discriminated and undiscriminated unions between objects. The former is a class that has a criterion for inclusion, such as a structural condition based upon type. Undiscriminated unions allow multiple types within a collection.

Finally, the Union Member describes objects within Union classes.

Expressions

Expressions are represented as trees, allowing relatively few structures to describe complex relationships. The Expression package uses a simple model with only four classes:

- Constant Node
- Element Node
- Expression Node
- Feature Node

The Constant Node, as the name implies, is used to represent constant values in an expression. The Expression Node is a hierarchical representation of an expression. The root of such a hierarchy is the value of the expression. The Expression Node has two subclasses, the Feature Node and the Element Node. The Feature Node is used to represent attributes or operators. The Element Node is any subclass of the Expression Node that is not a Feature Node, such as some other model type that can evaluate to an expression or value that can be used in an expression.

While these distinctions may seem academic at first, they are an important part of the interoperability goals of the CWM. Data warehousing tools may represent expressions in sometimes subtly different ways, and the Expression package provides a common representation for sharing expressions between these same tools.

Keys and Indexes

The use of keys and indexes is second nature to relational database designers. The basic concepts behind these two structures are the idea of unique identifiers and the relationship between keys. The unique identifier provides a way of precisely identifying an object and corresponds to a primary key (or in some cases, an alternate key). Relationships specify how one object relates to another and corresponds to the foreign key relationship in relational models. The classes used in the Keys and Indexes package are:

- Index
- Indexed Feature
- Key Relationship
- Unique Key

The Index class orders objects and is included in the CWM to provide a common representation of indexes. Although ANSI Standard SQL provides an alternate representation of indexes that could be used a common representation, the idea of keys and indexes are useful outside of relational databases and this class allows for their use in those other areas.

The Indexed Feature indicates the column or other attribute of a nonrelational object that is indexed by an instance of the Index class.

The Key Relationship class is used to represent foreign key relationships and depends upon Unique Keys, which in turn uniquely identify particular members of a class.

Software Deployment

The Software Deployment class is used to describe how software components, such as ETL tools, ad hoc query tools, and in the case of document warehousing, text analysis tools are used in the business intelligence environment. The main classes within this package are:

- Data Manager
- Data Provider

Data Managers are systems that control access to and maintain data, such as relational database management systems, multidimensional databases, and file systems.

Data Providers are client components that work with Data Managers to provide access to a data store. ODBC, SQL*Net, and JDBC are examples of data providers.

Other classes within the Software Deployment package include Deployed Component, Deployed Software System, Machine, Site, Provider Connection, and Site. These all serve to further describe the infrastructure of the data warehouse in terms of applications and the hardware on which they run.

Type Mapping

Type Mapping—the final class in the Foundation of the Common Warehouse Model—models the means by which data types can be translated between systems. The assumption behind this class is that data types are sufficiently similar across systems that it is possible to exchange data with some reformatting or mapping. There are only two classes in this package:

- Type Mapping
- Type Mapping System

The Type Mapping class specifies how a data type in one system is mapped to a data type in another. For example, the VARCHAR2 data type in Oracle might be mapped to the VARCHAR data type in SQL Server. The Type Mapping System is a collection of Type Mappings defined for a particular system.

These Foundation classes provide the basis for constructing the other classes within the CWM. Some classes are beyond the scope of this book, so the following sections will address only most relevant topics for document warehousing.

Resource Package

The Resource package contains the relational, multidimensional, record, and XML classes. The Relational class describes the basic elements of a relational database management system, including tables, columns, primary and foreign keys, procedures, triggers, constraints, and SQL queries. The Multidimensional class describes the data structures used in OLAP databases, such as hierarchies and dimensions, and OLAP operations, including aggregation and drill-down.

The Record class addresses simple data structures, encompassing both database-oriented records and programming language structures. The Record class is used primarily to describe older data sources, such as COBOL structures.

The XML class represents semistructured documents, using constructs such as attributes, contents, documents, element types, element content, element types, schema, and text. The most important is the schema, which contains declarations and definitions associated with a document, the element type (which defines elements used in a document), and text (which describes the value of an element).

Analysis Package

The Analysis package of the Common Warehouse Model includes several distinct packages—including transformation, OLAP, data mining, information visualization, and business nomenclature. The most important for our purposes are transformation, information visualization, and business nomenclature.

Transformations

The Transformation class describes ETL operations between relational, record, multidimensional, XML, data mining, and OLAP sources and targets. The three main constructs described by this package are links from data sources to targets, course-grained and fine-grained transformations, and the logical grouping of transformations into single groups of tasks. Figure 9.3 shows a logical flow of documents through transformations and to the document warehouse.

The main classes of the transformation package are:

- Transformation
- Data Object Set
- Transformation Task

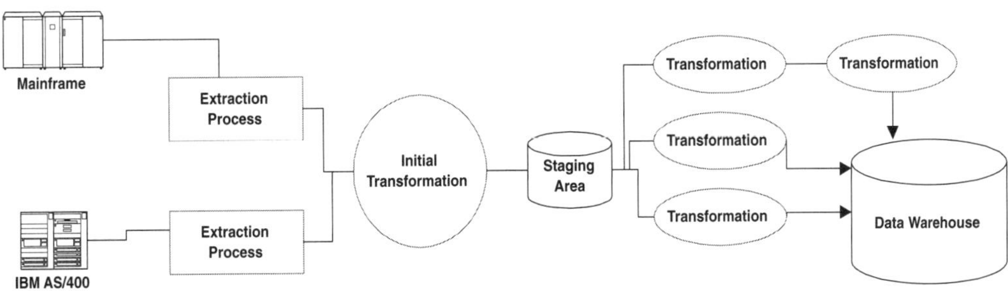

Figure 9.3 Transformation packages can encompass multiple types of sources and targets.

- Transformation Step
- Transformation Activity
- Precedence Constraint
- Step Precedence
- Transformation Map
- Feature Map

In both data warehousing and document warehousing, transformations need to be grouped in logical tasks that, in turn, may be dependent upon other transformation tasks. The CWM allows designers to describe these structures and dependencies using several different constructs. A transformation task is a set of transformations that must be completed together. These tasks are executed as transformation steps that are further organized by precedences and dependencies in structured groups called transformation activities.

Data object sets represent either sources or targets. Feature Maps express how to transform objects from source data objects into objects in target data objects.

Precedence Constraints and Step Precedences are used to control the flow of execution in ETL processes.

Information Visualization

Information visualization is the process of representing graphically or geometrically complex relationships between data elements. In document warehousing, visualization is especially important for complex and intricately connected hypertext documents. The primary purpose of visualization is to allow users to render the logical structure of a section of the data or document warehouse in a two-dimensional form. The CWM model provides four classes for information visualization.

- Rendered Object
- Rendered Object Set
- Rendering
- XSL Rendering

The Rendered Object represents a component in the data or document warehouse, such as a cell in a multidimensional cube or a hyperlinked document in a document warehouse. Rendered Object Sets are simply collections of rendered objects. Instances of the Rendering class describe how to map from the warehouse object to a two-dimensional graph or picture. XSL Rendering is a subclass of the Rendering class that is designed to support rendering using XSL, which could be used when depicting an object in an HTML document.

Business Nomenclature

Data warehouse and document warehouse users need to understand what resources are available in an organization's business intelligence environment. This includes knowing what information is in the repository, how it can be accessed, and where it came from, and this needs to be described in terms of the business, not technical, terms. The Business Nomenclature package provides the means to represent this type of metadata:

- Business Domain
- Concept
- Glossary
- Nomenclature
- Taxonomy
- Term
- Vocabulary Element

The Business Nomenclature package is one of the most important for document warehousing. These classes can be used to describe not only the structure of the document warehouse, but its contents as well.

The business domain represents a logical area of a business. Domains can be quite diverse, depending upon the industry. For example, a pharmaceutical company might require domains describing research and development that encompass genetics, chemistry, and biology, while it must also support a financial domain describing generally accepted accounting practices and principles.

Vocabulary elements are divided into two types: Concepts and Terms. Concepts represent ideas in a business domain. Terms are words or phrases that represent business concepts in a particular context. The context is defined in terms of a concept that is referenced by a term. Concepts can be thought of as preferred terms since they represent a common form of an idea that can be expressed using different terms. Terms are organized into two types of nomenclature classes: Glossaries and Taxonomies. A glossary is an unordered collection of terms. Taxonomies, sometimes called ontologies, are hierarchical organizations of terms.

In addition to these classes, the Common Warehouse Metamodel defines several relationships between classes. The Synonym to Preferred Term relationship links commonly used terms that mean the same thing to a single term. This is especially useful for minimizing the number of terms that need to be represented in a taxonomy or glossary. The Wider to Narrower relationship provides for navigation from a general term to a more specific. Related terms link terms to other terms, providing for horizontal relationships between terms in addition to the vertical, or hierarchical, relationships defined in taxonomies.

Management

The management areas of the Common Warehouse Metamodel can be subdivided into two sections: warehouse processes and warehouse operations. The former deals primarily with transformation operations, while the latter deals with day-to-day operations of the warehouse.

Warehouse Processes

Warehouse processes are specific events that result in the execution of a transformation activity. The CWM distinguishes three types:

- Scheduled
- External
- Internal

Scheduled transformation activities happen at a particular time, for example at midnight on August 15, 2000, or at regular intervals, for example every 24 hours.

External events are caused by some event outside of the warehouse, while internal processes are triggered by other events within the course of warehouse operations.

Warehouse Operations

Warehouse operations, at least in terms of the Common Warehouse Model, deal with three types of events:

- Transformation Executions
- Measurements
- Change Requests

Transformation executions record the results of the ETL activities, including when a transformation activity ran, whether or not it was successful, and how much of the ETL operations was actually completed.

Measurements allow data warehouse and document warehouse managers to track the growth and other metrics of the warehouse. Within the document warehouse, these measurements could be rates of growth of documents classified using particular categories in a taxonomy. Inordinate growth or lack of growth in particular topics could indicate the need to restructure the taxonomy to better classify documents. It could also indicate the need to adjust search parameters to better populate the warehouse in domains that are not well represented by documents in the repository.

Change requests track changes and proposed changes to the warehouse structure. Changes to the operations, such as changes to search targets in the document warehouse, are tracked separately.

Knowledge Management Based on the Open Information Model

The Open Information Model (OIM), like the Common Warehouse Metamodel, was a nonproprietary standard designed to model the metadata needs of data warehouses. Unlike the original CWM, the OIM extended its coverage beyond the warehouse to include a wide range of information systems, and related operations including:

- Analysis and design
- Components and objects
- Database and warehousing
- Knowledge management

Analysis and Design submodel addresses object-oriented design and processes and the software development life cycle. The Objects and Components submodel deals with software components and specifies metadata to support component reuse. The Database and Warehousing submodel covers many of the same areas as the Common Warehouse Model, such as relational and multidimensional database, records sources, and transformations. The Knowledge Management submodel is the most interesting from the perspective of document warehousing and will be the sole focus of our attention in this section.

Knowledge Management

The core focus of the Knowledge Management submodel is capturing business terminology—semantic relationships between objects in a business domain—and mapping these constructs to storage structures. Mapping linguistic phrases to data storage structures allows users to manipulate databases with natural language front ends rather than with SQL or SQL-based tools. It must be noted that this type of natural language processing is different from the core operations in text mining and document warehousing.

Document warehousing and text mining address problems in dealing with large groups or corpuses of text. Text analysis operations such as feature extraction, summarization, clustering, and classification use techniques from corpus linguistics, an area that emphasizes rough analysis of large texts. Natural language front ends, on the other hand, deal with relatively short pieces of text, such as:

```
Show me all the salespersons whose actual sales were less than their quota.
```

In this case, the linguistic processor must translate the English statement into a SQL SELECT statement that returns the specified information. This mapping from natural to data manipulation language requires precise mappings and a detailed understanding of the structure of a database. The Knowledge Management metadata specified in the OIM provides the basis for that understanding.

The Knowledge Management submodel specifies three elements:

- Entities
- Relationships
- Dictionaries

Entities name a category, such as document, author, publisher, or topic. These categories in turn have instances such as *OLAP Solutions* (Thomsen 1997) and multidimensional modeling. Entities usually correspond to a database table or one or more columns in a table.

Relationships indicate associations between entities, such as Erik Thomsen is the author of *OLAP Solutions* (John Wiley & Sons 1997). Associations are specified by verbs that define relationships. These relationships can also be modified by other entities. These additional entities are indicated by prepositions in natural language statements. For example, Erik Thomsen writes books on multidimensional modeling. The Knowledge Management submodel uses a construct called phrasings to represent different ways of expressing the same relationship. The following sentences say the same thing but use different phrasings:

- Alan Greenspan is Chairman of the Federal Reserve Board.
- The Chairman of the Federal Reserve Board is Alan Greenspan.
- The Federal Reserve Board is chaired by Alan Greenspan.

The last element in the Knowledge Management submodel is Dictionaries. Dictionaries are collections of words with support for both regular and irregular entries. Regular entries follow general grammatical rules, for example the past tense of *design* is *designed*. Irregular entries identify words that do not follow general grammatical rules, for example the past tense of *eat* is *ate*.[1]

[1] Actually, these irregular verbs do follow grammatical rules, just not the one commonly used today. For example, verbs that have been around since Old English; that is, English spoken from about the eight to the eleventh centuries, follow grammatical rules from that period. At that time, English was a highly inflected language, and verb tense was indicated by changing vowels (and sometimes other letters) rather than by adding an *–ed* to the end of the word, so ran becomes run instead of ranned.

The role of the Knowledge Management submodel will be limited in document warehousing to providing the same type of natural language front end to a document warehouse that it provides for other database applications.

The data warehousing metadata standard, the Common Warehouse Metamodel, provides a solid foundation upon which we can construct a metadata infrastructure for the document warehouse. Since document warehousing has an especially elaborate semantic context, we will need to go beyond data warehousing standards to include a resource discovery standard, the Dublin Core, to fully accommodate the metadata needs of the document warehouse.

Dublin Core

The Dublin Core is a metadata standard designed to support resource discovery. It does not presuppose a particular subject matter area or specific type of data like some metadata standards. A directorate located at the Online Computer Library Center in Dublin, Ohio, develops the Dublin Core standard, which was initiated in 1995. Although it came from a library science and cataloging perspective, the Dublin Core is becoming a de facto standard on the Internet resource metadata across disciplines.

Simple Dublin Core

The Simple Dublin Core is a set of fifteen elements that use attribute value pairs to describe a resource, such as a document. The fifteen elements are:

Title	Format
Creator	Identifier
Subject	Source
Description	Language
Publisher	Relation
Contributor	Coverage
Date	Rights
Type	

All fifteen data elements are optional for any data source, and each can occur an unlimited number of times. Data elements are all represented as character strings.

The Title element is simply the formal name of the resource. Although multiple occurrences are allowed, this element is usually only specified once.

The Creator element is the person, group, or other organization responsible for the document. The list of creators for a single document can include both persons and organizations.

The Subject element is usually a list of terms from a controlled vocabulary that describes the contents of the document. Digital libraries might include terms from the Dewey Classification System or related standard for shared documents. A corporation managing an intranet should use terms from a corporate thesaurus when specifying subjects. Searches will often use the subject metadata to identify the actual contents of a document. This element is one of the most important for improving the precision of keyword searches.

Descriptions are not limited to controlled vocabularies but can include summaries, tables of contents (for long documents), or other concise means of providing more details about the contents of a document than is available from the subject element.

Like a Creator, the Publisher is the person or organization responsible for publishing the document. Again, both persons and organizations can be included together in the same metadata set.

Contributors make substantive additions to the content of a document, in addition to creators.

Date elements define the time of significant events in the life of a document, such as the creation and publication. The Dublin Core Initiative recommends following the ISO 8601 profile, which uses the YYYY-MM-DD format. The Date element is frequently repeated but qualifiers are used to distinguish different events. Some of the most common are:

- Creation Date
- Publication Date
- Last Modified Date

The Type element describes the general category or genre of a document. The Dublin Core Initiative recommends using a controlled vocabulary such as the Dublin Core Types, which include:

- Text
- Image
- Sound
- Dataset
- Software

- Interactive
- Event
- Physical Object

Obviously, the text type is the most important in the document warehousing arena.

The Format element describes the way in which the document is stored and represented within a file. This element generally contains terms from the Internet Media Type (MIME) list of computer media. This information is generally used to determine the type of software needed to use a document, such as Microsoft Word, Adobe Acrobat Reader, or a simple text editor.

Identifiers provide a unique identifier for a resource. The values of these elements should always be defined in accordance with a formal standard, such as Universal Resource Indicators (URI, which includes Universal Resource Locators [URL]). Multiple identifiers may be included if they are of different types, such as an International Standard Book Number (ISBN) or Digital Object Identifier (DOI).

The Source element is used to specify where a document came from. Using a formal standard is the best approach here as with the Identifier. If a source is an internal server, then using the Universal Naming Convention or other system that can uniquely identify a directory within a networked file system is recommended.

The Language element describes the language of the text of the document. The Dublin Core Initiative recommends using the ISO 639 two-character standard abbreviations for this element. The values of this element sometimes use the ISO 3,166 two-letter country code as a suffix. For example, a document written in England would use *en-uk* to designate English as spoken in the United Kingdom.

The Relation element can be used to indicate that a document is related to another document. Ideally a URI is used to identify the related resource, making it easy for a document retrieval program to collect related documents as well as the original target.

The Coverage element is often used to specify a geographic location, jurisdiction, or time period. Again, using a controlled vocabulary allows for the greatest interoperability. The Dublin Core Initiative recommends using terms from the Thesaurus of Geographic Names for locations. Again, the use of standardized terms will improve interoperability.

Finally, the Rights element describes the legal rights held over the document by its creators or publishers. Sometimes this element contains the name of a service providing management of the owner's rights.

Qualified Dublin Core

Sometimes it is necessary or useful to provide additional information to more precisely describe a resource. To support this requirement, the simple Dublin Core can be augmented with two types of qualifiers: value qualifiers and element qualifiers.

Value identifiers are used to describe the vocabulary, encoding scheme, or language used to describe the metadata. Note, that the language specification does not apply to the document, but to the metadata itself. Thus, a single set of metadata descriptors can include subjects and descriptions in multiple languages. This also allows document warehouse designers the opportunity to provide machine-translated versions of the metadata along with the original metadata when supporting a multilingual user group. The SCHEME qualifier is used to specify a particular restricted vocabulary or other standard. For example, to indicate the subject, using the Library of Congress catalog, one could specify:

```
<META=DC.Subject, CONTENT=(SCHEME=LOC) … >
```

Element qualifiers narrow the definition of an element. Dates, for example, frequently require further classification. By default, the Date element specifies the creation date of the document. The following are commonly used to indicate precisely which date is specified by a Data element.

- Last Modified
- Published
- Expired
- Available
- Verified
- Accepted
- Data Gathered

To this standard list, we could add Date Translated and Translation Verified when machine translation is used.

In addition to specifying more precise meanings of elements with qualifiers, we can also specify them by subelements of the form `<element>.<subelement>`. For example, the data qualifiers can also be specified as:

- DC.Date.Created
- DC.Date.LastModified

- DC.Date.Published
- DC.Date.Expired
- DC.Date.Available
- DC.Date.Verified
- DC.Date.Accepted
- DC.Date.DataGathered

Subelements are also used in the Relation element. These include:

- Inclusion Relations
  - DC.Relations.IsPartOf
  - DC.Relations.HasPart
- Version Relations
  - DC.Relations.IsVersionOf
  - DC.Relations.HasVersionOf
- Mechanical Relations
  - DC.Relation.IsFormatOf
  - DC.Relation.HasFormat
- Reference Relations
  - DC.Relation.References
  - DC.Relation.IsReferencedBy
- Creativity Relations
  - DC.Relation.IsBasisOf
  - DC.Relations.IsBasedOn
- Dependency Relations
  - DC.Relations.Requires
  - DC.Relations.IsRequiredBy

The Dublin Core Initiative does not recommend adding new data elements because it decreases the interoperability of the standard. Since document warehouses are primarily intraorganizational systems, interoperability is less of an issue. When weighed against the added value of including new metadata elements, such as those concerning language translation, the interoperability concerns are not as relevant.

Adapting Metadata Standards to Document Warehousing

Now that we have an understanding of metadata standards, it is time to discuss how these will operate within the document warehouse environment and what benefits they will provide. The following sections will describe specific metadata structures and processes. At each step, we will define metadata needed in the warehouse in terms of the metadata elements specified within one of the standards discussed in this chapter.

Since the structure of the Dublin Core has been described in detail in Chapter 6, the main focus of the section on content metadata will be on collecting and storing the metadata.

The section on technical metadata will focus on controlling the collection and text analysis of documents as they are loaded into the document warehouse. Elements from the Resource and Analysis packages of the Common Warehouse Metamodel will play a prominent role in this section.

Following the technical metadata section, we will examine how business metadata can be represented using pieces of the Analysis packages of the Common Warehouse Metamodel.

Finally, in the last section of the chapter, we will present an example of how to use transformation metadata to drive the text analysis processes that occur after documents have been collected.

Content Metadata

The Dublin Core is the foundation for content metadata in the document warehouse. Although the Dublin Core standard is very specific about the semantics of the metadata that should be kept about a resource, it does not define a single syntax for expressing this information within a document. It also does not define how the metadata should be stored although several common options exist. In this section we look into the process of collecting and storing Dublin Core metadata.

Collecting Dublin Core Metadata

Traditionally in data warehousing, metadata is created either as part of the design, development, and maintenance phases of a project or generated as a by-product of a warehousing process, such as ETL data. In document warehousing, we ideally collect metadata along with the contents of the documents that interest us. The Dublin Core metadata can be included in documents using either the Dublin Core Structured Values encoding or the XML-based RDF format.

Dublin Core Structured Values

The Dublin Core Structured Values (DCSV) allows metadata to be embedded within an HTML document using META tags. The DCSV standard is a recommendation of the Dublin Core initiative for serializing metadata as a text string. The standard was designed to allow multiple occurrences of values and to minimize the use of restricted characters in HTML.

The DCSV recognizes two types of strings, labels, and values. Labels indicate the name of the metadata element being represented, such as DC.Creator or DC.Date.Published. Values are simply the data associated with the element, such as *John Smith* or *2000-09-25*. Three punctuation marks are used:

- Equal signs (=): Separate labels and values
- Semicolons (;): Separate values
- Dot (.): Indicate hierarchical structure

For example, the metadata for a document entitled "Top Ten Text Mining Mistakes" by Mary Smith and published November 18, 2000, is encoded in DCSV as:

```
"DC.Title=Top Ten Text Mining Mistakes; DC.Creator=Mary Smith;
DC.Date.Published=2000-11-18".
```

When used with the HTML META tag, the SCHEME term can be used to specify that DCSV is the encoding method.

While this representation has the advantage of being human readable and easily implemented within HTML, the Resource Descriptor Format uses an XML-based encoding to overcome the limitations of HTML-based encoding schemes.

Resource Descriptor Format

The Resource Descriptor Format (RDF) is a standard developed by the World Wide Web Consortium to store resource metadata. RDF was developed, in part, with the goal of providing a comprehensive method for representing the Dublin Core. The Dublin Core is primarily concerned with the semantics of metadata, defining a specific set of elements and their meanings. The RDF is more of a syntax specification for implementing the semantics defined by others, such as the Dublin Core. Like the Dublin Core, the RDF is based upon attribute value pairings. Since RDF is built upon XML and avoids the limits of HTML, we can expect widespread adoption of this method.

A simple set of metadata can be represented as follows:

```
<?xml version="1.0"?>
  <rdf:RDF
       xmlns:rdf=http://www.w3.org/1999/02/22-rdf-syntax-ns#
       xmlns:dc="http://purl.org/dc/elements/1.0/" >
    <rdf:Description rdf:about="http://www.tmnonsite.com/top10.doc">
         <creator> Mary Smith</creator>
```

```
        <title> Top Ten Text Mining Mistakes </title>
        <date> 2000-11-18 </date>
    </rdf:Description>
  </rdf:RDF>
```

The code begins with a specification of the XML version used followed by a list of name spaces used in the description. In this example, two namespaces are specified, one for RDF (xmlns:rdf=http://www.w3.org/1999/02/22-rdf-syntax-ns#) and one for Dublin Core (xmlns:dc=http://purl.org/dc/elements/1.0/). The RDF description identifies the file to which the following elements apply. If Dublin Core qualifiers were used as well, the document would include the qualifier namespace, http://purl.org/dc/qualifiers/1.0/.

The Dublin Core namespace defines element names, such as creator, title, and date. (Since XML is case sensitive, the element tags must be in lowercase since that is how they are defined in the RDF namespace. For a complete list of elements, see http://purl.org/dc/elements/1.0/.

Storing Dublin Core Metadata

Both the DCSV and RDF formats of the Dublin Core can be stored along with documents in the document warehouse, but this is not recommended. Instead, extracting the data and keeping it in a relational database is the preferred method for several reasons.

First, other types of document warehouse metadata, such as process and business metadata, are kept in the relational database. For both ease of use and ease of management, a single type of metadata repository should be used.

Second, if left in either the DCSV format or the semistructured RDF format, the metadata would need to be parsed each time it is needed.

Third, when stored in a relational table, the metadata can be indexed as one would index other data in the warehouse. This is especially important with commonly searched on elements such as Subject.

Technical Metadata

Technical metadata deals with document warehouse processes. In this section, we will look at four examples of how to use metadata to control document warehouse processes. In the course of our discussion, we will introduce relational data models for implementing metadata models based upon the Common Warehouse Metamodel.

The three document warehouse processes covered are:

- Controlling document loads in the warehouse
- Prioritizing items in multiple processing queues
- Summarizing documents

Controlling document loads will show how to use metadata to define what should be added to a warehouse—for example, the entire document, a summary, or just a URL. Since not all document searches have the same priority, prioritizing searches within and across search queues will also be controlled with metadata. Finally, as an example of how to control text analysis operations with metadata, we will discuss how to control which documents are summarized when loading into the warehouse.

Controlling Document Loads in the Warehouse

The first step in processing documents starts with moving documents from the staging area where the search processes left them, as shown in Figure 9.4. Metadata about document sources drive what documents are retrieved, while document targets define where they are loaded in the staging area. One way of partitioning the staging area is according to the operations that will be performed upon the documents in them. For example, documents that all need to be translated may go to one part of the staging area, while documents that will have features extracted will move to another. Of course, multiple operations can be performed on a single set of documents. To do this we simply associate a transformation activity with a directory of the staging area.

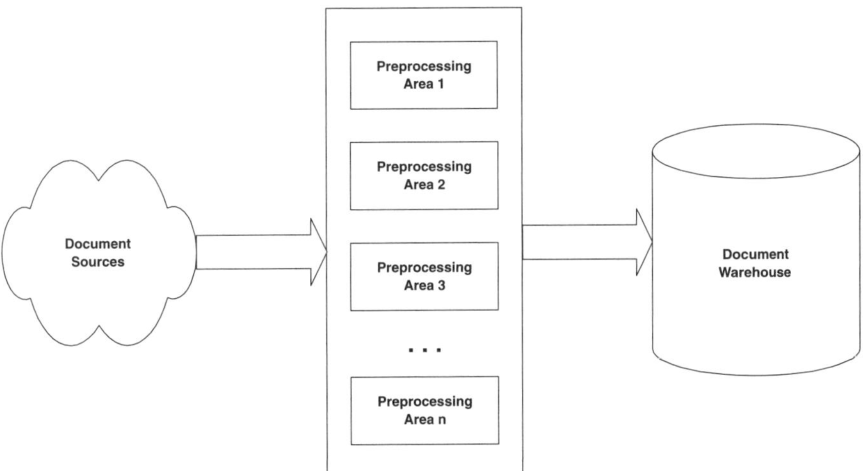

Figure 9.4 Multiple sources are partitioned in the staging area according to preload processing tasks.

Linking an area of the staging area to a single transformation activity eases the management of the preload processing. Since the staging area is most likely a directory in a file system, we do not have the power of a relational database at our disposal for manipulating files and selecting only those that meet some criteria. The real work, instead, comes with defining the transformation activity. As Figure 9.5 shows, the logical model for all preload tasks can be modeled using data sources, data targets, transformation activities, and related entities.

The Document Source entity describes the source of documents—a Web site, a search criteria for an Internet search engine, or a directory or file specification for a local file system. The Document Target associated with a Document Source specifies the directory in the staging area that will house the documents retrieved. Multiple document sources may be associated with a single document target, thus implementing the idea of partitioning in the staging area.

Multiple Transformation Activities can be associated with a Document Target. A Transformation Activity is a logical set of steps that is carried out to perform a logical task, such as translating a document or thematically indexing a text. Activities are defined as multiple Transformation Steps, since the same logical task may require the execution of multiple programs. For example, a file may need to be reformatted, or HTML tags may need to be removed before the text is sent on for linguistic processing.

A Transformation Step may have multiple parameters associated with it. Summarization transformations will require a specification describing the summary. For example, a summary could be a percentage of the size of the original document or it may be a fixed number of sentences. A reformatting program will probably map from multiple sources to multiple targets, such as from Portable Document Format (PDF), Microsoft Word, and HTML to plaintext or XML.

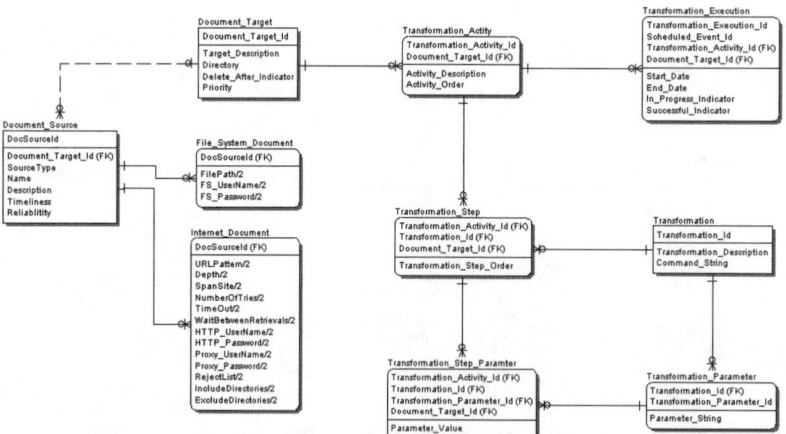

Figure 9.5 Logical model for representing metadata about preload activities.

Transformation Executions record information about the actual running of a transformation, thus providing a history of the execution of a particular Transformation Activity.

To control the loading of a set of documents, do the following:

- Define the Document Target area of the staging area.
- Define one or more Transformation Activities for the Document Target.
- Define a Schedule Event for each Transformation Activity.

The Document Target area will receive documents from one or more document search tasks. The Transformation Activities will specify the exact operations to apply to the text, and the Schedule Event will control how frequently the Transformation Activities execute.

Under this scenario, all Document Targets are treated equally, since the only ordering among steps is with regard to the Transformation Activities that are applied within a Document Target. We will now describe how to create multiple processing queues.

Prioritizing Items in Multiple Processing Queues

In the previous section, we assumed that all transformation activities were executed together, but in some circumstances, we may want to partition the staging area along another dimension to indicate the relative importance of some documents. To do this we will use the Priority attribute associated with the Document Target.

Using just one more attribute provides enough information to develop a multilayered processing structure. As Figure 9.6 shows, the multiple transformation queues can be assigned different priorities. Low-volume, high-priority parts of the staging area can be handled by one process, perhaps with a higher operating system priority than the other queues, while the higher-volume, less-important documents are sent through a low-priority process.

The queues themselves are relatively straightforward to implement. A Perl script that calls a series of transformation activities (themselves Perl scripts driven by metadata in the database) after collecting a list of files in a document target directory is all that is needed to implement a queue. The top-level script can either continuously look for new files or suspend execution for a period of time and then check for new files.

Once the queue processing is in place, defining the tasks associated with controlling document loads is the last step to implementing prioritized queues.

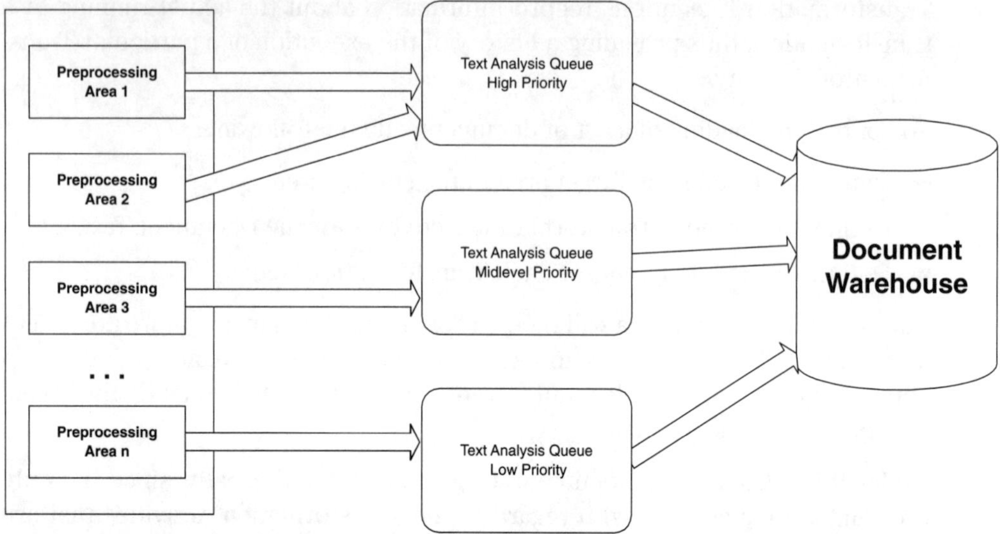

Figure 9.6 Multiple processes are used to implement different priority level queues.

Summarizing Documents

The process of summarizing documents is a common task in document warehousing, yet the process is complex enough to warrant a wide range of parameters. With so many options for configuring this text analysis process, document summarizing makes an ideal example for describing the use of parameters in transformation processing.

The summarizing process is a single transformation step within a, possibly larger, transformation activity. The Transformation Step has an associated Transformation Step record that defines exactly what program to run to create the summary. For example, when using the IBM Intelligent Miner for Text tool suite, the command line for running the summarizer is

```
imzsum <parameter>*  <input file>
```

where <parameter>* indicates a list of zero or more parameters, and the <input file> specifies the file in the staging area to be summarized.

The steps to creating a document summary are then:

- Define a Transformation Activity.
- Define a Transformation Step associated with the transformation for summarizing a document.
- For each parameter to the summarization, create a Transformation Parameter.

By way of example, here are a few of the parameters that can be specified along with a summarization transformation:

- Boundary definition associated with a document type (for example, in cases where only parts of a document should be summarized)
- Extraction options, such as extracting names, abbreviations, and other terms
- Methods for weighting terms; for example, frequency-based, information-based, or inverse-frequency-based
- Length of summary, either in sentences or as percentage of total original document
- Output format options, for example, plaintext or HTML
- Summarization of multiple documents or a single document

By collecting the set of parameters specified for a summarization task along with the basic command line string, a single invocation command string can be created and executed with a shell script.

Business Metadata

Business metadata does less to help administrators run a document warehouse than to help both end users and technical staff to understand what is in the warehouse. A great deal of information about the contents of the warehouse can be found in content metadata, such as the Dublin Core set of attributes, but that does not provide enough information. Specifically, it does not provide information about:

- Quality and reliability
- Access control
- Version and expiration control

Quality metadata provides information about a source of documents, such as a Web site or internal directory. These metrics tend to be rough indications of the timeliness and accuracy of the information available from a source. Access control describes how information is shared among warehouse users. Clearly, sensitive documents, such as negotiation notes and confidential agreements, must not be widely distributed. Finally, version and expiration control address how multiple versions of a document are handled within the warehouse and how long documents are kept in the repository.

Quality: Timeliness and Reliability

The value of a document is directly proportional to its quality. Quality, in turn, is a function of the rate at which information is provided and how quickly a reported event is made known. Reliability, on the other hand, indicates the accuracy of the information provided in a text.

Information associated with timeliness and reliability is kept in the Document Source entity in the metadata model. This will raise issues with regard to what constitutes a document source. For example, is the top level of a Web site the entire source? In many cases it is, and this does not cause problems. There are cases, however, in which the type of information itself better indicates the quality of the source. For example, an Internet news service might provide very timely, comprehensive coverage of political issues but only moderate or poor analysis of financial news stories. In such a case, the document source metadata would have to distinguish between the different areas of the Web site.

Access Control

The need for access control implies the need for an added entity in the document data model to represent document groups. As Figure 9.7 depicts, documents can belong to multiple groups, and users may have accesses to one or more groups. Again, this is a logical representation with a number of possible implementations. The full details of access control will be presented in Chapter 10.

One implementation is to use built-in security features of the RDBMS. For example, users or roles can be granted privileges to views that limit the scope

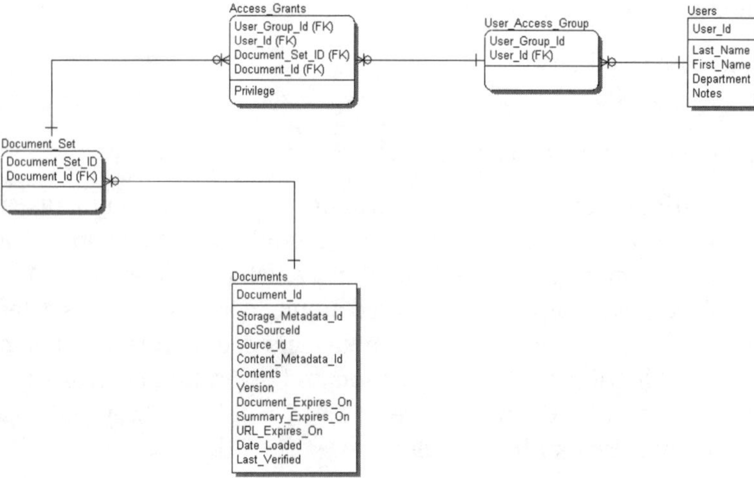

Figure 9.7 Documents can be in multiple groups that are accessed by multiple users.

of access to documents. A new development related to this is the virtual database, which limits access to records according to their content without the need for explicit views. This will be discussed fully in the next chapter.

When database security mechanisms are not sufficient or flexible enough, custom security can be developed. These generally require restricting access to tables to stored procedures, which in turn implement a custom security scheme. When this approach is used, the document and user groups described in Figure 9.7 need to be added to the document warehouse data model.

Versioning

The support for multiple document versions requires the ability to uniquely identify distinct versions of a document. Several techniques can be used to distinguish document versions, including:

- Timestamping
- Difference comparisons
- Naming conventions

Timestamping requires us to track the creation time of a document on its original source system. This time is different from the time at which it is created in either the staging area or the document warehouse. Retrieving the creation time or modification time of a document is supported by some crawlers, such as wget, and should be used on a regular basis. Using timestamps, we can determine if a file that already exists in the document warehouse is a newer version. If it is, we may replace the existing version in the warehouse, create a new version and maintain both copies, or ignore the newer version and keep the warehoused version. Since timestamping is so easily implemented and quickly checked, this is the preferred method for version control.

Timestamps of course can be manipulated and, in theory at least, lead to duplicates in the document warehouse. Given the unlikelihood of this actually happening along with the minimal adverse impact of an occasional duplicate, this does not warrant much attention for document warehouse designers. (At least not relative to all of the other tasks at hand). If, however, there is a need to determine if two files are identical, one could use difference comparison programs such as diff to compare them. The extra time required to perform this operation is not generally warranted.

Naming conventions are useful only within an organization, where naming standards can be enforced. For example, project status memos may always have the same name but be placed in a directory named for the project, and the date of the status memo may be appended as a suffix on the file name. In this case, we are actually dealing with distinct documents. Explicit version numbers in

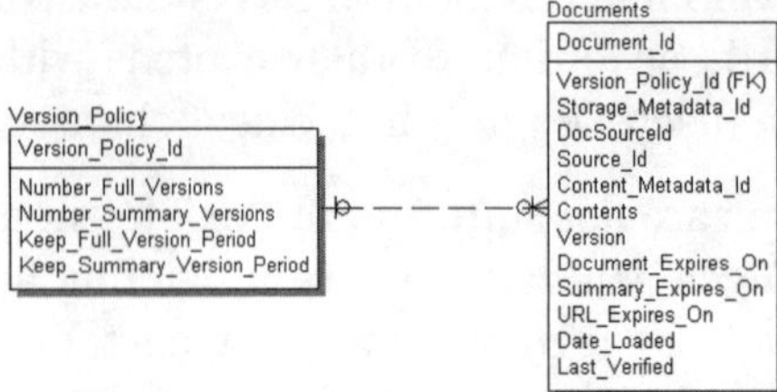

Figure 9.8 Version control policies can apply to multiple documents.

file names can signify the rendition of a particular document but the chances for errors in this method are relatively high. Although the practice of embedding versions into naming conventions is common, it is not recommended for version control.

Once a method for determining versions has been decided on, one must represent the version control policy in metadata. As Figure 9.8 shows, this policy includes the number of versions to keep, the content to keep for each version (that is, full text, summary, or URL or pathname), and the time period for which to keep each version.

Conclusions

Metadata is essential to controlling the complex array of options available in the document warehouse. Content metadata, implemented using Dublin Core semantics, will improve the precision of searches. Adapting the Common Warehouse Metamodel metadata standard to document warehousing provides the foundation for a flexible control architecture that supports many different strategies and policies regarding text analysis as well as access and version control. Without explicit metadata, the procedures for maintaining the document warehouse will be embedded in a series of document loader scripts and essentially inaccessible to the nonprogrammer. The goal of document warehousing is to provide not only access to the business information currently locked in text but to also a full understanding of the life cycle of that information and how it is acquired. Metadata is the key to meeting that objective. In the next chapter we will examine another key objective, maintaining the integrity of the document warehouse.

CHAPTER 10

Ensuring Document Warehouse Integrity

The integrity of the document warehouse—or information system for that matter—does not happen by accident. Ensuring the integrity of the warehouse means that we maintain it in a state consistent with the objectives that sponsors, designers, and users had in mind when it was implemented. These objectives require that we ensure adequate levels of quality control, protect the contents of the warehouse from tampering, and secure privileged information so that it is not used in ways contrary to the information owner's wishes. In this chapter, we will examine the specific techniques available to document warehouse designers and administrators for meeting these objectives, specifically:

- Information stewardship and quality control
- Security options
- Privacy protection

Information stewardship, as described by Larry P. English in *Improving Data Warehouse and Business Information Quality: Methods for Reducing Costs and Increasing Profits* (English 1999), is the willingness to take responsibility for the integrity of an organization's information resources without taking ownership of those same resources. Since there are so many distinct steps in collecting, organizing, and using information in the document warehouse, no single person or position can claim total ownership of a document. Some are responsible for finding and extracting documents, others are charged with ensuring the quality of the text analysis, and still others assess the accuracy and relative value of information to the organization. The following section on information stewardship and quality control will describe the steps needed to maintain the quality of the document warehouse.

Security is required in any information system. Document warehouses depend upon both file system and database security mechanisms. In this chapter, our primary concern will be on controlling two types of access. First, we need to control access to the staging area so that only documents placed there by known document warehouse processes are added to the repository. Second, access to the database that houses the actual documents and associated metadata might need to be controlled in one of several ways. Options for limiting access to sensitive documents will be described along with the benefits and drawbacks of each.

Privacy protection is a common concern in business intelligence. While this issue is less pressing when dealing with applications like competitive intelligence systems, it will come into play when organizations collect textual information about individual customers or clients. Correspondence, detailed responses to surveys, and specialized questionnaires, such as medical history forms, can all contain sensitive information. Furthermore, each individual document or piece of text might not contain protected information but taken together, a collection of documents can indicate further information that the person did not mean to disclose. With sophisticated feature extraction programs, it is possible to distill even long text into short lists of key facts. Simply applying this type of analysis over a set of texts about a single individual can provide enough facts to reliably deduce information not explicitly disclosed. The last key topic of this chapter will address privacy concerns, discuss the means of implementing privacy controls, and finally discuss some of the emerging standards and policies for protecting privacy.

Information Stewardship and Quality Control

The key to information stewardship and quality control is managing the quality at three critical control points:

- Document search and retrieval stage
- Text analysis stage
- Content control stage

At each stage a different type of quality control must occur. During the first stage, our primary concern is with the search and retrieval process. For example, some questions at this stage include: Are we getting the volume of documents expected? and How long do extraction processes run? At the text analysis stage the focus is on ensuring that all analysis processes run successfully and the results meet our quality standards. As we will see, different types of analysis require different amounts of quality control. The final stage, content control, is actually an ongoing process. This responsibility rests with domain experts who can assess the relative value of documents and more importantly, the accuracy of the content. Figure 10.1 shows the three stages in context of the entire document warehouse.

Since each stage requires a different type of quality control, no one person is likely to perform all three types. No single person can claim ownership of a set of documents within the warehouse, and for this reason, the idea of stewardship best reflects the roles assumed by those working on quality control issues.

Document Search and Retrieval

The first point of quality control occurs when documents are collected and staged for later processing. Here, we are not concerned with the content of specific documents and focus instead on the quality of the retrieval process itself.

Although we treat search and retrieval as a single control point, it is best to consider them separately when developing measures to assess the quality of these operations.

Assessing the Quality of Searching

During the search process, we work with a set of search patterns that have been provided in the document warehouse. These patterns may be file-system-based

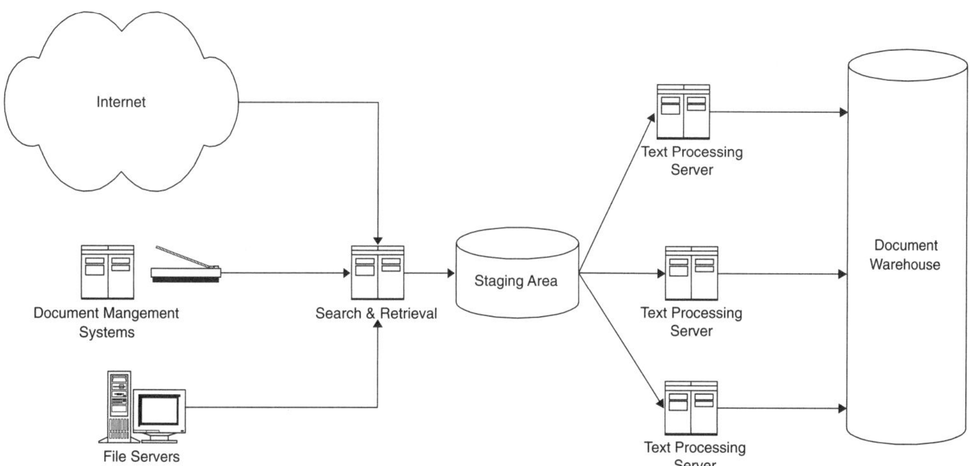

Figure 10.1 Three distinct points provide the key opportunities for quality control.

(for example, /legal/contracts/pending/*.doc indicates all Word documents corresponding to pending contracts that the legal department is creating). Patterns can also be Internet-based. In the case of HTTP searches, a pattern could be a search engine plus a search criteria, such as

```
http://www.altavista.com/cgi-bin/query/q?=%22text mining%22
```

which searches for documents with the phrase *text mining* using the AltaVista search engine. Given these patterns, the properties of the search process we should measure include:

- Time required to execute each search
- The number of documents found in each search
- The effectiveness of the search

The time required to execute each search should be relatively low when using Internet search engines. Total search time should remain a small percentage of the total time spent in search and retrieval. This measure should only become a concern if it rises about a few percentage points of the total search and retrieval process time and would then most likely indicate a network performance issue, not a search engine problem.

A more important measure of search quality is the number of documents found. Depending upon the search and the search engine, the most significant documents may be in the first tens of documents, or the first hundreds for very broad searches. With the relatively low precision of most search engines, the quality of a search degrades quickly after the most significant documents have been listed. This is in part due to the persistent problems of synonymy (different words with the same meaning) and polysemy (one word with multiple meanings).

The number of documents found, combined with an assessment of the value of these documents provides the single most important quality measure, the effectiveness of the search. The effectiveness is a simple measure:

```
Number of Useful Documents / Number of Documents Retrieved
```

This measure is calculated for each search pattern.

The number of useful documents must be provided by end users and analysts involved in the content analysis stage. For simplicity, we are assuming a simple binary relation here, either the document was useful or it was not. A more realistic measure would include several possible values such as:

- Useful
- Moderately useful
- Marginally useful
- Not useful

With multiple values, the effectiveness measure becomes slightly more complicated. First, we calculate the effectiveness for each possible value. For example:

- Effective Useful = Number of Useful Documents / Number of Total Documents Retrieved
- Moderately Useful = Number of Moderately Useful Documents / Number of Total Documents Retrieved
- Marginally Useful = Number of Marginally Useful Documents / Number of Total Documents Retrieved
- Not Useful = Number of Not Useful Documents / Number of Total Documents Retrieved

Now to calculate the effectiveness of the search we weight each value. Intuitively, we are looking for a measure that will increase as the number of useful documents increases but not increase when useless documents are retrieved. In the case of the binary-valued measures, if we found 100 documents and 50 were useful and 50 were not useful, the effectiveness measure should be 50 percent. To realize a similar effect with multiple values, we will need to weight each value. Continuing with the four value criteria just discussed, let us assume the following weights: Useful is 1.0, Moderately Useful is 0.67, Marginally Useful is 0.33, and Not Useful is 0.0. Now if the 100 retrieved documents were rated as 40 Useful, 20 Moderately Useful, 15 Marginally Useful, and 25 Not Useful, we would calculate the effectiveness measure as:

```
Effectiveness = (40 * 1.0) + (20 * 0.67) + (15 * 0.33) + (25 * 0)
```

or, 58.35 percent. The results meet with our intuition for this measure, that is, that it should increase according to the usefulness of the documents in the set.

With these two measures, the time it takes to execute a search and the effectiveness of a search, we can define baseline objectives for search quality and monitor future performance against those baseline measures. If search time increases significantly, or more likely, if effectiveness drops, then document warehouse administrators or users will need to change search patterns to improve effectiveness ratings.

Improving Search Effectiveness

Four factors can decrease search effectiveness:

- Poor precision of a search engine
- Broad search criteria
- Poor-quality content of a site
- Inappropriate time intervals between searches

In the first case, the search engine may suffer from poor precision and return too many hits. A search engine can provide hundreds or thousands of hits to a query, and the more hits that are used to drive the retrieval process, the lower the effectiveness rating will drop. This is virtually inevitable because the documents most likely to be useful will appear early in the hit list. Reducing the number of hits that are used to drive the retrieval process will increase effectiveness. Also, some search engines will do better than others, at least for some topics. If agribusiness news is of primary interest, use a specialty engine such as www.joefarmer.com instead of a general-purpose search engine.

We have all seen the product of using a broad search criterion—thousands of hits are returned. These tend to be good hits in the sense that they reflect what was sought. Improving search criteria can be as simple as adding more keywords, using Boolean expressions and other operators to improve precision, or using specialty features of some search engines, such as limiting a search to a particular set of Web sites.

The poor-quality content of a site is beyond the control of a document warehouse. In this case, there is no choice but to find another source or refine the search pattern to focus only on topics within a Web site that are highly effective. For example, searching a financial news source for articles on new drug treatments for diabetes may prove useful for investment analysis but useless for scientific interests. Sites should be targeted for searching on the basis of their overall quality, but when searching, we must remember to distinguish a particular site's area of expertise from its ancillary interests.

Another possible cause of poor usefulness is poor timing of searches. The value of information is time-dependent so searching for information at a weekly or monthly interval when it should be retrieved at a daily interval will reduce effectiveness. For example, general reports on stock market activity weeks after they occur are of little use to most of us. In this case, changing the frequency of searches may improve effectiveness, although that change may need to be combined with changes to search patterns to make significant improvements.

Retrieval Process Integrity

The second piece of document search and retrieval quality control focuses on the retrieval process. At this point, our primary concern is not with what was retrieved but how well it was retrieved. The key processes to measure are:

- Server timeouts
- Incomplete downloads
- Time to retrieve

- Number of documents retrieved
- Size of documents retrieved

Problems with these factors can be caused at several points as shown in Figure 10.2.

Retrieval Measures

Server timeouts occur when a request is sent to a Web server, and it cannot respond within a predefined period of time. Timeouts are an indication of an overtaxed server. Two options for dealing with the problem are to increase the length of time the crawler waits for a response from a server or to try to retrieve from the server at another time. Obviously avoiding peak traffic periods is the ideal but that might not always be realistic. For example, if a decision support system requires frequent updates—for example, on an hourly basis—then the window of opportunity for retrieving information is limited to less than one hour. If timeouts occur too frequently with a single source and changes in time-out periods and retrieval times do not improve the situation, then alternate sites might have to be found.

Like server timeouts, incomplete downloads can be caused by problems on the source system or with the network. Again, we cannot solve the problem within the confines of the document warehouse, we can at best adjust retrieval parameters to increase the number of attempts at finishing a download before failing.

The number of documents retrieved is not an important measure by itself, but when combined with others can provide essential information. Using the number of documents retrieved along with the number of total attempts made to download documents provides a measure of how effective the basic retrieval process actually is. The size of documents retrieved along with the number of documents can provide an average document size by site. We can specify ideal target numbers for these measures. Knowing effective retrieval rates and average document size can however provide a baseline for monitoring future performance.

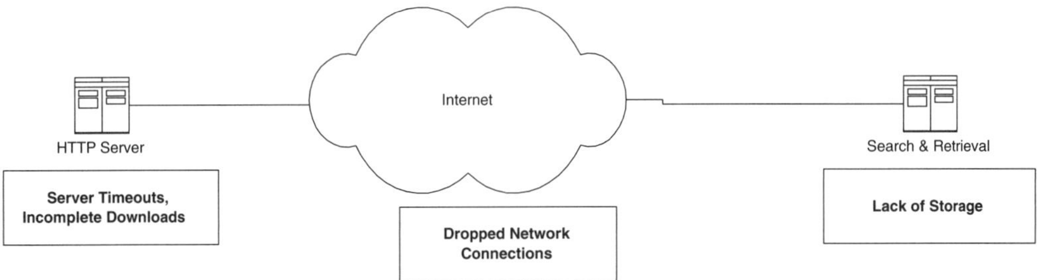

Figure 10.2 Retrieval problems can have several causes.

Retrieval Validation

A crawler that is allowed to span sites can quickly move from intended domains, so reviews of crawler logs is an important step in quality control for two reasons. First, crawlers that wander too far will retrieve too many irrelevant documents and lower effectiveness measures. Second, these irrelevant documents will take up bandwidth, storage space, and text analysis resources. By reviewing crawler logs, such as the one shown in Figure 10.3, we can ascertain important information about where the crawler has been and how much time was spent at particular sites.

```
—10:26:07—  http://www.crtinc.com:80/
            => `www.crtinc.com/index.html'
Connecting to www.crtinc.com:80... connected!
HTTP request sent, awaiting response... 200 OK
Length: unspecified [text/html]

    OK -> .......... .

10:26:07 (11.45 MB/s) - `www.crtinc.com/index.html' saved [12007]

Loading robots.txt; please ignore errors.
—10:26:07—  http://www.crtinc.com:80/robots.txt
            => `www.crtinc.com/robots.txt'
Connecting to www.crtinc.com:80... connected!
HTTP request sent, awaiting response... 404 Not Found
10:26:07 ERROR 404: Not Found.

—10:26:07—  http://www.crtinc.com:80/images/fp_background.gif
            => `www.crtinc.com/images/fp_background.gif'
Connecting to www.crtinc.com:80... connected!
HTTP request sent, awaiting response... 200 OK
Length: 19,655 [image/gif]

    OK -> ......... .........                                  [100%]

10:26:07 (18.74 MB/s) - `www.crtinc.com/images/fp_background.gif' saved
[19655/19655]

—10:26:07—  http://www.crtinc.com:80/images/spacer.gif
            => `www.crtinc.com/images/spacer.gif'
Connecting to www.crtinc.com:80... connected!
HTTP request sent, awaiting response... 200 OK
Length: 73 [image/gif]

    OK ->                                                      [100%]

10:26:07 (71.29 KB/s) - `www.crtinc.com/images/spacer.gif' saved [73/73]

—10:26:07—  http://www.crtinc.com:80/images/fp_collage.jpg
            => `www.crtinc.com/images/fp_collage.jpg'
Connecting to www.crtinc.com:80... connected!
```

```
HTTP request sent, awaiting response... 200 OK
Length: 8,514 [image/jpeg]

    OK -> ........                                          [100%]

10:26:07 (8.12 MB/s) - `www.crtinc.com/images/fp_collage.jpg' saved
[8514/8514]

—10:26:07—  http://www.crtinc.com:80/images/fp_who_how.gif
           => `www.crtinc.com/images/fp_who_how.gif'
Connecting to www.crtinc.com:80... connected!
HTTP request sent, awaiting response... 200 OK
Length: 973 [image/gif]

    OK ->                                                   [100%]

10:26:07 (950.20 KB/s) - `www.crtinc.com/images/fp_who_how.gif' saved
[973/973]

—10:26:07—  http://www.crtinc.com:80/how_to_find_us/index.html
           => `www.crtinc.com/how_to_find_us/index.html'
Connecting to www.crtinc.com:80... connected!
HTTP request sent, awaiting response... 200 OK
Length: unspecified [text/html]

    OK -> .......... .
```

Figure 10.3 A sample wget log shows the details provided by crawlers.

Tracking the quality of document search and retrieval requires that we monitor several points within the extraction and staging processes. Using feedback from users and domain experts on the usefulness of documents, we can determine the effectiveness of our search. While a site that provides many useful documents is ideal, if it provides too many useless documents, the overall quality of the document warehouse will suffer. As problems appear with regard to effectiveness, search patterns that drive the search and retrieval process may need to be modified. Also, the search process itself must be monitored to ensure that computer and network resources are used efficiently. Crawler behavior needs to be monitored to ensure that they do not go off on tangents, collecting documents of little interest to warehouse users.

There are no absolute measures for the quality of search and retrieval but baselines will serve the same purpose. When a document warehouse is completely configured and operating according to design, then baseline measures should be taken of key measures such as document retrieval effectiveness and average number of documents downloaded per time interval. Using these baseline measures, warehouse administrators will be able to track trends in the warehouse operations that may require attention and adjustment.

Text Analysis

Text analysis is the process of extracting information and transforming text to make its information content more accessible to end users or other text analysis programs.

At this stage of quality control, there are three main factors that should be measured.

- The number of transformations that executed
- The quality of the transformation
- The amount and types of editing required

The first issue, the number of transformations that executed, is tracked using transformation execution records saved in the database. The quality of transformations is determined by user assessment. Not all types of text analysis need the same level of quality checking. When the automated text analysis processes do not perform adequately, as is often the case in machine translation, the results must be edited to preserve the quality of the results or the text analysis processes.

Tracking Transformation Execution

The key to tracking the successful execution of transformations is to compare what *should have executed* with *what did execute*. As Figure 10.4 shows the Transformation Execution entity records the results of execution of a particular transformation. The Scheduled Event entity defines when the execution should occur. The Scheduled Event entity supports three different types of time specifications, Point in Time, Custom Calendar, and Interval. The first provides the means to specify a frequency and a recurring period, such as a day of the week or every other month. The Custom Calendar provides a list of days when the transformation is executed, while the interval defines the period of time between executions.

The Transformation activity defines a transformation on a document target. For example, all files downloaded from the U.S. Department of Agriculture dealing with grain production projections might be placed into a single document target. The transformations defined for this document target might include file conversion, summarization, and thematic indexing. When the execution of this transformation activity is complete, the success indicators are updated. Tracking transformation execution then becomes a matter of comparing the Scheduled Event with the Transformation Executions. (An outer join between the Scheduled Event table and the Transformation Execution table will ensure that all scheduled events appear in a report, even if the corresponding execution record is not found).

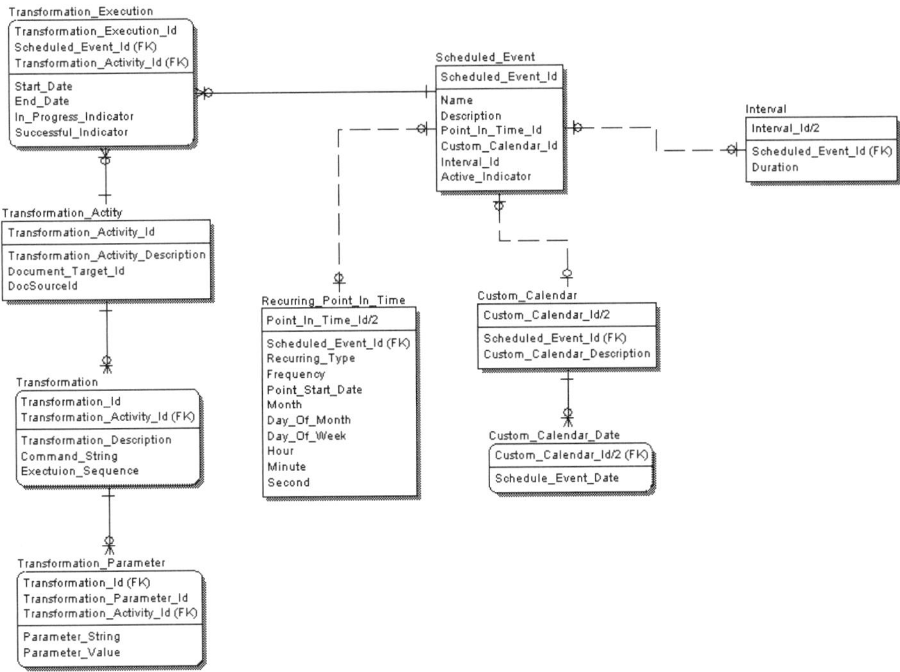

Figure 10.4 Transformation execution is tracked according to scheduled events and transformation activity executions.

Quality of Transformations

Knowing that a transformation executed is not enough of a quality check when dealing with text. In the data warehousing realm, if a correctly programmed or configured transformation runs then we can be fairly confident that the results are accurate. When dealing with numeric data, our transformations are algorithmic, that is they execute a sequence of steps that result in a specific output. For example, we often aggregate a set of numbers or extract a substring from a character array or the lookup of a key value from a dimension table. Text analysis transformations are different. The operations applied frequently rely on heuristics—or rules of thumb—that often perform well but may not in some cases. Take summarization, for example: Some techniques look for key phrases such as *In conclusion* to identify important sentences. This usually works well, but it could also result in using a sentence such as *In conclusion we can note three things*. This is a low information value sentence, while, presumably, the following sentences in the original text actually carry important content. To ensure that our heuristic-based transformations perform well enough to meet the needs of the document warehouse, we will need to monitor the quality of the text analysis transformations.

Sampling Levels

Not all transformations need the same level of monitoring. We can roughly divide transformations into three areas, depending on the reliability of the heuristics behind the transformations. The three groups are:

- Light sampling
- Moderate sampling
- Significant reviewing

Light sampling is limited to text analysis operations that work very well in general or are too complex to warrant the time and resources required to review them. We would include summarization in the first category. In general summarization works well when at least 20 percent of the original text is extracted as the summary. Using a summarizing tool from any of the major text analysis tool suites (for example, IBM Intelligent Miner for Text, Oracle interMedia Text, Megaputer's TextAnalyst, among others), the 20 percent extraction rate will produce high-quality results. More quality review is required if the extraction factor is changed. Some tools allow users to specify a fixed number of sentences to be extracted. This can result in poor summaries for long texts if the number of sentences is too low. Also, if we drop below a 10 percent extraction rate, we risk losing significant information in moderate to long texts, although most major tools will still extract the major topics.

The second category of transformations that require only limited review are those that depend upon complex operations, such as clustering. All clustering algorithms create a representation for a document, such as a weighted feature vector, and then calculate the similarity of documents based upon some type of distance measure between the feature vectors (or other representation scheme). Once the differences are calculated, a document is placed in a cluster that minimizes the difference in similarity measures between documents in a cluster and maximizes the difference between documents in different clusters. Clearly, we do not need to recalculate the similarity measures (nor would we want to). The purpose of reviewing clustering is to assess the overall quality of the results. If the clusters do not meet our intuitive expectations of how the documents should be grouped together, then other clustering algorithms could be tried. (See Chapter 13 for a discussion of various clustering algorithms.)

In general, during the early stages of document warehouse implementation, operations such as summarization and clustering will need reviewing to ensure that parameters (for example, extraction rate in summarization) are set appropriately and that the best algorithms are used (for example, binary or hierarchical clustering) for the particular needs of the warehouse. After that stage, these transformations should require only occasional review.

Some text analysis operations require a more involved review process. Feature extraction tools provide the means to precisely extract names, relations, and terms from text but these tools are especially dependent upon linguistic heuristics and customized dictionaries. The output of these tools should be monitored with particular interest in:

- Names of persons
- Multiword business terms
- Geographic locations

Since feature extraction programs use rules of thumb such as:

```
The phrase 'CEO of' is preceded by the name of the CEO and followed by
the name of the company
```

There is the possibility that a person's name is not parsed correctly or that the name of the company may be missing a word or include too many words. If there are problems with feature extraction transformations, first identify what types of features are causing problems (for example, relations, names, or terms). If possible create or modify custom dictionaries, sometimes called authority dictionaries, that cover domain-specific words.

Similarly, thematic indexing may not be as precise as desired. Thematic indexing depends upon taxonomies and thesauri for its basic information, so problems in thematic indexing can be addressed by adding custom thesauri or modifying a taxonomy. If too many documents are indexed under the same theme, such as *financial news*, then more refined terms need to be added to the taxonomy. Another problem occurs if some themes are not captured. For example, we would expect an article about the International Monetary Fund to be classified under *international organizations*, *monetary policy*, and several others. If it is not, then synonyms should be added to the thesaurus to ensure that domain-specific terms are adequately covered.

Any machine translation will require heavy review. As discussed in Chapter 10, machine translation systems commonly use word substitution and basic phrase rewrite rules to perform mappings from one language to another. Frequently, technical or domain-specific terms will not be defined in the translation dictionary. At other times, the rewrite rules, which are just heuristics, do not produce grammatically correct translations. This is not too much of a problem since readers can still get a rough idea of the contents of a document.

Creating Samples

A full discussion on creating adequate sample sizes for statistically significant quality control is beyond the scope of this book, and the reader is referred to Chapter 6 in Larry English's *Improving Data Warehouse and Business Information*

Quality (English 1999) for an introduction to the process. When sampling for document warehouse quality reviews there are a few factors to keep in mind.

First, the documents and transformation outputs are not uniform. Many statistical sampling techniques assume that you are working with a homogeneous data set, such as customer records or sales transactions. In document warehousing, not all documents are the same, and we may be willing to tolerate more errors in some types of documents than in others. Samples should be based upon domain-specific groupings, such as financial analysis documents, scientific reports, or internal memos.

Second, many traditional quality control techniques assume that one can measure the number of errors in a record. For example, if single record had a last name misspelled, a primary address out of date, and a phone number with an invalid area code, then the record would have three errors. It is more difficult to definitively say how many errors a summary has or whether or not a document that is classified correctly but not in the most precise category should count as an error.

Finally, a sample size of thirty is generally considered the smallest set that can provide meaningful results but larger sizes are necessary if there is greater variation in quality in the entire set of documents.

Correcting and Editing Process

The correcting and editing process may be a significant part of a document warehouse process or not exist at all. This step is the last stage in transformation quality control before documents are loaded into the warehouse.

In general, the manually intensive nature of this type of operation will be limited to correcting machine translations. Even here, as long as a rough translation provides enough information for document warehouse users, the need for extensive retranslation is limited. If human translation is required, machine-aided translation (MAT) applications can improve the efficiency of the operation. Remember, even if a human being is creating a translation, we do not need a perfectly grammatical revision, just one that meets the quality needs of the reader.

Text analysis operations transform documents from closed objects to feature-rich entries in the document warehouse. Summarization, thematic indexing, clustering, and machine translation all extract or reexpress valuable information in ways that are more easily accessed and manipulated by document warehouse users. The quality control operations described previously will help to ensure that these transformations meet their objectives. Regardless of the quality of translations and thematic indexing, if the document does not have anything of value to say, then we have not added benefit.

Content Validation

The final type of quality control is content validation. At this point in the process, we can assume that the other two stages of quality control that occur during document search and retrieval and text analysis, reliably provide the documents we have targeted for inclusion in the warehouse. We can also assume that the main transformations, such as summarization, thematic indexing, and translation have been performed adequately.

Now, the question is: So what do we have to show for that work? The essential issues to address at this point are:

- Are the contents of the documents true?
- Are the documents timely?
- Are the document contents useful?

The first and foremost question about a document is: Are the contents true? This is not as much of a problem when dealing with internal documents as when dealing with external documents, but some issues still occur. First, documents frequently go through multiple drafts before a finalized version is made. The question of content veracity then becomes more of an issue of understanding the differences between a work in progress and final copy. Documents from the Web should be assessed according to their source. Some sources, such as federal government publications and well-known news sources (for example, the *Wall Street Journal*, *Financial Times*, and *Washington Post*) have strong incentives to maintain the veracity of their publications. Documents from these types of sources not only do not need verification, they may in fact serve as the basis for verifying other sources. Other sources, such as trade publications, commercial Web sites, and industry studies can offer a wealth of information that requires only moderate reviewing. (See Chapter 16 for a list of some of these sources.) Helen Burwell's *Online Competitive Intelligence* (Burwell 1999) is an excellent source of reliable sites for gathering information on commercial operations. In general, when crawlers return documents from unknown sources, a domain analyst should review the contents.

Timeliness is another factor and is, fortunately, easier to address. If documents provide reliable information but it is not loaded into the document warehouse in time, then adjusting the frequency of loads and the priority with which the source site is searched should alleviate any problems in timeliness.

Finally, we need to ask if the contents are useful. The information drawn from documents may be true and timely but do they provide decision makers with the raw material to do their jobs? Of course, some documents may be added because they might prove useful in the future, such as background material on a nation's economy, culture, and political system, assuming that the nation is a potential site for future business or factory location. There is, however, no need to clutter the warehouse with material of no value to the organization.

Content quality control is much more subjective than either document search and retrieval or text analysis quality control. Elaborate quality measures can be developed for content quality control but that is not necessary. As long as the veracity and timeliness meet minimum requirements, and the document warehouse is able to target the types of topics of interest to users, then we can assume that we have sufficient quality controls. User needs change constantly, and our goal is not to make a perfect document warehouse, just a useful one. Trying to act as gatekeepers with high thresholds for entry in a dynamic business environment will be costly. If the document warehouse provides access to the information users need, if it takes less time to get that information than it did when the documents were scattered across platforms and sources, and if the users can trust what they find, then the objectives of document warehousing have been met.

Security

The second pillar of document warehouse integrity is security. The goals of document warehouse security are to ensure that documents loaded into the warehouse are not tampered with, either in the warehouse or in the staging area prior to text analysis. Security also controls access to sensitive documents. Some users will want the benefits of an integrated repository without allowing others to see their work. Lawyers, human resources professionals, and financial analysts often work with confidential information that can only be distributed among a limited group of individuals. This section will address these needs by examining the use of:

- File system security mechanisms
- Database roles and privileges
- Programmatic access control
- Virtual database security

We will discuss file system security only briefly before focusing on protecting the staging area, namely database roles and privileges. We will discuss them and the data modeling implications of their use to control document access in the warehouse. Programmatic access controls give warehouse administrators more flexibility than roles and privileges but have their own drawbacks, which will be discussed. Finally, a new security technique, the virtual database, has been introduced by Oracle. Although other RDBMS do not support this, it is such a powerful feature that Oracle users should at least be aware of how to use in the document warehouse.

File System Security

For document warehousing, file system security is especially important in the staging area. It is here that documents first enter the warehouse. Staging areas should be structured so that documents requiring different types of text analysis or security protection are in separate directories. Writing files to the staging area should be limited to search and retrieval processes and to users authorized to manually submit documents to the warehouse. Reading files in the staging area should be limited to text analysis processes and other operations associated with the document warehouse.

Database Roles and Privileges

Roles and privileges are commonly used to limit access to tables and views. These methods work well in models that have separate tables for distinct entities. For example, a financial system might have customer, address, invoice header, invoice line, and product tables. In this case, it is easy to grant access to the customer and address tables to employees who might need to add, delete, or update customer information, such as salespersons or telemarketers. These same employees, however, have no need to change invoices, which are presumably generated on the basis of orders placed and items shipped. So, at the table level, it is a simple matter to control who has the ability to read or change information in the database.

Programmatic Access Control

Generic data models are not quite so simple. For example, if we use a basic model for documents, as shown in Figure 10.5, then we will not have the luxury of a single table for each type of document.

In a model such as this, we have a simple document structure in which a document is composed of one or more subdocuments. The one-to-many relation to itself on the document realizes the hierarchical structure of documents. That is that documents have subsections that in turn can have subsections, and so on. This type of hierarchy is especially important when dealing with semistructured texts, such as XML or SGML documents, in which case the structuring entities in the document correspond to a single row in the document table.

All documents—whether they are news stories, project plans, marketing proposals, or labor negotiation position papers—can be stored within the document table. Using standard database roles and privileges that operate at the

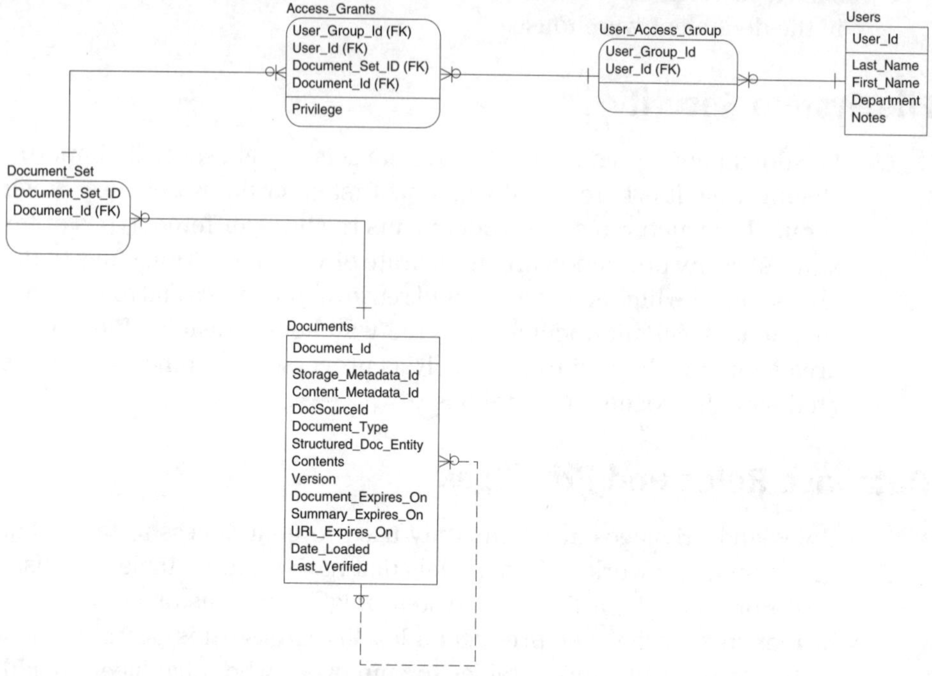

Figure 10.5 A generic data model maximizes flexibility but increases the complexity of security management.

table level will not provide sufficiently fine-grained access control in this scenario. The usual solution in these cases is to deny access to the table to all users and grant access only to stored procedures that execute particular functions on behalf of users. The stored procedures are designed to provide fine-grained access by taking into account the user executing the procedure. For example, a lookup on documents can be limited by first determining what user groups a user belongs to, then finding the access privileges granted to that group for particular sets of documents. At that point, only documents in sets that the user is allowed to access are returned.

The most significant drawback of this approach is that the joins are costly. However, if we do not partition the documents at storage time, by using separate tables, we have to partition them at query time, and this results in a more elaborate query that depends upon separate tables for security information.

Virtual Database Security

Virtual databases are a security construct introduced in Oracle 8*i*. Normally, database-specific features are outside of the scope of this book, but a brief discussion is provided here for two reasons: First, it is a flexible alternative to programmatic access control. Second, Oracle 8*i* is used in many data warehouses, and the native text management features provided by Oracle interMedia Text make it a likely database platform for those interested in document warehousing.

Virtual databases limit a user's view of data in a table according to a security policy defined by an applications administrator. A security policy includes a function that produces a selection criteria (essentially a WHERE clause predicate) that is implicitly added to all queries on a table. For example, if a user is allowed to view any documents except contract and negotiation texts, then a policy would be defined to return a statement such as

```
NOT (DOCUMENT_TYPE = 'CONTRACT')AND
NOT (DOCUMENT_TYPE = 'NEGOTIATION')
```

With that policy in place a query such as

```
SELECT
     Contents
FROM
     Documents;
```

is actually executed as

```
SELECT
     Contents
FROM
     Documents
WHERE
NOT (DOCUMENT_TYPE = 'CONTRACT')
 AND
NOT (DOCUMENT_TYPE = 'NEGOTIATION');
```

In addition to these data-driven controls, virtual databases implement context-driven controls that use application-specific attributes defined by application developers and administrators. These attributes are created and set only through the use of trusted packages. The right to execute these trusted packages in turn is restricted to security administrators.

Implementing security in a document warehouse is a multilayered task. Access to staging areas must be controlled along with access to the document repository within the warehouse. No single security mechanism—such as operating system controls or database management system privileges—can do it all. When generic models are used for document storage, the additional burden is placed on developers to limit access to sensitive documents without impeding the general use of the document warehouse.

Privacy

Privacy has been a subject of public debate in the United States at least since the Supreme Court formally promulgated the right in the 1965 ruling of *Griswald v. Connecticut* (381 U.S. 479, 85 S.Ct. 1678, 14 L.Ed.2d 510 [1965]). The advent of e-business and the ability to collect large quantities of detailed behavioral data on individuals has pushed the privacy debate to the forefront of public discourse again. For many document warehouse applications, privacy may not be an issue. Organizations that track their own internal documents and publicly distributed documents from the Internet will not need to concern themselves with this issue. However, when personnel, medical, legal, and other sensitive information about individuals is stored in the warehouse, privacy becomes an issue.

For the rest of this section, we will assume that we are dealing with sensitive documents and not public information like the lead story in this morning's *New York Times*.

Contracts between Document Owners and the Warehouse

When confidential information is added to a document warehouse, there is an implicit (if not explicit) contract between the document owner and the warehouse administrators. The document owner, such as an attorney or personnel officer, is charged with protecting the contents of the texts yet must allow documents to be added to the warehouse because of the business value provided by the warehouse. We, as the document warehouse designers, cannot assume that we control the content of the warehouse, nor can we dictate how the contents are used. In order to protect the document owners and the organization in general, document warehouse administrators must work within some privacy boundaries, such as:

- Document owners define policies for controlling access to documents.
- Document owners are stewards for information contained in documents and are thus responsible to protect the interest of third parties.
- The document warehouse is a repository for integrating information, but not all information is equally accessible.
- Warehouse administrators should minimize the opportunities to abuse confidential information.

If the need for privacy protection is not apparent, here is another point to consider.

Is Privacy the Third Rail of Business Intelligence? Protecting Individuals and Organizations

Privacy protections are not just an optional feature of a document warehouse but an essential requirement. Individuals want privacy, and businesses that have ignored privacy concerns have often ended up changing privacy policies after public rebuke.

The Pew Internet and American Life Project surveyed Americans to assess their opinions regarding online privacy. Document warehousing is of course not the same as using the Web to buy a car or find medical information, but the survey results are just as informative about how individual expect businesses and governments to treat their private information. Here are some of the most telling facts published in *Trust and Privacy On-Line: Why Americans Want to Rewrite the Rules* (Rainie, et al. 2000).

- 86 percent of Internet users favor privacy policies that require companies to ask for permission to use their personal information.
- 54 percent find Web site tracking of user actions is a harmful invasion of privacy even if it is used to provide better matching to a user's interest.
- 94 percent of Internet users want privacy violators punished.
- More users are concerned about business and strangers getting personal information (84 percent) than about credit card theft (68 percent), downloading a virus (54 percent), or finding false or inaccurate news reports (49 percent).

Anecdotal evidence also indicates that the public's heightened concern about privacy is working its way into business and legal practices.

- When online retailer Toysmart.com proposed selling its customer data as part of a bankruptcy plan, in violation of their privacy policy stated to customers, the Federal Trade Commission stopped the proposed transaction.
- The Office of Management and Budget had to issue a ban on the use of cookies on federal Web sites after the National Drug Control Policy office was discovered to have used cookies to track users' drug-related information requests.
- The Internet marketing firm DoubleClick faced a barrage of lawsuits following an announcement of its linking a database of 50 million Internet users' habit profiles to names and addresses *after* it specifically stated that the information would be kept anonymous.

As much as some might want it to go away, privacy is as much a fabric of business intelligence as data integrity and security. In the long-term interests of our organizations, clients, and customers, document warehouse designers and developers would do well to recognize the need to accommodate privacy as an actual system requirement from the start and not just an add-on later on.

Conclusions

Maintaining the integrity of the document warehouse serves both the organization and its customers. Quality control ensures that the document warehouse meets users' expectations and needs. Security will prevent tampering and misuse, while privacy protections will ensure that customers and other interested parties are not inadvertently harmed by our business intelligence practices. And just in case we still think we can collect personnel information in return for providing better service—forget it, over half of the Internet users in the Pew Internet and American Life Project survey did not buy it.

When it comes to quality, security, and privacy, balance is the operative word. We cannot have perfect data or totally secure systems or excessive privacy controls and still function in a business intelligence environment. There are no hard and fast rules in this arena, only general principles, such as respect your clients' and customers' concerns and try to accommodate them when designing your warehouse.

We will next turn our attention to choosing tools for building the document warehouse.

CHAPTER 11

Choosing Tools for Building the Document Warehouse

Building a document warehouse requires a set of tools not often found in data warehousing environments. These range from search and retrieval tools, such as crawlers, to text analysis and metadata tools for extracting information from text. Of course relational databases will play a central role as well, but those applications will not be covered here since RDBMSs are not new to most readers, but for those interested in an in-depth discussion of relational databases, I recommend C. J. Date's *An Introduction to Database Systems* (1999). This chapter will consider three general types of tools:

- Text analysis tools
- Supplemental tools
- Search and retrieval tools

By far, the most important of these is text analysis tools, since they perform the core operations of document warehousing. There are also several different approaches to this problem, and we will examine three in detail. In general, text analysis tools will focus on text mining, but also include preprocessing tools that are required in a production environment. Supplemental tools include end user support tools, such as visualization applications that improve the ease of use of the document warehouse. Finally, search and retrieval tools will be discussed. Text analysis programs will make up the bulk of this section, but we will also take a brief tour of portable open source programming languages such as Perl and Python. The extensive file management and related tasks that are required in document warehousing makes these tools essential.

This chapter will be of most use to designers and developers who are responsible for choosing and integrating tools. Each of the three main topics is treated independently, so sections that may not apply to you—such as visualization tools—can be safely skipped.

In each section, we will delve into details of particular programs or the algorithms behind the programs to demonstrate differences in architectural design and their implications for the document warehouse. The purpose of this chapter is not to provide a tutorial on any of these tools; rather, it is to highlight differences between representative tool suites and discuss the implications of the differences for the document warehouse. By the end of the chapter, readers should be familiar with different approaches to tackling common text analysis tasks and the benefits and limitations of each approach.

Choosing Text Analysis Tools

Text analysis tools can be roughly divided into two groups: text preprocessing tools and text mining tools. In the former group, we have character set conversion, reformatting, and translation tools. The text mining tool collection includes the other text analysis applications we have discussed: summarization, feature extraction, clustering, classification, question answering, thematic indexing, and keyword searching. We will also include tools that support the creation of taxonomies and thesauri in this group. In some cases, many of these tools are bundled together, as with IBM Intelligent Miner for Text and Oracle interMedia Text. Rather than try to separate out particular features, such as thematic indexing in Oracle Text, and compare it to a comparable feature in another tool set, we will examine tool suites as vendors offer them. This makes the examination more realistic and avoids the problem of having to tease out application features that are sometimes interdependent.

This section will include an examination of three text analysis tools:

- IBM Intelligent Miner for Text
- Oracle interMedia Text
- Megaputer TextAnalyst

These applications were chosen because they use three different architectures. The IBM tools are independent programs that can be easily controlled and executed from command shells or scripts. The Oracle interMedia Text tool set is integrated into the relational database, providing several advantages, particularly for querying. Next, Megaputer's tool provides programmable COM objects that can be embedded within custom applications to provide text mining services. TextAnalyst also provides an end-user interface for navigating a semantic network developed during processing. Each of these tools approaches the problem of text analysis from a different perspective. IBM Intelligent Miner for Text provides the greatest breadth of tools with an emphasis on information retrieval (IR) techniques. Oracle interMedia Text approaches the problem from the perspective of augmenting traditional relational databases with storage and search capabilities for text. Finally, Megaputer has developed a text analysis tool that can easily be embedded into other applications allowing developers to provide text analysis features outside of a traditional IR or database platform. Each tool will be described from an architectural perspective with a discussion of specific features that highlight the strengths or each tool. Following that, we will then compare the three and provide a discussion of the disadvantages of the various approaches and offer some guidelines for choosing among the three.

The Purpose of This Chapter

The following discussion of tools is not a tutorial on any of these systems. The purpose of this chapter is to discuss different approaches vendors have taken to addressing the needs of text analysis systems. Knowledge-based systems, neural networks, and statistically oriented techniques have been used in many different domains and text analysis is just one of them. By the end of this section, readers should have an understanding of the benefits and limits of each approach. A secondary goal is to introduce some of these tools, since they may be unfamiliar to many readers. Upon completing this section, you should also have a sense of what it is like to actually use these tools. Of course features will change and new tools will be introduced but the basic architectural approaches described here will continue to be used as they have been used for at least the last two decades. Please go to the companion Web for this book (www.wiley.com/compbooks/sullivan) for links to a broader array of vendors and related resources.

Although these three tools can meet many text analysis needs, other specialized tools may be of use in some document warehouse environments. We will briefly discuss three:

- AltaVista Discovery
- Inxight's Hyperbolic Tree
- Teragram's language analysis tool set

AltaVista Discovery is a personal text management and search tool. Inxight's Hyperbolic Tree provides visualization capabilities useful for navigating complex document collections. Finally, Teragram's language analysis tool set provides low-level linguistic functionality that may be required in some text analysis applications. While many document warehouses will function well without this type of specialized tool, each one of these offers a solution to particular text management problems that can crop up both within and outside of a document warehouse.

Statistical/Heuristic Approach

The IBM Intelligent Miner for Text suite uses a statistical and heuristic approach to text analysis. The suite includes several programs that can be run independently of each other from a command line or a shell script. The suites comprise five groups of programs:

- Language identification tool
- Feature extraction tool
- Summarizer
- Topic categorization tool
- Clustering tools

Some of these groups consist of a single program, such as the summarizer, and others consist of multiple programs, such as the language identification tool and the clustering tools. The following sections will describe each tool group and demonstrate common operations.

Language Identification

With the exception of the language identification program, all other programs in the IBM Intelligent Miner for Text suite work with English language documents only. When we are dealing with multilingual texts, language identification is a logical first step.

Language identification works by analyzing patterns in a text. Common word patterns, including prefixes and suffixes such as *anti-*, *post-*, *-ism*, and *-ing*, can indicate that a document is written in English. Applications that use statistical pattern matching such as this must be trained using sample documents that have been correctly labeled with the source language. Text Miner is configured with patterns for the most common languages but can be trained for use with others. As with many statistical and heuristic applications, language identification is not absolute. The IBM tool weights language identification on a scale of 0 to 1, where 1 indicates certain identification.

Even in cases where a human could readily identify the language of a text, automated tools are less certain. For example, the first few pages of this chapter were identified as English with a weight of 0.685. The other possible languages, listed in Table 11.1, are far less likely candidates.

When training a statistical tool, such as the language identification program, be sure to provide enough examples to allow the program to discover patterns that can distinguish the target language from other languages already identified by the tool. Also, be sure to train and test the tool with different sets of documents. Testing with the same set of documents that is used to train a statistical identification program can skew the results and lead you to believe the program will perform better in a production environment than it actually will.

Feature Extraction Tool

The feature extraction tool included in the IBM tool suite actually extracts several different types of features including:

- Terms
- Names
- Relations
- Multiword terms
- Date and time expressions

To find these features, the tool uses a combination of language-specific heuristics and lookup techniques to find significant terms. Language-specific heuristics, or rules of thumbs, are patterns that often occur in texts. For example the pattern:

<Proper Name> <Title> <Organization Name>

will match *Joe Smith director of sales and marketing Text Management, Inc.* since *Joe Smith* is identified as a proper name, and a noun phrase followed by *Inc.* is most likely the name of a company. The noun phrase between these two is tagged as the person's title within the company.

Table 11.1 Language Identification Based upon Statistical Analysis Uses Weighted Measures

LANGUAGE IDENTIFICATION	WEIGHT
French	0.393
Catalan	0.374
Dutch	0.344
Danish	0.331
Portuguese	0.328

Not all names or terms are obvious, and heuristics, unlike algorithmic approaches, are not guaranteed to generate correct answers all of the time. Lookup references, in the form of authority dictionaries and residue dictionaries, are used to improve overall performance. Authority dictionaries contain terms in both the canonical form and its variants, and appropriate feature types. Authority dictionaries are used for preprocessing lookups to map terms that may be incorrectly classified (see Figure 11.1). For example the term Alpha Beta Gamma in the following sentence is incorrectly identified as a person by statistical and heuristic processing.

Alpha Beta Gamma, the fraternity on Main Street, was closed by the administration.

(Actually, the feature extraction tool labeled the term as "PERSON?" indicating that the identification might be incorrect.)

If an authority dictionary had an entry indicating that Alpha Beta Gamma is an organization, then the feature would be correctly classified before the tool's heuristic and statistical techniques were applied. In this way, phrases that might later trip up the core feature extraction program are eliminated from analysis.

A similar problem can arise when terms are not analyzed correctly after the core feature extraction processing has been completed. Residue dictionaries are used in such cases to identify complex features that have not been categorized by the heuristic methods.

Let's now turn to a simple example to understand the type of information provided by this program. Assume we need to extract features from the following story:

> Alpha Text Management, Inc., announced today its intention to acquire Beta Morphological Industries for an undisclosed sum. Beta Morphological is known for its state of the art morphology and text preprocessing applications embedded in several leading Web content analysis tools. Alpha Text Management, founded in 1998 by computational linguists with venture capital backing, has moved aggressively in the field of automated competitive and market intelligence. The acquisition of Beta Morphological Industries is Alpha's third such acquisition this year. Officials from neither company could be reached for comment on this story.

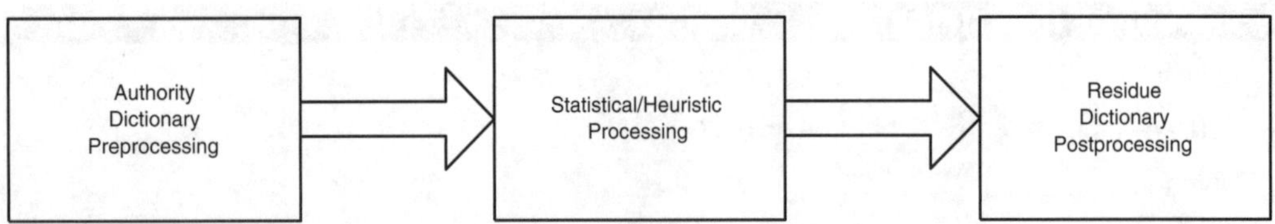

Figure 11.1 Authority dictionaries are used to preprocess text, while residue dictionaries handle features not identified after normal text analysis.

When directed to extract only names, the tool provides the following output:

```
NC     3     Alpha Text Management     ORG
NC     3     Beta Morphological Industries     ORG
NC     1     Web     OTHER
```

Each line consists of basic type information; in this case NC indicates that the term is a name (N) and that the term shown is the canonical (C) form. The numeric value is the number of times the term appeared in the text. Here we should note that the tool includes variations of the canonical form in the count. Alpha Text Management, Inc., is considered a variant of Alpha Text Management, so they are both included in the count of the occurrences of the term. The third entry on each line is the canonical form of the term followed by the category. In this case, both companies are correctly identified as organizations. The term Web is correctly identified as the name of an object and classified as OTHER because it is not the name of a person, place, or organization.

Some other possible categories for terms are:

- **Ordinal.** An ordinal number such as "1st" or second
- **Cardinal.** A cardinal number such as 38 or 2001
- **Percent.** A percentage, such as 10%
- **Date.** A date in either numeric (02/15/2001) or text form, such as "February 15, 2000"
- **Money.** A reference to an amount of money, such as $100,000
- **Uname.** A name
- **Person.** A name of a person, such as Franklin Roosevelt
- **Place.** A city, state, or country
- **Org.** The name of an organization, such as a company or institution
- **Other.** A name that is not a person, organization, or place
- **Uabbr.** An abbreviation such as FBI

When the feature extraction program processes the sample text processing all types of features, and not just names, the following are the results:

```
WC     1     acquire     UWORD
WC     2     acquisition         UWORD
NC     3     Alpha Text Management     ORG
WC     1     analysis     UWORD
WC     1     announce     UWORD
WC     1     application         UWORD
WC     1     art     UWORD
WC     1     automate     UWORD
WC     1     backing     UWORD
```

```
NC    3    Beta Morphological Industries     ORG
WC    1    capital      UWORD
WC    1    comment      UWORD
WC    1    company      UWORD
WC    1    competitive          UWORD
WC    1    computational      UWORD
WC    1    content      UWORD
WC    1    embed      UWORD
WC    1    field      UWORD
WC    1    found      UWORD
WC    1    intelligence      UWORD
WC    1    intention      UWORD
WC    1    known      UWORD
WC    1    leading      UWORD
WC    1    linguist      UWORD
WC    1    market      UWORD
WC    1    morphology      UWORD
WC    1    move      UWORD
WC    1    neither      UWORD
WC    1    official      UWORD
WC    1    preprocess      UWORD
WC    1    reach      UWORD
WC    1    state      UWORD
WC    1    story      UWORD
WC    1    sum      UWORD
WC    1    text      UWORD
WC    1    tool      UWORD
WC    1    undisclosed      UWORD
WC    1    venture      UWORD
NC    1    Web      OTHER
WC    1    year      UWORD
```

Since the tool provides a standard output format and several parameters for controlling the type of feature processing performed, it is a relatively simple matter to load the results into a database.

Summarizer

The summarizer tool in the IBM Intelligent Miner for Text suite performs summarization by extraction using a combination of heuristics.

Prior to executing the actual summarization program, the feature extraction tool is run to identify structural boundaries between words, sentences, and documents. Terms extracted from the text are then compared to a reference vocabulary that includes statistics on word frequencies.

The tool is configured with a reference vocabulary for common text but you can improve summarization performance in specialized fields by creating a specialized reference vocabulary. The feature extraction tool can be used to create a specialized reference vocabulary based on a set of sample documents. When deciding what documents to include in the training set, ensure that all important terms are included in the sample but that terms are not over-represented. For example, if the terms *pulmonary artery* and *aorta* are equally important and equally common in the general literature of the domain, then one should not appear in the training set significantly more frequently than the other. The problem is that word importance is (at least by default) calculated in part based upon inverse word frequency in the training set. Words that appear frequently are considered less important that those that occur infrequently. Keeping exact word counts are not necessary when compiling a sample set, just be sure to create a representative sample of the types of text you expect to summarize.

Summaries are built on the basis of word rankings. A word rank is calculated on the basis of several factors. First of all, words must pass a minimum importance test. Words are considered worth ranking if:

- The word appears in the title, headings, or captions.
- The word occurs more frequently in the document than in the reference vocabulary.

The relative frequency of a word in a document compared to its frequency in the reference vocabulary is known as the word salience measure. The default formula for calculating the salience measure is

```
Frequency of word in text * inverse document frequency
```

The inverse document frequency simply reflects how well a word can help discriminate between topics in a document set. As the number of times a word appears i n a set of documents increases, the inverse document frequency decreases.

In addition to word rankings based upon frequency, this summarization tool also considers a words position. Words close to the beginning of a paragraph are ranked more highly than those later in a paragraph. In the case of long paragraphs, the final sentence is given a higher ranking than it normally would have. Words can also be ranked according to the position of the paragraph in which they occur, so that words in early paragraphs are ranked higher than others.

For example, consider the following news release from the U.S. Food and Drug Administration (www.fda.gov/oc/po/firmrecalls/RomanDist8_00.html) regarding a product recall.

> State Agriculture Commissioner Announces Fish Recall
>
> NEWS RELEASE
>
> State Agriculture Commissioner Announces Fish Recall
>
> Brooklyn, NY - August 9, 2000 - State Agriculture Commissioner Nathan L. Rudgers announced today that uneviscerated processed fish has been voluntarily recalled

by its distributor Roman Enterprises & Sons, 27 Story Street, Brooklyn, New York. This product, labeled in Russian, was discovered by Department food inspectors during an inspection of a large public warehouse facility in Brooklyn, New York. Food samples analyzed at the New York State Food Laboratory confirmed that the fish had not been eviscerated prior to processing.

The product may be contaminated with *Clostridium botulinum* spores which can cause Botulism, a serious and potentially fatal food-borne illness.

The sale of this type of fish is prohibited under New York State Agriculture and Markets regulations because *Clostridium botulinum* spores are more likely to be concentrated in the viscera than any other portion of the fish. Uneviscerated processed fish has been linked to outbreaks of botulism poisoning.

Consumers who have this product are advised not to eat it.

According to the distributor, the product was imported into the United States by BP International. It is sold to grocery stores in large cardboard boxes that weigh approximately 20 pounds. Distribution records indicate the product has been sold to grocery stores in the Metropolitan New York City area, Massachusetts and Pennsylvania. New York Agriculture and Markets food inspectors are continuing their investigation.

Symptoms of Botulism include blurred vision, general weakness, poor reflexes, difficulty swallowing and respiratory paralysis.

Using the summarization tool with default settings and the predefined reference vocabulary results in the following summary:

```
  State Agriculture Commissioner Announces Fish Recall
Brooklyn, NY - August 9 , 2000 - State Agriculture Commissioner Nathan L.
The product may be contaminated with Clostridium botulinum spores which
can cause Botulism, a serious and potentially fatal food-borne illness.
The sale of this type of fish is prohibited under New York State Agriculture
and Markets regulations because Clostridium botulinum spores are more likely
to be concentrated in the viscera than any other portion of the fish.
```

While capturing the gist of the news release, it failed to include the name of the company and the specific product recalled. This example highlights one of the most significant problems with summarization by extraction—that is, that the importance of a fact in a text is not always reflected in the frequency with which particular terms are used. Again, we see here that while heuristics work well most of the time, they are not guaranteed to produce the accuracy we may be accustomed to with the algorithmic approaches of data warehousing. In light of this type of shortcoming in automatically generated summaries, the original full-length text should be made easily available along with its summary.

As noted at the beginning of this section, tools are constantly changing. Most commercially available summarization tools use sentence extraction, but work on knowledge-based summarization may lead to tools that can summarize by first abstracting the meaning of text and then generating a summary. Hahn and Mani (2000) describe the architecture of a summarization by abstraction system.

Topic Categorization

Unlike other tools in the suite, the topic categorization program must be trained before it can be used. The basic process of training the tool involves providing a set of documents about a particular topic or composing a logical group, such as a group of news stories of interest to an analyst. Like other programs in the suite, this tool uses statistical techniques along with morphological analysis to develop a profile or a category scheme describing a topic. These category schemes are then used as the basis for analyzing and categorizing other documents.

The benefit of this approach is that the topic categorization tool can be easily trained for a particular application. This type of design does not require a semantic representation, such as a taxonomy, to perform its work.

Let's look at an example in the area of consumer product safety. Assume that we are interested in monitoring news releases on product recalls and warnings as well as investigative reports from news agencies. We will also assume that we are looking for a rough categorization into three areas:

- Food products
- Cosmetic products
- Drugs and medications

To support this, we must first create three sets of training documents that represent each of the three areas. The sets should be large enough to provide reasonable coverage of the topics. They must also provide enough detail to generate discriminating feature sets for each topic. If a topic's set of training documents is too small, it could result in a discriminating criteria that are too broad and, therefore, lead to over-generalized categorizations.

Clustering

Clustering, like categorization, divides a group of documents into distinct sets. Unlike categorization, though, it does not require a training phase for a fixed set of categories. Instead, documents are grouped according to their similarity to each other. The IBM tool supports two types of clustering: hierarchical and binary relational.

Hierarchical Clustering

Hierarchical clustering, as the name implies, groups documents using a tree structure, with a single root, leaf nodes, and intervening levels. The hierarchical clustering algorithm begins by putting each document in a set into its own cluster. It then combines each of these singleton clusters with the cluster most similar to it, resulting in a second level of clusters with one-half as many clusters as the leaf node level. This process of combining clusters continues until only a single root node is left, which includes all documents in the collection (see Figure 11.2).

The similarity measure is the most important determinant in the formation of the resulting clusters. The hierarchical clustering tool supports two types of similarity measures, lexical affinities and linguistic features. Lexical affinities are groups of words that frequently appear together, such as:

- Data warehousing
- Securities and Exchange Commission
- Coronary artery
- Interstate highways
- North American Free Trade Agreement

Lexical affinities, sometimes called collocations, are generated for each document collection, so a predefined thesaurus is not required. The advantage of this approach is that, although additional processing is required before the core clustering operation can begin, the lexical affinities are specific to the documents being clustered. Prior to generating the list of lexical affinities, some basic morphological analysis is performed to improve the quality of the results.

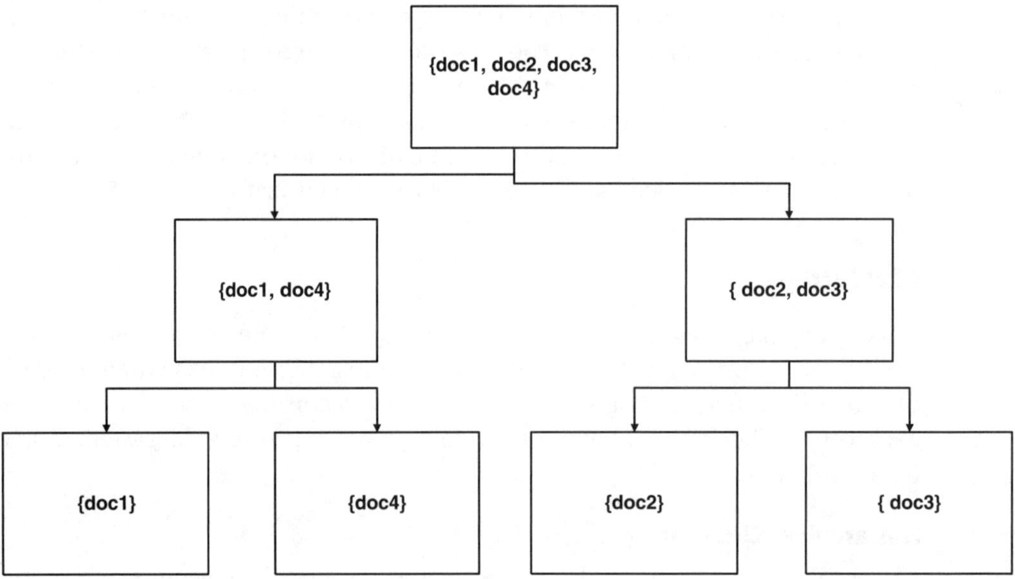

Figure 11.2 Hierarchical clustering results in a tree structure organization of documents.

The other similarity measure provided in the tool is based upon linguistic features. With this measure, the feature extraction program is used to identify key areas, such as names and terms. With this approach, one can cluster documents on the basis of specific types of information in them, rather than on all the text. For example, clustering can be performed on the basis of persons, places, and organizations, so that documents about particular companies, executives, or public officials are more likely to be grouped together than when lexical affinities are used.

Which similarity measure is used does not affect the shape of the resulting tree; hierarchical clustering always generates a binary tree. The results, especially for large document sets can be somewhat unwieldy to navigate, so a splicing operation is often used to merge some of the clusters. The basic idea is that similar clusters can be merged without losing much in the way of discrimination between document topics.

Binary Relational Clustering

Binary relational clustering differs from hierarchical clustering in several significant ways.

- The cluster structure is flat, not hierarchical.
- Documents are included in only one cluster.
- Each cluster tends to represent a single topic.
- Clusters are linked together by shared features that have been defined using the feature extraction tool.

As Figure 11.3 shows, binary relational clustering generates constellations of documents.

Like hierarchical clustering, the similarity measure used influences the resulting clusters. In binary relational clustering, users can specify one of three methods for calculating similarity. All are based on the use of descriptors, or features that represent a document. (Again, these features are defined using the feature extraction tool.)

The first measure gives more weight to features that appear in a wide range of documents. This tends to generate clusters based on common topics. The second measure gives more weight to features that appear infrequently. This tends to generate more clusters than the first measure, but the clusters are centered on more specific topics.

The third measure gives slightly less weight to wide-ranging descriptors than descriptors that appear in few documents. This tends to reduce the influence of common topics, without leading to large numbers of narrowly focused clusters.

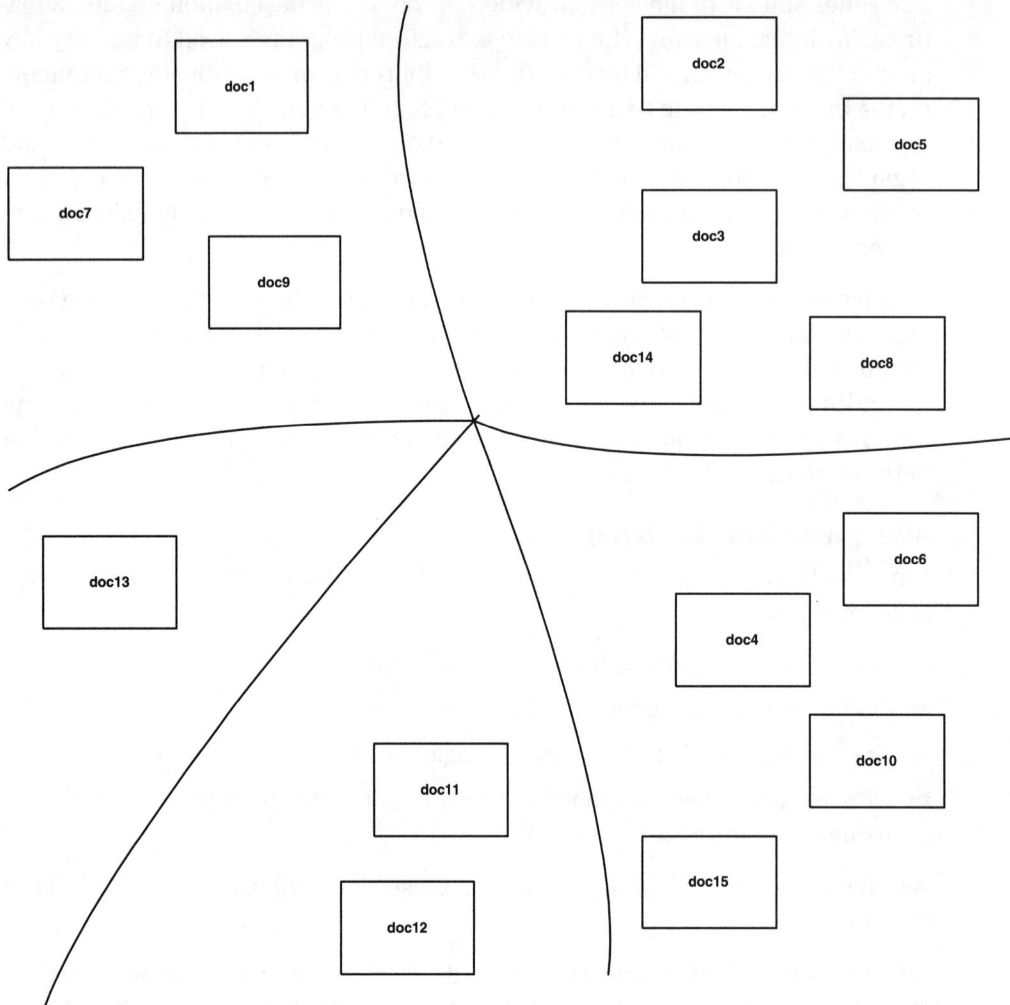

Figure 11.3 Binary relational clusters partition a document collection on the basis of shared features.

Working with IBM Intelligent Miner for Text

The architecture of the IBM tool suite is file-oriented. Input is provided to each tool as a stream of files or as a file containing fully qualified pathnames. The results of the analysis tools are output as streams of semistructured text that is easily manipulated. This combination of file-oriented input and output (as opposed to the database-oriented structure we will see in Oracle interMedia Text) makes the tool suite amenable to the type of command-line processing often found in UNIX environments. That is, one program pipes its output to another program, which in turn pipes it to another program, and so on until a complete task is accomplished.

The next tool we will consider, Oracle interMedia Text, uses a fundamentally different approach to text analysis.

The Knowledge-Based Approach

Oracle interMedia Text takes a knowledge-based approach to text analysis and extends standard relational database tools to include text manipulation operators. Unlike IBM Intelligent Miner for Text, which operates on files, the Oracle tool is integrated directly into the relational database engine. One benefit of this approach is that one can easily work with both the contents of documents and structured metadata at the same time. For example, one can easily query for documents that contain particular phrases (content) that originated from a particular source (metadata).

The differences between Oracle's and IBM's text analysis tools extend far beyond where documents are stored or how commands are executed. The interMedia Text tool requires little preprocessing for document formats or character set conversion since much of the required functionality is built into the tool. We also gain the benefits of a relational database, including transaction control and record locking as well as fine-grained security controls. On the other hand, loading documents into the database for processing is more complicated. Also, Oracle Text does not provide the types of clustering programs found in IBM Intelligent Miner for Text.

The key operations we will examine about Oracle interMedia Text are:

- Loading
- Indexing
- Searching

The tool offers several different approaches for loading documents into the database. This was not an issue with Intelligent Miner for Text, since all processing with that tool was done via the file system. Indexing is essential for efficient text searching, and two types are supported: full-text indexing and thematic indexing. Finally, we will examine the types of operators provided by Oracle Text for keyword and thematic searching, including fuzzy, stem, and proximity operators.

Loading Documents into the Database

When we think of loading data into a data warehouse, we usually are less concerned with the format of the data than the quality and referential integrity of the information. Also, we have so many good options for loading data, from native loaders, to ODBC drivers to full-blown ETL tools. In document warehouse environments this is not the case. First, although it is conceivable to load some text through ODBC drivers, high volumes of formatted text are best loaded with other techniques. Second, ETL tools have focused on solving extraction, cleansing, merging, and aggregating data, while capturing enough metadata to meet the needs of ETL administrators. This leaves us for the most part with platform-specific tools. Oracle provides several data types for storing documents, from VARCHAR2 for short pieces of text to a few different types for binary large objects (BLOB). For more on the appropriate use of each data type refer to Oracle documentation. (This is an important issue, but changes can be made in each release of the database, and the documentation will have the best, most up-to-date information. For example, the LONG RAW data type was often used in Oracle 7 for documents, but that data type should not be used in Oracle 8*i* and is supported only for migration purposes.) Instead of further discussion on data types, our focus here will be on the tools for loading documents into the database. The options provided are:

- SQL Insert
- SQL*Loader
- PL/SQL package for loading LOBs

The SQL Insert statement is used only for short, almost trivial pieces of text. For example, if we have a table called documents, with two columns (an ID and a short text column), then the following command can be used to add records:

```
INSERT INTO documents
VALUES (2873, 'Short pieces of text such as this are easy to load.')
```

The other three options are more interesting and useful in a document warehouse. SQL*Loader is a familiar tool to data warehouse practitioners and others who have had to get large quantities of data into Oracle. The ctxload program is an interMedia Text specific tool. Oracle also provides a package of procedures designed for working with large object data types that can be used to load BLOBs from files.

The SQL*Loader program works well when metadata has been extracted or otherwise defined for documents. For example, if we kept basic metadata along with the contents of a document in a single table, we could use SQL*Loader to populate the following table:

```
CREATE TABLE docs AS
     (doc_id          INTEGER,
      main_subject     VARCHAR2(100),
      publish_date     DATE
      language          VARCHAR2(3)
      content          BLOB);
```

SQL*Loader uses a configuration file (called a control file) to specify how the documents (or any data) should be loaded. A loader file for this might look like:

```
LOAD DATA
INFILE  'docs_to_load.dat'
INTO TABLE docs
APPEND
FIELDS TERMINATED BY ','
(doc_id     SEQUENCE (MAX,1)
 main_subject,
      publish_date,
 language,
 file_name FILLER CHAR(80),
  content  LOBFILE(file_name) TERMINATED BY EOF)
```

The most interesting lines in this control file are the last two: the file_name filed will take on the pathname of the file to load, while the content column of the docs table will actually get the text in the document specified by file_name. The control file will find the information about the documents in a file called docs_to_load.dat that would look something like this:

```
Debt, 01/02/2000, ENG, /docs/finance/debt/debt_faq.htm
Debt, 01/03/2000, ENG, /docs/finance/debt/debt_instruments.htm
Investment, 01/03/2000, ENG, /docs/finance/invest/debt_faq.htm
Investment, 01/05/2000, ENG, /docs/finance/invest/debt_faq.htm
Monetary Policy, 01/05/2000, ENG, /docs/monetary/fed_reserve1.htm
Monetary, 01/05/2000, ENG, /docs/monetary/fed_reserve2.htm
Monetary, 01/08/2000, GER, /docs/monetary/duetch_bank.htm
Regulations, 01/02/2000, ENG, /docs/reg/chemical1.htm
Regulations, 01/03/2000, ENG, /docs/reg/chemical2.htm
Regulations, 01/03/2000, ENG, /docs/reg/chemical3.htm
Regulations, 01/05/2000, ENG, /docs/reg/biohazard1.htm
Regulations, 01/05/2000, ENG, /docs/reg/biohazard2.htm
Regulations, 01/05/2000, ENG, /docs/reg/fire3.htm
```

The SQL*Loader program bridges the file-based staging area in a document warehouse and the database repository that actually provides the core services of the document warehouse. If more programmatic control is required, the DBMS_LOB package provides a LOADFROMFILE procedure to load text from a PL/SQL program.

Up to this point, we have discussed document loading assuming that text is stored directly in the database in a BLOB column, but this is not necessarily the case. Oracle interMedia Text supports six different methods of storing documents, although all are still managed by the database. These options are:

- Direct storage
- Master-detail table storage

- Nested table storage
- File storage
- URL-based storage
- User-defined procedure

Direct storage loads the contents of a document into a single row of a database table. The master-detail storage option allows documents to be broken down into multiple detail rows with document-level detail kept in a master table. Nested table storage makes use of Oracle's nested table data structure. When the file storage option is used, only the file name is stored in the database, and the contents remain in an operating system file. Similarly, the URL-based storage scheme leaves the content on the Internet or an intranet and keeps only the URL in the database. The last storage option allows developers to specify a storage procedure that creates text at index time.

When URL-based storage is used, Oracle's built-in crawler manages the retrieval of documents. The crawler can be configured according to several parameters including:

- Timeout
- Number of simultaneous threads
- Maximum document size
- HTTP proxy
- FTP proxy

The timeout parameter specifies how long the crawler will wait for a response from the targeted HTTP server. The number of simultaneous threads provides an upper bound on the number of threads the crawler will create to retrieve documents. Maximum document size limits the size of files that will be retrieved. The proxy parameters allow one to define a hostname and port number for proxies that are to be used for each protocol.

Indexing in Oracle interMedia Text

Indexing in Oracle interMedia Text is a more complex operation than in many tools, and this is due to the fact that more features are available within this tool than in others. To successfully index documents within Oracle Text, the following database objects need to be configured:

- Filter objects
- Lexer objects
- Wordlist objects

- Section groups
- Thematic indexes

Each of these objects controls a different element of the indexing operation. Not surprisingly, the database-oriented text analysis tool provides the most comprehensive indexing options. Note, other options related to the storage location of indexes and some system-defined parameters also need to be configured, but they do not directly affect text analysis, so they will not be discussed here.

Filter Objects

Filter objects control how word-processing and other formatted documents are handled by Oracle Text. Formatted documents are stored in their native format but converted to plain text or HTML format before indexing. The three basic types of filters provided are:

- Character set filter
- Inso filter
- User-defined filter

The character set filter is used when documents use a character set different from the character set defined for the database. The specified filter is used to translate documents into the database character set.

The Inso filter is used to convert most document format types.. It accommodates most word-processing, spreadsheet, database, and presentation formats. Many text mining tools, including IBM Intelligent Miner for Text and Megaputer's TextAnalyst, assume that the text presented for analysis has already been converted into a suitable format.

Using a user-defined filter allows developers to perform custom filtering on documents before they are indexed. High-level scripting languages with rich text manipulation features, such as Perl, can be used in cases where some preprocessing needs to be performed and has not been done before the documents were loaded into the database. While most preprocessing should be done prior to loading, there are cases where it makes sense to filter documents after loading. For example, a file may contain rendering information that should be maintained for display purposes but should not be passed through the indexing engine.

Lexer Objects

Lexer objects control how words and sentences are demarcated. In the case of English and most Western European languages (in fact most languages that use a single byte character set), a basic lexer will suffice. It is the responsibility of the lexer to define the beginnings and ends of tokens that are then passed on to the indexing engine for processing. (The lexer performs a similar role to a lexical analyzer in a compiler.)

For multibyte languages, including the most popular Asian languages, specialized lexical analysis is required since word boundary cues found in single byte languages are unavailable in those cases. Oracle interMedia supports seven character sets for Chinese, three for Japanese, and two for Korean.

The lexer object is used to define properties for language-specific options. For example, compound nouns (that is, nouns made up of more than one word) are written as a single word in German, so *federal bank* in English is written as *Bundesbank* in German. Oracle interMedia Text can be configured through a lexer object to index only the compound noun (*Bundesbank*) or to index each component noun (*Bundes* and *bank*) along with the compound noun.

Wordlist Objects

Wordlist objects are used to specify how stemming and fuzzy matches are performed when searching text. Stemming is the process of extracting the root from a word. For example, the stem of children is child, and the stem of bought is buy. When multiple languages may be kept in a data warehouse, Oracle Text can be set to automatically detect the language and stem it correctly. Again, this differs from the IBM design approach, in which language identification is done with a separate tool that is invoked separately from other text analysis operations. Oracle Text can stem several Western languages, including English, Spanish, French, Dutch, German, and Italian.

Fuzzy matches provide automatic expansion of a term to include similarly spelled terms. This is most useful when misspellings are common. Fuzzy matching is supported for several Western languages as well as for Chinese, Japanese, and Korean.

Section Groups

Section groups provide a powerful mechanism for limiting the range of a search at the cost of making indexing more complex. Sections are defined by HTML and XML tags that are specified within a query. For example, searching for *morphology* in a Title section would be specified with the clause

```
morphology WITHIN TITLE
```

and would match the text

```
<TITLE> The Role of Morphology in Text Mining </TITLE>
```

but not

```
<BODY>
     Morphology plays a critical role in several text mining operations …
<BODY>
```

With support for section groups, one does not need to decompose semistructured documents when they are stored in the database to gain some of the benefits of using a markup language. Without this section group indexing, the previous query would have to be rephrased to something along the lines of:

```
Entity_type = 'TITLE'  AND contains(doc, 'morphology')
```

Thematic Indexing

Oracle Text provides a taxonomy of concepts, called a knowledge base, that is used to support thematic indexing. By default, thematic indexing is done along with keyword indexing. The knowledge base category configured with Oracle interMedia Text spans six broad areas:

- Science and technology
- Business and economics
- Government and military
- Social environment
- Geography
- Abstract ideas and concepts

The knowledge base provides a semantic representation for a broad range of terms, using standard thesaurus relations, including broader terms, narrower terms, and related terms. For example, a broader term for *Internet technology* is *computer networking*, and narrower terms for *retail trade industry* are *convenience stores*, *department stores*, and *supermarkets*. While these categories are useful for general thematic indexing, domain-specific applications may require a domain-specific thesaurus.

The knowledge base can be extended with one or more domain-specific thesauri. This option provides some of the same advantages found in statistical categorization programs, like that used in IBM Intelligent Miner for Text. With statistical approaches, sample documents provide the terms used for categorization, and statistical functions provide the measures used to determine category labels. By extending the knowledge base, additional terms can be provided for categorization but rather than use statistics to determine appropriate labels, relationships between terms are used.

Thesauri used in interMedia follow the ISO-2788 standard for single-language thesauri. A thesaurus consists of a defined vocabulary made up of terms, known as indexing terms. Indexing terms can be single words or multiple words, in which case they are known as compound terms. As a means of supporting synonyms, the ISO standard distinguishes between preferred and nonpreferred terms. A preferred term is the one consistently used to describe a concept, while a nonpreferred term is a synonym or quasisynonym of a preferred term. Documents are indexed using preferred terms, but nonpreferred terms provide links from documents that use nonpreferred terms to the standardized vocabulary of preferred terms. For example, the preferred term for a small logical unit of computer code may be *procedure*, and a nonpreferred term for the same concept may be *subroutine*. Therefore, documents with the term *subroutine* are indexed as if the term *procedure* had been used instead. Preferred and nonpreferred is only one relation between terms in a thesaurus.

The most commonly used relationships are broader term, narrower term, and related term, denoted by BT, NT, and RT, respectively. The taxonomy shown in Figure 11.4 can also be implemented using the following thesaurus:

```
Data Warehouse
  BT database application
Object Database
  BT database system
Relational Database
  BT database system
Database system
  BT database
Database Application
  BT database
  NT OLTP
  NT OLAP
```

The knowledge base provided with Oracle Text covers a wide range of topics but is not suitable for classifying documents limited to a narrow domain that uses a rich vocabulary of its own, such as scientific, technical, and legal areas. In these cases, augmenting the Oracle Text knowledge base with a domain-specific thesaurus will greatly improve the discrimination between documents.

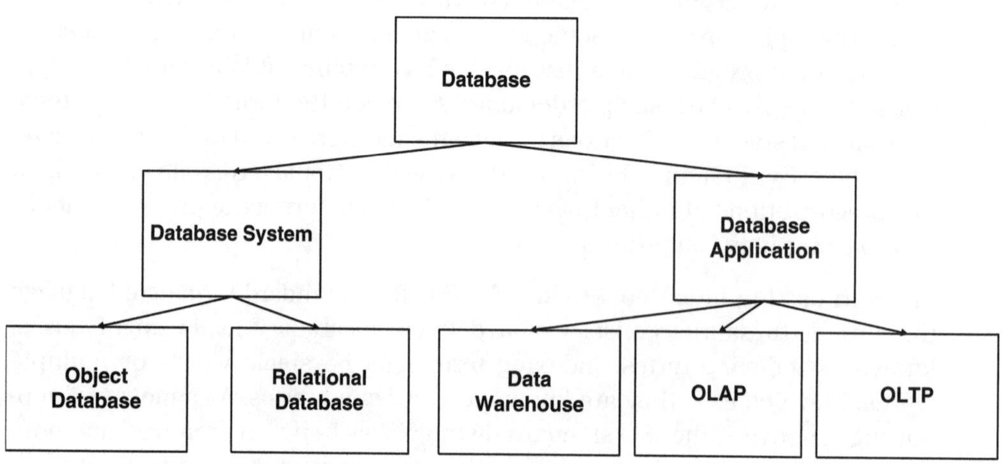

Figure 11.4 The hierarchical structure described in the sample thesaurus.

Searching in Oracle Text

Searching for documents with Oracle Text does not require a separate search engine since document indexing, both keyword and thematic, is integrated directly into the relational database engine. The basic function upon which queries are built is the CONTAINS function, and to a lesser degree, the SCORE function. This section will introduce some of the most important operators used in Oracle Text since these operators are one of the most important distinguishing characteristics of this tool.

The CONTAINS function is a SQL function used in WHERE clauses of SELECT statements to specify what documents should be retrieved. The CONTAINS function returns a numeric weight representing the frequency of the term in the text. The SCORE function is used to return the weight for any purpose other than comparison and selection. For the purpose of the following examples, let's assume we have a table defined with the following statement:

```
CREATE TABLE docs
     (doc_id          INTEGER          PRIMARY KEY,
      title           VARCHAR2(500),
      doc_content     CLOB)
```

Also, assume that the title and doc_content rows have been indexed with text indexes. To retrieve the document IDs of all documents containing the term *Federal Reserve* in the main body of the text, we would use the following query:

```
SELECT doc_id
FROM docs
WHERE CONTAINS(doc_content,'Federal Reserve') > 0
```

Similarly, we can restrict our search to the title of documents and return both the document primary key and the actual weight by using the following query:

```
SELECT doc_id, SCORE(1)
     FROM docs
     WHERE CONTAINS(title,'Federal Reserve', 1) > 0
```

The SQL used by Oracle has been extended to support a series of text-oriented operators beyond CONTAINS and SCORE to provide for more complex searching. These additional operators include:

- ABOUT
- ACCUMULATE
- BROADER TERM
- NARROWER TERM
- PREFERRED TERM
- RELATED TERM

- FUZZY
- STEM
- SOUNDEX
- TRANSLATION TERM
- TRANSLATION TERM SYNONYM
- NEAR
- WITHIN

ABOUT Operator and Thematic Searching

The ABOUT operator is used for thematic and keyword searching. A query for documents about securities markets such as:

```
SELECT doc_id
      FROM docs
      WHERE CONTAINS(doc_content,ABOUT('securities markets') > 0
```

This query returns documents containing the terms *stock market* and *bond market* as well as *mutual funds* because these three terms are defined as narrower terms in the knowledge base.

Multiple-Term Searching

At times, we need to find documents that may contain any one of several terms, and the documents should be ranked according to the highest score of all matching terms. The ACCUMULATE operator (written as a comma) serves this purpose. The following query returns documents that contain *acid*, *protein*, or *monosaturated*.

```
SELECT doc_id
      FROM docs
      WHERE CONTAINS(doc_content,'acid, protein, monosaturated') > 0
```

Broader, Narrower, and Preferred Terms

Thematic indexing allows Oracle Text to work with the thesaurus implicitly on a user's behalf. When a user wishes more control over the search process, the three thesaurus term operators,

BT (broader term)

NT (narrower term)

PT (preferred term)

are used. The broader and narrower term operators expand a query to include more general or specific terms. The operator also allows users to specify how far up or down the hierarchy the expansion processes should go. For example the clause

```
NT('marine transportation',1)
```

expands to

```
'boats and ships', 'steamship', 'waterways'
```

because these three terms are one level down in the hierarchy defined by the default thesaurus. Similarly, the broader term operator returns terms higher up in the hierarchy. For example, the clauses

```
BT('law enforcement')
BT('legal proceedings')
BT('courts')
```

all return the term *law* because it is the most specific term more general than those specified. If the first clause was changed to BT('law enforcement', 2) then it would expand to *law* and *government* because of the position of *government* in the thesaurus.

Unlike the broader and narrower operators, the preferred term operator always returns a single term. This operation is a straightforward substitution, so if *stock* is the preferred term for *equity*, then the clause

```
PT('equity')
```

is replaced by *stock* before a query is actually executed. In addition to working with the thesaurus, operators are provided to manipulate morphological features of words.

Manipulating Word Forms: Fuzzy, Stem, and Soundex Operators

The fuzzy, stem, and soundex operators allow searches to adapt to variations in word forms due to misspellings and inflections.

The fuzzy operator is useful when misspellings are frequent in a document collection. This operator effectively expands a term to include similarly spelled words.

The stem operator, on the other hand, expands the search to include words that have the same root word as the search term. For example,

```
SELECT doc_id
     FROM docs
     WHERE CONTAINS(doc_content,'$sing') > 0
```

returns documents with the words sing, sang, and sung.

The SOUNDEX operator expands a term search to include words that sound similar but are spelled differently. The SOUNDEX operator works only with English language text.

Multilingual Searching

Oracle Text supports multilingual searching through the use of specialized thesaurus that contain translations for particular terms. For example, a thesaurus with the following entries will allow expanded searching of German texts, using English terms.

```
Government
     German: Regierung
money
     German: Geld
policy
     German: Politik
```

The following sample query will return all documents containing the German terms for money:

```
SELECT doc_id
FROM docs
WHERE CONTAINS(doc_content,TRN(money,German)) > 0
```

The thesaurus can contain multiple translations for the same terms, so a single multilingual thesaurus can support several languages.

The translation term synonym (TRSYN) operator uses the translation operator to expand a query to include foreign equivalents for a term as well as synonyms for the term and foreign equivalents for the synonyms.

Proximity Searching

Searching for terms can be limited to particular areas of text in two ways, using the NEAR operator and using the WITHIN operator.

The NEAR operator specifies that the target terms must be within a specified number words to match. For example, the clause

```
NEAR{(monetary, policy), 5)
```

specifies that a match occurs when the word monetary is within five words of policy.

While the NEAR operator works with words, the WITHIN operator limits searches to predefined sections, sentences, and paragraphs. This operator is especially useful when working with structured documents. For example, the following query targets documents that have the phrase *monetary policy* in the heading section.

```
SELECT doc_id
FROM docs
WHERE CONTAINS(doc_content,'monetary policy WITHIN Heading') > 0
```

Working with Oracle Text

Working with Oracle Text is fundamentally different from working with either IBM Intelligent Miner for Text or Megaputer's TextAnalyst. Oracle's tools are integrated into the relational database so that large bodies of text are treated, in some ways, as just another data type. The text manipulation tools provided by Oracle Text are directed to getting text into the database, to indexing by keywords and by themes, and to searching text.

One obvious advantage of this approach is that relational data, such as metadata about the author, publication dates, copyrights, and other elements of the Dublin Core, can be stored right along with the contents of the documents. This, in turn, makes searching by content as well as metadata relatively straightforward. Oracle Text's rich set of operators extend SQL to allow users to develop complex query options. Whereas IBM Intelligent Miner for Text provides many tools for extracting features and clustering documents, Oracle has put the emphasis on more database-oriented features.

Now we will turn to a third architecture, the COM architecture used by Megaputer's TextAnalyst program. This third application provides an example of yet another approach to dealing with the problem extracting business intelligence from large collections of text.

Neural Network Approach: Megaputer's TextAnalyst

Our final example of a text analysis application is Megaputer's TextAnalyst. Like Oracle Text, this tool is designed for easy information retrieval and textbase navigation. Like IBM Intelligent Miner for Text, this product provides support for a range of text mining operations without a predefined knowledge base. The basis for Text Analyst's processing is a neural network technique that analyzes preprocessed text to develop a semantic network. The semantic network provides the core information required for clustering, summarizing, and navigating document collections.

Our discussion of TextAnalyst will begin with an overview of the text analysis process followed by a review of analysis performed on the sample news release on a fish product recall presented earlier in the chapter. Next, we will discuss how TextAnalyst supports the following operations:

- Textbase navigation
- Clustering
- Summarization
- Natural language information retrieval

Finally, we will examine some features of the COM object implementation of TextAnalyst.

TextAnalyst Processing

TextAnalyst uses a three-step process for compiling text mining information about a collection of documents.

- Preprocessing
- Statistical analysis
- Renormalization

As Figure 11.5 shows, these steps are performed sequentially, beginning with preprocessing.

The first phase is the only language-dependent operation in TextAnalyst's processing. During preprocessing, stop words are eliminated since they provide no semantic information. Next, the roots of the remaining words are identified so that the subsequent statistical analysis and renormalization phases have to deal only with a canonical form of words. With the text reduced to only semantically important words in standard form, TextAnalyst moves into a statistical analysis phase.

During statistical analysis, TextAnalyst calculates correlation weights between words. Words that appear together frequently (referred to as lexical affinities in IBM Intelligent Miner for Text) have higher weights than words that appear together infrequently. A graph data structure, such as that in Figure 11.6, holds the correlation weights between words.

The final phase of processing is called renormalization. During this stage, the weights between words are adjusted to reflect the strength of the relationship between the words in a sentence. Iterative adjustments are made to the weights until a stable set of weights is found that reflects the most important words and word combinations in the text.

We will now look at a specific example, using the news release presented earlier in the chapter.

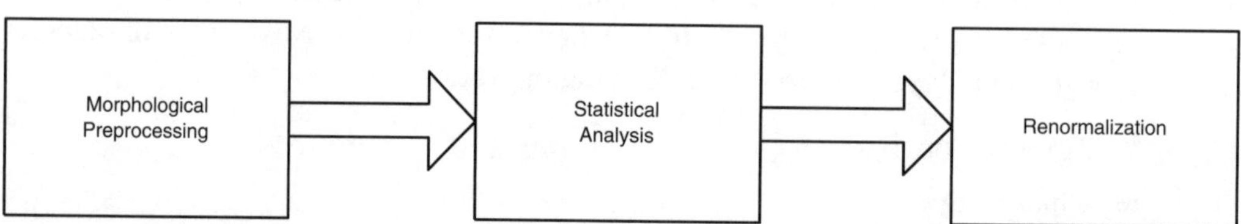

Figure 11.5 TextAnalyst uses a three-step process to build linguistic information about a document collection.

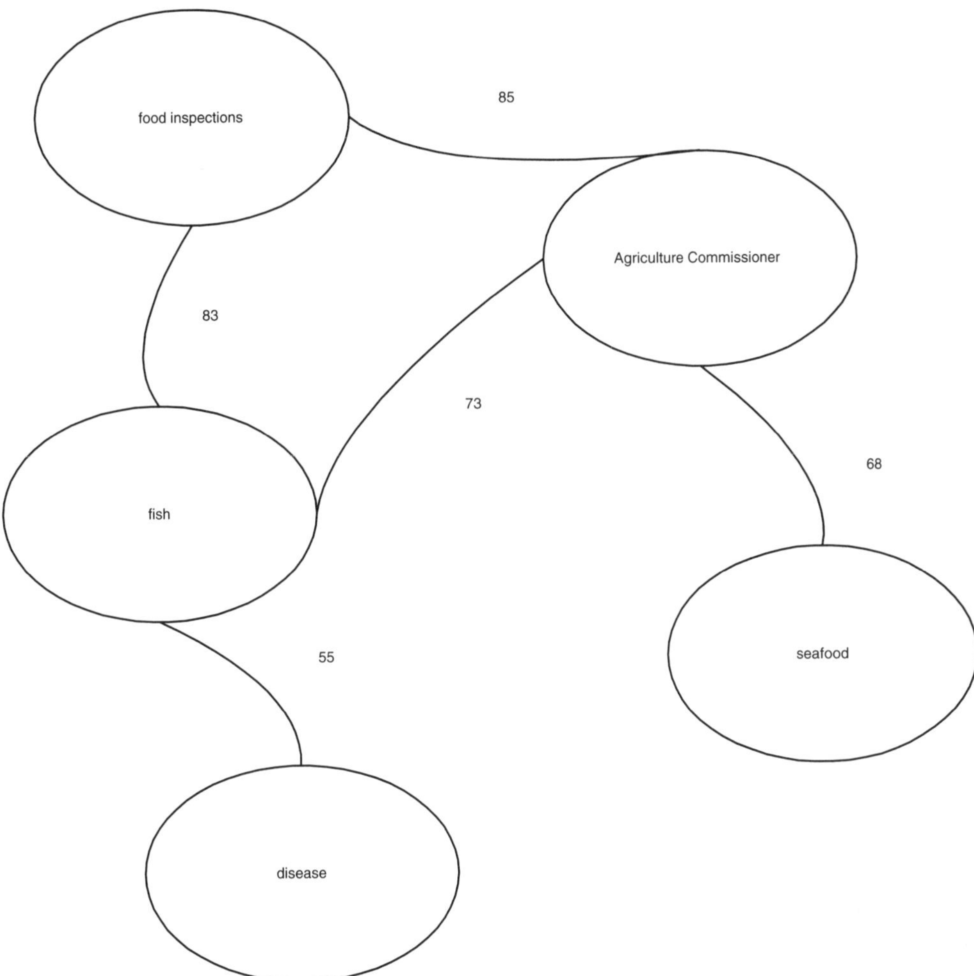

Figure 11.6 A graph data structure is used to store the correlation weights between terms.

TextAnalyst Example

The three-stage processing is preformed automatically by TextAnalyst when a document is loaded into the Megaputer application. Developers have more control when using the ActiveX objects directly but that will be discussed later. For the purpose of this example, we will focus solely on the TextAnalyst end user program. Figure 11.7 shows an example of the application after analyzing the fish recall news release.

The semantic network in TextAnalyst is the foundation upon which other operations depend. As Figure 11.7 shows, the semantic network (shown in the

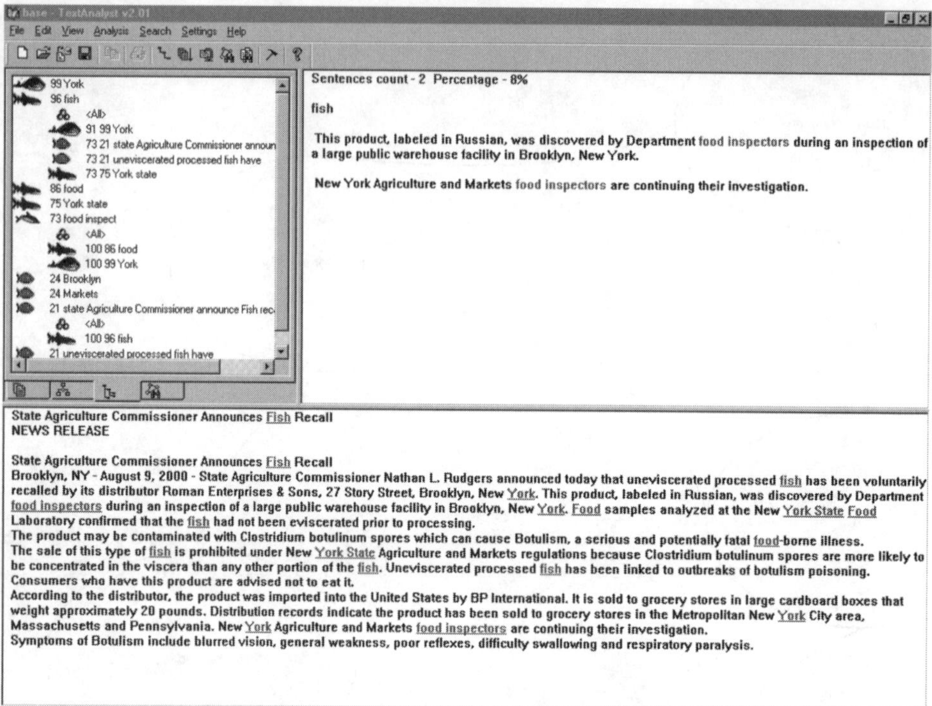

Figure 11.7 Browsing the semantic network by word selects related sentences from the text.

upper-left pane) consists of words and terms linked to other words and terms according to weight of terms. Multiword terms are identified on the basis of the frequency with which they co-occur. In this example important terms include *State Agriculture Department Announces Fish Recall*, *food inspector*, and *uneviscerated processed fish has*. Unlike IBM Intelligent Miner for Text, which does not usually include verbs outside of noun phrases in person, place, and organization terms, this tool did not terminate the first multiword term at *State Agriculture Department* or the last with *uneviscerated processed fish*. This is understandable since TextAnalyst uses a strictly mathematical approach, after preprocessing, to formulate the semantic network, whereas the IBM tool includes language-specific heuristics. The benefit of the IBM approach is that identifying terms can be done more cleanly; however, the tool is restricted to English language texts. If the feature extraction program were to be used with other languages, then the heuristics would need to be redesigned for the target language. Megaputer has chosen to limit language-specific operations to the preprocessing stage, thus allowing for more adaptability in later stages.

There is no single correct approach to this type of term identification or feature extraction. Each design described above has advantages and disadvantages. When choosing among tools, it is essential to understand the approach taken by the tool toward linguistic analysis since any design choice will ultimately lead to limitations in the tool. Given that any tool has inherent limitations, one of our jobs as document warehouse designers and text miners is to find the most appropriate tool for our specific application.

Note that this statistical analysis is performed after preprocessing and that initial processing excludes certain common words so those words are not subject to the frequency analysis. Notice that while *York State* is identified as a semantically relevant term, *New York State* is not because the word *new* was not available during the statistical analysis. This is not an uncommon problem with statistical techniques.

This error is just another example of a case where heuristic processing, in this case stop word elimination, improves results in most but not all cases. The alternative to this approach is to embed more knowledge about terms, such as that found in the Oracle Text knowledge base. The price in that case, though, is lack of flexibility. The domains suitable for analysis using the Oracle interMedia Text are constrained by the limits of the knowledge base. The tradeoff between breadth and accuracy of analysis is a ubiquitous phenomenon in text mining and not easily avoided.

TextAnalyst Summarization

Like most summarization programs, this one uses weights based upon individual words and multiword terms to calculate a sentence weight and then extract the most relevant sentences. Using the default threshold of 90 for semantic weight, only a single sentence is extracted for the summary.

> Food samples analyzed at the New York State Food Laboratory confirmed that the fish had not been eviscerated prior to processing.

This is the single most relevant sentence in the short text but it still does not capture the full scope of the news story. Simply decreasing the semantic threshold to 85 produces a much more thorough summary:

> This product, labeled in Russian, was discovered by Department food inspectors during an inspection of a large public warehouse facility in Brooklyn, New York.
>
> Food samples analyzed at the New York State Food Laboratory confirmed that the fish had not been eviscerated prior to processing. The sale of this type of fish is prohibited under New York State Agriculture and Markets regulations because Clostridium botulinum spores are more likely to be concentrated in the viscera than any other portion of the fish.
>
> New York Agriculture and Markets food inspectors are continuing their investigation.

Again, as in the case of IBM Intelligent Miner for Text, a critical piece of information is missing, the name of the product or manufacturer. Not until the threshold is dropped to 50 will the sentence with the key information about the distributor be included. Although it is apparent to us that this is a critical piece of information, it is still not included because the only semantically important words identified by TextAnalyst in that sentence are fish and York. Since each appears only once, the sentence is scored with a relatively low semantic weight. Again, heuristics could be added to improve some results, such as always include the first and last sentences of a short text, but like all rules of thumb, sometimes they apply and sometimes they do not.

A more reliable approach to capturing critical information is to use directed summarization techniques. These entail first identifying the type of story, in this case a product recall, and then extracting essential information, such as the names of the product and manufacturer, date of the recall and lot numbers or other identifying product information. System such as these are knowledge-intensive and require significant custom development even when tools such as Megaputer Text Analyst, IBM Intelligent Miner for Text and Oracle interMedia Text are available.

A third approach, and one adopted by Megaputer, is to provide the means to interrogate a text collection using natural language to find answers to particular questions not captured in a summary.

Question Answering

Another feature of TextAnalyst, especially useful with navigating large document collections, is the ability to ask questions using a natural language format. For example, using the example text, we could pose the question,

> Who distributed the fish?

The results to this query are shown in Figure 11.8 and include the first sentence of the text:

> State Agriculture Commissioner Nathan L. Rudgers announced today that uneviscerated processed fish has been voluntarily recalled by its distributor Roman Enterprises & Sons, 27 Story Street, Brooklyn, New York.

Processing questions is similar to processing sentences in documents. Words in the question are scored according to their relationship with other words. Based upon the results of that scoring, similar sentences are extracted from the source text. The intuition for this approach is straightforward. A question is a sentence with a placeholder (identified by terms such as who, what, when, and where) and some selection criterion, such as *distributed the fish*. The selection criterion provides the means of filtering sentences to find matches. The assumption is that at least one of the top matches will contain the answer targeted by the placeholder in the question.

As with other text processing operations, question answering does not entail a full semantic analysis resulting in an elaborate representation of the meaning of a question. Rather, statistical techniques combined with the neural-network-generated semantic network, provide likely answers to the question. Since these are heuristic techniques, finding the correct answer is not guaranteed, but

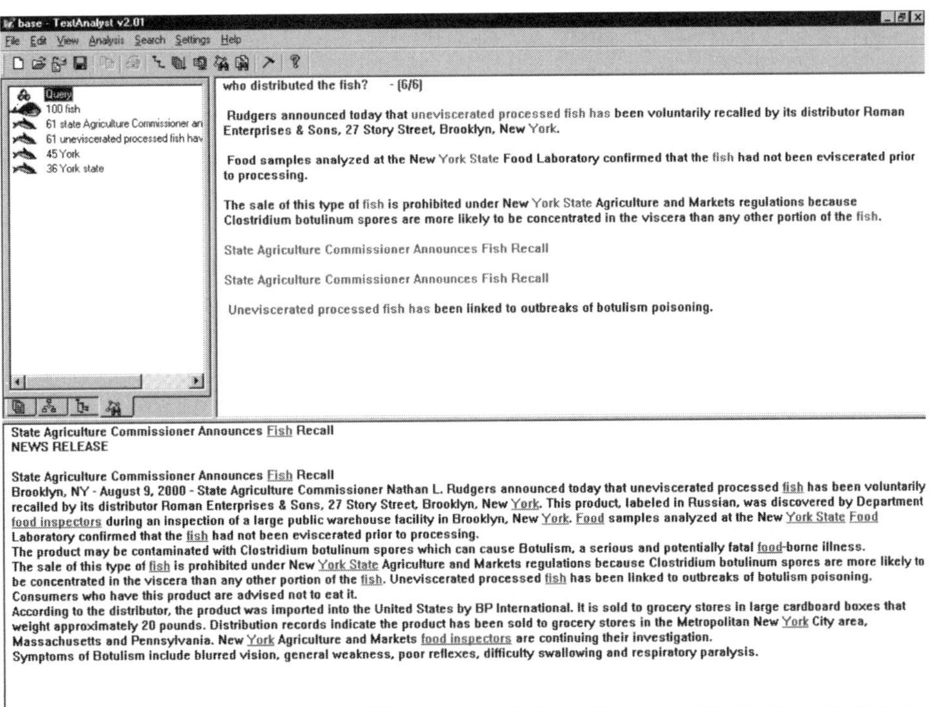

Figure 11.8 TextAnalyst supports natural language queries for searching for particular answers.

it is highly likely that you will find the answer, or something close, in many cases.

Working with the ActiveX Components

In addition to the end-user tool used in the previous sections, custom applications can be designed using ActiveX text analysis components. The components provide the means to build, manipulate, and extract information from the semantic network.

There are advantages to this type of model. First, targeted text analysis applications can be delivered directly to clients. For example, rather than summarizing documents and storing document summaries in a warehouse, the summarization task could be done locally at a client computer as a document is loaded from the Web or the document warehouse. Second, a semantic browsing application can be custom designed for a document warehouse. Semantic processing can be done on a server, while client applications navigate semantic networks.

Having addressed some of the main features of three text analysis tools, it is now time to examine them from a comparative analysis perspective.

There Is More Than One Way to Mine Text

This chapter has provided somewhat cursory overviews of three text analysis tools. Each tool was chosen because it reflected a distinct design approach to the problem of text mining. Our next task is to provide a more thorough direct comparison of these tools to assess their most appropriate use. The purpose of this chapter is to understand how to evaluate the applicability of a tool to a particular set of requirements. Three key areas will be compared with each tool:

- Component versus integrated framework architecture
- Performance versus knowledge-based analysis
- Repository architecture

The first set of comparisons will be made on how the text mining tools are integrated with each other and how well they work with third-party tools. The performance versus knowledge debate goes right to the heart of some of the tradeoffs discussed throughout this section. Finally, the repository architecture section will ask how well the tool supports the long-term management of the results of its own analysis.

Reusable Components versus Integrated Framework

At one end of the component spectrum, we have Megaputer's TextAnalyst with its ActiveX suite of objects for dealing with text and semantic analysis. At the other end of the spectrum resides Oracle's interMedia Text, which is fully embedded into a relational database engine. In the middle, and actually closer to Megaputer's TextAnalyst, is IBM's Intelligent Miner for Text. With an emphasis on understanding the implications of design choices in these tools, we can safely conclude the following.

First, that Megaputer's TextAnalyst is appropriate for applications requiring embedded text analysis, although the choice of an ActiveX framework restricts this tool to Microsoft platforms. The ease with which the ActiveX components can be integrated using common programming tools, such as Visual Basic, C++, and Python, make this a likely choice for both application-server-based and client applications.

IBM's Intelligent Miner for Text provides a suite of independent applications. The key to integration with these tools is a relatively standardized output format that is understood by applications in the collection. This, for example, makes it a relatively simple matter to exploit the feature extraction tool for use in document clustering or summarization. Also, with a semistructured output format, the tools all lend themselves to shell-level programming integration with third-party tools and custom applications. The format also makes it a relatively simple matter to store the results of analysis in a relational database, such as DB2 or Oracle, and therefore to integrate text analysis with other business intelligence operations.

If you work with Oracle interMedia Text, it is presumed that you are already working with the relational database as well. Although documents can be stored outside the database, and referenced through either a fully qualified pathname or a URL, all processing is controlled from within the database. In some cases, this architecture is more restrictive than those of the other tools we have considered because of the initial cost of implementing a full relational database management system for text analysis. When only small amounts of text will be analyzed, then more component-oriented tools are more appropriate. For large-scale document collections, the benefits of database integration are more pronounced. First, the documents and related metadata can be stored and queried together. Second, text indexing is fully integrated into the database, so the query optimizer can use statistics about both structured and long object (such as CLOB for text) columns when formulating a query execution plan. Third, SQL has been extended to support a range of text-specific selection criteria such as proximity searches, multilingual searches, thematic searches, and word variation searches.

The key measure when choosing among these tools from an integration perspective is determining how much the control and results of text analysis need to be integrated with other applications.

Performance- versus Knowledge-Based Analysis

Two broad-based approaches have been used in the development of intelligent systems, performance-based and knowledge-based approaches. In the former case, designers are concerned with the effective behavior of the system and not necessarily with the means used to obtain that behavior. This is the "airplanes do not flap their wings" school of thought. It follows from this design philosophy that just because humans process information in one way, that method may not be the best approach for artificial systems. Statistical techniques are probably the most common performance-based class of algorithms. Knowledge-based systems on the other hand use explicit representations of knowledge, such as the meaning of words, the relationship between facts, and rules for drawing conclusions in particular domains. Common knowledge representation schemes include inference rules, semantic networks (including taxonomies or ontologies), and logical propositions. The three tools we have examined represent both types of approaches.

Thesaurus-Driven Processing

Oracle Text is the most knowledge-oriented of the three tools. The thesaurus provided in the tool drives thematic classification of documents. With a predefined set of terms and well-defined relationships between terms, such as "stock is a narrower term for financial investment," there is no need for the statistical analysis of a corpus as with IBM Intelligent Miner for Text and Megaputer's Text-Analyst. With a taxonomy-dependent analysis tool, designers may need to create a domain-specific taxonomy to get the level of document discrimination needed for their application. For example, grouping terms such as *retroviral vector*, *fatty acid*, and *antigen binding protein* under biochemistry may be fine for most of us, but not for a genetics researcher. Building taxonomies is a difficult process and can be somewhat automated by using tools such as Semio's taxonomy-building tool or with IBM Intelligent Miner for Text using a technique described in Müller, et al. (1999). Taxonomies, however, are only one kind of knowledge representation scheme; pattern matching rules are also used extensively in text mining.

Pattern Matching Rules

Heuristics are often represented as pattern matching rules. Examples of such rules include:

- If this is the first sentence in the document, then include it in the summary.
- If the first two words of the sentence are *in conclusion* then add the sentence to the summary.
- If a noun phrase ends in *Inc* or *Co* then classify the entire noun phrase as an organization.
- When the phrase *north of* is encountered, classify the closest noun phrases before and after the phrase as locations.

Clearly these types of rules can be easily represented using IF-THEN conditions and regular expression pattern matching.

Like taxonomies, which need to be domain-specific to be most effective, text analysis heuristics tend to be language-specific. Adopting a text mining tool to additional languages, then, requires the development of another language-specific rule base.

It should be noted that most tools combine performance-oriented techniques with knowledge-based techniques in an attempt to balance the flexibility and adaptability of statistical techniques with the domain- and language-specific functionality provided by thesauri and heuristics. Choosing between a more statistically oriented tool and a knowledge-based tool depends upon the domain of interest. Rapidly changing or broad areas, such as genetics research, are better accommodated by performance-based systems that can adapt to new terms and classification schemes. Relatively stable areas, that is domains where the vocabulary is not constantly growing, such as corporate finance or political risk analysis, are well handled by taxonomy-driven systems. The best of both worlds can be realized by using taxonomies that can be automatically adjusted to accommodate new terms. We have not realized 100 percent automation in this area and will not likely realize it soon, but semiautomated methods have been successfully developed.

Repository Architecture

The final dimension we will consider for comparing text analysis tools is the use of repositories. The goal of text mining is to extract valuable pieces of textual information from documents and other natural language sources. The goal of document warehousing is to utilize text mining tools to target text-based business intelligence information and integrate it with numeric-oriented data warehouse information. Text mining benefits can be achieved with any of the tools, but document warehousing is not equally well supported.

Oracle Text's tight integration with the relational database provides the most extensive support for repository operations, including a wide-ranging query capability.

IBM's Intelligent Miner for Text does not include a relational database engine but the output from the various text analysis tools is semistructured, or in a fixed format that makes it easy to load the results into relational tables.

Megaputer's TextAnalyst is not geared for tight integration with databases, but it does provide its own storage mechanism, unlike IBM Intelligent Miner for Text. The ActiveX architecture, however, provides a wide range of flexibility for programmatic control so that a lack of direct support for relational database does not preclude using the tool with a database.

Picking the Tool for the Job

As we noted at the beginning of this section, the best tool for any job is a function of the requirements of the task at hand. Here is a quick checklist of features to consider when evaluating text analysis tools:

- Is direct integration with relational databases required?
- What core text mining features are required?
  - Is feature extraction required?
  - Is thematic indexing required?
  - Do documents need to be clustered?
- How are domain-specific terms supported?
  - Are statistical analysis tools used to evaluate sample texts or is a domain-specific thesaurus required?

    - Does the vocabulary of the domain change frequently?
- Is multilingual processing required?
    - Is multilingual searching required?
    - Is lexical analysis required for multiple languages?
    - What language-specific indexing is required? For example, do the root nouns of compound nouns in German need to be indexed individually?
- Will other applications use the results of text analysis operations?
    - Do the other applications share a common database?
    - Can the data be piped into other applications using IO redirection?
    - How much programmatic control is required?

How you answer these questions will determine which main text analysis tool you should use for document warehousing or other text mining projects.

Choosing Supplemental Tools

In addition to the main text analysis tools we have described, many computational linguistic–oriented tools are now available that can supplement broad suites of text mining tools. These additional tools include end-user search tools, visualization tools, and low-level computational linguistic tools for solving a specific text analysis problem. We will now look at three representative tools:

- AltaVista Discovery
- Inxight's Hyperbolic Tree
- Teragram's language analysis tool set

AltaVista Discovery provides users with an indexing tool that spans both internal and Internet-based document sources. Inxight's Hyperbolic Tree is an example of a visualization tool that aids users in navigating richly linked hyperlinked documents. Finally, Teragram's set of tools includes programs to perform morphological analysis, text generation, and related operations.

End-User Indexing Tools: AltaVista Discovery

Our primary focus in this book is on collecting, analyzing, and storing text in a manner that allows that allows users to exploit the business intelligence value of documents. This goal can be realized in many ways, and how the products of text mining operations are presented to users is quite varied. AltaVista Discovery takes a distributed and file-oriented approach to managing text, and places control of what is indexed and analyzed in the hands of end users and not a centralized document warehouse.

The purpose of AltaVista is to allow users to search and index both local and targeted Internet files. In addition, the tool provides a summarization feature and hooks into the AltaVista search engine, allowing users to quickly find similar documents.

Searching can be limited to specific areas, such as a user's documents, browsed Web pages, or the entire Web. The tool also provides advanced Boolean searches along with date restrictions on documents.

Using AltaVista Discovery is a simple process. Several of its features, including a built-in summarization tool, automatic indexing of selected Web sites, the ability to search both local and Internet file systems, and the ability to search for similar documents, make it a useful tool for end users, providing some of the features of a document warehouse with localized control.

Another useful feature of AltaVista Discovery is a hyperbolic tree viewer that allows users to quickly see the macrostructure of a hyperlinked group of documents.

Navigating Hyperlinked Texts: Inxight's Hyperbolic Tree

The hyperbolic tree viewer developed by Inxight allows users to quickly focus on a particular area of a complex web of documents, while still maintaining a representation of surrounding context.

Some of the most important features of this tool, are:

- Color-coding of nodes and links by document type
- Text box descriptions of contents
- Thumbnail images of documents
- Visual indicators of quantity, such as the amount of text in a document
- Spotlighting target nodes

Visual cues, such as color-coded nodes and links can be useful when used with categorization and classification routines. For example, documents classified as political risk analysis stories could be one color, while international finance articles are another. Text box descriptions and thumbnail images can aid a user in quickly determining if a document is one the user has seen before and is now searching for. Visual indicators of quantity can be in the form of thermometers (bars filled in proportionally to the quantity measured) or wafers (lines emanating from a node as in Figure 11.1). Spotlighting is another technique for helping users find particular documents. When a user searches for a group of documents, those that meet the search criteria can have links to them modified (for example, with a diamond at the end of the link) so users can quickly find search results in the hyperbolic tree format.

Since hyperlinked documents are so vital to intelligent information retrieval, the number of links between documents in a particular area can be quite large. Navigating these document spaces is much more difficult than manipulating the page, column, row structure found in OLAP tools for navigating multidimensional cubes. The hyperbolic tree construct is a useful mechanism for presenting and exploring the hyperlinked structures found in document warehousing.

Building from the Ground up: Basic Linguistic Tools

By far, most document warehousing applications are best built using suites of text mining tools that combine basic linguistic operations into logical operations, such as feature extraction, summarization, and clustering. Sometimes, however, one might need a specialized tool or more programmatic control of text mining operations. In these cases, low-level linguistic analysis tool sets may be required. Here, we will consider the types of tools available for the do-it-yourself text miner. (For a more complete list of such tools and tool vendors, see the companion Web site for this book.)

When working with text mining components you can expect to find both preprocessing and text analysis tools.

The preprocessing category includes:

- Text normalizers
- Tokenizers
- Part of speech taggers
- Morphological analyzers
- Full text indexing
- Unicode and multilingual support

Text normalizes put words and terms into standard form for later analysis. Normalization can include reformatting names and dates—for example, Bill Clinton and William Clinton can be recognized as the same term and put into a canonical form, such as William Clinton. Dates can also be reformatted to a standard date format.

Tokenizers demarcate the beginning and ends of words and sentences. These tools use punctuation, white spaces, and other indicators to create a clean stream of words for later processing. Different tokenizers are required for Western and Asian languages because of the different type of alphabetic systems used by each type of language.

Feature extraction programs and other pattern matching systems frequently depend upon part of speech information. For example, in the following sentences, the word *Will* can be either a proper noun or an auxiliary verb:

> Will Johnson has been appointed Chief Operating Officer of Alpha Industries, Inc.
>
> Will Bob Johnson be appointed Chief Operating Officer of Alpha Industries, Inc?

Part of speech taggers can use both lexical and syntactic clues to correctly identify the role played by each word in a sentence.

Morphological analyzers identify the root form of words—for example, the root of *children* is *child*. These tools also provide information about the tense and number of verbs and the number and, depending upon the language, the gender of nouns.

Full text indexing tools provide the basic operations and data structures required to find text patterns quickly. Many will also provide phonetic searching and word variation operations, such as soundex functions.

Multilingual support for different character sets is important for applications that deal with the complex processing required for languages such as Japanese, Chinese, and Korean. Each of these languages can be encoded in several formats, and determining a sequence of words in these languages is more difficult than in Western languages.

In addition to these preprocessing tools, text analysis tools are frequently available as independent components. When needed, document warehouse designers can find separate tools for:

- Summarization
- Categorization and classification
- Feature extraction

These tools, like the preprocessing tools, are generally available with proprietary application programming interfaces (APIs) and thus require more custom coding than higher-level tool suites or embedded tools such as Megaputer's TextAnalyst, IBM Intelligent Miner for Text, or Oracle Text.

Choosing Web Document Retrieval Tools

Web crawlers and related tools are an important element in the document warehouse toolkit. When choosing, or developing, document retrieval tools, there are at least four areas to consider:

- Performance
- Supported protocols (HTTP, FTP, Gopher, etc.)

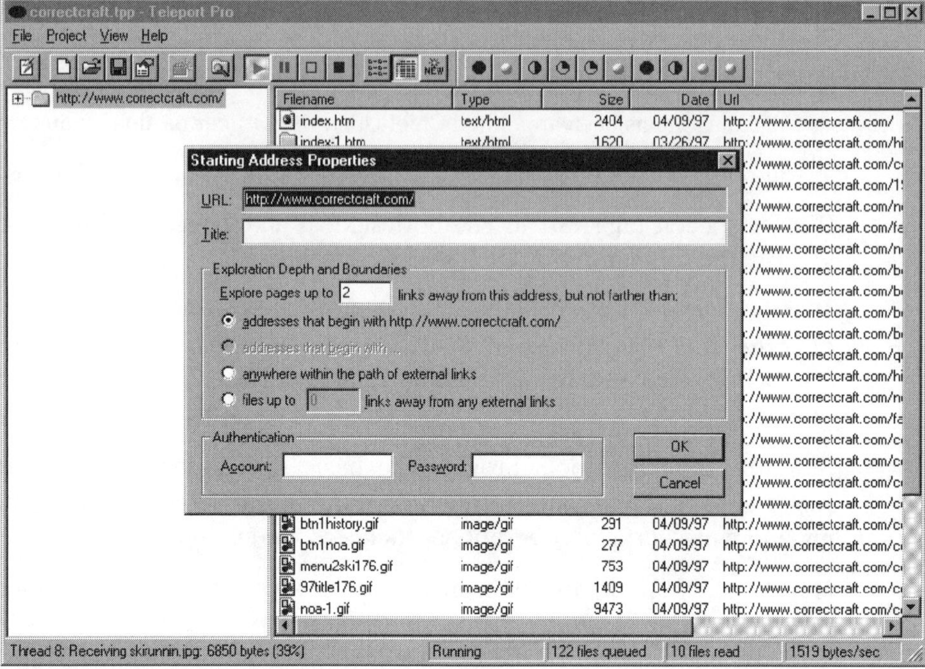

Figure 11.9 Teleport Pro provides several useful features—including a graphical interface, load balancing, and a scheduler.

- Search control
- Distributed processing

Performance is a key measure, as is support for multiple protocols. The expressiveness of search criteria, such as what document types to include and exclude, how much to retrieve, and how long to attempt to connect to a server are all part of search control.

Another, less common, feature of search tools allows crawler users to balance the load they place on servers. Some tools, such as Teleport, shown in Figure 11.9, can manage retrievals from multiple servers, thus distributing the load on servers. Although a similar load reduction scheme can be simulated by delaying successive requests to a single server, those strategies delay any processing on the searching machine.

As text mining tools become more mature, retrieval software becomes more integrated. Oracle Text supports URLs in the database, rather than entire texts. The documents are then retrieved as needed for processing or retrieval. IBM Intelligent Miner for Text also includes a Web crawler. Regardless of whether you use an embedded crawler or a third-party tool, the four key areas outlined previously should play a role in the choice of a search and retrieval tool.

Conclusions

Choosing document warehousing tools is no small task. It includes choosing text analysis tools, supplemental products such as visualization tools, and Web crawling tools. Text analysis tools offer the broadest range of options—ranging from statistical to knowledge-based to neural network approaches—and consequently are the most complex tools. Text analysis tools will change over time as new features are added and improvements are made in performance, although the range of approaches will remain relatively stable for the time being, building upon the three theoretical foundations described here. The need for supplemental tools will vary by application. In some cases, visualization is essential for navigating large document sets, but in other cases having low-level control over the text analysis process warrants the use of tool sets such as Teragram's. Finally, Web crawlers are the pipeline to the document warehouse and will find a place in any large-scale text mining operation.

We will conclude Part Two with an overview of building the document warehouse, including checklists that cover design, architecture, and maintenance issues within the document warehouse.

CHAPTER 12

Developing a Document Warehouse: A Checklist

The first eleven chapters of this book introduced the architecture and processes of document warehousing. In this chapter, we will review the basic steps in constructing a document warehouse and specifically look into five key issues:

- What to store
- Where to store documents and metadata
- What text mining services are needed
- How to populate the document warehouse
- How to maintain the warehouse

What to store is determined during the requirements gathering phase of the project. Similarly, determining what text processing services are provided by the document warehouse is done during the requirements stage. Once the content and the operations have been defined, we must decide how the documents and related metadata will be stored. Getting documents and transforming them prior to loading them into the warehouse will take considerable attention. Finally, we must have a maintenance plan in place to ensure that the quality of the warehouse does not degrade over time.

This chapter will not introduce new ideas or discuss particular text mining techniques. It does concisely describe the main points to keep in mind when developing a document warehouse. Each section will consist of a discussion of some of the most important parts of the five issues listed above, followed by a list of the steps, tasks, processes, and other operations that need to be addressed in the document warehouse process. Of course, not all steps will apply in all cases, and an indication will be provided of optional or conditional steps.

Step 1: What Should Be Stored?

The first step in document warehousing is identifying what types of documents should be available in the warehouse, locating where the data will come from, identifying the type of metadata needed, profiling user interests, and finally understanding how the document warehouse will be integrated with a data warehouse. Figure 12.1 shows some of the many different types of documents that can be stored in the document warehouse.

Understanding User Needs

Understanding user needs requires a focus on the business problem that is to be solved by the warehouse and a knowledge of where the appropriate information is to be found. Here are the main steps to understand user needs:

- Identify the target use for the document warehouse. If multiple uses are anticipated, apply these steps for each use. Some possible uses are: automatic document routing, market analysis, competitive intelligence, and augmenting the data warehouse.
- For each target use, identify key document types needed. These may include internal memos, status reports, project plans, marketing plans, contracts, negotiation notes, minutes of meetings, advertising material, and other marketing collateral material. External documents should also be included. These can include government reports such as monthly employ-

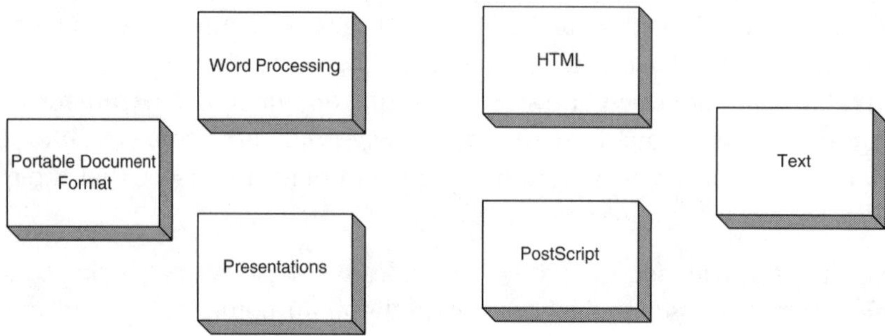

Figure 12.1 There are many possible types of documents to store in the warehouse.

ment reports, grain and cattle reports, import and export data, speeches by regulators, and safety or other regulatory notices.

- Understand the timing requirements of each document type. Does this document have only a limited useful time span? Detailed reports of stock market activity during a day may be of interest within a day or two of the report's creation, but of little value after that.
- Understand the quality control issues related to a document type. Fraudulent press releases have caused radical shifts in some companies' financial values, at least for short periods of time. It is unlikely that all documents in a warehouse can be verified with primary sources but some may warrant it.
- Identify the structure of the document types. Is XML or SGML used? If so, include the document type definition with the project documentation on each semistructured document type.
- For extremely large documents, will only portions of the document be required? If so and if the document is semistructured, define the entities that will be extracted and stored in the document warehouse. If parts will be extracted but the document does not use a markup language, define patterns to look for in the document to identify the beginning and end of interesting sections.

When this step is complete, you should have one or more target uses for the document warehouse, a list of document types, and a solid understanding of the nature of the documents.

Defining Document Sources

The next task is to identify the sources of the documents identified in the previous step. The steps involved here depend, at least to some degree, on the type of document source. Here are the steps to follow when defining document sources:

- Identify the potential sources for the needed documents. Be as specific as possible. These can include file servers, document management systems, or the Internet.
- For document types available on file servers, such as contracts, personnel memos, and other internal texts, identify precise paths and file search patterns for each type. For example, all *.doc documents in the \\HR_Serv7\Personnel_Recs\Marketing_Dept\ Performance_Appraisals directory might be evaluations of members of the marketing department that need to be included.
- Identify the frequency with which the document sources need to be periodically checked.

- Determine how new documents will be identified. Are timestamps and file names enough? In rare cases more elaborate checks, such as message digests, might be needed to determine if something has changed.
- Document access requirements for the process of copying files from the source.
- Understand any additional security requirements expected of the document warehouse for each document type. For example, contracts and other negotiation-related documents may have a limited distribution.
- In the case of document management systems, how will documents be extracted? Three standards, the Open Document Management API, the Document Management Alliance, and the WebDAV standards, are used for document management.
- List the types of Internet resources that will provide documents, such as HTTP servers, FTP servers, Gopher servers, and WAIS.
- Determine what sites should be searched. This list could be extensive and include sites provided by news organizations, government agencies, market analysis firms, industry watchdog groups, professional associations, and others.
- Determine what hub Web sites provide information related to the business area. Hub Web sites can be extremely broad, such as Yahoo!, or more focused on a particular topic.
- For each Internet site, determine what files types should be downloaded. Typically, HTML, portable document format (.pdf), word-processing documents (.doc), presentations (.ppt), spreadsheets (.xls), and PostScript (.ps) files are prime candidates for inclusion.

In addition to understanding document sources, metadata needs to be addressed as well.

Metadata

Tasks related to metadata, at this point, center around defining a content metadata schema, determining how metadata will be handled and stored within the document warehouse, identifying key pieces of information to control the search and retrieval process, and, finally, addressing quality control issues. Here are tasks to consider when specifying metadata:

- Define the metadata stored for each document. Decisions should be made to include at least as much as the Dublin Core standard.
- Determine how the metadata will be stored: embedded in the document, as is often done with Web documents, or as a separate entity in the document

warehouse. The latter is the preferred method since it allows for greater flexibility when using a relational database.

- Define the metadata required to control searching and retrieving documents from the identified sources. This can include proxy information, login identifiers and passwords, and priority specifications.
- For each document source, identify quality control metadata. Some sites are better than others in terms of content, others in terms of reliability, and still others in terms of timeliness.

User Profiles

Representing user interests is probably the most challenging area in document warehousing. In many instances, user profiles may not be needed or warranted. In cases where they are desired, be sure to at least consider the following tasks:

- First, identify users who can benefit from profiling. These include users with several interests and those who are not adequately served by classification and routing schemes.
- Group users according to similar interests. Define prototype profiles for these users that can be specialized at a later point.
- Assess how much feedback users are willing to provide. For those willing to provide limited feedback, a one-time checklist of interests is probably the best approach. If some are willing to provide more extensive feedback, including ranking the utility of many documents as to how well these meet their needs, then more elaborate machine-learning-based techniques might be warranted.
- Note particular areas of interest and the granularity of these interests. For example, are users interested in retail marketing, or are they interested in retail marketing of home electronics or retail marketing of car stereos? The types of interests that users have will guide the granularity of taxonomies and thesauri later on in the document warehousing processes. To adequately meet the needs of the users, we will need to classify documents according to user-defined areas of interest and that, in turn, requires that our taxonomies and classification schemes represent those specific interest areas.

Integration with the Data Warehouse

Data warehouses deal primary with numeric data, while document warehouses store text. Integrating the two requires building some common ground. Here are some points to remember when integrating data and document warehouses:

- Taxonomies are one way to integrate data and document warehouses through the use of shared terminology. If the data warehouse has been built, be sure to include in the document warehouse taxonomy the terms used in descriptive dimensions (if you are using a multidimensional model) or other descriptive entities (if you are using a normalized model).

- Remember when searching for text to explain a measured event in the data warehouse (for example, declining sales of a particular product line in a specific quarter) that the root of the problem may have occurred at an earlier time. Do not just search within the same time frame as the problem found in the data warehouse.
- Nonstandard terminology that is used in a data warehouse should be included in the document warehouse taxonomy as a specification of a more general standard term.

Understanding what to store begins with understanding user needs. Where to find documents that meet these needs comes next, followed by a design for document stores, metadata, and user profiling. Integration with data warehouses should also be considered from the beginning and not patched in at a later point as an afterthought. The following section moves into the issues confronted when deciding where to store text.

Step 2: Where Should It Be Stored?

Documents are rarely stored right in a document warehouse repository without some initial processing. Instead of having a single logical storage area for documents, up to three may actually be required, as shown in Figure 12.2. They are:

- Staging area
- Preprocessing area
- Document repository

The staging area is used by the retrieval agents and crawlers as the initial drop-off point for documents and Web pages. Preprocessing areas are functional areas for storing documents that require reformatting, language translation, character set mapping, or transformations before they can be passed on to analysis tools for processing. The document repository is the main storage area for the documents and associated metadata.

When working on storage area issues, these points need consideration:

- Documents retrieved by crawlers and other programs should be separated into distinct directories based upon the type of processing they will need.
- Regularly review crawler logs when search patterns are used with search engines. Some sites with valuable content can link to sites with marginally valuable content, at least from your perspective, and these sites can link to

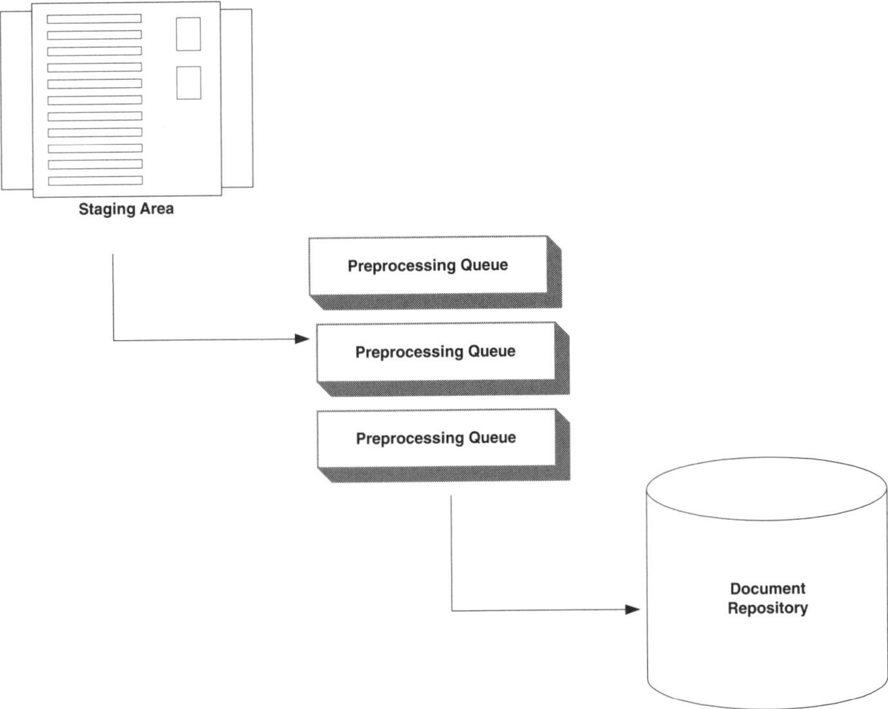

Figure 12.2 Document warehouses can have up to three distinct storage areas.

sites with useless content. The document warehouse could easily become home to a large number of useless documents.

- Unlike data warehousing, we are not sure that we want to load everything that comes from a search and retrieval operation. Delete files from the staging area that are obviously outside the domain of interest.
- If international sources may be used as document sources, be sure to include a language identification step. Many text analysis tools work only with one or two languages. Most work with English, and others, such as Megaputer's Text Analyst, have morphological analyzers for other languages. (Megaputer also provides a Russian version of Text Analyst).
- Many tools now support Unicode; if yours do not, be sure to check for Unicode documents and convert them to ASCII if necessary.
- If you expect to have many different document formats in the warehouse, consider purchasing a tool that handles file conversions between all popular document formats. Inso Corporation provides such a tool. As text analysis tools become more mature, these conversion features are being built into the tools. AltaVista Discovery and Oracle's interMedia Text both seamlessly support multiple document formats.

- Create separate processes to manage separate preprocessing operations, such as character set conversion and reformatting.
- Define transformations in a relational database structure in such a way that scripts (written in shell scripting languages, such as Perl, Python, or other portable languages) can execute the commands at regularly scheduled intervals.
- Decide upon the level of translation quality needed in the document warehouse. If rough automated translations are enough, then no additional checks are required. If high-quality translations are required, then once the automatic translation has been done, the original document and the translation should be queued for human review.
- If machine translation does not provide the quality required, consider using machine-aided translation tools, such as online dictionaries, to improve human translation efficiency.
- Determine what type of storage mechanism will be used for the document repository. For staging and preprocessing, a file system works well. The document repository could use either a file system, database system, or combination of the two. Some tools, such as IBM Intelligent Miner for Text, are file-system-centric, reading text from files and rendering results as structured text streams. Oracle's interMedia Text is integrated directly into the relational database but supports storing documents outside the database. In general, a database storage solution will provide more features, such as flexible role-based security, than a file system one.
- Metadata should always be stored in a relational database.
- Semistructured documents have a hierarchical structure that fits well into object-oriented database models. If unstructured documents are kept in the warehouse or if the document warehouse will be integrated with a data warehouse built on a relational database, then a relational database should be used for the document warehouse.
- Design security and privacy controls in from the beginning. Users can be grouped according to needs, and documents should be grouped according to access controls required.
- Develop quality control procedures to review documents, and Web sites and other document sources.

Step 3: What Text Mining Services Should Be Used?

Text mining services are numerous and varied. Not all document warehouses will need every type of text analysis service but most will require some version of the two main types of services. These are direct text analysis services (such as summarization and feature extraction) that provide output used by end users and support services that provide essential tools or information for the direct services. Support operations include creating taxonomies and training classification tools. As Figure 12.3 shows, direct services build upon support services. Some direct services are:

- Full text indexing
- Thematic indexing
- Feature extraction
- Summarization
- Clustering
- Question answering
- Classification and routing

Support services include:

- Training classification programs
- Creating taxonomy
- Creating thesauri

The following are points to guide the selection and implementation of text mining services.

Indexing Services

Indexing can be based upon both full text and topics described in documents.

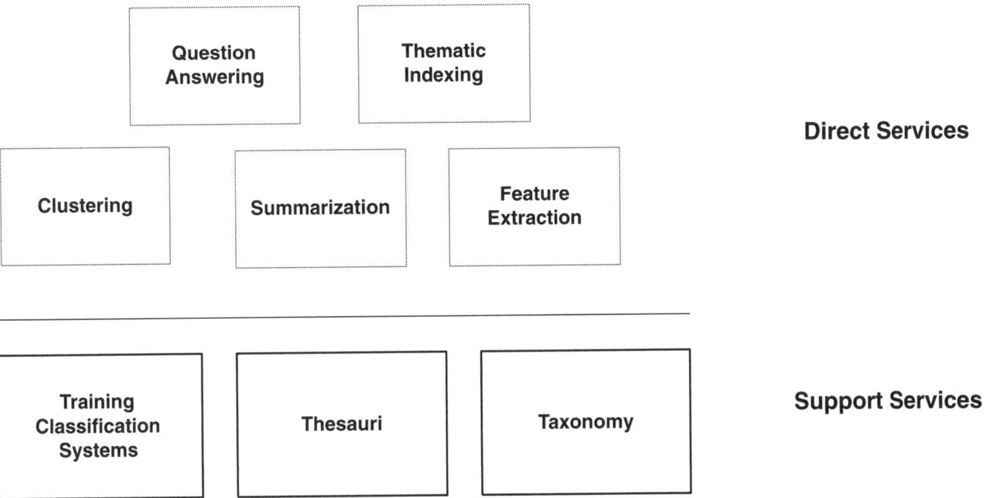

Figure 12.3 Direct text analysis services depend upon support services.

- Always provide support for full text searches.
- If the document warehouse will route documents to interested readers (this can be done by either pushing the documents to a user or adding the document to a group of documents that the reader has access to), then implement thematic indexing.

Feature Extraction

Determine the type of features that should be extracted and if additional resources, such as authority dictionaries, are required.

- For feature extraction programs, determine what types of features will be extracted. Some examples are:

  Relations

  Name

  Term

  Pattern
- Create authority dictionaries for feature extraction tools, with terms and names specific to your business.
- If the feature extraction tool provides a mechanism for complex feature types, configure it for your business requirements. These are sometimes called residue directories.

Summarization

Summarization tasks generally revolve around setting parameters for the summarization process and determining when summarization should be applied.

- Define summarization criteria, such as the percentage of the original text extracted in the summary or the number of sentences to extract. These criteria may be different for different document types.
- Do not attempt to summarize short or ungrammatical texts, such as e-mails. Feature extraction is more likely to provide useful information.
- For each document type, determine how long the document, summary, and reference will be kept in the warehouse.

Document Clustering

Multiple types of clustering can be supported in the document warehouse. Here are some points to keep in mind with regard to clustering:

- Determine if clustering will be used to support similarity searching.

- There are several types of clustering, including:

  Hierarchical

  Binary

  Fuzzy partitions

  Self-organizing maps

- Use hierarchical clustering when users will navigate from general to more specific topics. Binary clustering will keep each document in a separate cluster and works well when there is little overlap between clusters. Fuzzy partitions recognize the fact that in some document collections, one cannot make hard and fast distinctions between clusters. With fuzzy partitions, documents are members of all clusters, but to differing degrees. Finally, self-organizing maps work well in document collections with a wide range of topics that can be reduced to two-dimensional maps. Internet listserv messages have been successfully clustered with this technique.

Question Answering

When supporting question answering, consider:

- Use question answering when users want a more natural, language-oriented interface.
- Determine the types of questions users need answered. Are they direct answers to questions such as, "Where is the headquarters of IBM?" or are they process-oriented questions such as, "How do I create a batch of acetate product 7893?"
- Based upon the type of questions, choose an appropriate tool. In the case of direct questions, a feature-extraction-like question-answering tool will work, while process-oriented questions are best answered with entire documents that are likely to contain the explanation the user is seeking.

Classification and Routing

When automatic classification and routing is required, consider doing the following:

- Define the classification scheme. Each classification term should be documented with the name of the term and a brief description of the term. Descriptions should clearly differentiate terms.
- If classification will be based upon statistical pattern analysis, then collect sample documents for each distinct classification area. Ensure that training documents cover the full range of the topic.

- Develop a feedback mechanism for users to report misclassified documents. Correct classification will not occur 100 percent of the time, but if successful classification drops below 60 percent, then retrain the classification program. (Human beings can generally classify documents correctly about 70 percent of the time). Broaden the training set of documents and include the misclassified documents identified by users, ensuring that they are correctly labeled for the classification training program.

Building Taxonomies and Thesauri

In specialized domains, taxonomies or custom thesauri may need to be constructed or acquired. In those cases, consider:

- When thematic indexing is used, determine if a general taxonomy is suitable or if a specialized taxonomy is required. If the answer to this question is not obvious, provide classifications of sample documents to users based upon the taxonomy provided with your text analysis tool. Ask the following questions: Are documents sufficiently differentiated? Do too many documents end up in one classification? Are many categories left with few, if any, documents?
- If documents are not sufficiently differentiated, change the taxonomy to include specializations of the overused term. For example, if the term *financial instrument* is overused, it could be specialized with the terms *money*, *stocks*, *bonds*, *commercial paper*, and so forth.
- Consider eliminating terms if few documents are classified under those terms. This is an indication of overspecialization in the taxonomy.

Even within general areas of text analysis services, such as summarization, classification, and building taxonomies, the steps required will vary with the tool used. Summarization requires very little configuration on the part of the document warehouse administrator. Classification, however, can require significant preparation in terms of identifying classification categories and developing training set samples.

Once the document warehouse has been designed and the tools and text services identified, the next step is populating the repository.

Step 4: How Should the Warehouse Be Populated?

Populating the warehouse is generally done from internal file systems, document management systems, and the Internet. Figure 12.4 depicts the need for

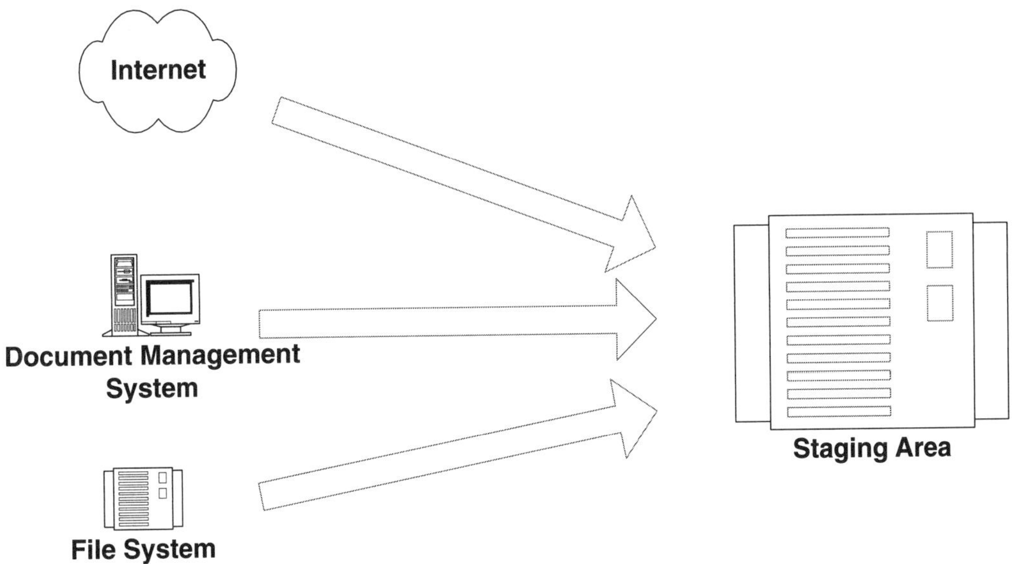

Figure 12.4 Populating the warehouse requires multiple search and retrieval processes.

multiple processes to collect documents from various types of sources. Here are the points to watch out for when developing the document warehouse analog to the data warehouse extraction process.

Crawlers

Crawlers can be configured to meet the needs of many different retrieval scenarios:

- Crawlers can easily retrieve large numbers of documents if limits are not placed on retrieval commands. If a crawler is allowed to span Web sites, do not recursively search lower than five levels.
- Provide a means for users to manually add documents to the warehouse. Ideally, users should add documents to the staging areas appropriate for each document type so that they are preprocessed and analyzed correctly. A generic staging area can be provided for user-supplied documents that provides basic preprocessing, including character set conversion, formatting, and machine translation. Rather than using a fixed set of transformations for this generic staging area, transformation can be based upon simple tests. For example, only documents over a certain size will be summarized, but presentation slides will not be summarized in any case.

- If your crawler provides an option for it, set a limit on the cumulative size of documents retrieved.
- Check the robot.txt file on Web sites to ensure that a crawler is not used on a server that does not allow them.
- When possible, extend the time between requests to the same server to minimize the demands placed on Web sites being searched.
- Use timestamping to prevent duplicate copies of documents from being included in the warehouse.

Searching

Since the document warehouse supports a range of search criteria, the following criteria should be considered.

- Become familiar with the syntax of searches for search engines that will be used in the warehouse.
- When using keyword searches, use as many specific terms as possible to improve the precision of the search.
- Use the "find similar" feature of search engines to find documents related to a prototype document. Documents ranked highly useful by end users make good prototypes.
- Find similar documents to top documents returned by keyword searches to expand the breadth of the search.
- When defining search patterns, control for escape characters, such as quotation marks, that have to be specified by using a character code. The Perl module, URI::Escape provides the uri_escape function that reformats a URL using only legal characters.
- For each search, define the number of documents that will be retrieved for the search and how many levels should be recursively searched. When general searches are specified, use caution when searching beyond the Web site of the original document returned by the search engine.
- Use a scripting language for retrieving documents from internal sources. Perl and Python are excellent choices. Both provide a wealth of file manipulation operations that are useful for this task.
- Schedule search and retrieval operations for nonpeak hours.

Once the warehouse has been created and populated, the workload shifts to maintenance.

Step 5: How Should the Warehouse Be Maintained?

The key operations for maintaining the document warehouse focus on quality control, maintaining user profiles, and controlling access and meeting other security and privacy concerns. Unlike data warehousing, where we can assume that if a data source is identified by an end user it has relevant data, document sources can produce useless as well as important content in the document warehouse. The review process is the critical step in monitoring and controlling the content of the warehouse and should not be overlooked Consider the following steps in your quality control plan:.

- Quality management is essentially a manual process. Develop a review process that includes sampling documents in the warehouse and assessing the value of the documents to the enterprise's needs in business intelligence.
- Utilizing user reviews, track the quality of document sources and eliminate or minimize the use of poor-quality sites.
- Review search and retrieval logs to ensure that processes do not run for an unusually long period of time, retrieve an unusually large number of documents, or take up an inordinate amount of storage.
- Review security and privacy requirements with document owners. If copies of sensitive documents are kept in the warehouse, review lists of users with access to the documents.
- Review user profiles and adjust search and retrieval programs according to user interests. If some areas are of particular interest, then increase the resources dedicated to finding those topics. Similarly, reduce the effort spent finding little-used document types.

Conclusions

Developing and maintaining a document warehouse is a multifaceted project. As with any application, the needs of the end user must be understood. Trying to meet all possible needs at once will lead to an overloaded document warehouse that does not meet its objectives. Using automated retrieval mechanisms, such as crawlers and search engines, the document warehouse can be quickly populated with rich sources of textual information. Preprocessing is a rather unglamorous but essential step in document warehousing. If documents are not in appropriate formats, languages, or character sets, the results could be useless. Also, use quality control measures to ensure that the content provided in the warehouse continues to meet the needs of the enterprise and that the text analysis services used in the warehouse are targeted to particular business intelligence needs. Following the steps outlined previously will help to ensure that the document warehouse is built according to business objectives and maintained in manner that will allow it to continue to meet those objectives.

This concludes the document warehousing section of the book, and we will now turn our attention to the details of text mining and how we can apply text mining techniques to operational, business intelligence, and related needs of an organization.

PART THREE

Text Mining

CHAPTER 13

What Is Text Mining?

Text mining is the art and science of extracting information and knowledge from text. As we shall see in this chapter, the role of the document warehouse is to provide a structured repository for conducting text mining and related business intelligence operations. The practice of text mining builds upon a number of related disciplines that we have encountered earlier in this book, in particular:

- Information retrieval (IR)
- Computational linguistics
- Pattern recognition

After providing a formal definition of text mining, we will examine in detail the particular contributions each of these disciplines has made to the practice of text mining. This section is designed for those interested in the details and algorithms of these domains—those who do not feel the need to look under the hood of text mining may want to skip it. Next, we will discuss how to conduct text mining operations using a data mining process model—the Cross-Industry Standard Process Model for Data Mining (CRISP-DM)—as a guide. With an understanding of the nature of text mining and how to practice it, we will turn our attention to explaining how document warehouses support text mining. The chapter will end with a brief look into some applications of text mining in the business environment.

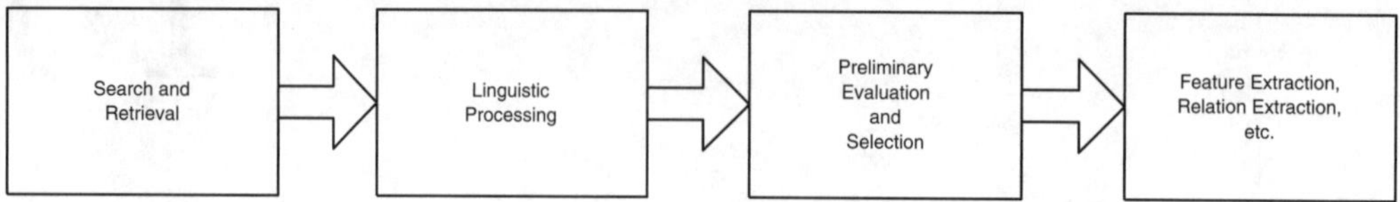

Figure 13.1 Extracting business intelligence from text requires several steps, each dependent upon a distinct technology or approach.

The process of text mining builds upon the other preliminary tasks we have addressed in the first part of this book. As Figure 13.1 shows, extracting the business intelligence value of text requires several steps, beginning with the compilation of a document collection. That operation is followed by the linguistic processing of the documents in the collection, the evaluation and exploration of those documents, and then the extraction of features and relationships from a target set of documents relative to a particular business problem.

Defining Text Mining

Text mining is a relatively new discipline and, like many new areas of inquiry, is hard to pin down with a generally agreed-upon definition. In fact, if you were to look through research and commercial application literature, you could find several different definitions. We will consider two commonly used classes of definitions. Each of these represents a different perspective on text mining and can include a number of variations.

The first definition is the broadest, and identifies text mining with any operation related to gathering and analyzing text from external sources for business intelligence purposes. This encompasses both Web farming as defined by Richard D. Hackathorn (1999) and the practice of document warehousing developed here. Web farming is the process of searching for external sources of information related to an area of interest. Web farming is a useful practice and can provide much useful information but it is not text mining in the most precise sense of the term.

The second class of definitions defines text mining as the discovery of previously unknown knowledge in text. This definition takes the mining metaphor more seriously by looking for nuggets of information that can be logically grouped to allow users to draw conclusions that had not been made previously. One example of this type of text mining involves searching through scientific literature to find links between related studies. A text mining researcher found that magnesium deficiencies may be related to migraines by extracting features from a broad-ranging set of medical research literature on migraines and nutrition. Some of the extracted nuggets, as described in (Hearst 1999) include:

- Stress is associated with migraines.
- Stress can lead to a loss of magnesium.
- Calcium channel blockers prevent some migraines.
- Magnesium is a natural calcium channel blocker.
- Spreading cortical depression (SCD) is implicated in some migraines.
- High levels of magnesium inhibit SCD.
- Migraine patients have high platelet aggregability.
- Magnesium can suppress platelet aggregability.

Although this series of facts was discovered by using text mining techniques, the magnesium link to migraines has received support from clinical research as well.

The core of this type of text analysis operation is the extraction of key features—such as the fact that magnesium blocks calcium channels—and then the linking of those features into logical causal or relational chains. As Figure 13.2 shows, researchers and analysts can only keep abreast of limited areas of knowledge, whether we are talking about migraine research or marketing analysis. Unfortunately, these knowledge workers sometimes miss important facts because they do not have time to read material in related areas. The benefit of text mining is that we can discover chains of logical and causal

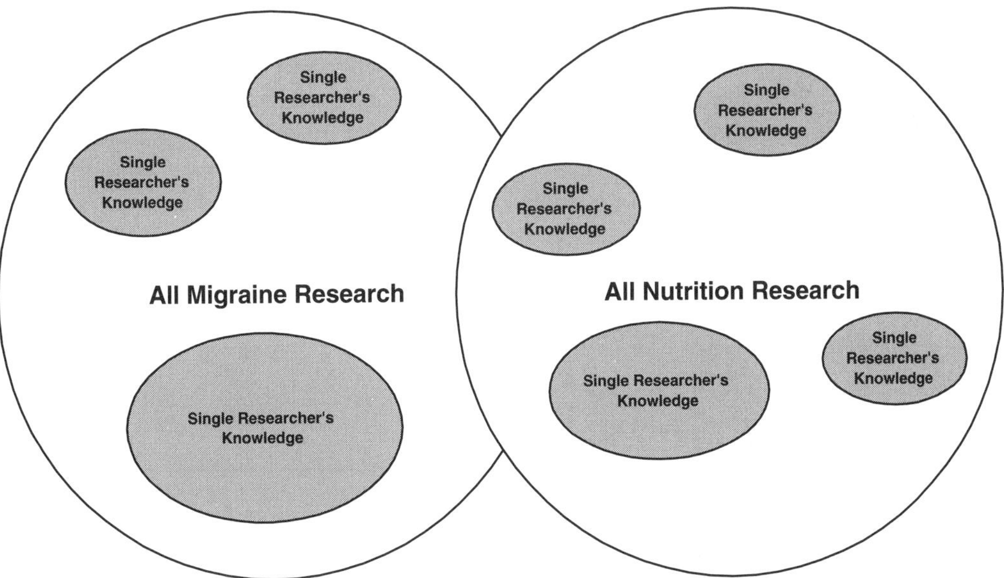

Figure 13.2 No one can know entire domains of research. Spanning multiple domains is even more difficult.

connections in large document collections (for example, medical research literature) that no human could possibly analyze on his or her own.

The product of this second and stricter definition of text mining is the discovery of facts that no one knew before. The product of the broader, information-retrieval-based definition is the identification and delivery of text to users searching for particular topics. In this case, no new knowledge is discovered but existing information is made known to someone who was previously unaware of it. So, although I may not know what the chairman of the Federal Reserve Board said about interest rates and productivity, I can find that information by using information retrieval techniques.

In this work, we will use the broader definition of text mining with the understanding that the goal of the process includes both making existing information available to decision makers and discovering new knowledge through analysis of extracted features. The formal definition of text mining is:

> Text mining is the process of compiling, organizing, and analyzing large document collections to support the delivery of targeted types of information to analysts and decision makers and to discover relationships between related facts that span wide domains of inquiry.

From this definition, we can see that several supporting operations are required in text mining. First, relevant documents must be identified in large collections of potentially relevant texts. This problem has been addressed by information retrieval research. Second, business information must be identified in the text. This is done by using both computational linguistics and natural language processing techniques. Finally, patterns and relationships within the core, extracted information must be found. This type of analysis is the province of data mining and machine learning. In the next section, we will look at how each of these related disciplines supports the text mining processes. Since some related material has been discussed in the context of document warehousing (for example, the summarization and categorization of documents), it will not be repeated here. Instead, we will take a lower-level look into other areas and discuss the building blocks of each so we may have a better understanding of the potential and limits of text mining.

Foundations of Text Mining

Text mining did not emerge from an intellectual vacuum but grew from a number of related disciplines that developed techniques useful for solving the problem of extracting business intelligence from text. Four of the most important are described below, followed by a discussion of how they interrelate to solve the problems faced in text mining.

Information Retrieval

Information retrieval (IR) has developed models for representing large collections of text that lend themselves to finding documents about particular topics. IR is a broad field with many subject areas but our primary interest is in how to represent and identify documents about a particular set of topics. We will look at two methods, the vector space model and latent semantic indexing. The first is a basic representation scheme used in many IR techniques. The second has been developed in response to some of the limitations of the vector space model, particularly the problems of synonymy and polysemy.

When discussing both the basic vector space model and latent semantic indexing, we will use some basic concepts from trigonometry and linear algebra. These are provided for the interested reader but can be skipped without loss of continuity in the general explanation. We will delve into the details because they provide a foundation for understanding document collections as a geometric space and documents as points in that space. Since similar documents tend to cluster together, we can envision groupings as in Figure 13.3.

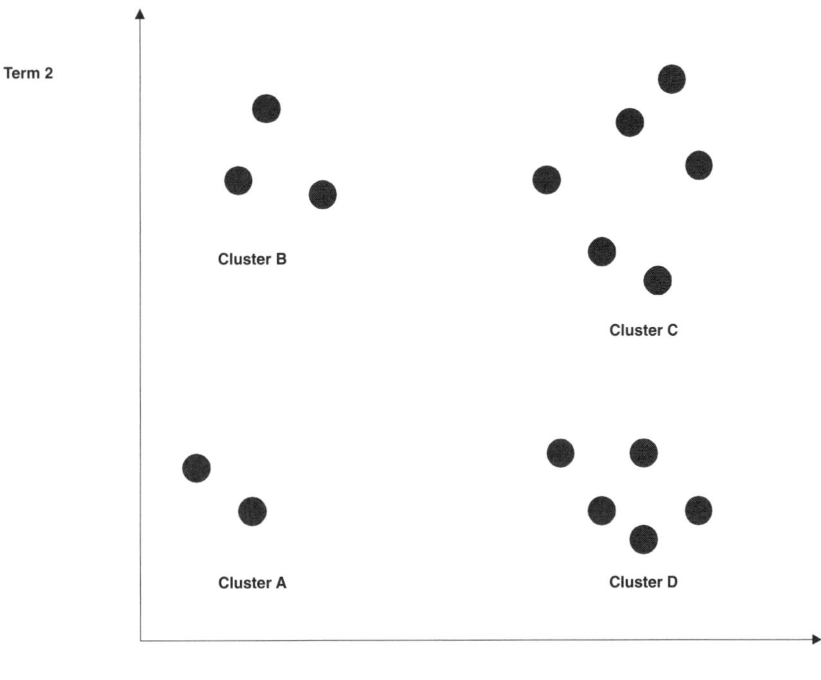

Figure 13.3 Document clusters can form around similar documents. IR techniques work well for finding documents within clusters.

Some of the greatest potential value of text mining techniques lies in spanning multiple clusters. For example, researchers working on migraines may tend to read literature in one cluster, while nutritionists tend to read another, and neither is aware of the common ground between them. With the aid of a text mining process model and text mining algorithms for extracting common features, readers can expand the sweep and effectiveness of text-based research.

Efficient Document Representation: Vector Space Model

The vector space model efficiently addresses three problems in information retrieval:

- Representing documents
- Representing queries
- Finding documents that meet a query's criteria

The vector space model solves the first two problems using the same geometric representation. The solution to the third problem follows naturally from the representation scheme, as we shall now see.

Representing Documents in a Vector Space

One of the basic problems addressed by IR is to efficiently retrieve documents that meet the criteria of a specific query. Ideally, a query should be represented in a form similar to the representation of the documents that are searched. For example, if a query is a simple list of keywords such as:

```
magnesium AND calcium AND migraine
```

then we would want documents to be represented in a similar manner, such as:

```
document 1:  magnesium AND zinc AND hypertension
document 2:  migraine AND sleep deprivation
document 3:  hypertension AND sodium AND calcium
```

The advantage of this approach is that an IR system does not need to compile a query down into an execution plan as we have to in relational database queries. Instead, the query can be executed by comparing a list of keywords. While the spirit of this naive approach is the basis of most IR searches, such a linear search is far too inefficient. A better approach is to search for all keywords at once. So instead of searching for *magnesium*, *calcium*, and *migraine* sequentially, we should do it in a single operation. This, however, requires that we first reduce the three-term representation of the query to a single object representation, and the way to do this is with a vector space model.

Consider a simple example. Let us assume that we are interested in documents about migraines and magnesium. At the very least we have four possible combinations that can describe documents:

- About migraines and about magnesium
- About migraines and not about magnesium
- Not about migraines and about magnesium
- Not about migraines and not about magnesium

We can map these two-term combinations into points on a two-dimensional grid. In this example, the documents are represented by a pair of numbers, one for *migraines* and one for *magnesium*. If *migraines* is present, then the first number is a 1; otherwise it is a 0. Similarly, if the term *magnesium* is in the document, then the second number is a 1; otherwise it is 0. Thus, a document with the terms *migraine* and *magnesium* is represented as (1,1), and a document without *migraines* but with *magnesium* is represented as (0, 1).

Now, let's move to the next level of complexity. Assume that we can measure the relative frequency of the terms *migraine* and *magnesium*. If *migraine* appears more frequently than *magnesium*, then the corresponding number should reflect that weight. When the document is primarily about magnesium, its number will be greater. Figure 13.4 shows how two such documents can be mapped to a two-dimensional grid. The document closer to the migraine axis has a value of (0.8, 0.3), while the document closer to the magnesium axis has a value of (0.2, 0.75).

Additional terms can be added to the model by adding another dimension to the geometric representation. Figure 13.5 shows a three-dimensional space that can now model the relative weight of the term *calcium* in addition to the terms *migraine* and *magnesium*. Now, the numeric representation of these documents becomes a list of three numbers, such as (0.5, 0.63, 0.25).

This pattern of adding dimensions to represent additional terms can be continued as many times as needed. Since we cannot easily represent higher dimensions on two-dimensional surfaces, we will have to use algebraic notation for these higher-dimensional models. If we needed to model four terms, then we would use (weight of term 1, weight of term 2, weight of term 3, weight of term 4), and for n distinct terms we would use (weight of term 1, weight of term 2, weight of term 3, ... , weight of term n).

Representing Queries in a Vector Space

Regardless of how many dimensions we use, an important benefit of this approach to representing documents is that a query can be represented using the

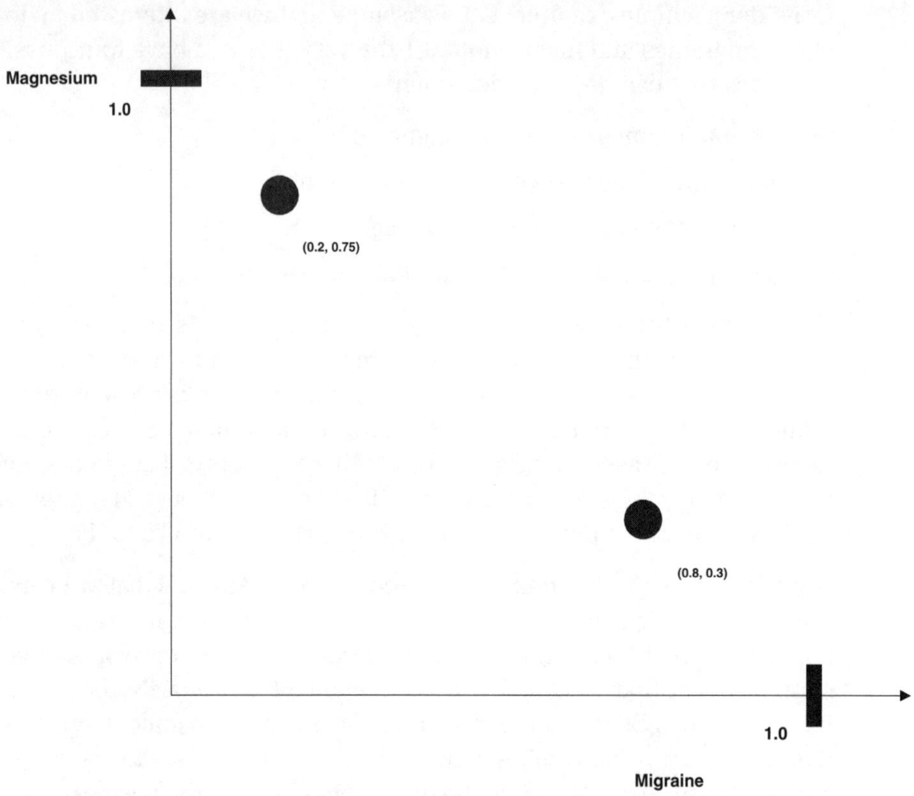

Figure 13.4 Relative weights can be modeled using real number values to represent the presence of a term in a document.

same method. Let us assume that we have indexed a collection of documents using 100 terms. Term 1 is *migraine*, term 2 is *magnesium*, term 3 is *calcium*, term 4 is *platelet*, term 5 is *hypertension*, term 6 is *steroid*, and so on to term 100. For any given document, many of the term weights will be 0. For example, the documents in Table 13.1 vary in topics, and the term vectors reflect that.

In the case of documents, the weight of terms can be calculated by using several different measures, most of which are based upon the terms' frequency in the document and overall frequency in the entire document collection. A query is usually just a series of terms. (Actually, this is a gross simplification, since we are not even considering a simple operation such as NOT or any of the other Boolean, proximity, or search operators used in an IR system. However, we can safely work within this assumption since our intent here is to explain the vector space model and not to specify exactly how an IR system functions.)

A query for all documents about migraines and hypertension could be expressed as a vector with nonzero values in the first and fifth coordinate positions, such as:

```
(0.8, 0, 0, 0, 0.8, 0,0,0,0,0, ....)
```

The weights of each term could be adjusted by using operators to indicate the relative importance of each term. If hypertension is three times more important than migraines to the user, then the query

```
migraine AND hypertension * 3
```

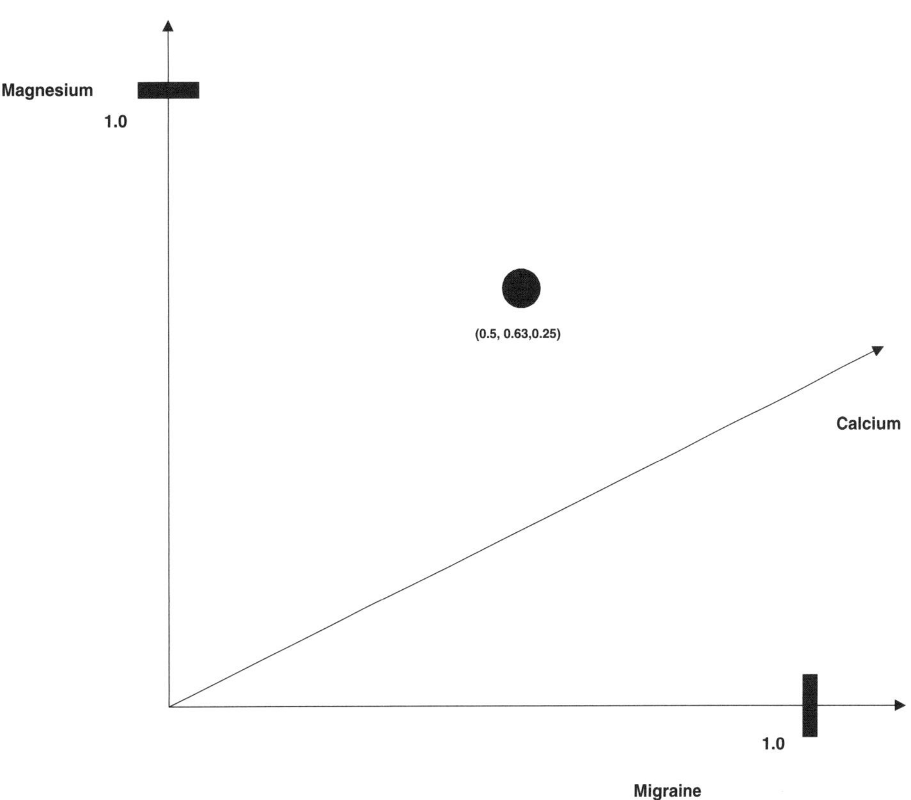

Figure 13.5 Adding an additional dimension allows us to model the relative weight of another term.

Table 13.1 Term Vectors Indicate the Relative Weight of Significant Terms in Individual Documents

DOCUMENT TOPIC	TERM VECTOR
Migraine, magnesium, platelet	(0.85, 0.75, 0, 0.6,0,0,0,0,0,0,......)
Platelets, hypertension	(0,0,0,0.93,0.64,0,0,0,0,0,0,0,......)
Calcium, hypertension	(0,0,0.87,0,0.87,0,0,0,0,0,0,0,......)
Migraine, steroid, calcium	(0.75,0,0.48,0,0,0.82, ...)

(using Oracle interMedia Text syntax) would be mapped into a vector such as:

```
(0.33, 0, 0, 0, 1.0, 0,0,0,0,0, ....)
```

Now we have the means to represent documents on the basis of the relative frequency of the terms. The vector space model does not require any particular measure of frequency, only that documents about similar topics should fall near each other. It is this element of the vector space model that makes the retrieval of similar documents relatively straightforward.

Document Retrieval in the Vector Space Model

Since the vector space model is a geometric representation of documents and queries, it is not surprising that the way we measure how well a document matches a query also has a geometric interpretation. As Figure 13.6 shows, documents and queries can be understood as points in an n-dimensional space, where n is the number of indexed terms. Like frequency measures, there is no single approach to measuring similarity. One simple approach is to calculate the Euclidean distance between two points.

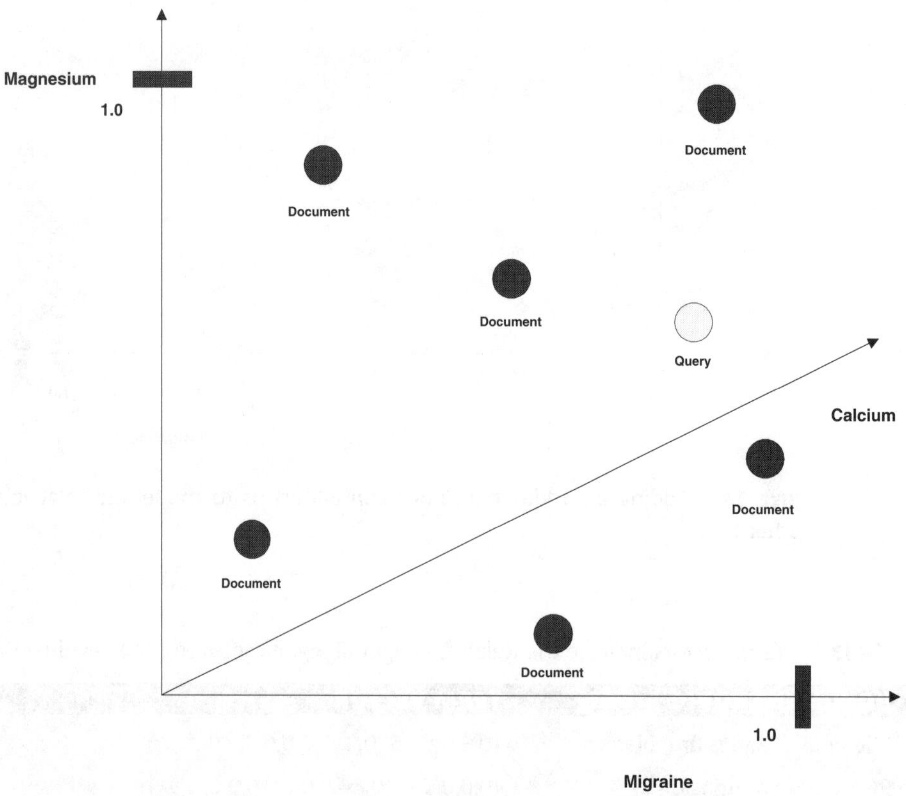

Figure 13.6 In the vector space model, documents are reduced to points representing the intersection of key words and terms.

From early algebra, we recall that the distance between two points (x_1,y_1) and (x_1,y_1) is calculated as the square root of $(x_1 - x_2)^2 + (y_1 - y_2)^2$. Another, and more common technique in IR for calculating similarity requires a little trigonometry. Rather than calculating the distance between points, we work with the angle between lines that can be drawn from the origin of the vector space to the points representing the documents and queries. Figure 13.7 shows how we can think of documents and queries as lines, or vectors, and not just as points in a space.

The most common angle measurement used as a similarity measure, is the cosine of the angle between two vectors, where each vector is a line from the origin of the space to the point specified by the feature weights. This idea is best explained with an example. To keep the diagrams simple, we will work with a two-dimensional space. Figure 13.8 shows a space where we can map documents about migraines and magnesium. We have three documents in our collection with the following weights:

```
Doc1 = (0.8, 0.2)
Doc2 = (0.5, 0.5)
Doc3 = (0.3, 0.4)
```

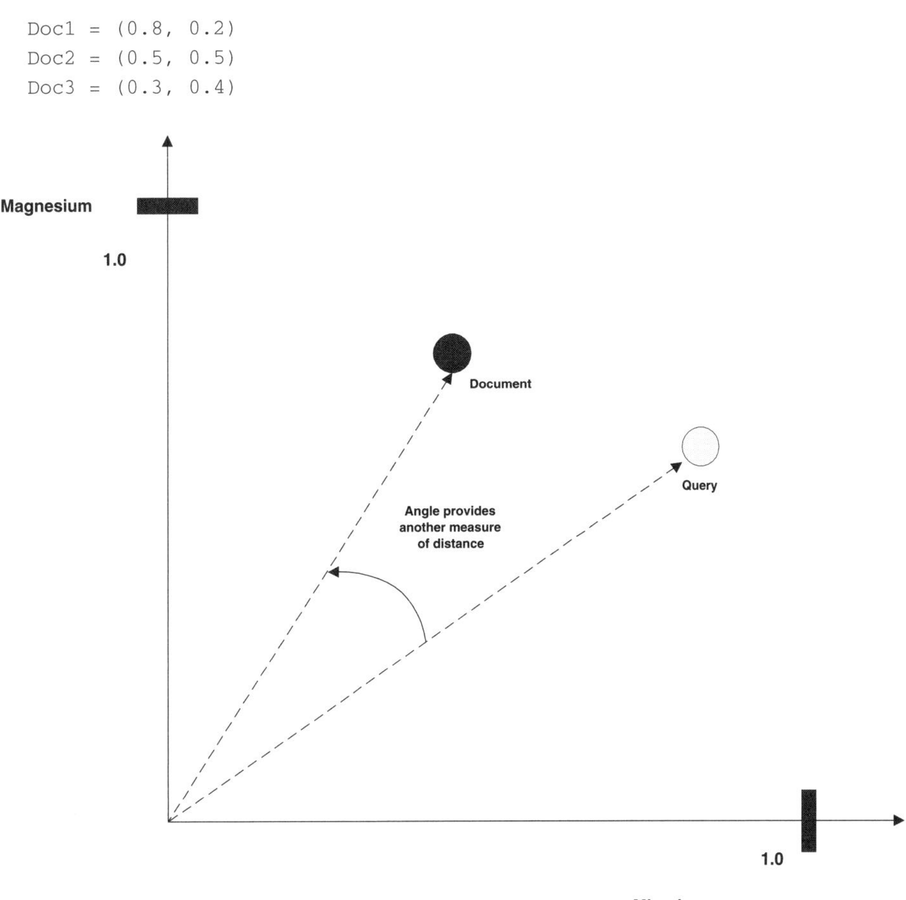

Figure 13.7 When we think of documents and queries in terms of lines, instead of just points, we can work with properties between lines, such as their angle, to develop other similarity measures.

where the first weight is the relative frequency of the term *migraine*, and the second weight is the relative frequency of *magnesium*.

Now let's add a query. We will use

```
Query1 =  (1.0, 1.0)
```

as our query, since we are looking for documents that are equally about migraines and magnesium. Figure 13.9 shows the addition of the query.

Now, let's add a little more notation. First, we will denote the length of the line, or vector, representing a document as || DocN ||, where N is the document's number. Second, we will refer to the first coordinate of the document or query as DocN(1) or QueryN(1) and the second coordinate as DocN(2) or Query1(2). For example, referring to the three document vectors listed earlier, Doc1(1) = 0.8, Doc2(2) = 0.5, and Query1 (1) = 1.0. Finally, let us call the angle between the Query and any document DocN as SN, for example S1, S2, and S3 since these are measures of similarity. Figure 13.10 shows where these angles occur.

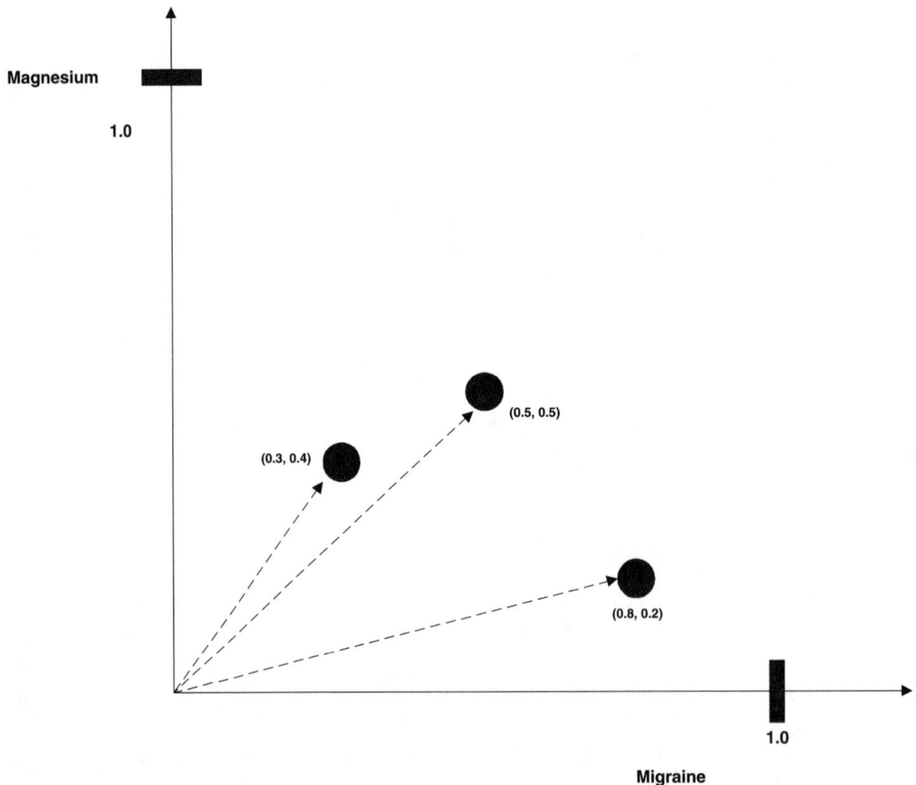

Figure 13.8 This diagram depicts the representation of three documents about migraines and magnesium.

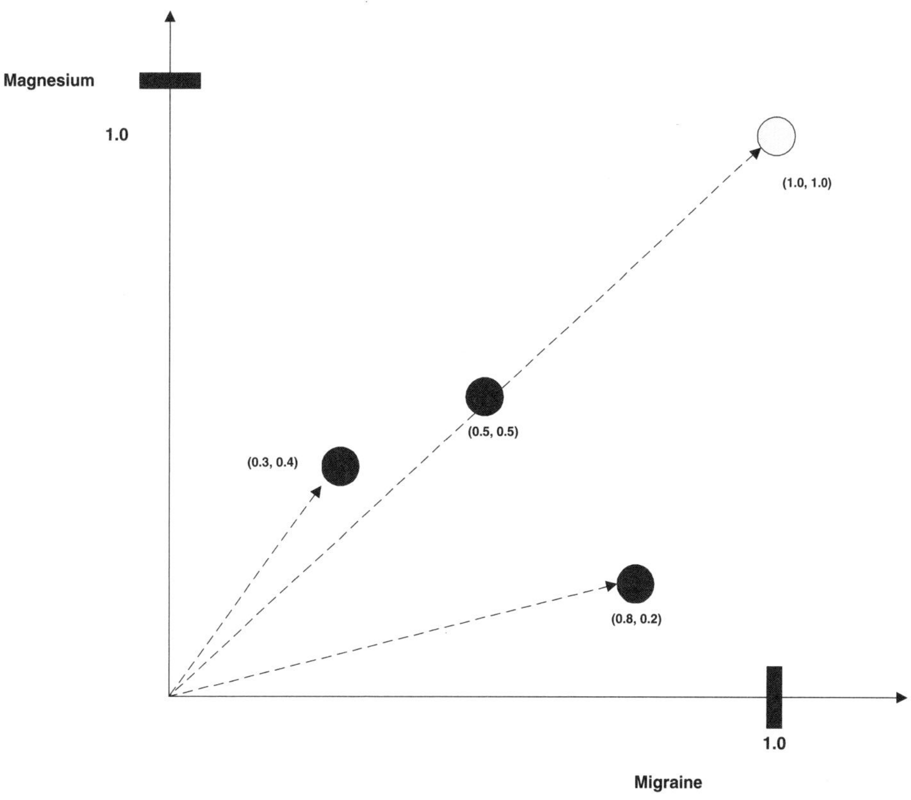

Figure 13.9 Queries are represented as vectors as well in the vector space model.

It is finally time for the real work. To calculate the cosine of angle S1, we use the formula:

```
cos S1 = [Doc1(1)*Query(1)] + [Doc1(2)*Query(2)]
         ___________________________________________
                      ||Doc1|| * ||Doc2||
```

To determine which documents to return as a result of the query, we would calculate the cosine of the angle between the query and each document. Then either all documents with a cosine over a predefined threshold or a fixed number of documents would be returned.

We have now discussed two basic similarity measures, each of which can return either a fixed number of documents or only those documents whose similarity to the query exceeds some threshold. Intuitively, these models seem reasonable, but in practice they can run into problems when we need to index a large number of terms.

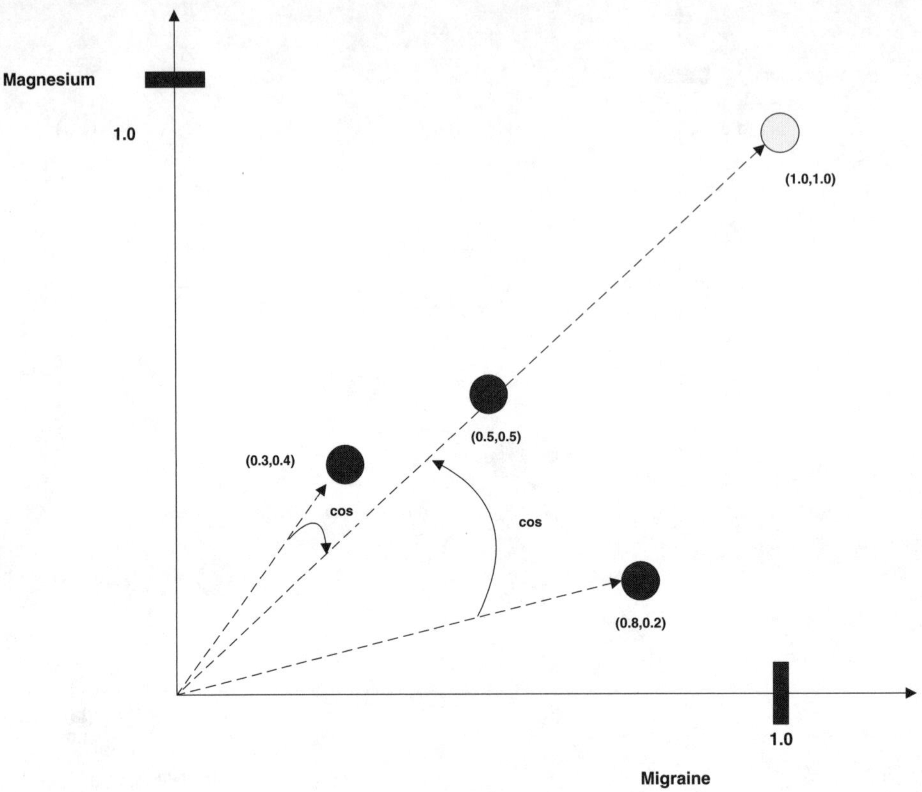

Figure 13.10 The cosines of the angles between the query and each document are often used as similarity measures.

Limits of the Vector Space Model

In production environments, it is not uncommon to deal with thousands or tens of thousands of distinct terms, many of which are not used in any given document. The result is that the dimensional models are extremely sparse in some areas; for example there are few documents that cover three widely different areas at once, such as migraines, microbreweries, and foreign policy. At the same time, there are areas where documents will tend to cluster such as around migraines and pain relief or monetary policy and inflation. This clustering of terms provides the opportunity to take on two different types of problems with the vector space model.

First, if we create a dimension for each distinct term used in a document collection, we will have to work with thousands or tens of thousands of terms. Even when we remove extremely frequent words (stop words), we can still have an extremely high number of dimensions to deal with.

The second problem we address is actually composed of the two ubiquitous issues of synonymy (the existence of multiple words that mean the same thing) and polysemy (the fact that a single word can have multiple meanings). One approach to reducing the number of dimensions also minimizes the effect of synonymy and polysemy at the same time. The name of this apparent silver bullet technique is latent semantic indexing.

Latent Semantic Indexing

A long-recognized problem in information retrieval is that users look for documents about a particular concept, while IR systems index documents by particular terms. It therefore falls on the user to map the desired concept into appropriate terms. Deerwester and colleagues (Deerwester, et al. 1990) identified three core problems with this approach.

- Incomplete indexes
- No automatic method to address polysemy
- Poor support for co-occurring words

The first problem, that of incomplete indexes, stems from the fact that indexes usually contain far fewer terms than users expect to use when querying the document collection. The lack of terms in the index stems from the fact that the documents themselves often do not contain the terms that users expect to be available to them. In some cases the terms may be in the document but are not indexed because they do not pass a filtering criteria used by the IR system.

Multiple meanings of words can be dealt with in a couple of ways. First, controlled vocabularies can be specified so that words with multiple meanings are eliminated or severely reduced in number. This obviously creates more work for IR system developers, who have to formulate the controlled vocabulary, as well as for users, who have to learn or at least reference the vocabulary when using the system. A second approach is to require users to specify additional terms to disambiguate polysemous words. For example, if a user searches for documents with the word *draft*, they would also have to specify one or more terms such as:

Document, proposal, white paper

Conscription, military, war

Withdrawal, check

With these additional terms, the IR system can distinguish whether the meaning of *draft* is a preliminary version of a document, an order of conscription into military service, or a bank transaction. This approach places additional work on the user, who has to recognize polysemous words and find additional terms related to the target meaning.

A third problem that has been addressed in some text mining systems, such as Megaputer's TextAnalyst, is that terms that frequently appear together are not treated differently from terms that rarely appear together. The term *organic* frequently occurs with *compound* and *chemistry*, and their occurrence in the same document should be weighted more heavily than terms that do not appear as frequently, such as *stereo* and *desktop*. The scoring of these terms can produce skewed results to unknown degrees (see Deerwester, et al. 1990).

Latent semantic indexing addresses these three problems by getting at the underlying meaning, or latent semantics, of documents. It should be pointed out right from the beginning that latent semantic indexing does not use the semantic content of words or concepts but rather statistical and linear algebraic techniques to find clusters of terms. These clusters of terms represent concepts, such as organic chemistry, information systems, fiscal policy, political risk analysis, and data resource quality. These clusters are not predefined but are calculated on the basis of techniques that estimate the likelihood of the occurrence of one term, given another term.

Let's look at an example. Table 13.2 shows a list of documents down the side and a list of index terms across the top. Each cell represents the presence or absence of the term in the document. For simplicity, we will assume that the weights are binary—if the term appears at all in the document, then the weight is 1; otherwise it is 0.

The terms *debt* and *deficit* appear together in documents 1, 3, 4, and 6. The terms *debt*, *deficit*, and *federal* appear together in documents 1 and 3. If a user queries for the terms *federal deficit*, then documents 1 and 3 match. If the user then queries for *federal debt* and *deficit*, then documents 1, 3, 4, and 6 match, but document 5 does not. Clearly document 5 is about the topic of deficit spending, bonds, which are used to fund deficit spending, and taxes, which are used to pay the interest on bonds that fund the deficit, which in turn become debt. In our trivial example, a human evaluator would have probably considered docu-

Table 13.2 The Co-Occurrence of Significant Terms in a Document Used to Determine Semantically Related Terms

DOC	DEBT	DEFICIT	FEDERAL	FISCAL	BONDS	TAXES
Doc 1	1	1	1	0	0	0
Doc 2	0	0	1	0	0	1
Doc 3	1	1	1	0	1	1
Doc 4	1	1	0	0	1	0
Doc 5	0	1	0	0	1	1
Doc 6	1	1	0	1	1	1

ment 5 a match to the user's query, but it failed to match the query because the document did not mention the term *debt*. Latent semantic indexing provides something of a middle ground between automatic term indexing, which misses documents that should be returned, and human evaluation that works with conceptual models of document topics. In latent semantic indexing, concepts are statistically approximated by finding terms that occur frequently together, such as *federal*, *deficit*, and *debt*. In a basic vector space model, these three terms require three dimensions, as shown in Figure 13.11.

Given that the three terms occur so frequently together, we can approximate the three dimensions with a single dimension, or a line. As Figure 13.12 shows, a document with the *federal-deficit-debt* term collection is at position one; documents without the concept are at position 0.

Of course we lose some accuracy when we reduce the number of dimensions, because documents that have only two of the terms will still appear at the same point on the line as those documents that have all three terms. This lack of accuracy is exactly what we want from latent semantic indexing. Just because a document does not have the term *debt* does not mean the document is not about the

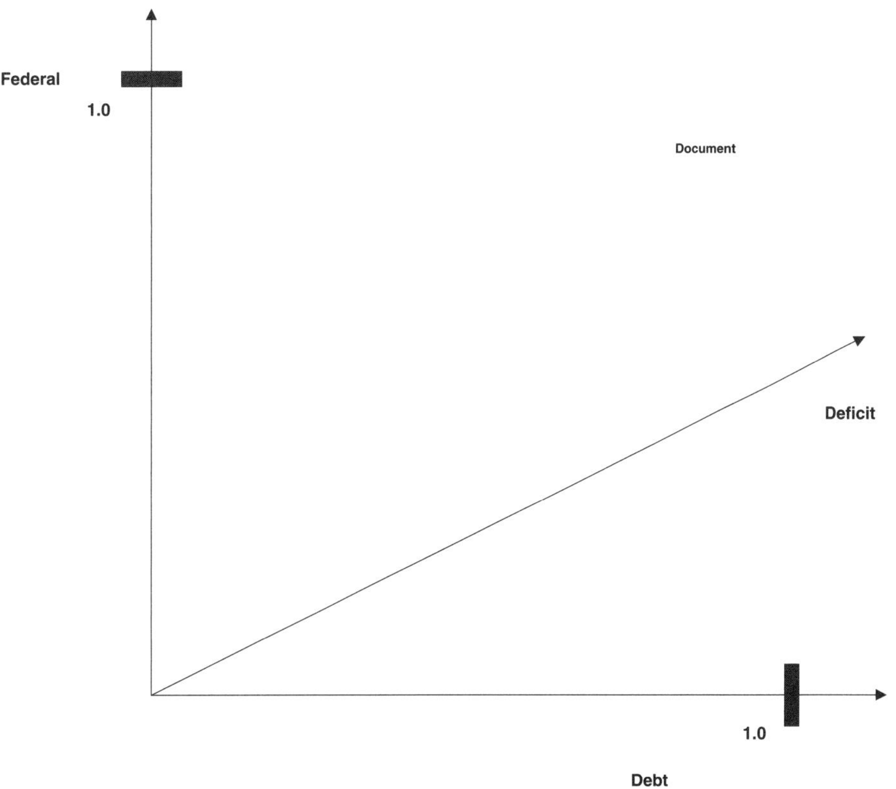

Figure 13.11 Basic vector space models use one dimension for each term, even if documents tend to cluster around a single point.

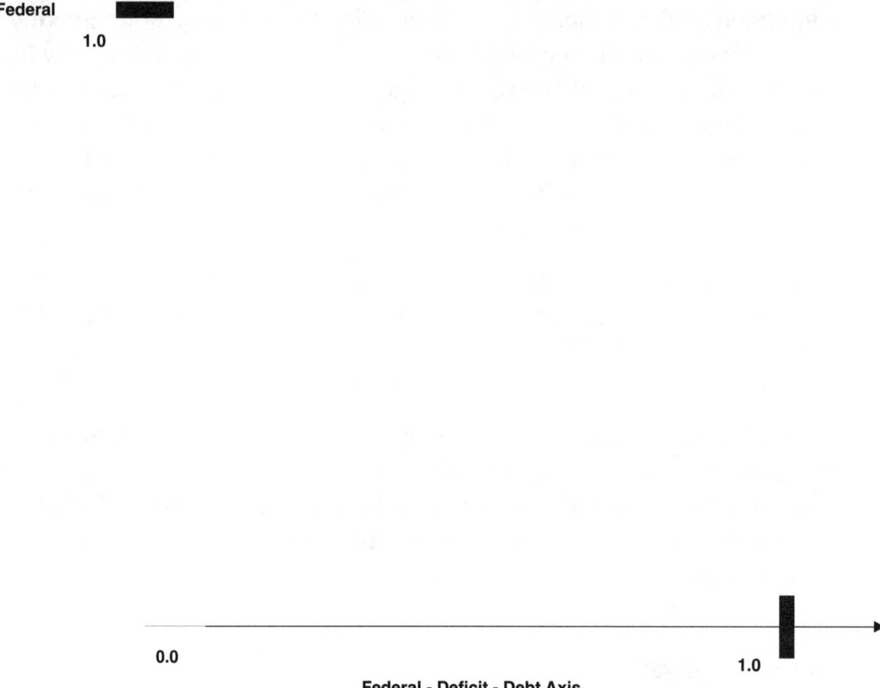

Figure 13.12 Reducing the number of dimensions allows us to approximate concepts such as federal deficit and debt.

federal debt and deficit spending. By reducing dimensions, we have minimized the impact of a missing term. We have also implicitly addressed the polysemy problem since dimensions are reduced to groups of statistically linked terms. In the example, we have grouped *debt* together with *federal* and *deficit*, so we know immediately that we are not dealing with corporate or personal debt. Depending upon the documents in the collection, though, we may also have reduced dimensions representing corporate debt and personal debt as well.

Reducing the number of dimensions we have to represent has obvious implications for IR system efficiency. Less space is required for indexes. More calculations are required to find the reduced dimensions but the benefits significantly outweigh the extra computational costs.

A detailed discussion of how we choose to group dimensions is outside the scope of this work but the interested reader is referred to Deerwester, et al. (1990) for an overview of latent semantic indexing and to Landauer and Dumais (http://lsa.colorado.edu/papers/plato/plato.annote.html) for a discussion of latent semantic analysis from a cognitive science perspective. Roughly, latent semantic indexing operates like a least squares method used in statistics to approximate linear relationships while minimizing total error. (Approximating a reduced dimension representation from a higher dimension one is a common problem. Techniques from linear algebra, such as singular value decomposition [SVD], have been developed to create these approximations. See Strang [1980] for more on SVD and least squares.)

Information Retrieval in the Text Mining Process

Information retrieval is the first step in text mining. The goal of this phase of the process is to find documents that may be of use in solving a problem at hand. Document warehousing search and retrieval operations are like a funnel, channeling documents into the warehouse without much concern for their content. An IR system acts like a first-round filter on these documents, providing them to users researching a particular problem. The goal of IR systems is to find targeted documents, but it does not address problems with the volume of text that an end user must read to extract information from these documents. Having dealt with the problem of finding documents of interest, and minimizing the problems of synonymy and polysemy by using variations of the basic vector space model, we shall now turn our attention to that problem of filtering text further to provide readers with even more targeted information.

Computational Linguistics and Natural Language Processing

Information retrieval can give users sets of documents so large that they cannot read all of them, and thus they run the risk of missing essential information. Fortunately, work in computational linguistics and natural language processing has provided a set of fundamental analysis tools. With these tools, we can delve into the structure of texts to extract even more targeted information.

Throughout our discussion of document warehousing, we have examined core operations that are performed on text: summarization, feature extraction, clustering, and categorization. When discussing document warehousing, we were primarily concerned with the benefits of these operations and understanding how basic algorithms work. Now, we will look at some of the details glossed over in early chapters. In particular we will examine:

- Types of morphological analysis
- Part of speech tagging
- Pattern detection

We will look into both derivational and inflectional morphology and discuss how this type of analysis supports part of speech tagging. Identifying parts of speech is critical step in feature extraction and pattern detection because heuristics, or rules of thumb, for identifying important phrases often depend upon knowing the parts of speech of particular words. Finally pattern detection is discussed as one of the core outcomes of text mining. Later, we will see how patterns can be used to link complementary sets of documents, such as those dealing with different areas of scientific research or economic and political news stories to find useful information that has not been explicitly stated in a single place.

Atom-Smashing Linguistics Style: Morphological Analysis

In Chapter 2, we discussed how morphological analysis is used to understand the structure of words. For most of this book, we have considered words as the most basic unit of analysis, much as chemists consider atoms the basic units of study for their work. When we need to address word variations, we often referred to finding the root of a word, for example, for the purpose of calculating word frequencies or term weights in a document. Therefore, we could treat all of the following the same for frequency analysis purposes:

- Eat
- Ate
- Eaten

Morphological analysis can provide us with even more information than the root of a word, if we know where to look.

Before going any farther, we need to define a couple of important terms. A word is the smallest linguistic unit that can stand on its own in a grammatical way. Words can be made up of morphemes, which are the smallest units that can carry a meaning or a serve a grammatical purpose. Some common morphemes are shown in Table 13.3.

These morphemes cannot stand alone grammatically and must be attached to another morpheme to function. Words are composed of morphemes. In many languages, but not all, morphemes are concatenated together to create new words. For example:

Table 13.3 Some Common Morphemes

MORPHEME	MEANING
Re-	To do again
Un-	Negated or reversed operation
Anti-	Against or opposed to
-ism	A belief system
-ed	In the past tense

anti + establish + ment

becomes *antiestablishment.*

So from a text mining perspective, we are more interested in morphemes, the meaning-bearing elements, than words, the stable grammatical forms that appear in text. With that in mind, let's look into the three different ways of grouping morphemes.

- Bound and free morphemes
- Content and function morphemes
- Inflectional and derivational morphemes

Bound and Free Morphemes

In the *antiestablishment* example, we see two different types of morphemes, bound and free. Bound morphemes, such and *anti-* and *–ment*, cannot occur on their own. *Establish,* on the other hand, can stand as a word and is a type of free morpheme. Free morphemes can be root words, but bound morphemes cannot. Bound morphemes are, instead, referred to as affixes, which are of two types (at least in English), prefixes and suffixes.

Content and Function Morphemes

Another dimension along which we categorize morphemes is content and function. Content morphemes carry meaning independently of how words are expressed in a grammar and are usually root words. *Text* is a content morpheme because it refers to a specific thing, while *–ual* is not, although they both appear in the word *textual.* The role of *–ual* is to turn the noun *text* into an adjective so that it can be used in a phrase such as *a textual description.* This second kind of morpheme is a referred to as a function morpheme, and it serves a grammatical purpose.

Inflectional and Derivational Morphemes

Another distinction between morphemes is whether they are inflectional or derivational. Derivational morphemes make new words. For example, changing a verb into a noun, such as when we change *pay* into *payment*, is done by the addition of a derivational morpheme (*-ment*) to the root morpheme (*pay*). Inflectional morphemes do not create new words, but inflect the root word to meet some grammatical requirement, such as making the singular version of a word plural. Turning *computer* into *computers* is done with an inflectional morpheme.

After the Smash: Examining the Pieces

After morphological analysis, we are left with the morphemes that make up the words that in turn make up the text we are processing. So what? Well the morphemes are not ends in themselves; what we really want is two things:

- To be able to identify root words for frequency analysis
- To be able to identify or tag each word with a part of speech and other grammatical information

The content morphemes give us the root words for frequency analysis. The combination of content and function morphemes allows us to identify parts of speech and other grammatical features of each word. This, in turn, allows us to build heuristics for extracting features and identifying useful patterns.

The process of adding morphological information to words is called tagging. One morphological analyzer, developed for the Penn Treebank Project (http://morph.ldc.upenn.edu/Catalog/docs/treebank2/c193.html) uses the following set of tags:

- CC Coordinating conjunction
- CD Cardinal number
- DT Determiner
- EX Existential there
- FW Foreign word
- IN Preposition or subordinating conjunction
- JJ Adjective
- JJR Adjective, comparative
- JJS Adjective, superlative
- LS List item marker
- MD Modal
- NN Noun, singular or mass
- NNS Noun, plural
- NNP Proper noun, singular
- NNPS Proper noun, plural
- PDT Predeterminer
- POS Possessive ending
- PRP Personal pronoun
- PRP$ Possessive pronoun
- RB Adverb
- RBR Adverb, comparative
- RBS Adverb, superlative
- RP Particle

- SYM Symbol
- TO To
- UH Interjection
- VB Verb, base form
- VBD Verb, past tense
- VBG Verb, gerund or present participle
- VBN Verb, past participle
- VBP Verb, non-third person singular present
- VBZ Verb, third person singular present
- WDT Wh-determiner
- WP Wh- pronoun
- WP$ Possessive wh- pronoun
- WRB Wh- adverb

Morphological analysis becomes the basis for part of speech tagging, and that tagging, in turn, brings us one step closer to our goal of extracting target information from text.

Part of Speech Tagging

Part of speech tagging is the process of explicitly labeling words and terms in a text with their part of speech as well as with other grammatical information. For example,

> This is a sentence.

is tagged in the following way:

```
This/DT is/VBZ a/DT sentence/NN
```

identifying *This* and *a* as determiners, *is* as a verb, and *sentence* as a noun. Let's now consider a more realistic example.

The following is an excerpt from a U.S. Federal Trade Commission news release on identify theft (www.ftc.gov/opa/2000/09/idthefttest.htm). The opening paragraph is:

> The Federal Trade Commission said today that features of certain legislation—some passed into law, some pending could help the consumer victims of identity theft. In FTC testimony before the House Committee on Banking and Financial Services, Betsy Broder, Assistant Director of the Bureau of Consumer Protection told Committee members, "The Commission has made great strides in assisting consumers and law enforcement to combat identity theft, but recognizes that much remains to be done."

When tagged using the PennTree Bank set of markers, the paragraph becomes:

> The/DT Federal/NNP Trade/NNP Commission/NNP said/VBD today/NN that/IN features/NNS of/IN certain/JJ legislation/NN -/: some/DT passed/VBN into/IN law/NN ,/, some/DT pending/VBG -/: could/MD help/VB the/DT consumer/NN victims/NNS of/IN identity/NN theft./NN/* In/IN FTC/NNP testimony/NN before/IN the/DT House/NNP Committee/NNP on/IN Banking/NNP and/CC Financial/NNP Services/NNPS ,/, Betsy/NNP Broder/NNP ,/, Assistant/NNP Director/NNP of/IN the/DT Bureau/NNP of/IN Consumer/NNP Protection/NNP told/VBD Committee/NNP members/NNS ,/, "The/NNP/* Commission/NNP has/VBZ made/VBN great/JJ strides/NNS in/IN assisting/VBG consumers/NNS and/CC law/NN enforcement/NN to/TO combat/VB identity/NN theft/NN ,/, but/CC recognizes/VB that/IN much/RB remains/VBZ to/TO be/VB done."/NNS/*

Note that common words, such as *said*, *today*, and *pending* are correctly identified. This is not surprising since some taggers use dictionary lookups to first identify known words and then use output from morphological analysis to determine appropriate tags. In some cases, statistics on surrounding words are used as well to identify unknown words. In practice, part of speech taggers work with very high accuracy—above 96 percent.

The output of part of speech tagging continues the process of building toward our final goal of information extraction. With the annotated text (that is, the original text plus tags), we can now move on to pattern matching.

Pattern Matching and Information Extraction

Pattern matching is the process of searching for predefined sequences in text. Unlike pattern matching with regular expressions in programming languages, this type of pattern recognition works with words as well as morphological and syntactic properties. We will consider two different levels of pattern matching:

- Word and term matching
- Relevancy signatures

Word and term matching is the simplest of the three approaches and has been used successfully in the migraine research example discussed below. The other approach, relevancy signatures, was developed by Ellen Riloff and Wendy Lehnert (1994) and builds upon both morphological and syntactic information provided by a part of speech tagger.

As we shall see, word and term matching is easier to implement than the other approaches but requires significant manual intervention. Riloff and Lehnert's techniques were developed for use with automated feature extraction programs. Both methods have a role in text mining, and we shall discuss that further in the next section when we consider example applications of these techniques.

Word and Term Matching

By now we are all familiar with the limits of keyword searching and the problems of poor precision and recall due to polysemy and synonymy. So why consider something as simple as term matching? The answer lies in a change in the application of this technique. Rather than use it simply to search for specific terms in a single document, it can be used to build up correlations between terms in a group of documents. These correlations can then form the basis for discovering causal chains and other relationships between concepts expressed in a document collection.

Consider a researcher looking into oil prices and their influence on other markets. The terms *oil*, *crude oil*, and *home heating oil* will have high correlations with other terms such as:

- Per barrel
- OPEC (Oil Producing Exporting Countries)
- Benchmark Brent
- Light sweet crude

These terms, in turn, will have high correlation with other terms such as:

- Natural gas
- Gulf Coast
- Refining
- Heavy Louisiana Sweet
- Mexico
- Venezuela

What we can see is that a starting term, A (*oil*) is correlated with a set of other terms, B (*per barrel*, *OPEC*, and so on), and those terms are in turn are correlated with another set of terms, C (*natural gas*, *Gulf Coast*, *refining*, and so on). We can quickly move from one term to a wide group of other terms. When we hit terms about large geographic areas, such as *Mexico*, *Venezuela*, and the *Gulf Coast*, the potential number of correlated terms is enormous. To deal with the combinatorial explosion, we can use two basic techniques:

- Threshold specification
- Term elimination

Threshold specification specifies that there must be a minimum correlation between two terms before they are included in the list of related terms. This is easily done using only statistical techniques. Term elimination requires a more elaborate mechanism.

Term elimination removes terms on the basis of some criteria other than correlation weights. Swanson and Smalheiser (1991) used a list of stop words in their work to identify words that did not appear useful. Many words on these types of stop lists are prepositions, conjunctions, determiners, and other words that serve a grammatical function but do not carry content. A second approach uses the output of a part of speech tagger and eliminates word categories that are not considered relevant. In many cases, only nouns are needed for this type of noun correlation operation. We shall see later, in more feature-extraction-oriented operations, that verbs are required to identify relationships (such as smoking causes cancer), and prepositions are used in appositive phrases (such as Mary Jones, CEO of Alpha Industries).

Approaches similar to those used by Swanson and Smalheiser can be implemented with Megaputer's TextAnalyst. Figure 13.13 shows a collection of documents about consumer protection and credit cards from www.consumer.gov/idtheft and www.ftc.govs/os/2000/idtheft/htm. As we can see, we can move from the term *credit card* to *theft*, to *identity theft*, and then to *victim*. In normal circumstances, we do not usually associate the term *credit card* with the idea of a victim, but in this case, the concept of identity theft links the two. For example, some of the sentences extracted from the document set inform us about the existence of several important entities. These include legislation called the Identity Theft and Assumption Deterrence Act, a commission (in this case the Federal Trade Commission) that seems to be responsible for enforcing related legislation, and a centralized complaint and service center that exists for victims of identity theft.

Recognizing the serious nature of identity fraud and the long term ramifications to its victims, the Identity Theft and Assumption Deterrence Act

I appreciate the opportunity to present the Commission's views on the important issue of identity theft, and describe to you the Commission's efforts to help victims, alert industry and equip law enforcement to deal with this harrowing crime.

Consumers feel particularly vulnerable knowing that no matter how careful they are, they may nonetheless become identity theft victims.

The second way in which the Act addresses the problem of identity theft is by focusing on consumers as victims.

(4) In particular, the Act provides for a centralized complaint and consumer education service for victims of identity theft and gives the responsibility of developing this function to the Commission.

Figure 13.13 Information about identity theft was extracted while analyzing documents about consumers and credit card protection.

This type of analysis is useful, for example, if you are trying to discover different ways in which credit card users can become victims of crimes. In general, when an analyst has two concepts that may be related but the relationship is unknown, this type of text mining operation can shed light on the relationship, as seen in Figure 13.14.

Of course, this is a simple example and real-world problems are more complex, but they are still amenable to this type of business intelligence operation. A methodology, or process model, will be described shortly that supports the more extensive and iterative process of finding these conceptual links in larger scale document collections.

The advantage of using this approach is that it supports the exploration of large collections of documents, whereas the other two techniques we will now discuss are single-document-oriented.

Relevancy Signatures

The relevancy signature algorithm was developed in response to the problem that although some keywords are good indicators of relevance in almost all situ-

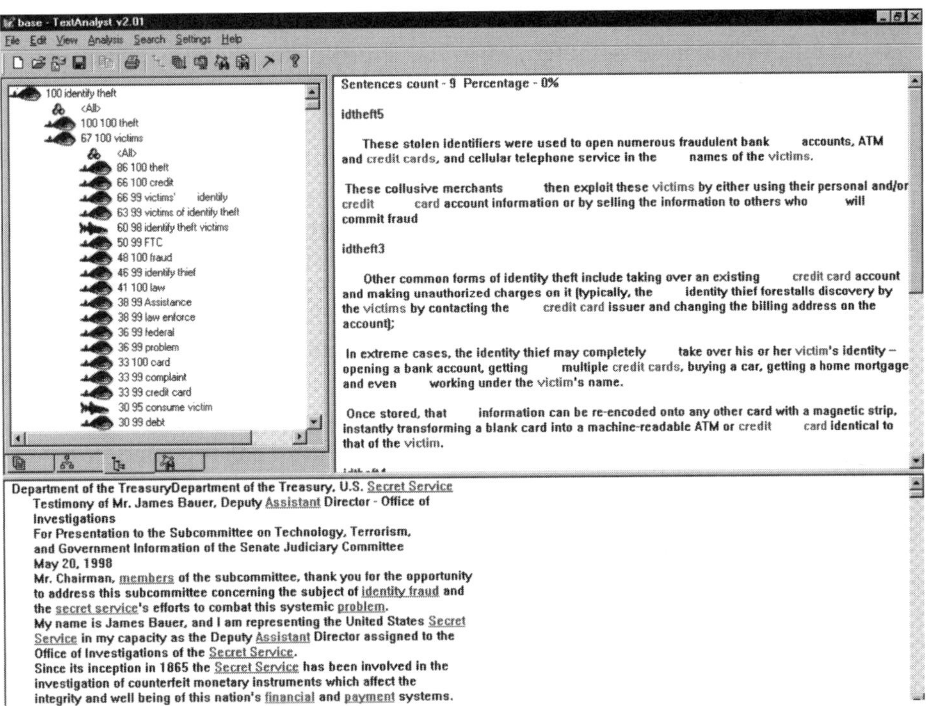

Figure 13.14 Text mining for word patterns and links between them can find links between terms when intermediary concepts provide strong links.

ations, many terms are good indicators only in certain contexts. Since context is not within the scope of keyword searches, precision is sacrificed. For example, Riloff and Lehnert (1994) noted that when working on extracting information about terrorist incidents, the word *dead* is not a good indicator of a terrorist act. For example, simply searching for *dead* could return stories about military conflicts or traffic accidents as well as those about terrorism. They did, however, find that *was found dead* is a good indicator, especially when the news story originated in a country or region suffering from a history of terrorism.

One way to describe context is to use proximity operators, word correlations, or other statistical techniques. This has been done in some cases, such as by Dillon (1983) and Fagan (1989), but even these techniques can run into problems. For example, stemming (that is, removing inflectional elements from a word) can reduce the effectiveness of matching. Riloff and Lehnert found that in the case of terrorism, the singular form *assassination* was a good indicator that the news story was about a terrorist act, while the plural form, *assassinations*, was not. In the latter case, *assassinations* usually referred to the problem of assassinations in general rather than to a specific event. As with keyword searching, relevancy signatures can avoid some of the shortcomings of proximity, word correlations, and other statistical techniques.

A signature, in Riloff and Lehnert's terminology, is a pair consisting of a word and a concept associated with that word. The signature (dead, $found-dead-passive$) represents all passive forms of *found dead*, *was found dead*, *were found dead*, and *had been found dead*. The pattern search for these passive forms is triggered by the word *dead* in the text. A relevancy signature is a signature highly correlated with a particular topic, such as terrorism. A candidate signature is considered a relevancy signature if it occurs frequently in a document collection and is highly correlated with a particular topic—that is, documents that contain the phrase are relevant at least, say, 85 percent of the time.

Relevancy signatures improve the performance of word and term matching by taking into account morphological and syntactic properties. The basic relevancy signature algorithm can be improved by keeping even more context information. Work with the relevancy algorithm has revealed that it is susceptible to false hits when dealing with metaphorical language (for example, *stock market crash* versus *airline crash*) or when additional semantic attributes are required. For example, an attack by a rebel is a terrorist incident but an attack by a mad dog is not. Augmented relevancy algorithms use semantic features, such as type of agent or a person's position in government.

The augmented relevancy algorithm improved performance by using local context around keywords. Specifically, it improved precision by reducing the number of false hits. It did not, however, improve recall. The basic problem lay in the fact that not all keywords specified in relevancy signatures occur in relevant stories. This is the same problem that motivated the move away from a basic vector space model to the latent semantic indexing approach in information retrieval.

Relevancy signatures are a class of heuristics used to extract targeted information from text. These heuristics are generalizable—that is, they can be adapted for different patterns in a range of domains. Recall, from our discussion of document warehousing tools in Chapter 12, that the IBM Intelligent Miner for Text, has a feature extraction program that has some similarities to this type of pattern matching.

Looking for Some Middle Ground: IBM's Feature Extraction Tool

The feature extraction tool in the IBM tool suite uses a fixed set of heuristics, although it can be augmented with authority and residual dictionaries to improve feature identification. This tool lies somewhere between the two general techniques that we have outlined here. It can be used to extract words and terms and, thus, is useful for compiling lists of relevant terms for word and pattern matching. It is also useful for extracting relationships between terms. These are generalized patterns that do not have the specificity of relevancy signatures but are useful nonetheless in text mining.

Extracting relationships can significantly reduce the amount of text a user needs to read when assessing whether or not a document is relevant. More importantly for our immediate text mining concerns, it can reduce text to a series of relationships that themselves represent the key concepts in a document.

Discovering Knowledge in Text: Example Cases

Discovering knowledge in text requires that we apply the techniques and algorithms we have just described. In this section, we will consider an example of knowledge discovery in text. The example is based upon the work of Don R. Swanson and Neil R. Smalheiser (Swanson and Smalheiser 1991) and deals with scientific discoveries about the causes and cures of migraines. Swanson and Smalheiser's work is important for the method employed to conduct the search for relevant text. Their project did not use extensive morphological analysis, although it probably would have benefited from it.

Knowledge Discovery in Complementary Research

Complementary areas of research are domains that cover distinct issues but when combined produce useful information. Swanson coined the term (Swanson 1991) when discussing scientific research but we can easily find complementary areas within our own field of information technology as depicted in

Figure 13.15. For example, database designers develop techniques for designing relational database, assess the benefits and drawbacks of different levels of normalization, and create methodologies to conduct their practice of data modeling. Complementary to database design, we have database administration. Database administrators are concerned with the efficient and reliable performance of database management systems. Topics that concern them include managing storage and CPU resources, planning for recovery in case of a failure, and configuring and tuning production databases. Clearly, combining these two areas can yield useful information. Designers who understand the physical implementation of their models can design better applications. For example, data warehouse designers who understand the purpose of rollback segments and transaction logging can avoid the overhead of those features during data loads, since they are frequently not necessary in a decision support environment. That fact is one that bridges the world of design, where requirements and models dominate, and the world of database administration, where the particulars of a database management system take precedence.

Although data modeling and database administration are distinct practices, there is a great deal of overlap. Data modelers often use knowledge of the specific implementation features of a database to boost performance. Similarly, database administrators are familiar with data modeling and design, especially with respect to how design choices affect performance. In fact, it is not uncommon for data modelers and database administrators to read the same trade magazines, attend the same conferences, and work closely together on development projects. This overlap is not always the case, however.

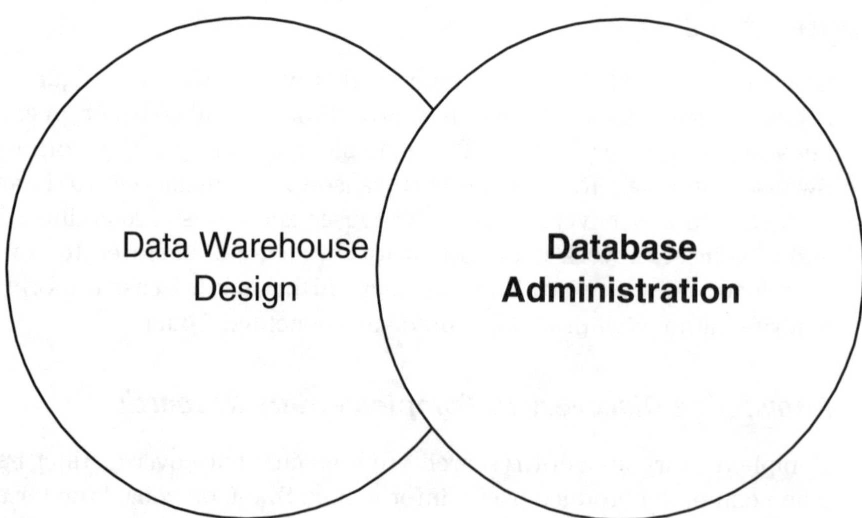

Figure 13.15 Useful information can be extracted by working in complementary domains.

Complementary but Disjoint Domains

Some complementary research areas, particularly in science, are disjoint—that is, the work in one area is not known, at least not well known, in the other area. The problem with complementary but disjoint (CBD) structures is that the practitioners in each field are relatively unaware of the work in the other's field.

This lack of familiarity can occur in any field, and information technology is no exception. Until the early 1990s, information retrieval and natural language processing were distinct domains with little overlap. Information retrieval focused on the problems of storing and retrieving homogeneous document collections. The tools of the trade were primarily statistical and probabilistic approaches to representing document topics and user queries. At the same time, natural language processing tended to focus on problems in sentence level syntax and semantics, with some work on discourse. The latter area tended to work only on single documents, not the large collections that information retrieval addressed. Within natural language processing, the chief means of tackling the understanding problem were linguistic and cognitive models of language processing. Early on in the field there was some debate over the primacy of syntax versus semantics but the idea of using statistical or probabilistic techniques did not receive much attention. Information retrieval and natural language processing were complementary but disjoint domains until the focus of natural language processing shifted to corpus linguistics (that is, linguistics about large texts or collections of text). At that point the benefits of sharing techniques with information retrieval researchers became apparent, and the past decade has seen much more mutual referencing and adaptation of each area's techniques by the other.

The benefits of sharing information between information retrieval and natural language processing practitioners became apparent when the focus of the latter changed. Since it was such a broad shift and the work of IR researchers was so well known, it was relatively easy to exploit information retrieval. In narrower domains, such as migraine research, the common interests and possible links to other fields is much more difficult to discover. It is here that text mining can help.

Text Mining in Complementary and Disjoint Domains

Swanson and Smalheiser's work in migraine research demonstrates the applicability of the CBD model of scientific discovery. In this section, we will concern ourselves primarily with the text mining element of the process and seek to understand two distinct processes:

- For a given domain, find a set of possible complementary domains.
- Given two domains, find plausible useful links between the two.

The first step can begin in several ways, such as by analyzing terms that co-occur between domains. The second process requires a solid understanding of the two domains to eliminate implausible connections.

In the migraine research, Swanson began with migraines as his source domain and set out to find a complementary or target domain. The first step was to search a medical literature database for all articles about migraines. The titles of these articles were then used to extract a list of unique words used in the titles, exclusive of stop words. These words that co-occurred with *migraine* were the candidate terms for searching for a complementary literature. These candidate terms included:

- Platelets
- Allergic
- Aggregation
- Sodium
- Channel
- Calcium
- Cerebrospinal
- Inflammatory
- Vasospasm

In addition to eliminating stop words, broad terms were eliminated—terms such as *drugs*, *evidence*, *treatment*, and *studies*. This list was compiled on the basis of knowledge of the domain, although, inverse frequency measures could have been used as well. In that case, terms that appeared frequently throughout the document collection would have been eliminated because they provided little discriminatory power, which is exactly what the researchers were looking for.

With the list of terms set, the medical database was searched again using the pruned list of co-occurring words. The list was further pruned in a second step to keep only words that occurred with *migraine* more frequently than they occurred in the document set in general. Whereas the first round of pruning used the relative frequency of the candidate term in the document collection as a whole, the second round eliminated words on the basis of the relative frequency of only terms in that occur in all titles containing the word migraine.

With a list of reduced terms, a human evaluator then reviewed the list to eliminate other terms that might be too broad or biologically implausible. This human interaction in the middle of the search process is a common element in both data mining and text mining. These processes are searches for information over extremely large data or document sets. Some tasks, such as frequency analysis are best left to applications, while more knowledge-intensive steps, such as the final refinement of the candidate word list, are best left to humans.

The final word list was then used to search the medical database. This search list was referred to as the list of B words. The titles containing B words were returned and used to produce a list of unique terms that appeared in these titles. This list was referred to as the list of A words. The list of A words included:

- Magnesium
- Hormone
- Salt
- Pyridoxine
- Pressure
- Lipids
- Hypertension
- Cholesterol
- Membrane

Each A word, such as magnesium, was then linked to the B word, such as vasospasm, that co-occurred with it.

To further prune the list of A words, because combinatorial growth can result in an unmanageable list of words, words were eliminated on the basis of their probabilistic occurrence with one of the B words. This is similar to the pruning step, in which some candidate B words were eliminated on the basis of their probabilistic occurrence with *migraine*. Terms that were too broad to be useful, such as *hormone*, *pressure*, *lipids*, and *membrane* were eliminated as well.

Finally, a human being evaluated the list of A words to find terms that appeared to be the best candidates for a complementary literature. In the case of migraines, *magnesium* ranked highest, and that became the complementary domain of research.

Once the complementary domain was identified, it was time to move to the next step: finding plausible and useful links between the two domains. This was done by organizing documents, or in this case, titles of documents, from both the source domain (migraines) and the target domain (magnesium) according to B words in the title. For example, the B word *prostaglandin* occurred in the following phrases from articles, the first from the target literature and the second from the source literature:

> Magnesium ions control prostaglandin reactivity of venous smooth muscles …
>
> Migraine attacks: Alleviation by an inhibitor of prostaglandin synthesis …

At this point, the text mining component of the operation ended. Logical, or at least plausible, connections between the source and target domains had been found and now human evaluation was needed to assess the results.

We have spent a significant amount of time looking into the process details of one text mining project for several reasons. First, it demonstrates the use of some basic feature extraction techniques. In this case, the focus was on single word terms with relatively low frequency in the document collection as a whole. Second, it makes clear the multiple steps that are necessary in text mining. There is no single text mining application that will produce intelligible pieces of information. Finally, and most importantly, it shows that human interaction is required. Text mining is not a fully automated process but, like data mining, it is an interactive process for exploring text-based resources.

In the next section, we will examine a process model for conducting text mining. Fortunately, we do not have to build this model from scratch since such a model for data mining already exists.

Text Mining Methodology: Using the Cross-Industry Process Model for Data Mining

Any task that is repeated multiple times and by more than one person can benefit from a methodology for conducting the process. Data mining practitioners recognized that fact and developed the Cross-Industry Process Model for Data Mining, also known as CRISP or CRISP-DM. The initial model was developed by a consortium of practitioners from NCR, the computer manufacturer; Integrated Solutions Limited, a data mining tool vendor now part of SPSS; Daimler Chrysler, the automobile manufacturer; and OHRA Verzeking en Bankk Groep, BV, an insurance firm based in the Netherlands. The goal of the consortium was to develop a model, independent of any particular data mining tool or algorithm, that supported the knowledge discovery process. The specific objectives of the group were to make the data mining process:

- Faster
- More efficient
- More reliable
- More manageable
- Less costly

The CRISP-DM model achieves these goals by addressing critical stages in the data mining process, including:

- Business understanding
- Data understanding
- Data preparation
- Modeling
- Evaluation
- Deployment

As Figure 13.16 shows, the CRISP-DM process model is a cyclical process but can branch to different phases, depending upon what is learned at each step.

Although CRISP-DM was developed with numeric data mining in mind, the basic process is suitable for text mining as well. The basic steps, such as business understanding, data understanding, and evaluation address similar issues and have similar implementation requirements in both data mining and text mining. Data preparation is less demanding in text mining but it is certainly still

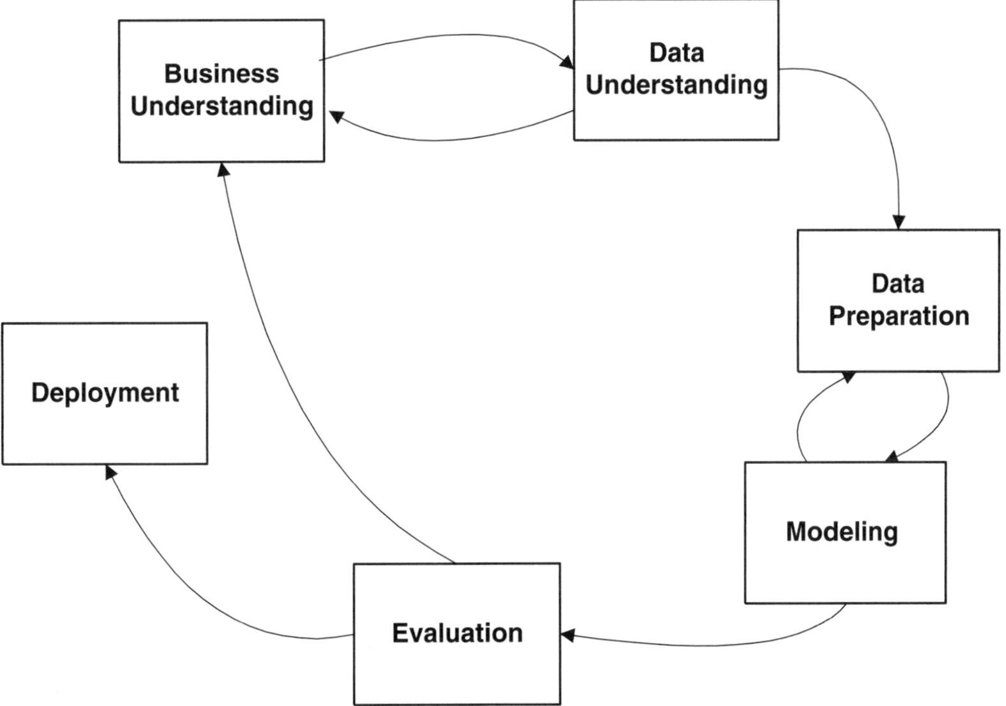

Figure 13.16 The CRISP-DM process model is not a linear, waterfall type of process model, but cyclical with multiple branching points.

a requirement. Modeling is the point at which data mining and text mining processes diverge most, but still basic principles hold across both processes.

In the following sections, we discuss each stage of CRISP-DM in detail. Then we will evaluate its applicability to text mining and discuss differences and adaptations that can be made in the text mining realm.

Business Understanding

The initial stage, business understanding, deals with formulating the business requirements and developing an approach to addressing those requirements through data mining techniques. The CRISP-DM model specifies four steps in the business understanding stage:

- Determine business objectives
- Assess situation
- Determine data mining goals
- Produce project plan

The first step in this process is to understand what the business users really want. This is usually described in terms of the business's overall market and business situation. Although there may be a single primary business objective, such as identifying why a subpopulation of customers has been leaving for the competition, there may be secondary objectives as well, such as identifying the cause of reduced sales to customers in a particular region. A third, and vitally important, element of this process is defining the success criteria for the project. This is essential to ensuring that the correct problems are identified and studied.

After a preliminary assessment of the business objectives has been made, data miners move to assessing the situation. This is a much more detail-oriented stage than the first step. Here the objective is to develop an inventory of resources, such as domain experts, data sources, and computing resources. The final list of requirements is formulated at this point along with any known constraints. Constraints can be:

- Chronological: Must be complete in 90 days.
- Legal: Privacy policy restricts use of particular pieces of data.
- Technical: Maximum size of data set.
- Personnel: Domain experts are only available for two weeks.

In addition to constraints, the model calls for explicitly listing risks that could delay the project or lead to project failure. A two-part glossary should be constructed that includes terminology from the domain being analyzed as well as data mining terminology. The objective of this step is to share project-oriented knowledge as widely as possible. Finally, during assessment a cost benefit analysis should be done.

The third step is defining the data mining goals. Unlike a business goal, which states a business objective, such as reducing the number of customers who leave for the competition (this is called churning), a data mining goal is an operational definition of the goal. In the case of customer churning, the goal may be to predict the likelihood of churning, given a customer's buying patterns over the past six months, location, bill paying history for the past six months, and demographic profile.

The fourth and final step in the business understanding stage is the development of a project plan. This should include time schedules, resource requirements, dependencies, and other factors that can influence the outcome of the project. An initial assessment of the tools and techniques is done at this stage as well, to ensure that the project is not limited in its use of essential algorithms or approaches.

Data Understanding

During the data understanding stage, the primary focus is on acquiring and evaluating the data sets that will be mined. This stage consists of four steps:

- Collect data
- Describe data
- Explore data
- Verify data quality

These are familiar steps to data warehouse practitioners, and, as we shall see, many of the same concerns that confront data miners have parallels in data warehousing.

During the data collection stage, data is extracted from source systems and loaded into a repository or analysis tool. Integration with other data sources may also be required at this time. An important output of this stage is a list of problems encountered during the data loads, which can be used to aid future projects working with the same data sets.

The description of the data should include the format of the data, the number of records loaded, and brief descriptions of each attribute.

Next, explore the data using simple statistics, reporting, and visualization techniques. Subsets of the data should be grouped and their properties understood. For example, what is the distribution of customers by location, how do sales transactions break down by time of day and what product categories are sold in each store? The initial output from this process may not address the specific data mining goals but they might help formulate hypotheses about patterns in the data.

Finally, a data quality assessment should be conducted. This step includes ensuring that the data set adequately represents the area being studied. For example, if you are interested in churn patterns for customers with a particular class of service plans, then the data should include customers from all plans in that class. Also, the data should not be skewed along some other dimension, such as location. Even if the data set has customers from all service plans in the target class, the customers should not be from just the Northeast region if you are trying to understand churn patterns across the country.

Data Preparation

Once a preliminary assessment of the data has been done, it is time to prepare the data for use with data mining tools. The five steps of this stage are:

- Select data
- Clean data
- Construct data
- Integrate data
- Format data

The first step in this stage is identifying data to include in analysis. Most data mining tools expect a single table or file of data, so data selection becomes a case of identifying the rows (records) and columns (attributes) that will be analyzed. For data sets that are too large to analyze with a given tool, statistical sampling can be used to select rows. Choosing columns is more difficult since, in many cases, we do not know which attributes or set of interacting attributes correlate with a particular outcome. For example, when analyzing churn, should all demographic information be included or should some be eliminated so billing history information can be used? If the wrong attribute is eliminated, the data mining process will miss existing patterns in the larger data set.

The next step is cleaning the selected data. This can be done in several ways. Default values can be substituted for missing values. Referential integrity checks can be used to identify invalid codes that are then replaced with either default values or best-guess values.

Once the data is clean, derived values need to be calculated. In many cases, derived values are limited to calculations within a single record. For example, if a sales transaction record has total sales revenue and total cost of goods sold attributes, then gross margin can be calculated as the difference of those two. In some cases, entire records can be added to the data set as well.

Step four in data preparation is data integration. This situation applies only when there are multiple data sources, such as sales transactions, store information, and demographic data. After additional data has been derived—for example, total sales by product and by store—it can be integrated with regional demographic data about each store.

The fifth step in data preparation is reformatting the data to meet the needs of the data mining tool. At this point, no new data is introduced and the meaning of the data is not changed, only the syntactic properties of the data change. For example, product codes may be changed from a list of alphabetic abbreviations to a bit mask suitable for a neural network, or the order of records in the data set might be randomized to meet the requirement of a data mining algorithm.

At this point in the process, the data has been identified, cleaned, integrated, and reformatted for use with a data mining tool. The next step is to develop a model for mining this data.

Modeling

The modeling stage is what many would consider the real data mining process. It is certainly the most interesting. This stage breaks down into four steps:

- Selecting the modeling technique
- Generating a test design
- Building the model
- Assessing the model

Selecting a modeling technique means identifying a particular approach and algorithm to meet a data mining goal. For example, if the goal involves making predictions based upon classification information, then one could use a decision tree algorithm, such as C4.5, or train a neural network with the back propagation algorithm.

Once the model is built and executed, we need a way of testing its accuracy and validity. During the second step of this stage a test design is developed for just that purpose. This usually involves dividing the data set into training and testing subsets. The training subset is used for step three, building the model. Once the model has been developed and trained, for example, the neural network stops making significant changes to weights within the model, then the test set can be used and the output of the model measured using a predefined attribute, such as error rate in classification tasks.

Data miners assess models by looking at technical criteria, such as error rates in classification, while domain experts evaluate it in terms of its descriptive properties. For example, a model that predicts that customers with four or more children in a particular socioeconomic category are likely to churn might fit with an expert's understanding of the problem. Similarly, a prediction about churning based on the day of the week that a product was purchased might be suspect in the expert's eyes.

Evaluation

The evaluation stage follows the modeling process and consists of three steps:

- Evaluate results
- Review process
- Determine next steps

When evaluating the results of the modeling stage, the entire set of results is assessed in terms of the business objectives that drive the data mining project. This is different from earlier evaluation steps that looked at a specific part of the project, such as data quality or error rates in model output. Also, during this stage, unanticipated outputs of the model are examined in more detail.

After the model has been assessed and it appears to meet the business objectives, it is time to review the data modeling process. The purpose of this step is to document unanticipated issues that arose during the process and to summarize the process in general for future reference.

The last step of evaluation is to determine the next steps of the project, specifically, should the project continue through to deployment or should a previous phase be revisited? For example, domain experts may want to expand the data set to include other attributes that may shed more light on some results found in the current iteration of the process.

Deployment

The deployment stage is the final component of the CRISP-DM process model. In this four-step stage the model is put into production use. The steps at this point are:

- Plan deployment
- Plan monitoring and maintenance
- Produce final report
- Review project

Plan deployment is simply a formal documenting of the steps required to roll the model out for production use. Similarly, the monitoring and maintenance plan outlines how the model will be maintained—for example, how often the model should be rerun with the latest data. The final report and project review provides an opportunity to assess and document the findings of the project as a whole.

Adopting the CRISP-DM to Text Mining

Many of the steps outlined in the CRISP-DM model are applicable to text mining with little variation. We will now consider each step in detail and identify significant differences.

Business Understanding in Text Mining

Business understanding is identical in both processes. In fact, this is a general step in any type of development or analysis project that we undertake in organizations. Within a text mining context, we still need to address particular business problems, such as:

- What is the state of the new construction project?
  - What legal processes are pending?
  - Which permits have been applied for and received?
  - What documentation has been received on financing?
  - What are other financing options?
  - How viable are the subcontractors seeking the business?
- What is our competition planning?
  - Are they moving into new territories?
  - How have they expanded their product line?
  - What distributors and VARs have signed on with them?
- How can we use this new adhesive compound developed in our labs?
  - Have similar products been patented?
  - What problems exist with available adhesives in its category?
  - What is our production capacity if we were to produce this commercially?

These are the types of business problems that initially drive the need for text mining.

Data Understanding in Text Mining

When it comes to data understanding, data mining and text mining share similar requirements but with different types of data. In text mining, the first question is what type of text and documents are required to address the business issues:

- Can we get by with only internal documents?
- If external documents are needed, where should they come from?

- Are known sources enough or do we need to discover other content providers?
- How frequently is content available, daily, weekly, monthly, and so on?
- Are these sources publicly accessible and, if not, what is the cost of obtaining them?
- What is the source language of the text? Will rough machine translations serve the needs of the project, or will a human translator be required?

As in data mining, data preparation requires a significant proportion of the entire project's time and resources.

Data Preparation in Text Mining

The data preparation process is still required but the specific tasks are fundamentally different from those in data mining. To begin with, text mining does not have to deal with missing values, referential integrity, or merging multiple data sources into a single table or file. On the other hand, text mining still has plenty of preparation tasks, including:

- Character set conversion
- File format conversion
- Machine or human translation
- Metadata extraction
- Clustering
- Classification
- Summarization
- Feature extraction

With these tasks complete, the process moves to the first major point of difference between data mining and text mining.

Mining, Not Modeling, for Text

The modeling stage of CRISP-DM does not have a close analog in text mining. Data mining is fundamentally a search for patterns and properties that hold over a large set of data. Text mining is the search for particular pieces of information related to a given topic with the objective of finding a set of these pieces, that together provide insight or new knowledge to the text miner. This type of process does not function in a "produce a data set, execute a chosen algorithm, and evaluate the results" fashion. The first steps of text mining include finding a document set to work with, such as a document warehouse and the World Wide Web. IR techniques are used to limit the document set and then feature extraction and summarization programs reduce the total amount of text even more. Users evaluate this reduced set and, in the process, learn new information that can lead to several outcomes:

- The user formulates new hypothesis about the business problem at hand.
- The user discovers a piece of information that needs to be explored further.
- Inconsistencies between documents are found and may need to be resolved.
- The user decides to reduce the document set even further to focus on a particular set of facts.

In some cases, multiple iterations of a process may occur. For example, Swanson extracted key terms as features from article titles a few times and in each case reduced the set of features by applying restrictions and filtering criteria at different times.

Whereas data mining leads to a model, such as a list of classification rules, a trained neural network, or a segmentation of a data set, the product of text mining is discrete pieces of textual information related to a business domain.

Evaluation and Deployment

The evaluation process in CRISP-DM is relatively generic and could apply to many different types of analysis. The key questions—once information has been extracted by the text mining process—are:

- Are these facts relevant to the business objective?
- Are the facts actually true?
- What pieces of information are missing that increase the risk of acting on these facts?

Depending upon how these questions are answered, the user may decide to continue to mine for other pieces of information.

The deployment, however, is somewhat different. What is gained by text mining are pieces of information that are shared with others and drive business decisions? There is no executable application and no mathematical model describing a business process. Deployment, then, reduces to sharing the new information or knowledge and acting upon this newfound information.

Text Mining Applications

Text mining is a collection of techniques and processes that lend themselves to solving a range of problems. We have seen a detailed example of how it can be used in science to discover plausible links between nutrient deficiencies and migraines. Projects are also underway to use text mining techniques to discover facts in genetics and protein research. (See Rigoutsos IBM Pattern discovery servers, software, and downloadable content at www.research.ibm.com/bioinformatics/). In Chapters 15, 16 and 17, we will concentrate on business-related topics, including internal operations, customer relationship management, and competitive intelligence.

Knowing Your Business

If we take Socrates' admonition, "know thyself" to heart, we can start our discussion of text mining with its application to the internal operations of our own businesses. Any sufficiently large organization will have processes that are repeated over and over again, from invoicing and payroll management to manufacturing processes and service delivery. Most business intelligence analysts' and decision makers' resources have been limited to information extracted from online transaction processing systems. These provide plenty of details about the number and type sales, whether or not production quotas have been met, and quality control measures. Text mining applications can provide a new dimension for these users. Some applications they could use are:

- Project management tracking, using status reports, project documentation, and customer communications
- Personnel management, using skills tracking, performance appraisals, OSHA regulations, and labor contracts
- Marketing plan development based upon details of past plans, advertising options, and market research
- Compliance tracking for government reporting about safety, materials handling, environmental controls, and other operations

Of course a business does not exist in a vacuum, and the market at large, and the business climate of suppliers and customers are also areas worth monitoring.

Knowing Your Customer

Customer relationship management is garnering much attention in the business world. With the advent of e-commerce and the ability to track details of customer browsing as well as buying patterns, businesses can learn more about their customers than ever before. The collection and sharing of customer data by businesses provides the means for even more detailed understanding of customers. Again, as in the case of understanding one's business, text mining can provide even more insight about customers.

One of the limits of current customer relationship management systems is that they focus on numeric and character data. How much was purchased? What types of products were purchased? Are cross-selling techniques effective with this customer? When does this person shop? What is not addressed are questions such as:

- What are the salient features of the Web pages that this customer spends the most time browsing or reading?
- How can customer complaints be automatically classified and routed to the right person to reduce the period between the time the complaint is made and when it is resolved?
- For commercial customers, what is happening in their market? What pressures are they responding to?

This last question is representative of a whole class of business issues in market intelligence, also known as competitive intelligence, that look into significant changes in a market, either in the demand for or supply of products and services in that arena. This too is another fertile area for text mining applications.

Knowing Your Competition and Market

The need to know what your competition is up to and where the market is going is as old as business itself. The Web and fee-for-service providers can supply a wealth of information about both your competitors and your market. Some of the areas that text mining applications can help with are:

- Major capital expansions by competitors
- Changes in the regulatory environment
- New alliances and partnerships
- New product introductions
- Monitoring patents

Targeted searches can be used to keep abreast of competitors' activities by regularly updating the document warehouse with news stories, press releases, patent applications, and other general information about competitors. Financial details can be extracted from the Security and Exchange Commission's EDGAR database, at least for U.S. companies, as well as from other sources. (XBRL, an XML-based business reporting language is gaining acceptance, so the job of extracting detailed financial information should become easier.) The document warehouse can thus become the source of information for automatic notifications about competitor's activities as well as the initial source of data for iterative, interactive text mining operations.

Conclusions

Text mining builds on the work of other fields—information retrieval, computational linguistics, and data mining. Information retrieval gets us going by making the first pass at reducing the potentially unmanageable set of text content available to us from the Web and other sources. Using IR techniques to hone in on text related to particular business objectives and issues, we can use computational linguistic techniques, such as feature extraction and summarization, to reduce the amount of content we are dealing with even further. These techniques do not work most effectively in a totally automated system. Human intervention is required. Heuristics will only go so far before a rich understanding of the domain, whether it is migraine research or the marketing of sports shoes, is needed to help focus the search for salient information.

It is this interaction of automated techniques and human judgement that necessitates the need for a sound process model to guide the text mining process. Rather than start from scratch, text miners would do well to adopt the Cross-Industry Process Model for Data Mining as a guiding methodology. Although there are differences between data mining and text mining, the process model is general enough to guide text mining operations.

In the next few chapters, we will turn our attention away from individual text mining techniques and process descriptions and discuss applications of text mining to three broad classes of business problems: internal operations, customer relationship management, and competitive intelligence.

CHAPTER 14

Know Thyself: Using Text Mining for Operational Management

In this chapter, we will turn our attention to applying text mining techniques to the operational management of organizations. We will look at several different aspects of organizational management, including the use of documents as communication channels within an enterprise. These document-oriented communication channels will be examined from several different perspectives, including:

- The needs of standard operations versus ad hoc projects
- The use of enterprise document management systems (EDMSs) to manage these processes
- The integration of EDMSs with document warehouses
- Specific steps to support text mining for operational management

First, we must make a distinction between two types of operations within any organization. First, there are regular processes that are developed to meet the core objectives of an organization, such as manufacturing lawn mowers, developing new drugs, marketing services to potential clients, or educating students. The second type of processes are one-time projects, such as building a new plant, installing an enterprise resource planning system, litigating a law suit, or merging with another company. Of course, in many organizations, projects are so common that project management has become a regular process and is managed like other standard operating procedures, but the projects themselves are still driven by ad hoc needs, and the particulars of each project are different. As we shall see, the standard process versus ad hoc distinction will be reflected in how these two types of processes make use of text mining operations.

We cannot discuss text mining within large organizations without understanding document management systems and the types of needs they meet. Text analysis for operational management begins with information retrieval (IR) from document management systems long before we can apply text mining techniques. The relationship between EDMSs and document warehouses parallels the relationship between online transaction processing (OLTP) systems and data warehouses (that is, they are one of the primary sources of information for the document warehouse). Successfully integrating these two systems is a critical step toward supporting text mining for internal operations.

Next, we will consider the need for text mining and other text analysis techniques in operational management, for both standard processes and ad hoc projects. Standard operating procedures generate similar types of communications repeatedly. This may be production run reports, quality control test results, employee evaluations, or reports to regulatory agencies. Over time, a large number of these documents will sometimes be compiled in a single repository, such as an EDMS, and in other cases they will be distributed throughout the organization. In either case, this collection of documents can provide the raw material for text mining operations, searching for as yet unknown patterns in the organization's operations. Within the realm of projects, text analysis can support the research tasks of a project. For example, during a merger a company may need detailed market information for the Federal Trade Commission (FTC) to demonstrate that the proposed union will not hamper competition in a particular area. Cross-project analysis can also lead to insights about overlapping projects, duplicated efforts, or even conflicting objectives.

The chapter will conclude with a discussion of specific techniques that can be applied to both standard operations and projects within an organization. These include:

- Summarization
- Visualization techniques
- Classification and routing
- Feature extraction

Summarization and visualization are used to identify relevant documents efficiently. Classification and routing are used to automatically notify interested end users about significant events. These operations, in turn, depend upon feature extraction methods to reduce text to a minimum and identify the most salient features.

Ultimately, the goal of using text analysis, and text mining techniques in particular, is to refine and make more efficient the communication channels that already exist within an organization.

Operations and Projects: Understanding the Distinct Needs of Each

Any nontrivial organization will have repeatable processes. One of the great advances in the industrial age was the creation of the assembly line. This advance allowed a process to be broken down into its constituent tasks and ordered in such a way as to maximize the efficiency of each task. This is one of the best examples of managing repeatable processes. The key characteristics of repeatable processes are:

- The process can be broken down into subprocesses.
- There is a well-defined order of subprocesses.
- The entire process is understood at the organizational level, if not at individual levels.
- The process has a specific beginning and ending point.
- The process is executed over and over again as part of the organization's basic operations.

The first characteristic of a nontrivial repeatable process is that it can be broken down into subprocesses. Sure, using a stapler or running a photocopying machine is a repeatable process without subprocesses, but it is also too simple to be of interest to us. For our purposes, we are concerned with the core business processes of an organization, and any of these can be divided into logical steps or components.

A well-defined order is essential. Invoices are sent from Accounts Payable before Accounts Receivable can expect to receive payments. The chassis of an automobile must be assembled before the body is put on a car. Some processes are not as linear. We saw in the last chapter that data mining and text mining operations using the Cross-Industry Process Model for Data Mining (CRISP-DM) can move from one stage to one of several others, depending upon the findings of the current stage. What is important here is that all possible transitions from one subprocess to another are defined in advance, as shown in Figure 14.1 for some document warehousing operations.

The staff of some enterprises may debate the next characteristic. Organizations understand the overall process, even if a single individual does not. This means that for complex processes, such as assembling an aircraft, no one person

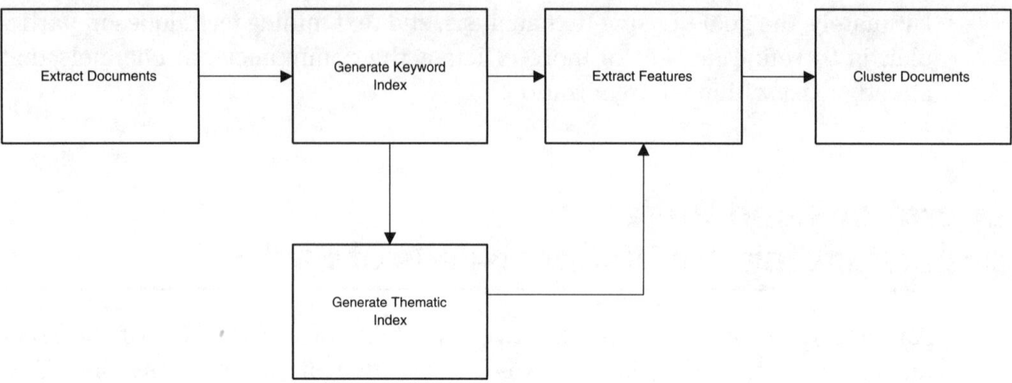

Figure 14.1 Well-defined order does not require a linear order.

knows the entire process, but there is a set of individuals in the enterprise that collectively understand it. This is one of the factors that drives the use of documents as a communication channel. Operational processes are often too complex for anyone to understand but at any point in the process, someone may need to understand what happened or will happen at another stage.

Repeatable processes have a specific starting and ending point. For example, raw materials delivered to a plant is the start of a manufacturing process, and the shipping of the finished product is the end. This contrasts with projects, which often have informal beginnings, such as:

- The recognition of a problem
- The formation of an informal team to solve the problem
- The recognition that the problem cannot be solved with the current options
- Management approval to create a project to solve the problem

For example, users might complain that the response time of a database server is declining. A system support person might work with a database administrator and network engineer to isolate the problem. They discover that the problem is that the number of users has grown faster than expected, and both the server and the network are at capacity. The database administrator recognizes the need to cluster another server, while the network engineer sees the need to resegment the network and perhaps install a storage area network to meet the performance objectives of the various applications. The tasks are clearly outside the realm of normal operations (at least for most organizations) and result in initiating a project.

The final characteristic of a repeatable process is, as the name implies, that it occurs repeatedly. Whether the operation is to generate payroll, write software, or resolve customer complaints, it will occur over and over again.

Let's now contrast these characteristics with projects. We have seen in the example of the database server that projects are initiated when something out of the ordinary occurs. Projects, like repeatable processes, can often be broken down into subprojects or tasks. Projects may or may not have well-defined order, for example, the database administrator may be analyzing log files while the network engineer monitors traffic patterns, and the next step is dependent upon what they find. Another difference is that the subjects of projects are not necessarily well understood. For example, no one in a company may be an expert on mergers, occupational safety education, or text mining, even though there is a need for that knowledge. This lack of full understanding also leads to the fact that projects may not have well-defined ending points. Of course if funding runs out, the project ends but it could end without a resolution to the problem. Finally, projects are often one-time or very infrequent operations. In some cases, projects end without changing the operational landscape significantly. For example, if a plant is built to manufacture the same products that are manufactured in other plants or if an additional server is added to a network, operations will continue much as before. At other times, projects evolve into new standard operating procedures. Take data warehousing projects for instance. Once built, the data warehouse often continues to grow, requires maintenance, and becomes a production system within an organization.

Why should we care about these characteristics? It is these characteristics that determine how text mining operations can support operational management.

In the case of standard operating procedures, we are not concerned with learning new information about a particular problem or researching competitors operations. The key value of text mining is in monitoring operations. This can include examining performance evaluations or other personnel documentation for key concepts such as poor performance, harassment issues, and conflicts of interest. Within the context of customer relationship management, we would want to look for complaints about particular areas of operations, such as fulfillment, quality control, and customer contacts. In contrast to these relatively fixed types of queries, project-oriented operations have a much broader range of topics of interest.

Projects by their nature do not require monitoring of a fixed set of documents. The types of operations required depend upon the problem at hand. Information retrieval techniques can solve many problems, such as searching a technical support database for a solution to a software installation problem, researching vendor options for hardware performance problems, or searching the Web for a legal firm versed in mergers as well as your industry in general.

For more targeted operations, such as developing a competitive intelligence profile of your competitors before launching a new product line or searching for applications for a new chemical compound with unusual properties, more precise techniques, such as feature extraction are required. In both the case of standard operating procedures and the case of projects, we need to start our text analysis operations with internal documents.

Enterprise Document Management Systems

Enterprise Document Management Systems (EDMS) have emerged as a solution to the document-tracking problem that arises in many organizations. Attending to the day-to-day operations of an organization requires an awareness of key events throughout the enterprise. The size and diversification of organizations limit how well informal communication channels can meet the information-sharing needs of a company. In a small three- or four-person business it is possible to keep abreast of all essential operations and projects with conversations at the coffeepot. As organizations grow, formal procedures are implemented to ensure that information is available to all those who will need it, including coworkers, managers, business partners, attorneys, and accountants. The formal procedures almost always entail the use of documents. The solution to one problem—maintaining communication channels—creates another—managing all the documents used for intraorganizational communications.

Benefits of Enterprise Document Management Systems

Like their numeric OLTP counterparts, EDMS applications are used primarily to store, edit, and retrieve particular documents. EDMS are repositories of potentially valuable sources for text-based information needed for business intelligence operations, if we can only get at it in a manageable form. The objectives of an EDMS overlap with those of document warehousing and text mining. In his book *Document Management for the Enterprise: Principles, Techniques and Applications*, Michael J. D. Sutton outlines several objectives for enterprise document management systems (Sutton 1996):

- Increased efficiency and effectiveness
- Increased productivity by optimally using documents
- Increased consistency of classification, indexing, and retrieval of documents
- Increased sharing of documents
- Preservation of decision and accountability trails
- Automated retention and disposal procedures for documents

Increased efficiency and productivity are common objectives with document warehousing. The classification and indexing of documents is a primary goal of document warehousing, although within the text analysis framework, this is an automated process, not the usual manual process found in EDMS operations. Since the document warehouse is a decision support platform, sharing of documents is a fundamental means of meeting that objective. The last two objectives—preservation of audit trails and retention schedule management—are outside of the scope of document warehousing. As Figure 14.2 shows, EDMSs support OLTP operations, not business intelligence tasks.

Although EDMS and document warehouses share similar objectives, the means by which they meet those objectives differ.

Limits of Enterprise Document Management Systems

Enterprise document management systems are limited in their utility for decision support operations. Some of the specific shortcomings of EDMS are:

- Treat documents as an atomic unit
- Store homogeneous collections
- Support information retrieval, not text mining
- Limited semantic metadata
- Not always historically complete

A central idea behind document warehousing is that documents are the ideal level at which to work with text. First of all, ideas within documents are related and generally form a cohesive whole. Because of this, if one piece of information in a document is of interest to a reader, there are probably other facts of interest as well. Second, documents provide a context for understanding a statement. For example, if a text mining program extracted the text nugget

Document Management Systems	Document Warehouse
Large Number of Users Frequent Updates Not Historical Keyword-Driven Queries Manually Generated Metadata Fixed Classification System	Small to Moderate Number of Users Regular Bulk Loads Rich Historical Record Integrated with Data Warehouse Manual and Auto Generated Metadata Flexible Classification

Figure 14.2 Document management systems are transaction-oriented, unlike document warehouses, which are decision-support-oriented.

"Alpha Beta Industries shares will drop 15 percent," a reader would want to know:

- Where did it come from?
- When was it written?
- Could it be verified?
- What was the reason behind the projection?
- Do others agree with this forecast?

Hyperlinks from a document, such as one with the fictional earnings estimate, provide an extended context for understanding the extracted fragment. Third, documents provide detail required to understand correlations between concepts found in text mining operations. For example, in one text mining project, (Loh, et al. 2000), a high correlation was found between corruption and the name of a particular politician from a large Brazilian city. Was this due to the fact that the politician was combating corruption in government or because he was under investigation for corruption? (It was the latter.) Without the additional information lost during the feature extraction process, we cannot know critical details.

Although EDMSs support documents, we cannot get inside of them, as shown in Figure 14.3. This problem is partially solved by including manually entered metadata, but that does not provide the semantic richness that is available in a document warehouse.

A second limitation is that documents in an EDMS tend to be of a similar type—for example, they might be performance evaluations, contacts, press releases,

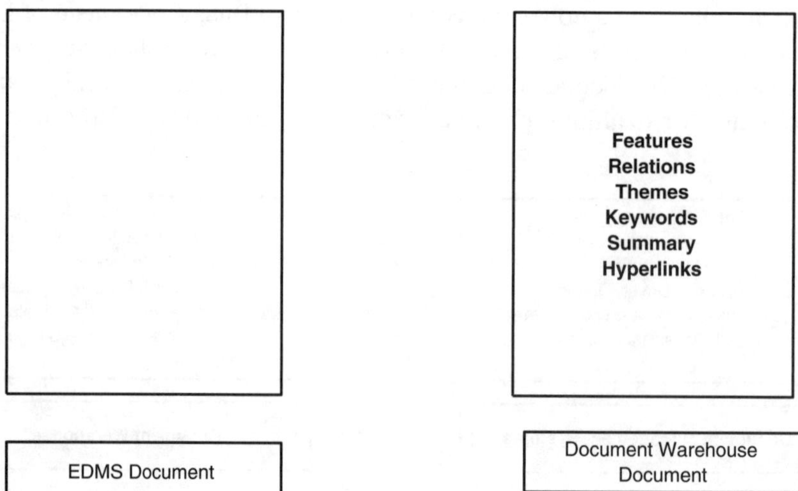

Figure 14.3 Easy access to context is an essential element in successful text mining.

audit reviews, procurement files, or policies and procedures. A document warehouse makes no presumption about the types of documents stored in the warehouse, where they are physically stored, or their format. This flexibility allows us to store just about any text-bearing object in the warehouse without worrying about predefined classification schemes. With this flexibility, externally generated documents can be easily added to the warehouse.

Another point is that EDMS systems support only information retrieval (IR) and not text mining. The job of IR systems is to identify documents that match a query and return them to the user; they do not provide further analysis. Within the document warehouse, IR is one step in the full text analysis process as depicted in Figure 14.4.

The metadata provided in EDMS applications is not as semantically rich in the document warehouse. Again turning to *Document Management for the Enterprise: Principles, Techniques and Applications* (Sutton 1996), we find that some metadata attributes found in EDMS include:

- Author
- Subject/Title
- Project Number
- File Number
- Document Type
- Version Identifier
- Date/Time Authored

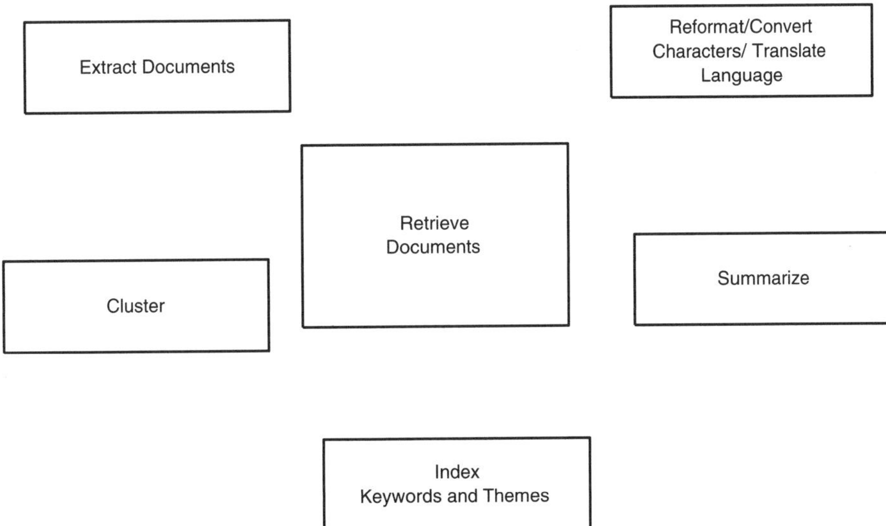

Figure 14.4 IR is one of many text analysis steps in document warehouses.

Within the document warehouse, we would want access to summaries; key persons, places, and organizations mentioned; relations between entities; and the relative weight of dominant themes within the document. As we can see from Sutton's list, many of the attributes support a fixed organizational structure, such as file number, project number, and document type.

The final limit of an EDMS is that it is not historically complete, but actually a document warehouse might not be historically complete either. Some external documents, such as news briefs, might be important in the short term but not worth retaining for the long run. In general though, document warehouses will be more likely to store documents for a greater period of time than an EDMS.

Again, it should be noted that these are shortcomings from the business intelligence perspective. EDMS applications are not designed for business intelligence any more than a screwdriver is designed to hammer nails. Like the OLTP systems that support sales, accounting, and production control, enterprise document management systems are not designed for dealing with ad hoc queries or aggregate analysis. Fortunately, there is a way to address this problem: integrate the EDMS with a document warehouse.

Integrating Document Management with Document Warehousing

The integration of enterprise document management systems with document warehouses will sound very familiar to those familiar with the extraction, transformation, and load process in data warehousing. The steps include:

- Identifying internal sources of documents
- Extracting documents from their source systems
- Transforming and reformatting as necessary

Internal sources can be identified as a function of the system's requirements. In general, internal documents will be found either in document management systems, in file systems, or increasingly in Web-based content management systems.

Document Extraction

Extracting documents will likely be the most time-consuming part of the integration operation. The exact nature of the extraction process will depend upon the source of the documents. We will consider three general classes of document sources:

- File systems

- Document management systems
- Web-based content management systems

As we shall see, each of these has distinct characteristics.

File System Extraction

As we noted in Chapter 7, file systems are relatively easy to work with, especially if a well-developed scripting language is available. Some key points to remember when working with file systems are:

- Many file systems do not support versioning (OpenVMS is an exception), so date and time stamps often must be used to determine the most recent version of a document.
- Depending upon file extensions to identify document types is not reliable. Certainly, most documents with a .doc extension are word-processing documents, and HTML documents often have .htm or .html extensions, but these conventions are not enforced.
- The process that copies files from file systems to the data warehouse should have only read access to source directories to minimize security risks.
- Separate processes should be used to copy files from sensitive areas, such as contracts or the human resources area, to minimize the possibility that the files will be read by someone other than the extraction process.
- Use any available operating system options to restrict the user accounts associated with extraction processes. For example, login to these accounts should be limited to only times when the processes will be running, such as between midnight and 3 A.M.
- Always log summary information about the extraction processes to the document warehouse database.

Some of these considerations also apply to document management systems.

Extracting from Document Management Systems

When extracting from an EDMS, the first step is to identify the export protocol. Some of the common standards are:

- Open Document Management API (ODMA)
- Document Management Alliance (DMA)
- WebDAV

These standards are discussed in Chapter 6, and the details will not be repeated here. The point to remember is that these standards were developed to promote interoperability between document management systems. If you have the choice between using one of these standards and a proprietary method, using the standard will minimize the amount of ETL code that must be rewritten if the EDMS is changed. Some other points to consider are:

- Many EDMS applications provide security and access controls. Not only will these affect the extraction process, but as much security information as possible should be extracted as well. The document warehouse will need to provide equivalent levels of access control.
- A decision will need to be made about extracting multiple versions. Will all versions be extracted and maintained or only the most recent? Should drafts be included in the document warehouse?
- Use EDMS metadata as much as possible. Document management systems do not follow the Dublin Core but the information could still prove useful in information retrieval operations.
- EDMS applications are production systems. Extractions will have to be timed to minimize the impact on production.

Some of the problems once solved by document management systems are now addressed by more generalized content management systems that bring many EDMS functions to the Web.

Extracting from Content Management Systems

While content management systems can be considered a type of EDMS because they fulfill many of the same roles, they are primarily Web-oriented tools. These tools allow users to organize documents hierarchically, specify keywords and other basic metadata, and search for documents using basic information retrieval technology.

Unlike traditional document management systems, content management systems are tightly integrated into the Web, and this makes integration with a document warehouse much easier. Here are some points to keep in mind when working with content management systems and document warehouses together:

- Documents are easily accessible through the Web. Only document metadata, including summaries and extracted features, should be stored in the document warehouse.
- Since content managers often use databases, some popular crawlers will not find documents within these systems. Tools are beginning to emerge that support what has been termed deep linking—that is, linking to documents within a database. Most deep linking tools require site-specific wrappers to work and so are not generalizable to other sites.

- Content managers provide for access controls. As with file and document management systems, ensure the extraction process has adequate access to find relevant documents.

The extraction process is highly dependent upon the document source system. Although we are primarily concerned with internal documents in this chapter, Web-oriented tools, such as content managers, are becoming integral components of document management strategies.

This concludes our discussion of the extraction process for supporting internal operations. We will now turn our attention to the types of text analysis we can expect to utilize in this domain.

Steps to Effective Text Mining for Operational Management

We will begin our discussion on the steps to effective text mining for operational management by assuming that we have a populated document warehouse at our disposal. Our next objective is to utilize this decision support resource for creating a more detailed understanding of standard operations as well as projects. The steps toward this goal include:

- Defining the type of information we need
- Specifying a process for extracting that information

The first step is obvious. We need to identify what we are looking for, and this could include: indicators of personnel problems, quality control issues, background information for a research project, or customer complaints.

Specifying a Process for Extracting Information

The second step is more challenging. Here, we must determine the best way to extract the information we need. At one end of the spectrum, we could simply use IR techniques to retrieve all documents with keywords. In the case of personnel monitoring, an HR director may want to know of all cases where the term *harassment* is used in an evaluation, reprimand, or other HR document. To reduce the amount of text that the reader must deal with, IR techniques could be combined with automatic summarization. These options will provide satisfactory results for the limited number of documents one would have to read in such cases. When a larger result set is likely in our searches, the feature extraction techniques should be applied. In the case of customer communications, we may find high degrees of correlation between the names of particular products and commonly used complaint terms. How we use these techniques will also depend upon whether we are dealing with repeated processes or ad hoc projects.

Text Analysis for Process Monitoring

In the case of process monitoring, an auto-alert mechanism can be utilized. Let's consider again the case of the HR director watching for harassment incidents. A simple query, such as the following, could return the summarized version of HR documents that deal with harassment.

```
SELECT
      doc_id, summary
FROM
      documents
WHERE
      CONTAINS(ABOUT('harassment'))>0
AND
      load_date >= :last_load_date;
```

Here, we use the Oracle interMedia Text syntax. The ABOUT operator uses a thematic index to search for documents that make reference to *harassment* or similar terms, such as *aggravate*, *irritate*, or *haze*. The exact terms that would cause a document to be indexed under harassment are specified in the thesaurus used during thematic analysis. The CONTAINS function returns the relative weight of the specified theme in each document, so that only documents about harassment are returned.

The query itself could be implemented as a trigger but a better approach is to use a queue of queries that are executed after each load, as depicted in Figure 14.5. With this approach, system designers and end users have more control over when queries are executed and the priority of each query. It also eases maintenance since triggers do not grow into unmanageable sizes.

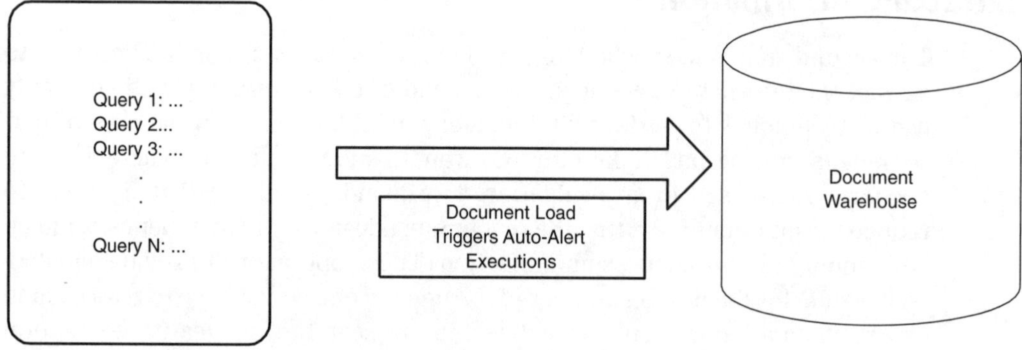

Figure 14.5 An auto-alert queue should be used to manage regular text monitoring operations.

Text Mining for Ad Hoc Analysis

Auto-alerts of this sort are not useful for ad hoc analysis. When dealing with project-oriented operations, the process is more interactive and less well defined. The best that can be provided are some basic principles for interactive text mining operations. These include:

- Begin with broad-ranging information retrieval. Do not be concerned with retrieving a large document set at this point. The main objective here is to ensure a high recall rate. We do not want to miss relevant documents, and we will use other techniques to improve precision by weeding out extraneous documents.
- Next, apply clustering techniques to divide the document set into manageable groups. This step may require that a feature extraction program be run first to provide the basis for grouping the documents.
- If hierarchical clustering is used, try to identify branches of the cluster that are outside your domain of interest. Pruning branches at this point will reduce the feature set we will have to work with later.
- Analyze the contents of each cluster, perhaps using summaries. At this stage, we are still exploring the set of documents trying to understand the range of topics covered by the document set.
- If key topics are missing or too many irrelevant topics are included in the document set, narrow the information retrieval queries used in the first step and repeat the exploration process. When this step is completed, you will have a relatively high-precision set of documents. The next step depends upon your objective.
- If an overall understanding of the domain is your objective, review document summaries and explore hyperlinked documents as necessary. This would be the case, for example, when an attorney is becoming familiar with a legal case or a market analyst is trying to assess the company's position relative to a particular market.
- If a detailed understanding of the relationship of certain topics is required, then feature extraction and analysis come next. This would be the case if an analyst were looking for patterns across documents, such as consistent complaints about a line of products or from a particular region. Analyzing features can be done using statistical or data mining techniques. For example, how frequently do the terms *broken* and *electronic* or *handheld* occur? This association does not denote a causal relationship, and more analysis of text is required if a pattern is discovered.

As Figure 14.6 shows, text mining is frequently a cyclical process that often leads to new searches for other types of information.

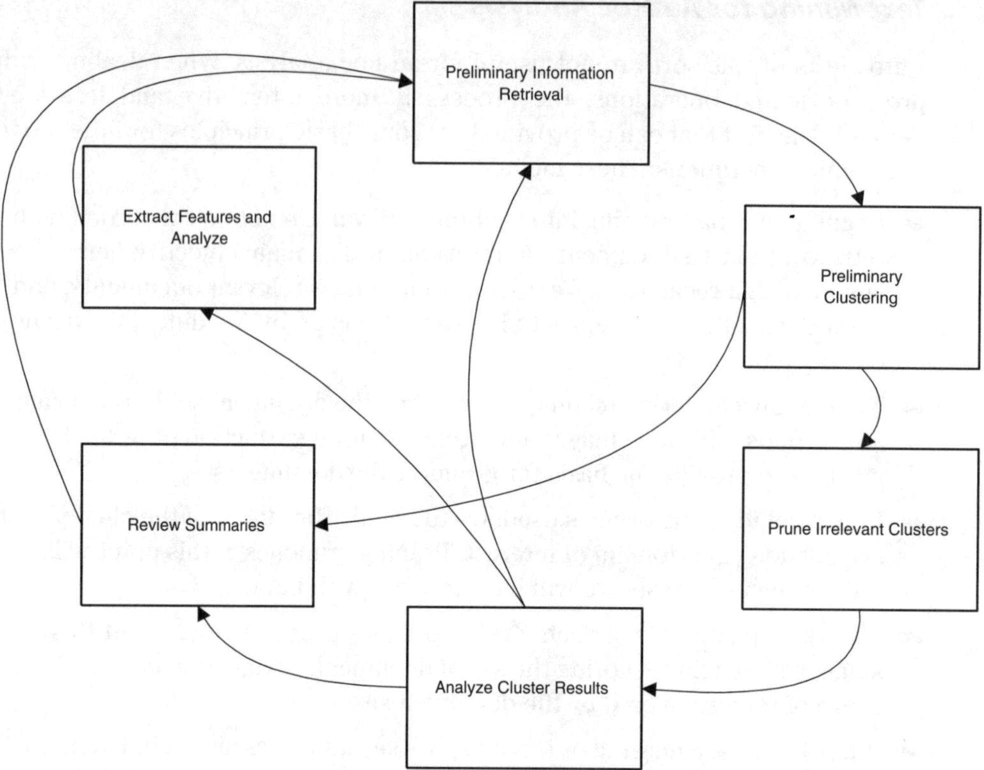

Figure 14.6 Text mining is an interactive process, driven at each stage by the findings of the previous step.

Meeting Wide-Ranging Organizational Needs

Whether we are dealing with standard operating procedures or ad hoc projects, the document warehouse can support a wide range of needs. One of the key advantages of a document warehouse is that, like the enterprise document management system, it can be exploited across the organization. When building a document warehouse to improve internal operations remember one simple principle: build at the department level and share at the enterprise level.

First, why build at the department level? This is the easiest place to start. Starting a document warehouse is not a trivial process, and simplifying organizational issues will only help the project. At a department level, one can still find a wide range of documents to work with, especially in areas such as law and marketing. This will give project staff already familiar with the domain an opportunity to use their knowledge to help learn text mining operations. Working within a single department will also minimize domain-specific tasks, such as developing a custom thesaurus. Since the structure of a document warehouse does not impose restrictions on the type or content of documents that are included, the risk of creating a department-specific document warehouse that will not adapt to other areas is minimized.

Next, why share across the enterprise? This will provide the biggest payback. Any of us used to working within a particular department sometimes have a hard time imagining that our documents or information could be of use to anyone else. The rapid and vigorous adoption of data warehousing has dispelled some of those ideas. Furthermore, as repositories, such as document and data warehouses are used, they tend to generate expectations for more information than is actually in the warehouse, thus driving the growth of the warehouse.

Starting with a department level warehouse and extending it to include other areas means that the document warehouse can grow to meet the needs of the entire organization.

Conclusions

Meeting the operational needs of an organization requires an understanding of both standard operating processes and ad hoc projects. The former is best served by monitoring operations that can alert managers and analysts to potential problems early in their development. Projects, by their very nature, can cover a wide range of needs. In this case, interactive exploration of a document warehouse can provide background information or raw material for a detailed analysis of a particular problem, such as customer complaints about a product. Regardless of which of the two types of operations one focuses on, the document warehouse built at the department level and then extended incrementally to other areas can grow to meet the text analysis needs of an organization.

In the next chapter we will examine ways that text mining can be used to support customer relationship management.

CHAPTER 15

Knowing Your Business-to-Business Customer: Text Mining for Customer Relationship Management

Customer relationship management (CRM) is the practice of understanding all aspects of a business's dealings with its customers. Traditional CRM typically focuses on transaction-oriented data, such as purchase and payment records that shed light on the types of products that interest the customer the most. This strategy works well in consumer markets, especially when internal data, such as purchase history, is combined with demographic and sociographic information acquired from third parties. When dealing with the business-to-business market, though, we have even more options for obtaining information about our customers. Certainly, we still have internal data at our disposal but we also have news stories, financial statements, regulatory agency reports, and market news about customers. This wealth of additional information presents opportunities to extend the reach of customer relationship management research into another dimension by using text mining. To develop a rich CRM model of our customers, we will move beyond transactional data and look into:

- Customers' needs for products and services
- Customers' markets
- Customer's strategy

As Figure 15.1 shows, while transactional data can provide a 360-degree view of a customer, adding another dimension, in this case text analysis, can provide an even richer, more complex view of your customers' operations, needs, and long-term plans.

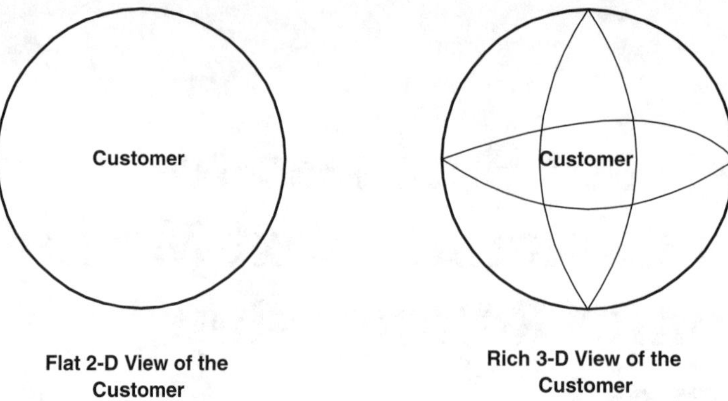

Figure 15.1 A transaction-data-oriented 360-degree view does not provide the full view of a customer.

A customer's initial need for products and services can be determined, in large part, from purchasing history. Data mining techniques can help to identify purchasing cycles (when particular products are bought), associative patterns (what products are purchased together), and clusters of similar customers (how customers can be grouped by similarity). However, looking only at past transactions as a basis for future expectations makes an implicit assumption that the causes for those past purchases will continue into the future. For example, a customer that ordered $3 million in electronics equipment last year might have done so to meet the requirements of a government contract that is now complete. How much can we reasonably expect this client to purchase next year? Without an understanding of the client's market and its position in the market, it is impossible to accurately estimate.

This chapter will include some of the low-level programming details that arise when working with large collections of documents. We will introduce several Perl programs that provide the glue we need to link all the programs we work with in the document warehouse environment. Those not interested in the coding aspects can easily skip the program descriptions without loss.

Understanding Your Customer's Market

Understanding a customer's market requires familiarity with at least three areas:

- Competition
- Industry trends
- Market conditions

Your customer's competition may also be your customers, and this may provide some insight into the competitive advantages and disadvantages of each. Even when competitors of your customers are not also your customers, understanding their practices can shed light on the needs of your customers. Industry trends are more useful for long-term analysis. If new housing construction is increasing, then this will have secondary effects on other markets related to home building, such as mortgages, homeowner's insurance, furniture, and local government real estate tax rolls. Finally, market conditions will influence the purchasing patterns of customers. Interest rates have a direct affect on investment and capital expansion. For international clients, currency exchange rates, import and export regulations, and political changes at home can all factor into business decisions.

Understanding your customer's short-term tactics and long-term strategy is yet another element of the full understanding of your customer. In the next chapter, "Know Your Competition: Text Mining for Competitive Intelligence," we will examine in detail ways to assess the tactics and strategies and monitor the activities of competitors. Those same techniques can be applied to your customer's competitors and thus extend your understanding of your customer.

In the next section, we will delve into ways to know your customer through text analysis techniques and then move on to understanding your customer's markets and some of the influences on those markets. Finally, we will conclude with a discussion of an example illustrating the development of a customer intelligence profile that can move you from a two-dimensional 360-degree understanding to the richer three-dimensional spherical understanding of the factors that affect your customers.

Before going any farther, we should clarify some terminology. Throughout this chapter, we will be discussing two different types of markets. The first is yours, the one the company building the CRM application lives with every day. For example, for IBM, HP, and Compaq, one of these markets is the high-end UNIX server market. The second type of market is the one the customer operates in on a regular basis. For example, customers using high-end UNIX servers operate in chemical manufacturing, insurance, food distribution, power generation, and hundreds of other markets. Within this chapter, we will refer to the first market as the business's market and the second as the customer's market.

Developing a Customer Intelligence Profile

The objective of this section is to define what it is we should know about our customers and how we can learn it by developing a customer intelligence profile. The essential tasks of answering both the what and the how questions can be addressed by three distinct types of documents:

- Internal resources
- Client communications
- External sources

The most easily accessed source of information is, of course, internal documentation, such as proposals, contracts, communications, project plans, and other information shared with the client. Another equally valuable source is internal documents about the market in which the business operates and other documents that are used only internally and not shared with customers and clients.

Client communications can include letters, e-mails, and other correspondence. These can be especially useful for spotting issues before they become the subject of formal documents, such as project reviews or contracts.

External sources are any information sources outside of the business's or the customer's organization. These can provide a wealth of information and include:

- Business news sources
- Press releases
- Regulatory agencies filings
- Patents and trademarks
- Trade association publications

Each of these sources provides a different perspective on a customer. Business news sources will report on significant and unusual events, both favorable and unfavorable, while press releases are controlled by the customer and serve to notify the market and investors of significant events in the business. Regulatory agency reports provide a wealth of information about how well a business is complying with rules governing specific areas of operations, such as environmental pollution controls or worker safety. Patents, trademarks, and trade associations can provide more detailed information about an enterprise.

It is obvious that there is a wealth of information available, in addition to conventional CRM sources; the questions now are how to get at it and how to analyze it. Here are the basic steps, which we have seen before:

- Define document sources
- Identify processing requirements
- Retrieve documents
- Load and analyze documents
- Assess the results

These basic steps are probably well understood at this point, so we will move right into an example of a text-oriented customer relationship process.

Sample Case of B-to-B Customer Relationship Management

In this example, we will assume that our company provides goods and services to the chemical manufacturing industry and that our customers include Dow Chemical, Dupont, BASF, and other major companies in the industry. We will now walk through the process of gathering and analyzing information on our customers. First, we will work with internal documents and describe in concrete detail, the steps required to gather, preprocess, and analyze the documents. We will then move on to external documents and discuss the steps to extract business intelligence from them as well. As we work through each task, we will describe how to perform the task for a particular tool. Although this is not a tutorial on any of these tools, there is no better way to get a realistic sense of what is actually involved in text analysis operations.

Getting the Information I: Internal Sources

As we have seen in the previous chapter, internal information can be stored in file systems, document management systems, and Web-based content management systems. In this section, we will look at how to efficiently work with file systems to gather customer-related documents and identify key topics described in the text of the documents. The basic steps are to:

- Identify internal sources
- Determine preprocessing requirements
- Develop retrieval and transformation programs
- Load the documents into the document warehouse
- Perform text analysis operations

We will now look into the details of each step. In the case of retrieving and loading, we will look at simple sample programs to help describe the basic structure common to these types of operations.

Identifying Internal Sources

The first step is to define exactly what types of documents we want. For purposes of understanding our customers, let's assume that the key internal documents we need are contracts, proposals, and product specification reports that describe the particular requirements for a product, such as parts machined to a certain tolerance or lubricants within a certain range of viscosity.

Identifying Processing Requirements

Next, we need to understand any preprocessing requirements. First, we need to make sure the document is in a format accessible to our text mining tools. Microsoft Word and other word-processing documents are no problem for Oracle interMedia Text because it uses a format filter, but other tools, such as IBM Intelligent Miner for Text and Megaputer TextAnalyst, expect text files. This conversion is a relatively easy task. One can either use a third-party filter, such as Inso's, or write a basic conversion program using the source tool. For example, Microsoft Word makes much of the tool's functionality available to programmers through OLE objects, so one can write a program in Visual Basic, Visual C++, or Python that reads a document and saves it as a text file.

Retrieving Documents Examples

The next two steps, retrieving and transforming documents, can often be combined into a single step. Scripting languages such as Perl and Python support many types of file manipulation. One of the most useful is a technique called globbing. Globbing is the process of expanding a file name pattern as the UNIX shell would. For example, in Perl, the line

```
glob("r:/legal/contracts/*.doc")
```

will return all word-processing documents in the r:\legal\contracts\ directory. This is usually used to drive a loop within a Perl program that is retrieving and loading documents. A common pattern using glob is:

```
while (defined($fname = glob($fpattern))) {
     open (SOURCE, $fname)

#   Perform transformations here, e.g.,
     # strip HTML tags, etc.
     …

#   Write file to target directory if using a file oriented
     #  tool or insert into database if using db oriented tool.
     …}
```

The first line of the while loop does a lot of work. Let's start with the innermost part. The $fpattern is a scalar variable, which means that it holds a single value, unlike a list or an array, which may have multiple values. In this case, $fpattern would most likely be passed as a command-line argument that specifies the pattern identifying a group of files to load. When used with the glob function, the pattern "m:/marketing/pr/*.doc" would get the press release word-processing documents, while "s:/sales/presentations/*.ppt" would retrieve all PowerPoint documents in the presentations subdirectory of the sales department. Defined is a Boolean function that is used to determine when glob has returned all files specified by the pattern. Once all the file names have been returned, glob returns undefined.

The next line is executed once for each file name returned by glob and attempts to open the file. Now, in most real programs, the open statement is followed by a command such as:

```
|| die "Can't open source file: $!"'
```

The double bars (||) is a shorthand notation for OR and indicates "if the open fails, perform the following command." The die command terminates the program and writes the specified message to the standard error stream. Since we do not want to terminate the program because of an error with a single file, the more likely scenario in document warehousing is to skip that file and write a message to a log file. We will, however, use the die command in later scripts.

Document Loading Example

Now let's turn to the loading process. The actual load process is dependent upon whether the documents will reside in directories or in a database. In the former case, we still want to add metadata to the database while copying files to the target directory. When loading into a database, we have two basic options, using a database-specific loader program, such as Oracle SQL*Loader, Microsoft SQL Server, a bulk copy program and IBM DB2 Load-Utility, or a generic programmatic tool, such as Perl's database-independent interface (DBI) module.

When we are using a directory-based repository, we will either copy files to a document warehousing directory or leave them in their original locations and build lists of files that are used to drive the analysis process. The first method is easily implemented and will not be considered any further, but we will look into the latter method in this section. We will also describe how to use a scripting language, such as Perl, to minimize the work required to use database-specific loading tools.

Building File Lists for Text Analysis

Some tools, such as IBM Intelligent Miner for Text, work with individual files but also take file lists as input. In this case, the loading process can be reduced to simply building a file with a list of file names. The following code shows the basic elements of a Perl script that can be used to create such a file. Note that it uses the glob function again so file name patterns can be used to specify a group of files to include in the file name list.

```
# Demo File List Generator: filelist.pl
#      This script creates a file with the names of files that
#      match the specified pattern. This is useful for tools like
#      IBM Intelligent Miner for Text which can take a list of files
#      as input for processing. Note, that the output file is
#      opened in append mode so this can be called multiple times
#      with different patterns.
#
# First, name the command line arguments
#  1. First is the name of the target file to write to.
#  2. Next is the file name pattern to search for.
#
$outfile = $ARGV[0];
$pattern = $ARGV[1];

# Open the target file in append mode
open (TARGET, ">> $outfile") || die "Can't open target file: $!";

# For each file name that matches the pattern,
# write it to the output file specified in the command line.
while (defined($fname = glob($pattern))) {
                 print TARGET $fname . "\n";
                 }
```

The benefits of using a script like this are twofold. First, it is portable. One could also use shell scripts to do the same process but if you need to pull files from both Windows NT and UNIX systems, using a Perl script will minimize the amount of code that you might need to change when it's used on the different platforms. Second, Perl is a rich programming language, so additional features, such as error logging are easily added.

Using the script is straightforward. First, call the script with each set of files that should be included in analysis and then invoke the text analysis program. For example, to extract the features from all contracts and press releases using the feature extractor included in IBM Intelligent Miner for Text, we would:

```
filelist infile.txt  r:/legal/contracts/*.txt
filelist infile.txt  m:/marketing/pr/*.txt
imzxrun -f C -x n -I -o outfile.txt  infile.txt
```

The first two lines add file names to infile.txt, which is then used in the third line to run the feature extraction program (imzxrun.exe). The imzxrun command options include –f C, which indicates that only the cannonical form of the terms should be used. The –x n command option forces names of persons, places, and organizations to be extracted. Finally, the –I option indicates that the input file contains a list of file names and is not the source text, and the –o option specifies where to pipe the extractor's output. The next step would be to load the infile.txt file into a database for further analysis, and we will cover that step later in this chapter.

Building Custom Loader Scripts

As we noted, when loading documents into a database, one of the options is to use the proprietary loader tool supplied with the database. In this section, we will consider the Oracle loader tool, SQL Loader. Most loader tools use a control file plus data file model. The data file contains the data to load into the database, while the control file describes the contents of the data file and specifies where each element is to be loaded. So, although we will only consider one tool here, the basic principles apply in general to most relational database loading tools.

Rather than go into great detail about the structure of SQL Loader files, we will work from an example and explain as much as needed. The goal here is not to become proficient in writing SQL Loader control files, but to discuss how to quickly generate the data files that will identify the documents that are to be loaded into the document warehouse.

First, let's assume that we are working with a table created with the following statement:

```
CREATE TABLE customer_docs (
          doc_id                NUMBER    PRIMARY KEY,
          doc_text              CLOB,
          doc_modified_date     DATE,
          doc_loaded_date       DATE);
```

In this simple table, the doc_id is a unique identifier created at load time, and the doc_text column is large object type for text. The doc_modified_date is the date the document was last modified, and doc_loaded_date will contain the date and time the document is loaded into the warehouse.

Now, we need to build a control file that specifies how to map the data from the data file to the table. For the customer_docs table, we'll use the following control file:

```
LOAD DATA
INFILE 'docs_to_load.txt'
INTO TABLE customer_docs
APPEND
FILEDS TERMINATED BY ','
(doc_id SEQUENCE (MAX, 1),
 doc_modified_date,
 doc_type,
 doc_loaded_date SYSDATE,
 ext_fname FILLER CHAR(80),
 doc_text LOBFILE(ext_fname) TERMINATED BY EOF)
```

The file named docs_to_load.txt will hold the raw data to append to the customer_docs table. The primary key will be generated on the fly, but the source file will contain the document's last modified date and document type along with the name of the document to load. The name is loaded into the temporary variable ext_fname, and the text is loaded into the doc_text LOB file. The data file looks like:

```
10-5-2000, CONTRACT, r:\legal\contracts\acme_may5.doc
15-5-2000, CONTRACT, r:\legal\contracts\acme_may15.doc
23-5-2000, CONTRACT, r:\legal\contracts\acme_may23.doc
17-5-2000, CONTRACT, r:\legal\contracts\brz_may17.doc
18-5-2000, CONTRACT, r:\legal\contracts\brz_may18.doc
10-6-2000, CONTRACT, r:\legal\contracts\clnd_jun10.doc
15-7-2000, CONTRACT, r:\legal\contracts\clnd_jul15.doc
23-10-2000, CONTRACT, r:\legal\contracts\drw_oct23.doc
17-11-2000, CONTRACT, r:\legal\contracts\drw_nov17.doc
18-10-2000, CONTRACT, r:\legal\contracts\elft_oct18.doc
```

Now, creating this file is essential to the loading process but we do not want to construct this by hand, so once again, it is time to build a Perl script. The following script does the trick.

```
#  DEMO: SQL Loader Data File Generator
#       This generates a data file that is used with Oracle SQL
#     Loader to load documents into a database. The data file
#     generated by this script is actually loaded by a SQL Loader
#     command and a schema specific control file.
#
# Load package to get file statistics
use File::stat;

# Three arguments are passed:
#        1. a regular expression describing the files to load, e.g.,
#        /usr/legal/*.doc
#       2. a file type indication, e.g., Contract, News, Press
#         Release, etc.
#      3. Output file for results

$pattern = $ARGV[0];
$doctype = $ARGV[1];
$outfile = $ARGV[2];

open (OUT, ">$outfile") || die "Can't open output file. $!";

# For each file in meeting the specified pattern in the glob call
while (defined($filename = glob($pattern))) {

    # Get some basic file statistics like last modification time.
    $sb = stat($filename);

    # Get modification time and reformat for database.
   ($sec, $min, $hour, $mday, $mon, $year, $wday, $yday, $isdst)
      = localtime $sb->mtime ;
```

```
# Write the load spec to the data file.
print OUT  $mday . "-" . $mon . "-" . ($year+1900),", ",
  $doctype,", ",$filename, "\n";

   }
```

The script starts with a command to load a module that provides access to file statistics. The script is invoked with three parameters on the command line, a file name pattern, the type of documents to load, and an output file.

The open command opens the output file for writing. Next, the while loop iterates over each file name returned by the glob function. For each file, statistics are collected, but for this example we are only using the modified date and time of the file (mtime). The final line formats the data, in this case the modified date, document type, and file name, and writes it to the output file.

In a production environment, we would most likely add other metadata in addition to the modification date, such as the author or owner and the file format.

Scripting languages such as Perl are essential to document warehousing. The techniques described here work for both internal and external documents and for both database-oriented and file-oriented warehouses. In these examples, globbing provides access to a large number of files using a simple syntax. Scripts also make it easy to construct data files that are used with proprietary loader programs such as SQL Loader. Since Perl, and similar languages, such as Python, provide modules for specific functions, such as collecting file statistics, working with the Internet, accessing databases, and calling external programs such as file filters, they are ideal platforms for building transformation and load programs as well.

The thrust of this section has been on working with internal documents, but now we will turn our attention to external documents and gathering information on our customers' markets.

Getting the Information II: External Documents

We work with external documents in customer relationship management to understand our customers' markets and to anticipate their near-term needs. We can break down the problem into three subproblems to construct a customer intelligence profile:

- Understanding industry trends
- Understanding market conditions
- Understanding the customer's competition

Industry trends are broad changes in the market that will affect the ways in which companies manufacture and deliver products, the ways in which companies work with each other, and how they are regulated. Market conditions are short-term phenomena that vary, for the most part, outside of the control of any single company. Interest rates, trade embargoes, currency exchange rates, and other economic and political factors can influence the short-term, and sometimes long-term, decisions of customers. Finally, customers probably expend a lot of resources to keep abreast of their competition's activities. With an understanding of their customers' competitive advantages and disadvantages, a business can better meet the needs of their customers.

Let's assume that we are interested in understanding each new area of investment, research, and development, and we've decided to gather documents from the following sources:

- Company Web sites
- Financial reports, such as Security Exchange Commission (SEC) filings
- Industry news sources
- Financial news sources

Since we will want to keep up to date on these sources, we will use a command-line crawler that we can run under a UNIX cron job or with the Windows NT AT command. An interactive tool that provides a scheduling mechanism will also meet our needs. For our example, we'll use GNU's wget utility.

Once we have the documents in hand we'll need to find out the most important topics covered in those texts. In particular, we will want to see the most frequently mentioned products, locations, and companies, by company. We'll use two techniques for this. First, we'll extract features, load them into a relational database, and explore the results using SQL. The alternative is to use an interactive browser to explore the connection between topics. For this we will use Megaputer's TextAnalyst.

Collecting External Documents

To get our well-rounded view of the chemical industry we'll start by downloading the press releases from the major manufacturers, Dow, Dupont, and BASF, using the following command:

```
wget -A  *.html, *.htm -nd -r -l 5 -nv  www.basf-
ag.basf.de/en/news/presse
wget -A *.html, *htm -nd -r -l 5 -nv www.dow.com/dow_news/index.html
wget -A  *.html,*.htm -nd -r -l 5 -nv www.dupont.com/corp/whats-
new/releases/index.html
```

These commands will retrieve the press releases from each of these companies. The wget program can take a wide range of options but we used just a few. The –A option specifies the file types to accept. In this case, we want only HTML files. Since these documents are being run through a text analysis program, there is no need to waste bandwidth downloading images. The –nd option tells wget to ignore the directory structure of the Web site when creating the local copy of the files. The –r options indicates that the directory structures of the Web site should be traversed recursively, while the –l option sets the maximum number of levels that will be traversed. Finally, the –nv option turns off most of wget's logging messages.

To get a sense of what is happening in the chemical industry from a broader perspective, we will use several industry-wide sites, such as:

- bizspacechemicals.com: A chemical industry technology site
- www.neis.com: Chemical Industry Home Page
- www.chemonnet.com: Chemical Industry Portal
- www.cnionline.com: Chemical News & Intelligence
- www.chemistryindustry.com: ChemClub.com, a source for events, publications, and news

As with customer sites, we will use wget to gather the documents we need, and once we have them we'll begin our preliminary analysis.

Preliminary Document Analysis

At this stage, we have gathered documents and are ready to perform basic preprocessing. Since the text we have collected is all in English and in HTML format, we do not need any special machine translation preprocessing. Next, we'll move on to the basic text analysis, which in this case can take on two forms:

- Extracting features
- Developing a semantic net of related terms

Figure 15.2 shows how we can decide between the two techniques. For the first process, we will discuss the use of IBM Intelligent Miner for Text, while Megaputer's TextAnalyst will be used to create a semantic net of terms.

Let's start with our analysis of example documents.

Analysis I: Feature Extraction

After downloading files with wget, we now have a directory filled with the HTML files found at the site. We want to use IBM Intelligent Miner for Text to

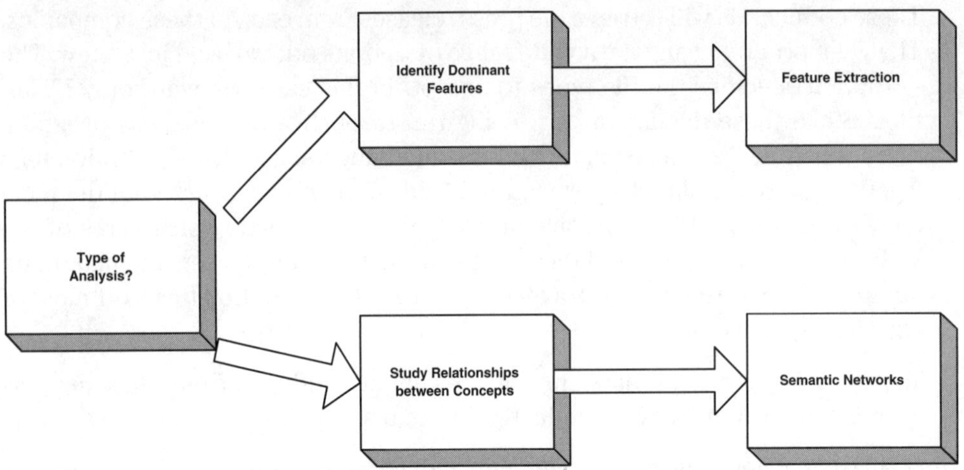

Figure 15.2 The objectives of the analysis phase drive the technique used.

extract the features, so we need to build a file listing all the documents we have retrieved; therefore, we will use the filelist.pl program listed earlier. The result should be simply a list of HTML files. Generating a list of files given a pattern, such as r:/legal/contracts/*.doc is a simple matter with a shell script in either UNIX or Windows NT. A simple Perl script, such as the following, will also do.

```
# First, name the command line arguments.
#  1. First is the name of the target file to write to.
#  2. Next is the file name pattern to search for.
$outfile = $ARGV[0];
$pattern = $ARGV[1];

# Open the target file in append mode.
open (TARGET, ">> $outfile") || die "Can't open target file: $!";

# For each file name that matches the pattern,
# write it to the output file specified in the command line.
while (defined($fname = glob($pattern))) {
                print TARGET $fname . "\n";
                }
```

Lets assume that we have created a list of file names in filelist.txt. To run the feature extraction program over those files and save the results to extract_feat.text, use the following command:

```
imzxrun -f C -x n -o extract_feat.txt -I filelist.txt
```

The output from this command will look like this:

```
<IMZ ID>chem_pr.txt</IMZ ID>
<IMZ CONTENT>
```

```
NC    7     Alpha Beta Chemical    PERSON?
NC    1     Director of Technology for Gamma Chemical Computing ORG
NC    2     Gamma   UNAME
NC    2     Gamma Chemical UNAME
NC    3     Gamma Chemical Computing      UNAME
NC    2     Gamma Chemical Computing System      UNAME
NC    1     John Jones     PERSON?
NC    1     Mary Smith     PERSON?
NC    1     New Technologies      ORG
</IMZ CONTENT>
<!---->

.
.
.
```

The output is a structured format where the features of each record are output using the <IMZ CONTENT> entity. This entity is preceded by an <IMZ ID> entity with the file name of the source document. Our main concern is the lines prefixed with NC. Each line contains in the second column the number of times the feature occurred in the document. Since we used the –f C option, each occurrence of a term is converted to its canonical form before being counted. The third column list the terms themselves, and the final column indicates the type of feature. The command to run the feature extractor included the –x n option, so only the names of persons, places, organizations, and other entities are included.

Next, we need to load this information into a database for further analysis, such as finding the top ten places mentioned by Alpha Beta Chemical or the top twenty names of objects, such as chemicals or products. For this task, we will once again use a Perl script.

The following scripts takes as arguments a source file with the extracted features and the name of the company associated with the documents. After some preliminary housekeeping, a connection is made to the database using DBI. The DBI module uses drivers for specific databases but otherwise provides a common interface to relational databases. Once a connection is established, an INSERT statement is prepared. By creating and parsing the statement outside the loop, the program will avoid the work of creating an execution plan for the statement with each iteration. Bind variables, represented as question marks, are used as placeholders for the actual values inserted into the table.

After preparing the statement, the feature file is opened and read. Each line that contains a feature record—that is, each line that is preceded by NC—is split up using tab characters as delimiters, and each value is assigned to a variable. Perl, like Python, allows multiple assignments in a single statement as in the case of

```
($nc, $count, $term, $type) = split('\t');
```

where four variables are assigned at once. The variables are then bound to the placeholders using the sth→bind_param function, and the execute statement actually performs the insert operation.

```
# FEATURE_LOAD.PL - This demonstration program loads features
# extracted by the IBM Intelligent Miner for Text into a
# relational database for further analysis.

use DBI ;          # Load the DBI Module


# Rename the command line arguments.
#  The first is the name of the customer company.
#  The second is the source file with the extracted features.
#  The source for this program is the output from imzxrun.
my $company = $ARGV[0];
my $source = $ARGV[1];

# Set up a connection to the database. DBI supports a range
# of drivers, in this case we'll load it into a DB2 database.
my $dbh = DBI->connect("dbi:DB2:DocWarehouse","textmgr","textminer") ;

# Parse the INSERT statement once and use parameters for the attributes
# to be inserted. Some DBI drivers may not support parameters so this
# may not work with other drivers.
my $sth = $dbh->prepare("
                  INSERT INTO DOC_FEATURES
                        (term, company, frequency)
                      VALUES
                        (?, ?, ?)
                     ");

#  Open the feature file for reading.
open (SOURCE, $source) || die ("Can't open file: $!");

# Now, for each line in the source file
while (<SOURCE>) {
     # check if the line starts with NC, if so, add the
     # feature, otherwise ignore the line. In a production
     # program, we'd want to track the file ID but we'll
     # ignore that here.
    if (/^NC/){
        # First, clean up the end of line character.
        chomp;

        # Break the attributes into terms, splitting on the
        # tab character
          ($nc, $count, $term, $type) = split('\t');

             # Bind parameters to the INSERT statement.
             # First, the term
```

```
        $sth->bind_param(1, $term);

        # Next the name of the company
        $sth->bind_param(2, $company);

        # And third, the number of times the term
        # appeared in this document
        $sth->bind_param(3, $frequency);

        # Finally, execute the insert.
        $sth->execute;
        }
    }
```

With the terms and their frequencies loaded, it is now a simple matter of using SQL or an ad hoc query tool to examine the most frequent terms by company and how often terms used by one company are also used by another. If we are willing to make the load operation more complex, we could add other information such as the name and date of the source document. This would allow us to determine the number of distinct documents mentioning a feature and the time range over which those documents were issued. This would help us better understand seasonal variations or if many of the companies are mentioning the same terms at roughly the same time, changes in the market.

Rather than use a database to analyze the key features of documents, we could also use a visual exploration tool, such as Megaputer's TextAnalyst.

Analysis II: Exploring Documents with Semantic Nets

While using SQL with extracted features is an excellent way to get a quick handle on the basic issues described in a document set, exploring and linking concepts provides an alternate method. Exploring does not provide, at least not easily, quickly calculated statistics, such as how many times a particular term appeared. It does provide the means to navigate around terms that frequently appear together and thus explore the relationships between concepts. In Figure 15.3 we can see how key terms are related.

Browsing and drilling down through levels of related concepts helps us to understand the broader landscape of a set of documents better than the basic feature extraction does. When developing a customer intelligence profile, it is important to segregate documents by source. With that set up, we can easily analyze subsets of the document collection by source or at least by general topic, such as market and competition. In the chemical industry example, we would want to keep customers separate as well as third-party sources, such as news stories. We can always combine groups of documents, such as internal documents and customer press releases, to try to detect overlap in key areas.

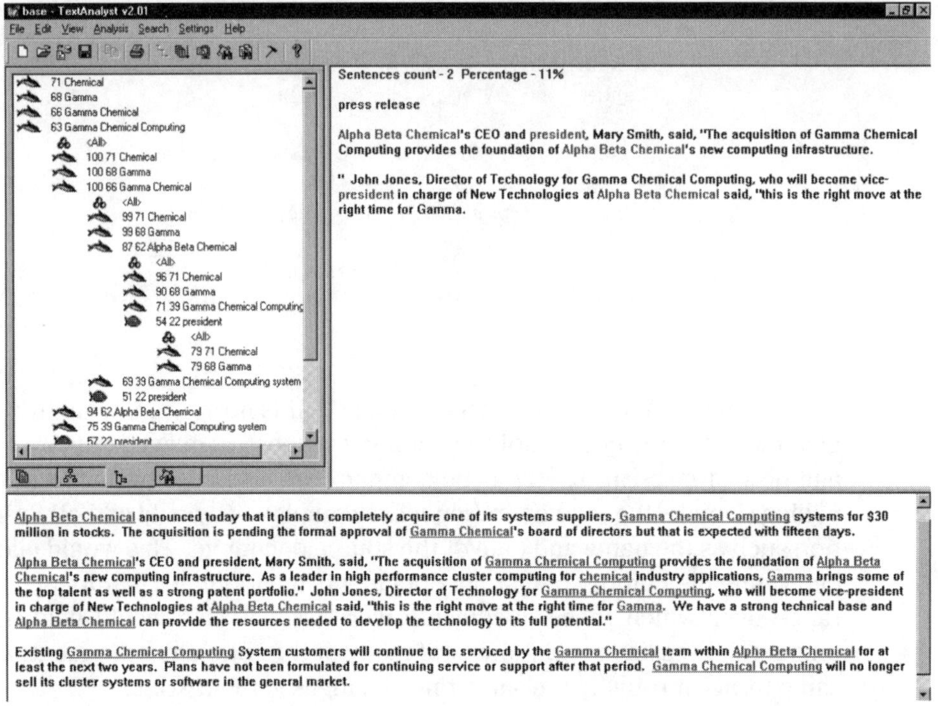

Figure 15.3 Analyzing press releases from chemical manufacturers can show a wide range of relationships.

Since analysis occurs automatically at document load time, it is important to perform preprocessing before opening the files in TextAnalyst.

When using HTML documents with TextAnalyst, we first need to strip out the HTML tags. The current version of TextAnalyst (version 2) does not automatically remove HTML tags, although support is planned for this operation in a later versions. If we do not strip out the HTML tags, they will be analyzed along with the content, resulting in something like the output shown in Figure 15.4.

In any case, this is not a problem because a short Perl script will do the trick. Regardless of whether or not TextAnalyst automatically removes tags, we would want an HTML-to-text conversion script. Here is a basic one to do the job.

```
# HTML2TXT.PL - HTML to text converter. This program takes an HTML
# file and strips out HTML tags. The first argument to
# program is the name of the HTML file to convert and the
# second is the output file.

# It's a short program, but let's use mnemonic names anyway.
```

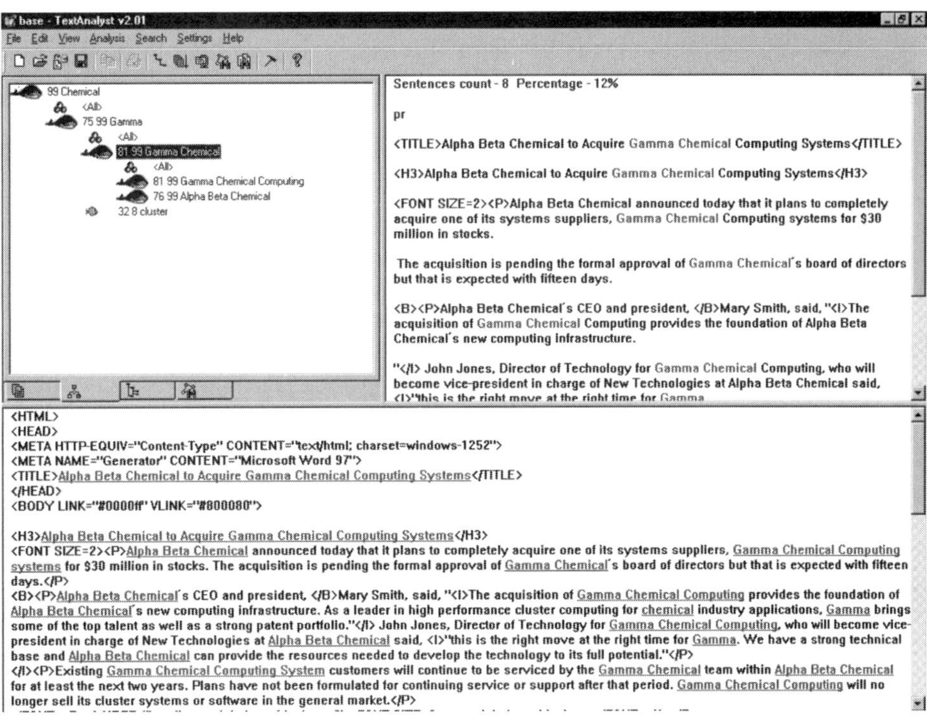

Figure 15.4 Without removing HTML tags, we will not get the results we expect.

```
my $source = $ARGV[0];
my $target = $ARGV[1];

# Open our two files and stop if there are any problems.
open (SOURCE , "<$source") || die "Can't open source file: $!";
open (TARGET , ">$target") || die "Can't open target file: $!";

# Loop over each line in the source file
# 1. Substitute a space for character strings
#    beginning with a < and ending with a >, using
#    a lazy search (i.e., stop at the first closing
#    bracket, not the last).
# 2. Print the current line ($_) with the substitution
#    to the output file.
while (<SOURCE>) {
   s/<.+?>/ /g;
   print TARGET $_;
   }
close($source);
close($target);
```

Once the HTML files are cleaned up, we can load them into TextAnalyst. We noted in Chapter 13 that TextAnalyst has a COM interface, so we can develop programs to perform much of the analysis we are interested in, but here we will use the interface provided with the tool. Loading files is simply a matter of opening them in a standard Windows dialog box.

When documents are loaded, the application automatically performs morphological analysis and builds the semantic net.

When an interesting relationship is found, it can be explored in three ways. First, one can drill into it to find other terms. Following links in this way is analogous to drilling down in an ad hoc query tool from higher levels within a hierarchy to lower levels.

A second technique is to find an interesting term and then examine the context in which it is found. For example, focusing in on the term *countries* can lead to a discussion of the number and location of the countries with which this firm deals.

Finally, summaries can provide insight into the most important terms and how they relate all at once. Summaries are built using the most important sentences in a text and those sentences are chosen, in large part, based up the number of key terms in those sentences.

Navigating through the set of most prevalent terms and drilling down to find related but less prevalent terms can help you understand key concepts surrounding your customer's tactics, strategy, and market conditions.

Conclusions

When operating in a business-to-business environment, we have a wealth of textual information about our customers at our disposal. Rather than settle for only the information that can be supplied from internal transactional systems, companies can develop a richer model of their customers by analyzing both their internal documents and external sources of information. Developing customer intelligence profiles can be done with the text analysis tools and techniques we have discussed throughout this book. Using simple techniques such as feature extraction, navigation of semantic maps, and document summarization can help you to identify key concepts that are important to your customers and to the market in which they operate.

In the next chapter, we will take a closer look at a problem similar to customer intelligence profiling—competitive or market intelligence—and expand further on how applying text analysis techniques can help you develop a richer understanding of your own market and your company's position in it.

CHAPTER 16

Text Mining for Competitive Intelligence

Knowing your own strengths and weaknesses and understanding your customers' are critical to your organization's success. Unless you operate under monopolistic conditions, you have competitors who are vying for the same market you are. Knowing your competition by gathering and analyzing competitive intelligence is a key to successful business strategy. Larry Kahaner, a leading competitive intelligence consultant and writer, defines competitive intelligence as "a systematic program for gathering and analyzing information about your competitors' activities and general business trends to further your own company's goals" (Kahaner 1996).

In this chapter, we will discuss how to apply the techniques developed throughout this book to the problem of competitive intelligence. We will begin with a detailed description of competitive intelligence tasks, including the development of competitive intelligence profiles and the identification of information sources. Since so much information about companies can be found from financial sources, we will discuss how to extract information from structured financial documents, particularly those using the eXtensible Business Reporting Language (XBRL). This will require a short diversion into methods of processing XML but will quickly return to how it can be applied to XBRL documents. We will then discuss how to use the text analysis, and text mining techniques in particular, to develop a competitive intelligence system. Finally, we will turn to examples of competitive intelligence in retail markets, manufacturing, financial services, and the health care industry.

Competitive Intelligence versus Business Intelligence

The term business intelligence (BI) is well understood in the IT community, especially among data warehouse practitioners but competitive intelligence (CI) is not as commonly recognized. While the two topics share some common characteristics, they are distinct.

First, business intelligence is inwardly directed. BI systems are often built on top of data warehouses. The data warehouse, in turn, is populated with data from one or more production systems that track areas such as manufacturing processes, payables and receivables, employee information, and sales and marketing data. These sources are all internal and describe only the operations of a single company. CI, on the other hand, has an external focus. Competitive intelligence systems draw information from news sources, regulatory agencies, public records, environmental and consumer watchdog groups, annual reports, speeches, competitor's marketing material, and other external information sources.

Second, a great deal of raw business intelligence information is available in structured form (that is, structured from a database perspective). Production information from an enterprise resource planning system will have the same basic format next week as it did last week. Similarly, other sources of BI information will provide reasonably well-defined data that remains consistent for long periods of time. Competitive intelligence information is often textual and not structured according to traditional data modeling rules, although it does have a coherent and intelligible structure of its own. (See Chapter 2 for more of a discussion on the myth of unstructured text).

BI data is extracted from its sources and transformed by algorithmic processes before loading into the warehouse. The algorithmic operations ensure that data in the warehouse will fit expected formats, use only codes from standardized lists, and have values within known ranges. CI comes from a variety of external sources, each of which may use different file formats, use different terms to describe the same concept and have varying degrees of quality and veracity. We can reasonably expect to find CI information in word-processing documents, presentations, Portable Document Format files, PostScript files, and text files, including HTML and XML documents. Terminology will vary by source as well. A document on a new organic solvent found at the Chemical Abstracts Service (www.cas.org) will sound decidedly different from a story at a financial news service about the same discovery. Of course, BI systems are subject to data entry errors (although most extraction, transformation and load processes catch the most serious mistakes), but for the most part we can depend upon the quality of internal data when data quality control procedures are in place. (See Larry English's *Improving Data Warehouse and Business Information Quality: Methods for Reducing Costs and Increasing Profits* [English 1999] for a discussion of this topic). Forecasts, budgets, and other estimates are relatively easy to identify within BI systems because they are usually coded as such. In fact budget systems often support multiple projection scenarios. Depending upon the application, this type of information might be needed in the warehouse where it is kept alongside actual expenditures for comparison purposes. Analyzing text to determine if the discussion is about an actual event or a projection can be difficult. The time period of some documents is obvious. Earnings estimates are future projections. Market summary reports discuss recent history, perhaps the same day's activities. Key phrases such as *industry analysts expect ...* and *Alpha Analysts predict a 15% decline in ...* tell readers that the document they are reading is a forecast and not a reporting of fact. Unfortunately, key terms such as *expect* and *predict* can often be lost in feature extraction programs and, to a much lesser degree, in automatically generated summaries. For this reason, CI system users will need access to both the processed and the original content to verify and understand the complete picture portrayed by the analyzed text. BI users rarely need to move from data warehouse data back to the original production systems.

The third difference centers on the use of competitive and business intelligence. BI is often used operationally to identify tactical level details. Which regions showed a decreasing profit margin over the last three quarters? What is the average number of serious defects by production line? What are the top ten best selling consumer electronics components in the Northeast region? Data warehouses can answer these questions and help a business understand how to fine-tune operations, perhaps by identifying weakness in the sales force, detecting patterns in quality control problems, and targeting cross-selling opportunities. BI information can also work at the strategic level. Executives need the same type of information, perhaps at a more aggregate level, to identify trends in sales and production on a larger scale. With an understanding of long-term trends across the company, decision makers can rationally allocate resources to profitable lines, while scaling back or eliminating unprofitable ones. But executives do not look just at internal numbers. To make strategic decisions, one needs to understand competitors, markets, and external factors, such as government regulations and political events. It is at the strategic level that CI complements traditional business intelligence to give decision makers a more complete picture of the world in which their firms operate.

Competitive intelligence, like business intelligence, needs to be structured and organized in such a way as to make the information accessible to those who need it, and for that we will use competitive intelligence profiles.

Competitive Intelligence Profiles

Before we begin the process of gathering information on competitors, we need to define some organizing principles or else we could find ourselves searching, retrieving, and loading documents that do not meet our requirements. CI organization develops by addressing the following points:

- Defining the target competitors
- Completing a strengths, weaknesses, opportunities, and threats (SWOT) assessment
- Answering specific research questions
- Augmenting document collection with analysis

Knowing your competitors is the first step in gathering competitive intelligence. In some industries, such as automobile or aircraft manufacturing, this is a simple matter if we look only at broad markets, such as automobile sales. In addition to making cars, General Motors also sells car parts, and in that market General Motors is not competing against other auto manufacturers but against parts manufacturers. The barriers to entry in that industry are substantially less than in the automobile market so new firms can enter more easily. The pharmaceutical industry provides a similar example. While developing and testing new drugs is a complex process, often left to large pharmaceutical companies, smaller firms are often formed to develop and market a single drug or exploit a single technology, such as genetic engineering, to improve the manufacturing process for some class of drugs. Clearly, the Goliaths of an industry should not be concerned only with the other Goliaths. In fact, it is often the Davids of the industry that were created to take advantage of a niche market or technology that the larger firms have not yet exploited, that require monitoring.

A basic form of analysis is called SWOT for strengths, weaknesses, opportunities, and threats. The strengths of a company are its best attributes, from a competitive standpoint. These can include patented technologies, a skilled labor force, corporate brands, and financial security. Weaknesses are just the opposite of strengths and can include labor disputes, process control problems, poor distribution channels, and expiring patents. Opportunities are external conditions that the company can exploit for its advantage. These can include pending favorable legislation, increased market demand, decreasing taxes and tariffs, or the expiration of competitor's patents in key technologies. Threats, like opportunities, are external to the company and cover litigation, political unrest, particularly for multinational corporations, and increasing energy costs. Using SWOT, we can form our competitive intelligence profile of a company and drive the information-gathering process. In addition to answering the four basic

SWOT questions (that is, what are the company's strengths, what are the company's weaknesses, and so on) about the company as a whole, we can also look into different dimensions of the company. We could apply SWOT to the firm's financial position, its manufacturing base, its intellectual property portfolio, or its public image and brand recognition. SWOT provides a high-level assessment of a competitor's position in a market and can also identify more specific issues that require further investigation.

Specific research questions often address changes in competitor's activities, especially in marketing and research and development. Major changes in either of these areas can indicate a change in strategic thrust. A pharmaceutical company that compiles patents for drugs to treat rheumatoid arthritis will clearly be making a move into that market. Sometimes the indications are less obvious. A retail store chain might be considering a shift away from home appliances to focus more on consumer electronics. This shift may not be reflected in press releases but there may be indications in investor reports to the Securities and Exchange Commission and, even more likely, in their advertising and marketing literature. Shifts like that can be identified, at least in part, by detecting changes in dominant terms mentioned in company literature and third-party news sources.

Another piece of a CI profile is the analysis conducted by the users of the collected information. As Larry Kahaner warns, it is easy to fall into the trap of collecting information, the easiest part of competitive intelligence, without conducting the analysis (Kahaner 1997). SWOT is a high-level analysis of the competition and a good place to start. More detailed analysis, such as the implications of particular competitor activities on your strategy or the ability of the competitor to meet its objectives, needs to be done by someone with in-depth knowledge of the industry. For example, after gathering and analyzing content from multiple sources and making a preliminary SWOT assessment, we may find three competitors with strong intellectual property and sound financial foundations that appear to be moving into our market. Further details are needed to understand how this will affect our organization. When will the competitor threaten our market share? Does our competitor have the distribution channels to deliver the products to key geographic regions? How will they compete, by price, quality, service, or some combination of the three? What should our company's reaction be? Will our competitor's actions force us to move up the introduction or increase the production of new products? Adding this type of analysis is essential because the goal of CI is to provide knowledge of competitors and markets so decision makers can adapt to and take advantage of market opportunities in a rational manner. Adding analytic assessments to the CI document collection will add to the value of the raw material and provide what decision makers really need, intelligence and not just data.

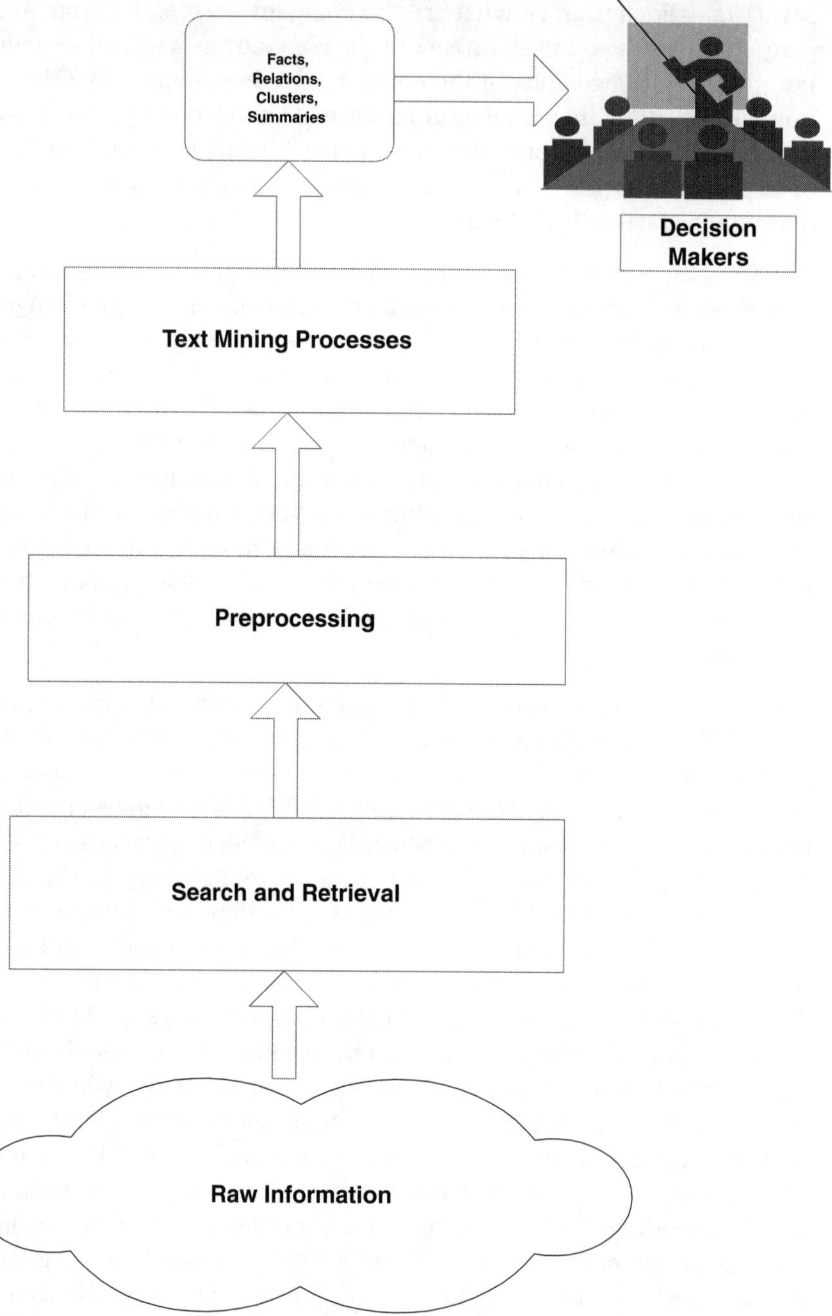

Figure 16.1 Competitive intelligence can be enhanced with automated text analysis, but human analysis is still required to generate truly useful intelligence.

Competitive intelligence profiles of competitors consists of several distinct parts. There is the raw material that is gathered from a variety of sources. Text analysis techniques, especially, feature extraction, clustering, and summarization, can be used to reduce the amount of material an analyst must review. Building on the extracted information, analysts build high-level SWOT assessments that can then provide the starting point for more targeted analysis, such as an investigation of the competitor's moves into a particular market and what it means for our firm. As Figure 16.1 shows, the text-based raw material at the bottom of this process continues to be distilled until it reaches the top where decision makers have the facts and analysis they need to chart a course of action.

Identifying Information Sources

Identifying sources of information for competitive intelligence is easy. Choosing the best sources is much more difficult and requires knowledge about the particulars of your industry and market conditions. In this section, we will discuss some general-purpose resources for corporate, financial, and government news. In the process, we will see that these sources lead to other, more targeted sources.

For someone just starting in competitive intelligence, Helen P. Bruwell's book *Online Competitive Intelligence: Increase Your Profits Using Cyber-Intelligence* (Bruwell 1999) is a treasure trove of Web-based resources. The books covers thousands of sources, including newspapers, trade and industry publications, market research reports, scientific and technical publications, government databases, public records, and financial reporting services.

Identifying information sources should first begin with compiling a list of your competitors. As we discussed earlier, for some industries this is straightforward, especially for highly specialized products such as advanced medical equipment and microprocessors. In other cases, you may find competitors through a few different types of sources, including:

- Corporate directories
- Web directories
- Financial report filings
- Patent and trademark databases

Corporate directories, such as the *Thomas Register of American Manufacturers* (www.thomasregister.com), list basic information about companies. These directories often have both free and fee-based services, with the latter providing more detail.

Web directories, such as Yahoo!, Excite, and Google can also help to pinpoint companies working in the same area as your company. These Web directories also have noncorporate sources, including academic and research sites, as well as commercial Web sites. To narrow the search to just commercial sources, financial report sites are very useful. The Security and Exchange Commission's (SEC) EDGAR database provides access to many documents filed with the SEC.

SEC filings and annual reports in particular can provide much more than financial information, especially in the Business section of the document. Of course the company will not spell out its strategy in detail in these documents, but they do want to provide enough information to comply with SEC regulations as well put their best foot forward for investors. Often we can find basic information on the company's products and development history, market, competition, intellectual property, and relationship with key vendors or alliances with other firms. Full text searches of the EDGAR database can be done from third-party sites such as 10K Wizard (www.tenkwizard.com), which also provides a slightly more flexible search interface. As Figure 16.2 shows, a user can search by keyword.

In this case, a search for diabetes in the health services industry resulted in about fifty hits. The details of one of those are shown in Figure 16.3.

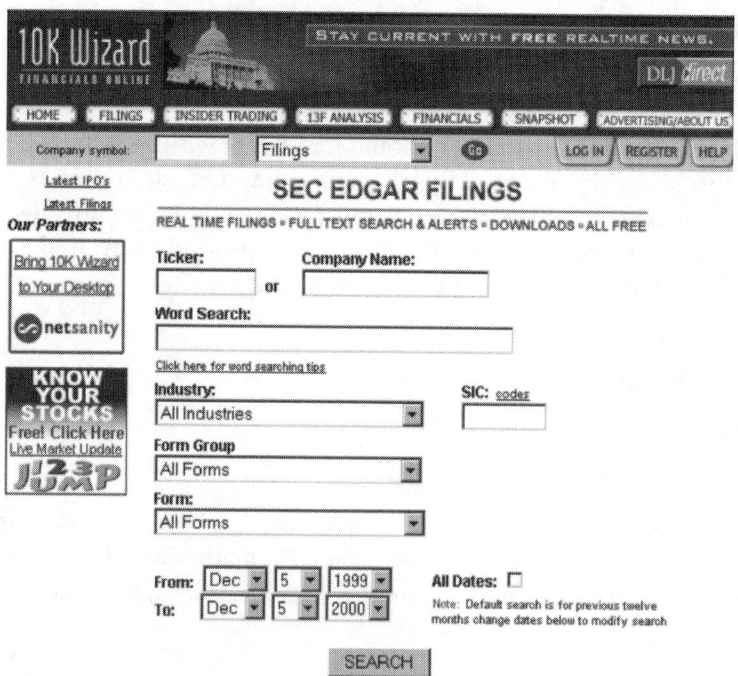

Figure 16.2 10K Wizard provides flexibility in searching the EDGAR database.

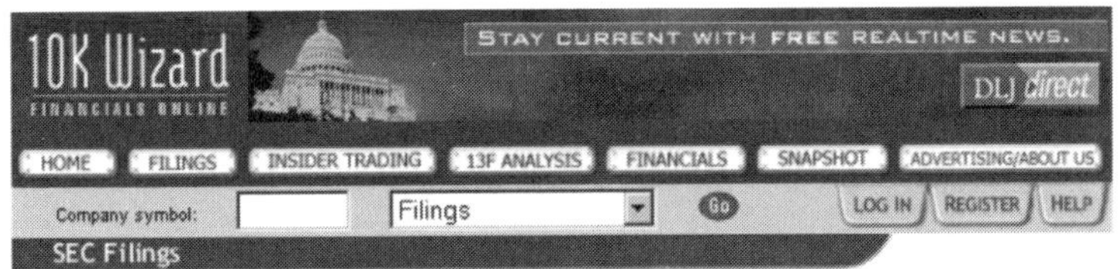

Word Search Results For: diabetes

Click the high-lighted links below to go to that section of the filing

(or click HERE to go directly into filing.)

Back to search results

RENAL CARE GROUP INC filed this 10-K on 03/30/2000.

certain practice management and administrative services to 21 physician practices with a total of 73 physicians. As of December 31, 1999, there were 263 nephrologists affiliated with the Company's outpatient dialysis centers. In addition, the Company operates a business providing wound and diabetic care services. Because of the chronic nature of ESRD and the fact that many ESRD patients also have diabetes , many of Renal Care Group's dialysis patients also have needs for wound care services. Renal Care Group is a Delaware corporation that commenced business in February 1996, with the simultaneous acquisition (the "Combination") of Kidney Care, Inc. and Medical Enterprises Ltd., D.M.N. Professional Corporation, Tyler Nephrology Associates, Kansas Nephrology Association, and Renal Care Grou

al executive offices are located at 2100 West End Avenue, Suite 800, Nashville, Tennessee 37203, and its telephone number is (615) 345-5500. 2 3 INDUSTRY OVERVIEW End-Stage Renal Disease ESRD is a state of advanced kidney failure. ESRD is irreversible and ultimately lethal. It is most commonly a result of complications associated with diabetes , hypertension, certain renal and hereditary diseases, aging and other factors. In order to sustain life, ESRD patients require either dialysis for the remainder of their lives or a successful kidney transplant. By the end of 1997, dialysis was the primary treatment for approximately 72% of all ESRD patients, and the remaining 28% of ESRD patients had a functioning kidney transplant. Acc

Figure 16.3 Search results from a 10K Wizard search provide enough context in this case to identify the services provided by this firm.

Another way to identify competitors is to search patent databases. The U.S. Patent and Trademark Office (www.uspto.gov) provides a full text database of all U.S. patents since 1790, including current classifications as well as classifications at the time of issue. For example, if your firm is developing new diabetes testing kits, you should know what techniques have already been patented and, more importantly, who else is doing work in this area. The patents include references to other patents (a good starting point for other searches), the exact patent claims, and a detailed description of the invention.

In the age of a global economy, one cannot assume that all related products will be in the U.S. Patent Office database. The Japanese Patent Office (www.jpo-miti.go.jp/homme.htm) and the European Patent Office (www.european-patent-office.org) can also be used to identify competition. Unlike the U.S. Patent Office, which does not make patent applications public until they have been approved, the European Patent Offices make information available at the time of application, so you may be able to find competitors months earlier by using the European Patent Office's records.

The patent offices provide these databases as a public service, and they are not designed for large, bulk downloads. If a crawler is used to gather patent information, make sure that search criteria is as specific as possible to reduce the number of hits. Also, if your crawler has a feature to control the time between requests to the same server, set it to a reasonably high value, such as every 60 to 90 seconds to spread out your requests.

Once we have identified and retrieved the documents that interest us, we must analyze the contents. For the most part, we have assumed that we were working with free-form text, but this is not always the case, especially in competitive intelligence. Financial reports, for example, contain descriptive text that can provide information about topics ranging from strategic moves to short-term weaknesses. Since accounting practices are generalized across industries, financial reports are generally well structured, and we can easily target particular pieces of information, such as the description of a company acquired in a merger. The advent of the XBRL, an XML standard, makes the job of targeting information in financial reports a straightforward task. As we shall see in the next section, parsing XML files can be done with a relatively small amount of code thanks to open source libraries freely available to developers.

XML Text Processing Operations

In Chapter 2, we saw that the Extensible Markup Language (XML) can be used to structure documents and that we can use that structure to identify the pieces of information of most interest to us. In this section, we will look more closely at how we actually extract information from XML data sources and pass that text on to text analysis tools or a database for storage. First, we will discuss three methods for working with XML files. They are:

- SAX
- DOM
- Pyxie

SAX, or the Simple API for XML, is an event-driven model for parsing XML files. DOM, the Document Object Model, provides a hierarchical model of navigating around documents. Finally the Pyxie approach is based upon a Python-centric open source project initiated by Sean McGrath to minimize the work involved in working with the logical and structural elements of XML. (The Pyxie project's Web site is www.pyxie.org. McGrath's book *XML Processing with Python* provides a detailed discussion of Pyxie and numerous examples and is highly recommended for anyone working with XML in document warehousing and text mining [McGrath 2000].) After discussing the alternate methods of working with XML, we will move on to discussing XBRL. XBRL is an XML standard for financial reporting. As the standard is adopted by more firms, we will encounter it more frequently when conducting competitive intelligence research. We may very well come across other XML standards in particular business arenas but XBRL will apply across industries, so we will use it for the examples in this chapter.

XML Interface Models

The two most common APIs for working with XML documents are SAX and DOM.

When XML was first introduced a number of parsers were developed to work with XML documents, and the lack of standards soon led to the development of the Simple API for the XML standard, first released in May 1998 (version two was released in May 2000). The purpose of the SAX standard was to provide a model for serialized, event-driven processing of XML documents. This approach is best when dealing with documents in a stream processing style. For example, our need to extract data from an XML document, pass it through to text mining tools, and store the results in a database fits into the stream processing style. This approach does not work as well when one needs to manipulate the contents of a document.

The World Wide Web Consortium (www.w3.org) has developed the DOM as a processing model for tree-oriented views of documents. Rather than focusing on an event basis, as in SAX, the DOM model assumes that the entire document is available during the entire course of processing. For example, an application can navigate down several levels from the root of the document, move forward and backward to sibling nodes and up and down through parent and child nodes.

These standards are language-independent, and implementations of both the SAX and DOM specifications are available for several languages, including C++, Java, Perl, and Python. A third approach, Pyxie, was developed as a Python-specific interface. The goals of Pyxie are to (McGrath 2000)

- Provide a natural Python API
- Support SAX and DOM on top of core Pyxie
- Support both tree- and event-driven processing models
- Keep the notation simple

Each of the core objectives has been realized. Although Pyxie started as Python-oriented standard, it has since been adopted for use with Perl as well. (Since Sean McGrath published Pyxie, Matt Sergeant has developed a XML::PYX module for Perl. Oled A. Parasrchenko has also released XML::Parser::PyxParser to allow developers the ability to work with Pyxie and Perl SAX.) The SAX-like event-driven models and the DOM tree-oriented model are supported by different interfaces. Keeping the notation simple has been accomplished by focusing only on the structural and control elements and disregarding the markup-oriented information, an approach borrowed from the Element Structure Information Set (ESIS) standard developed in SGML.

In this book, we will use the Pyxie library for Python XML processing for one simple reason, it is the easiest to use. Coding is quick and the result is quite readable.

PYX Notation

The key to simplifying XML processing with Pyxie is the PYX notation. Rather than use tags as in XML, the PYX notation expresses basic elements by placing each distinct element on a line with a type indicator. The following codes are used:

(Start tag

) End tag

\- Character data

A Attribute

? Processing instruction

Translation programs from XML to PYX and from PYX to XML are provided in the Pyxie library. Two XML to PYX translators are included, xmln and xmlv. The first uses a nonvalidating parser, and the second uses a validating parser. The programs are designed to work easily with other line-processing utilities, such as grep and awk, as well as with programming languages such as Perl and Python.

Let's consider the following simple XML file we first saw in Chapter 2:

```
<?xml version="1.0"?>
          <MarketingStatus>
             <ReportDate>April 10, 2000</ReportDate>
             <MarketingPeriod> Q1, 2000</MarketingPeriod>
             <Region>Northeast</Region>
             <Status>
             This quarter has seen a significant shift in marketing
             efforts away from . . .
             </Status>
            <MarketCondition>
             The market for our products in the Northeast is undergoing
             significant change with the introduction of
              alternate technologies . . .
              </MarketCondition>
             <MarketCondition>
               Another factor affecting the region is . . .
            </MarketCondition>
            <CompetitiveActivity>
              Our main competitor has launched a campaign targeted at
```

```
            . . .
            </CompetitiveActivity>
      </MarketingStatus>
```

This is translated into PYX notation using the xmln program. From the command line, this is as simple as:

```
xmln   ms000410.xml > ms000410.pyx
```

The resulting content is:

```
(MarketingStatus
-\n
-
(ReportDate
-April 10, 2000
)ReportDate
-\n
-
(MarketingPeriod
- Q1, 2000
)MarketingPeriod
-\n
-
(Region
-Northeast
)Region
-\n
-
(Status
-\n
-             This quarter has seen a significant shift in marketing
efforts away from . . .
-\n
-
)Status
-\n
-
(MarketCondition
-\n
-             The market for our products in the Northeast is undergoing
significant change with the introduction of
-\n
-              alternat-e technologies . . .
-\n
-
)MarketCondition
-\n
-
(MarketCondition
-\n
-               Another factor affecting the region is . . .
```

```
-\n
-
)MarketCondition
-\n
-
(CompetitiveActivity
-\n
-            Our main competitor has launched a campaign targeted at . . .
-\n
-
)CompetitiveActivity
-\n
-
)MarketingStatus
```

(The \n is the PYX notation for the newline character.)

The PYX notation is easy to work with using the regular expression pattern matching provided in Perl and Python but the Pyxie library provides a more extensible method. (Actually, there are three distinct methods, but we will use only one. See *McGrath's XML Processing with Python* for a full discussion of the others.)

Simple Pyxie Example

We'll start with a simple sample program that simply prints the phrase *Starting Market Conditions* whenever the parser encounters the start of a MarketCondition element.

```
#  PYX1.py - Simple program to demonstrate
#     1.     Basic Python syntax and program structure
#     2.     Pyxie class xDispatch
#     3.     Simple XML processing with Pyxie
# get basic system functions and the Pyxie classes
import sys
from pyxie import *
# First, create a derived class from xDispatch to implement
# the processing logic for this type of XML document.
class parseHandler(xDispatch) :
    def start_MarketCondition(self, etn, attrs):
        print "Starting Market Conditions: "
# In a realistic example, other event handlers would go here
# . . .

#     This is the equivalent of a main program.
#     Create an instance of the parseHandler class
#     then invoke the parser on the contents of the XML file
#     after it has been translated from XML to PYX.
p = parseHandler()
p.Dispatch(File2PYX(sys.argv[1]))
```

There are basically three parts to the program. Following the initial comments, the first two lines of code import external modules needed in the program. Next, a class called parseHandler is defined as a specialization of the Pyxie class xDispatch. For this program, we define a single event handler called start_MarketCondition within the class. The event handler is called whenever a MarketCondition entity is encountered in the file. Unlike the SAX API, which uses events such as startElement, endElement, StartDocument, and endDocument, the Pyxie interface uses start and end events for each entity type. The result is that the code is clear and easily understood. The third and final section does two things. First, an instance of the parseHandler class is created. Second, the Dispatch method, inherited from the xDispatch class, is invoked with the results of the File2PYX function. This function takes an XML file name as the argument and returns the corresponding PYX translation. When this program is executed on the above example, the output is:

```
Starting Market Conditions:
Starting Market Conditions:
```

Now let's add a few more details and discuss a general model for extracting targeted pieces of data out of an XML file and getting it into the document warehouse.

A More Realistic Pyxie Example

The following example expands upon the previous simple Python program that used Pyxie to parse a XML file. In this example, we have added more event handlers and a database connection for saving extracted data. Although more realistic than the last example, this is still less complicated than one you will probably write for most XML files. The purpose here is to show as simply as possible the basic steps required to get targeted information from XML files and into the document warehouse.

Here is the new script:

```
import sys
from pyxie import *
import odbc, dbi
# First, create a derived class from xDispatch
class parseHandler(xDispatch) :
     def __init__(self,fo) :
          xDispatch.__init__(self,fo)
          self.MC = []
          self.CharAccum = []
     def start_MarketCondition(self, etn, attrs):
          self.CharAccum = []
     def end_MarketCondition(self, etn):
          self.MC.append ( string.join(self.CharAccum))
     def characters(self,str):
          self.CharAccum.append (PYXDecoder(str))
```

```
    # Name the command line arguments for readability
    xml_file = sys.argv[1]
    db_connect = sys.argv[2]
    # Parse the XML files and accumulate the data to be saved
    p = parseHandler(File2PYX(sys.argv[1]))
    p.Dispatch()

    # Save the accumulated data to the database
    #       open a connection to the database
    db = odbc.odbc(db_connect)
    cur = db.cursor()
    for txt in p.MC:
         # build the string to insert the data
         sql_str = "INSERT INTO docs (text) VALUES (' " + txt + "')"
         #actually do the INSERTing
         cur.execute(sql_str)
    #       clean up object handles
    cur.close
db.close
```

The first change is that we need to import modules to support an ODBC connection to the database.

Next, the parseHandler class has changed. It is still a subclass of xDispatch but new methods have been included. The first is the __init__ method. All classes in Python support an initialization method such as this. The first thing this one does is to call the initialization method of the parent class, xDispatch. In the previous program, we did not have our own initialization method for parseHandler so the parent class was used. The method then initializes two class variables, MC and CharAccum. MC is a list used to hold the contents of the MarketConditions entities encountered in the XML files. The CharAccum is a list that is used to accumulate characters as they are encountered in the XML stream. In non-object-oriented programming languages, this would probably be implemented as a global variable because it is used across methods within the class. As we see, the start_ and end_ entity methods control the initialization of CharAccum and how its contents are used.

The start_MarketCondition simply initializes the CharAccum list. If CharAccum were used to collect the contents of other entities, such as the MarketingPeriod, Status, or CompetitiveActivity, then their corresponding start_ methods would also initialize the class variable.

The end_MarketCondition converts the list of characters into a string, joining them together before assigning the value to the MC class variable. Since CharAccum can be used for multiple entities, each end_ method must save the string that has accumulated since the beginning of the entity.

Most of the work in this program is actually done by the characters method. This method collects the characters between the start and end entities. The PYXDecoder is called on the string to handle special characters such as newline and tabs.

Following the class definition, variables were added to make the code more readable. The sys.argv[] method of referencing command-line variable can become confusing as the number of arguments grows.

Invoking the parser has not changed but after that some code has been added to connect to a database and save the accumulated market condition strings. Again, this is a simplified example. In a production environment, we would probably have accumulated a number of different elements from the file and inserted all of them along with metadata about the source file.

The basic pattern of using Pyxie to extract XML data elements is a four-step process.

- Initialize a class variable to accumulate text for each particular entity type along with an accumulator variable.
- Define a characters method to append strings to the accumulator variable as they are encountered in the XML data stream.
- Define a start_ method for each entity to accumulate and initialize the accumulator variable. Define an end_ method for each entity to assign the accumulated text the class-level variable for the entity.
- After the instance of the Pyxie xDispatcher subclass has been invoked, store the data in a database, or if further file-level processing is required, print it to standard output so that it can be piped to the next program.

As I mentioned earlier, this event-driven code is only one technique supported by Pyxie; the two others are a tree-driven technique and a hybrid event- and tree-driven approach. When parsing small to medium-sized documents, the tree-driven approach will often require the least amount of coding. The hybrid approach is more efficient than the tree-driven method but requires slightly more coding (McGrath 2000). In general, the event-driven approach used here requires more coding than the other two Pyxie techniques but provides the most control. For more details on the Pyxie library and the associated open source project, see www.pyxie.com.

Armed with a minimal coding tool for working with XML, we can take on even larger XML standards such as the XBRL.

Getting Financial Information from XBRL Documents

XBRL is a comprehensive public domain XML standard developed for describing financial statements from both public and private companies. The standard is built upon current accounting practices, so one will not find additional information in XBRL documents that is not normally required by generally accepted principles and practices. It will, however, make the information in financial documents much more accessible. With 80 percent of major U.S. public companies providing some financial information on the Internet, anyone involved in competitive intelligence will want to access the contents of those financial documents, and XBRL will make the task much easier.

Development of the standard began in 1998, and it was first known as XFRML. The XBRL Project Committee began under the auspices of the American Institute of Certified Public Accountants and now has over thirty companies participating in the development of additional standards. One of the key elements of the standard is a comprehensive taxonomy of terms.

The taxonomy covers a wide range of topics including:

- Document information
- Entity information
- Accountant's Report
- Balance Sheet
- Income Statement
- Statement of Comprehensive Income
- Statement of Stockholder's Equity
- Cash Flows
- Notes to Financial Statements
- Supplemental Financial Information
- Financial Highlights
- Management Discussion and Analysis

For the most part, these sections deal with primarily numeric data, and the one of most interest to competitive intelligence practitioners, Management Discussion and Analysis, has not been fully developed yet. The Notes to Financial Statements, however, can contain useful details on credit risks, litigation, mergers, and other financial matters that can indicate areas that require further exploration. For example, the following two items show the contents of two paragraphs describing the acquisition of the Telenor Financial Systems company. (This is taken from one of the XBRL Project Committee's samples, available at www.xbrl.org/us/gaap/ci/2000-07-31/Sample/Viewer.htm. Copyright © 2000 XBRL.ORG [AICPA] All Rights Reserved. www.XBRL.org/legal/)

```
<item type="ci:purchaseAccounting.nameAndDescriptionOfAcquiredCompany">On
May 1, 1998, the Company acquired certain assets and assumed certain lia-
bilities of Telenor Financial Systems, a software provider of sophisti-
cated multinational consolidations and budgeting solutions. The purchase
price was paid in cash and totaled $4,406,000. The acquisition was
accounted for as a purchase and accordingly, the net assets acquired were
```

```
recorded at their estimated fair values at the effective date of the
acquisition. The allocation included $1,680,000 to in-process research
and development, $990,000 to intangible assets, $1,681,000 to goodwill
and $55,000 to the fair value of net tangible assets.</item>

<item type="ci:purchaseAccounting.nameAndDescriptionOfAcquiredCompany">The
$1,680,000 related to acquired in-process research and development, as
determined by an independent third party appraisal, was charged against
income in fiscal 1998 as the underlying research and development projects
had not yet reached technological feasibility. The Company's consolidated
financial statements include the results of Telenor Financial Systems from
May 1, 1998. The results of operations prior to May 1, 1998, were not
material to the consolidated financial statements; accordingly, pro forma
financial disclosures are not presented.</item>
```

The same statement from which this example was taken also has a great deal of numeric data that is probably of interest as well to a competitive intelligence analyst. The numeric data will not be addressed here other than to say that the same techniques used to extract targeted textual data from XML documents will work as well with numeric data.

We will now turn to some concrete examples to see how one goes about conducting competitive intelligence analysis using financial reports, news stories, corporate Web sites, regulatory reports, and other sources as well.

The Practice of Competitive Intelligence

Before starting in with concrete examples, let's first recap where we have been in this chapter. We first discussed the differences between business intelligence and competitive intelligence and discovered that CI is a highly text-oriented operation. Next, we discussed some organizing principles for conducting CI research, including analysis of the strengths, weaknesses, and opportunities of and threats to a company. We then moved on to discuss the different sources of CI information that are available, particularly on the Web. We have just concluded a slight diversion from CI proper into the details of extracting information from XML and XBRL documents since those will be so important in CI analysis.

Now, it is time to pull the pieces together with an overview of how to conduct CI in three different industries:

- Health care
- Manufacturing
- Financial services

In the health care example, our goal will be to determine what companies are developing new procedures and products for diabetes testing. In the manufacturing area, we will look at the financial standing of a particular competitor, using XBRL reports. Finally, in the financial services example, we will discuss how to gather information on a range of competitors to perform a market-oriented analysis.

Competitive Intelligence in Health Care: Patent Analysis

Some aspects of the health care industry seem more akin to high-technology industries than the medical profession as we often think of it. This is due to the rapid pace of technical advances in medical technology. Companies in this industry can make huge investments in a single product line for little or no return if a competitor can beat them to market, patent a particular process, or even take advantage of their intellectual property. Patent searches can help us to understand patterns of technology use in a several ways.

The patent search process is also a technique for conducting SWOT analysis. Knowing the owners of key patents is important to understanding the strengths and weaknesses of competitors. Patent expirations can also present opportunities for other companies that are ready to move into the market that may have been open only to the patent holder.

Patents as a CI Information Source

First, patents will disclose the general areas a company is researching and developing. Although you may be aware of the activity of some of your competitors, you might not even know that others exist. Patent searching will identify those as yet unknown companies.

Second, patent applications make reference to other patents that influenced the current work or provide some foundation for the patent under consideration. Patterns of citation can emerge in patents for a particular industry and provide some indication of how a company is developing or exploiting technology. Pioneers in a new field will frequently cite their own patents, while imitators will cite the work of others. Kahaner discusses pioneer versus imitator strategies as well as teaching versus protecting strategies in *Competitive Intelligence: How to Gather, Analyze and Use Information to Move Your Business to the Top* (Kahaner 1996) and should be consulted for a more thorough discussion of patent analysis in competitive intelligence.

Third, the activity level of patent applications can indicate emerging technologies. As industries mature, patent activity will decrease. If one needs to understand the maturity of a technology, the number of patents issued over time is a useful, albeit rough, indicator.

The information provided in patents may not be available anywhere else. Companies are required to disclose how an invention works in a patent application and that alone can provide valuable information even if you do not directly compete with the patented product. Unfortunately, this disclosure requirement often leads inventors to try to obfuscate as much critical detail as possible but patent searching can still prove a valuable tool.

The Patent Search Process

The patent search process begins by identifying a source of patent data. Some of the major sources of patent information are:

- The U.S. Patent and Trademark Office (www.uspto.gov)
- The European Patent Office (www.european-patent-office-org)
- The Japanese Patent Office (www.jpo-miti-go.jp, English version)
- World Intellectual Property Organization (www.wipo.int)

Other patent offices around the world can be found at www.jpo-miti.go-jo/linke/tuekey.htm. Occasionally, you may find a technology-specific patent search service that can sometimes improve the precision of searches. For example, the DNA Patent Database from Georgetown University's Kennedy Institute for Ethics and the Foundation for Genetic Medicine provides free access to the full text of all DNA patents issued in the United States. For this example, we will use the U.S. Patent Office for examples.

In the following example, we will use a three-step process. First, a search is made for a broad topic such as diabetic testing. A brief description of the patent is retrieved and key terms are extracted along with key attributes of the patents, such as assignee, inventor, date of application, and date the patent was awarded. Second, a CI analyst reviews the key terms to determine the most important terms that arise in the search. These terms are likely indicators of essential elements of the technology. The CI analyst then identifies the most interesting patents and retrieves the full text of the patents along with the bibliographic details of cited patents in the third step of the process. At this point, the description of the invention is extracted and summarized and the features of the cited patents' abstract are extracted. The cited patents will expand the set of essential terms and give the analyst a broader and more in-depth understanding of the particular technology under study. The process is cyclical, with each in-depth analysis of a patent leading to a survey of cited patents that in turn can lead to an in-depth study of yet another patent.

The first step is to search the U.S. Patent Office (www.uspto.gov) Web site's database of patents for the terms *diabetes* and *testing* for the time period

1999–2000. Much older patents can searched too, but they are probably of no interest to us in this example. The result is a set of 34 patents, ranging from patents dealing with genetic diabetes tests to a reminder devices for blood self-testing. The patent information is then downloaded for analysis in the second step of the analysis.

Patent information is available in bibliographic and full-text form. The bibliographic format contains a title, an abstract, inventors, assignee, application number filed date, classification, cited references, and other references. The full text format includes those same fields as well as description of the patent claim and a detailed description of the invention. Here for example is the description of a test method for determining a risk of diabetic complications. (U.S. Patent 6.074,822).

> A test method and test kit for determining a risk of diabetic complications based upon abnormal aldose reductase genetic material expression is described. Cells isolated from a patient which exhibit elevated levels of aldose reductase genetic material expression at pathophysiologic levels of glucose (about 20 mM) which can occur commonly in the cells of diabetic patients are evaluated based upon a level of expression of DNA or RNA in the cells with the glucose at the pathophysiologic level. The cells can be used to isolate DNA or RNA for a probe which detects the abnormal aldose reductase gene expression. The method can be used to determine when particular aldose reductase inhibitors can be effective for a particular patient.

When this abstract, along with the bibliographic information is run through a feature extraction program, the key terms that are extracted include:

aldose reductase

aldose reductase gene

aldose reductase gene expression

aldose reductase genetic material expression

diabetic nephropathy

diabetic patient

pathophysiologic level

These terms briefly indicate the scope of the patent is genetic testing based upon aldose reductase to identify diabetic conditions. At this point, though, we are especially interested in understanding general approaches to the problem of diabetes testing so we collect the set of patents together and run extract features from the entire set to find key terms. Table 16.1 shows some of the most prominent terms.

Table 16.1 The Frequency of Terms in Patents Can Indicate Their Relevance to Particular Domains

NUMBER OF OCCURRENCES	TERMS
18	Implantable glucose sensor
10	Artificial Organs
8	Miniaturized Glucose Sensor
7	Blood glucose
6	Analytical Chemistry
6	Glucose sensor
6	Needle-Type Glucose Sensor
6	Soc Artif Intern Organ
5	Diabetic dog
5	Electroenzymatic Glucose Sensor
5	Implantable sensor
4	Biomedical Engineering
4	Blood constituent
4	Blood Glucose Monitoring System
4	Clinical Chemistry
4	Diabetic Retinopathy
4	Electrocatalytic Glucose Sensor
4	Implantable Electrochemical Glucose Sensor
4	Implanted Glucose
4	Implanted Microfabricated Glucose Sensors
4	Oxygen Sensor
4	Subcutaneous Glucose Concentration
4	Subcutaneous Glucose Sensor
4	Subcutaneous Tissue
4	Vivo Evaluation
4	Whole Blood
4	Wick technique
3	Artificial endocrine pancreas
3	Automated Feedback Control
3	Counter electrode
3	Electrochemical sensor

In this list we will see the entire range of types of terms we can expect. First, there are the obvious ones, such as *blood glucose* and *whole blood*. Second, we have the extraneous ones that are terms not directly related to our search but are possibly useful, such as the term *Soc Artif Intern Organ*, referring to the journal of the Society of Artificial Internal Organs. These terms can provide clues to other possible sources of information. Third, and most importantly, are the terms that indicate the technical information we are looking for. In this example, the terms

- Implantable glucose sensor
- Miniaturized glucose sensor
- Needle-type glucose sensor
- Electroenzymatic glucose sensor
- Implantable sensor

seem to indicate that small implantable sensors are getting significant attention but needle-type sensors are also an area of active research and development. The term electroenzymatic describes the functional mechanism behind some of these sensors.

The next step is to examine patents with these terms more closely. Searching for patents using the term *electroenzymatic glucose sensor* returns five hits. We know these are relevant patents so we move to the next step, summarizing the descriptions of the patent to learn more details about the technology. A summary from one of the relevant patents (U.S. Patent 6,122,536) is as follows:

> The present invention is an implantable sensor and system capable of measuring, controlling, monitoring, and reporting blood constituent levels. In one aspect of the invention, the implantable device comprises at least one source of radiation from infrared through visible light, arranged to direct the radiation at the tissue.
>
> In another aspect of the invention, the implantable device comprises at least two sources of radiation from infrared through visible light, arranged to direct the radiation at the tissue.
>
> In another of its aspects, the present invention includes a device for both measuring and controlling the level of a blood constituent in a mammal, and comprises an implantable infrared source and sensor module for directing infrared radiation through vascular tissue such as, but not limited to, an artery, a vein, a vascular membrane, or vascular tissue.
>
> The sensor module senses the infrared radiation after it has passed through the tissue and generates an output signal representative of the sensed infrared radiation.
>
> In another aspect of the invention, an implantable oxygenation, hemoglobin, and perfusion sensor is provided to obtain frequent objective data on patients with chronic illnesses such as heart failure and respiratory failure.
>
> Patients would be monitored for changes in hemoglobin oxygen saturation (pulse oximeter), hemoglobin concentration (infrared measurement), and changes in tissue

> perfusion (analysis of the photoplethsmograph waveform) for the purpose of detecting cardiovascular decompensation early so that the physician can manage the problem as an outpatient.
>
> In another aspect of the invention, the implantable device comprises at least one radiation source consisting of at least two discrete spectral bands lying somewhere within the infrared through visible spectrum, arranged to direct the radiation at the tissue.

The summary describes multiple aspects of the invention, and in the processes discloses fundamental technical approaches to the problem of glucose level testing. To most of us the details here may sound foreign, but to a CI analyst in the health care industry phrases such as detecting *infrared radiation through vascular tissue* may bring to mind other applications addressed in the CI analyst's company. It may also indicate an approach that the analyst's company has not considered.The CI analyst can go through summaries for all the product descriptions and extract features from the full patent applications of the most relevant patents. That alone may not provide enough information but at that point other patents cited in the application can be analyzed. Fortunately, the U.S. Patent Office includes URLs to cited patents in patent applications, so it is a simple matter to retrieve cited patents and perform feature extraction operations on them. The process can continue on from the cited patents, finding relevant ones, reviewing summaries of cited patents, and extracting features of cited patents from those cited patents, and so on. Patent analysis is a powerful tool for competitive intelligence. The information available in patent applications often cannot be found elsewhere, and the fact that related patents are cited means that a single patent can provide a starting point to researching the application of a particular technology. The information derived from patent research can provide a wealth of information for SWOT analysis, especially when patents are searched for an entire domain and not just for a single company. In addition to the technical innovations and intellectual property of a company, the financial condition of a firm is a key element of SWOT analysis. In the next section, we will look at how XBRL documents can provide insights into the financial condition of competitors.

Competitive Intelligence in Manufacturing: Financial Analysis

Financial analysis requires more than numbers. Of course the numeric details of financial statements are essential for assessing the health of a company. As we shall see in this section, financial reports can contain valuable textual information as well. Using a fictitious manufacturing firm, Alpha Beta Gamma Industries, we will take advantage of XBRL documents to discover details of the company's financial status.

XBRL Annual Report

Publicly traded companies in the United States are required to file annual reports with the Security and Exchange Commission. When published in XBRL format, the document comprises several sections, including document information, company information, accounting firm information, financial details, and most importantly for us, notes on the financial report. In these notes we can find information on mergers and acquisitions, pending litigation, management estimates, and other information of interest to investors, and competitors, alike.

Below is an excerpt of an annual report in XBRL format. This example shows only a sample of the details that can be found in the Notes section of the report. Other sections, such as Document Information, Balance Sheet, Income Statement, and Cash Flows are not shown here. (For a complete example of an XBRL annual report, visit the XBRL Web site at www.xfrml.org/Sample/Viewer.htm.)

```
<group type="statements.notesToFinancialStatements" period="1999-12-31">
<!--NOTE 1-->
<group id="NOTE01.001" type= "notesToFinancialStatements.summaryOfSig-
nificantAccountingPolicies">
<item type= "summaryOfSignificantAccountingPolicies.natureOfBusiness">
The Company designs,  manufactures and markets innovative medical
devices ...">
</item>
<item type="notesToFinancialStatements.dependency">
The Company uses independent parties to manufacture for the Company, on
a contract basis, ....</item>
<item type= "summaryOfSignificantAccountingPolicies.managementEstimates-
keyEstimates-">
Actual results could differ from these estimates.</item>
<item type= "summaryOfSignificantAccountingPolicies.consolidation-policy-">
The  Company's  customers  include  OEMs,  end  users,   retailers  and
distributors. Revenue,  less reserves for returns, is generally recog-
nized upon shipment to the customer.</item>
<item type="abg:notesToFinancialStatements.warrantyCosts">A one-year
limited warranty is generally provided on the Company's AlphaBetaCheck
devices. Certain OEM customers have a three-year limited warranty on the
Company's AlphaBetaCheck ...</item>
<group id="NOTE02.001" type= "notesToFinancialStatements.acquisitions">
<item type="notesToFinancialStatements.acquisitions">
On August 1, 1999,  the Company  purchased a majority  interest in Tau
Omega Industries ...</item>
<item type="notesToFinancialStatements.acquisitions">
The  transaction  was accounted for as a purchase;  and, on net tangible
assets ....</item>
<item type="notesToFinancialStatements.acquisitions">
Upon  completion  of the Tau Omega Industries  acquisition,  the  Com-
pany  immediately expensed $20.3 million representing purchased in-
process technology that has not yet reached  technological  feasibility
and has no alternative  future use.
```

```
<item period="1997-12-31">10334</item>
</group>
<group id="NOTE03.001" type= "notesToFinancialStatements.lossContingen-
cies">
<item type="notesToFinancialStatements.lossContingencies">
On September 10, 1999, a purported class action lawsuit, Sullivan  et
al. v. AlphaBetaGamma  Industries,  was filed against the Company in the
Superior  Court of Virginia, New Castle County. The suit alleges that a
defect in the Company's AlphaBetaChecker harmed patients ....</item>
</group>
```


From the Notes section, we can see several important facts about the company:

- The company subcontracts at least some of the manufacturing to other firms.
- The firm provides a longer warranty to some OEMs than to end users.
- Alpha Beta Gamma Industries acquired Tau Omega Industries.
- The company is facing a class action lawsuit.

Each of these facts can lead to further points of investigation. For example, who subcontracts to Alpha Beta Industries? Could the subcontractor have been responsible for faulty devices that led to the lawsuit? If so, does our company use the same subcontractors? What technology was retired by the acquiring firm? Could this indicate a shift to a competing technology? How should our company respond to a shift away from the technology developed by Tau Omega? And the list goes on.

In the case of annual reports, the items delineated by XBRL entities are small enough to be reviewed individually without summarization. However, if a large number of these documents were analyzed together, then feature extraction could be used across the same types of notes. For example, all notes relating to acquisitions or loss contingencies could be analyzed together to determine repeating terms that could indicate a strategic thrust in a particular area or a significant legal liability.

Since XBRL is an XML standard, the Pyxie library for Python described earlier in the chapter is an ideal tool for extracting targeted entities from XBRL documents.

In our next example, we shall see how text analysis techniques can be applied to broad market issues, external to all companies, that can affect strategic planning.

Competitive Intelligence in Financial Services Market: Market Issue Analysis

Innovations in information technology have fueled the growth of financial services. One area in particular, stock markets, has seen radical changes in the way business is conducted. Individuals can trade online without a broker, vast amounts of information is available to the public that was once only available to professional traders and other financial specialists, and perhaps most important, trading options have been extended through the use of off-market trading.

In the past, buy and sell orders have been placed in single markets, or exchanges. This means that a buyer or seller knows there is only one price for a stock at any given time. The Nasdaq exchange is not a single point for buyers and sellers but a dealer market in which market makers compete for buy and sell orders. The Nasdaq provides the best bid and best offer quotations across market makers and provides for automatic execution of orders between them. In 1996, the Securities and Exchange Commission gave electronic communications networks (ECNs) access to the Nasdaq system and required both market makers and ECNs to post their best quotes and bids on Nasdaq. A problem may arise though because there is no requirement that trades within an ECN or a market maker be at the best prevailing bid or offer across all market makers and ECNs (Securities Industry Association, Comment Letter, May 5, 2000. www.sia.com/legal_regulatory/htm/market_fragmentation.html). For example, a person buying stock A on ECN 1 will pay the best offer price on ECN 1, say, $20 per share. Another person executing the same purchase on ECN 2 will pay the best offer price on that ECN, which might be $25. The result is a fragmentation of the market prices, and the cost of a stock becomes, in part, determined by how the trade is executed. This problem, known as market fragmentation, has generated a great deal of debate in the securities industry.

From a competitive intelligence perspective, market fragmentation is an external factor that can represent an opportunity or a threat, depending upon your position as a service provider in the market. If you are an ECN, then reduced regulations can present new opportunities. Older established exchanges may see the rise of ECNs as a threat to more traditional trading methods. Finally, regulators, are questioning what, if any action, should be taken to address the problem of fragmentation. A great deal has been written on this, and if you are a financial services analyst and need to get a handle on the debate, then some text analysis is needed.

Let's assume that you have already identified a number of sources for information on this issue. These can include:

- Government agencies, such as the Securities and Exchange Commission and the Federal Reserve
- Professional associations, such as the Securities Industry Association
- Financial news sources such as the *Wall Street Journal*, *The Economist*, and CNNfn
- Research groups such as the Heritage Foundation

The collection will likely consist of regulations, speeches by regulators, commentary, open letters, and economic analyses as well as opinions and perspectives of members of the ECN and securities industry. With a collection of sources in hand, preprocessed and ready for analysis, the next step is to decide how to proceed. One option is to use feature extraction. This often works well when we are learning about a new area but in this case we can assume that the analyst understands all the basic concepts and would not discover anything new by reviewing key terms and concepts. Since we are dealing with a presumably sizable document collection, clustering is one way to help bring some order to the collection.

To quickly review, the clustering process groups similar documents on the basis of key features. In the case of hierarchical clustering, we can start at a single root node that encompasses all documents in the collection and then drill down into more specific subsets of documents. Each layer down brings us to a smaller and narrower set until we reach the bottom of the hierarchy where each node represents a single document. With binary relational clustering, the entire document set is partitioned into some number of distinct groups with no hierarchical relationship.

For this application, we will use hierarchical clustering. As Figure 16.4 shows, a small group of documents on market fragmentation can be grouped along logical

		access,informed		
sim:0 market,stock market,nasdaq act,security	sim:105 market,stock market,nasdaq exchange,stock	sim:0 market,nasdaq share,traded maker,market		THENAS~1.TXT
		sim:370 market,stock exchange,stock stock,traded	sim:0 exchange,stock maker,market stock,traded	SECEXP~1.TXT
			sim:0 market,stock chairman,sec stock,traded	LEVITT~1.TXT
	sim:49 derivative,instrument financial,instrument funds,money	sim:0 funds,money amended,rule exemptive,funds		21837.txt
		sim:0 derivative,instrument financial,instrument commodity,instrument		33-7386.txt
		sim:0 offers,security exchange,security act,security		33-7282.txt
		sim:0 equity,market market,nasdaq guilty,proven		angel1.txt
		sim:0 broker,dealers improve,price fragmented,market		COMMEN~3.TXT

Figure 16.4 Hierarchical clustering can provide a quick overview of the logical structure of a document collection.

lines. The first level down from the root breaks into stock exchanges, derivative instruments, and equity markets. The next level down includes equity markets, a node on dealers and brokers as well as one on proposed rules, disclosure, and executing.

The practice of competitive intelligence requires a number of distinct types of text-based information. Patents for example provide clues about a company's research and development efforts as well as their strategic investments in intellectual property. Looking into the details of financial statements can also provide insights into what is happening within a company, particularly if mergers, lawsuits, and special relationships with third parties are discussed. Finally, we must remember that no company operates in a vacuum. The opportunities and threats that a company may face are created by market conditions that CI analysts must be aware of. In each of these cases, text analysis and text mining techniques can be brought to bear to help manage document collections and extract valuable information from that collection.

Conclusions

Competitive intelligence is as important to a company as internally directed business intelligence. Just as data warehousing has provided the foundation to meet the business intelligence needs of firms, document warehousing and text mining techniques can be applied to the competitive intelligence needs of those same companies. In some cases, we will deal with free-form text from speeches and news reports, and in other cases we have the advantage of working with semistructured documents, such as XBRL reports. We can easily extract targeted information from XML-based documents by using XML APIs such as SAX and Pyxie. We have seen, through the three sample scenarios that a wealth of information is available to competitive intelligence researchers, that preprocessing programs can be quickly developed with freely available scripting languages, and that code libraries and text mining tools can extract and distill the information we need.

In the next chapter, we will turn our attention to broader issues of document warehousing and text mining. Specifically, we will look into how we go about choosing our tools and what tradeoffs and limitations we can expect from the current generation of applications.

CHAPTER 17

Text Mining Tools

In this chapter, we will discuss some criteria for choosing tools and then look into the limits of text mining tools. Since we have discussed many document warehousing and text mining tools throughout the book, we will not cover specific details here. Rather, our objective in this chapter is to develop criteria for choosing among tools and understanding the tradeoffs of our choices.

Since text mining addresses knowledge discovery in large document collections, tools must address a range of needs not directly related to text mining including:

- Document retrieval
- Document storage
- Character set document conversion
- Language translation

We have labeled these as preprocessing tasks, and while they are not technically text mining operations, they are required to get us where we are going, so they will be briefly discussed below. We will examine specific text mining operations, such as feature extraction, clustering, and textbase navigation, and we will discuss the specific features we should expect from tools supporting those operations.

Once we have reviewed tool selection criteria, we will look at the limits of these tools so that we can understand what can reasonably be expected from the current state of the art in text mining.

Criteria for Choosing Tools

In this section, we will divide the criteria for tool selection into two areas, preprocessing tools and text mining tools.

Preprocessing Tools

We choose preprocessing tools on the basis of several needs:

- Where are source documents located?
- What character sets and file formats are used?
- Will text mining operations be integrated with other operations, such as data warehousing?

In some cases, the appropriate tool can be determined on the basis of only one of these questions but in other cases, two or more criteria may come into play when making a decision.

Source Document Location

Getting the text to mine is the first step in document warehousing and text mining. As we discussed in part one of this book, we can consider three general sources:

- Local area file systems
- Document management systems
- Internet

When working with local area file systems, we generally have two choices for document retrieval: the first is operating system or shell scripting languages, and the second is general-purpose scripting languages. The first option is sometimes the easiest. The tool is readily available and probably well understood by enough staff members to begin using the operating system command language immediately. The drawback is lack of portability. This is less of an issue for UNIX shell scripts but clearly a problem for Win32, OpenVMS, and other proprietary platforms. The second option is almost always a better choice. General-purpose scripting languages, particularly Perl and Python, are ideal choices for working with local area file systems. The tools have been ported to most commercially available platforms, provide much of the functionality of shell scripting languages, and also have extensive libraries of extra code useful for many preprocessing tasks.

Extracting text from a document management system (DMS) requires the use of an API- or DMS-specific extraction tool. Depending upon the platform, many APIs use a C call interface or a COM object interface, or both. C, of course, is a viable option in both cases but requires significantly more coding than Perl or Python.

Whatever tool we use for Internet file retrieval should have solid support for both the HTTP and FTP protocols. Automatically retrieving a large number of documents from a single site can strain the Web server, so many sites post rules for the use of automate retrieval in a robots.txt file in the root directory of the site. When using a crawler, choose one that accommodates the robot exclusion protocol. Some tools, such as Tennyson Maxwell Information System's Teleport Pro, use a dynamic balancing algorithm to spread out requests across multiple servers and thus minimize the impact on any single server. This and similar features are definitely a desirable option in a Web retrieval tool.

A scripting language will almost certainly come into play when retrieving documents. These languages provide the glue for tying together multiple operations, so it is worth briefly discussing the two best options, Perl and Python.

Perl: Practical Extraction and Report Language

Larry Wall developed Perl as a reporting tool for the UNIX operating system. It quickly grew beyond its original scope as a reporting tool to become a full-blown portable programming language. Perl is freely available from many sites on the Web, including www.perl.com. Perl has grown in popularity in part because it is so useful for CGI applications for the Web, but also because it fits the needs of many system administration tasks. System managers often perform many basic maintenance operations using Perl instead of shell scripting languages. These tasks frequently entail file manipulation, and Perl's extensive support for file management and regular expression matching minimize the amount of coding required to build such applications.

One of the best features of Perl is the extensive library of Perl modules that extend the functionality of Perl. Located at www.perl.com/CPAN, the Comprehensive Perl Archive includes modules for:

- Development support
- Operating system interfaces
- Networking and interprocess communication
- Extended data types
- Database interfaces
- User interfaces

- Extended file support
- Parsing and searching
- Internationalization
- Web, HTMK, PTTP, CGI, and MIME support

The Perl archive is a good place to start when looking for programs to perform many of the preprocessing operations we have discussed, such as conversion, crawling, and reformatting.

A common criticism of Perl is that its syntax is difficult to understand. Like C, it supports auto increment operators and other shortcut operations not found in many other languages but Perl does not stop there. For example, when a line is read from a file, it is automatically assigned to the variable $_. The condition (<INFILE>) means "keep reading from the file associated with the handle INFILE until reaching the end of file, and copy the contents of the current line into the $_ variable." Until you have used Perl for a while, these and similar constructs seem a little strange.

Perl is an actively developing language. Support for object orientation is now included. The language also has a very active community of developers supporting and extending the tool. Perl will no doubt be a widely used tool in document warehousing and text mining.

Python: Object-Oriented Scripting

The Python scripting language, like Perl, is a very high-level language that provides extensive support for operating system and file operations. In this book, we have used Python primarily for XML processing but it could have been used for any Perl program as well. (Truth be told, the reverse is true too, we could have used Perl for the XML parsing instead of Python.) Python was developed by Guido van Rossum around 1990 and is actively supported by a developer community at home at www.python.org. (Guido van Rossum is no doubt a British comedy fan since the language is named after the *Monty Python's Flying Circus*, not the snake.)

Like Perl, Python is often used for system administration tasks, but since it was designed from the ground up as a fully object-oriented language, it is useful for many system development tasks. It too supports file manipulation and regular expressions, so it is an excellent tool for preprocessing tasks. Python's syntax is well structured and easy to follow, which is a primary advantage over Perl.

Choosing between Perl and Python is like choosing a favorite flavor of ice cream. Some people will swear by one language, while their colleagues will swear by the other, with both sides often including detailed reasons why one is better than the other. Recognizing that the choice is really about a tool to help us accomplish our document warehousing and text mining projects, the choice should boil down to efficiency. Since both languages will meet the needs in this area, there is no "better" choice. Simply choose based on the aesthetics of the language or choose the one that requires the least typing, or use any other arbitrary reason. Of course you could, as we have done in this book, use both.

Character and File Formats

When dealing with multiple character sets, we need tools that can translate between them when possible. Many text analysis tools assume they are dealing with ASCII files, so some Unicode characters are not recognized. A conversion tool is the best option in this case but if the need arises, you may be able to develop an application using a scripting language. For example, Python provides the encode() function to convert between encodings but of course, not all Unicode characters can be converted to ASCII. If you need to work with Unicode directly, then Perl's extensive support for Unicode's regular expressions may be of use in those cases.

Whether or not we can convert a file to ASCII may be irrelevant. Some text mining tools only work with specific languages. Many work with English and often European languages, and few provide support for Chinese, Japanese, and Korean. The latter three require Unicode to represent the logograms and syllabaries of the corresponding writing systems, but until there are text mining tools for those languages, the character conversion issue will not need to be addressed.

When it comes to dealing with file formats, we have three options. First, we can use product-specific conversion tools. For example, Microsoft Office products provide COM interfaces to their products' functionality, so one can develop custom applications to convert from application-specific file formats to text files. Second, a general conversion utility, such as Advanced Computer Innovations' WordPort, can be used to translate multiple formats. Finally, some applications, such as Oracle interMedia Text provide automatic format detection and conversion.

There are two specific criteria to keep in mind when dealing with character and file formats: First, ensure that your text mining tools can analyze the language used in the document collection. If they do not, there is no point worrying about converting Unicode characters. Second, if the document collection contains a number of different file formats, consider using a tool with automatic format identification and conversion, or use a general file conversion utility. Consider writing your own conversion program when you use only a small number of different file formats.

Integrated Operations

Another point to keep in mind when selecting tools is how well integrated the document warehouse and text mining operations will be with other business intelligence applications. To take advantage of integrating text and numeric data, you will need a database that supports both.

Major database vendors have enhanced their relational database products with add-on features for text. Many have extended their relational engines using user-defined types, functions, and indexes. While this provides the greatest flexibility for adding new features, this approach does not provide the performance that could be gained if text were natively supported in the database. Thuderstone's Texis and Oracle interMedia Text are designed for both relational data and text, and therefore they can take advantage of better optimization of queries that reference both text and relational attributes. A more detailed look into the design choices that database vendors have to make is in order.

Indexing Text versus Indexing Relational Data

The first point that database vendors need to address is that relational data is indexed differently from text. Relational data, such as integers, floats, chars, and varchars, are usually indexed using balanced trees, or b-trees. Figure 17.1 shows a simple b-tree that indexes Table 17.1.

Without an index, we could use a full table scan to search for employee 7 and find the record within four steps. That process is fine for trivial tables such as this but not when we are dealing with thousands or millions of rows. Using a b-tree index, we can radically reduce the amount of time required to find a record. As Figure 17.1 shows, just by traversing two nodes we can get to our target record with the b-tree index. The impact is even more dramatic when dealing with larger tables. With only ten steps through a b-tree, we can find any of thousands of rows.

Bitmap indexes are used in some data warehousing applications where there are a relatively small number of possible values compared to the number of rows containing those values. For example, a table with hundreds of thousands of U.S. customer addresses could use a bitmap index for a State column since there are only about fifty possible values. Gender and age range categories are also good candidates for bitmap indexes. The advantage of bitmap indexes is

Table 17.1 Relational Data

EMPLOYEE ID	LAST NAME	FIRST NAME	NUMBER
1	Jones	Bob	127
3	Smith	Mary	188
5	Connors	Robert	207
7	Hickmen	Nicole	135

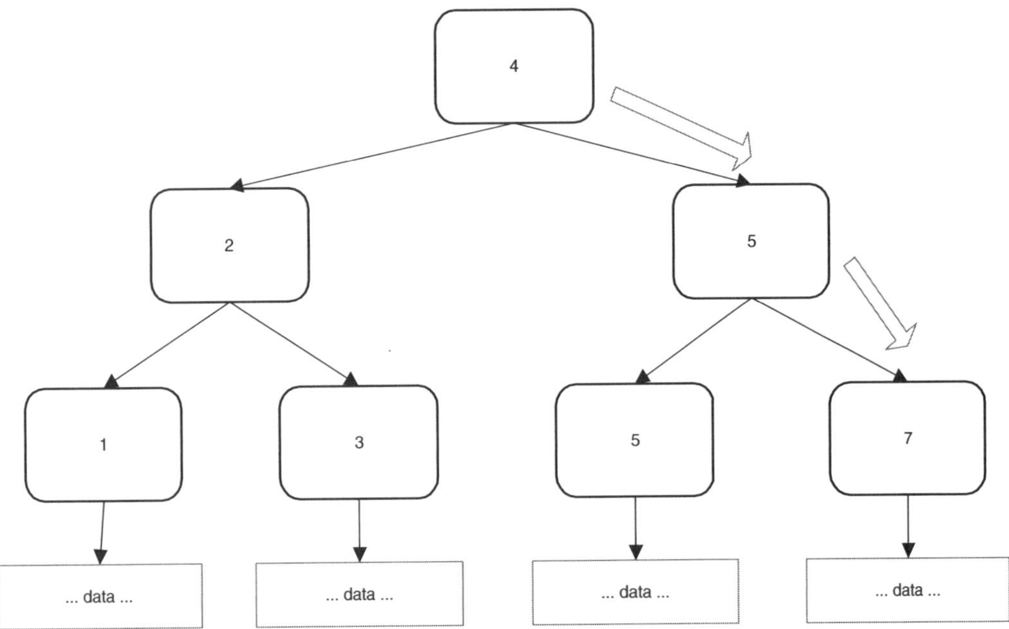

Figure 17.1 A b-tree index allows one to rapidly find any record in roughly the same amount of time as any other record.

that Boolean operations can be performed very quickly. Consider the data in Table 17.2.

Assume that we have a bitmap index on the State, Gender, and Age Range columns. The State index would consist of approximately fifty binary columns with one row for each row in the source table. Only one column will be set to 1 for any given row, the others will be all 0. Similarly for the gender column, we would have two columns, or three if we want to include unknown, and again only one column per row would be set to 1; the others would be 0. Boolean operations such as Gender = 'F' and State = 'MA' then become a matter of bitmap comparisons. This description of bitmap indexes is highly simplified.

Table 17.2 Example of Common Demographic Data Found in a Data Warehouse

LAST NAME	ADDRESS	CITY	STATE	GENDER	AGE RANGE
Pughee	15 Main St.	Springfield	MA	M	31-40
Mandell	123B N. Pamet	Wolfson	WI	F	21-30
Woddall	3214 Brock Ave	Alexandria	VA	M	31-40
Johnson	7781 Winchester Dr.	San Jose	CA	F	31-40

These indexes are often compressed for efficiency, so there is more to the comparison than explained here. Still, the general principle of how bitmap indexes are used is reflected here.

With regard to text, though, neither b-tree nor bitmap indexes meet our needs. With text, we are not looking at the body of text as a single atomic unit, as we are with relational data, such as a person's name or the number of sales transactions in a region last quarter. Instead, we want to operate on the contents of the text, looking for documents that contain several terms, or some terms and not others, or two or more terms in close proximity to each other. These types of operations require an inverted index.

An inverted index is used to list the location of each significant term in a document collection. For each term, the inverted index maintains a list of documents that contain the term along with the offset of the location of the term. The index does not contain commonly used words, often called stop words, such as *the*, *was*, and *do*. Each term entry in the inverted index looks something like this:

Term 1 → ({doc 1, offset 1}, {doc 12, offset2}, {doc 12, offset 3}, … {doc n, offset m})

Therefore, if you want to find all documents containing the term *publishing*, the text retrieval engine would look up the term *publishing* in the index and return the list of documents found there. For queries containing multiple terms, such as *publishing* AND *computer*, both terms would have to be found in the index. With both terms' list of documents, the retrieval engine would then find the intersection of the two lists of documents. Proximity searches such as *text* NEAR *mining* require the same mechanism as the AND operation plus an additional check of the offsets to calculate the distance between the terms. Supporting additional features such as fuzzy searches, soundex operations, and thematic indexes requires additional support but the basic mechanism is the same.

Although inverted indexes are significantly different from the b-tree and bitmap indexes we are accustomed to in the relational database world, they can operate together.

Performance Consideration in Text and Relational Indexing

The single most important consideration when working with both text and relational indexes is how the two are used together. Consider the following example:

```
SELECT doc_id, title
FROM   docs
WHERE
    author = 'Chomsky'
AND
     CONTAINS(abstract,'syntax') > 0;
```

This query selects the document identifier and title of all documents that are written by Chomsky and contain the word *syntax*. Now, although the author's name is a text field, it can easily be accommodated using a varchar data type, so the author column can be indexed using b-tree indexes. The abstract column however, will contain an arbitrarily long piece of text and, therefore, is indexed using an inverted index. How will the optimizer execute this query? Well, as is usually the case, it depends.

If the b-tree and inverted indexes are native to the database system, then information about both will be available to the optimizer. In that case, the optimizer will likely determine which of the two selection criteria will return the fewest rows and use that first to generate the initial result set. Then the second criteria would be applied to the initial result set to find the set of all rows satisfying both criteria. Textbases that are built to support text retrieval as well as relational attributes work like this.

On the other hand, if the b-tree index is native to the RDBMS but the inverted text index is an extension to the core engine, then it is not available to the optimizer. In this case, the optimizer works on the relational indexes to find a set of rows that meet the relational criteria, and a separate text selection process identifies the rows that satisfy the text search criteria. The results of the two processes are then joined to find the set of rows that meet both criteria.

Clearly, the need to introduce a join will slow down the process. The separation also eliminates the possibility that the optimizer can exploit particular patterns across the two types of indexes. The net result is that textbases with native support for inverted indexes can deliver better performance than relational databases that add on text support outside of the database engine.

Database Selection Criteria

For many data warehouse operations, choosing a database is often a matter of choosing among commonly used databases, such as IBM DB2, Oracle, Microsoft SQL Server, and those of specialty data warehouse vendors such as Red Brick. When document warehousing becomes a significant factor in database selection, then other vendors, such as Thunderstone, should be considered. Textbases, such as Thunderstone's Texis, provide a robust SQL language that has been augmented to deal with text queries, much like that provided by Oracle Text. Since it is designed for native support of text like Oracle interMedia Text, the optimizer has access to inverted indexes as well as the b-tree indexes used for relational data. Choosing a database for document warehousing and text mining operations entails a number of considerations.

First, consider the extent to which text is integrated with nontext attributes. The strongest commercial databases have been built to support transaction processing and more recently for data warehouses. If your current database supports text as an extension, and performance is not meeting your requirements, then a database that supports both text and nontext operations should be considered.

Second, although databases often do not provide native support for text, they have been designed for high-performance data warehousing and transaction processing. Some of the performance enhancements such as partitioning and parallel query optimization can prove useful in text-oriented operations as well.

Finally, the introduction of a new type of RDBMS to get native text support must be weighed against the costs of supporting another database system. Textbases will be tuned differently, have different configuration requirements, and may entail different maintenance procedures, all of which could be unfamiliar to existing staff.

Which database is chosen will have the greatest impact on searching and on embedded text mining operations but text mining tools are also independent applications in their own right.

Text Mining Tool Selection

Extracting information from text can be done in several ways, and the types of text analysis and text mining tools need for an application will vary. The main types of tools to consider are:

- Clustering
- Categorization
- Feature extraction
- Summarization
- Textbase navigation
- Visualization

Each type of tool extracts a different type of information from text. Clustering makes explicit the relationship between documents, while categorization identifies the key topics of a document. Feature extraction is used when we need to know the people, organizations, places, and objects mentioned in text. Summarization extends the principle of feature extraction by focusing on entire sentences rather than on nouns and phrases. Textbase navigation allows us to understand the relationship between terms in a set of documents. Finally, thematic indexing is useful when we want to be able to work with topics rather than keywords. In the following section, we will examine specific features we should expect from each type of tool and the types of problems for which the tool is best suited.

Clustering Tools

There is no single type of clustering. The most common are hierarchical, binary relational, and fuzzy. To quickly review, hierarchical clustering creates a tree with all documents in the root node and a single document in each leaf node. The intervening nodes have multiple documents and become more and more specialized as they get closer to the leaf nodes. Binary relational clustering partitions the documents into a flat structure in which each document is placed in only one set. Fuzzy clustering takes a different approach. With fuzzy clustering all documents are included in all clusters, but to varying degrees.

When choosing a clustering tool, consider how documents are grouped. All clustering is based upon a similarity measure, but the question is which one. One approach is to group documents that share lexical affinities—that is, words that frequently appear together such as *text mining* and *business intelligence*. This results in clusters that are written using similar terminology. Another approach is to group documents on the basis of extracted features. This puts a greater emphasis on the objects described and referenced in a text than on the word patterns used to describe them. Ideally, a clustering tool will offer two or more similarity measures.

You should also consider the types of clustering algorithms used. Hierarchical clustering is useful when you are exploring a new document collection and want to get a handle on the overall contents of the collection. This approach lets you start with the forest and quickly drill down into the trees. Binary clustering can, on the other hand, sometimes produce nonintuitive results. For example, why was the article about an airline pilots' strike put in with stories about airports instead of with other labor dispute articles? Using hierarchical clusters, the airline pilots' strike article would be with both airport and labor dispute stories in the top levels of the hierarchy before separating. Fuzzy clustering provides an even better solution. The airline pilots' strike would be with both airport stories and labor disputes, but with differing degrees of membership. The airline pilots' story could be in the airport cluster with a weight of 0.7 but in the labor dispute cluster with a weight of 0.68. With both hierarchical clustering and fuzzy clustering, the user working with the output of the algorithm will decide the level of the hierarchy that is appropriate to work at or the minimum weight to consider when working with documents in a particular group. This will maximize the chance of understanding the relationship between the documents and minimize the possibility of missing significant texts because they were placed in an unexamined cluster.

To summarize, look for a clustering tool that offers either hierarchical or fuzzy clustering in addition to basic binary relational clustering. Also, try to use one that allows for multiple similarity measures. These will allow the greatest freedom for end users to explore the relationship between documents.

Categorization

Categorization tools are used to identify the main topics of a document. When choosing a categorization tool, here are a few things to keep in mind:

- Configuring or training the categorizer
- Number of categories identified per document
- Weighting schemes

The first criterion deals primarily with how much work is involved in setting up the tool, while the last two criteria address issues with the tool's output.

Configuring or Training a Categorizer

The set of categories that can be applied to a document set can be either preconfigured or left to the tool's user to establish. The obvious advantage of a preconfigured categorization tool is that you can use it right out of the box. This may be acceptable in some cases, particularly when dealing with broad topics, such as news stories. If the domain of the documents is highly specialized, such as software patents, legal briefs, or medical texts, then a specialized list of categories should be used.

There are two ways to create the classifications. First, a thesaurus can be created that defines a set of domain-specific terms and the relationships between them. The most common relationships are broader term, narrower term, synonym, and related term. (The last is something of a catch-all relationship that indicates that a richer semantic relationship actually exists between the terms but cannot be directly represented in the thesaurus.) The categorizer can then determine the topics of the text on the basis of the frequency of domain-specific words in the text. For large domains, such as medicine, creating a rich thesaurus is an enormous task, and the benefit is often not worth the effort.

Alternately, a categorizer can be trained with sample documents. A set of examples representing each category is presented to the categorizer, which then statistically analyzes linguistic patterns, such as lexical affinities and word frequencies, to produce a statistical signature for each category. The categorizer applies the statistical signatures to documents to find the closest matches. The benefit of this approach is that the labor-intensive process of developing a thesaurus is avoided.

Number of Categories Identified per Document

Like any text analysis operation at this point in time, categorization is not a foolproof process. To minimize the effects of mistaken classification, multiple categories should be identified for a text. Returning to our airline pilots' strike example, articles about that story should probably be classified under both air transportation and labor issues. Multiple classifications allow the same article to be routed to readers interested in different stories or indexed under multiple topics for future reference.

The number of categories provided is less important than the fact that a tool can generate multiple categories. Setting either a maximum number of topics per document or a minimum weight for a topic are useful methods.

Topic Weighting Schemes

One subtle but important point to remember about weights is the range of documents to which they apply. If one document is about labor disputes with a weight of 0.80 and air traffic with a weight of 0.70, and a second document is about the airline industry with a weight of 0.65 and air traffic with a weight of 0.50, then can we say that the first document is about air traffic more than the second? Not necessarily. In some tools, the relative weights of topics take into account only a single document and the topics' relationship to each other, so cross-document comparison does not work. In these cases, we could at least rank the topics from highest weight to lowest and compare them on that basis.

A tool that offers interdocument-based rankings as well as intradocument-based rankings is the ideal categorization tool.

Feature Extraction

Feature extraction tools generally work well at identifying noun phrases, and in many cases can even determine whether the noun phrase is a person, place, organization, or other object. Some features to consider when choosing such a tool are:

- Specialized support for preprocessing and postprocessing, such as authority and residual references.
- Canonical forms
- Frequency

The first item does not deal directly with the feature extraction algorithm but can be used to improve overall performance. Both canonical forms and frequency measures are provided by the core algorithm.

Preprocessing and Postprocessing

Feature extraction algorithms can use dictionaries to identify some terms and linguistic patterns to detect others. For example, the name of a company, such as MyE-Biz, may not be in a dictionary but a feature extraction program could determine it is a noun and probably a significant term. Pattern recognition algorithms often use a technique called Hidden Markov Models (HMM). These models can be trained to detect patterns in a stream of objects. For example, a noun phrase followed by a verb phrase is often followed by another noun phrase as in *John saw the ball.* By training with enough examples, HMMs can learn a large number of patterns with very good accuracy. These HMMs can then be used to detect unrecognized terms on the basis of where they fall in a string of words. While HMMs work in many cases, they cannot catch every term.

Rather than try to train an HMM beyond the point of diminishing return, feature extraction tools should provide users with the option of identifying significant terms in a text before the feature extraction algorithm is run. In this way, difficult terms are labeled before the feature extraction program is run, and thus it does not have to try to determine if the word or phrase is significant. It is not always possible to identify a term before other terms around it have been labeled. In this case, a postprocessing operation could act as a cleanup operation to label leftovers.

Canonical Forms and Frequency

Users should have the option of extracting canonical, or standard, forms of words and phrases. The terms *Chairman of the Federal Reserve Board*, *Fed Chairman*, and *Chairman of the Fed* should all be identified as the same term. This makes indexing, retrieval, and frequency analysis much more accurate.

In addition to identifying key terms and features, the tool should indicate the number of times each term appears in a document. This can be combined with automatically generated categories to provide a more fine-grained classification of documents.

Summarization Tools

Summarization tools often allow users to define a number of parameters, including the number of sentences to extract or a percentage of the total text to extract. These can be experimented with to determine the best settings for a particular application.

Tools that offer finer-grained parameter tuning are welcome. For example, when summarizing news stories or press releases, the first sentence is almost always significant, yet it does not always appear in a summary. Ideally, a user should be able to indicate that the first sentence should always be included. Also, some phrases indicate important points, such as *in conclusion*. Allowing users to specify key phrases that should be more heavily weighted than others could improve summarization performance in some cases.

Textbase Navigation

Textbase navigation is the ability to move about in a document collection by examining related topics. For example, when studying extracted sentences that contain the phrase *inflation*, we should be able to quickly move to documents or sentences containing related phrases such as *monetary policy*. Figure 17.2

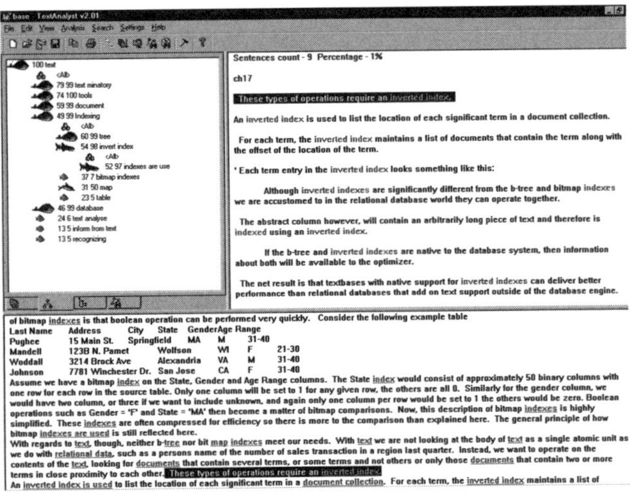

Figure 17.2 Textbase navigation is an important exploratory process.

shows an example from this chapter that illustrates the relationship between the terms *index* and *inverted index*.

Textbase navigation tools are especially useful in research across complementary but disjoint domains, such as the nutrition and migraine research example from Chapter 15.

There are two key criteria for assessing textbase navigation. The first is the ability to see related terms in context. When we notice that two terms seem to keep occurring together, we will likely start formulating a hypothesis about their relationship. Seeing multiple examples of the context around the terms can help assess the quality of the hypothesis. The second criterion is the ability to quickly move from one pair of terms to another. For example, if pursing *inflation* and *monetary policy* does not seem meet our needs, we should be able to quickly move to *inflation* and *fiscal policy* or *inflation* and *trade deficit* or any number of other possible combinations.

Textbase navigation is a useful tool for exploring large document collections. Like clustering and feature extraction, it quickly helps to identify key concepts and additionally shows some of the relationships between key concepts.

Visualization

We saw in Chapter 13 that document collections can be thought of geometrically, with documents represented as points in a multidimensional space. While that abstraction works well for behind-the-scenes document indexing and retrieval, it does not help with user interfaces. Visualization tools have been developed that build upon the feature extraction or key term indexing to provide a graphical representation of document collections. Figure 17.3, for example, shows a visual layout of about 1,000 patents dealing with PC/MCIA card technology using Cartia's ThemeScape.

The advantage of such tools is that main themes or concepts can be quickly identified by their prominence on the map. Related but less dominant themes can then be found by drilling down into the main themes, providing a tool analogous to the drill-down features of OLAP tools. Visualization tools also make it easy to identify the location of specific documents within a document map, as seen in Figure 17.4, again using Cartia's ThemeScape.

Visualization techniques reduce the representations of document collections to two or three dimensions. While there is a risk of losing information with this type of compression, in practice the procedures generally work quite well. For example, latent semantic indexing, described in Chapter 13, can reduce the number of dimensions by identifying clusters of terms that represent concepts, such as *federal*, *debt*, and *taxes*. Self-organizing maps, introduced in Chapter 11,

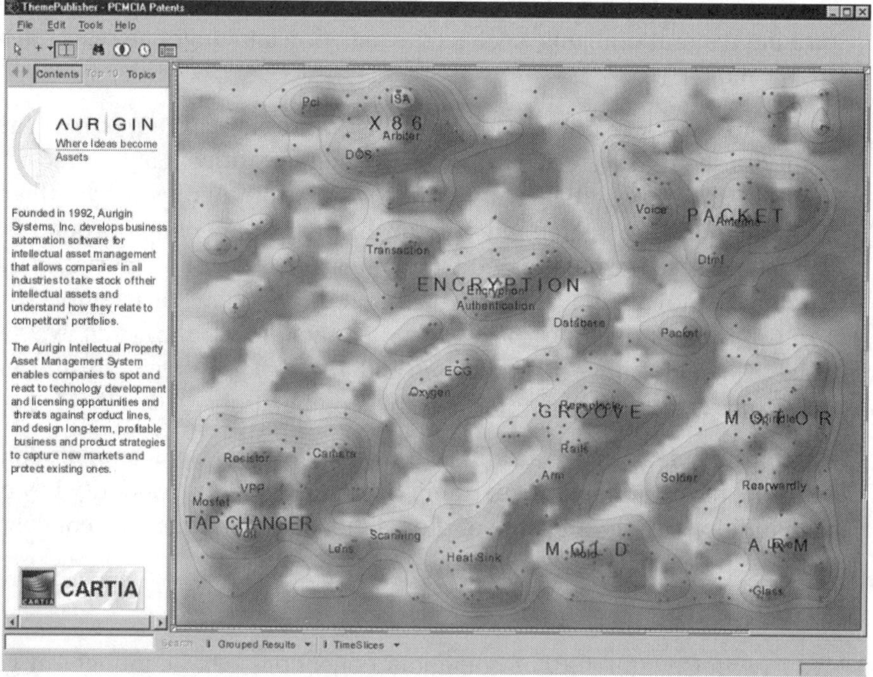

Figure 17.3 Multidimensional models of document collections can be reduced to topographical maps.

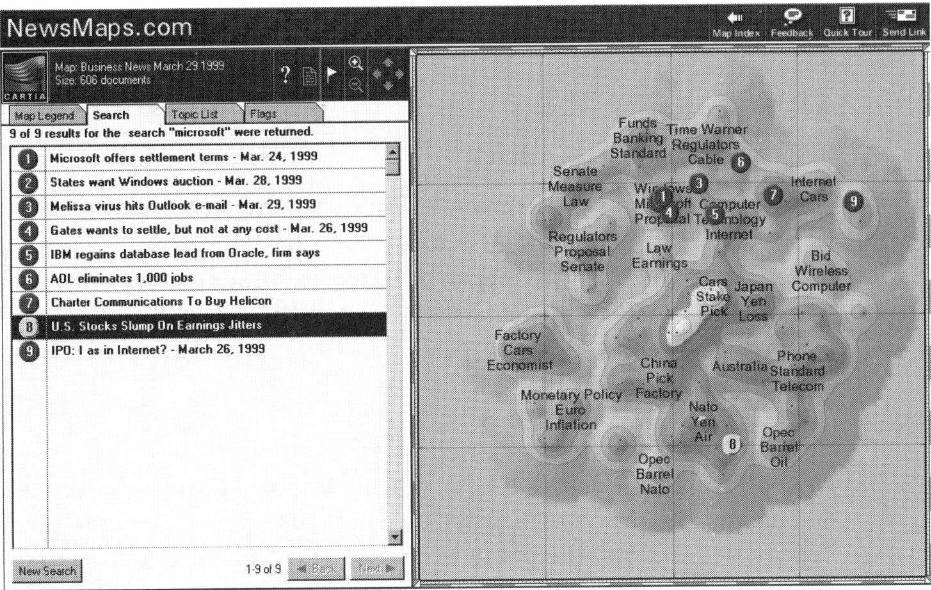

Figure 17.4 Knowing where a document is located within a visualization map can help identify its key themes quickly.

provide an even more dramatic reduction by mapping high-dimensional spaces into two-dimensional grids.

In the first part of the chapter, some basic criteria were outlined for choosing text mining tools. Using these guidelines, we can begin to determine which tools on the market will best meet our needs from a feature perspective as well as from a performance requirements perspective. There are, however, limits to how much we can expect from text mining tools. The art and craft of computational linguistics is constantly developing on a number of different research fronts but many challenges remain. We will now briefly turn our attention to some of those limits.

Still Looking for a Silver Bullet: The Limits of Text Mining

Text mining techniques are essential for dealing with the massive quantities of text that are available to us today. They are not, however, the silver bullet that can lay to rest once and for all the challenges of finding useful texts and discovering knowledge in extremely large document collections such as the Web. Some of the most significant limitations of text mining center on fundamental issues in computational linguistics that are still not adequately understood, including:

- Discourse analysis
- Rich semantic relationships

Discourse analysis is the study of the structure of texts and is beyond the ability of current techniques. Rich semantic relationships capture more than simple relationships such as broader and narrower term. We can discuss what we would like from these techniques but we have to live without those capabilities for now.

Discourse Analysis

Discourse analysis describes the logical structure of texts. In semistructured documents, the structure is explicit, an entity is opened, attributes and subentities are defined, and the entity is closed. Natural language discourse is much more complex. In some texts, such as this book, the beginning of major sections, such as chapters, contain a brief explanation of how that section is structured. So instead of having a separate language for describing structure, as in SGML and XML, the same language that describes document structure is used to constitute the content of the document as well. So instead of seeing something like:

```
<Chapter>
   <Chapter Outline>
   <Chapter Topic>
     Criteria for selecting text mining tools.
   </Chapter Topic>
   <Chapter Topic>
     Limits of text mining techniques>
   </Chapter Topic>
   </Chapter Outline>
   <Chapter Content>
     In this section we will divide the criteria for tool selection …
   </Chapter Content>
 …
</Chapter>
```

In this chapter, we will discuss some criteria for choosing tools and then look into the limits of text mining tools.

With an adequate computational model of discourse, we could describe the structure of texts. This would entail recognizing introductions that describe the content of a text, identifying the central thesis, recognizing lines of argument in the work, discerning examples, and finding other rhetorical and pedagogical devices. If we could recognize these macrolevel structures beyond the sentence, then we could better summarize a document for beginners. More importantly, we could extract the main points of an argument and juxtapose them with arguments from other documents or build chains of reasoning across documents.

To fully support discourse analysis, we need much richer semantic models than those available today.

Semantic Models

How to represent meaning has been a fundamental problem in Artificial Intelligence since its inception. Some of the most studied techniques have been logic, production rules, semantic networks, cases, and neural networks. These techniques have all be successfully applied in many applications but we still do not know how to deal with the kinds of large amounts of diverse knowledge we need to read a newspaper or understand a competitor's moves in the market.

Text mining techniques are certainly more than string manipulation and regular expression matching but we are still missing some fundamental capabilities. Sure, we can build toy programs to extract bits of information from text, such as

> The Federal Reserve Board will increase interest rates.

and represent it in a logical form such as

> interest_rates(rising).

which, when combined with rules (and a suitable rule engine) such as

> If interest_rates(rising) then bond_prices(falling).

allows us to conclude that bond prices will be falling. Our problem, though, is not dealing with single bits of information in well-structured domains but with massive quantities of text covering a many areas of interest that influence each other in a rich array of ways.

Some projects have been undertaken to develop large-scale encyclopedic knowledge bases, such as CYC (www.cyc.com), but they have not yet been integrated into commercial text mining tools. On a smaller scale, but perhaps more significant, projects such as WordNet, a large-scale semantic net of the English language, is available for text analysis operations. The incorporation of WordNet or a similar knowledge base into commercial tools could provide a significant advance in the ability to intelligently process text.

The challenges in discourse analysis and large-scale semantic representations are formidable and for the time being beyond the scope of our current commercially available text mining capabilities.

Conclusions

Choosing text mining tools is best done with an appreciation for the options available to us as well as the limits before us. Many different preprocessing tools are at our disposal, from basic utilities, such as file conversion programs, to portable scripting languages. We should have no problem getting documents and preparing them for text analysis. Things are a little more difficult when we move into text mining tools. The techniques applied are more complex than in the preprocessing phase and the features that concern us are more specialized, such as the choice between lexical-affinity-based clustering and feature-based clustering. Nonetheless, with just a few basic criteria we can distinguish among the commercial tools available for common text mining operations such as clustering, categorization, feature extraction, summarization, and textbase navigation. As powerful and as useful as these tools are, they do not understand text. Complex analysis related to the structure of discourse and the nature of large-scale semantic relationships is beyond the reach of contemporary tools, but inroads are being made and, no doubt, the text mining landscape will look radically different ten years from now.

For information on the latest text mining tools, see this book's companion Web site. The rapid pace of development in text mining tools will guarantee that some of the shortcomings of current tools will be addressed in a relatively short period of time.

PART FOUR

Conclusions

CHAPTER 18

Changes in Business Intelligence

Business intelligence is no longer limited to numeric reports and graphs. Text plays a more central role in providing decision makers with a more expansive model of business intelligence than it has in the past. In this final chapter, we will review the overall picture of the structure and role of the document warehouse, the need for text mining services, and applications for this technology. We will also compare fundamental differences between document warehousing and data warehousing and the respective benefits of each. Finally, we will briefly look at how document warehousing and text mining techniques may evolve to meet the demands of text-based business intelligence.

Business Intelligence and the Dynamics of Organizations

In the past, executives and analysts were the sole users of business intelligence (BI) systems. The exclusivity of the BI club was even reflected in our names for these tools that included "executive information systems." Those days are gone. Management philosophies have changed, and more and more individuals are involved in organizational decision making. The types of decisions that need to be made and how they are made are also changing. Astute observers of innovation have recognized that good companies, following rational decision making processes can fail in the face of some types of technological changes.

Navigating the turbulent waters of organizational and market change requires more than looking at production quotas and sales figures from the data warehouse. Decision makers need access to every possible business intelligence resource, including text, and that is why we need document warehouses.

The role of the document warehouse is to provide a repository for text-based business intelligence information and, working in parallel with the data warehouse, provide a full range of information to decision makers. As Figure 18.1 shows, business intelligence depends upon appropriately analyzed text and numeric information.

The benefits of data warehousing are well understood. A data warehouse provides a historical, integrated view of an organization's operations. For the most part, data warehouses are internally directed in scope. That is, most of the information is internally generated, and it describes internal processes such as sales, manufacturing, inventory management, and quality control. Using a data warehouse, managers and can better understand how particular segments of an organization's operations is doing. Rather than simply knowing that sales are declining in the last quarter, a manager or analyst can pinpoint particular regions, product lines, or divisions in the company that are primarily responsible for shifting sales. Like the organizations that use business intelligence systems, the systems themselves must adapt to continue to meet their objectives. We will now briefly outline three broad types of changes that occur in organizations and markets and look at ways in which business intelligence systems can incorporate text to meet these latest needs:

- Changing decision makers
- Changing technologies
- Changing strategies

The highly centralized, hierarchically managed organization seems as out of place now as the centrally controlled, command economies of mid- and late-twentieth-century Eastern Europe. Decision making and operational responsibility in many organizations has devolved to those closer to the actual production and services of the business. Technological innovation is nothing new but the pace of innovation is so rapid that it is difficult to keep up with so many changes. Not only that, but also we must recognize that not all innovations can be assessed and managed in the same ways. Finally, organizations need to change strategies to adapt to new market conditions. Managing the process of strategy creation and implementation cannot be done simply by measuring how well a company is implementing its current strategy. Business intelligence systems must provide information about the environment in which a company functions as well as about the company's internal operations.

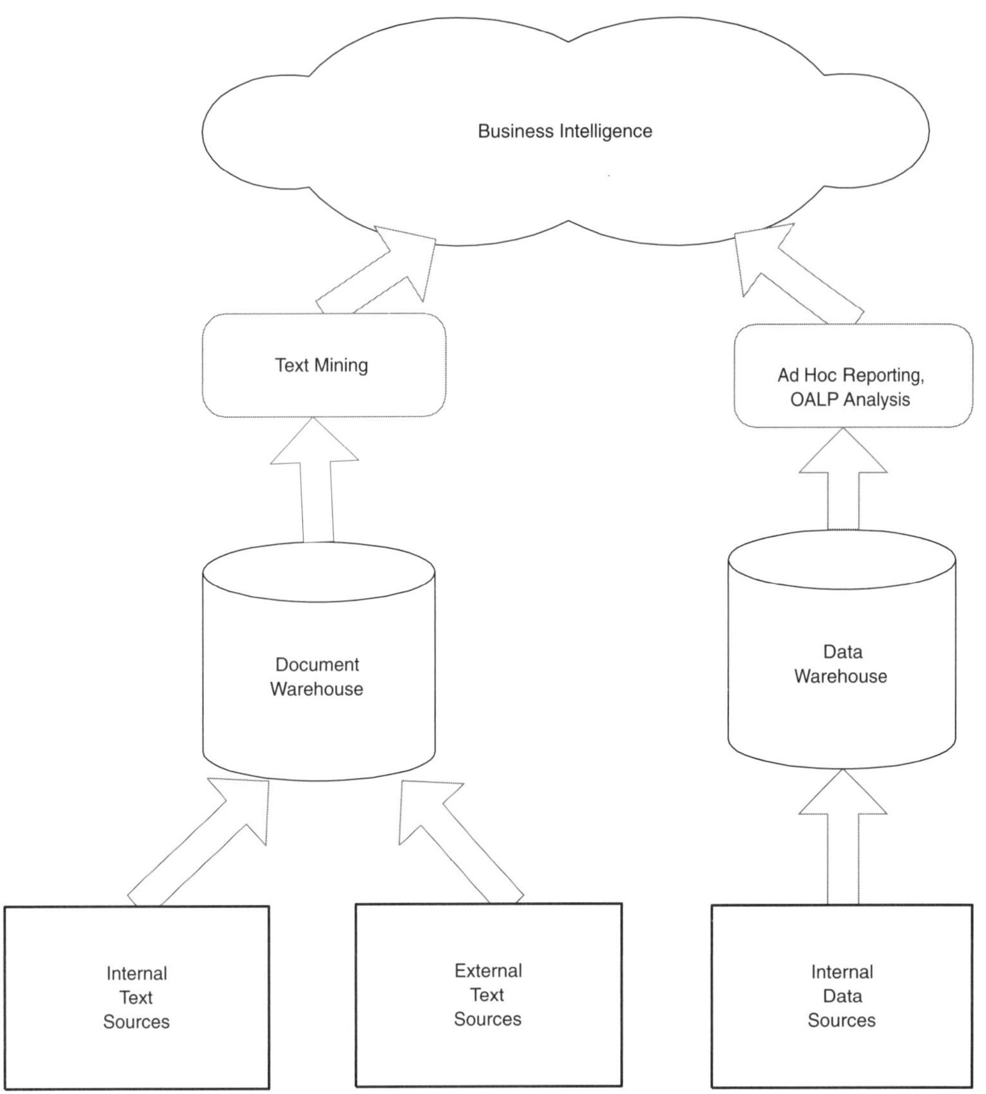

Figure 18.1 Both and text and numeric information are required for a full understanding of a business environment.

Changing Decision Makers

Management practices have shifted from hierarchical, highly structured models to more decentralized models that move decision making to front-line workers and provide frequent feedback on performance to those directly involved with production. The advent of the data Webhouse (Kimball and Merz 2000) as another variant of the data warehouse is a response to the massive need for data warehousing services. Decision support is no longer the province of executives and managers isolated from day-to-day or minute-to-minute production or service operations. If you are involved in business operations, you need business intelligence about those operations. Just as these new decision makers need to understand internal processes, they also need to understand wider organizational needs and objectives laid out in internal documents, press releases, and news or other market reports.

Changing Technologies

Just as those on the front lines of production and service operations need more information than they have had in the past, so too, executives and managers need more intelligence than in the past. Consider, for example, the problem of emerging technologies. Innovations abound that improve performance of established products. These innovations, called sustaining technologies (Christensen 2000), allow producers to continue to improve their offerings in ways that matter most to their customers, such as with longer mean time between failures, greater shelf life, or faster speeds. Other types of innovations underperform existing technologies in mainstream markets but provide advantages to small segments of the market. These are called disruptive technologies and are more difficult to understand and manage. Clayton Christensen notes that the emergence of personal computers, offroad motorcycles, transistors, and digital photography all radically changed their respective markets, even though they did not immediately capture significant market interest (Christensen 2000).

According to Christensen, companies that do not recognize the role of disruptive technologies can fall into the innovator's dilemma, which can be explained in this way: Disruptive technologies do not meet the needs of the company's best customers because the technologies provide improvements in areas that those same customers do not rank very highly, and therefore the company does not feel they warrant investment. The result is that by not investing in these technologies, the company eventually loses market position when the disruptive technology begins to meet changing customer needs more effectively than the older, sustaining technologies. The prospect can seem pretty bleak. "If good management practice drives the failure of successful firms faced with disruptive technological change, then the usual answers to companies' problems—planning better, working harder, becoming more customer-driven, and taking a longer-term perspective—all exacerbate the problem. Sound execution, speed to market, total quality management, and process reengineering are similarly ineffective" (Christensen 2000). Fortunately, as Christensen points out, there are ways to deal with disruptive technologies.

Among the principles that must be followed is understanding that customers and investors ultimately control the flow of resources in an organization. Keeping abreast of the changing expectations of customers and investors is a process that must be incorporated into business intelligence systems. Second, disruptive technologies take hold in emerging markets where there is little or no quantitative data. Depending on numbers just won't work. "Companies whose investment processes demand quantification of market sizes and financial returns before they can enter a market get paralyzed or make serious mistakes when faced with disruptive technologies. They demand market data when none exists and make judgments based upon financial projections when neither revenues or cost can, in fact, be known" (Christensen 2000). Before we can measure a market or a process, we must understand it or at least be able to make judgements about how it will evolve. This type of market or technology assessment will come from analyzing news stories, industry analysis reports, patents, and market analysis.

Changing Strategies

Broadly speaking, organizations make two types of decisions: tactical and strategic. Tactical decisions are short range, operationally focused decisions. These can include deciding on the best way to implement part of the manufacturing process, defining the criteria for which customers to include in a new directed marketing effort, and deciding how to argue a particular point in a labor negotiation. Strategic decisions on the other hand, have a much broader impact. These decisions determine the overall objectives of an organization with respect to the current market conditions. Will a company continue to compete in a particular market, should it make a partnership with another firm to improve its position in a particular vertical market, and how should the company respond to new, sweeping regulations are all examples of strategic decisions faced by organizations. Data warehouses and other internally focused decision support platforms are excellent means for improving tactical decision making. Since their focus is on internal operations and processes, they do not provide all the information that is needed for strategic decision making, and this is where the document warehouse comes into play.

Strategic decision making entails a number of steps:

- Framing the strategy problem
- Identifying alternatives
- Evaluating alternatives

Organizational needs are the impetus to appropriately frame strategic problems. The problem could be slowing sales in a particular product line, a need to cut costs to meet earnings projections, or even a change in a competitor's strategy. The types of problems that can drive strategy changes are widely varied, but they must all be put into a context. For example, the slumping sales could be due to a quality control problem, the need to cut costs could be an investor relation's problem, and the change in a competitor's activity could be seen as a marketing problem. Once the context for the problem is framed, managers can move onto identifying alternatives, the first point where document warehousing can provide significant support in this process.

With a frame of reference in mind, decision makers can make use of past experience. Has this problem or something similar been faced in the past? If so, what was done, and how effective was it? These and related questions are examples of case-based or analogical reasoning and are aptly supported by document warehousing techniques. For example, a document warehouse containing both competitive intelligence information and internal marketing, production, and strategy documents can be queried for examples of similar changes in competitor behavior, such as the introduction of low-cost alternatives, expansion into new markets, or strategic alliances with shared vendors or distributors. Of course, past effectiveness is no guarantee of future success, so even if a similar case is found, it needs to be thoroughly evaluated.

Evaluating strategic alternatives, according to George Day (Day 1994), entails a number of steps:

- Assessing market opportunity
- Assessing competitive advantage
- Understanding the prospects for successful implementation
- Deciding if the risks are acceptable
- Determining if projected financial results will be achieved.

Reviewing the details of each of these steps is beyond the scope of this book, but you may refer to Day's paper for more information. Here, we will simply note that the answers to these questions require significant information that is neither internally generated nor available in numeric form. That is, these are ideal problems for a document warehouse.

Market opportunities come from changes in the needs of customers or changes in the abilities of competitors to meet those needs.

The competitive advantage a firm holds is a function of proprietary methods and technologies as well as the ability, or inability, of other firms to provide to provide suitable substitutes for products and services. Since other companies inevitably find ways to meet or overcome a competitive advantage, innovators are forced to constantly add features to distinguish their products. This rapid innovation and feature bloating can result in products that overreach beyond market demand, leading to customers' changing the key dimensions on which they make purchase decisions. This, in turn, provides an opportunity for disruptive technologies to take hold in the market and establish themselves as a dominant technology. As Figure 18.2 shows, these market trends can lead to fundamental changes in the established positions of dominant firms.

To successfully implement a new strategy, a firm must have both the skills and the resources to meet its objectives. An inventory of skills and knowledge does not fit easily into the relational structures of traditional database systems. Using the expressive richness of language is the best, and perhaps only, way for organizations to record, access, and analyze key intangible assets, such as process knowledge. Even a wealth of industry knowledge and proprietary skills cannot guarantee success.

Risk comes in many forms. Global corporations face political, monetary, and market risks every day but when a company makes a change in strategy it exposes itself to new types of risks it has not experienced before. Again numeric measures from past practices are not a sufficient guide in this area. Knowledgeable executives and analysts will be studying and assessing risks in new areas, and the raw material for this process is text. Again, a data warehouse will not meet this need, but a document warehouse can.

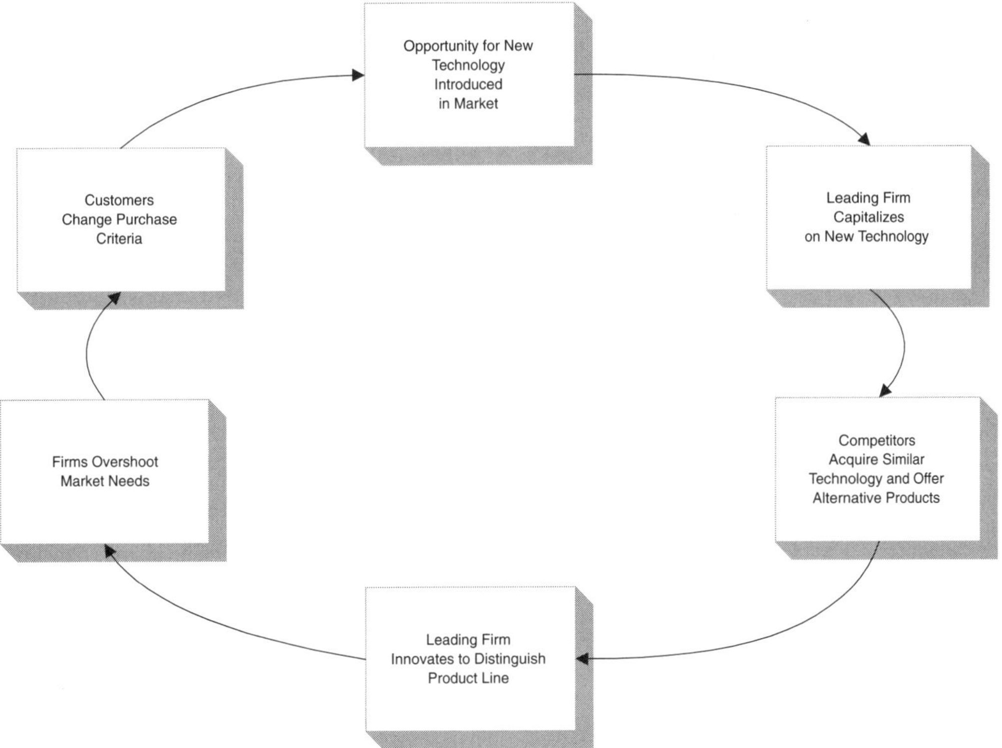

Figure 18.2 The cycle of change in how customers make purchasing decisions.

The final criterion for evaluating alternate strategies, as outlined by George Day, is assessing whether or not expected financial returns will be realized. For most firms, this boils down to estimating the increase in shareholder value. This of all five criteria is the most quantitative but even here, numbers are not enough. Any assessment of return on investment will take into account market demand, changes in competitors' activities, and the potential for substitute products and services from competitors. This information can best be derived from rich, textual market analysis, competitive intelligence portfolios, and a sound understanding of opportunities and threats in a market.

The changing face of business intelligence is driven by need. Decision makers are changing, they are no longer a relatively small set of individuals within an organization but could include almost anyone with management responsibility. To manage in rapidly changing markets, it is no longer enough to understand your own internal processes when the market and the technologies that shape the market are continually evolving in response to innovation driven by competitive pressures. Understanding the dynamics of today's markets also requires that executives, managers, and other decision makers be ready to adopt new strategies as needed. This is the environment in which business intelligence systems now operate. To meet the needs of business intelligence system users, we BI designers and developers need to adopt document warehousing and text mining technologies to meet the needs of our own customers, the decision makers.

Meeting BI Needs with the Document Warehouse and Text Mining

Clearly the business intelligence needs of organizations are not going to be met by numbers or internal sources alone. Data warehousing has served tactical and some strategic decision making, and now with the inclusion of text in the business intelligence process, that support will meet even more needs. Supporting text-based business intelligence requires the introduction of new tools and processes into the decision support environment. These, by no means, will displace our current tool set; they will compliment it. As we see in Figure 18.3, our goal is to expand the breadth and scope of business intelligence, and to do that we must build upon what we already have.

The Process of Document Warehousing

We will now review the core processes of the document warehouse and discuss how each component supports business intelligence operations. The key steps of document warehousing are:

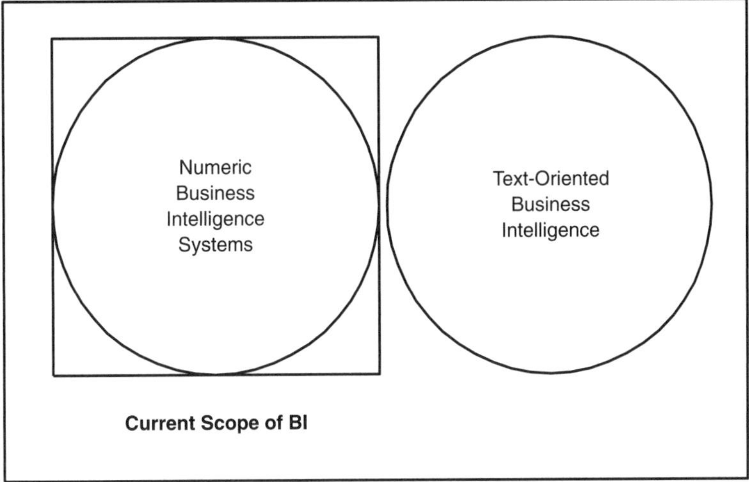

Figure 18.3 Internal, numeric decision support systems are vital, but we must add text-based information sources to meet additional decision support needs.

- Identifying document sources
- Document retrieval
- Preprocessing operations
- Text analysis operations
- Managing document warehouse metadata
- Supporting end-user text mining operations

Throughout the first half of this book, we have developed these ideas in detail. We will now cover them here to tie together these separate steps, and will discuss how they serve to further our goal of expanding the scope of business intelligence.

Identifying Document Sources

Identifying document sources requires significant effort on the part of end users and analysts familiar with particular domains of interest. The critical success factors in this stage are, first, to ensure that topics of interest are adequately covered. Broad topics, such as biotechnology, are difficult to cover in depth. In these cases, it is best to begin with document sources from a wide range of subareas, such as genetic engineering, bioinformatics, and genetic patent law. Working from the broad base of text information, users can identify more precise areas of interest and identify sources of specific information. For example, a health care analyst working in disease management may focus in on new diabetes screening techniques after discovering features shared by descriptions of existing screening techniques and a recently patented low-cost method for manufacturing key agents for the screening process. Once a narrow area has been identified, then targeted sources, such as patents and scientific journals, can be comprehensively explored.

Document Retrieval

The document retrieval processes can actually be three distinct processes, depending upon the document sources. These include:

- Internal file systems
- Document management systems
- The Internet

Internal file systems are easy to work with, especially when using a cross-platform scripting language such as Perl or Python. Security access is a dominant concern, and no single process should be given access to all relevant servers or directories. Access controls within the document warehouse will need to balance confidentiality requirements with the interest in sharing and integrating as much information as possible. Of course, the organizational and metadata support provided in most file systems is limited, but document management systems have met those needs in many cases.

From the perspective of the document warehouse designer, document management systems offer perhaps the most organized and metadata-rich document source. Extracting documents from document management systems is more complex than simply working with file systems but standardized application programming interfaces (API) make extraction programs more portable than those based on earlier, proprietary techniques. By drawing documents from internal file systems and document management systems, business intelligence users have access to the semantic content of texts, just as data warehouse users have access to content of transactions from transaction processing systems.

The Internet is, of course, the largest source of text for the document warehouse. The Internet is also the most difficult document source with which to deal. Crawlers, agents, and other retrieval tools must be carefully configured so as not to search uncontrollably through hyperlinked documents. Controls must not only limit the amount of text returned to the document warehouse but also screen poor-quality information. Metadata about document sources is the best way to control what sites are searched as well as to provide quality control information to users reading Internet-based documents or information extracted from the Internet.

Preprocessing Operations

The next step in the document warehouse pipeline after retrieving documents is preprocessing. This step does not directly support business intelligence operations but is akin to transformations in the extraction, transformation, and load processes of data warehousing. The output of preprocessing operations is text that has been reformatted and translated to a target form suitable for the text analysis tools that will operate on the text next.

Text Analysis Operations

Text analysis operations are the heart of the document warehouse process. It is here that we reduce the raw text to facts, features, and summaries of relevant information. This is also the point at which full text indexing and thematic indexing occurs. Clustering, or grouping related documents together, is another key operation that is included within the realm of text analysis operations.

Reducing the amount of text that a user must read to find relevant information is a key objective of document warehousing, and it is accomplished by distilling a document down to its most important components through summarization techniques. Categorizing documents, so that they can be automatically routed to interested users, and indexing by themes for later searching by topic also reduce the number of documents a reader must wade through.

When dealing with extremely large numbers of related documents, feature extraction is another effective way of getting information to users without their having to read irrelevant texts. For example, consider a researcher investigating the types of proteins created by a new set of genes and looking for links with a particular disease, such as hypertension, diabetes, or glaucoma. If the researcher had access to the main terms that occurred frequently in research publications on the genes, then he or she could match them with terms occurring frequently in disease state research and find evidence of links between the two domains. As we saw in Chapter 13, this process was used to find links between nutrition and migraines.

Finally, grouping similar documents together, especially in a hierarchical manner, can help researchers and analysts hone in on particular areas of interest without wading through irrelevant texts simply because they may contain some of the same terms. Other techniques, such as fuzzy clustering, take into account that we cannot always make clear rules for deciding if a document belongs in one group or another.

These and other text analysis techniques are built upon a number of different approaches. Some tools use statistical techniques that analyze the frequencies with which terms occur together. These tools are useful in areas that use specialized vocabularies, such as scientific and technical disciplines. By training these tools with sample documents from a domain, they can effectively classify other texts from the same domain. Instead of opting for statistical approaches, other tools use knowledge-based techniques first developed for Artificial Intelligence applications. Knowledge-based tools include databases of facts, relations, and word meanings used to categorize, summarize, and distill meaning from texts. Other tools focus on identifying the significance of relationships between words. Neural networks, for example, have been used to build semantic networks of weighted correlations between words. These techniques will prove useful when exploring complimentary but disjoint areas of research. There is no single best approach. Depending upon your objectives, some tools will work better than others. No matter your choice of tools, integrating the tools with the document warehouse is, in large part, done with metadata.

Managing Document Warehouse Metadata

Metadata drives the document warehouse. Information about documents in the warehouse, technical operations, and business requirements are all embedded in metadata. As we discussed in Chapter 9, the three types of metadata are:

- Content metadata
- Technical metadata
- Business metadata

Content metadata succinctly describes the key subjects of a document. Technical metadata on the other hand serves to control document warehouse processes, such as document retrieval. Business metadata addresses issues such as quality control and user access to documents. Effectively employing these types of metadata can significantly ease the administration of the document warehouse.

Content metadata will come from at least two sources. Some documents will contain metadata information. As Web sites become more complex, site designers are turning to metadata to help manage and control their content. Metadata can also be extracted from document management systems. In both cases, the predefined metadata may not be as comprehensive as is needed in the document warehouse. In these cases, feature extraction, categorization, and summarization techniques can augment existing metadata to round out our metadata requirements.

Technical metadata deals primarily with document searching, retrieval, and processing. Determining the files to copy from internal file servers, the documents to extract from document management systems, and topics to search on the Internet are all controlled by document warehouse technical metadata. Preprocessing operations, such as machine translation and format conversion, can also be controlled by metadata, although sometimes these requirements are determined on the fly. Document warehouses support a number of distinct text analysis operations. Not all of these techniques are required for every document, and technical metadata can be used to determine which operations should be applied to which documents. Some documents, such as e-mails, do not require summarization. Newsgroup messages may only be useful in a broader context, such as a cluster of related documents. Controlling which text analysis operations are applied to which documents is the province of technical metadata.

While content metadata is about what is inside of documents, and technical metadata describes how to process those documents, business metadata is less fixed. In general, business metadata deals with quality control assessments and user access to documents.

The quality control issue focuses on the reliability and timeliness of an information source. These are two distinct dimensions and should be treated as such. For example, a source that provides carefully researched and verified information on the securities market is almost certainly reliable, but at the cost of timely reporting. Other sources may rush to break an important event in the market at the risk of acting prematurely. Which is more valuable? That depends on how you balance your need for rapid access to information with your need for accurate information. Of course, the two are not necessarily mutually exclusive, but in practice, the more we get of one characteristic the more we risk getting less of the other.

Access control in transactional systems is easily implemented. The need is so pervasive that relational database management systems regularly provide a robust collection of security control mechanisms to manage the creating, reading, updating, and deleting of transactional records. Data warehouse security is more complex. Users might be restricted to viewing detail data from their own regions or product lines but have access to aggregate-level measures that cross reporting centers. Document warehouse access control can be more complex still. In some cases, access is based upon the source of the document. For example, notes on pending labor negotiations or legal briefs from ongoing litigation should not be publicly available in the document warehouse. Since these types of documents come from controlled sources, as opposed to Internet searches, they can be easily identified and protected. A less obvious problem is that sometimes a potential breach of security or confidentiality is not a function of a single document but of a collection of documents. A single document may not outline a new overall marketing strategy, but a document warehouse user might be able to piece together 90 percent of the plan by examining a wide range of documents available in the document warehouse. Of course, this type of piecing together of information from a wide range of disparate sources is one of the objectives of document warehousing, so preventing it is somewhat counterproductive, to say the least.

Supporting End-User Text Analysis Operations

Users have both short-term and long-term interests that should be supported within the document warehouse. While short-term interests are best addressed by allowing users to easily execute ad hoc queries or navigate a visual representation of salient themes, long-term interests are best handled with explicit definitions of a user's area of interest.

Creating and maintaining explicit representations of long-term interests requires four components:

- A language for describing interests
- A data store for these descriptions
- A means of creating the interest specifications
- A method for using the interest specification to drive the search process

With each component in place, the document warehouse can adequately support user's text analysis operations.

Languages for Describing User Interests

Languages for describing user interests can range from the extremely simple to the full expressiveness of natural languages. The problem with the simplest representations, such as a list of keywords, is that they generally lead to poor precision and recall. Poor precision is the result of words having multiple meanings. So if a user is interested in the aviation industry, and a representation of his or her interest includes the word *fly*, then documents about winged insects might also be retrieved. Using multiple keywords with each query reduces the likelihood of that kind of obvious mistake. Poor recall is the result of having many words at our disposal for describing a single concept, such as *flight*, *aviation*, and *aerospace technology*. Solving this problem with simple representations requires including synonyms for each key word. Thesauri provide the best option for representing synonyms in text analysis systems, and standardized formats for thesauri make these resources tool independent.

More complex representations based upon first order logic have been used in Artificial Intelligence and database applications. (See *Readings in Artificial Intelligence and Databases* [Muylopolous et al. 1989] for more on this topic.) The advantage of extending the representation scheme beyond simple lists of terms is that more complex concepts can be represented. If we stick to the simplest form of logic, propositional logic, then we can build expressions using Boolean operators such as:

```
(aviation AND propulsion) OR (airline AND jet)
```

To this representation we can add the quantification that allows us to describe whether certain expressions apply in all cases or only sometimes. For the most part, this additional functionality is not needed in document warehousing, and the additional computational overhead is prohibitive.

The most complex way of describing interests is through natural language, but that cannot meet our needs. Our goal in document warehousing is to make natural language texts accessible by reducing the complexity of their representations.

This end is best served by a simple term-based representation augmented with weights to describe relative importance. A variation on this is the use of sample documents to represent topics that interest a reader. These documents can then be reduced to key terms and concepts along with an indication of the relative importance of each in the document set.

Data Stores for User Interests

Data stores for readers' interests support either key terms plus weights or prototypical documents. In both cases, the essential features of the data structure are that they provide efficient access to an interest description and that the description itself be easily mapped into search query.

The term plus weight representation can easily meet these needs in many cases although search engines may require different syntax for specifying the weight of each term. Document prototypes can also be used with search engines that support a find similar document feature. Both representations are also capable of representing multiple sets of interests for each user.

Creating Interest Specifications

Interest specifications can be created explicitly or implicitly. In the first case, users define key terms and concepts of interest to them. The advantage of this approach is ease of implementation. Users can choose terms from a predefined thesaurus or taxonomy and make subjective assignments of importance to each one. Implicit creation of a user interest specification requires that the document warehouse track the user's queries to discover key terms. Ideally, the user would also provide feedback on how well each document that was returned by a query actually met his or her needs. With enough feedback, machine learning and data mining algorithms can be used to determine appropriate sets of terms and their weights without user intervention.

Using Interest Specifications

The final piece of effectively using interest specifications is to tie them to search and routing functions in the document warehouse. Each distinct interest specification can drive a single search operation, both for internal and for external documents. They can also be used to filter existing documents in the document warehouse and route newly acquired documents to users likely to need the information in those documents.

Document warehousing is a multifaceted operation. Document sources must be identified, documents need to be retrieved and prepared for later processing. Text analysis operations can range from full text and thematic indexing to clustering and summarization. The type of analysis performed on each document can vary and is controlled by a metadata maintained in the document warehouse. In addition, users' long-term interests should be represented in such a way as to support the document search process as well as users' own text mining operations. With the document warehouse in place, we now have the ability to exploit text mining for business intelligence operations.

Text Mining for Decision Support

Decision support is moving beyond the limits of numeric data. Document warehouses are the structured repositories of documents and related metadata that provide the foundation upon which text-based business intelligence operations are built. Document warehouses are specifically designed to support text mining—that is, the process of extracting targeted information from text. Since text mining is a relatively new field with a wide range of definitions, we have adopted the following as our working definition:

> Text mining is the process of compiling, organizing, and analyzing large document collections to support the delivery of targeted business information to analysts and decision makers and to discover relationships between related facts that span wide domains of inquiry.

This definition helps us to understand the range of operations that are entailed in text mining, but solid examples of applied text mining are perhaps the best illustration of how text mining can be used in organizations to enhance their business intelligence operations. In this book, we looked into three example applications of text mining:

- Operations management
- Customer relationship management
- Competitive intelligence

Our discussion of operations management looked into using text mining techniques to better understand what is happening within a business's core processes. Customer relationship management is often thought of in terms of integrating customer records to personalize services for those customers. Unfortunately, text is rarely considered a source of potential information to further that personalization process. Text mining with a document warehouse should demonstrate that a more in-depth perspective on customers, particularly business customers, could be attained. Finally, competitive intelligence and market research can be as important to managing a business as knowing the details of internal operations. The ability to analyze large volumes of text in this area can provide a competitive advantage to those who take on the challenge.

Text Mining and Operational Management

Operational management encompasses both standard operating processes and ad hoc projects. In the first case, text mining can best be applied to standard operating processes from a monitoring perspective. For example, status reports, production reports, and other regularly produced documents can be summarized and routed according to their contents to appropriate mangers. Ad hoc projects, by their nature, vary in scope and duration. Text mining is best used to help solve particular problems such as: Why did severe quality control problems occur with a particular production batch? or What is the range of complaints with regard to a newly introduced product line? In both standard operating processes and ad hoc projects, text can be used to delve beneath numeric measures to look into why something has occurred.

Text Mining and Customer Relationship Management

When addressing the customer relationship management needs of business customers, we have the opportunity to use documents to help us better understand customers. In particular we can look into:

- Customer's needs for products and services
- Customer's market
- Customer's strategy

While past purchasing patterns can provide an indication of future purchases, it is risky to assume that demand will stay relatively constant. Markets can become flooded with a product, dramatically reducing prices for that product, which in turn reduces the demand for the raw materials or components of that product. The market for computer memory has seen this type of fluctuation when production outstrips demand. In other cases, customers might make large purchases to meet one-time needs, such as to build a fixed number of commercial jets for an airline.

In a broader context, businesses can monitor their customers' markets to better understand the changing needs of those customers. This can be especially important when a customer's markets are adapting to new technologies that could radically change their means of production or the demand for their products. Similarly, the customer's strategy may change in response to market dynamics. For example, a customer could shift from being a low-cost producer to being a best-cost producer of higher-quality versions of their products. Knowing how this could affect your customer's purchasing patterns or needs can help your business adapt earlier than if it simply waited to see the effect of the strategic changes show up in operational data.

Text Mining and Competitive Intelligence

A third application that is ripe for text mining is automated competitive intelligence gathering and analysis. Business intelligence and competitive intelligence differ in three significant ways.

First, business intelligence is generally inward-directed and driven by data from operational systems. Competitive intelligence, on the other hand, draws information from a wide range of external sources. These can include news sources, regulatory agencies, public records, environmental and consumer watchdog groups, annual reports, speeches, and even competitors' marketing material.

A second difference is that business intelligence systems are fed from database-structured sources, such as operational applications like enterprise resource planning systems. Competitive intelligence is highly textual, so its sources are linguistically structured and thus require a different approach and a different set of tools.

A third difference between business intelligence and competitive intelligence is that the former is often used for tactical decisions, while the latter can help shape strategic decisions. Strategic management focuses on how a company operates in the macroenvironment, which includes competitors, markets, and regulatory atmosphere. At this level, measures of internal operations cannot directly help understand a company's strengths, weakness, opportunities, and threats with regard to others in the market. Intelligence on competitors' objectives and strategies, however, can support strategic decision making.

Harnessing the potential for text mining in competitive intelligence centers around four activities:

- Defining the target competitors
- Completing a strengths, weaknesses, opportunities, and threats (SWOT) assessment
- Answering specific research questions
- Augmenting document collection with analysis

Defining target competitors is not always as easy or obvious as it may first appear. Companies that offer multiple products and services can have multiple types of competitors in several different markets. Competitors may vary by location as well as by product line. Competitors are not always obvious. When Amazon.com first offered books for sale through the Web, it probably was not considered the competitor to brick and mortar bookstores it has now become. With the lower barriers to entry that e-business sometimes offers and the potential for disruptive technologies to take hold unexpectedly, just knowing who your competitors are can be a project in itself.

Developing a SWOT assessment can also be supported with text mining operations. Strengths and weaknesses are, in many cases, a function of market demand. Possessing the infrastructure to produce high-quality, low-cost products is a definite strength when demand for the product is high. Carrying the cost of owning the same production facilities after demand for the products has dropped is a weakness. Similarly opportunities and threats depend upon a company's position in the market. Here again, understanding market trends and alternate technologies can improve strategic management by providing early warnings of shifting weakness and threats and provide advance intelligence on potential opportunities.

Just as operational management needs support for ad hoc projects, strategic management needs support for one-time research projects. These may spin off from recognized changes in market trends or changes in the regulatory environment. They can also arise as effects of other strategic decisions, such as the decision to acquire or merge with another company.

Finally, the internal analysis conducted through the use of the document warehouse will in turn create other competitive intelligence and strategic management documents that should be included in the document warehouse. Collections of assessments will provide a yet higher level of strategic analysis for other users of the document warehouse.

Decision making can change in light of the advances in text mining and document warehousing. Executives, managers, and analysts are no longer limited to numeric measures of internal operations. Richly descriptive texts covering topics from the release of new products and the patenting of new technologies to proposed regulations and indicators of political risk in international markets can be made available to readers in a targeted fashion. Of course, the information is available without text mining or document warehousing, but finding it and wading through irrelevant material without these tools is often prohibitive. The result is that a shift in our mind set about decision support is in order. We can now support strategic decisions as well as tactical ones and cull intelligence from internal and external texts as well as from numeric measures of internal operations.

Shifting Emphasis of BI

The inclusion of text in decision support operations is a fundamental change in business intelligence operations. Not only have the types of decision support systems changed but the tools and techniques have changed as well. This shift in emphasis can be seen along three different dimensions:

- Text versus numbers
- Heuristics versus algorithms
- Distributed versus centralized sources

Each of these dimensions identifies a different mode of meeting the intelligence needs of decision makers.

Text, Not Just Numbers

If nothing else, the goal of this book is to argue for the inclusion of text-based resources in decision support environments. With somewhere between 60 percent and 80 percent of all business information kept in text, it is irresponsible to ignore it. Numeric systems have served us well and will continue to do so. It is hard to imagine any modern organization not utilizing production metrics to manage operations. Data warehousing techniques, and especially dimensional models, are mainstays of business intelligence systems, and their value is beyond question. What can and should be the question is: Are these the only techniques that are needed to provide a rich, robust decision support environment? Clearly the answer is no. Without support for text analysis, we cannot provide access to vast amounts of information that might be needed for strategic as well as operational decision making.

Heuristics, Not Just Algorithms

Many of the techniques described throughout the book will not guarantee correct results 100 percent of the time. Heuristics, or rules of thumbs, are frequently used in Artificial Intelligence systems that deal with complex environments and wide arrays of inputs. This is certainly the case with text analysis. We learned after nearly thirty years of intensive research that developing a program that can fully understand natural language is still a long way off. We also know that information retrieval (IR) systems, at best, peak between 60 percent and 70 percent when measured for precision and recall. That level seems to be something of a glass ceiling that we have not been able to break through. This is not a theoretical limit by any means, it is just a practical observation.

Knowing the limits of both linguistic-based natural language processing approaches and the more statistically oriented IR techniques should not dissuade us from using these tools. Document warehousing and text mining are techniques to support decision makers, not replace them. Heuristic techniques that reduce the amount of text a user must read and improve the precision and recall of his or her searches are useful, pragmatic tools in their own right and can be employed to make business intelligence operations more efficient.

Distributed Intelligence, Centralized Management

Business intelligence and competitive intelligence cannot be found in a single source. An enterprise resource planning system may contain vast amounts of data about internal operations and future projections but even this cannot meet all the needs of decision makers. Strategies can be formulated with broad objectives in mind, but bits and pieces of information gathered from diverse sources can shape both those objectives and how they are realized. Information from financial news sources, vertical industry portals, government agencies, and patent offices around the world can all provide small pieces to a very large strategic puzzle.

The role of the document warehouse is to bring these distributed pieces together and to make them available from a single, centralized source. Document warehouses do not need to duplicate entire documents but only metadata about those documents; thus, a document warehouse could be distributed over an organization's internal network as well as across the Internet. Through centralized management, users can have fast, efficient access to germane documents that are distributed across multiple platforms.

The shift in emphasis with document warehousing and text mining is a shift both in what users can expect from their business intelligence systems and in the types of tools and techniques that we apply to meet these users' needs. As noted above, these techniques are not foolproof but at least we can look forward to a continuous stream of improved products as the demand for text mining increases.

Next Steps: Where Do We Go from Here?

Significant improvements in document warehousing and text mining will come from a several different arenas. We will stick to the most likely area to yield radical improvements, advances in knowledge representation.

Knowledge representation is a difficult but well-researched area of artificial intelligence. The goal of this subfield of AI is to develop efficient and expressive means of describing both declarative and procedural knowledge. Let's pull that last sentence apart one step at a time.

First, a knowledge representation scheme is efficient if a program can manipulate it in such a way as to find facts and reason over those facts in a reasonable period of time. A scheme is expressive if we can represent sufficiently complex ideas to convey the meaning of a text. For example, propositional logic can express ideas such as, show documents that are either about aviation and propulsion or about jet airlines with the following:

```
(aviation AND propulsion) OR (airline AND jet)
```

We cannot express conditions on this statement or make statements about this expression in propositional logic though. For example, we cannot say that there exists at least one document about aviation and propulsion nor can we make modal statements, such as there could be a document about jet airlines. For the most part, these limits do not effect us in the basic types of text mining we have addressed here. As we move to more complex operations, such as representing projections and conjectures as well as facts, it is important to be able to distinguish between the two. In addition to efficiency and expressiveness, we need to consider advances in how different types of knowledge are represented.

Declarative knowledge is a statement of fact or belief. It is raining; if interest rates rise, bond prices will fall; and the Labor Party will lose control of Parliament in England are all examples of declarative knowledge. Procedural knowledge, however, is knowledge about how to perform a process such as identifying a handwritten character or estimating the semantic network representing correlations between key terms in a document set. Accomplishing these tasks often cannot be described using a series of facts and requires, in effect, programming code. We will see more declarative knowledge representation schemes as variations of first order logic and propositional logic are incorporated into database systems. The theoretical underpinnings of both relational databases and logic programming are similar enough that combining the two is a natural extension of both. Procedural knowledge will make inroads through the greater use of neural networks in language processing. Some tools, such as Megaputer's TextAnalyst, already build upon a neural network to accomplish tasks that cannot be done as efficiently or effectively with statistical or rule-based approaches.

Researchers have been compiling tools and techniques for dealing with language for the past thirty to forty years, and we are now reaping the benefits. As work continues in this area, we will certainly see more effective means of dealing with text, and the result will be tools that more effectively summarize, classify, and cluster texts as well extract facts and reason over those facts.

Conclusions

Our ability to communicate through language has always distinguished us from other creatures. We are now at the point where we can use machines to manipulate languages—in a crude but effective manner—to help us manage our businesses and organizations. Text is anything but unstructured, and we have the tools to analyze that structure and produce valuable business intelligence. By integrating document warehousing and text mining into our decision support environments, we will add new information sources that have been previously unavailable to executives, managers, and analysts. The scope of business intelligence can move beyond numbers and operational data into text and strategic information. There is no going back now.

Conclusions

APPENDIX A

Templates

Document Warehouse Requirements Template

Preliminary Document Descriptions

1. What is the subject domain of the document warehouse?

2. What are the sources of documents for this domain?

   Internal sources?

   External sources?

For each source, the level of grammatical structure should be noted. For example, government reports, news articles, and formal internal documents are grammatical, while e-mails tend to be less structured grammatically. Also, note any quality control issues with each document source.

3. For each source or document type, how frequently should the documents be loaded?

4. For each source or document type, what operations/transformations should be performed, including:

   Character code conversion

   Format conversion

   Language identification

   Classification

   Summarization

   Feature extraction

   Metadata extraction

5. For each source or document type, how time-sensitive is the information?

6. What is the priority level of each source or document type?

7. How should document warehouse information be presented?

   Publish or deliver directly to end user

   Publish to intranet portal

   Include in taxonomy-based browsing (e.g., Yahoo!-like structure)

   Ad hoc querying

   Similarity searches

Document Warehouse Architecture Template

1. Software tools (note: some tools such as crawlers and conversion tools may be integrated into text analysis tools)

   Retrieval tool, such as a Web crawler

   Scheduling tool

   Character code identification tool

   Format conversion tool

   Text analysis tools

   End-user access tools

   Commercial tools (e.g., AltaVista Discovery)

   Custom tools

2. Describe how the document warehouse will be integrated with the following:

   Data warehouse

   Document management

   Intranet portal

3. Hardware and networking infrastructure:

   Retrieval and preprocessing servers

   Text analysis servers

   Database and or textbase servers

   Network bandwidth availability

Document Warehousing Testing and Evaluation Template

1. Objective measures. The following evaluation criteria should be examined by document type or source.

   How many documents were successfully loaded?

   How many documents were correctly stored?

   What percentage of metadata was accurately collected?

   What percentage of documents was rejected because of errors?

   Character set conversion errors?

   Format errors?

   Language issues?

2. Subjective measures. The following criteria are based on end-user assessments. Most measures can be graded using the following scale: incorrect, some inaccuracies but usable, and correct.

   How well are the documents summarized?

   How well are the documents categorized?

   How well are the documents clustered?

   How well are the documents translated?

APPENDIX B

Tools and Resources

Active State

www.activestate.com

Active State offers Perl and Python distributions for the Win32 and Linux platforms as well as toolsets such as the Perl Dev Kit, VisualPerl, VisualPython, and Komodo, multi-language integrated development environment.

AltaVista Discovery

discovery.altavista.com

AltaVista Discovery is a personal text management tool for indexing favorite Web sites, browsed Web pages, local and network files, and e-mails, automatically summarizing Web pages, and finding similar pages to one currently displayed in the browser. The tool is offered for free by AltaVista.

Aurigin Systems Innovation Asset Management

www.aurigin.com

The Aurigin Innovation Asset Management system is designed to support patent portfolio management. This tool includes visualization tools such as Cartia's Themescape and InXight's Hyperbolic Tree. It also provides structured access to the U.S. and European patent offices' data.

Cartia Themescape

www.cartia.com

A visualization tool for organizing document collections on the basis of content. Themescape produces a topographical map describing the range and relationship of concepts within a document collection.

CRISP—Cross-Industry Platform for Data Mining

www.crisp.org

The process model developed by the founding members of the CRISP consortium is a good starting point for a text mining process model. Data mining and text mining use different tools and have different objectives, but share fundamental similarities as well. The CRISP-DM documentation is well worth reading by anyone interested in text or data mining.

dtSearch

www.dtsearch.com

dtSearch provides desktop LAN and Web versions of its text search tool that supports Boolean, proximity, thesaurus-based, and fuzzy searches. The tool is available for both NT and RedHat Linux platforms.

Edgar Database of Securities and Exchange Filings

www.sec.gov/edgarhp.htm

The U.S. Security and Exchange Commission database of public company filings. This is a solid source of publicly available information on publicly traded companies in the United States. Some more user-friendly services, such as 10K Wizard (www.tenkwizard.com), provide a better interface.

Excalibur Technologies RetrievalWare

www.excalib.com

RetrievalWare provides indexing and searching over a wide range of content sources, including file servers, groupware systems, relational databases, and document management systems.

Fulcrum KnowledgeServer

www.hummingbird.com

Fulcrum KnowlwedgeServer is a text management tool that provides a Web interface, multiple document types, linguistic analysis, similar retrieval and document summarization, and agent-based delivery. It is an NT-based solution. Hummingbird also provides a suite of document management tools, including DOCSFusion, CyberDOCS, and PowerDOCS.

Glimpse

webglimpse.org

Glimpse is an indexing and query system for searching UNIX file systems quickly. Webglimpse is a spider that manages files to be searched.

ht://Dig

www.htdig.org

A World Wide Web indexing and searching system for a small domains or intranets. Source code is licensed under the GNU Public License.

IBM Intelligent Miner for Text

www-4.ibm.com/software/iminer/fortext

A suite of text mining tools including:

- Text searching
- Language identification
- Topic categorization
- Feature extraction
- Clustering
- Summarization

This is a high-end suite of products that uses statistical techniques to analyze document collections. Training is required for topic categorization and additional languages in the language identification module.

InfoGist

www.infogist.com

InfoGist offers a program called infoFinders for searching the Web, news, subscription services, and the Usenet.

InMagic DB/Text

www.inmagic.com

DB/Text is a file-based text database capable of supporting terabyte-level textbases. The tool started in the library and collections market but has moved into other bibliographic-oriented applications such as patent databases.

Inxight Hyperbolic Tree

www.inxight.com

Inxight's Hyperbolic Tree is used in a number of text-management-oriented tools, including AltaVista Discovery and Aurigin's Innovation Asset Management program. This is an ideal tool for providing users a quick way to navigate complex networks of linked pages or documents. Inxight also offers other tools such as a categorizer, feature extractor, and summarizer.

Isearch

www.etymon.com/searchIsearch is an open source tool for indexing and searching text documents that supports full text and field-based searching, relevance ranking, multiple file formats, and Boolean queries. The tool does not handle large, highly structured collections, but a companion product, AmberFish from Etymon, does.

LexiQuest

www.lexiquest.com

Founded in 1979 as Erli SA in France, LexiQuest develops products such as Leximine, a classification and categorization tool, and LexiRespond, a search engine support tool to improve precision through semantic analysis.

Megaputer

www.megaputer.com

Megaputer developed the TextAnalyst text mining tool. Although it runs only on Win32 platforms, this is one of the best tools to use whether you are just starting out or need sophisticated feature extraction and term relationship maps. TextAnalyst comes with an interface so you can begin using it immediately, or you can use the COM interface for custom application development.

Mohomine's MohoPlatform

www.mohomine.com

MohoPlatform is a suite of tools for locating online resources, extracting features from the resources, and classifying the results into customizable directories.

Oracle interMedia Text

www.oracle.com

With the release of Oracle 8*i*, Oracle interMedia Text has been integrated directly with the RDBMS' query optimizer, unlike its predecessor Oracle

ConText. The tool includes the Inso file filter for loading many common file formats, thematic indexing, automatic summarization, and a rich selection of search operations. Given Oracle's popularity in the data warehouse market, interMedia will surely play a significant role in document warehousing.

Perl.Com

www.perl.com

This site, sponsored by O'Reilly Publishing, is command central for the Perl language. One of the most important resources here is CPAN, the Comprehensive Perl Archive Newtork (www.perl.com/CPAN). At CPAN you can find just about any Perl material you will need.

Perl Mongers

www.perl.org

This site is one of several excellent sources of Perl information on the Web.

Python.Org

www.python.org

The official Python Web site, www.python.org, is home to news about Python, topic guides, a tutorial, documentation, development tools, and, of course, the latest version of Python.

Search Engine Watch

www.searchenginewatch.com

Search Engine Watch is a Web site dedicated to the search engine industry. The site offers a regular newsletter, in-depth information on the search engine business and reviews, ratings, and tips.

Semio Taxonomy

www.semio.com

Semio Taxonomy partially automates the process of building taxonomies or directories for portals and other text-rich applications.

Solutionsoft's Perl Builder

www.solutionsoft.com

Solutionsoft offers a fully integrated development environment for Perl development, including interactive debugger.

Tennyson Maxwell Information System's Teleport Pro

www.tenmax.com

Teleport Pro is an award-winning spider that provides a visual interface, a scheduler, and load balancing of requests to minimize burden on servers.

Teragram Language Technologies

www.teragram.com

Teragram offers a wide range of products useful in text analysis, including:

- Language and character set identification
- HTML parsing and text extraction
- Text normalization
- Word and sentence tokenizer
- Part of speech tagging
- Morphological stemming
- Pattern retrieval
- Full text indexing

APIs support client/server environments as well as Java and Perl. These tools offer relatively low-level analysis features, so expect to do more programming with these than if you used an integrated tool. On the plus side, Teragram programs are used in by AltaVista, which has greater demand than just about any document warehouse.

Thomas Register

www.thomasregister.com

The *Thomas Register* provides basic information on American manufactures searchable by company name, product or service, and brand name. Registration is required but basic information is free of charge.

Thunderstone Texis

www.thunderstone.com

Thunderstone's Texis is a comprehensive text retrieval and publishing system based on a text-relational database. Unlike other database systems that add on text support through a general extension model, such as Informix DataBlade architecture, Texis was built to handle both text and traditional relational data types from the ground up. The database has been used in high-volume, high-content Web sites and includes a Web development package called Web Script.

UMBC AgentWeb

agents.umbc.edu

UMBC AgentWeb is a good starting point for learning about agents. This site includes many links to software, companies, courses, and conferences dedicated to agents.

U.S. Patent and Trademark Office

www.uspto.gov

This is the site to go to for U.S. patent information, and if you are conducting competitive intelligence, you will want to visit this site. If you are dealing in a specialized field (for example, chemistry and life science patents), then third-party vendors, such as Derwent Thompson Scientific (www.derwent.com), can provide additional information. Also be sure to visit the Japan Patent Information Organization (www.japio.or.jp/welcome2.html for the English version) and the European Patent Office (www.european-patent-office.org).

VantagePoint

www.thevantagepoint.com

VantagePoint develops patent analysis software with a number of visualization tools. The applications use the Derwent World Patent Database. Depending upon your level of involvement with competitive intelligence, this tool may be worth consideration.

XML Spy

www.xmlspy.com

XML Spy is an integrated development environment for XML. This vendor's tool set includes support for XML editing, validation, schema creation, and XSL editing transformation.

APPENDIX C

Basic Document Warehouse Data Model

Documents and Metadata Data Model

Note, these scripts can be downloaded from the companion Web site.

```
CREATE TABLE Content_Metadata (
       Content_Metadata_Id  INTEGER NOT NULL,
       Creator              VARCHAR2(100) NULL,
       Subject              VARCHAR2(100) NULL,
       Title                VARCHAR2(100) NULL,
       Description          VARCHAR2(100) NULL,
       Publisher            VARCHAR2(100) NULL,
       Contributor          VARCHAR2(100) NULL,
       Published_Date       DATE NULL,
       Revised_Date         DATE NULL,
       Type                 VARCHAR2(100) NULL,
       Format               VARCHAR2(100) NULL,
       Language             VARCHAR2(100) NULL,
       Rights               VARCHAR2(100) NULL
);

CREATE UNIQUE INDEX XPKContent_Metadata ON Content_Metadata
(
       Content_Metadata_Id
);
```

```
ALTER TABLE Content_Metadata
       ADD  ( PRIMARY KEY (Content_Metadata_Id) ) ;


CREATE TABLE Content_Relations (
       Document_Id          INTEGER NOT NULL,
       Object1              VARCHAR2(100) NULL,
       Object2              VARCHAR2(100) NULL,
       Relation             VARCHAR2(100) NULL
);

CREATE UNIQUE INDEX XPKContent_Relations ON Content_Relations
(
       Document_Id
);

CREATE INDEX XIF11Content_Relations ON Content_Relations
(
       Document_Id
);


ALTER TABLE Content_Relations
       ADD  ( PRIMARY KEY (Document_Id) ) ;


CREATE TABLE Document_Features (
       Document_Id          INTEGER NOT NULL,
       Taxonomy_Id          INTEGER NOT NULL,
       Feature_Weight       NUMBER(10,4) NULL
);

CREATE UNIQUE INDEX XPKDocument_Features ON Document_Features
(
       Document_Id,
       Taxonomy_Id
);

CREATE INDEX XIF4Document_Features ON Document_Features
(
       Document_Id
);

CREATE INDEX XIF5Document_Features ON Document_Features
(
       Taxonomy_Id
);
```

```
ALTER TABLE Document_Features
       ADD  ( PRIMARY KEY (Document_Id, Taxonomy_Id) ) ;


CREATE TABLE Document_Source (
       DocSourceId            INTEGER NOT NULL,
       SourceType             VARCHAR2(100) NULL,
       URLPattern             VARCHAR2(500) NULL,
       FilePath               VARCHAR2(500) NULL,
       Depth                  INTEGER NULL,
       SpanSite               VARCHAR2(1) NULL,
       NumberOfTries          INTEGER NULL,
       TimeOut                INTEGER NULL,
       WaitBetweenRetrievals INTEGER NULL,
       HTTP_UserName          VARCHAR2(100) NULL,
       HTTP_Password          VARCHAR2(100) NULL,
       Proxy_UserName         VARCHAR2(100) NULL,
       Proxy_Password         VARCHAR2(100) NULL,
       FS_UserName            VARCHAR2(100) NULL,
       FS_Password            VARCHAR2(100) NULL,
       RejectList             VARCHAR2(500) NULL,
       IncludeDirectories     VARCHAR2(500) NULL,
       ExcludeDirectories     VARCHAR2(500) NULL,
       Search_Engine          VARCHAR2(100) NULL
);

CREATE UNIQUE INDEX XPKDocument_Source ON Document_Source
(
       DocSourceId
);


ALTER TABLE Document_Source
       ADD  ( PRIMARY KEY (DocSourceId) ) ;


CREATE TABLE Documents (
       Document_Id            INTEGER NOT NULL,
       Storage_Metadata_Id    INTEGER NULL,
       DocSourceId            INTEGER NULL,
       Source_Id              INTEGER NULL,
       Content_Metadata_Id    INTEGER NULL,
       Contents               LONG RAW NULL,
       Summary                LONG RAW NULL,
       Version                INTEGER NULL,
       Document_Expires_On    DATE NULL,
       Summary_Expires_On     DATE NULL,
       Date_Loaded            DATE NULL,
       Last_Verified          DATE NULL
);
```

```
CREATE UNIQUE INDEX XPKDocuments ON Documents
(
       Document_Id
);

CREATE INDEX XIF10Documents ON Documents
(
       Storage_Metadata_Id
);

CREATE INDEX XIF6Documents ON Documents
(
       Content_Metadata_Id
);

CREATE INDEX XIF7Documents ON Documents
(
       Source_Id
);

CREATE INDEX XIF8Documents ON Documents
(
       DocSourceId
);


ALTER TABLE Documents
       ADD  ( PRIMARY KEY (Document_Id) ) ;


CREATE TABLE Source (
       Source_Id             INTEGER NOT NULL,
       Name                  VARCHAR2(100) NULL,
       Description           VARCHAR2(100) NULL,
       Timeliness            VARCHAR2(100) NULL,
       Reliablitity          VARCHAR2(100) NULL,
       Main_URL              VARCHAR2(500) NULL,
       Internal_Source_Indicator VARCHAR2(1) NULL,
       External_Source_Indicator VARCHAR2(1) NULL,
       Source_Type           VARCHAR2(100) NULL,
       Purge_Multiple_Versions VARCHAR2(1) NULL
);

CREATE UNIQUE INDEX XPKSource ON Source
(
       Source_Id
);
```

```
ALTER TABLE Source
       ADD  ( PRIMARY KEY (Source_Id) ) ;


CREATE TABLE Storage_Metadata (
       Storage_Metadata_Id  INTEGER NOT NULL,
       Store_Entire_Document_Indicato VARCHAR2(1) NULL,
       Store_Summary_Indicator VARCHAR2(1) NULL,
       Store_URL_Indicator  VARCHAR2(1) NULL,
       Store_Pathname_Indicator VARCHAR2(1) NULL,
       Prune_Full_Doc       VARCHAR2(1) NULL,
       Prune_Full_Doc_After INTEGER NULL,
       Prune_Summary        VARCHAR2(1) NULL,
       Prune_Summmary_After INTEGER NULL,
       Keep_Full_Translations VARCHAR2(1) NULL,
       Keep_Summarized_Translations VARCHAR2(1) NULL,
       Translation_Review_Required VARCHAR2(1) NULL
);

CREATE UNIQUE INDEX XPKStorage_Metadata ON Storage_Metadata
(
       Storage_Metadata_Id
);


ALTER TABLE Storage_Metadata
       ADD  ( PRIMARY KEY (Storage_Metadata_Id) ) ;


CREATE TABLE Taxonomy (
       Taxonomy_Id          INTEGER NOT NULL,
       Name_2               VARCHAR2(100) NULL,
       Description_2        VARCHAR2(500) NULL
);

CREATE UNIQUE INDEX XPKTaxonomy ON Taxonomy
(
       Taxonomy_Id
);

CREATE INDEX XIF3Taxonomy ON Taxonomy
(
       Taxonomy_Id
);


ALTER TABLE Taxonomy
       ADD  ( PRIMARY KEY (Taxonomy_Id) ) ;
```

```
ALTER TABLE Content_Relations
       ADD   ( FOREIGN KEY (Document_Id)
                              REFERENCES Documents ) ;


ALTER TABLE Document_Features
       ADD   ( FOREIGN KEY (Taxonomy_Id)
                              REFERENCES Taxonomy ) ;


ALTER TABLE Document_Features
       ADD   ( FOREIGN KEY (Document_Id)
                              REFERENCES Documents ) ;


ALTER TABLE Documents
       ADD   ( FOREIGN KEY (Storage_Metadata_Id)
                              REFERENCES Storage_Metadata ) ;


ALTER TABLE Documents
       ADD   ( FOREIGN KEY (DocSourceId)
                              REFERENCES Document_Source ) ;


ALTER TABLE Documents
       ADD   ( FOREIGN KEY (Source_Id)
                              REFERENCES Source ) ;


ALTER TABLE Documents
       ADD   ( FOREIGN KEY (Content_Metadata_Id)
                              REFERENCES Content_Metadata ) ;


ALTER TABLE Taxonomy
       ADD   ( FOREIGN KEY (Taxonomy_Id)
                              REFERENCES Taxonomy ) ;
```

Automated Searching Data Model

```
DROP TABLE Search_Command_Parameter CASCADE CONSTRAINTS;

CREATE TABLE Search_Command_Parameter (
       Parameter_Id          INTEGER NOT NULL,
       Search_TooI_Id        INTEGER NOT NULL,
       Search_Commmand_Id    INTEGER NOT NULL,
       Parameter_Value       VARCHAR2(50) NULL
);
```

```
CREATE UNIQUE INDEX XPKSearch_Command_Parameter ON Search_Command_Param-
eter
(
       Parameter_Id,
       Search_TooI_Id,
       Search_Commmand_Id
);


ALTER TABLE Search_Command_Parameter
       ADD  ( PRIMARY KEY (Parameter_Id, Search_TooI_Id, Search_Comm-
mand_Id) ) ;


DROP TABLE Search_Command CASCADE CONSTRAINTS;

CREATE TABLE Search_Command (
       Search_Commmand_Id   INTEGER NOT NULL,
       Search_TooI_Id       INTEGER NOT NULL,
       URL                  VARCHAR2(500) NULL,
       Priority             INTEGER NULL,
       Description          VARCHAR2(100) NULL,
       Start_Date           DATE NULL,
       End_Date             DATE NULL,
       Frequency            INTEGER NULL,
       Last_Executed        DATE NULL
);

CREATE UNIQUE INDEX XPKSearch_Command ON Search_Command
(
       Search_Commmand_Id,
       Search_TooI_Id
);


ALTER TABLE Search_Command
       ADD  ( PRIMARY KEY (Search_Commmand_Id, Search_TooI_Id) ) ;


DROP TABLE Parameter CASCADE CONSTRAINTS;

CREATE TABLE Parameter (
       Parameter_Id         INTEGER NOT NULL,
       Search_TooI_Id       INTEGER NOT NULL,
       Purpose              VARCHAR2(100) NULL,
       Parameter_String     VARCHAR2(50) NULL,
       Optional_Indicator   VARCHAR2(1) NULL,
       Sort_Order           INTEGER NOT NULL
);
```

```
CREATE UNIQUE INDEX XPKParameter ON Parameter
(
       Parameter_Id,
       Search_TooI_Id
);

CREATE UNIQUE INDEX XParameterSortOrder ON Parameter
(
       Sort_Order
);


ALTER TABLE Parameter
       ADD  ( PRIMARY KEY (Parameter_Id, Search_TooI_Id) ) ;


DROP TABLE Search_Tool CASCADE CONSTRAINTS;

CREATE TABLE Search_Tool (
       Search_TooI_Id        INTEGER NOT NULL,
       Name                  VARCHAR2(50) NOT NULL,
       Description           VARCHAR2(100) NOT NULL,
       Command_Line          VARCHAR2(50) NOT NULL
);

CREATE UNIQUE INDEX XPKSearch_Tool ON Search_Tool
(
       Search_TooI_Id
);


ALTER TABLE Search_Tool
       ADD  ( PRIMARY KEY (Search_TooI_Id) ) ;


ALTER TABLE Search_Command_Parameter
       ADD  ( FOREIGN KEY (Search_Commmand_Id, Search_TooI_Id)
                             REFERENCES Search_Command ) ;


ALTER TABLE Search_Command_Parameter
       ADD  ( FOREIGN KEY (Parameter_Id, Search_TooI_Id)
                             REFERENCES Parameter ) ;


ALTER TABLE Search_Command
       ADD  ( FOREIGN KEY (Search_TooI_Id)
                             REFERENCES Search_Tool ) ;
```

```
ALTER TABLE Parameter
       ADD  ( FOREIGN KEY (Search_TooI_Id)
                              REFERENCES Search_Tool ) ;
```

Metadata Schema Objects

```
DROP TABLE Transformation_Step_Parameter CASCADE CONSTRAINTS;

CREATE TABLE Transformation_Step_Parameter (
       Transformation_Activity_Id INTEGER NOT NULL,
       Transformation_Id    INTEGER NOT NULL,
       Transformation_Parameter_Id INTEGER NOT NULL,
       Document_Target_Id   INTEGER NOT NULL,
       Parameter_Value      VARCHAR2(500) NULL
);

CREATE UNIQUE INDEX XPKTransformation_Step_Parameter ON
Transformation_Step_Paramter
(
       Transformation_Activity_Id,
       Transformation_Id,
       Transformation_Parameter_Id,
       Document_Target_Id
);

CREATE INDEX XIF10Transformation_Step_Parameter ON
Transformation_Step_Parameter
(
       Transformation_Id,
       Transformation_Parameter_Id
);

CREATE INDEX XIF8Transformation_Step_Parameter ON
Transformation_Step_Parameter
(
       Transformation_Activity_Id,
       Transformation_Id,
       Document_Target_Id
);


ALTER TABLE Transformation_Step_Parameter
       ADD  ( PRIMARY KEY (Transformation_Activity_Id,
Transformation_Id, Transformation_Parameter_Id, Document_Target_Id) ) ;
```

```
DROP TABLE Transformation_Step CASCADE CONSTRAINTS;

CREATE TABLE Transformation_Step (
       Transformation_Activity_Id INTEGER NOT NULL,
       Transformation_Id     INTEGER NOT NULL,
       Document_Target_Id    INTEGER NOT NULL,
       Transformation_Step_Order INTEGER NULL
);

CREATE UNIQUE INDEX XPKTransformation_Step ON Transformation_Step
(
       Transformation_Activity_Id,
       Transformation_Id,
       Document_Target_Id
);

CREATE INDEX XIF13Transformation_Step ON Transformation_Step
(
       Transformation_Activity_Id,
       Document_Target_Id
);

CREATE INDEX XIF9Transformation_Step ON Transformation_Step
(
       Transformation_Id
);


ALTER TABLE Transformation_Step
       ADD  ( PRIMARY KEY (Transformation_Activity_Id,
Transformation_Id, Document_Target_Id) ) ;




DROP TABLE Transformation_Execution CASCADE CONSTRAINTS;

CREATE TABLE Transformation_Execution (
       Transformation_Execution_Id INTEGER NOT NULL,
       Scheduled_Event_Id    INTEGER NOT NULL,
       Transformation_Activity_Id INTEGER NOT NULL,
       Document_Target_Id    INTEGER NOT NULL,
       Start_Date            DATE NULL,
       End_Date              DATE NULL,
       In_Progress_Indicator VARCHAR2(1) NULL,
       Successful_Indicator VARCHAR2(1) NULL
);
```

```
CREATE UNIQUE INDEX XPKTransformation_Execution ON Transformation_Execution
(
       Transformation_Execution_Id,
       Scheduled_Event_Id,
       Transformation_Activity_Id,
       Document_Target_Id
);

CREATE INDEX XIF12Transformation_Execution ON Transformation_Execution
(
       Transformation_Activity_Id,
       Document_Target_Id
);


ALTER TABLE Transformation_Execution
       ADD  ( PRIMARY KEY (Transformation_Execution_Id,
Scheduled_Event_Id, Transformation_Activity_Id, Document_Target_Id) ) ;



DROP TABLE Transformation_Activity CASCADE CONSTRAINTS;

CREATE TABLE Transformation_Activity (
       Transformation_Activity_Id INTEGER NOT NULL,
       Document_Target_Id   INTEGER NULL,
       Activity_Description INTEGER NULL,
       Activity_Order       INTEGER NULL
);

CREATE UNIQUE INDEX XPKTransformation_Activity ON Transformation_Activity
(
       Transformation_Activity_Id,
       Document_Target_Id
);

CREATE INDEX XIF14Transformation_Activity ON Transformation_Activity
(
       Document_Target_Id
);


ALTER TABLE Transformation_Activity
       ADD  ( PRIMARY KEY (Transformation_Activity_Id,
Document_Target_Id) ) ;


DROP TABLE Transformation_Parameter CASCADE CONSTRAINTS;
```

```
CREATE TABLE Transformation_Parameter (
       Transformation_Id     INTEGER NOT NULL,
       Transformation_Parameter_Id INTEGER NOT NULL,
       Parameter_String      VARCHAR2(50) NULL
);

CREATE UNIQUE INDEX XPKTransformation_Parameter ON Transformation_Param-
eter
(
       Transformation_Id,
       Transformation_Parameter_Id
);

CREATE INDEX XIF11Transformation_Parameter ON Transformation_Parameter
(
       Transformation_Id
);


ALTER TABLE Transformation_Parameter
       ADD  ( PRIMARY KEY (Transformation_Id,
Transformation_Parameter_Id) ) ;


DROP TABLE Transformation CASCADE CONSTRAINTS;

CREATE TABLE Transformation (
       Transformation_Id     INTEGER NOT NULL,
       Transformation_Description VARCHAR(100) NULL,
       Command_String        VARCHAR2(100) NULL
);

CREATE UNIQUE INDEX XPKTransformation ON Transformation
(
       Transformation_Id
);


ALTER TABLE Transformation
       ADD  ( PRIMARY KEY (Transformation_Id) ) ;



DROP TABLE Internet_Document CASCADE CONSTRAINTS;

CREATE TABLE Internet_Document (
       DocSourceId           INTEGER NOT NULL,
       URLPattern_2          VARCHAR2(500) NULL,
       Depth_2               INTEGER NULL,
       SpanSite_2            VARCHAR2(1) NULL,
```

```
        NumberOfTries_2         INTEGER NULL,
        TimeOut_2               INTEGER NULL,
        WaitBetweenRetrievals_2 INTEGER NULL,
        HTTP_UserName_2         VARCHAR2(20) NULL,
        HTTP_Password_2         VARCHAR2(20) NULL,
        Proxy_UserName_2         VARCHAR2(20) NULL,
        Proxy_Password_2        VARCHAR2(20) NULL,
        RejectList_2            VARCHAR2(500) NULL,
        IncludeDirectories_2 VARCHAR2(500) NULL,
        ExcludeDirectories_2 VARCHAR2(500) NULL
);

CREATE UNIQUE INDEX XPKInternet_Document ON Internet_Document
(
        DocSourceId
);

CREATE INDEX XIF2Internet_Document ON Internet_Document
(
        DocSourceId
);


ALTER TABLE Internet_Document
        ADD  ( PRIMARY KEY (DocSourceId) ) ;


DROP TABLE File_System_Document CASCADE CONSTRAINTS;

CREATE TABLE File_System_Document (
        DocSourceId             INTEGER NOT NULL,
        FilePath_2              VARCHAR2(500) NULL,
        FS_UserName_2           VARCHAR2(20) NULL,
        FS_Password_2           VARCHAR2(20) NULL
);

CREATE UNIQUE INDEX XPKFile_System_Document ON File_System_Document
(
        DocSourceId
);

CREATE INDEX XIF3File_System_Document ON File_System_Document
(
        DocSourceId
);


ALTER TABLE File_System_Document
        ADD  ( PRIMARY KEY (DocSourceId) ) ;
```

```
DROP TABLE Document_Source CASCADE CONSTRAINTS;

CREATE TABLE Document_Source (
       DocSourceId           INTEGER NOT NULL,
       Document_Target_Id    INTEGER NULL,
       SourceType            VARCHAR2(50) NULL,
       Name                  VARCHAR2(100) NULL,
       Description           VARCHAR2(500) NULL,
       Timeliness            VARCHAR2(10) NULL,
       Reliablitity          VARCHAR2(10) NULL
);

CREATE UNIQUE INDEX XPKDocument_Source ON Document_Source
(
       DocSourceId
);

CREATE INDEX XIF15Document_Source ON Document_Source
(
       Document_Target_Id
);


ALTER TABLE Document_Source
       ADD  ( PRIMARY KEY (DocSourceId) ) ;


DROP TABLE Document_Target CASCADE CONSTRAINTS;

CREATE TABLE Document_Target (
       Document_Target_Id    INTEGER NOT NULL,
       Target_Description    VARCHAR2(100) NULL,
       Directory             VARCHAR2(500) NULL,
       Delete_After_Indicator VARCHAR2(1) NULL,
       Priority              VARCHAR2(10) NULL
);

CREATE UNIQUE INDEX XPKDocument_Target ON Document_Target
(
       Document_Target_Id
);


ALTER TABLE Document_Target
       ADD  ( PRIMARY KEY (Document_Target_Id) ) ;
```

```
DROP TABLE Custom_Calendar_Date CASCADE CONSTRAINTS;

CREATE TABLE Custom_Calendar_Date (
       Custom_Calendar_Id_2 INTEGER NOT NULL,
       Schedule_Event_Date  DATE NULL
);

CREATE UNIQUE INDEX XPKCustom_Calendar_Date ON Custom_Calendar_Date
(
       Custom_Calendar_Id_2
);

CREATE INDEX XIF4Custom_Calendar_Date ON Custom_Calendar_Date
(
       Custom_Calendar_Id_2
);


ALTER TABLE Custom_Calendar_Date
       ADD  ( PRIMARY KEY (Custom_Calendar_Id_2) ) ;


DROP TABLE Custom_Calendar CASCADE CONSTRAINTS;

CREATE TABLE Custom_Calendar (
       Custom_Calendar_Id_2 INTEGER NOT NULL,
       Scheduled_Event_Id   INTEGER NULL,
       Custom_Calendar_Description VARCHAR2(100) NULL
);

CREATE UNIQUE INDEX XPKCustom_Calendar ON Custom_Calendar
(
       Custom_Calendar_Id_2
);

CREATE INDEX XIF3Custom_Calendar ON Custom_Calendar
(
       Scheduled_Event_Id
);


ALTER TABLE Custom_Calendar
       ADD  ( PRIMARY KEY (Custom_Calendar_Id_2) ) ;
```

```
DROP TABLE Interval CASCADE CONSTRAINTS;

CREATE TABLE Interval (
       Interval_Id_2          CHAR(18) NOT NULL,
       Scheduled_Event_Id     INTEGER NULL,
       Duration               INTEGER NULL
);

CREATE UNIQUE INDEX XPKInterval ON Interval
(
       Interval_Id_2
);

CREATE INDEX XIF1Interval ON Interval
(
       Scheduled_Event_Id
);


ALTER TABLE Interval
       ADD  ( PRIMARY KEY (Interval_Id_2) ) ;




DROP TABLE Recurring_Point_In_Time CASCADE CONSTRAINTS;

CREATE TABLE Recurring_Point_In_Time (
       Point_In_Time_Id_2     INTEGER NOT NULL,
       Scheduled_Event_Id     INTEGER NULL,
       Recurring_Type         VARCHAR2(20) NULL,
       Frequency              INTEGER NULL,
       Month                  INTEGER NULL,
       Day_Of_Month           INTEGER NULL,
       Day_Of_Week            INTEGER NULL,
       Hour                   INTEGER NULL,
       Minute                 INTEGER NULL,
       Second                 INTEGER NULL
);

CREATE UNIQUE INDEX XPKRecurring_Point_In_Time ON
Recurring_Point_In_Time
(
       Point_In_Time_Id_2
);

CREATE INDEX XIF2Recurring_Point_In_Time ON Recurring_Point_In_Time
(
       Scheduled_Event_Id
);
```

```
ALTER TABLE Recurring_Point_In_Time
       ADD  ( PRIMARY KEY (Point_In_Time_Id_2) ) ;


DROP TABLE Scheduled_Event CASCADE CONSTRAINTS;

CREATE TABLE Scheduled_Event (
       Scheduled_Event_Id   INTEGER NOT NULL,
       Name                 VARCHAR2(50) NULL,
       Description          VARCHAR2(100) NULL,
       Point_In_Time_Id     INTEGER NULL,
       Custom_Calendar_Id   INTEGER NULL,
       Interval_Id          INTEGER NULL
);

CREATE UNIQUE INDEX XPKScheduled_Event ON Scheduled_Event
(
       Scheduled_Event_Id
);


ALTER TABLE Scheduled_Event
       ADD  ( PRIMARY KEY (Scheduled_Event_Id) ) ;
```

Bibliography

Ananyan, Sergei. 2000. "Text Mining Applications and Technologies." www.megaputer.com/DOWN/Presentations/TextAnalyst.zip.

Application Development Trends. February 2000. "Development Snapshot: Warehouse Data of the Future."

Apte, Chidanand, Fred Damerau, and Sholom M. Wiess. July 1994. "Automated Learning of Decision Rules for Text Categorization." *ACM Transactions on Information Systems*. Vol. 12, No. 3.

Barton, G., R. C. Berwick, and E. S. Ristad. 2000. *Computational Complexity and Natural Language*. Cambridge, MA: MIT Press.

Beazley, David M. 2000. *Python Essential Reference*. Indianapolis, IN: New Riders.

Berger, Adam, Rich Caruana, David Cohn, Dayne Freitag, and Vibhu Mittal. 2000. "Bridging the Lexical Chasm: Statistical Approaches to Answer-Finding." *Proceedings of the 23rd Annual International ACM SIGIR Conference on Research and Development in Information Retrieval*.

Berger, Adam, and Vibhu O. Mittal. 2000. "OCELOT: A System for Summarizing Web Pages." *Proceedings of the 23rd Annual International ACM SIGIR Conference on Research and Development in Information Retrieval*.

Bharat, Krishna, and Monika R. Henzinger. 1998. "Improved Algorithms for Topic Distillation in a Hyperlinked Environment." *Proceedings of SIGIR '98*.

Burnard, L., and C. M. Sperberg-McQueen. 1995. "TEI Lite: An Introduction to Text Encoding Interchange." www-tei.uic.edu/orgs/tei/intros/teiu5.tei.

Burwell, Helen P. 1999. *Online Competitive Intelligence: Increase Your Profits Using Cyber-Intelligence*, Tempe, AZ: Facts on Demand Press.

Chakrabarti, Soumen, Byron Dom, Prabhakar Raghavan, Sridhar Rajagopalan, Davide Gibson, and Jon Kleinberg. 1998. "Automatic Resource Compilation by Analyzing Hyperlink Structure and Associated Text." www7.scu.edu.au/programme/fullpapers/1898/com1898.html.

Cheng, Jie, David Bell, and Weiru Liu. 1998. "Learning Bayesian Networks from Data: An Efficient Approach Based on Information Theory." http://cs.ualberta.ca/~jcheng/report98.ps.gz.

Chomsky, Noam. 1957. *Syntactic Structures.* The Hauge: Mouton & Company.

———. 1965. *Aspects of the Theory of Syntax.* Cambridge, MA: MIT Press.

———. 1975. *Reflections on Language.* New York: Pantheon Books.

Christensen, Clayton M. 2000. *The Innovator's Dilemma.* New York: HarperCollins.

Chuang, Shui-Lung, Hsiao-Tieh Pu, Wen-Hsiang Lu, and Lee-Feng Chien. 2000. "Auto-Construction of a Live Thesaurus from Search Term Logs for Interactive Web Search" *Proceedings of the 23rd Annual International ACM SIGIR Conference on Research and Development in Information Retrieval.*

Chuang, Wesley T., and Jihoon Yang. 2000. "Extracting Sentences for Text Summarization: A Machine Learning Approach" *Proceedings of the 23rd Annual International ACM SIGIR Conference on Research and Development in Information Retrieval.*

Chen, Hsinchum. 1995. "Machine Learning for Information Retrieval: Neural Networks, Symbolic Learning and Genetic Algorithms."
http://ai.pba.azrizona.edu/ papers/mlir93/mlir93.html.

Cole, R., ed. *Survey of the State of the Art in Human Language Technology.* 1998. Edinburgh, Scotland: Edinburgh University Press.

CRISP-DM Consortium. 1999. *CRISP 1.0 Process Model and Users Guide.* www.crisp-dm.org.

Date, C. J. 1999. *Introduction to Database Systems, 7th ed.* Reading, MA: Addison-Wesley.

Day, George S. 1994. "Evaluating Strategic Alternative." Liam Fahey and Robert M. Randall, *The Portable MBA in Strategy.* New York: John Wiley and Sons.

Decker, Keith, Victor Lesser, M. V. Nagendra Prasad, and Thomas Wagner. 1995. "MACRON: An Architecture for Multi-agent Cooperative Information Gathering." *Proceedings of the CIKM Workshop on Intelligent Information Agents.* ftp://dis.cs.umass.edu/pub/macron.ps.

Deerwester, Scott, Susan T. Dumais, George W. Furnas, Thomas K. Landauer, and Richard Harshman. 1990. "Indexing by Latent Semantic Analysis." *Journal of the American Society for Information Science.* Vol. 41, No. 391.

Descartes, Alligator, and Tim Bunce. 2000. *Programming the Perl DBI.* Cambridge, MA: O'Reilly.

Dillon, M. 1983. "FASIT: A Fully Automatic Syntactically Based Indexing System" *Journal of American Society for Information Science.* Vol. 34, No. 2.

Dodge, Gary, and Tim Gorman. 1998. *Oracle 8 Data Warehousing: A Hands-on Guide to Designing, Building and Managing Oracle Data Warehouses.* New York: John Wiley and Sons.

Dublin Core Metadata Initiative. "Dublin Core Metadata Element Set, Version 1.1: Reference Description." http://www.purl.org/DC/dcouemcts/rec-dces-19990702.htm.

Dumias, Susan, and Hao Chen. 2000. "Hierarchical Classification of Web Content." *Proceedings of the 23rd Annual International ACM SIGIR Conference on Research and Development in Information Retrieval.*

English, Larry P. 1999 *Improving Data Warehouse and Business Information Quality: Methods for Reducing Costs and Increasing Profits.* New York: John Wiley and Sons.

Fagan, J. 1989. "The Effectiveness of Nonsyntactic Approach to Automatic Phrase Indexing for Document Retrieval." *Journal of American Society for Information Science.* Vol. 40, No. 2.

Fensel, Dieter, Stefan Decker, Michael Erdmann, and Rudi Studer. 1998. "Ontobroker: How to Enable Intelligent Access to the WWW." *Proceedings of the American Association for Artificial Intelligence.*

Fillmore, C. 1968. "The Case for Case." E. Bach and R. Harms, eds. *Universals of Syntactic Theory.* New York: Holt, Rinehart and Winston.

Fox, Susannah, Lee Rainie, John Horrigan, Amanda Lenhart, Tom Spooner, and Cornelia Carter. August 2000. "Trust and Privacy Online: Why Americans Want to Rewrite the Rules." Technical report from The Pew Internet & American Life Project.

Gause, Donald. C. and Gerald M. Weinberg. 1989. *Exploring Requirements: Quality Before Design.* New York: Dorset House.

Giménez, Mario J., Mira I. and Mikel L. Forcada. April 1998. "Understanding Commercial Machine Translation Systems for Evaluation, Teaching, and Reverse Engineering: the Treatment of Noun Phrases in Power Translator Deluxe." *Machine Translation Review.* No. 7. www.bcs.org.uk/siggroup/sg37.htm.

Gough, Roger. 2000. "Perl for Oracle Developers." *Proceedings of the Oracle Development Tools User's Group.*

Hackathorn, Richard D. 1999. *Web Farming for the Data Warehouse: Exploiting Business Intelligence and Knowledge Management.* San Francisco, CA: Morgan Kaufmann Publishers, Inc.

Hahn, Udo, and Inderjeet Mani. November 2000. "The Challenges of Automatic Summarization." *IEEE Computer.* Vol. 33, No. 11.

Hatzivassiloglou, Vasileios, Luis Gravano, and Ankineedu Maganti. 2000. "An Investigation of Linguistic Features and Cluster Algorithms for Topical Document Clustering." *Proceedings of the 23rd Annual International ACM SIGIR Conference on Research and Development in Information Retrieval.*

Hausser, Roland. 1998. *Foundations of Computational Linguistics.* New York: Springer-Verlag.

Hay, David C. 1996. *Data Model Patterns: Conventions of Thought.* New York: Dorset House Publishing.

Hearst, Marti A. 1999. "Text Data Mining." www.sims.berkeley.edu/~hearst/talks/dm-talk/textfile.html.

———. 1999. "Untangling Text Data Mining." www.sims.berkeley.edu/~hearst/papers/ac199/ac199-tdm.html.

Hobbs, Jerry R., Douglas Appelt, John Bear, David Isreal, Megumi Kameyama, Mark Stickel, and Mabry Tyson. "FASTUS: Extracting Information from Natural Language Texts." http://www.ai.sri.com/natural-langauge/projects/fastus-schabes.html.

Hobbs, Lilian, and Susan Hillson. 2000. *Oracle 8i Data Warehousing.* Boston: Digital Press.

St. Laurent, Simon. 1999. *XML: A Primer, 2nd ed.* New York: M&T Books.

Hoch, Rainer. 1997. "Using IR Techniques for Text Classification in Document Analysis." www.dfki.uni-lk.de/dfkidok/publications/RR/94/19/abstract.html.

Hull, David. 1994. "Improving Text Retrieval for the Routing Problem Using Latent Semantic Indexing." *SIGIR '94.* Association of Computing Machinery.

IBM Corporation. 1998. Intelligent Miner for Text: Text Analysis Tools version 2.3.

Inmon, W. H. 1995. "What Is a Data Warehouse?" *Prism.* Vol. 1, No. 1.

Iwayama, Makoto. 2000. "Relevance Feedback with a Small Number of Relevance Judgements: Incremented Relevance Feedback versus Document Clustering." *Proceedings of the 23rd Annual International ACM SIGIR Conference on Research and Development in Information Retrieval.*

Joshi, Anupam, Karuna Joshi, and Kaghu Krishnapuram. 1999. "On Mining Web Access Logs." www.csu.umbc.edu/~ajoshi/web-mine/tr1.ps.gz.

Kahaner, Larry. 1996. *Competitive Intelligence: How to Gather, Analyze, and Use Information to Move Your Business to the Top.* New York: Simon and Schuster.

Kambil, Ajit, and Mark Ginsburg. June 1998. "Public Access Web Information Systems: Lessons from the Internet Edgar Project." *Communications of the ACM.* Vol. 41, No. 47.

Kimball, Ralph. 1996. *The Data Warehouse Toolkit.* New York: John Wiley and Sons.

Kimball, Ralph, Laura Reeves, Margy Ross, and Warren Thornthwaite. 1998. *The Data Warehouse Lifecycle Toolkit.* New York: John Wiley and Sons.

Kimball, Ralph, and Richard Merz. 2000. *The Data Webhouse Toolkit: Building the Web Enabled Data Warehouse.* New York: John Wiley and Sons.

Klavans, Judith L., and Philip Resnik. 1996. *The Balancing Act: Combining Symbolic and Statistical Approaches to Language.* Cambridge, MA: MIT Press.

Klein, Fred. 1999. "TR05: Machine Translation—Mystery, Misery or Miracle." www.tc-forum.org/toictrtr05mach.htm.

Knight, Kevin. November 1999. "Mining Online Text." *Communications of the ACM*. Vol. 42, No. 11.

Koch, George, and Kevin Loney. 1997. *Oracle 8: The Complete Reference*. New York: Osborne Oracle Press.

Kohonen, Teuvo. 1984. *Self-Organization and Associative Memory*. New York: Springer-Verlag.

Koller, Daphene, and Mehran Sahami. "Hierarchically Classifying Documents Using Very Few Words." *Proceedings of the International Conference on Machine Learning*.

Kosala, R., and H. Blockeel. June 2000. "Web Mining Research: A Survey." *SIGKDD Explorations*. Vol. 2, No. 1.

Kosko, Bart. 1993. *Fuzzy Thinking: The New Science of Fuzzy Logic*. New York: Hyperion.

Kuflik, Tsvi, and Peretz Shoval. 2000. "Generation of User Profiles for Information Filtering—Research Agenda." *SIGIR 2000*.

Landauer, Thomas K., and Susan T. Dumais. 1996. "A Solution to Plato's Problem: The Latent Semantic Analysis Theory of Acquisition, Induction and Representation of Knowledge." http://lsa.colorado.edu/papers/plato/plato.annote.html.

Lanquillon, Carsten, and Ingred Renz. 1999. "Adaptive Information Filtering: Detecting Changes in Text Streams." *Association for Computing Machinery CIKM '99*.

Lawrie, Dawn, and Daniela Rus. 1999. "A Self-Organized File Cabinet." *Association of Computing Machinery CIKM '99*.

Leavitt, Neal. August 2000. "What Ever Happed to Object-Oriented Databases?" *IEEE Computer*. Vol. 33, No. 8.

Lewis, David D., and Karen Sparck Jones. January 1996. "Natural Language Processing for Information Retrieval." *Communiations of the ACM*. Vol. 39, No. 1.

Lin, Shian-Hua, Chi-Shenbg Shih, Meng Chang Chen, Jan-Ming Ho, Ming-Tat Ko, and Yueh-Ming Huang. 1998. "Extracting Classification Knowledge of Internet Documents with Mining Term Associations: A Semantic Approach." *Association of Computing Machinery SIGIR '98*.

Lin, Xia, Dagobert Soergel, and Gary Marchionini. 1991. "A Self-Organizing Semantic Map for Information Retrieval." *Association for Computing Machinery*.

Loh, S., L. K. Wives, and J. P. de Oliveira. June 2000. "Concept-Based Knowledge Discovery in Texts Extracted from the Web." *SIGKDD Explorations*. Vol. 2, No. 1.

Lucyk, Blaine. October 2, 2000. "Controlling the Digital Deluge: IBM Content Manager." *DB2 Magazine*.

Lutz, Mark. 1996. *Programming Python*. Cambridge, MA: O'Reilly.

Lyles, Marjorie A. 1994. "Identifying and Developing Strategic Alternatives." Liam Fahey and Robert M. Randall eds. *The Portable MBA in Strategy*. New York: John Wiley and Sons.

Manning, Christopher D., and Hinrich Schutze. 1999. *Foundations of Statisitical Natural Language Processing*. Cambridge, MA: MIT Press.

Marcus, Mitchell, Beatrice Santorini, and Mary Ann Marcinkiewicz. "Building a Large Annotated Corpus of English: The Penn Treebank." http://morph.ldc.upenn.edu/Catalog/docs/treebank2/cl93.html.

Maria, Nuno, and Mario J. Silva. 2000. "Theme-Based Retrieval of Web News." *Proceedings of the 23rd Annual International ACM SIGIR Conference on Research and Development in Information Retrieval.*

Marsh, S., and Y. Masrour. 1997. "Agent Augmented Community Information—The ACORN Architecture." www.iit.nrc.ca/~steve/pubs/ACORN/CASCON97/CASCON97.pdf.

McGrath, Sean. 2000. *XML Processing with Python*. Upper Saddle River, NJ: Prentice Hall.

Mikheev, Andrei. 2000."Document Centered Approach for Text Normalization." *Proceedings of the 23rd Annual International ACM SIGIR Conference on Research and Development in Information Retrieval.* New York: Association for Computing Machinery.

Mitchell, Tom. November 1999. "Machine Learning and Data Mining." *Communications of the ACM*. Vol. 42, No. 11.

Muylopolous, John, and Michael L. Brodie. 1989. *Readings in Artificial Intelligence and Databases*. San Mateo, CA: Morgan Kaufmann Publishers, Inc.

Narayanan, V. K., and Liam Fahey. 1994. "Macroenvironmental Analysis: Understanding the Environment Outside the Industry." *The Portable MBA in Strategy*. New York: John Wiley and Sons.

Nasraoui, Olft, Hichem Frigui, Anupam Joshi, and Raghu Krishnapuram. 1999. "Mining Web Access Logs Using Relational Competitive Fuzzy Clustering Algorithm Based on a Robust Estimator." Viror.wiwi.uni-karlsruhe.de/webmining/ bib/pdf/Nasraoui199b.pdf.

Object Management Group. 2000. "Data Warehousing, CWM and MOF Resource Page." www.omg.org/technology/cwm/.

Oracle Corporation. interMedia Text 8.1.6. http://technet.oracle.com.

Pinker, Steven. 1994. *The Language Instinct: How the Mind Creates Language*. New York: HarperPerennial.

Reiterer, Harald, Gabriela Mussler, Thomas H. Mann, and Siegfried Handschuh. 2000. "INSYDER—An Information Retrieval Assistant for Business Intelligence." *Proceedings of the 23rd Annual International ACM SIGIR Conference on Research and Development in Information Retrieval.* New York: Association for Computing Machinery.

Riloff, Ellen, and Wendy Lehnert. July 1994. "Information Extraction as a Basis for High Precision Text Classification." *ACM Transactions on Information Systems*. Vol. 12, No. 3.

Rissland, Edwina L., and Jody J. Daniels. 1995. "Using CBR to Drive IR." *International Joint Conference on Artificial Intelligence 1995.*

Sacco, Giovanni M. May/June 2000. "Dynamic Taxonomies: A Model for Large Information Bases." *IEEE Transactions on Knowledge and Data Engineering*. Vol. 12, No. 3.

St. Laurent, Simon. 1999. *XML: A Primer, 2nd edition*. New York: M&T Books.

St. Pierre, Margaret, and William P. LaPlant, Jr. 1998. "Issues in Crosswalking Content Metadata Standards." www.niso.org/crsswalk.html.

Schwartz, Randal L., and Tom Christiansen. 1997. *Learning Perl, 2nd ed.* Cambridge, MA: O'Reilly.

Semio Corporation. "Products and Solutions: Semio Taxonomy Service." www1.semio.com/products/service.html.

———. "Products and Solutions: The Semio Solution." www.semio.com/products/solution.html.

Siever, Ellen, Stephen Spainhour, and Nathan Patwardhan. 1999. *Perl in a Nutshell: A Desktop Quick Reference*. Cambridge, MA: O'Reilly.

Spitzer, Tom. January 1997. "Textbases Deliver Web Results." *Internet Systems*. www.dbmsmag.com/970i06.html.

Stalont, G. 1989. *Automatic Text Processing*. Reading, MA: Addison-Wesley.

Stockes, Nicola, Paula Hatch, and Joe Carthy. 2000. "Lexical Semantic Relatedness and Online New Event Detection." *Proceedings of the 23rd Annual International ACM SIGIR Conference on Research and Development in Information Retrieval*.

Strang, Gilbert. 1980. *Linear Algebra and Its Applications*. Orlando, FL: Academic Press.

Sullivan, Dan. April 10, 2000. "Beyond the Numbers." *Intelligent Enterprise*, Vol. 3, No. 6.

———. September 8, 2000. "Eye on the Competition." *Intelligent Enterprise*, Vol. 3, No. 14.

Sullivan, Patrick H. 2000. *Value-Driven Intellectual Capital: How to Convert Intangible Corporate Assets into Market Value*. New York: John Wiley and Sons.

Susac, Denis. 1999. "Text/Web Mining." http://ai.about.com/compute/ai/library/weekly/aa102899.htm.

Sutton, Michael J. D. 1996. *Document Management for the Enterprise: Principles, Techniques, and Applications*. New York: John Wiley and Sons.

Swanson, Don R. 1991."Complementary Structures in Disjoint Science Literatures." *Proceedings of the 14th International ACM/SIGIR Conference*.

Swanson, Don R., and N. R. Smalheiser. 1991. "An Interactive System for Finding Complementary Literatures: A Stimulus to Scientific Discovery." *Artificial Intelligence*.

Thomsen, Erik. 1997. *OLAP Solutions: Building Multidimensional Information Systems*. New York: John Wiley and Sons.

Thunderstone Corporation. "Detailed Information about the Texis Document-RDBMS." www.thunderstone.com/jump/texisdetail.html.

Tkach, Daniel, ed. 1998. "Technology Text Mining: Turning Information Into Knowledge: A White Paper From IBM." www-4.ibm.com/software/data/iminer/fortext/download/whiteweb.html.

TSA Consulting. 2000. "Automatic Generation of Metadata Based on Concepts within the Document." www.klarity.com.au/.

Valeds-Perez, Raul E. November 1999. "Discovery Tools for Science Apps" in *Communications of the ACM*. Vol. 42, No. 11.

van Riemsdijk, Henk, and Edwin Williams. 1986. *Introduction to the Theory of Grammar.* Cambridge, MA: MIT Press.

van Rijsbergen, C. J. 1979. *Information Retrieval.* www.dcs.gla.ac.uk/Keith/Preface.html.

W3C. *Document Object Model (DOM) Level 2 Specification.* www.w3.org/TR/2000/REC-DOM-Level-2-Core-20001113/.

W3C. *Resource Description Format (RDF).* http://www.w3.org/RDF/.

Wall, Larry, Tom Christiansen, and Jon Orwant. 2000. *Programming Perl.* 3rd edition. Cambridge, MA: O'Reilly.

Weinsetin, Peter. 1997. "Seed Ontologies: Growing Digital Libraries as Distributed Systems." *Association for Computing Machinery Digital Library '97.*

Widyantoro, Dwi H., Thomas R. Ioerger, and John Yen. 1999. "An Adaptive Algorithm for Learning Changes in User Interests." *Association of Computing Machinery CIKM '99.*

Wilks, Yorick A., Brian M. Slator, and Louise M. Guthrie. 1996. *Electric Words: Dictionaries, Computers and Meaning.* Cambridge, MA: MIT Press.

Xanalys Corporation. 2000. "Text Mining White Paper." www.xanalys.com/intelligence_tools/products/text_mining_text.html.

Xia Lin, Dagobert Soergel, and Gary Marchionini. 1991. "A Self-Organizing Semantic Map for Information Retrieval."

Glossary

Agent An agent is a software component designed to execute a task in a distributed environment and to operate with minimal user input. Agents can be programmed to interact with other agents and move within a distributed environment according to predefined rules and particular conditions of its environment.

Artificial Intelligence (AI) AI is the discipline dedicated to developing machines that can exhibit high-level cognitive functions, such as diagnosing diseases, planning complex operations, and understanding natural language.

Cluster A cluster is a group of related documents, and clustering is the process of grouping documents on the basis of some similarity measure. The main types of clustering are binary, hierarchical, and fuzzy.

Competitive intelligence (CI) CI is the practice of gathering information about the tactical and strategic actions of competitors as well as information about market conditions and related government regulations.

Computational linguistics This discipline bridges computer science and linguistics by addressing issues in the computational aspects of human languages.

Document warehouse A document warehouse is an integrated repository of documents and document metadata designed to support text-based decision support.

Feature extraction Feature extraction is the process of finding facts and relations in text.

Full text indexing Full text indexing is the process of identifying all words in a document, with the exception of stop words, and creating a mapping from words to documents with those words.

Fuzzy logic Fuzzy logic is a branch of deductive logic that deals with rules of reasoning that provide for nonexclusive outcomes. For example, using fuzzy logic, one can conclude that a proposition is somewhat true and somewhat false.

First order logic Rules of deductive reasoning that include quantification.

Hypernyms Hypernyms are words that describe a superclass of another word, for example, vehicle is a hypernym of car and airplane.

Hyponyms Hyponyms are words that instantiate a higher class of objects, for example, convertibles, sedans, and station wagons are all hyponyms of automobile.

Keyword indexing Keyword indexing is the process of identifying the most important and discriminating words in a document set and mapping from those words to individual documents containing those words.

Morphology Morphology is the study of the structure of words and rules for transforming between particular structures.

Natural language Natural languages are languages spoken by humans, as opposed to artificial languages, such as mathematical and musical notation, and programming languages.

Neural network Neural networks are a computational model based upon biological nervous systems rather than digital computers and Boolean algebra. Neural networks are composed of simple processing elements that produce an output signal based upon a set of inputs and a combination rule. Neural networks have been successfully used in a wide range of applications, many of which have not been efficiently solved with symbolic computational methods.

Perl Perl is an open source programming language combining features of C, awk, sh, Basic, and extensive support for text and operating system operations. Perl has been ported to many platforms.

Precision This is a measure of how well information retrieval systems select documents meeting a query. The more documents returned that are unrelated to a query, the lower the precision.

Polysemy Is the characteristic of having multiple meanings.

Python Python is an open source programming language based upon object-oriented design principles. Like Perl, Python is available on many platforms and supports rapid application development.

Recall This is a measure of how well information retrieval systems find all documents that meet a query. The more documents that are not returned but actually meet the query criteria, the lower the recall.

Semantics Semantics is the area of linguistics dealing with the meaning of words and expressions.

Stopwords Stopwords are words ignored in full text indexing because they occur so often that they provide no discriminating information.

Summarization Summarization is the process of reducing the amount of text in a document while still retaining its key meanings.

Synonyms Synonyms are words or terms with similar meanings, for example car and automobile.

Syntax Syntax is an area of linguistics dealing with the structure of word phrases and sentences.

SGML Standard Generalized Markup Language is a predecessor of XML and HTML. The complexity of this markup language has limited its adoption.

Text mining Text mining is the process of automatically extracting information from large collections of documents.

Thematic indexing Thematic indexing is the process of finding key concepts within a document set and developing a map from concepts to documents expressing those concepts.

XML The Extensible Markup Language was developed to solve the limitations of SGML, primarily its complexity, and has been widely adopted for both Web publishing and data exchange.

INDEX

D

G

H

I

K

L

Q

R

S

T

U